PROGRAMMING WITH
MICROSOFT® VISUAL BASIC® 2017

EIGHTH EDITION

PROGRAMMING WITH MICROSOFT® VISUAL BASIC® 2017

DIANE ZAK

Australia • Brazil • Canada • Mexico • Singapore • United Kingdom • United States

Programming with Microsoft® Visual Basic®
2017, **Eighth Edition**
Diane Zak

SVP, GM Science, Technology & Math: Balraj S. Kalsi

Product Director: Kathleen McMahon

Product Team Manager: Kristin McNary

Associate Content Developer: Brianna Vorce

Associate Product Manager: Kate Mason

Senior Director, Development: Julia Caballero

Product Assistant: Jake Toth

Marketing Director: Michele McTighe

Marketing Manager: Stephanie Albracht

Senior Production Director: Wendy Troeger

Production Director: Patty Stephan

Senior Content Project Manager: Jennifer K. Feltri-George

Art Director: Diana Graham

Cover image(s): saemilee/DigitalVision Vectors/ Getty Images

Cover Designer: Lisa Buckley

Unless otherwise noted all screenshots are courtesy of Microsoft Corporation

Open Clip art source: OpenClipArt

Unless otherwise noted, all content is © Cengage.

For product information and technology assistance, contact us at **Cengage Learning Customer & Sales Support, 1-800-354-9706**

For permission to use material from this text or product, submit all requests online at **www.cengage.com/permissions**.
Further permissions questions can be e-mailed to **permissionrequest@cengage.com**

Library of Congress Control Number: 2017940681

Softcover ISBN-13: 978-1-337-10212-4
LLF ISBN: 978-1-337-68573-3

Cengage
200 Pier 4 Boulevard
Boston, MA 02210
USA

Cengage Learning is a leading provider of customized learning solutions with employees residing in nearly 40 different countries and sales in more than 125 countries around the world. Find your local representative at **www.cengage.com**.

To learn more about Cengage Learning, visit **www.cengage.com**

Purchase any of our products at your local college store or at our preferred online store **www.cengagebrain.com**

Notice to the Reader

Publisher does not warrant or guarantee any of the products described herein or perform any independent analysis in connection with any of the product information contained herein. Publisher does not assume, and expressly disclaims, any obligation to obtain and include information other than that provided to it by the manufacturer. The reader is expressly warned to consider and adopt all safety precautions that might be indicated by the activities described herein and to avoid all potential hazards. By following the instructions contained herein, the reader willingly assumes all risks in connection with such instructions. The publisher makes no representations or warranties of any kind, including but not limited to, the warranties of fitness for particular purpose or merchantability, nor are any such representations implied with respect to the material set forth herein, and the publisher takes no responsibility with respect to such material. The publisher shall not be liable for any special, consequential, or exemplary damages resulting, in whole or part, from the readers' use of, or reliance upon, this material.

Printed at CLDPC, USA, 04-21

Brief Contents

Contents

Preface

Programming with Microsoft Visual Basic 2017, Eighth Edition uses Visual Basic 2017, an object-oriented language, to teach programming concepts. This book is designed for a beginning programming course. However, it assumes that students are familiar with basic Windows skills and file management.

Organization and Coverage

Programming with Microsoft Visual Basic 2017, Eighth Edition contains 13 chapters that present concepts along with hands-on instruction; it also contains five appendices (A through E). In the chapters, students with no previous programming experience learn how to plan and create their own interactive Windows applications. GUI design skills, OOP concepts, and planning tools (such as Planning Charts, pseudocode, and flowcharts) are covered in the book. The chapters show students how to work with objects and write Visual Basic statements such as If...Then...Else, Select Case, Do...Loop, For...Next, and For Each...Next. Students also learn how to create and manipulate variables, constants, strings, sequential access files, classes, and arrays. In Chapters 11 and 12, students learn how to create SQL Server databases and then use them in applications. They also learn how to use Structured Query Language (SQL) to access specific fields and records from the database and also to create calculated fields. Chapter 13 shows students how to create both static and dynamic Web Site applications.

Appendix A contains a summary of the GUI design guidelines mentioned in the chapters. Appendix B contains additional topics that can be covered along with (or anytime after) a specified chapter. Appendix C teaches students how to locate and correct errors in their code. The appendix shows students how to step through their code and also how to create breakpoints. The Visual Basic 2017 Cheat Sheet contained in Appendix D summarizes important concepts covered in the chapters, such as the syntax of statements, methods, and so on. The Cheat Sheet provides a convenient place for students to locate the information they need as they are creating and coding their applications. Appendix E contains Case Projects that can be assigned after completing specific chapters in the book.

Approach

Each chapter in *Programming with Microsoft Visual Basic 2017, Eighth Edition* contains two lessons titled Focus on the Concepts and Apply the Concepts. Each lesson has its own set of objectives. The Focus lessons concentrate on programming concepts, using examples along with sample applications designed to reinforce the concepts being taught. The Apply the Concepts lessons show students how to apply the concepts from the chapter's Focus lesson in different ways. The Apply lessons also expand on the concepts taught in the Focus lesson. Both lessons provide tutorial-style steps that guide the student on coding, running, and testing applications. Each sample application allows the student to observe how the current concept can be used before the next concept is introduced.

Features

Programming with Microsoft Visual Basic 2017, Eighth Edition is an exceptional textbook because it also includes the following features:

READ THIS BEFORE YOU BEGIN This section is consistent with Cengage Learning's unequaled commitment to helping instructors introduce technology into the classroom. Technical considerations and assumptions about hardware, software, and default settings are listed in one place to help instructors save time and eliminate unnecessary aggravation.

YOU DO IT! BOXES These boxes provide simple applications that allow students to demonstrate their understanding of a concept before moving on to the next concept.

OPTION STATEMENTS All applications include the Option Explicit, Option Strict, and Option Infer statements.

START HERE ARROWS These arrows indicate the beginning of a tutorial steps section in the book.

FIGURES Figures that introduce new statements, functions, or methods contain both the syntax and examples of using the syntax. Including the syntax in the figures makes the examples more meaningful, and vice versa.

 TIP These notes provide additional information about the current concept. Examples include alternative ways of writing statements or performing tasks, as well as warnings about common mistakes made when using a particular command and reminders of related concepts learned in previous chapters.

SUMMARY Each chapter contains a Summary section that recaps the concepts covered in the chapter.

KEY TERMS Following the Summary section in each chapter is a list of the key terms introduced throughout the chapter, along with their definitions.

REVIEW QUESTIONS Each chapter contains Review Questions designed to test a student's understanding of the chapter's concepts.

New to This Edition!

NEW CHAPTERS All of the chapters in the book have been revamped. A list of the changes made to the chapters is available via the optional MindTap for this text.

LESSONS Each chapter is divided into two lessons: Focus on the Concepts and Apply the Concepts. Each lesson has its own set of objectives. The Focus lessons introduce programming concepts, which are illustrated with code examples and sample applications. The Apply lessons show students how to apply the concepts from the chapter's Focus lesson in different ways. The Apply lessons also expand on the concepts taught in the Focus lesson. Both lessons provide tutorial-style steps that guide the student on coding, running, and testing applications. The applications allow students to observe how the current concept can be used before the next concept is introduced.

MINI-QUIZ BOXES Mini-quiz boxes are strategically placed to test students' knowledge at various points in the chapter. Answers to the quiz questions are printed upside down in the boxes, allowing students to determine whether they have mastered the material covered thus far before continuing with the chapter.

SQL SERVER DATABASES AND SQL   The book includes two chapters (Chapters 11 and 12) on SQL Server databases and SQL.

NEW EXERCISES   The Review Questions in each chapter are followed by Exercises, which provide students with additional practice of the skills and concepts they learned in the chapter. The Exercises are designated as INTRODUCTORY, INTERMEDIATE, ADVANCED, ON YOUR OWN, and FIX IT. The ON YOUR OWN Exercises encourage students to challenge and independently develop their own programming skills while exploring the capabilities of Visual Basic 2017. Students are given minimum guidelines to follow when creating the ON YOUR OWN applications. The FIX IT Exercises provide an opportunity for students to detect and correct errors in an application's code.

APPENDICES   Appendix A summarizes the GUI design guidelines mentioned in the chapters, making it easier for the student to follow the guidelines when designing an application's interface. Appendix B contains additional topics that can be covered along with (or anytime after) a specified chapter. Appendix C teaches students how to locate and correct errors (syntax, logic, and run time) in their code. The appendix shows students how to step through their code and also how to create breakpoints. Appendix D contains a Cheat Sheet that summarizes important concepts covered in the chapters, such as the syntax of statements, methods, and so on. The Cheat Sheet provides a convenient place for students to locate the information they need as they are creating and coding their applications. Appendix E contains Case Projects that can be assigned after completing specific chapters in the book.

 UPDATED VIDEOS   These notes direct students to videos that accompany many chapters in the book. The videos explain and/or demonstrate one or more of the chapter's concepts. The videos have been revised from the previous edition and are available via the optional MindTap for this text.

Steps and Figures

The tutorial-style steps and figures in the book assume you are using Microsoft Visual Studio Community 2017 and a system running Microsoft Windows 10. Your screen may appear slightly different in some instances if you are using a different version of Microsoft Windows.

Instructor Resources

The following teaching tools are available for download at our Instructor Companion Site. Simply search for this text at sso.cengage.com. An instructor login is required.

INSTRUCTOR'S MANUAL   The Instructor's Manual that accompanies this textbook includes additional instructional material to assist in class preparation, including items such as Sample Syllabi, Chapter Outlines, Technical Notes, Lecture Notes, Quick Quizzes, Teaching Tips, Discussion Topics, and Additional Case Projects.

TEST BANK   Cengage Learning Testing Powered by Cognero is a flexible, online system that allows you to:

- Author, edit, and manage test bank content from multiple Cengage Learning solutions

- Create multiple test versions in an instant

- Deliver tests from your LMS, your classroom or wherever you want

POWERPOINT PRESENTATIONS This book offers Microsoft PowerPoint slides for each chapter. These are included as a teaching aid for classroom presentation, to make available to students on the network for chapter review, or to be printed for classroom distribution. Instructors can add their own slides for additional topics they introduce to the class.

SOLUTION FILES Solutions to the chapter applications and the end-of-chapter Review Questions and Exercises are provided.

DATA FILES Data Files are necessary for completing the computer activities in this book. Data Files can also be downloaded by students at CengageBrain.com.

MindTap

MindTap is a personalized teaching experience with relevant assignments that guide students to analyze, apply, and improve thinking, allowing you to measure skills and outcomes with ease.

- Personalized teaching: Becomes yours with a Learning Path that is built with key student objectives. Control what students see and when they see it. Use it as-is or match to your syllabus exactly—hide, rearrange, add, and create your own content.

- Guide students: A unique learning path of relevant readings, multimedia and activities that move students up the learning taxonomy from basic knowledge and comprehension to analysis and application.

- Promote better outcomes: Empower instructors and motivate students with analytics and reports that provide a snapshot of class progress, time in course, engagement and completion rates.

The MindTap for *Programming with Microsoft Visual Basic 2017* includes videos, study tools, and interactive quizzing, all integrated into a full eReader that contains the full content from the printed text.

Acknowledgments

Writing a book is a team effort rather than an individual one. I would like to take this opportunity to thank my team, especially Jennifer Feltri-George (Senior Content Project Manager), Prathiba Rajagopal (Senior Project Manager), Nicole Spoto (Quality Assurance), Alyssa Pratt (Senior Content Developer), Brianna Vorce (Associate Content Developer), and the compositors at SPi Global. Thank you for your support, enthusiasm, patience, and hard work. And a special thank you to all of the past and present reviewers, as well as to Sally Douglas (College of Central Florida), who suggested the YOU DO IT! boxes several editions ago.

Diane Zak

Read This Before You Begin

Technical Information

Data Files

You will need data files to complete the computer activities in this book. Your instructor may provide the data files to you. You may obtain the files electronically at CengageBrain.com and then navigating to the page for this book.

Each chapter in this book has its own set of data files, which are stored in a separate folder within the VB2017 folder. The files for Chapter 1 are stored in the VB2017\Chap01 folder. Similarly, the files for Chapter 2 are stored in the VB2017\Chap02 folder. Throughout this book, you will be instructed to open files from or save files to these folders.

You can use a computer in your school lab or your own computer to complete the steps and Exercises in this book.

Using Your Own Computer

To use your own computer to complete the computer activities in this book, you will need the following:

- A Pentium® 4 processor, 1.6 GHz or higher, personal computer running Microsoft Windows. This book was written and Quality Assurance tested using Microsoft Windows 10.

- Microsoft Visual Studio 2017 installed on your computer. (You need to install the .NET desktop development component to complete Chapters 1 through 12. You need to install the ASP.NET and web development component to complete Chapter 13.) This book was written and Quality Assurance tested using Microsoft Visual Studio Community 2017. At the time of this writing, you can download a free copy of the Community Edition at *https://www.visualstudio.com/downloads*.

To control the display of filename extensions in Windows 10:

1. Press and hold down the Windows logo key on your keyboard as you tap the letter x. (Or, right-click the Windows Start button on the taskbar.) Click Control Panel, click Appearance and Personalization, click File Explorer Options, and then click the View tab.

2. Deselect the Hide extensions for known file types check box to show the extensions; or, select the check box to hide them. Click the OK button and then close the Appearance and Personalization window.

To always display the underlined letters (called access keys) in Windows 10:

1. Press and hold down the Windows logo key on your keyboard as you tap the letter x. (Or, right-click the Windows Start button on the taskbar.) Click Control Panel and then click Appearance and Personalization.

2. In the Ease of Access Center section, click Turn on easy access keys, and then select the Underline keyboard shortcuts and access keys check box. Click the OK button and then close the Ease of Access Center window.

To start and configure Visual Studio to match the figures and tutorial steps in this book:

1. Use the steps on Pages 9 through 11 in Chapter 1.

2. If you are using the Professional or Enterprise editions of Visual Studio, you may also need to click Tools, click Options, expand the Text Editor node, expand the All Languages node, click CodeLens, and then deselect Enable CodeLens.

Figures

The figures in this book reflect how your screen will look if you are using Microsoft Visual Studio Community 2017 and a Microsoft Windows 10 system. Your screen may appear slightly different in some instances if you are using another version of either Microsoft Visual Studio or Microsoft Windows.

Visit Our Web Site

Additional materials designed for this textbook might be available at CengageBrain.com. Search this site for more details.

To the Instructor

To complete the computer activities in this book, your students must use a set of data files. These files can be obtained on the Instructor Companion Site or at CengageBrain.com.

The material in this book was written and Quality Assurance tested using Microsoft Visual Studio Community 2017 on a Microsoft Windows 10 system.

CHAPTER 1

An Introduction to Visual Studio 2017 and Visual Basic

In this chapter's Focus on the Concepts lesson, you will learn the definitions for many of the terms used by programmers. The lesson also introduces you to Microsoft's newest integrated development environment (IDE): Visual Studio 2017. The IDE contains the latest version of the Visual Basic programming language. You will use the IDE and language to create the applications in this book. As stated in the Read This Before You Begin section of this book, the steps and figures in this book assume you are using the Community edition of Visual Studio 2017. Your steps and screen might differ slightly in some instances if you are using a different edition of Visual Studio 2017.

In the Apply the Concepts lesson, you will apply the concepts covered in the Focus lesson. The Apply lesson is designed to help you get comfortable with both the Visual Studio IDE and the Visual Basic programming language.

■ FOCUS ON THE CONCEPTS LESSON

Concepts covered in this lesson:

- F-1 Computer programming terminology
- F-2 The programmer's job
- F-3 The Visual Basic programming language
- F-4 The Visual Studio IDE
- F-5 Assigning names to objects

F-1 Computer Programming Terminology

In essence, the word **programming** means *giving a mechanism the directions to accomplish a task*. When the mechanism is a computer, the directions are typically referred to as instructions. A set of instructions that tells a computer how to accomplish a task is called a **computer program** or, more simply, a **program**.

Programs are written by **programmers** using a variety of special languages called **programming languages**. Some popular programming languages are Visual Basic, C#, C++, and Java. In this book, you will write your programs using the Visual Basic programming language, which is built into Microsoft's newest integrated development environment: Visual Studio 2017. An **integrated development environment** (**IDE**) is an environment that contains all of the tools and features you need to create, run, and test your programs. You also will use the IDE to create graphical user interfaces for your programs. A **graphical user interface** (or **GUI**) is what the person using your program (referred to as the user) sees and interacts with while your program is running. The user interface and its program instructions are referred to as an **application**. Figure 1-1 shows the user interface and program instructions for the Good Morning application.

```
1    Public Class frmMain
2        Private Sub btnExit_Click(sender As Object, e As EventArgs) Handles btnExit.Click
3            Me.Close()
4        End Sub
5
6        Private Sub tmrGetUp_Tick(sender As Object, e As EventArgs) Handles tmrGetUp.Tick
7            ' Blink the message.
8
9            lblMessage.Visible = Not lblMessage.Visible
10       End Sub
```

Figure 1-1 Good Morning application

To run the Good Morning application:

START HERE

1. Use Windows to locate and then open the VB2017\Chap01 folder on your computer's hard disk or on the device designated by your instructor. Double-click **Good Morning.exe** in the list of filenames. (Depending on how Windows is set up on your computer, you might not see the .exe extension on the filename. Refer to the Read This Before You Begin section to learn how to show filename extensions.) The application's user interface appears on the screen with a blinking "It's time to get up!!!!" message.

2. Click the **Exit** button to close the application.

F-2 The Programmer's Job

When a company has a problem that requires a computer solution, typically it is a programmer who comes to the rescue. The programmer might be an employee of the company; or he or she might be a freelance programmer, who works on temporary contracts rather than for a long-term employer.

First, the programmer meets with the person (or people) responsible for describing the problem. This person might be the one who will eventually use the solution; or he or she might be a software developer, who serves as an intermediary between the user and the programmer. The software developer will meet with the user and then outline the problem specification for the programmer. After the programmer understands the problem, he or she will begin planning an appropriate solution. After the planning is complete, the programmer will translate the solution into computer instructions—a process called **coding**. The programmer then will test the program rigorously with sample data to make sure it works both correctly and to the user's satisfaction. Depending on the complexity of the problem, multiple programmers might be involved in the planning and coding phases. Programming teams often contain subject matter experts, who might or might not be programmers. For example, an accountant might be part of a team working on a program that requires accounting expertise.

F-3 The Visual Basic Programming Language

Visual Basic is an **object-oriented programming language**, which is a language that allows the programmer to use objects to accomplish a program's goal. In object-oriented programming, or **OOP**, an **object** is anything that can be seen, touched, or used. In other words, an object is nearly any *thing*. Programs written for the Windows environment typically use objects such as check boxes, list boxes, and buttons.

Every object in an object-oriented program is created from a **class**, which is a pattern that the computer uses to create the object. The class contains the instructions that tell the computer how the object should look and behave. An object created from a class is called an **instance** of the class and is said to be **instantiated** from the class. An analogy involving a cookie cutter and cookies is often used to describe a class and its objects: The class is the cookie cutter, and the objects instantiated from the class are the cookies. You will learn more about classes and objects throughout this book.

In the following set of steps, you will run two Visual Basic applications that employ many of the objects you will learn about in this book.

START HERE **To run the applications:**

1. If necessary, open the VB2017\Chap01 folder. Double-click **Payment.exe**. After a few moments, the Monthly Payment Calculator application shown in Figure 1-2 appears on the screen. (If some of the letters on your screen are not underlined, press the Alt key.) The interface contains a text box, a list box, buttons, radio buttons, and labels. You can use the application to calculate the monthly payment for a car loan.

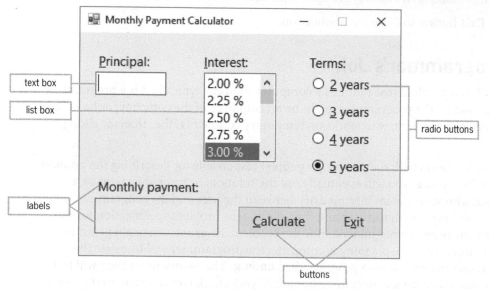

Figure 1-2 Monthly Payment Calculator application

2. First, you will use the application to calculate the monthly payment for a $15,000 loan at 3.5% interest for five years. Type **15000** in the Principal text box. Scroll down the Interest list box and then click **3.50 %**. Finally, click the **Calculate** button. The application indicates that your monthly payment would be $272.88. See Figure 1-3.

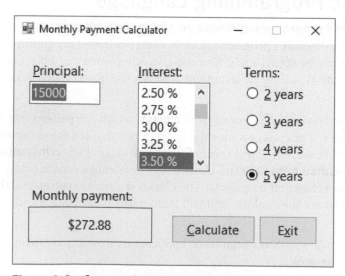

Figure 1-3 Computed monthly payment

3. Next, you will determine what your monthly payment would be if you borrowed $4,500 at 2.75% interest for four years. Type **4500** in the Principal text box, click **2.75 %** in the Interest list box, click the **4 years** radio button, and then click the **Calculate** button. The Monthly payment box shows $99.11.

4. Click the **Exit** button to close the application.

5. Now double-click **Einstein.exe**. (The file is located in the VB2017\Chap01 folder.) Click the **Show equation** button to display Einstein's famous equation. See Figure 1-4. The interface contains picture boxes and buttons. (If some of the letters on your screen are not underlined, press the Alt key.)

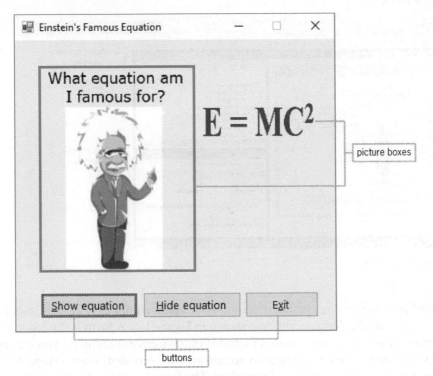

Figure 1-4 Equation shown in the interface

6. Click the **Hide equation** button to hide the equation, and then click the **Exit** button to close the application.

Mini-Quiz 1-1

1. What is a computer program?

2. What is a GUI?

3. What is the process of translating a solution into a computer program called?

4. In object-oriented programming, what is a class?

1) A set of instructions that tells a computer how to accomplish a task. 2) Stands for Graphical User Interface. It is what the user sees and interacts with when using an application. 3) Coding 4) A pattern used to instantiate (create) an object.

F-4 The Visual Studio IDE

The Visual Studio IDE contains many different windows, each with its own special purpose. The four windows you will use most often when designing your user interfaces are shown in Figure 1-5.

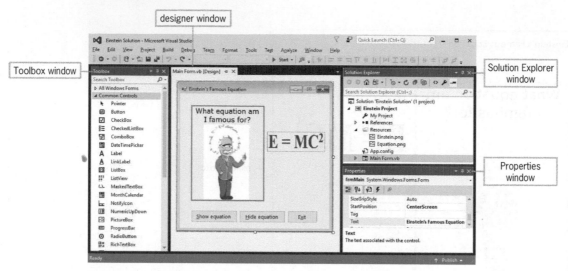

Figure 1-5   Visual Studio IDE

The **designer window** is where you create (or design) your application's GUI. A Windows Form object, or form, appears in the designer window shown in Figure 1-5. A **form** is the foundation for the user interface in an application created for the Windows environment. As you learned earlier, all objects in an object-oriented program are instantiated (created) from a class. A form, for example, is an instance of the Windows Form class. The form (an object) is automatically instantiated for you when you create a Windows Forms application in Visual Basic.

You use the **Toolbox window** to add other objects, called **controls**, to the form. Each tool listed in the Toolbox window represents a class. You add an object by clicking its corresponding tool (class) in the toolbox and then dragging it with your mouse pointer to the form. When you drag the tool to the form, Visual Basic creates (instantiates) an instance of the class (an object) and places it on the form. For example, the two picture box objects shown in Figure 1-5 were instantiated (created) by dragging the PictureBox tool from the toolbox to the form. Similarly, the three button objects were instantiated using the Button tool.

Each object has a set of attributes that determine its appearance and behavior. The attributes, called **properties**, are listed in the **Properties window** when the object is selected in the designer window. In Figure 1-5, the form is selected, and the names of its properties (such as StartPosition and Text), along with their values (CenterScreen and Einstein's Famous Equation), appear in the Properties window. You can use the Properties window to change the value of an object's property. For example, you can use it to change the form's Text property, which appears in the form's title bar, from Einstein's Famous Equation to Guess My Equation.

Windows applications in Visual Basic are composed of solutions, projects, and files. A solution is a container that stores the projects and files for an entire application. A project is also a container, but it stores only the files associated with that particular project. The **Solution Explorer** window displays a list of the projects contained in the current solution and the items contained in each project. The Solution Explorer window shown in Figure 1-5 indicates that the Einstein Solution contains the Einstein Project, which contains several items. The Einstein.png and Equation.png items are the names of files on your disk. These files contain the images that appear in the picture boxes on the form. The Main Form.vb item is also the name of a file on your disk. The Main Form.vb file stores the program instructions (**code**) that tell the three buttons how to respond when the user clicks them. You enter the code in the **Code Editor window**, which is shown in Figure 1-6.

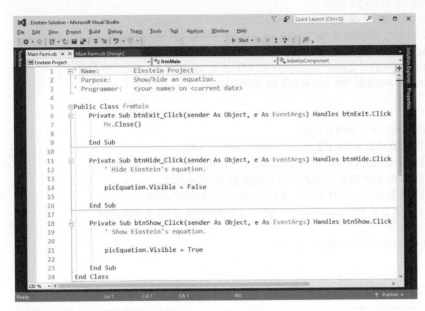

Figure 1-6 Code Editor window

At this point, you are not expected to understand the contents of the Code Editor window in Figure 1-6; you will learn about the contents in this chapter's Apply the Concepts lesson. However, briefly, the green lines of text are comments and are not executed by the computer when the application is run; they serve simply to internally document the program. The code on Lines 6 through 9 tell the computer to close (end) the application when the Exit button is clicked. The code on Lines 11 through 16 indicate that the computer should hide the equation picture box when the Hide equation button is clicked. The code on Lines 18 through 23 tell the computer to show the equation picture box when the Show equation button is clicked.

F-5 Assigning Names to Objects

As mentioned earlier, each object has a set of properties attached to it. One of the most important of these properties is the Name property. This is because you use the **Name property** to refer to the object in code. The code in Figure 1-6, for example, refers to objects named frmMain, btnExit, btnHide, btnShow, and picEquation. Figure 1-7 lists the rules and conventions this book will follow when naming objects. Typically, you assign names to only objects that are either coded or referred to in code.

Camel case refers to the fact that the uppercase letters appear as "humps" in the name because they are taller than the lowercase letters.

Naming rules (these are required by Visual Basic)
1. Each object must have a unique name.
2. Each name must begin with a letter and contain only letters, numbers, and the underscore character.

Naming conventions used in this book
1. Each name will begin with an ID of three (or more) characters that represents the object's type—for example, *frm* for a form, *btn* for a button, and *txt* for a text box.
2. The remaining characters after the ID will indicate the object's purpose.
3. Each name will be entered using camel case: the ID will be in lowercase, and the first letter in each subsequent word in the name will be capitalized.

Examples
frmMain	the main form in a project
btnExit	a button that ends the application when clicked
txtFirstName	a text box for entering a customer's first name
picEquation	a picture box that displays an image of an equation
lblTotalDue	a label that displays the total amount a customer owes
chkDiscount	a check box for specifying whether a customer gets a discount

Figure 1-7   Rules and conventions for naming objects

Mini-Quiz 1-2

1. Which window in the IDE lists the tools you can use to add objects to a form?

2. While designing an interface, which window in the IDE allows you to change the default value of an object's property?

3. Using the naming rules and conventions listed in Figure 1-7, which of the following are valid names and which are not? Explain why the names are not valid.

   a. lblTotal

   b. txtFirst.Name

   c. lblCity&State

   d. btnCalc Total

   e. txtFirstQuarter

1) Toolbox 2) Properties 3) Answers a and e are valid. Answer b is invalid because it contains a period. Answer c is invalid because it contains an ampersand. Answer d is invalid because it contains a space.

■ APPLY THE CONCEPTS LESSON

After studying this lesson, you should be able to:

- A-1 Start and configure Visual Studio Community 2017
- A-2 Create a Windows Forms application
- A-3 Manage the windows in the IDE
- A-4 Change a form file's name
- A-5 Change the properties of a form
- A-6 Save a solution
- A-7 Close and open a solution
- A-8 Add a control to a form
- A-9 Use the Format menu
- A-10 Lock the controls on the form
- A-11 Start and end an application
- A-12 Enter code and comments in the Code Editor window
- A-13 Print an application's code and interface
- A-14 Exit Visual Studio and run an executable file

A-1 Start and Configure Visual Studio Community 2017

In this Apply lesson, you will create the Einstein's Famous Equation application that you viewed in the Focus lesson. First, you need to start and configure Visual Studio Community 2017, which contains the Visual Basic language. (Keep in mind that your steps might differ slightly if you are using a different edition of Visual Studio 2017.)

To start Visual Studio Community 2017:

START HERE

1. Click the **Start** button on the Windows 10 taskbar. Locate and then click **Visual Studio 2017** in the Start menu.

2. Click **Tools** on the menu bar, click **Import and Export Settings**, select the **Reset all settings** radio button, click the **Next** button, select the **No, just reset settings, overwriting my current settings** radio button, click the **Next** button, click **Visual Basic**, and then click the **Finish** button. Click the **Close** button to close the Import and Export Settings Wizard dialog box.

3. Click **Window** on the menu bar, click **Reset Window Layout**, and then click the **Yes** button. When you start Visual Studio 2017, your screen will appear similar to Figure 1-8. However, your menu bar might not contain the underlined letters, called access keys. You can show/hide the access keys by pressing the Alt key on your keyboard.

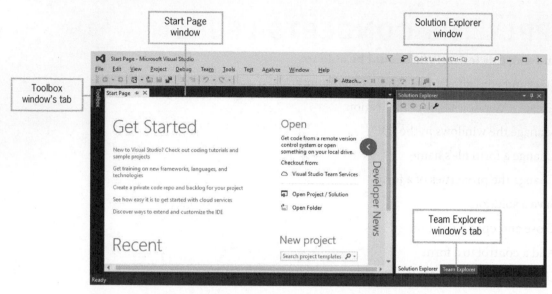

Figure 1-8 Microsoft Visual Studio Community 2017 startup screen

Next, you will configure Visual Studio Community 2017 so that your screen and tutorial steps agree with the figures and tutorial steps in this book. As mentioned in the Read This Before You Begin section of this book, the figures in this book reflect how your screen will look if you are using Visual Studio Community 2017 and a Microsoft Windows 10 system. Your screen might vary in some instances if you are using a different edition of Visual Studio or another version of Microsoft Windows. Do not worry if your screen display differs slightly from the figures.

START HERE ▶ **To configure Visual Studio 2017:**

1. Click **Tools** on the menu bar and then click **Options** to open the Options dialog box. Click the **Projects and Solutions** node. Use the information shown in Figure 1-9 to select and deselect the appropriate check boxes.

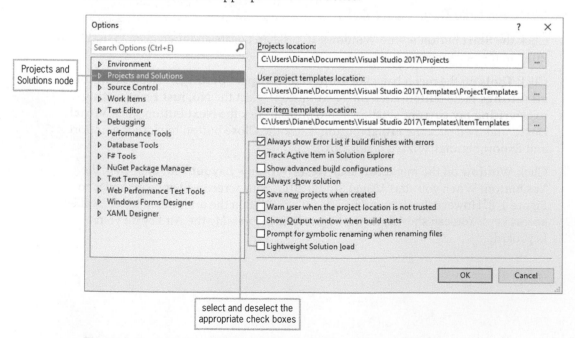

Figure 1-9 Projects and Solutions options in the Options dialog box

2. Expand the **Text Editor** node, expand the **Basic** node, expand the **Code Style** node, and then click **Naming**. Locate the **Types** row in the dialog box and then click the **list arrow** in its Severity column. See Figure 1-10.

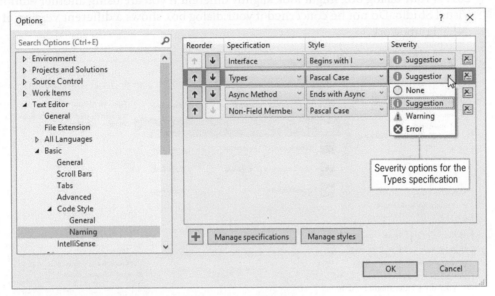

Figure 1-10   Naming options in the Options dialog box

3. Click **None** in the list. Then locate the **Non-Field Members** row and change its Severity column entry to **None**.

4. Click the **Code Style** node. Locate the **Qualify property access with 'Me'** row, click the **list arrow** in its Preference column, and then click **Prefer 'Me.'** Now locate the **Qualify method access with 'Me'** row and change its Preference column entry to **Prefer 'Me.'**

5. Scroll down the left column of the dialog box until you locate the Debugging node. Click the **Debugging** node and then deselect the **Step over properties and operators (Managed only)** check box. Also deselect the **Enable Diagnostic Tools while debugging** check box (if necessary) and the **Show elapsed time PerfTip while debugging** check box.

6. Click the **OK** button to close the Options dialog box.

   Note: If you change your default environment settings *after* performing the previous six steps, you will need to perform the steps again.

A-2 Create a Windows Forms Application

The Einstein's Famous Equation application will be a Windows Forms application, which is an application that has a Windows user interface and runs on a laptop (or desktop) computer.

To create a Windows Forms application:

START HERE

1. Click **File** on the menu bar and then click **New Project** to open the New Project dialog box. If necessary, click the **Visual Basic** node in the Installed Templates list, and then click **Windows Forms App (.NET Framework)** in the middle column of the dialog box.

2. Change the name entered in the Name box to **Einstein Project**.

3. Click the **Browse** button to open the Project Location dialog box. Locate and then click the **VB2017\Chap01** folder. Click the **Select Folder** button to close the Project Location dialog box.

4. If necessary, select the **Create directory for solution** check box in the New Project dialog box. Change the name entered in the Solution name box to **Einstein Solution**. Figure 1-11 shows the completed New Project dialog box in Visual Studio Community 2017. (Your dialog box might look slightly different if you are using another edition of Visual Studio. Do not be concerned if your dialog box shows a different version of the .NET Framework.)

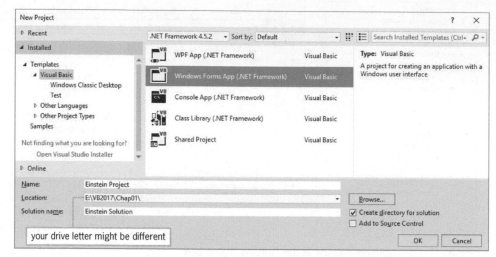

Figure 1-11 Completed New Project dialog box

5. Click the **OK** button to close the New Project dialog box. The computer creates a solution and adds a Visual Basic project to the solution. The names of the solution and project, along with other information pertaining to the project, appear in the Solution Explorer window. Visual Basic also automatically instantiates (creates) a form object, which appears in the designer window. See Figure 1-12.

You can size a window by positioning your mouse pointer on one of its borders until the mouse pointer becomes a sizing pointer (a horizontal line with an arrowhead at each end), and then dragging the border.

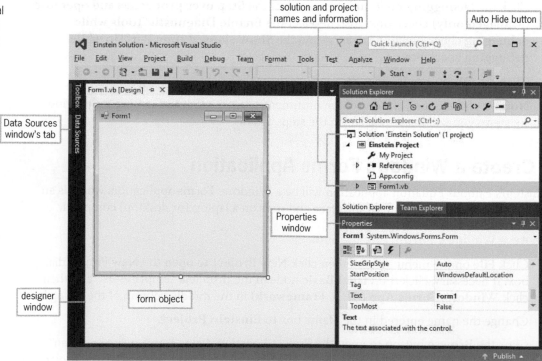

Figure 1-12 Solution and Visual Basic project

A-3 Manage the Windows in the IDE

In most cases, you will find it easier to work in the IDE if you either close or auto-hide the windows you are not currently using. You close an open window by clicking the Close button on its title bar. You will find the options for opening a closed window on the View menu. You auto-hide a window by using its Auto Hide button (refer to Figure 1-12), which is located on the window's title bar. The Auto Hide button is a toggle button: Clicking it once activates it, and clicking it again deactivates it. The Toolbox and Data Sources windows in Figure 1-12 are auto-hidden windows.

To close, open, auto-hide, and display windows in the IDE: START HERE

1. Click the **Close** button on the Properties window's title bar to close the window. Then click **View** on the menu bar and click **Properties Window** to open the window.

2. Click the **Team Explorer** tab. When the Team Explorer window appears, click the **Close** button on its title bar.

3. Click the **Auto Hide** (vertical pushpin) button on the Solution Explorer window. The Solution Explorer window now appears as a tab on the edge of the IDE.

4. To temporarily display the Solution Explorer window, click the **Solution Explorer** tab. Notice that the Auto Hide button is now a horizontal pushpin rather than a vertical pushpin. To return the Solution Explorer window to its auto-hidden state, click the **Solution Explorer** tab again.

5. To permanently display the Solution Explorer window, click the **Solution Explorer** tab and then click the **Auto Hide** (horizontal pushpin) button on the window's title bar. The vertical pushpin replaces the horizontal pushpin on the button.

6. On your own, close the Data Sources window.

7. If necessary, click **Form1.vb** in the Solution Explorer window. The name of the selected object (Form1.vb) appears in the Properties window's Object box. The Properties window also contains two columns of information. The left column, called the Properties list, displays the names of the selected object's properties. The right column contains the Settings boxes; each box displays the current value (or setting) of its associated property.

8. If the names listed in the Properties list do not appear in alphabetical order, click the **Alphabetical** button, which is the second button on the Properties window's toolbar. Figure 1-13 shows the current status of the windows in the IDE. Only the designer, Solution Explorer, and Properties windows are open; the Toolbox window is auto-hidden. (If necessary, close any other open or auto-hidden windows in the IDE.)

 To reset the window layout in the IDE, click Window on the menu bar, click Reset Window Layout, and then click the Yes button.

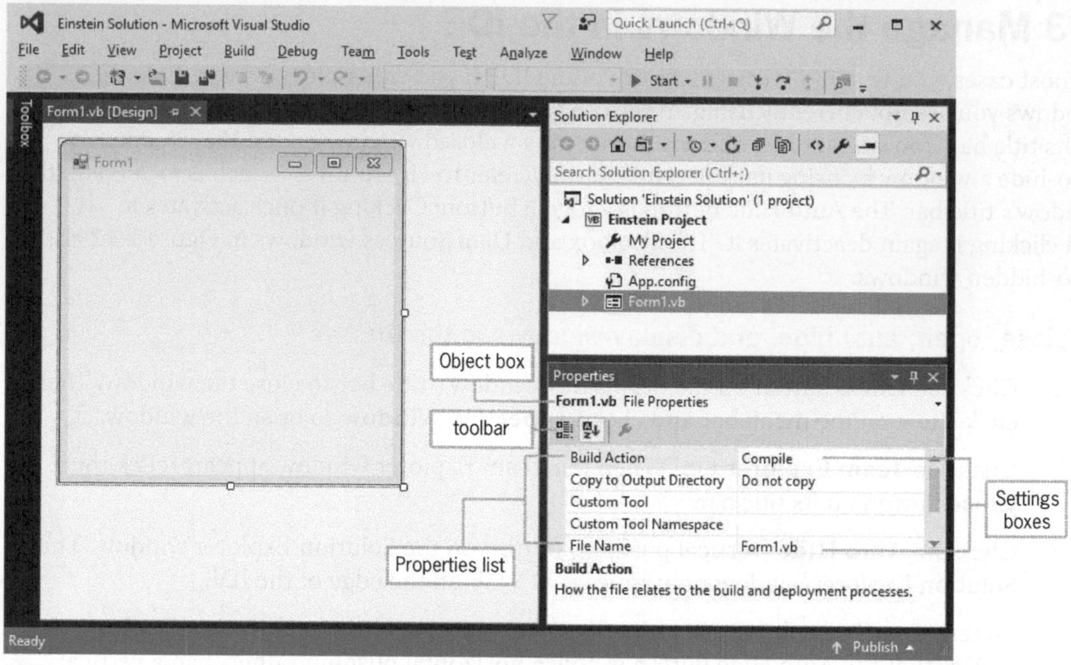

Figure 1-13   Current status of the windows in the IDE

A-4 Change a Form File's Name

The code associated with the first form included in a project is automatically stored in a file, referred to as a **form file**, named Form1.vb. It's called a form file because it contains the code associated with the form. All files with a .vb filename extension are also referred to as **source files** because they contain Visual Basic code. The code associated with the second form in the same project is stored in a file named Form2.vb, and so on. To help you keep track of the various form files in a project, you should give each a unique and meaningful name.

START HERE

To use the Properties window to change the form file's name:

> You can also change the File Name property by right-clicking Form1.vb in the Solution Explorer window and then clicking Rename on the context menu.

1. Click **File Name** in the Properties list for the Form1.vb file. Type **Main Form.vb** in the Settings box and press **Enter**. (Be sure to include the .vb extension on the filename; otherwise, the computer will not recognize the file as a source file.) Main Form.vb appears in the Solution Explorer and Properties windows and on the designer window's tab, as shown in Figure 1-14.

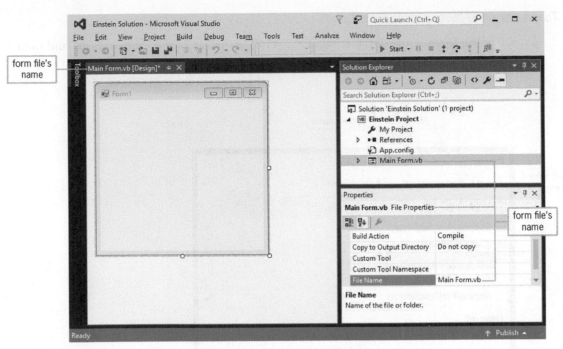

Figure 1-14 Form file's name shown in various locations

Mini-Quiz 1-3

1. Which menu provides options for opening a closed window in the IDE?

2. What is the name of the vertical pushpin button on a window's title bar?

3. What filename extension indicates that the file is a Visual Basic source file?

1) View 2) Auto Hide button 3) .vb

A-5 Change the Properties of a Form

In order to display the properties of a form in the Properties window, the form must be selected in the designer window. (It is easy to confuse a form file, whose File Name property you changed in the previous section, with a form. The form file is an actual file that resides on your disk and contains code, like the code shown earlier in Figure 1-6. The form is the object that appears in the designer window.)

START HERE
To display the form's properties:

1. Click the **form** in the designer window. Scroll to the top of the Properties list and then click **(Name)**. See Figure 1-15.

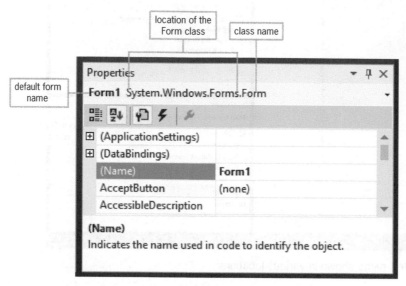

Figure 1-15   Partial list of the form's properties

The Object box in Figure 1-15 shows the text *Form1 System.Windows.Forms.Form. Form1* is the name of the form that appears in the designer window. The name is automatically assigned to the form when the form is instantiated (created). In *System.Windows. Forms.Form, Form* is the name of the class used to instantiate the form. *System.Windows.Forms* is the namespace that contains the Form class definition. A **class definition** is a block of code that specifies (or defines) an object's appearance and behavior. All class definitions in Visual Basic are contained in namespaces, which you can picture as blocks of memory cells inside the computer. Each **namespace** contains the code that defines a group of related classes. The *System.Windows.Forms* namespace contains the definition of the Windows Form class. It also contains the class definitions for objects you add to a form, such as buttons and text boxes.

The period that separates each word in *System.Windows.Forms.Form* is called the **dot member access operator**. Similar to the backslash (\) in a folder path, the dot member access operator indicates a hierarchy, but of namespaces rather than folders. In other words, the backslash in the path *E:\VB2017\Chap01\Einstein Solution\Einstein Project\Main Form.vb* indicates that the Main Form.vb file is contained in (or is a member of) the Einstein Project folder, which is a member of the Einstein Solution folder, which is a member of the Chap01 folder, which is a member of the VB2017 folder, which is a member of the E: drive. Likewise, the name *System.Windows.Forms.Form* indicates that the Form class is a member of the Forms namespace, which is a member of the Windows namespace, which is a member of the System namespace. The dot member access operator allows the computer to locate the Form class in the computer's main memory, similar to the way the backslash (\) allows the computer to locate the Main Form.vb file on your computer's disk.

Figure 1-16 lists the names and purposes of the most commonly used properties of a form. In the next several sections, you will change the default values assigned to many of the properties listed in the figure.

Name	Purpose
AcceptButton	specify a default button that will be selected when the user presses the Enter key
BackColor	specify the background color of the form
CancelButton	specify a cancel button that will be selected when the user presses the Esc key
ControlBox	indicate whether the form contains the Control box and Minimize, Maximize, and Close buttons
Font	specify the font to use for text
FormBorderStyle	specify the appearance and behavior of the form's border
MaximizeBox	specify the state of the Maximize button
MinimizeBox	specify the state of the Minimize button
Name	give the form a meaningful name (use frm as the ID)
StartPosition	indicate the starting position of the form
Text	specify the text that appears in the form's title bar and on the taskbar

Figure 1-16   Most commonly used properties of a form

The Name Property

Following the naming rules and conventions shown earlier in Figure 1-7, you will name the current form frmMain. The *frm* identifies the object as a form, and *Main* reminds you of the form's purpose, which is to be the main form in the application.

To change the form's name: START HERE

1. The form's Name property should be selected in the Properties window. Type **frmMain** and press **Enter**. The asterisk (*) on the designer window's tab indicates that the form has been changed since the last time it was saved.

The Font Property

A form's Font property determines the type, style, and size of the font used to display the text on the form. A font is the general shape of the characters in the text. Font sizes are typically measured in points, with one point (pt) equaling 1/72 of an inch. The recommended font for applications created for systems running Windows 10 is Segoe UI because it offers improved readability. Segoe is pronounced "SEE-go," and UI stands for user interface. For most of the elements in the interface, you will use a 9pt font size. However, to make the figures in the book more readable, some of the interfaces created in this book will use a slightly larger font size. In this case, for example, you will set the font size to 10.

To change the form's Font property: START HERE

1. Click **Font** in the Properties list and then click the **…** (ellipsis) button in the Settings box to open the Font dialog box.

2. Locate and then click **Segoe UI** in the Font box. Click **10** in the Size box and then click the **OK** button. (Do not be concerned if the size of the form changes. Also do not be concerned if the Font property shows 9.75pt rather than 10pt.)

The MaximizeBox, StartPosition, and Text Properties

You can use a form's MaximizeBox property to disable the Maximize button, which appears in the form's title bar; doing this prevents the user from maximizing the user interface while the application is running. The form's StartPosition property determines the form's initial position on the screen when an application is started. To center the form on the screen, you set the property to CenterScreen. A form's Text property specifies the text that appears in the form's title bar. Form1 is the default value assigned to the Text property of the first form in a project. For the current form, "Einstein's Famous Equation" would be a more descriptive value.

START HERE

To change the three properties:

1. Click **MaximizeBox** in the Properties list, click the **list arrow** button in the Settings box, and then click **False**.

2. Change the StartPosition property to **CenterScreen**.

3. Click **Text** in the Properties list, type **Einstein's Famous Equation** and then press **Enter**. Notice that Einstein's Famous Equation, rather than Form1, appears in the form's title bar.

Mini-Quiz 1-4

1. What character is the dot member access operator?

2. What is the recommended font type for Windows 10 applications?

3. Which of a form's properties determines the location of the form when the application is started?

4. To display the words ABC Company in a form's title bar, you need to set which of the form's properties?

1) a period 2) Segoe UI 3) StartPosition 4) Text

The Save All button looks like this:

A-6 Save a Solution

As mentioned earlier, an asterisk (*) on the designer window's tab indicates that a change was made to the form since the last time it was saved. It is a good idea to save the current solution every 10 or 15 minutes so that you will not lose a lot of your work if a problem occurs with your computer. You can save the solution by clicking File on the menu bar and then clicking Save All. You can also click the Save All button on the Standard toolbar. When you save the solution, the computer saves any changes made to the files included in the solution. It also removes the asterisk that appears on the designer window's tab.

START HERE

To save the solution:

1. Click **File** on the menu bar and then click **Save All**. The asterisk is removed from the designer window's tab, indicating that all changes made to the form have been saved.

A-7 Close and Open a Solution

Before learning how to add a control to the form, you will close the current Einstein Solution and open a partially completed one. You should always close a solution when you are finished working on it because doing so ensures that all of the projects and files contained in the solution are closed.

START HERE

To close the current solution and open a partially completed one:

1. Click **File** on the menu bar. Notice that the menu contains a Close option and a Close Solution option. The Close option closes the designer window in the IDE; however, it does not close the solution itself. Only the Close Solution option closes the solution.

2. Click **Close Solution**. The Solution Explorer window indicates that no solution is currently open in the IDE.

3. You can also use the File menu to open an existing solution. Click **File** and then click **Open Project** to open the Open Project dialog box. Locate and then open the VB2017\ Chap01\Partial Einstein Solution folder.

4. The names of solution files end with .sln. Click **Einstein Solution.sln** in the list of filenames and then click the **Open** button. (Depending on how Windows is set up on your computer, you might not see the .sln extension on the filename. Refer to the Read This Before You Begin section to learn how to show/hide filename extensions.)

5. The Solution Explorer window indicates that the solution is open. If the designer window is not open, right-click **Main Form.vb** in the Solution Explorer window and then click **View Designer**.

6. Expand the **Resources** node in the Solution Explorer window. See Figure 1-17. The interface contains a picture box and two buttons.

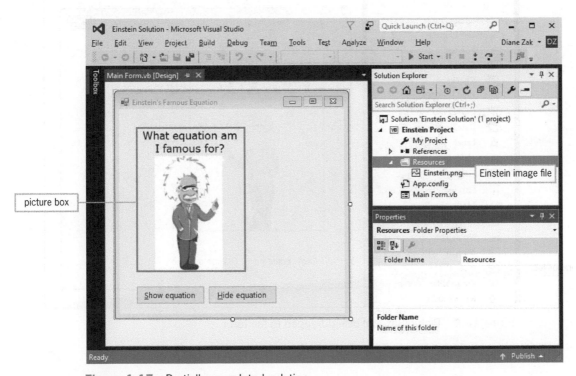

Figure 1-17 Partially completed solution

A-8 Add a Control to a Form

Two controls are missing from the interface shown in Figure 1-17: a picture box that displays Einstein's famous equation ($E = MC^2$) and an Exit button. You will add the picture box to the form first. You use a **picture box** to display an image on the form. In this case, the picture box will display the image stored in the VB2017\Chap01\Equation.png file. Figure 1-18 lists the most commonly used properties of a picture box.

Ch01-Adding a Control

Name	Purpose
Image	specify the image to display
Name	give the picture box a meaningful name (use pic as the ID)
SizeMode	specify how the image should be displayed
Visible	hide/display the picture box

Figure 1-18   Most commonly used properties of a picture box

START HERE

To add a picture box to the form:

1. Click the **Toolbox** tab and then click the Toolbox window's **Auto Hide** button. If necessary, expand the **Common Controls** node.

2. Click the **PictureBox** tool, but do not release the mouse button. Hold down the mouse button as you drag the tool to the form. See Figure 1-19.

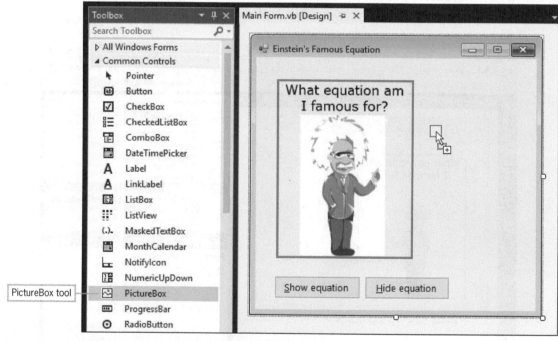

Figure 1-19   PictureBox tool being dragged to the form

3. Release the mouse button. The PictureBox tool (class) instantiates a picture box control (object) and places it on the form. The picture box's properties appear in the Properties list, and a box containing a triangle appears in the upper-right corner of the control. The box is referred to as the task box because when you click it, it displays a list of the tasks associated with the control. Each task in the list is associated with one or more properties. You can set the properties using the task list or the Properties window.

4. Click the **task box** on the PictureBox1 control. See Figure 1-20.

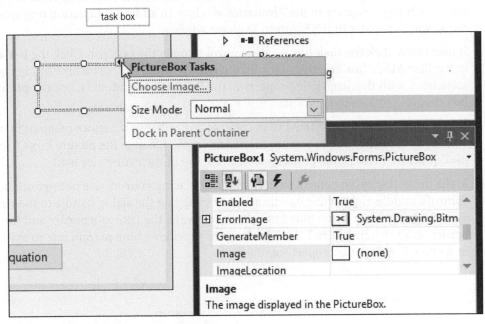

Figure 1-20   Open task list for a picture box

5. Click **Choose Image** to open the Select Resource dialog box. The Choose Image task is associated with the Image property in the Properties window.

6. To include the image file within the project itself, the Project resource file radio button must be selected in the dialog box. Verify that the radio button is selected, and then click the **Import** button to open the Open dialog box.

7. Open the VB2017\Chap01 folder. Click **Equation.png** in the list of filenames and then click the **Open** button. See Figure 1-21. (The Einstein.png file was already added to the project.)

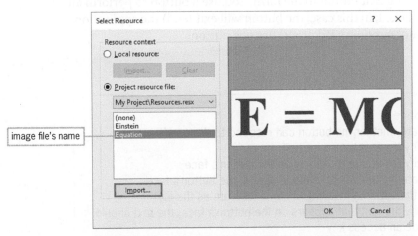

Figure 1-21   Completed Select Resource dialog box

8. Click the **OK** button. A small portion of the image appears in the picture box control on the form, and *Einstein_Project.My.Resources.Resources.Equation* (which indicates that the Equation.png file is stored in the project's Resources folder) appears in the control's Image property in the Properties window. In addition, Equation.png appears in the Resources folder in the Solution Explorer window.

9. If necessary, click the **task box** on the control to open the task list. Click the **list arrow** in the Size Mode box and then click **StretchImage** in the list. (The Size Mode task is associated with the SizeMode property in the Properties window.) Click the **picture box** control to close the task list.

10. The picture box will be referred to in code, so you will give it a more meaningful name. The three-character ID for picture box names is pic. Change the picture box's name to **picEquation**. (The Name property is near the top of the Properties list.)

11. Make the picEquation control slightly wider by placing your mouse pointer on the control's middle-right sizing handle and then dragging the sizing handle to the right. Stop dragging when a thin blue line appears between the control's border and the form's border, as shown in Figure 1-22. The designer provides a blue margin line to assist you in spacing the controls properly on the form.

blue margin line

$$E = MC^2$$

Figure 1-22   Result of dragging the sizing handle

12. Release the mouse button.

13. The picEquation control should not be visible when the interface appears on the screen after the application is started. Set the control's Visible property to **False**.

Now you will add the missing Exit button to the form. You use a button to perform an immediate action when clicked; in this case, the button will exit (end) the application. Figure 1-23 lists the most commonly used properties of a button.

Name	Purpose
Enabled	indicate whether the button can respond to the user's action
Font	specify the font to use for text
Image	specify the image to display on the button's face
ImageAlign	indicate the alignment of the image on the button's face
Name	give the button a meaningful name (use btn as the ID)
Text	specify the text that appears on the button's face; the text should include an access key

Figure 1-23   Most commonly used properties of a button

To add a button to the form:

1. Click the **Button** tool in the toolbox, and then drag the tool to the form. Position the tool to the right of the Hide equation button, using the blue margin and snap lines, as shown in Figure 1-24.

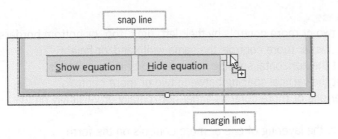

Figure 1-24 Correct position for the button control

2. Release the mouse button. The Button tool (class) instantiates a button control (object) and places it on the form. The button will be coded, so you will give it a more meaningful name. The three-character ID for button names is btn. Change the button's name to **btnExit**.

3. A button's Text property determines the text that appears on the button's face. As indicated earlier in Figure 1-23, the Text property should include an access key. You will learn about access keys in Chapter 2. For now, you just need to know that a button's access key allows the user to select the button by pressing the Alt key in combination with a character that appears in the Text property. You designate the character by preceding it with an ampersand. For example, to designate the letter x as the access key for an Exit button, you enter E&xit in the button's Text property. The access key will appear underlined on the button's face. Set the button's Text property to **E&xit**.

4. Now drag the Exit button's bottom sizing handle down slightly until the underline below the letter x is visible, and then release the mouse button.

5. Auto-hide the Toolbox and Properties windows.

6. Click **File** on the menu bar and then click **Save All**. (Or you can click the Save All button on the Standard toolbar.)

Mini-Quiz 1-5

1. What is the three-character ID used when naming picture boxes?

2. What is the three-character ID used when naming buttons?

3. What is the purpose of an access key?

4. What character is used to designate an access key?

1) pic 2) btn 3) It allows the user to access a control using the Alt key in combination with the control's access key. 4) &

A-9 Use the Format Menu

Visual Basic's Format menu provides many options that you can use when designing your user interface. Figure 1-25 lists each option and explains its purpose

Option	Purpose
Align	align two or more controls by their left, right, top, or bottom borders
Make Same Size	make two or more controls the same width and/or height
Horizontal Spacing	adjust the horizontal spacing between two or more controls
Vertical Spacing	adjust the vertical spacing between two or more controls
Center in Form	center one or more controls either horizontally or vertically on the form
Order	specify the layering of one or more controls on the form
Lock Controls	lock the controls in place on the form

Figure 1-25   Format menu options

Before you can use the Format menu to change the alignment or size of two or more controls, you first must select the controls. You should always select the reference control first. The **reference control** is the one whose size and/or location you want to match. The reference control will have white sizing handles, whereas the other selected controls will have black sizing handles. In the next set of steps, you will use the Format menu to adjust the Exit button's height (if necessary) to match the height of the Hide equation button. You will also use it to align the top border of the Exit button (if necessary) with the top border of the Hide equation button.

Ch01-Format Menu

START HERE ▷

To adjust the Exit button's height and top border:

1. Click the **Hide equation** button (the reference control) and then Ctrl+click the **Exit** button. Click **Format**, point to **Make Same Size**, and then click **Height**.

2. Next, click **Format**, point to **Align**, and then click **Tops**.

3. Click the form's **title bar** to deselect the selected controls.

A-10 Lock the Controls on the Form

A locked control can be deleted. It can be moved by setting its Location property.

After placing all of the controls in their appropriate locations, you should lock them on the form, which prevents them from being moved inadvertently as you work in the IDE. You can lock the controls by clicking the form (or any control on the form) and then clicking the Lock Controls option on the Format menu; you can follow the same procedure to unlock the controls. You can also lock and unlock the controls by right-clicking the form (or any control on the form) and then clicking Lock Controls on the context menu. When a control is locked, a small lock appears in the upper-left corner of the control.

START HERE ▷

To lock the controls on the form and then save the solution:

1. Right-click the **form** and then click **Lock Controls**. A small lock appears in the upper-left corner of the form. See Figure 1-26.

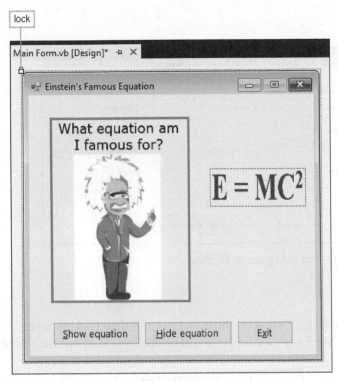

Figure 1-26   Completed interface with the controls locked on the form

2. Save the solution. Try dragging one of the controls to a different location on the form. You will not be able to do so.

A-11 Start and End an Application

Before you start an application for the first time, you should open the Project Designer window and verify the name of the **startup form**, which is the form that the computer automatically displays each time the application is started. You can open the Project Designer window by right-clicking My Project in the Solution Explorer window and then clicking Open on the context menu. Or, you can click Project on the menu bar and then click *<project name>* Properties on the menu.

To verify the startup form:

START HERE

1. Right-click **My Project** in the Solution Explorer window, and then click **Open** to open the Project Designer window.

2. Auto-hide the Solution Explorer window.

3. If necessary, click the **Application** tab to display the Application pane, which is shown in Figure 1-27. If frmMain does not appear in the Startup form list box, click the **Startup form** list arrow and then click **frmMain** in the list. (Do not be concerned if your Target framework list box shows a different value.)

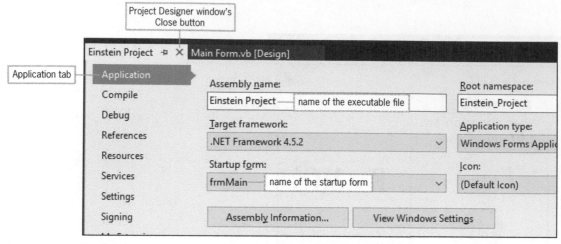

Figure 1-27 Application pane in the Project Designer window

The Start button looks like this:

▶ Start ▾

You can start an application by clicking Debug on the menu bar and then clicking Start Debugging. You can also press the F5 key on your keyboard or click the Start button on the Standard toolbar.

When you start a Windows Forms application from within the IDE, the computer automatically creates a file that can be run outside of the IDE, like the application files you ran in this chapter's Focus lesson. The file is referred to as an **executable file**. The executable file's name is the same as the project's name, except it ends with .exe. The name of the executable file for the Einstein Project, for example, is Einstein Project.exe. However, you can use the Project Designer window to change the executable file's name.

The computer stores the executable file in the project's bin\Debug folder. In this case, the Einstein Project.exe file is stored in the VB2017\Chap01\Einstein Solution\Einstein Project\ bin\Debug folder. When you are finished with an application, you typically give the user only the executable file because it does not allow the user to modify the application's code. To allow someone to modify the code, you need to provide the entire solution.

START HERE

To change the name of the executable file, and then start and end the application:

1. The Project Designer window should still be open. Change the filename in the Assembly name box to **My Einstein**. Save the solution and then close the Project Designer window by clicking its **Close** button. (If necessary, refer to Figure 1-27 for the location of the Close button.)

2. Click **Debug** on the menu bar and then click **Start Debugging** to start the application. (Or you can press the F5 key or use the Start button on the Standard toolbar.) See Figure 1-28. (Do not be concerned about any windows that appear at the bottom of the screen.)

form's Close button

disabled Maximize button

startup form

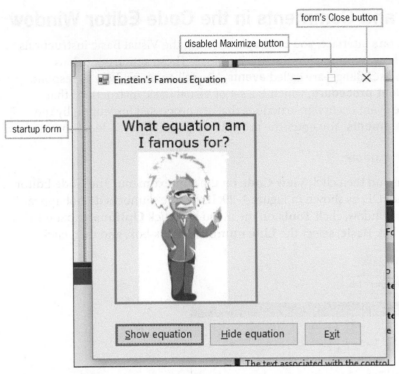

Einstein's Famous Equation

What equation am I famous for?

| Show equation | Hide equation | Exit |

Figure 1-28 Result of starting the Einstein application

3. Recall that the purpose of the Exit button is to allow the user to end the application. Click the **Exit** button. Nothing happens because you have not yet entered the instructions that tell the button how to respond when clicked.

4. Click the **Close** button on the form's title bar to stop the application. (You can also click the designer window to make it the active window, then click Debug on the menu bar, and then click Stop Debugging. Or you can click the Stop Debugging button on the Standard toolbar.)

 The Stop Debugging button looks like this: ■

Mini-Quiz 1-6

1. What menu provides options for centering two or more controls on the form?

2. To use the menu from Question 1 to make the btnCalc control the same size as the btnExit control, which of the two controls should you select first?

3. Why is it a good idea to lock the controls on the form?

4. What filename extension indicates that the file is an executable file that can be run outside of the IDE?

1) Format **2)** btnExit **3)** Doing so prevents you from inadvertently moving the control during design time. **4)** .exe

A-12 Enter Code and Comments in the Code Editor Window

After creating your application's interface, you can begin entering the Visual Basic instructions (code) that tell the controls how to respond to the user's actions. Those actions—such as clicking, double-clicking, and scrolling—are called **events**. You tell an object how to respond to an event by writing an **event procedure**, which is a set of Visual Basic instructions that are processed only when the event occurs. Instructions that are processed (executed) by the computer are also called **statements**. You enter the procedure's code in the Code Editor window.

START HERE

To open the Code Editor window:

1. Right-click the **form** and then click **View Code** on the context menu. The Code Editor window opens in the IDE, as shown in Figure 1-29. If the line numbers do not appear in your Code Editor window, click **Tools** on the menu bar, click **Options**, expand the **Text Editor** node, click **Basic**, select the **Line numbers** check box, and then click the **OK** button.

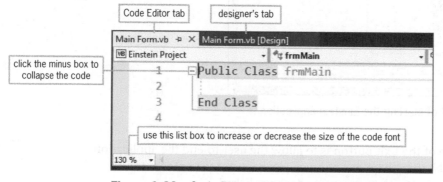

Figure 1-29   Code Editor window opened in the IDE

The Code Editor window in Figure 1-29 contains the Class statement, which is used to define a class in Visual Basic. In this case, the class is the frmMain form. The Class statement begins with the Public Class frmMain clause and ends with the End Class clause. Within the Class statement, you enter the code to tell the form and its objects how to react to the user's actions.

The Public keyword in the Class statement indicates that the class can be used by code defined outside of the class.

If the Code Editor window contains many lines of code, you might want to hide the sections of code that you are not currently working with. You hide a section (or region) of code by clicking the minus box that appears next to it. To unhide a region of code, you click the plus box that appears next to the code. Hiding and unhiding the code is also referred to as collapsing and expanding the code, respectively.

START HERE

To collapse and expand a region of code:

1. Click the **minus box** that appears next to the Public Class frmMain clause. Doing this collapses the Class statement, as shown in Figure 1-30.

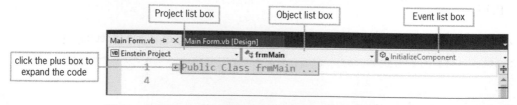

Figure 1-30   Code collapsed in the Code Editor window

2. Click the **plus box** to expand the code.

As Figure 1-30 indicates, the Code Editor window contains three dropdown list boxes named Project, Object, and Event. The Project box contains the name of the current project, Einstein Project. The Object box lists the names of the objects included in the user interface, and the Event box lists the events to which the selected object is capable of responding. To code the Exit button so that it ends the application when it is clicked by the user, you select btnExit in the Object list box and select Click in the Event list box.

To select the btnExit control's Click event:

START HERE

1. Click the **Object** list arrow and then click **btnExit** in the list. Click the **Event** list arrow and then click **Click** in the list. A code template for the btnExit control's Click event procedure appears in the Code Editor window. See Figure 1-31.

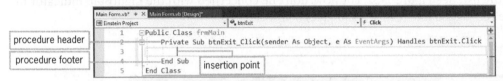

procedure header

procedure footer

insertion point

Figure 1-31   btnExit control's Click event procedure

The Code Editor provides the code template to help you follow the rules of the Visual Basic language. The rules of a programming language are called its **syntax**. The first line in the code template is called the **procedure header**, and the last line is called the **procedure footer**. The procedure header begins with the keywords `Private Sub`. A **keyword** is a word that has a special meaning in a programming language, and it appears in a different color from the rest of the code. The `Private` keyword in Figure 1-31 indicates that the button's Click event procedure can be used only within the class defined in the current Code Editor window. The `Sub` keyword is an abbreviation of the term **sub procedure**, which is a block of code that performs a specific task.

Following the `Sub` keyword is the name of the object, an underscore, the name of the event, and parentheses containing some text. For now, you do not have to be concerned with the text that appears between the parentheses. After the closing parenthesis is the following Handles clause: `Handles btnExit.Click`. This clause indicates that the procedure handles (or is associated with) the btnExit control's Click event. It tells the computer to process the procedure only when the btnExit control is clicked.

The code template ends with the procedure footer, which contains the keywords `End Sub`. You enter your Visual Basic instructions at the location of the insertion point, which appears between the Private Sub and End Sub clauses in Figure 1-31. The Code Editor automatically indents the lines between the procedure header and footer. Indenting the lines within a procedure makes the instructions easier to read and is a common programming practice. In the next section, you will enter an instruction that tells the btnExit object to end the application when it is clicked.

The Me.Close() Statement

The **Me.Close() statement** tells the computer to close the current form. If the current form is the only form in the application, closing it terminates the entire application. In the instruction, `Me` is a keyword that refers to the current form, and `Close` is one of the methods available in Visual Basic. A **method** is a predefined procedure that you can call (or invoke) when needed. To have the computer close the current form when the user clicks the Exit button, you enter the `Me.Close()` statement in the button's Click event procedure. Notice the empty set of parentheses after the method's name in the statement. The parentheses are required when calling some Visual Basic methods; however, depending on the method, the parentheses might or might not be empty. If you forget to enter the empty set of parentheses, the Code Editor will enter them for you when you move the insertion point to another line in the Code Editor window.

To code the btnExit_Click procedure:

1. You can type the Me.Close() statement on your own or use the Code Editor window's IntelliSense feature. In this set of steps, you will use the IntelliSense feature. Type **me.** (be sure to type the period, but don't press Enter). When you type the period, the IntelliSense feature displays a list of properties, methods, and so on from which you can select.

    Note: If the list of choices does not appear, the IntelliSense feature might have been turned off on your computer system. To turn it on, click Tools on the menu bar, click Options, expand the Text Editor node, click Basic, select the Auto list members check box, and then click the OK button.

2. Type **clo** (but don't press Enter). The IntelliSense feature highlights the Close method in the list. See Figure 1-32. For now, don't be concerned with the LightBulb indicator or the red jagged line (called a squiggle) below Me.clo.

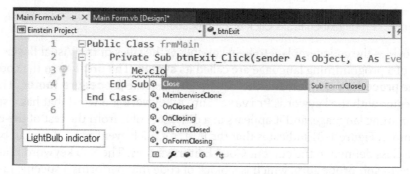

Figure 1-32   List displayed by the IntelliSense feature

3. Press **Tab** to include the Close method in the statement and then press **Enter**. See Figure 1-33.

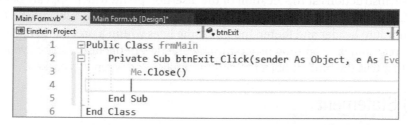

Figure 1-33   Completed btnExit_Click procedure

It is a good idea to test a procedure after you have coded it so you will know where to look if an error occurs. You can test the Exit button's Click event procedure by starting the application and then clicking the button. When the button is clicked, the computer will process the Me.Close() statement contained in the procedure.

START HERE

The Start
button looks
like this:

▶ Start ▾

To test the btnExit_Click procedure:

1. Save the solution and then click the **Start** button on the Standard toolbar (or press the F5 key). The user interface appears on the screen.

2. Click the **Exit** button to end the application.

Assignment Statements and Comments

Earlier in this chapter, you learned how to use the Properties window to set an object's properties during **design time**, which is when you are building the interface. You can also set an object's properties during **run time**, which occurs while the application is running; you do this by using an assignment statement. An **assignment statement** is one of many different types of Visual Basic instructions. Its purpose is to assign a value to something, such as to the property of an object.

The syntax of an assignment statement is shown in Figure 1-34 along with examples of using the syntax. In the syntax, *object* and *property* are the names of the object and property, respectively, to which you want the value of the *expression* assigned. The expression can be a keyword, a number, or a **string literal**, which is defined as zero or more characters enclosed in quotation marks. The expression can also be a calculation; you will learn how to assign calculations in Chapter 3. You use the dot member access operator (a period) to separate the object name from the property name. The operator indicates that the *property* is a member of the *object*. You use an equal sign between the *object.property* information and the *expression*. The equal sign in an assignment statement is called the **assignment operator**. When the computer processes an assignment statement, it assigns the value of the expression that appears on the right side of the assignment operator to the object and property that appear on the left side of the assignment operator.

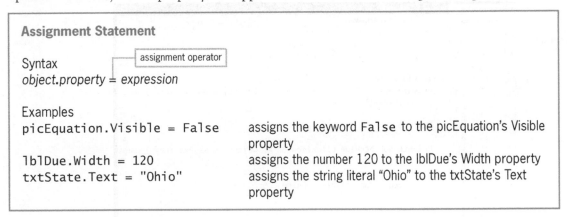

```
Assignment Statement

Syntax                    ┌─ assignment operator ─┐
object.property = expression

Examples
picEquation.Visible = False      assigns the keyword False to the picEquation's Visible
                                 property

lblDue.Width = 120               assigns the number 120 to the lblDue's Width property
txtState.Text = "Ohio"           assigns the string literal "Ohio" to the txtState's Text
                                 property
```

Figure 1-34 Syntax and examples of assigning a value to a property during run time

You will use assignment statements to code the btnShow_Click and btnHide_Click procedures. In each procedure, you will enter a comment that indicates the procedure's purpose. A **comment** is a line of text that serves to internally document a program. You create a comment in Visual Basic by placing an apostrophe (') before the text that represents the comment. The computer ignores everything that appears after the apostrophe on that line. Although it is not required, some programmers use a space to separate the apostrophe from the comment text; they also begin the comment text with a capital letter and end it with a period. You will use these conventions in this book.

To enter a comment and code in both procedures:

START HERE

1. Use the Object and Event boxes to open the code template for the btnShow object's Click event. Type **' Show Einstein's equation.** (be sure to type the apostrophe followed by a space) and press **Enter** twice.

2. Type **piceq** to highlight picEquation in the list and then press **Tab**. Type **.v** (a period followed by the letter v) to highlight Visible in the list and then press **Tab**. Type **=t** to highlight True in the list and then press **Enter**. The picEquation.Visible = True statement appears in the procedure.

3. Save the solution and then start the application. Click the **Show equation** button to display the image stored in the picEquation control, and then click the **Exit** button.

4. On your own, open the code template for the btnHide object's Click event. Type **' Hide Einstein's equation**. and press **Enter** twice. Now enter the picEquation.Visible = False statement in the procedure.

5. Save the solution and then start the application. Click the **Show equation** button to display the image stored in the picEquation control, and then click the **Hide equation** button to hide the image.

6. Now use the Show equation button's access key to show the image again. Press and hold down the **Alt** key as you tap the letter **s**, and then release the **Alt** key. The Alt+s combination tells the computer to process (execute) the statements contained in the button's Click event procedure.

7. Use the Hide equation button's access key (**Alt+h**) to hide the image, and then use the Exit button's access key (**Alt+x**) to end the application.

8. Click **immediately before the letter P** in Line 1 of the Code Editor window and then press Enter. **Enter** the additional comments shown in Figure 1-35. Replace <your name> and <current date> with your name and the current date, respectively.

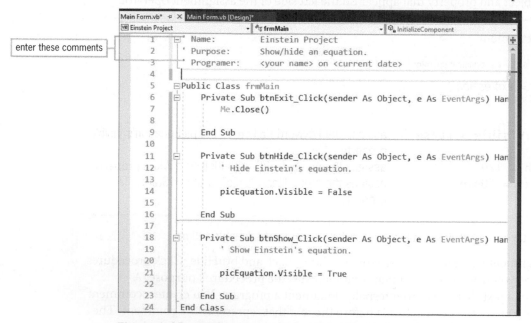

enter these comments

```
Main Form.vb*  ⧉ ✕  Main Form.vb [Design]*
VB Einstein Project                          ▾ ⚙ frmMain                           ▾ ⚙ InitializeComponent            ▾
    1       ' Name:          Einstein Project
    2       ' Purpose:       Show/hide an equation.
    3       ' Programer:     <your name> on <current date>
    4
    5     □Public Class frmMain
    6     □    Private Sub btnExit_Click(sender As Object, e As EventArgs) Han
    7              Me.Close()
    8
    9          End Sub
   10
   11     □    Private Sub btnHide_Click(sender As Object, e As EventArgs) Han
   12              ' Hide Einstein's equation.
   13
   14              picEquation.Visible = False
   15
   16          End Sub
   17
   18     □    Private Sub btnShow_Click(sender As Object, e As EventArgs) Han
   19              ' Show Einstein's equation.
   20
   21              picEquation.Visible = True
   22
   23          End Sub
   24     End Class
```

Figure 1-35 Additional comments entered in the Code Editor window

9. Save the solution.

A-13 Print an Application's Code and Interface

It is a good idea to print a copy of your application's code for future reference. To print the code, the Code Editor window must be the active (current) window. You might also want to print a copy of the user interface; you can do this using the Window's Snipping Tool, as long as the designer window is the active window.

To print the code and interface:

START HERE

1. The Code Editor window is currently the active window. Click **File** on the menu bar, and then click **Print** to open the Print dialog box. If your computer is connected to a printer, select the appropriate printer (if necessary) and then click the **Print** button; otherwise, click the **Cancel** button.

Ch01-Snipping Tool

2. Close the Code Editor window. Click the **Start** button on the Windows 10 taskbar. Click **Windows Accessories** on the Start menu and then click **Snipping Tool**. Click the **New** button. Hold down your left mouse button as you drag your mouse pointer around the form, and then release the mouse button. Click **File** on the Snipping Tool's menu bar and then click **Print**. If your computer is connected to a printer, select the appropriate printer (if necessary) and then click the **Print** button; otherwise, click the **Cancel** button. Close the Snipping Tool window without saving the snip.

3. Close the solution.

A-14 Exit Visual Studio and Run an Executable File

You can exit Visual Studio using either the Close button on its title bar or the Exit option on its File menu. You can run an application's executable (.exe) file by locating the file in the project's bin\Debug folder and then double-clicking it.

To exit Visual Studio and then run the My Einstein.exe file:

START HERE

1. Click **File** and then click **Exit**.

2. Open the VB2017\Chap01\Partial Einstein Solution\Einstein Project\bin\Debug folder, and then double-click the **My Einstein.exe** file. Test the application to verify that it works correctly.

Mini-Quiz 1-7

1. What is an event procedure?

2. What is a keyword?

3. If an application contains only one form, what Visual Basic statement tells the computer to end the application?

4. Write an assignment statement that assigns the keyword `False` to the btnPrint control's Enabled property.

5. In the Code Editor window, what character designates that the text that follows it is a comment?

1) A set of instructions processed only when its associated event occurs. **2)** A word that has a special meaning in a programming language. **3)** Me.Close() **4)** btnPrint.Enabled = False **5)** an apostrophe

Summary

- Programs are the step-by-step instructions that tell a computer how to perform a task.

- Programmers use various programming languages to communicate with the computer.

- Programmers are responsible for translating a problem's solution into instructions that the computer can understand.

- Programmers rigorously test a program before releasing the program to the user.

- An object-oriented programming language, such as Visual Basic, enables programmers to use objects (for example, check boxes and buttons) to accomplish a program's goal. An object is anything that can be seen, touched, or used.

- Every object in an object-oriented program is instantiated (created) from a class, which is a pattern that tells the computer how the object should look and behave. An object is referred to as an instance of the class.

- The four windows you use most often when designing your application's GUI are the designer window, Toolbox window, Solution Explorer window, and Properties window.

- Each tool in the toolbox represents a class.

- Each object has a set of properties that determines its appearance and behavior.

- Windows applications in Visual Basic are composed of solutions, projects, and files.

- You enter your application's program instructions in the Code Editor window.

- An object's name, which is entered in its Name property, can be used to refer to the object in code.

- To start Visual Studio 2017:

  Click the Start button on the Windows 10 taskbar. Locate and then click Visual Studio 2017.

- To change the default environment settings:

  Click Tools, click Import and Export Settings, select the Reset all settings radio button, click the Next button, select the appropriate radio button, click the Next button, click the settings collection you want to use, click the Finish button, and then click the Close button to close the Import and Export Settings Wizard dialog box.

- To reset the window layout in the IDE:

  Click Window, click Reset Window Layout, and then click the Yes button.

- To configure Visual Studio:

  Click Tools, click Options, click the Projects and Solutions node, and then use the information shown earlier in Figure 1-9 to select and deselect the appropriate check boxes. Next, expand the Text Editor node, expand the Basic node, expand the Code Style node, click Naming, and then change the Severity column in the Types and Non-Field Members rows to None. Click the Code Style node, and then change the Preference column in the Qualify property access with 'Me' and Qualify method access with 'Me' rows to Prefer 'Me.' Finally, click the Debugging node, deselect the Step over properties and operators (Managed only) check box, deselect the Enable Diagnostic tools while debugging check box, deselect the Show elapsed time PerfTip while debugging check box, and then click the OK button to close the Options dialog box.

- To create a Visual Basic 2017 Windows Forms application:

  Start Visual Studio 2017. Click File, click New Project, click the Visual Basic node, and then click Windows Forms App (.NET Framework). Enter an appropriate name and location in the Name and Location boxes, respectively. If necessary, select the Create directory for solution check box. Enter an appropriate name in the Solution name box and then click the OK button.

- To size a window:

  Position your mouse pointer on one of the window's borders and then drag the border.

- To close and open a window in the IDE:

  Close the window by clicking the Close button on its title bar. Use the appropriate option on the View menu to open the window.

- To auto-hide a window in the IDE:

  Click the Auto Hide (vertical pushpin) button on the window's title bar.

- To temporarily display an auto-hidden window in the IDE:

  Click the window's tab.

- To permanently display an auto-hidden window in the IDE:

  Click the window's tab to display the window, and then click the Auto Hide (horizontal pushpin) button on the window's title bar.

- The code associated with a form is stored in a form file whose filename ends with .vb. All files with a .vb filename extension are referred to as source files because they contain Visual Basic code.

- To set the value of a property:

  Select the object whose property you want to set and then click the appropriate property in the Properties list. Type the new property value in the selected property's Settings box, or choose the value from the list, color palette, or dialog box.

- To change the name of a form file:

  Set the form file's File Name property in the Properties window.

- To change an object's name:

  Set the object's Name property.

- To specify the type, style, and size of the font used to display text on the form:

  Set the form's Font property.

- To disable/enable the form's Maximize button:

  Set the form's MaximizeBox property.

- To specify the starting location of the form:

  Set the form's StartPosition property.

- To control the text appearing in the form's title bar:

  Set the form's Text property.

- To save a solution:

  Click File on the menu bar and then click Save All. You can also click the Save All button on the Standard toolbar.

- To close a solution:

  Click File on the menu bar and then click Close Solution.

- To open an existing solution:

  Click File on the menu bar and then click Open Project. Locate and then open the application's solution folder. Click the solution filename, which ends with .sln. Click the Open button. If the designer window is not open, right-click the form file's name in the Solution Explorer window and then click View Designer.

- To add a control to a form:

  Click a tool in the toolbox, but do not release the mouse button. Hold down the mouse button as you drag the tool to the form, and then release the mouse button. As demonstrated in the Ch01-Adding a Control video, you can also click a tool and then click the form. In addition, you can click a tool, place the mouse pointer on the form, and then press the left mouse button and drag the mouse pointer until the control is the desired size. You can also double-click a tool in the toolbox.

- To display a graphic in a control in the user interface:

  Use the PictureBox tool to instantiate a picture box control. Use the task box or Properties window to set the control's Image and SizeMode properties.

- To display a standard button that performs an action when clicked:

  Use the Button tool to instantiate a button control.

- An access key allows the user to select a control by pressing the Alt key in combination with the access key.

- To assign an access key to a button:

  In the button's Text property, precede the access key character with an ampersand (&).

- To select multiple controls on a form:

  Click the first control you want to select, and then Ctrl+click each of the other controls you want to select. You can also select a group of controls on the form by placing the mouse pointer slightly above and to the left of the first control you want to select, and then pressing the left mouse button and dragging. A dotted rectangle appears as you drag. When all of the controls you want to select are within (or at least touched by) the dotted rectangle, release the mouse button. All of the controls surrounded or touched by the dotted rectangle will be selected.

- To cancel the selection of one or more controls:

  You cancel the selection of one control by pressing and holding down the Ctrl key as you click the control. You cancel the selection of all of the selected controls by releasing the Ctrl key and then clicking the form or any unselected control on the form.

- To make two or more controls on the form the same size:

  Select the reference control and then select the other controls you want to size. Click Format on the menu bar, point to Make Same Size, and then click the appropriate option.

- To align the borders of two or more controls on the form:

  Select the reference control and then select the other controls you want to align. Click Format on the menu bar, point to Align, and then click the appropriate option.

- To lock/unlock the controls on a form:

  Click the form (or any control on the form), click Format, and then click Lock Controls. Or you can right-click the form (or any control on the form) and then click Lock Controls on the context menu.

- To verify or change the names of the startup form and executable file:

  Use the Application pane in the Project Designer window. You can open the Project Designer window by right-clicking My Project in the Solution Explorer window, and then clicking Open on the context menu. Or, you can click Project on the menu bar and then click *<project name>* Properties on the menu.

- To start and stop an application:

  You can start an application by clicking Debug on the menu bar and then clicking Start Debugging. You can also press the F5 key on your keyboard or click the Start button on the Standard toolbar. You can stop an application by clicking the form's Close button. You can also first make the designer window the active window, then click Debug, and then click Stop Debugging.

- When you start a Visual Basic application, the computer automatically creates an executable file that can be run outside of the IDE. The file's name ends with .exe.

- You tell an object how to respond to the user's actions by writing an event procedure, which can contain comments and Visual Basic statements.

- To open the Code Editor window:

  Right-click the form and then click View Code on the context menu.

- To show/hide the line numbers in the Code Editor window:

  Click Tools, click Options, expand the Text Editor node, click Basic, select/deselect the Line numbers check box, and then click OK.

- To collapse or expand a region of code in the Code Editor window:

  Click the minus box next to the region of code to collapse the code; click the plus box to expand the code.

- To display an object's event procedure in the Code Editor window:

  Open the Code Editor window. Use the Object list box to select the object's name, and then use the Event list box to select the event.

- To allow the user to close the current form while an application is running:

  Enter the `Me.Close()` statement in an event procedure.

- To turn on/off the IntelliSense feature in the Code Editor window:

  Click Tools, click Options, expand the Text Editor node, click Basic, select/deselect the Auto list members check box, and then click the OK button.

- During run time, you can use an assignment statement to assign a value to an object's property.

- All comments in the Code Editor window begin with an apostrophe.

- To print an application's code:

  With the Code Editor window the active window, click File on the menu bar and then click Print. Select the printer (if necessary) and then click Print.

- To print an application's interface:

  Make the designer the active window. Click the Start button on the Windows 10 taskbar, click Windows Accessories, and then click Snipping Tool. Click the New button. Drag your mouse pointer around the form and then release the mouse button. Click File, select the printer (if necessary), and then click Print.

- To exit Visual Studio:

  Click the Close button on the Visual Studio title bar. You can also click File on the menu bar and then click Exit.

- To run an application's executable (.exe) file outside of the IDE:

  Locate the file in the project's bin\Debug folder and then double-click it.

Key Terms

Application—a GUI along with its program instructions

Assignment operator—the equal sign in an assignment statement

Assignment statement—an instruction that assigns a value to something, such as to the property of an object

Camel case—used when entering object names; the practice of entering the object's ID characters in lowercase and then capitalizing the first letter of each subsequent word in the name

Class—a pattern that the computer uses to create (instantiate) an object

Class definition—a block of code that specifies (or defines) an object's appearance and behavior

Code—program instructions

Code Editor window—where you enter the program instructions (code) for your application

Coding—the process of translating a solution into a language that the computer can understand

Comment—a line of text that serves to internally document a program; begins with an apostrophe

Computer program—the directions given to computers; also called a *program*

Controls—objects (such as a picture box or a button) added to a form

Design time—occurs when you are building an interface

Designer window—used to create an application's GUI

Dot member access operator—the period used to indicate a hierarchy

Event procedure—a set of Visual Basic instructions that tell an object how to respond to an event

Events—actions to which an object can respond; examples include clicking and double-clicking

Executable file—a file that can be run outside of the IDE; the filename ends with the .exe extension

Form—the foundation for the user interface in a Windows Forms application; also called a *Windows Form object*

Form file—a file that contains the code associated with a Windows form

Graphical user interface—what the user sees and interacts with while your program is running; also called a *GUI*

GUI—graphical user interface

IDE—integrated development environment

Instance—an object created (instantiated) from a class

Instantiated—the process of creating an object from a class

Integrated development environment—an environment that contains all of the tools and features you need to create, run, and test your programs; also called an *IDE*

Keyword—a word that has a special meaning in a programming language

Me.Close() statement—tells the computer to close the current form

Method—a predefined procedure that you can call (invoke) when needed

Name property—assigns a name to an object; the name can be used to refer to the object in code

Namespace—a block of memory cells inside the computer; contains the code that defines a group of related classes

Object—anything that can be seen, touched, or used

Object-oriented programming language—a programming language that allows the programmer to use objects to accomplish a program's goal

OOP—object-oriented programming

Picture box—used to display an image

Procedure footer—the last line in a procedure

Procedure header—the first line in a procedure

Program—the directions given to computers; also called a *computer program*

Programmers—the people who write computer programs

Programming—the process of giving a mechanism the directions to accomplish a task

Programming languages—languages used to communicate with a computer

Properties—the attributes that determine an object's appearance and behavior

Properties window—lists an object's attributes (properties)

Reference control—the first control selected in a group of controls; this is the control whose size and/or location you want the other selected controls to match

Run time—occurs while an application is running

Solution Explorer—displays a list of the projects contained in the current solution and the items contained in each project

Source files—files that contain program instructions; in Visual Basic, the names of source files end with .vb

Startup form—the form that appears automatically when an application is started

Statements—Visual Basic instructions that are processed (executed) by the computer

String literal—zero or more characters enclosed in quotation marks

Sub procedure—a block of code that performs a specific task

Syntax—the rules of a programming language

Toolbox window—contains the tools used when creating an interface (each tool represents a class); referred to more simply as the *toolbox*

Review Questions

1. A(n) _____ is an environment that contains all of the tools and features you need to create, run, and test your programs.

    a. GUI   c. UDE
    b. IDE   d. user interface

2. When using an analogy involving a blueprint and a tree house, the _____ is the class, and the _____ is an object created from it.

    a. blueprint, tree house   b. tree house, blueprint

3. You create your application's user interface in the _____ window in the IDE.

    a. designer   c. GUI
    b. form   d. interface

4. Each tool in the toolbox represents a class from which an object can be instantiated.

    a. True   b. False

5. Which window is used to set the characteristics that control an object's appearance and behavior?

    a. Characteristics   c. Properties
    b. Object   d. Toolbox

6. Which window lists the projects and files included in a solution?

    a. Object   c. Properties
    b. Project   d. Solution Explorer

7. Which of the following is an invalid name for an object?

    a. picMy.Dog   c. lbl2017
    b. btnCalcSalesTax   d. All of the above are invalid names.

8. Which property controls the text displayed in a form's title bar?

    a. Caption   c. Title
    b. Text   d. TitleBar

9. Which property is used to give a form file a more meaningful name?

    a. File   c. Form Name
    b. File Name   d. Name

10. Which property determines the initial position of a form when the application is started?

    a. InitialLocation   c. StartLocation
    b. Location   d. StartPosition

11. Which property is used to disable the Maximize button on a form's title bar?

   a. ButtonMaximize

   b. Maximize

   c. MaximizeBox

   d. MaximizeButton

12. Which property is used to give a button control a more meaningful name?

   a. Application

   b. Caption

   c. Name

   d. Text

13. The text displayed on a button's face is stored in which property?

   a. Caption

   b. Label

   c. Name

   d. Text

14. When a form has been modified since the last time it was saved, what appears on its tab in the designer window?

   a. an ampersand (&)

   b. an asterisk (*)

   c. a percent sign (%)

   d. a plus sign (+)

15. Which option on the File menu closes the current solution?

   a. Close

   b. Close All

   c. Close Solution

   d. Exit Solution

16. What is the three-character extension appended to solution filenames in Visual Basic?

   a. .prg

   b. .sln

   c. .src

   d. .vbs

17. Which of the following can be accomplished using the Format menu?

   a. aligning the borders of two or more controls

   b. centering one or more controls horizontally on the form

   c. making two or more controls the same size

   d. All of the above.

18. When two or more controls are selected, how can you tell which one is the reference control?

   a. The reference control has white sizing handles.

   b. The reference control has black sizing handles.

   c. The reference control displays the number 1 in the left corner.

   d. You can't tell. You just need to remember which control you selected first.

19. Which statement terminates an application that contains only one form?

   a. `Me.Close()`

   b. `Me.Done()`

   c. `Me.Finish()`

   d. `Me.Stop()`

20. When you start a Windows Forms application in the IDE, the computer saves the application's executable (.exe) file in the _____ folder.

    a. project   c. project's bin\Debug

    b. project's bin   d. project's Debug\bin

21. Explain the difference between a form's Text property and its Name property.

22. Explain the difference between a form file and a form.

23. What does the dot member access operator indicate in the text *System.Windows .Forms.Label*?

24. Define the term "syntax."

25. How do you verify the name of the startup form?

Exercises

INTRODUCTORY

1. Create a Windows Forms application. Use the following names for the project and solution, respectively: Florist Project and Florist Solution. Save the application in the VB2017\Chap01 folder.

    a. Change the form file's name to Main Form.vb.

    b. Change the form's Name property to frmMain.

    c. Change the form's Font property to Segoe UI, 9pt.

    d. Change the form's MaximizeBox property to False.

    e. Change the form's StartPosition property to CenterScreen.

    f. Change the form's Text property to Florist Haven.

    g. Add a button to the form. Change the button's Name and Text properties to btnExit and E&xit, respectively. Position the button in the lower-right corner of the form.

    h. Add three picture boxes to the form. PictureBox1 should display the image stored in the Florist.png file, which is located in the VB2017\Chap01 folder. PictureBox2 and PictureBox3 should display the images stored in the Message.png and Hours.png files, respectively. Use the interface shown in Figure 1-36 as a guide when sizing and positioning the picture boxes.

    i. Lock the controls on the form.

    j. Code the Exit button and then add comments to the Code Editor window, as shown in Figure 1-36.

    k. Open the Project Designer window and verify the name of the startup form, which should be frmMain. Also change the name of the application's executable file to MyFlorist. Save the solution and then close the Project Designer window.

    l. Start the application and then test the Exit button.

    m. Print the application's code and interface, and then close the solution.

    n. Verify that the MyFlorist.exe file works correctly. (The file is contained in the VB2017\Chap01\Florist Solution\Florist Project\bin\Debug folder.)

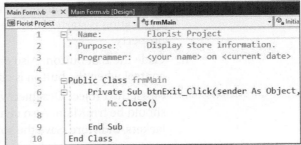

Figure 1-36 Interface and code for Exercise 1

2. If necessary, complete Exercise 1. Use Windows to rename the Florist Solution folder to INTRODUCTORY Florist Solution-Modified. Open the Florist Solution.sln file contained in the VB2017\ Chap01\Florist Solution-Modified folder. If necessary, open the designer window.

a. Change the name of the picture box that displays the hours to picHours.

b. The picHours control should not be visible when the application is started and the interface appears on the screen; set the appropriate property.

c. Unlock the controls and then modify the interface as shown in Figure 1-37. Change the buttons' names to btnShow and btnHide, and then lock the controls.

d. Code the Show hours and Hide hours buttons. The Show hours button should display the picHours control when the button is clicked; the Hide hours button should hide the picHours control.

e. Save the solution and then start the application. Test the buttons and then close the solution.

Figure 1-37 Interface for Exercise 2

3. Create a Windows Forms application. Use the following names for the project and INTRODUCTORY solution, respectively: Jackets Project and Jackets Solution. Save the application in the VB2017\Chap01 folder.

a. Change the form file's name to Main Form.vb.

b. Change the form's Name property to frmMain.

c. Change the form's Font property to Segoe UI, 9pt.

d. Change the form's MaximizeBox property to False.

e. Change the form's StartPosition property to CenterScreen.

f. Create the interface shown in Figure 1-38. The images in the picture boxes are stored in the BlackJacket.png and SizeChart.png files; both files are contained in the VB2017\Chap01 folder.

g. Lock the controls on the form. The picChart control should not be visible when the application is started and the interface appears on the screen; set the appropriate property.

h. Code the Exit button. Also code the Size chart button so that it displays the picChart control when the button is clicked. Include comments in the Code Editor window.

i. Open the Project Designer window and verify the name of the startup form, which should be frmMain. Also change the name of the application's executable file to JacketsAndMore. Save the solution and then close the Project Designer window.

j. Start and test the application. Close the solution and then verify that the JacketsAndMore.exe file works correctly.

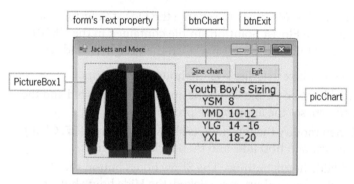

Figure 1-38 Interface for Exercise 3

INTERMEDIATE

4. Open the Colors Solution.sln file contained in the VB2017\Chap01\Colors Solution folder. If necessary, open the designer window. The interface contains one label control and two buttons. You can use a label control to display information that you do not want the user to change during run time. You will learn more about label controls in Chapter 2.

a. Add two buttons to the form, as shown in Figure 1-39, and then lock the controls on the form. Change the names of the buttons to btnGreen and btnRed; also change their Text properties.

b. Open the Code Editor window, which contains comments and the code for the btnBlue_Click and btnExit_Click procedures. The btnBlue_Click procedure assigns the string literal "Azul" to the Text property of the lblSpanish control. Start the application. Click the Blue button; the word Azul appears in the label control on the form. Click the Exit button.

c. Using the btnBlue_Click procedure as a guide, code the Click event procedures for the btnGreen and btnRed controls. (Hint: The Spanish words for Green and Red are Verde and Rojo, respectively.)

d. Save the solution and then start and test the application.

Figure 1-39 Interface for Exercise 4

INTERMEDIATE

5. If necessary, complete Exercise 4. Use Windows to rename the Colors Solution folder to Colors Solution-Modified. Open the Colors Solution.sln file contained in the VB2017\Chap01\Colors Solution-Modified folder. If necessary, open the designer window. Locate the btnBlue_Click procedure in the Code Editor window. In the line above the procedure footer, enter the following assignment statement: `lblSpanish.BackColor = Color.Blue`. Save the solution and then start the application. Click the Blue button; the word Azul appears in the label control and the control's background color changes to blue. Click the Exit button. Modify the code in the btnGreen_Click and btnRed_Click procedures so that each changes the label control's background color appropriately. Save the solution and then start and test the application.

INTERMEDIATE

6. Open the Emoji Solution.sln file contained in the VB2017\Chap01\Emoji Solution folder. If necessary, open the designer window. The interface contains one label control and one button. You can use a label control to display information that you do not want the user to change during run time. You will learn more about label controls in Chapter 2.

   a. Add five picture boxes to the form, as shown in Figure 1-40. Name the picture boxes picCrying, picHappy, picLove, picSad, and picTired. The picture boxes should display the images stored in the following files, which are contained in the VB2017\Chap01 folder: Crying.png, Happy.png, Love.png, Sad.png, and Tired.png.

   b. Lock the controls on the form. Open the Code Editor window, which contains comments and the code for the btnExit_Click procedure. When the user clicks the picCrying control, its Click event procedure should assign the string literal "I am crying." to the lblMessage control's Text property; code the procedure. (Hint: Refer to the examples shown earlier in Figure 1-34.)

   c. Using the messages included in Figure 1-40, code the Click event procedures for the remaining picture boxes. Save the solution and then start and test the application.

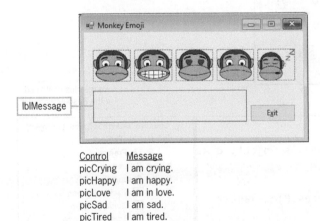

Control | Message
picCrying | I am crying.
picHappy | I am happy.
picLove | I am in love.
picSad | I am sad.
picTired | I am tired.

Figure 1-40   Interface and messages for Exercise 6

ADVANCED

7. If necessary, complete Exercise 3. Use Windows to rename the Jacket Solution folder to Jackets Solution-Modified. Open the Jackets Solution.sln file contained in the VB2017\Chap01\Jackets Solution-Modified folder. If necessary, open the designer window.

   a. Unlock the controls and then modify the interface, as shown in Figure 1-41.

   b. Change the name of the picture box that displays the jacket to picJacket. Name the four new buttons btnBlack, btnBlue, btnBrown, and btnRed.

   c. Each of the four color buttons will display an image of an appropriately colored jacket in the picJacket control. The different colored images are stored in the

BlackJacket.png, BlueJacket.png, BrownJacket.png, and RedJacket.png files, which are contained in the VB2017\Chap01 folder. In Exercise 3, you added the BlackJacket.png file to the project; now you need to add the other three files. Use the task box on the picJacket control to add the BlueJacket.png, BrownJacket.png, and RedJacket.png files to the project, and then close the Select Resource dialog box. (Do not be concerned that the jacket in the picJacket control is no longer the black one.) If necessary, expand the Resources node in the Solution Explorer window. Notice that the folder contains five .png files.

d. Lock the controls on the form. When the user clicks the Black button, the black jacket should appear in the picJacket control. Open the Code Editor window and then open the code template for the btnBlack_Click procedure. Enter the comment and assignment statement shown in Figure 1-41. The My in the statement refers to the current application, Resources refers to the Resources folder, and BlackJacket refers to the BlackJacket.png file within the Resources folder. The dot member access operator indicates that BlackJacket is a member of the Resources folder, which is a member of the current application.

e. Code the btnBlue_Click, btnBrown_Click, and btnRed_Click procedures. Save the solution and then start and test the application.

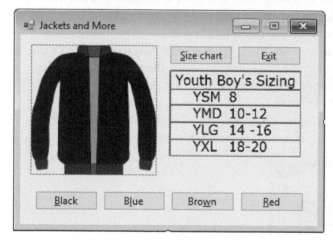

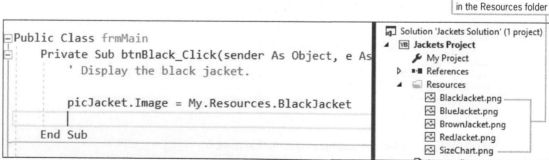

image files contained in the Resources folder

Figure 1-41 Interface and code for Exercise 7

ADVANCED

8. Create a Windows Forms application. Use the following names for the project and solution, respectively: Texting Project and Texting Solution. Save the application in the VB2017\Chap01 folder.

a. Change the form file's name to Main Form.vb. Change the form's Name property to frmMain, its Font property to Segoe UI, 9pt, its MaximizeBox property to False, its StartPosition property to CenterScreen, and its Text property to Text Message Symbols.

b. Create the interface shown in Figure 1-42. Use the Label tool to create the label control. However, you will not be able to size the label control until you complete Step c. Set each picture box's BorderStyle property to FixedSingle. The images in the picture boxes represent text message symbols. The images are stored in the BFF.png, BRB.png, IDK.png, LOL.png, SRY.png, and XO.png files, which are contained in the VB2017\Chap01 folder.

c. Change the label control's name to lblMeaning. Set its AutoSize property to False, its BorderStyle property to FixedSingle, its Font size to 18pt, and its TextAlign property to MiddleCenter. Delete the contents of its Text property. Now size the label control as shown in Figure 1-42.

d. Lock the controls on the form. Give the picture boxes and the Exit button meaningful names.

e. Code the Exit button.

f. When clicked, each picture box should assign the meaning of its associated symbol to the lblMeaning control's Text property. For example, the picture box that displays BFF should assign the message "Best friends forever" to the Text property. Code each picture box's Click event procedure. (If necessary, use the Internet to research the meaning of any symbols you do not recognize.)

g. Open the Project Designer window and verify the name of the startup form. Save the solution and then close the Project Designer window. Start and test the application.

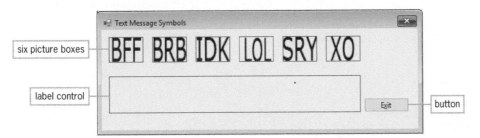

Figure 1-42   Interface for Exercise 8

9. Create a Windows Forms application. Use the following names for the project and solution, respectively: OnYourOwn Project and OnYourOwn Solution. Save the application in the VB2017\Chap01 folder. Design and code an application that adheres to the guidelines listed in Figure 1-43. Open the Project Designer window and verify the name of the startup form. Save the solution and then close the Project Designer window. Start and test the application. Print the application's code and interface.

ON YOUR OWN

> 1. The interface must contain at least two picture boxes. You can use your own image files, or you can download image files from openclipart.org. When downloading from openclipart.org, be sure to use the SMALL IMAGE (.PNG) button.
> 2. The interface must contain at least one button.
> 3. The interface can contain label controls; however, this is not a requirement.
> 4. Objects that are either coded or referred to in code should be named appropriately.
> 5. The Code Editor window must contain comments, the **Me.Close()** statement, and at least one assignment statement.

Figure 1-43   Guidelines for Exercise 9

FIX IT

10. Open the VB2017\Chap01\FixIt Solution\FixIt Solution.sln file. If necessary, open the designer window. The interface contains a picture box, two buttons, and a label control that displays the price of the parrot.

    a. Start the application. Click the Show price button, which should display the label control. Notice that the button is not working. Click the Exit button to end the application.

    b. Open the Code Editor window and then fix the code contained in the btnShow_Click procedure. Save the solution and then start the application. Click the Show price button to verify that it now displays the price of the parrot. Click the Exit button to end the application.

    c. Start the application again. This time, use the Exit button's access key (Alt+x) to end the application. Notice that the access key is not working. Click the Exit button to end the application.

    d. Which event procedure in the Code Editor window contains the Me.Close() statement? In which event procedure should the statement be entered? Delete the entire incorrect event procedure and then enter the Me.Close() statement in the correct one. Save the solution and then start the application. Test the Exit button by clicking it and also by using its access key.

CHAPTER 2

Planning Applications and Designing Interfaces

In this chapter's Focus on the Concepts lesson, you will learn the steps for planning a Windows Forms application. You will also learn how to design interfaces that follow the Windows standards, including assigning access keys and setting the tab order for the controls. In the Apply the Concepts lesson, you will use what you learned in the Focus lesson to plan an application and design its interface. You will also learn about label controls and text boxes.

■ FOCUS ON THE CONCEPTS LESSON

Concepts covered in this lesson:

- F-1 Planning a Windows Forms application
- F-2 Windows standards for interfaces
- F-3 Access keys
- F-4 Tab order

F-1 Planning a Windows Forms Application

Before you begin creating a Windows Forms application, you need to plan it. The steps listed in Figure 2-1 will help you accomplish this important task. In this lesson, you will use the steps to plan the Restaurant Tip application, which calculates a server's tip based on two amounts: the user's restaurant bill and the tip percentage.

Planning steps
1. Identify the application's purpose.
2. Identify the items that the user must provide.
3. Identify the items that the application must provide.
4. Determine how the user and the application will provide their respective items.
5. Draw a sketch of the user interface.

Figure 2-1   Steps for planning a Windows Forms application

The first step in the planning process is to identify the application's purpose. The purpose of the Restaurant Tip application is to calculate and display a server's tip. The second step is to identify the items that the user must provide for the application to accomplish its purpose. In this case, the user needs to provide the bill amount and the tip percentage. The third step is to identify the items that the application must provide. The Restaurant Tip application needs to provide the tip amount, as well as a button for the user to end the application.

Before continuing to Step 4 in the planning process, it is helpful to record the information from Steps 1 through 3 in a Planning Chart. You can create a Planning Chart by hand or use the table feature in a word processor. Figure 2-2 shows the information entered in the Restaurant Tip application's Planning Chart.

Planning Chart for the Restaurant Tip application

Purpose: Calculate and display a server's tip.

	How?
User-provided	
1. bill amount	
2. tip percentage	
Application-provided	
1. tip	
2. button for ending the application	

Figure 2-2   Planning Chart showing the information from Steps 1 through 3

The fourth step in the planning process is to determine how the user and the application will provide their respective items. This information will be recorded in the How? column of the Planning Chart. The two items listed in the User-provided section (bill amount and tip percentage) will need to be entered by the user. Visual Basic provides many different controls for getting user input, such as text boxes, list boxes, radio buttons, and check boxes; the Restaurant Tip application will use text boxes named txtBill and txtPercentage. (The three-character ID for text box names is txt.)

According to the Planning Chart, the application (rather than the user) is responsible for providing the tip item. The application will employ two controls to accomplish this task: a button named btnCalc and a label control named lblTip. (The three-character ID for label control names is lbl.) Label controls are used in an interface to display text that the user is not allowed to edit during run time, such as text that identifies other controls and text that represents the result of a calculation. The btnCalc control will calculate the tip and then assign the result to the lblTip control. It will perform these tasks when it is clicked, so you will code its Click event procedure. Assigning the tasks to a button allows the user to determine when the tasks are performed.

The Planning Chart also indicates that the application must provide a button for the user to end the application. You will name the button btnExit and code its Click event procedure so it ends the application when it is clicked. Figure 2-3 shows the completed Planning Chart for the Restaurant Tip application.

Planning Chart for the Restaurant Tip application

Purpose: Calculate and display a server's tip.

	How?
User-provided	
1. bill amount	user will enter in txtBill
2. tip percentage	user will enter in txtPercentage
Application-provided	
1. tip	btnCalc_Click will calculate and display in lblTip
2. button for ending the application	btnExit_Click will end the application

Figure 2-3   Completed Planning Chart for the Restaurant Tip application

F-2 Windows Standards for Interfaces

A company's standards for interfaces used within the company supersede the Windows standards.

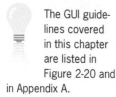

The GUI guidelines covered in this chapter are listed in Figure 2-20 and in Appendix A.

The final step in planning an application is to draw a sketch of your application's user interface. While the interface's design is open to creativity, there are some guidelines to which you should adhere so that it is consistent with the Windows standards. This consistency will give your interface a familiar look, which will make your application easier for users to both learn and use. The guidelines are referred to as graphical user interface (GUI) guidelines.

The first GUI guideline covered in this book pertains to the organization of the controls in the interface. In Western countries, the user interface should be organized so that the information flows either vertically (top to bottom) or horizontally (left to right). Related controls should be grouped together using either white (empty) space or one of the tools located in the Containers section of the toolbox. Examples of tools found in the Containers section include the GroupBox, Panel, and TableLayoutPanel tools. (You will learn about the GroupBox tool in Chapter 4.)

Figures 2-4 and 2-5 show two sketches of the Restaurant Tip application's interface. In Figure 2-4, the information is arranged vertically; in Figure 2-5, it is arranged horizontally. Both sketches contain the controls listed in the Planning Chart, and each of those controls is labeled so the user knows its purpose. For example, the "Bill:" label identifies the type of information to enter in the txtBill control. Likewise, the "Calculate tip" caption indicates the action the btnCalc control will perform when it is clicked.

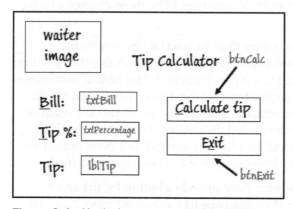

Figure 2-4 Vertical arrangement of the interface

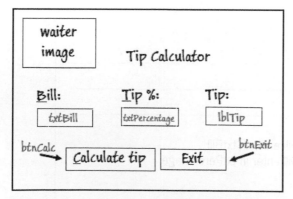

Figure 2-5 Horizontal arrangement of the interface

When positioning the controls in the interface, place related controls close to each other and be sure to maintain a consistent margin from the edges of the form. Also, it is helpful to align the borders of the controls wherever possible to minimize the number of different margins appearing in the interface. Doing this allows the user to more easily scan the information.

Guidelines for Identifying Labels and Buttons

The text contained in a label control that identifies another control's contents should be meaningful and left-aligned within the label. In most cases, an identifying label should consist of one to three words only and appear on one line. In addition, the identifying label should be positioned either above or to the left of the control it identifies. An identifying label should end with a colon (:), which distinguishes it from other text in the user interface (such as the heading text "Tip Calculator"). Some assistive technologies, which are technologies that provide assistance to individuals with disabilities, rely on the colons to make this distinction. The Windows standard is to use sentence capitalization for identifying labels. **Sentence capitalization** means you capitalize only the first letter in the first word and in any words that are customarily capitalized. All of the identifying labels in Figures 2-4 and 2-5 follow these Windows standards.

Buttons are identified by the text that appears on the button's face. The text is often referred to as the button's caption. The caption should be meaningful, consist of one to three words only, and appear on one line. For Windows 10 applications, the button's caption should be entered using sentence capitalization. If the buttons are stacked vertically, as they are in Figure 2-4, all the buttons should be the same height and width. If the buttons are positioned horizontally, as they are in Figure 2-5, all the buttons should be the same height, but their widths may vary if necessary. In a group of buttons, the most commonly used button typically appears first—either on the top (in a vertical arrangement) or on the left (in a horizontal arrangement).

Guidelines for Including Graphics

The human eye is attracted to pictures before text, so use graphics sparingly. Designers typically include graphics to either emphasize or clarify a portion of the screen. However, a graphic can also be used merely for aesthetic purposes, as long as it is small and placed in a location that does not distract the user. The interface for the Restaurant Tip application, for example, will contain a small image of a waiter in the upper-left corner of the form. The image will add a personal touch to the interface without distracting the user.

Guidelines for Selecting Fonts

As you learned in Chapter 1, an object's Font property determines the type, style, and size of the font used to display the object's text. You should use only one font type (typically Segoe UI) for all of the text in the interface, and use no more than two different font sizes. In addition, avoid using italics and underlining in an interface because both font styles make text difficult to read. The use of bold text should be limited to titles, headings, and key items that you want to emphasize.

Guidelines for Using Color

The human eye is attracted to color before black and white; therefore, use color sparingly in an interface. It is a good practice to build the interface using black, white, and gray first, and then add color only if you have a good reason to do so. Keep the following three points in mind when deciding whether to include color in an interface:

1. People who have some form of either color blindness or color confusion will have trouble distinguishing colors.

2. Color is very subjective: A color that looks pretty to you may be hideous to someone else.

3. A color may have a different meaning in a different culture.

Usually, it is best to use black text on a white, off-white, or light gray background because dark text on a light background is the easiest to read. Using a dark color for the background or a light color for the text is not recommended because a dark background is hard on the eyes, and light-colored text can appear blurry.

If you are going to include color in an interface, limit the number of colors to three, not including white, black, and gray. Be sure that the colors you choose complement each other. Although color can be used to identify an important element in the interface, you should never use it as the only means of identification; you should also include an identifying label for the colored control.

Mini-Quiz 2-1

1. What is the first step in the planning process for a Windows Forms application?

2. What type of control is used to display the result of a calculation?

3. What type of control is used to identify the contents of a text box?

4. Button captions should end with a colon. True or False?

1) Identify the application's purpose. 2) Label 3) Label 4) False

F-3 Access Keys

In the sketches shown earlier in Figures 2-4 and 2-5, the text in four of the controls contains an underlined letter. As you learned in Chapter 1, the underlined letter is called an **access key**, and it allows the user to select an object using the Alt key in combination with a letter or number. For example, you can select the Exit button in the Restaurant Tip application's interface by pressing Alt+x because the letter x is the Exit button's access key. Access keys are not case sensitive. Therefore, you can select the Exit button by pressing either Alt+x or Alt+X. If you do not see the underlined access keys while an application is running, you can show them temporarily by pressing the Alt key.

In an interface, you should assign access keys to each control that can accept user input, such as text boxes and buttons. The only exceptions to this rule are the OK and Cancel buttons, which typically do not have access keys in Windows applications. Access keys are important because they allow people with certain physical disabilities to interact with an application's interface.

You assign an access key by including an ampersand (&) in the control's caption or identifying label. If the control is a button, you include the ampersand in the button's Text property, which is where a button's caption is stored. If the control is a text box, you include the ampersand in the Text property of its identifying label. (As you will learn later in this lesson, you must also set the TabIndex properties of the text box and its identifying label appropriately.) As you learned in Chapter 1, you enter the ampersand to the immediate left of the character you want to designate as the access key.

Each access key in an interface should be unique. The first choice for an access key is the first letter of the caption or identifying label, unless another letter provides a more meaningful association. For example, the letter x is the access key for an Exit button because it provides a more meaningful association than does the letter E. If you cannot use the first letter (perhaps because it is already used as the access key for another control) and no other letter provides a more meaningful association, then use a distinctive consonant in the caption or label. The last choices for an access key are a vowel or a number.

Notice that the "Tip:" label in the sketches shown earlier in Figures 2-4 and 2-5 does not have an access key. This is because the label does not identify a control that accepts user input; rather, it identifies another label control (lblTip). Recall that users cannot access label controls while an application is running, so it is inappropriate to include an access key in their identifying labels.

F-4 Tab Order

Each control's TabIndex property contains a number, beginning with 0, that represents the order in which the control was added to the form. The TabIndex values determine the **tab order**, which is the order in which each control receives the **focus** when the user either presses the Tab key or employs an access key while an application is running. A control whose TabIndex is 4 will receive the focus immediately after the control whose TabIndex is 3, and so on. When a control has the focus, it can accept user input. Not all controls have a TabIndex property; a PictureBox control, for example, does not have a TabIndex property.

Most times you will need to reset the TabIndex values for the controls in an interface. To do this, you first make a list of the controls that can accept user input; the Restaurant Tip application's interface contains four of these controls. The list should reflect the order in which the user will want to access the controls. In the Restaurant Tip application's interface, the user typically will want to access the txtBill control first, followed by the txtPercentage control, the btnCalc control, and then the btnExit control. If a control that accepts user input is identified by a label control, you also include the label control in the list. (A text box is an example of a control that accepts user input and is identified by a label control.) You place the name of the label control immediately above the name of the control it identifies in the list. In the Restaurant Tip application's interface, the name of the txtBill control's identifying label should appear immediately above txtBill in the list. Likewise, the name of the txtPercentage control's identifying label should appear immediately above txtPercentage in the list. The names of the remaining controls in the interface should be placed at the bottom of the list and do not need to be in any specific order.

After listing the control names, you then assign a TabIndex value to each control in the list, beginning with the number 0. If a control does not have a TabIndex property, you do not assign it a TabIndex value in the list. You can tell whether a control has a TabIndex property by viewing its Properties list.

Figure 2-6 shows the list of controls and TabIndex values for the Restaurant Tip application; it also shows the interface's TabIndex boxes. You display the boxes by clicking the Tab Order option on the View menu. (The option is available only when the designer window is the active window.) You use the boxes along with the list you created to set the TabIndex values. Notice that the TabIndex value assigned to each text box's identifying label is one number less than the value assigned to the text box itself. This is necessary for a text box's access key (which is defined in its identifying label) to work correctly.

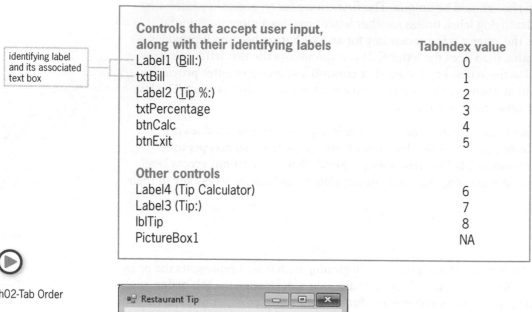

ChO2-Tab Order

identifying label and its associated text box

Controls that accept user input, along with their identifying labels	TabIndex value
Label1 (<u>B</u>ill:)	0
txtBill	1
Label2 (<u>T</u>ip %:)	2
txtPercentage	3
btnCalc	4
btnExit	5
Other controls	
Label4 (Tip Calculator)	6
Label3 (Tip:)	7
lblTip	8
PictureBox1	NA

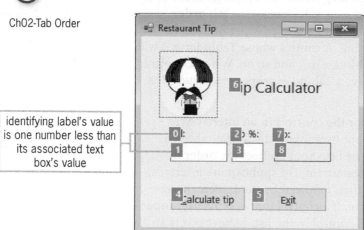

identifying label's value is one number less than its associated text box's value

Figure 2-6   List of controls and TabIndex values along with TabIndex boxes

START HERE

To observe how the application's access keys and TabIndex values work:

1. Use Windows to locate and then open the VB2017\Chap02 folder. Double-click **Tip.exe** in the list of filenames. The interface appears on the screen. The blinking insertion point in the txtBill control indicates that the control has the focus.

2. First you will verify the tab order. In Windows applications, the Tab key moves the focus forward, and the Shift+Tab key combination moves the focus backward. Press **Tab** to move the focus to the txtPercentage control, and then press **Shift+Tab** to move the focus back to the txtBill control.

3. Press **Tab**, slowly, three times. The focus moves to the txtPercentage control, then to the btnCalc control, and then to the btnExit control. Notice that when a button has the focus, a dotted rectangle appears inside its darkened border.

4. Next, you will verify that the access keys work correctly. Press **Alt+b** to move the focus to the txtBill control. Type **100**, press **Alt+t**, and then type **20**. Now press **Alt+c** (the Calculate tip button's access key) to calculate the tip. $20.00 appears in the lblTip control. Press **Alt+x** to end the application.

Mini-Quiz 2-2

1. To assign the letter P as the access key for a Print button, what value must be entered in the button's Text property?

2. If a text box's TabIndex value is the number 10, what TabIndex value should its identifying label have?

3. Which menu contains an option for displaying the interface's TabIndex boxes?

4. All controls have a TabIndex property. True or False?

1) &Print 2) 9 3) View 4) False

■ APPLY THE CONCEPTS LESSON

After studying this lesson, you should be able to:

- A-1 Create a Planning Chart for a Windows Forms application
- A-2 Design an interface using the Windows standards
- A-3 Add a label control to the form
- A-4 Add a text box to the form
- A-5 Set the tab order

A-1 Create a Planning Chart for a Windows Forms Application

For every purchase made at the Jacobson Furniture store, the store's cashiers manually calculate the amount of sales tax to charge the customer as well as the total amount the customer owes. The application you will create in this Apply the Concepts lesson will computerize both calculations. Figure 2-7 shows a sample of the manual calculations using the store's required sales tax rate, 5%.

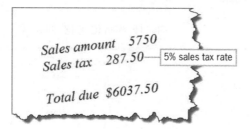

Sales amount   5750
Sales tax   287.50 — 5% sales tax rate
Total due $6037.50

Figure 2-7   Sample of manual calculations

As you learned in this chapter's Focus lesson, you should plan a Windows Forms application before you begin creating it. The first step in the planning process is to identify the application's purpose; in this case, the application needs to calculate and display the sales tax and total due amounts. The second step is to identify the items that the user must provide for the application to accomplish its purpose. The cashier at Jacobson Furniture needs to provide one item: the sales amount. The third step is to identify the items that the application must provide. The Jacobson Furniture application needs to provide the 5% sales tax and total due items as well as a button for the user to end the application. Figure 2-8 shows the results of the first three planning steps entered in a Planning Chart.

Planning Chart for the Jacobson Furniture application
Purpose: Calculate and display the sales tax and total due amounts.
How?
User-provided 1. sales amount
Application-provided 1. 5% sales tax 2. total due 3. button for ending the application

Figure 2-8   Planning Chart showing the results of the first three planning steps

The fourth step in the planning process is to determine how the user and the application will provide their respective items. The user-provided item (sales amount) will be entered in a text box named txtSales. The application will use a button named btnCalc to calculate the 5% sales tax and total due items. The button will also be responsible for displaying the result of the calculations in two label controls named lblTax and lblTotal. The button will perform these tasks when it is clicked, so you will code its Click event procedure.

The Planning Chart also indicates that the application must provide a button for the user to end the application. You will name the button btnExit and code its Click event procedure so it ends the application when it is clicked. Figure 2-9 shows the completed Planning Chart for the Jacobson Furniture application.

Planning Chart for the Jacobson Furniture application

Purpose: Calculate and display the sales tax and total due amounts.

	How?
User-provided	
1. sales amount	user will enter in txtSales
Application-provided	
1. 5% sales tax	btnCalc_Click will calculate and display in lblTax
2. total due	btnCalc_Click will calculate and display in lblTotal
3. button for ending the application	btnExit_Click will end the application

Figure 2-9   Completed Planning Chart for the Jacobson Furniture application

A-2 Design an Interface Using the Windows Standards

The final step in planning an application is to draw a sketch of the user interface. Figures 2-10 and 2-11 show two sketches of the interface for the Jacobson Furniture application. Both sketches follow the GUI guidelines covered in this chapter's Focus lesson. Each text box and button, as well as each label control that displays program output, is labeled so the user knows the control's purpose. The text contained in the identifying labels and button captions is entered using sentence capitalization. In addition, the identifying label text ends with a colon and is left-aligned within the label. The button captions and identifying labels appear on one line and do not exceed the three-word limit. Because the buttons in Figure 2-10 are stacked in the interface, each button has the same height and width. The buttons in Figure 2-11 also have the same height and width, even though the width of these buttons may vary if necessary. The most commonly used button (Calculate) is placed at the top of the button group in Figure 2-10 and at the left in Figure 2-11. Each control that can accept user input has an access key assigned to it. The Total due: label does not have an access key because it identifies the lblTotal control, which cannot accept user input.

Figure 2-20 and Appendix A contain a summary of the GUI guidelines covered in this chapter.

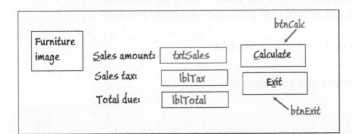

Figure 2-10   Vertical arrangement of the Jacobson Furniture interface

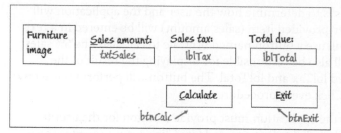

Figure 2-11 Horizontal arrangement of the Jacobson Furniture application

START HERE ▶ **To open the partially completed Jacobson Furniture application:**

1. Open the Jacobson Solution.sln file contained in the VB2017\Chap02\Jacobson Solution folder.

2. If the designer window is not open, double-click **Main Form.vb** in the Solution Explorer window.

Missing from the interface are three labels and a text box. You will add the missing controls in the following sections.

A-3 Add a Label Control to the Form

You use the Label tool to add a label control to a form. The purpose of a **label control** is to display text that the user is not allowed to edit while the application is running. As mentioned in this chapter's Focus lesson, label controls are used to identify other controls as well as to display the result of calculations made by the application. Figure 2-12 shows the most commonly used properties of a label control.

Name	Purpose
AutoSize	enable/disable automatic sizing; labels that display program output typically have their AutoSize property set to False; identifying labels should have the default property setting (True)
BackColor	specify the label's background color
BorderStyle	specify the appearance of the label's border; labels that display program output typically have their BorderStyle property set to FixedSingle; identifying labels should have the default property setting (None)
Font	specify the font to use for text
ForeColor	specify the color of the text inside the label
Name	give the label a meaningful name (use lbl as the ID)
Text	specify the text that appears inside the label; if the label identifies another control that can accept user input, the text should include an access key
TextAlign	specify the position of the text inside the label

Figure 2-12 Most commonly used properties of a label control

To add the missing label controls to the form:

START HERE

1. Drag a label control to the form. Position it to the left of the Total due: label and then release the mouse button. Change its Text property to **Sales tax:** and press **Enter**. This label control does not need an access key because it will identify another label control (the lblTax control), which cannot accept user input. In addition, the label control's name can stay at its default value (Label2) because none of its events will be coded and it will not be referred to in code.

2. Place your mouse pointer on the Sales tax: label and reposition the control as shown in Figure 2-13. When positioning controls, you should align their text using the pink snap (or text-alignment) line. Release the mouse button.

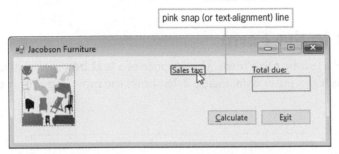

Figure 2-13   Correct position of the Sales tax: label

3. Drag another label control to the form. Position it to the left of the Sales tax: label and then release the mouse button. This label control will need an access key because it will identify a text box, which can accept user input. Change the label control's Text property to **&Sales amount:** and press **Enter**. The label control's name can stay at its default value (Label3) because none of its events will be coded and it will not be referred to in code.

4. Now place your mouse pointer on the label and reposition it as shown in Figure 2-14, and then release the mouse button.

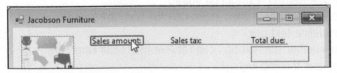

Figure 2-14   Correct position of the Sales amount: label

5. Drag another label control to the form. Position it below the Sales tax: label and then release the mouse button. Change its name to **lblTax**.

6. The lblTax control will display the sales tax amount calculated by the btnCalc control. As indicated earlier in Figure 2-12, label controls that display program output typically have their AutoSize and BorderStyle properties changed from the default values. Set the lblTax control's AutoSize and BorderStyle properties to **False** and **FixedSingle**, respectively.

7. Click **Text** in the Properties list, highlight **Label4** in the Settings box, press **Delete**, and then press **Enter** to remove the contents of the Text property. Click **TextAlign** in the Properties list, click the **down arrow** in the Settings box, and then click the **center button** to change the property to MiddleCenter.

8. The lblTax control should be the same size as the lblTotal control. Click the **lblTotal** control and then Ctrl+click the **lblTax** control. Use the Format menu to make the controls the same size, and then click the **form** to deselect the controls.

9. Reposition the lblTax control as shown in Figure 2-15, and then save the solution.

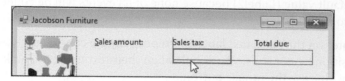

Figure 2-15 Correct position of the lblTax control

A-4 Add a Text Box to the Form

You use the TextBox tool to add a text box to a form. The purpose of a **text box** is to provide an area in the form where the user can enter data. Figure 2-16 shows the most commonly used properties of a text box.

Name	Purpose
BackColor	specify the text box's background color
CharacterCasing	while the text is being entered into the text box, specify whether the text should remain as typed or be converted to either uppercase or lowercase
Font	specify the font to use for text
ForeColor	specify the color of the text inside the text box
Name	give the text box a meaningful name (use txt as the ID)
MaxLength	specify the maximum number of characters the text box will accept
Multiline	specify whether the text box can span more than one line
PasswordChar	specify the character to display when entering a password
ReadOnly	specify whether the text can be edited
ScrollBars	indicate whether scroll bars appear on the text box (used with a multiline text box)
TabStop	indicate whether the text box can receive the focus when the user presses the Tab key
Text	get or set the text that appears inside the text box

Figure 2-16 Most commonly used properties of a text box

START HERE **To add the missing text box to the form:**

1. Drag a text box to the form. Position it below the $\underline{S}$ales amount: label and then release the mouse button. Change its name to **txtSales**.

2. Reposition the txtSales control as shown in Figure 2-17, and then release the mouse button.

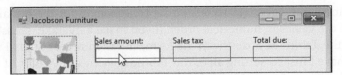

Figure 2-17 Correct position of the txtSales control

3. Use the Format menu to make the text box the same size as the lblTax control, and then click the **form** to deselect the controls.

4. Lock the controls on the form and then save the solution.

A-5 Set the Tab Order

As you learned earlier, the tab order is the order in which each control receives the focus when the user either presses the Tab key or employs an access key during run time. The tab order is determined by the TabIndex values of the controls in the interface. Because it is rare for the controls to be added to the form in the correct tab order, you typically will need to reset the TabIndex values after you have completed the interface. Recall that you begin by making a list of the controls that can accept user input. The list should reflect the order in which the user will want to access the controls. If a control that accepts user input is identified by a label control, you also include the label control in the list. Figure 2-18 shows the list of controls and TabIndex values for the Jacobson Furniture store's interface.

Controls that accept user input, along with their identifying labels	TabIndex value
Label3 (Sales amount:)	0
txtSales	1
btnCalc	2
btnExit	3
Other controls	
Label2 (Sales tax:)	4
Label1 (Total due:)	5
lblTax	6
lblTotal	7
PictureBox1	N/A

Figure 2-18 List of controls and TabIndex values

To set the tab order:

START HERE

1. Click **View** on the menu bar and then click **Tab Order**. The current TabIndex values appear in blue boxes on the form. (A picture box does not have a TabIndex property.) Click the blue box on the Sales amount: label. The number in the box changes to 0 and the box's color changes to white.

2. Click the blue box on the txtSales control. The number in the box changes to 1.

3. Use the information shown in Figure 2-19 to set the TabIndex values for the remaining controls. Be sure to set the values in numerical order. If you make a mistake, press the Esc key to remove the TabIndex boxes from the form, and then repeat Steps 1 through 3. When you have finished setting all of the TabIndex values, the color of the boxes will automatically change from white to blue, as shown in Figure 2-19.

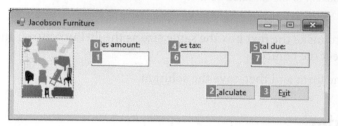

Figure 2-19   TabIndex boxes showing the correct TabIndex values

4. Press **Esc** (or click **View** and then click **Tab Order**) to remove the TabIndex boxes from the form.

5. Save the solution and then start the application. If the access keys do not appear in the interface, press the **Alt** key. When you start an application, the computer sends the focus to the control whose TabIndex is 0. In the current interface, that control is the Label3 (Sales amount:) control. However, because label controls cannot receive the focus, the computer sends the focus to the next control in the tab order sequence: txtSales. The blinking insertion point indicates that the text box has the focus and is ready to receive input from you.

6. Press **Tab** to move the focus to the Calculate button, and then press **Shift+Tab** to move the focus back to the Sales amount text box.

7. Now press **Tab**, slowly, two times. The focus moves to the Calculate button and then to the Exit button. Notice that when a button has the focus, a dotted rectangle appears inside its darkened border.

8. You can also move the focus using a text box's access key. Press **Alt+s** to move the focus to the text box.

9. Unlike pressing a text box's access key, which moves the focus, pressing a button's access key invokes the button's Click event. Press **Alt+x** to invoke the Exit button's Click event, which ends the application. (The btnExit_Click procedure has already been coded for you. You will learn how to code the Calculate button in Chapter 3.)

10. Close the solution.

Mini-Quiz 2-3

1. A text box's access key is defined in its identifying label. True or False?

2. Which property determines a label's border?

3. Which property specifies the alignment of the text inside a label control?

4. TabIndex values begin with the number 1. True or False?

1) True 2) BorderStyle 3) TextAlign 4) False

Summary

- To plan a Windows Forms application, perform the following five steps in the order shown:

    1. Identify the application's purpose.

    2. Identify the items that the user must provide.

    3. Identify the items that the application must provide.

    4. Determine how the user and the application will provide their respective items.

    5. Draw a sketch of the user interface.

- Use a label control to display text that a user is not allowed to edit during run time.

- Use a text box control to provide an area in the form in which a user can enter data.

- To assign an access key to a control, type an ampersand (&) in the Text property of the control or identifying label. The ampersand should appear to the immediate left of the character that you want to designate as the access key.

- Users cannot access label controls while an application is running, so it is inappropriate to include an access key in their identifying labels.

- To provide keyboard access to a text box, assign an access key to the text box's identifying label. Set the identifying label's TabIndex value so that it is one number less than the text box's TabIndex value.

- To employ an access key, press and hold down the Alt key as you tap the access key.

- To set the tab order, use the Tab Order option on the View menu to display the TabIndex boxes. (The Tab Order option is available only when the designer is the active window.) Set each control's TabIndex box to a number (starting with 0) that represents the order in which the control should receive the focus.

- When a control has the focus, it can accept user input.

- Use a label control's BorderStyle property to put a border around the control.

- Use a label control's AutoSize property to specify whether the control should automatically size to fit its current contents.

- Use a label control's TextAlign property to specify the alignment of the text inside the control.

- Figure 2-20 lists the GUI design guidelines covered in this chapter:

GUI design guidelines

1. *Organizing the interface:* Organize the user interface so that the information flows either vertically (top to bottom) or horizontally (left to right).
2. *Grouping controls:* Group related controls together using either white (empty) space or one of the tools from the Containers section of the toolbox.
3. *Identifying controls:* Use a label to identify each text box in the user interface. Also use a label to identify other label controls that display program output. The label text should be meaningful, consist of one to three words only, and appear on one line. Left-align the text within the label and position the label either above or to the left of the control it identifies. Enter the label text using sentence capitalization, and insert a colon (:) following the label text.
4. *Identifying buttons:* Display a meaningful caption on the face of each button. The caption should indicate the action the button will perform when clicked. Enter the caption using sentence capitalization. Place the caption on one line and use from one to three words only.
5. *Aligning buttons:* When a group of buttons are stacked vertically, all buttons in the group should be the same height and width. When a group of buttons are positioned horizontally, all buttons in the group should be the same height; their widths can vary if necessary. In a group of buttons, the most commonly used button is typically placed first in the group.
6. *Aligning control borders:* Align the borders of the controls wherever possible to minimize the number of different margins appearing in the interface.
7. *Using graphics:* Use graphics sparingly. If the graphic is used solely for aesthetics, use a small graphic and place it in a location that will not distract the user.
8. *Choosing font types, styles, and sizes:* Use only one font type (typically Segoe UI) for all of the text in the interface. Use no more than two different font sizes in the interface. Avoid using italics and underlining because both font styles make text difficult to read. Limit the use of bold text to titles, headings, and key items that you want to emphasize.
9. *Using color:* Build the interface using black, white, and gray. Only add color if you have a good reason to do so. Use white, off-white, or light gray for the background. Use black for the text. Limit the number of colors in an interface to three, not including white, black, and gray. The colors you choose should complement each other. Never use color as the only means of identification for an element in the interface.
10. *Setting the BorderStyle property:* Keep the BorderStyle property of text boxes at the default setting: Fixed3D. Keep the BorderStyle property of identifying labels at the default setting: None. Use FixedSingle for the BorderStyle property of labels that display program output, such as the result of a calculation. (Avoid setting a label control's BorderStyle property to Fixed3D because in Windows applications, a control with a three-dimensional appearance implies that it can accept user input.)
11. *Setting the AutoSize property:* Keep the AutoSize property of identifying labels at the default setting: True. In most cases, use False for the AutoSize property of label controls that display program output.
12. *Setting the TextAlign property:* Use the TextAlign property to specify the alignment of the text within a label control.
13. *Assigning access keys:* Assign a unique access key to each control that can accept user input. When assigning an access key to a control, use the first letter of the control's caption or identifying label, unless another letter provides a more meaningful association. If you cannot use the first letter and no other letter provides a more meaningful association, then use a distinctive consonant. As a last resort, use a vowel or a number.
14. *Setting the tab order:* Assign a TabIndex value (starting with 0) to each control in the interface, except for controls that do not have a TabIndex property. The TabIndex values should reflect the order in which the user will want to access the controls.
15. *Providing keyboard access to a text box:* Assign an access key to the text box's identifying label, and then set the identifying label's TabIndex value so it is one number less than the text box's TabIndex value.

Figure 2-20 GUI design guidelines covered in Chapter 2

Key Terms

Access key—the underlined character in an object's identifying label or caption; allows the user to select the object using the Alt key in combination with the underlined character

Focus—indicates that a control is ready to accept user input

Label control—the control used to display text that the user is not allowed to edit while an application is running

Sentence capitalization—the capitalization used for identifying labels and button captions; refers to capitalizing only the first letter in the first word and in any words that are customarily capitalized

Tab order—the order in which each control receives the focus when the user either presses the Tab key or employs an access key while an application is running

Text box—a control that provides an area in the form for the user to enter data

Review Questions

1. A button's caption should be entered using sentence capitalization.

   a. True   b. False

2. Which of the following statements is false?

   a. The text contained in an identifying label should be left-aligned within the label.

   b. An identifying label should be positioned either above or to the right of the control it identifies.

   c. Identifying labels should use sentence capitalization.

   d. Identifying labels should end with a colon (:).

3. Which property determines the tab order for the controls in an interface?

   a. SetOrder   c. TabIndex

   b. SetTab   d. TabOrder

4. A control's access key is specified in which of its properties?

   a. Access   c. Key

   b. Caption   d. Text

5. Which of the following specifies the letter D as the access key?

   a. &Display   c. ^Display

   b. #Display   d. D&isplay

6. Which of the following controls will provide an area in the form for the user to enter a name?

   a. button   c. text box

   b. label   d. All of the above.

7. What is the ID used for text box names?

   a. tex

   b. text

   c. txt

   d. None of the above.

8. What is the ID used for label control names?

   a. lab

   b. lal

   c. lbe

   d. None of the above.

9. How can the user access a button whose Text property contains Clea&r?

   a. Alt+r

   b. Ctrl+r

   c. Shift+r

   d. Esc+r

10. Label controls that display program output typically have their BorderStyle property set to _____.

    a. BorderSingle

    b. Fixed3D

    c. FixedSingle

    d. None

11. Identifying labels typically have their BorderStyle property set to _____.

    a. BorderSingle

    b. Fixed3D

    c. FixedSingle

    d. None

12. Text boxes should have their BorderStyle property set to _____.

    a. BorderSingle

    b. Fixed3D

    c. FixedSingle

    d. None

13. Label controls that display program output typically have their AutoSize property set to _____.

    a. Auto

    b. False

    c. NoSize

    d. True

14. Identifying labels typically have their AutoSize property set to _____.

    a. Auto

    b. False

    c. NoSize

    d. True

15. If a text box's TabIndex value is 12, its identifying label's TabIndex value should be _____.

    a. 11

    b. 12

    c. 13

    d. True

16. Which of the following should have their names changed to more meaningful ones?

    a. all controls that will be coded

    b. all controls that will be referred to in code

    c. the form

    d. All of the above.

17. Which property determines the position of the text inside a label control?

    a. Align

    b. Alignment

    c. AlignText

    d. TextAlign

18. Explain the method for providing keyboard access to a text box.

19. Define sentence capitalization.

20. Listed below are the five steps for planning a Windows Forms application. Put the steps in the proper order by placing a number (1 through 5) on the line to the left of the step.

    _____ Identify the items that the user must provide.

    _____ Identify the application's purpose.

    _____ Draw a sketch of the user interface.

    _____ Determine how the user and the application will provide their respective items.

    _____ Identify the items that the application must provide.

Exercises

1. Open the Amlie Solution.sln file contained in the VB2017\Chap02\Amlie Solution folder. If necessary, open the designer window. Organize the interface so that it follows the GUI design guidelines covered in this chapter. (The guidelines are summarized in Figure 2-20.) Save the solution and then start the application. Test the access keys, tab order, and Exit button and then close the solution.   INTRODUCTORY

2. Create a Windows Forms application. Use the following names for the project and solution, respectively: Moonbucks Project and Moonbucks Solution. Save the application in the VB2017\Chap02 folder. Change the appropriate properties of the form. Also, be sure to verify the name of the startup form. Use the Planning Chart shown in Figure 2-21 to build an appropriate interface. Code the Exit button. (You do not need to code the button that calculates and displays the two amounts.) Save the solution and then start the application. Test the access keys, tab order, and Exit button and then close the solution.   INTRODUCTORY

Planning Chart for the Moonbucks application	
Purpose: Calculate and display the increase and projected sales amounts.	
	How?
User-provided	
1. current sales amount	user will enter in txtCurrent
Application-provided	
1. 10% increase amount	btnCalc_Click will calculate and display in lblIncrease
2. projected sales amount	btnCalc_Click will calculate and display in lblProjected
3. button for ending the application	btnExit_Click will end the application

Figure 2-21   Planning Chart for Exercise 2

3. Create an application that calculates and displays the amount of a homeowner's property tax. The tax is 1.35% of the property's assessed value, which will be entered by the user.

    a. Prepare a Planning Chart for the application.

    b. Draw a sketch of an appropriate interface. Be sure to follow the GUI design guidelines covered in the chapter. The guidelines are summarized in Figure 2-20. (If you want to include an image in the interface, you can either use your own image file or download an image file from *openclipart.org*. When downloading from *openclipart.org*, be sure to use the SMALL IMAGE (.PNG) button.)

    c. Create a Windows Forms application. Use the following names for the project and solution, respectively: Tax Project and Tax Solution. Save the application in the VB2017\Chap02 folder. Change the appropriate properties of the form. Also, be sure to verify the name of the startup form.

    d. Use your Planning Chart as a guide when building the interface.

    e. Code the Exit button. (You do not need to code the button that calculates and displays the tax.) Save the solution and then start the application. Test the access keys, tab order, and Exit button and then close the solution.

4. Create an application that calculates and displays the area of a rectangle in both square feet and square yards. The user will provide the rectangle's length and width, both measured in feet.

    a. Prepare a Planning Chart for the application.

    b. Draw a sketch of an appropriate interface. Be sure to follow the GUI design guidelines covered in the chapter. The guidelines are summarized in Figure 2-20. (If you want to include an image in the interface, you can either use your own image file or download an image file from *openclipart.org*. When downloading from *openclipart.org*, be sure to use the SMALL IMAGE (.PNG) button.)

    c. Create a Windows Forms application. Use the following names for the project and solution, respectively: Area Project and Area Solution. Save the application in the VB2017\Chap02 folder. Change the appropriate properties of the form. Also, be sure to verify the name of the startup form.

    d. Use your Planning Chart as a guide when building the interface.

    e. Code the Exit button. (You do not need to code the button that performs the two calculations and displays the results.) Save the solution and then start the application. Test the access keys, tab order, and Exit button and then close the solution.

5. Create an application that calculates and displays two raise amounts, which are based on an employee's current salary. The current salary will be entered by the user. The two raise rates are 5% and 8%. In addition to the raise amounts, the application should also calculate and display the employee's new salaries. Include a button in the interface that the user can click to clear the user input and calculated results from the screen.

    a. Prepare a Planning Chart for the application.

    b. Draw a sketch of an appropriate interface. Be sure to follow the GUI design guidelines covered in the chapter. The guidelines are summarized in Figure 2-20.

(If you want to include an image in the interface, you can either use your own image file or download an image file from *openclipart.org*. When downloading from *openclipart.org*, be sure to use the SMALL IMAGE (.PNG) button.)

c. Create a Windows Forms application. Use the following names for the project and solution, respectively: Salary Project and Salary Solution. Save the application in the VB2017\Chap02 folder.

d. Use your Planning Chart as a guide when building the interface.

e. Code the Exit button. (You do not need to code the button that calculates and displays the raises and new salaries or the button that clears the user input and calculated results.)

f. Save the solution and then start the application. Test the access keys, tab order, and Exit button and then close the solution.

6. Kramden Inc. pays each of the company's salespeople the same expense allowance. Create an application that calculates and displays the total cost of these allowances, given both the number of salespeople and the expense allowance amount entered by the user.

INTERMEDIATE

a. Prepare a Planning Chart for the application.

b. Draw a sketch of an appropriate interface. Be sure to follow the GUI design guidelines covered in the chapter. The guidelines are summarized in Figure 2-20. (If you want to include an image in the interface, you can either use your own image file or download an image file from *openclipart.org*. When downloading from *openclipart.org*, be sure to use the SMALL IMAGE (.PNG) button.)

c. Create a Windows Forms application. Use the following names for the project and solution, respectively: Kramden Project and Kramden Solution. Save the application in the VB2017\Chap02 folder.

d. Use your Planning Chart as a guide when building the interface.

e. Code the Exit button. (You do not need to code the button that calculates and displays the total cost.)

f. Save the solution and then start the application. Test the access keys, tab order, and Exit button and then close the solution.

7. Create an application that calculates and displays the percentage of students receiving a grade of P (for Pass) and the percentage of students receiving a grade of F (for Fail). Before creating your Planning Chart, consider what information the user (in this case, the professor) will need to enter.

ADVANCED

a. Prepare a Planning Chart for the application.

b. Draw a sketch of an appropriate interface. Be sure to follow the GUI design guidelines covered in the chapter. The guidelines are summarized in Figure 2-20. (If you want to include an image in the interface, you can either use your own image file or download an image file from *openclipart.org*. When downloading from *openclipart.org*, be sure to use the SMALL IMAGE (.PNG) button.)

c. Create a Windows Forms application. Use the following names for the project and solution, respectively: Grade Project and Grade Solution. Save the application in the VB2017\Chap02 folder.

d. Build the interface and then code the Exit button. (You do not need to code the button that calculates and displays the percentages.)

e. Save the solution and then start the application. Test the access keys, tab order, and Exit button and then close the solution.

ADVANCED

8. Create an application that calculates and displays the percentage of the total sales made by each of the following three salespeople: Jim, Karen, and Martin. Before creating your Planning Chart, consider what information the user (in this case, the sales manager) will need to enter.

   a. Prepare a Planning Chart for the application.

   b. Draw a sketch of an appropriate interface. Include a picture box in the interface. Be sure to follow the GUI design guidelines covered in the chapter. The guidelines are summarized in Figure 2-20. (You can either use your own image file or download an image file from *openclipart.org*. When downloading from *openclipart.org*, be sure to use the SMALL IMAGE (.PNG) button.)

   c. Create a Windows Forms application. Use the following names for the project and solution, respectively: Sales Project and Sales Solution. Save the application in the VB2017\Chap02 folder.

   d. Build the interface and then code the Exit button. (You do not need to code the button that calculates and displays the percentages.)

   e. Save the solution and then start the application. Test the access keys, tab order, and Exit button and then close the solution.

ON YOUR OWN

9. Create a Windows Forms application. Use the following names for the project and solution, respectively: OnYourOwn Project and OnYourOwn Solution. Save the application in the VB2017\Chap02 folder. Plan and design an application of your choice. The only requirement is that you must follow the minimum guidelines listed in Figure 2-22. Before starting the application, be sure to verify the name of the startup form. Save the solution and then start and test the application.

1. The user must enter at least two items.
2. The application must provide at least one item.
3. The interface must contain at least two buttons. One of the two buttons must be an Exit button.
4. The interface can include a picture box, but this is not a requirement.
5. The interface must follow the GUI design guidelines covered in the chapter. The guidelines are summarized in Figure 2-20.
6. Objects that are either coded or referred to in code should be named appropriately.
7. The Code Editor window must contain comments and the `Me.Close()` statement.

Figure 2-22   Guidelines for Exercise 9

FIX IT

10. Open the VB2017\Chap02\FixIt Solution\FixIt Solution.sln file. If necessary, open the designer window. Start the application. Test the tab order and the access keys. End the application and then fix the problems you observed.

CHAPTER 3

Coding with Variables, Named Constants, and Calculations

In this chapter's Focus on the Concepts lesson, you will learn how programmers use two different types of memory locations when coding procedures: variables and named constants. You will also learn how to write an assignment statement that performs a calculation and then assigns the result to a variable. The Apply the Concepts lesson expands upon some of the concepts covered in the Focus lesson. More specifically, you will learn how different types of variables and named constants are used in applications.

▌FOCUS ON THE CONCEPTS LESSON

Concepts covered in this lesson:

- F-1 Pseudocode and flowcharts
- F-2 Main memory of a computer
- F-3 Variables
- F-4 TryParse method
- F-5 Arithmetic expressions
- F-6 Assigning a value to an existing variable
- F-7 ToString method
- F-8 Option statements
- F-9 Named constants

F-1 Pseudocode and Flowcharts

In Chapter 2 you learned how to plan a Windows Forms application and then design and build its user interface. Now you need to learn how to code the application. You code an application so that the objects in the interface perform their assigned tasks when the appropriate event occurs. The objects and events that need to be coded are listed in the application's Planning Chart along with their assigned tasks. The Planning Chart and user interface shown in Figure 3-1 are for an application that calculates the area of a circle. The chart indicates that two event procedures need to be coded: btnCalc_Click and btnExit_Click.

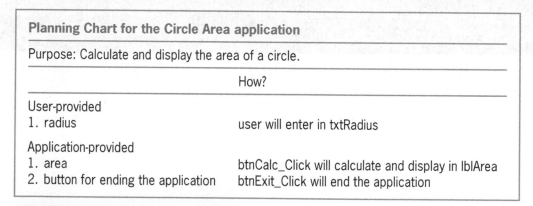

Planning Chart for the Circle Area application

Purpose: Calculate and display the area of a circle.

	How?
User-provided 1. radius	user will enter in txtRadius
Application-provided 1. area 2. button for ending the application	btnCalc_Click will calculate and display in lblArea btnExit_Click will end the application

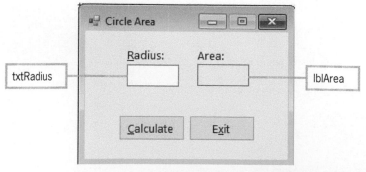

Figure 3-1   Planning Chart and user interface for the Circle Area application

It is important to plan a procedure before you begin coding it. Many programmers use planning tools such as pseudocode and flowcharts. **Pseudocode** uses short phrases to describe the steps a procedure must take to accomplish its goal. A **flowchart**, on the other hand, uses standardized symbols to illustrate a procedure's steps. Figure 3-2 shows the pseudocode and flowcharts for the procedures in the Circle Area application. When planning a procedure, you do not need to create both a flowchart and pseudocode; you need to use only one of these planning tools.

btnCalc_Click
1. declare variables
2. convert txtRadius.Text property to a number and store in a variable
3. calculate the area by multiplying pi by the radius squared (use 3.14159 for pi)
4. display the area in lblArea

btnExit_Click
end the application

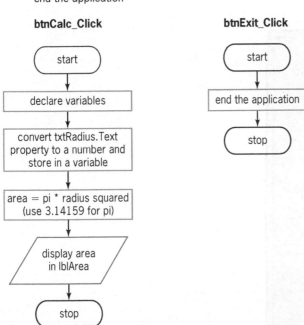

Figure 3-2 Pseudocode and flowcharts for the Circle Area application

The flowcharts in Figure 3-2 contain three different symbols: an oval, a rectangle, and a parallelogram. The oval symbol is called the **start/stop symbol**. The start and stop ovals indicate the beginning and end, respectively, of the flowchart. The rectangles are called **process symbols**. You use the process symbol to represent tasks such as ending the application and making calculations. The parallelogram in a flowchart is called the **input/output symbol**, and it is used to represent input tasks (such as getting information from the user) and output tasks (such as displaying information). The parallelogram in Figure 3-2 represents an output task. The lines connecting the symbols in a flowchart are called **flowlines**.

Programmers use the planning tool of their choice as a guide when coding the procedure. For example, according to both planning tools in Figure 3-2, the btnExit_Click procedure should end the application; you can code this procedure using the `Me.Close()` statement. Both planning tools for the btnCalc_Click procedure indicate that it has four tasks to perform; the concepts required to code the procedure are covered in this Focus lesson. Because the procedure will need to temporarily store values in the main memory of the computer, we will begin with that concept.

F-2 Main Memory of a Computer

The main memory of a computer is called **random access memory** or, more simply, **RAM**. When your computer is on, it uses RAM to temporarily store the items that are currently being used so that the computer's processor can quickly access them. Examples of items stored in RAM include the operating system (Windows), application programs (such as Visual Studio or the Circle Area application), and data (such as the radius entered in the txtRadius control or the area calculated by the application). When the computer is turned off, the contents of RAM are erased. (The operating system files and application program files still reside on your hard drive.)

Each memory location in RAM has a unique numeric address. It may be helpful to picture memory locations as lockers, similar to the ones shown in Figure 3-3. Like lockers, memory locations can be different sizes and hold different types of items. Unlike lockers, however, a memory location can store only one item at a time.

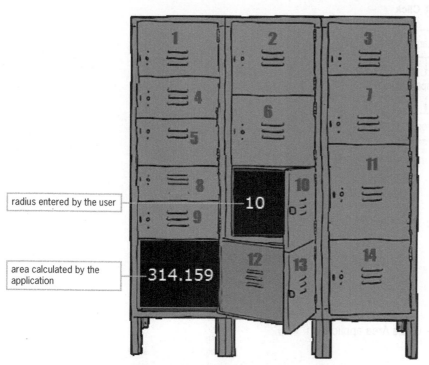

radius entered by the user

area calculated by the application

Figure 3-3 Locker illustration

Some of the locations in RAM are automatically filled with data while you use your computer. For example, when you start the Circle Area application, each program instruction is placed in a memory location, where it awaits processing. Similarly, when you enter the number 10 in the txtRadius control during run time, the computer stores your entry in a memory location. Your application can access the contents of the memory location by referring to the control's Text property, like this: txtRadius.Text.

Programmers can also reserve memory locations for their own use when coding a procedure. Reserving a memory location is more commonly referred to as **declaring a memory location**. There are two types of memory locations that a programmer can declare: variables and named constants. You will learn about variables first. Named constants are covered later in this Focus lesson.

F-3 Variables

A **variable** is a computer memory location where a programmer can temporarily store an item of data while an application is running. The memory location is called a variable because its contents can change (vary) during run time. Examples of data stored in variables include all of the user-provided items (from your Planning Chart) that will be included in a calculation, as well as the result of any calculation made by the application. Storing the data in a variable allows the programmer to control the preciseness of the data, verify that the data meets certain requirements, and save the data for later use within the application's code. It also makes your code run more efficiently because the computer can process data stored in a variable much faster than it can process data stored in the property of a control.

Most times you will use the **Dim statement** to declare a variable within the procedure that needs it. The statement assigns a name, a data type, and an initial value to the variable. The `Dim intQuantity As Integer` statement, for example, declares a variable whose name is `intQuantity`, data type is Integer, and initial value is the number 0. When the computer processes the Dim statement, it sets aside a section in its main memory and attaches the name `intQuantity` to it. An instruction within the procedure can then use the name to access the memory location, perhaps to store a different value in it, use its current value in a calculation, or simply display its value. Before viewing more examples of Dim statements, you will learn how to select appropriate data types and names for your variables.

Dim comes from the word *dimension*, which is how programmers in the 1960s referred to the process of allocating the computer's memory. *Dimension* refers to the size of something.

Selecting an Appropriate Data Type

A variable's data type indicates the type of data—for example, numeric or textual—the variable will store. It also determines the variable's size, which is the amount of memory it consumes. Visual Basic provides many different data types, but Figure 3-4 lists only the ones used in this book. Each data type in the list is a class, which means that each is a pattern from which one or more objects—in this case, variables—can be instantiated (created).

Data Type	Stores	Memory
Boolean	a logical value (True, False)	2 bytes
Decimal	numbers with a decimal place (29 significant digits) Range with no decimal place: $+/-79,228,162,514,264,337,593,543,950,335$ Range with a decimal place: $+/-7.9228162514264337593543950335$	16 bytes
Double	numbers with a decimal place (15 significant digits) Range: $+/-4.94065645841247 \times 10^{-324}$ to $+/-1.79769313486231 \times 10^{308}$	8 bytes
Integer	integers Range: $-2,147,483,648$ to $2,147,483,647$	4 bytes
String	text; 0 to approximately 2 billion characters	

Figure 3-4 Visual Basic data types used in this book

Variables assigned the Integer data type can store integers, which are positive or negative numbers that do not have any decimal places. If you need to store a number containing a decimal place, you would use either the Decimal or Double data type. The two data types differ in the range of numbers each can store and the amount of memory each needs to store the numbers. Calculations involving Double variables execute faster than those involving Decimal variables. However, calculations involving Decimal variables are not subject to the small rounding errors that may occur when using Double variables; this is due to the Decimal data type storing numbers with many more significant digits. In most cases, these small rounding errors do not create any problems in an application. One exception to this is when the application performs complex calculations involving money, where you need accuracy to the penny. In those cases, Decimal is the recommended data type.

Also listed in Figure 3-4 are the String and Boolean data types. The String data type can store from zero to approximately 2 billion characters. The Boolean data type stores Boolean (or logical) values: either True or False.

> The Boolean values (True and False) are named after the English mathematician George Boole.

Selecting an Appropriate Name

A variable's name, also called its identifier, should describe (identify) its contents. A good variable name is meaningful right after you finish a program and also years later when the program needs to be modified. The name allows the programmer to refer to the variable using one or more descriptive words, rather than its cryptic numeric address, in code. Descriptive words are easier to remember and serve to self-document your code. Figure 3-5 lists the rules and conventions this book will follow when naming variables.

Naming rules (these are required by Visual Basic)
1. Each variable declared in a procedure must have a unique name.
2. Each name must begin with a letter and contain only letters, numbers, and the underscore character.
3. The recommended maximum number of characters to use for a name is 32.
4. The name cannot be a reserved word, such as Sub or Double.

Naming conventions used in this book
1. Each name will begin with an ID of three (or more) characters that represents the variable's data type. The IDs are listed below.
2. The remaining characters after the ID will indicate the variable's purpose.
3. Each name will be entered using camel case: the ID will be in lowercase, and the first letter in each subsequent word in the name will be capitalized.

Data type	ID	Example
Boolean	bln	blnIsInsured
Decimal	dec	decSales
Double	dbl	dblTotalDue
Integer	int	intPopulation
String	str	strName

Figure 3-5   Rules and conventions for naming variables

Mini-Quiz 3-1

1. A user-provided item that will be used in a calculation should be stored in a variable. True or False?

2. The result of a calculation made by an application should be stored in a variable. True or False?

3. Which data types are appropriate for storing the number 4.5?

4. Which data type stores only whole numbers?

5. Which data type is appropriate for storing the name of a street?

6. Which of the following are valid names for variables: intAge, dblFirst&Qtr, decRate5, strFirst_Name, and dbl$Sales?

1) True 2) True 3) Decimal and Double 4) Integer 5) String 6) intAge, decRate5, and strFirst_Name

Examples of Variable Declaration Statements

Once you have chosen its data type and name, you can declare the variable in code. Figure 3-6 shows the Dim statement's syntax and includes several examples of using the statement. As mentioned earlier, a variable is considered an object in Visual Basic and is an instance of the class specified in the *dataType* information. The Dim intQuantity As Integer statement, for example, uses the Integer class to create a variable (object) named intQuantity.

Dim Statement

Syntax
Dim *variableName* **As** *dataType* [= *initialValue*]

Example 1
Dim intQuantity As Integer
Declares an Integer variable named intQuantity; the variable is automatically initialized to 0.

Example 2
Dim intCount As Integer = 1
Declares an Integer variable named intCount and initializes it to 1.

Example 3
Dim blnIsInsured As Boolean
Declares a Boolean variable named blnIsInsured; the variable is automatically initialized using the keyword False.

Example 4
Dim blnIsValid As Boolean = True
Declares a Boolean variable named blnIsValid and initializes it using the keyword True.

Example 5
Dim strMsg As String
Declares a String variable named strMsg; the variable is automatically initialized using the keyword Nothing.

Figure 3-6 Syntax and examples of the Dim statement

The square brackets in the syntax indicate that the "= *initialValue*" part of the Dim statement is optional. If it is omitted, which most times it is, the computer stores a default value in the variable. The default value depends on the variable's data type. A variable declared using one of the numeric data types (Integer, Decimal, and Double) is automatically initialized to the number 0. The computer automatically initializes a Boolean variable using the keyword `False`. String variables are automatically initialized using the keyword `Nothing`, which means they contain no data at all.

The btnCalc_Click procedure in the Circle Area application will require two variables: one for the radius (because it is a user-provided item that will be used in a calculation) and one for the area (because it is the result of a calculation made by the application). Both items may contain a decimal place, so you will use the Double data type for each. Meaningful names for both variables are `dblRadius` and `dblArea`.

START HERE

To begin coding the btnCalc_Click procedure:

1. Open the Circle Solution.sln file contained in the VB2017\Chap03\Circle Solution folder. If the designer window is not open, double-click **Main Form.vb** in the Solution Explorer window.

2. Open the Code Editor window and locate the btnCalc_Click procedure. Click the **blank line** immediately above the End Sub clause and then enter the following two Dim statements. Be sure to use the exact capitalization shown for the variable names. Press **Enter** twice after typing the second Dim statement. (For now, do not be concerned about the green squiggle that appears below each variable name after you press Enter.)

```
Dim dblRadius As Double
Dim dblArea As Double
```

3. Place your mouse pointer on the green squiggle below `dblArea`, as shown in Figure 3-7. A warning message box appears and alerts you that the `dblArea` variable has not been used yet. The squiggle will disappear when you include the variable name in another statement within the procedure.

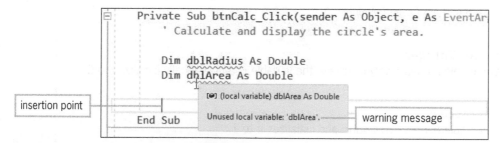

Figure 3-7   Dim statements entered in the btnCalc_Click procedure

Mini-Quiz 3-2

1. Write a Dim statement that declares a Decimal variable named `decSales`.

2. Write a Dim statement that declares a String variable named `strName`.

3. Write a Dim statement that declares a Boolean variable named `blnIsRegistered` and initializes it using the keyword `True`.

1) Dim decSales As Decimal 2) Dim strName As String
3) Dim blnIsRegistered As Boolean = True

F-4 TryParse Method

When the user enters data in a text box during run time, the computer stores the data in the control's Text property. Because the Text property can contain any characters—numbers, letters, and so on—it is treated as a string in Visual Basic. A **string** is simply a sequence of characters. Even when the Text property contains only numbers, it is still considered a string and cannot be used as is in a calculation; instead, it must be converted to its numeric equivalent. This explains why Step 2 in the btnCalc_Click procedure's pseudocode converts the txtRadius control's Text property to a number before using it in the area calculation.

One way of converting a string to a number is to use the **TryParse method**. Every numeric data type in Visual Basic has a TryParse method that converts a string to that particular data type. The Integer data type's TryParse method converts a string to an integer. Similarly, the Double data type's TryParse method converts a string to a Double number. Figure 3-8 shows the basic syntax of the method and includes examples of using it.

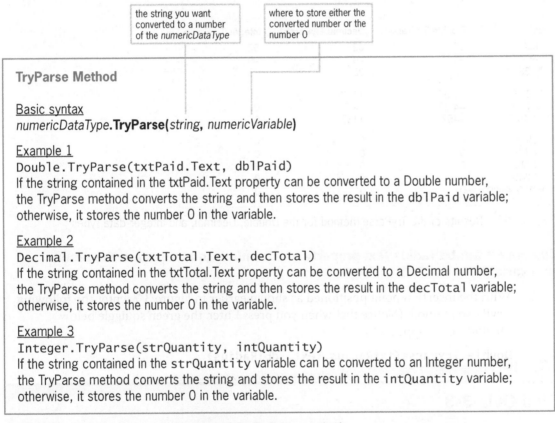

the string you want converted to a number of the *numericDataType*

where to store either the converted number or the number 0

TryParse Method

Basic syntax
numericDataType.**TryParse**(*string*, *numericVariable*)

Example 1
```
Double.TryParse(txtPaid.Text, dblPaid)
```
If the string contained in the txtPaid.Text property can be converted to a Double number, the TryParse method converts the string and then stores the result in the dblPaid variable; otherwise, it stores the number 0 in the variable.

Example 2
```
Decimal.TryParse(txtTotal.Text, decTotal)
```
If the string contained in the txtTotal.Text property can be converted to a Decimal number, the TryParse method converts the string and then stores the result in the decTotal variable; otherwise, it stores the number 0 in the variable.

Example 3
```
Integer.TryParse(strQuantity, intQuantity)
```
If the string contained in the strQuantity variable can be converted to an Integer number, the TryParse method converts the string and stores the result in the intQuantity variable; otherwise, it stores the number 0 in the variable.

Figure 3-8 Basic syntax and examples of the TryParse method

In this book, *numericDataType* in the syntax will be Integer, Decimal, or Double. The dot member access operator indicates that the TryParse method is a member of the *numericDataType* class. The method's **arguments**, which are the items within parentheses, represent information that the method needs to perform its task. The *string* argument is the string you want converted to a number of the *numericDataType*. The *string* argument is typically either the Text property of a control or the name of a String variable. The *numericVariable* argument is the name of a numeric variable where the TryParse method can store the number. The *numericVariable* must have the same data type as specified in the *numericDataType* portion of the syntax. For example, if *numericDataType* is Double, then the *numericVariable* must have been declared as a Double variable in its Dim statement.

The TryParse method parses its *string* argument to determine whether the string can be converted to a number. In this case, the term "parse" means to look at each character in the string. If the string can be converted to a number, the TryParse method converts it and then stores the number in the variable specified in the *numericVariable* argument; otherwise, it stores the number 0 in the variable. For example, the statement `Double.TryParse("15.65", dblPay)` will store the number 15.65 in the `dblPay` variable because the *string* "15.65" can be converted to a Double number. The statement `Double.TryParse("ABC", dblPay)`, however, will store the number 0 in the `dblPay` variable because the *string* "ABC" cannot be converted to a Double number.

Figure 3-9 shows how the TryParse method of the Double, Decimal, and Integer data types would convert various strings. As the figure indicates, the three methods can convert a string that contains only numbers. They can also convert a string that contains a leading sign as well as one that contains leading or trailing spaces. In addition, the Double.TryParse and Decimal.TryParse methods can convert a string that contains a decimal point or a comma. However, none of the three methods can convert a string that contains a dollar sign, a percent sign, a letter, a space within the string, or an empty string.

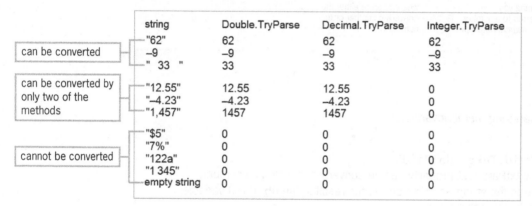

	string	Double.TryParse	Decimal.TryParse	Integer.TryParse
can be converted	"62"	62	62	62
	−9	−9	−9	−9
	" 33 "	33	33	33
can be converted by only two of the methods	"12.55"	12.55	12.55	0
	"−4.23"	−4.23	−4.23	0
	"1,457"	1457	1457	0
cannot be converted	"$5"	0	0	0
	"7%"	0	0	0
	"122a"	0	0	0
	"1 345"	0	0	0
	empty string	0	0	0

Figure 3-9 Results of the TryParse method for the Double, Decimal, and Integer data types

START HERE

To convert the txtRadius.Text property to a number and then store the result in a variable:

1. With the insertion point positioned as shown earlier in Figure 3-7, enter the following TryParse method. (Notice that when you press Enter, the green squiggle below `dblRadius` disappears.)

   `Double.TryParse(txtRadius.Text, dblRadius)`

Mini-Quiz 3-3

1. Write a TryParse method that converts the contents of the txtAge.Text property to an integer, storing the result in the `intAge` variable.

2. If the txtTax.Text property contains $57.25, what number will the `Decimal.TryParse(txtTax.Text, decTax)` method store in the `decTax` variable?

3. If the txtTax.Text property contains 6.89, what number will the `Decimal.TryParse(txtTax.Text, decTax)` method store in the `decTax` variable?

4. Write a TryParse method that stores the `strSales` variable's value in the `dblSales` variable.

1) Integer.TryParse(txtAge.Text, intAge) 2) 0 3) 6.89
4) Double.TryParse(strSales, dblSales)

Step 3 in the procedure's pseudocode calculates the circle's area. Before you can code this step, you need to learn how to write arithmetic expressions in Visual Basic.

F-5 Arithmetic Expressions

Most applications require the computer to perform at least one calculation. You instruct the computer to perform a calculation using an arithmetic expression, which is an expression that contains one or more arithmetic operators. Figure 3-10 lists the most commonly used arithmetic operators available in Visual Basic, along with their precedence numbers. It also includes several examples of using the operators. The precedence numbers indicate the order in which the computer performs the operation in an expression. Operations with a precedence number of 1 are performed before operations with a precedence number of 2, and so on. However, you can use parentheses to override the order of precedence because operations within parentheses are always performed before operations outside parentheses.

Operator	Operation	Precedence
^	exponentiation (raises a number to a power)	1
−	negation (reverses the sign of a number)	2
*, /	multiplication and division	3
\	integer division	4
Mod	modulus (remainder) arithmetic	5
+, −	addition and subtraction	6

Note: You can use parentheses to override the normal order of precedence. For instance, in the 6 / (2 + 4) example, the parentheses indicate that the addition should be performed before the division.

Examples	Results
7 ^ 2	49
6 / 2 + 4	7
6 / (2 + 4)	1
33 \ 5	6
33 Mod 5	3

Figure 3-10 Most commonly used arithmetic operators

> The expression 7 ^ 2 is equivalent to 7 * 7. Similarly, the expression 7 ^ 3 is equivalent to 7 * 7 * 7.

Although the negation and subtraction operators use the same symbol (a hyphen), there is a difference between them. The negation operator is a unary operator, which means it requires only one operand. The expression −10 uses the negation operator to turn its one operand (the positive number 10) into a negative number. The subtraction operator, on the other hand, is a binary operator; this means it requires two operands. The expression 8 − 2 uses the subtraction operator to subtract its second operand (the number 2) from its first operand (the number 8).

The **integer division operator** (\) divides two integers and then returns the result as an integer. Using this operator, the expression 9 \ 4 results in 2, which is the integer result of dividing 9 by 4. (If you use the standard division operator [/] to divide 9 by 4, the result is 2.25 rather than 2.) You might use the integer division operator in a procedure that determines the number of quarters, dimes, and nickels to return as change to a customer. For example, if a customer should receive 77 cents in change, you could use the expression 77 \ 25 to determine the number of quarters to return; the expression evaluates to 3.

The **modulus operator** (sometimes referred to as the remainder operator) also divides two numbers, but the numbers do not have to be integers. After dividing the numbers, the modulus operator returns the remainder of the division. For example, the expression 9 Mod 4 equals 1, which is the remainder of 9 divided by 4. A common use for the modulus operator is to determine whether a number is even or odd. If you divide the number by 2 and the remainder is 0, the number is even; if the remainder is 1, the number is odd.

Some of the arithmetic operators, such as the addition and subtraction ones, have the same precedence number. When an expression contains more than one operator having the same priority, those operators are evaluated from left to right. In the expression 45 − 20 / 5 + 15, the division is performed first, then the subtraction, and then the addition. The result of the expression is the number 56, as shown in Example 1 in Figure 3-11. You can use parentheses to change the order in which the operators in the expression are evaluated, as shown in Example 2. The parentheses tell the computer to perform the addition first, then the division, and then the subtraction; the result is 44 rather than 56.

Example 1		Example 2	
Expression: 45 − 20 / 5 + 15		Expression: 45 − 20 / (5 + 15)	
Division first	45 − 20 / 5 + 15	Addition first	45 − 20 / (5 + 15)
Subtraction next	45 − 4 + 15	Division next	45 − 20 / 20
Addition last	41 + 15	Subtraction last	45 − 1
Answer:	56	Answer:	44

Figure 3-11   Expressions containing more than one operator having the same precedence

Ch03-Arithmetic Operators

The arithmetic expressions you enter in your code should not contain commas or special characters, such as the dollar sign or percent sign. To include a percentage in an arithmetic expression, you must use its decimal equivalent. For example, to multiply 30 by 5%, you would use the expression 30 * 0.05 (rather than 30 * 5%).

Arithmetic expressions can also contain numeric variables, as shown in the examples in Figure 3-12. The computer uses the value stored inside the variable when evaluating the expression. The expression in Example 4 could be used to calculate the area in the Circle Area application.

Expressions Containing Numeric Variables

Example 1
```
dblSalary * 0.04
```
Multiplies the contents of the `dblSalary` variable by 0.04.

Example 2
```
intAge + 1
```
Adds 1 to the contents of the `intAge` variable.

Example 3
```
decSales − decDiscount
```
Subtracts the contents of the `decDiscount` variable from the contents of the `decSales` variable.

Example 4
```
3.14159 * dblRadius ^ 2
```
Squares the contents of the `dblRadius` variable and then multiplies the result by 3.14159. The expression is equivalent to `3.14159 * dblRadius * dblRadius`.

Figure 3-12   Examples of expressions containing numeric variables

Mini-Quiz 3-4

1. Evaluate the following expression: 6 / 2 * 3 + 4.
2. Evaluate the following expression: 3 * 2 ^ 4 − 6.
3. Evaluate the following expression: 55 \ 5 * 6 Mod 3.
4. Evaluate the following expression: 45 − (20 / 5 + 15).
5. Write an expression that multiplies the value stored in the dblTotal variable by 15%.

1) 13 2) 42 3) 1 4) 26 5) dblTotal * 0.15

F-6 Assigning a Value to an Existing Variable

In Chapter 1 you learned how to use an assignment statement to assign a value to a control's property while an application is running. An assignment statement is also used to assign a value to a variable during run time; the syntax for doing this is shown in Figure 3-13. In the syntax, *expression* can contain items such as numbers, string literals, object properties, variables, keywords, and arithmetic operators. When the computer processes an assignment statement, it evaluates the *expression* first and then stores the result in the *variable*. Keep in mind that a variable can store only one value at any one time. When you assign another value to a variable, the new value replaces the existing one.

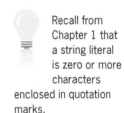 Recall from Chapter 1 that a string literal is zero or more characters enclosed in quotation marks.

Assigning a Value to an Existing Variable

Syntax ———— [assignment operator]
variable = *expression*
Note: The *expression*'s data type should be the same as the *variable*'s data type.

Example 1
intYear = 2019
Assigns the integer 2019 to the intYear variable.

Example 2
strCity = "Charleston"
Assigns the string literal "Charleston" to the strCity variable.

Example 3
strState = txtState.Text
Assigns the string contained in the txtState control's Text property to the strState variable.

Example 4
dblRate = 0.25
Assigns the Double number 0.25 to the dblRate variable.

Example 5 ———— [changes the number's type from Double to Decimal]
decRate = 0.03D
Converts the Double number 0.03 to Decimal and then assigns the result to the decRate variable.

Example 6
dblNewPay = dblCurrentPay * 1.1
Multiplies the contents of the dblCurrentPay variable by the Double number 1.1 and then assigns the result to the dblNewPay variable.

Figure 3-13 Syntax and examples of assigning a value to a variable

As noted in the figure, the *expression*'s data type should be the same as the *variable*'s data type. The statement in Example 1 assigns an integer to an Integer variable, and the statement in Example 2 assigns a string literal to a String variable. Notice that string literals are enclosed in quotation marks, but numbers and variable names are not. The quotation marks differentiate a string literal from both a number and a variable name. In other words, "2019" is a string literal, but 2019 is a number. Similarly, "Charleston" is a string literal, but Charleston (without the quotation marks) would be interpreted by the computer as the name of a variable. When the computer processes a statement that assigns a string literal to a String variable, it assigns only the characters that appear between the quotation marks; it does not assign the quotation marks themselves.

The statement in Example 3 assigns the string contained in the txtState control's Text property to a String variable. Example 4's statement assigns the Double number 0.25 to a Double variable named dblRate. In Visual Basic, a number that has a decimal place is automatically treated as a Double number.

The decRate = 0.03D statement in Example 5 shows how you convert a number of the Double data type to the Decimal data type, and then assign the result to a Decimal variable. The D that follows the number 0.03 in the statement is one of the literal type characters in Visual Basic. A **literal type character** forces a literal to assume a data type other than the one its form indicates. In this case, the D forces the Double number 0.03 to assume the Decimal data type.

The dblNewPay = dblCurrentPay * 1.1 statement in Example 6 multiplies the contents of the dblCurrentPay variable by the Double number 1.1 and then assigns the result to the dblNewPay variable. Notice that the calculation appearing on the right side of the assignment operator is performed first, and then the result is assigned to the variable whose name appears on the left side of the operator.

You are now ready to code Step 3 in the btnCalc_Click procedure's pseudocode (shown earlier in Figure 3-2). Recall that Step 3 calculates the circle's area. The procedure will assign the area to the dblArea variable.

START HERE

To calculate the circle's area and then assign it to a variable:

1. In the blank line below the Double.TryParse method, enter the following assignment statement:

```
dblArea = 3.14159 * dblRadius ^ 2
```

Mini-Quiz 3-5

1. Write a statement that assigns the number 2.5 to the dblNum variable.

2. Write a statement that assigns the number 9.99 to the decPrice variable.

3. Write a statement that assigns the name Jim to the strFirst variable.

4. Write a statement that adds together the values stored in the dblDomestic and dblInternational variables, assigning the result to the dblTotal variable.

1) dblNum = 2.5 2) decPrice = 9.99D 3) strFirst = "Jim"
4) dblTotal = dblDomestic + dblInternational

F-7 ToString Method

The last step in the btnCalc_Click procedure's pseudocode displays the circle's area in the lblArea control. You do this using an assignment statement that assigns the number stored in the **dblArea** variable to the lblArea.Text property; however, you first must convert the number to a string. (Recall that the Text property stores only strings.) You can use the ToString method to make the conversion. All of the numeric data types have a ToString method for this purpose. The ToString method also allows you to **format** the value, which means to specify the number of decimal places and the special characters (such as a dollar sign, percent sign, or thousands separator) to display.

The ToString method's syntax is shown in Figure 3-14 along with examples of using the method. In the syntax, *numericVariable* is the name of a numeric variable. The **ToString method** formats a copy of the value stored in the numeric variable and then returns the result as a string. The optional *formatString* argument specifies the format you want to use.

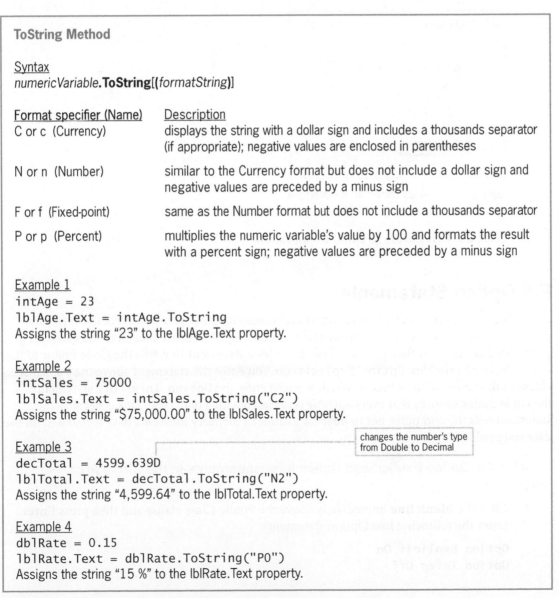

ToString Method

Syntax
numericVariable.**ToString**[(*formatString*)]

Format specifier (Name)	Description
C or c (Currency)	displays the string with a dollar sign and includes a thousands separator (if appropriate); negative values are enclosed in parentheses
N or n (Number)	similar to the Currency format but does not include a dollar sign and negative values are preceded by a minus sign
F or f (Fixed-point)	same as the Number format but does not include a thousands separator
P or p (Percent)	multiplies the numeric variable's value by 100 and formats the result with a percent sign; negative values are preceded by a minus sign

Example 1
```
intAge = 23
lblAge.Text = intAge.ToString
```
Assigns the string "23" to the lblAge.Text property.

Example 2
```
intSales = 75000
lblSales.Text = intSales.ToString("C2")
```
Assigns the string "$75,000.00" to the lblSales.Text property.

Example 3
```
decTotal = 4599.639D                    changes the number's type
                                        from Double to Decimal
lblTotal.Text = decTotal.ToString("N2")
```
Assigns the string "4,599.64" to the lblTotal.Text property.

Example 4
```
dblRate = 0.15
lblRate.Text = dblRate.ToString("P0")
```
Assigns the string "15 %" to the lblRate.Text property.

Figure 3-14   Syntax and examples of the ToString method

The *formatString* argument must take the form "*Axx*", where *A* is an alphabetic character called the format specifier and *xx* is a sequence of digits called the precision specifier. The format specifier must be one of the built-in format characters. The most commonly used format characters are listed in Figure 3-14. When used with one of the format characters listed in the figure, the precision specifier controls the number of digits that will appear after the decimal point in the formatted string.

START HERE

To display the area with a comma (if necessary) and two decimal places:

1. In the blank line below the calculation statement, enter the following assignment statement:

   ```
   lblArea.Text = dblArea.ToString("N2")
   ```

2. Save the solution and then start the application. Type **5.5** in the Radius box and then click the **Calculate** button. See Figure 3-15.

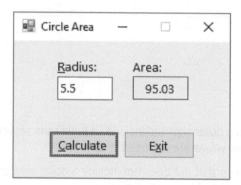

Figure 3-15   Area shown in the interface

3. Click the **Exit** button to end the application.

F-8 Option Statements

A variable's declaration statement is important because it allows you to control the variable's data type; it also makes your code more self-documenting. To ensure that all of the variables in your code have been declared, Visual Basic provides a statement that tells the Code Editor to flag any undeclared variables: `Option Explicit On`. You enter the statement above the Public Class clause in the Code Editor window. When you also enter the `Option Infer Off` statement, the Code Editor ensures that every variable is declared with a data type. This is because the statement tells the computer not to infer (or assume) a memory location's data type based on the data assigned to it.

START HERE

To enter the Option Explicit and Option Infer statements in the Circle Area application:

1. Click the **blank line** immediately above the Public Class clause and then press **Enter**. Enter the following two Option statements:

   ```
   Option Explicit On
   Option Infer Off
   ```

Earlier in this Focus lesson, you learned that the data type of the value assigned to a memory location should be the same as the data type of the memory location itself. If the value's data type does not match the memory location's data type, the computer uses a process called **implicit type conversion** to convert the value to fit the memory location. For example, when processing the statement `Dim dblLength As Double = 9`, the computer converts the integer 9 to the Double number 9.0 before storing the value in the `dblLength` variable. When a value is converted from one data type to another data type that can store either larger numbers or numbers with greater precision, the value is said to be **promoted**. In this case, if the `dblLength` variable is used subsequently in a calculation, the results of the calculation will not be adversely affected by the implicit promotion of the number 9 to the number 9.0.

On the other hand, if you inadvertently assign a Double number to a memory location that can store only integers, the computer converts the Double number to an integer before storing the value in the memory location. It does this by rounding the number to the nearest whole number and then truncating (dropping off) the decimal portion of the number. When processing the statement `Dim intScore As Integer = 78.4`, for example, the computer converts the Double number 78.4 to the integer 78 before storing the integer in the `intScore` variable. When a value is converted from one data type to another data type that can store only smaller numbers or numbers with less precision, the value is said to be **demoted**. If the `intScore` variable is used subsequently in a calculation, the implicit demotion of the number 78.4 to the number 78 will probably cause the calculated results to be incorrect.

With implicit type conversions, data loss can occur when a value is converted from one data type to a narrower data type, which is a data type with less precision or smaller capacity. You can eliminate the problems that occur as a result of implicit type conversions by entering the `Option Strict On` statement above the Public Class clause in the Code Editor window. When the `Option Strict On` statement appears in an application's code, the computer uses the type conversion rules listed in Figure 3-16. The figure also includes examples of these rules.

Type Conversion Rules

1. Strings will not be implicitly converted to numbers.

   Incorrect: `dblRadius = txtRadius.Text`
   Solution: `Double.TryParse(txtRadius.Text, dblRadius)`

2. Numbers will not be implicitly converted to strings.

   Incorrect: `lblArea.Text = dblArea`
   Solution: `lblArea.Text = dblArea.ToString("N2")`

3. Wider data types will not be implicitly demoted to narrower data types.

   Incorrect: `decRate = 0.05`
   Solution: `decRate = 0.05D`

4. Narrower data types will be implicitly promoted to wider data types.

   Correct: `dblAverage = dblTotal / intNum`

Figure 3-16   Rules and examples of type conversions

According to the first rule, the computer will not implicitly convert a string to a number. As a result, the Code Editor will issue the warning message "Option Strict On disallows implicit conversions from 'String' to 'Double'" when your code contains the statement `dblRadius = txtRadius.Text`. As you learned earlier, you can use the TryParse method to explicitly convert a string to the Double data type before assigning it to a Double variable. The appropriate TryParse method to use in this case is shown in Figure 3-16.

According to the second rule, the computer will not implicitly convert a number to a string. Therefore, the Code Editor will issue an appropriate warning message when your code contains the statement `lblArea.Text = dblArea`. As Figure 3-16 indicates, you can use the ToString method to explicitly convert the number stored in the `dblArea` variable to a string before assigning it to the lblArea.Text property.

The third rule states that wider data types will not be implicitly demoted to narrower data types. A data type is wider than another data type if it can store either larger numbers or numbers with greater precision. Because of this rule, a Double number will not be implicitly demoted to the Decimal or Integer data types. If your code contains the statement `decRate = 0.05`, the Code Editor will issue an appropriate warning message because the statement assigns a Double number to a Decimal variable. As Figure 3-16 shows, you can use the literal type character D to convert the Double number to the Decimal data type.

According to the last rule listed in Figure 3-16, the computer will implicitly promote narrower data types to wider data types. This means that when processing the statement `dblAverage = dblTotal / intNum`, the computer will implicitly promote the integer stored in the `intNum` variable to Double before dividing it into the contents of the `dblTotal` variable. The result, a Double number, will be assigned to the `dblAverage` variable.

START HERE

To enter the Option Strict statement in the Circle Area application:

1. Insert a blank line below the `Option Explicit On` statement. Type **Option Strict On**, but don't press Enter.

If a project contains more than one form, the three Option statements should be entered in each form's Code Editor window.

Note: Rather than entering the Option statements in the Code Editor window, you can set the options using either the Project Designer window or the Options dialog box. However, it is strongly recommended that you enter the Option statements in the Code Editor window because doing so makes your code more self-documenting and ensures that the options are set appropriately. The steps for setting the options in the Project Designer window and the Options dialog box are included in the Summary section.

F-9 Named Constants

In addition to declaring variables in a procedure, you can also declare named constants. Like a variable, a **named constant** is a memory location inside the computer. However, unlike the value stored in a variable, the value stored in a named constant cannot be changed while the application is running. Named constants make code more self-documenting and easier to modify because they allow you to use meaningful words in place of values that are less clear. The named constant dblPI, for example, is much more meaningful than the number 3.14159, which is the value of pi rounded to five decimal places. Once you create a named constant, you then can use the constant's meaningful name (instead of its less clear value) in the application's code. Using a named constant to represent a value has another advantage: If the value changes in the future, you will need to modify only the named constant's declaration statement, rather than all of the program statements that use the value.

You declare a named constant using the **Const statement**. The statement's syntax is shown in Figure 3-17 along with examples of using the statement. In the syntax, *expression* is the value you want to store in the named constant, and it must have the same data type as the named constant itself. The expression can contain a number, a string literal, another named constant, or an arithmetic operator; however, it cannot contain a variable or a method. To differentiate the name of a constant from the name of a variable, many programmers uppercase all of the characters that appear after the three-character ID in a constant's name.

Const Statement

Syntax
Const *constantName* **As** *dataType* = *expression*

Example 1
`Const dblPI As Double = 3.14159`
Declares `dblPI` as a Double named constant and initializes it to the Double number 3.14159.

Example 2
`Const intMAX_SPEED As Integer = 70`
Declares `intMAX_SPEED` as an Integer named constant and initializes it to the integer 70.

Example 3
`Const strTITLE As String = "Vice President of Sales"`
Declares `strTITLE` as a String named constant and initializes it to the string literal "Vice President of Sales".

> changes the number's type from Double to Decimal

Example 4
`Const decRATE As Decimal = 0.05D`
Declares `decRATE` as a Decimal named constant and initializes it to the Decimal number 0.05.

Figure 3-17   Syntax and examples of the Const statement

To use a named constant in the Circle Area application:

START HERE

1. Click the **blank line** immediately above the first Dim statement and then press **Enter**. In the blank line, type the following Const statement, but don't press Enter.

    Const dblPI As Double = 3.14159

2. Change 3.14159 in the calculation statement to **dblPI**.

3. Save the solution and then start the application. Type **5.5** in the Radius box and then click the **Calculate** button to display the circle's area, which is 95.03.

4. Click the **Exit** button to end the application. Figure 3-18 shows the application's code. Close the Code Editor window and then close the solution.

```
1  ' Name:          Circle Project
2  ' Purpose:        Calculate and display the circle's area.
3  ' Programmer:     <your name> on <current date>
4
5  Option Explicit On
6  Option Strict On
7  Option Infer Off
8
9  Public Class frmMain
10     Private Sub btnCalc_Click(sender As Object, e As Even
11         ' Calculate and display the circle's area.
12
13         Const dblPI As Double = 3.14159
14         Dim dblRadius As Double
15         Dim dblArea As Double
16
17         Double.TryParse(txtRadius.Text, dblRadius)
18         dblArea = dblPI * dblRadius ^ 2
19         lblArea.Text = dblArea.ToString("N2")
20
21     End Sub
22
23     Private Sub btnExit_Click(sender As Object, e As Even
24         Me.Close()
25     End Sub
26  End Class
```

Figure 3-18   Circle Area application's code

Mini-Quiz 3-6

1. Write a statement that displays the decPrice variable's value in the lblPrice.Text property. The value should contain a dollar sign and two decimal places.

2. Write a statement that displays the dblRate variable's value in the lblRate.Text property. The value should contain a percent sign and no decimal places.

3. Write a statement that displays the intQuantity variable's value in the lblQuantity.Text property.

4. If Option Strict is set to On, how will the computer evaluate the intPrice * 1.05 expression?

5. Write a statement that declares a named constant whose value is 0.12 and name is dblRATE.

YOU DO IT 1!

Create an application named You Do It 1 and save it in the VB2017\Chap03 folder. Add a text box, a label, and a button to the form. The button's Click event procedure should store the contents of the text box in a Double variable named dblCost. It then should display the variable's contents in the label. Enter the three Option statements above the Public Class clause in the Code Editor window, and then code the procedure. Save the solution and then start and test the application. Close the solution.

YOU DO IT 2!

Create an application named You Do It 2 and save it in the VB2017\Chap03 folder. Add a text box, a label, and a button to the form. Enter the following three Option statements above the Public Class clause in the Code Editor window: Option Explicit On, Option Strict Off, and Option Infer Off. In the button's Click event procedure, declare a Double variable named dblNum. Use an assignment statement to assign the contents of the text box to the Double variable. Then, use an assignment statement to assign the contents of the Double variable to the label. Save the solution and then start and test the application. Stop the application. Finally, change the Option Strict Off statement to Option Strict On and then use what you learned in this Focus lesson to make the necessary modifications to the code. Save the solution and then start and test the application. Close the solution.

APPLY THE CONCEPTS LESSON

After studying this lesson, you should be able to:

- A-1 Determine a memory location's scope and lifetime
- A-2 Use procedure-level variables
- A-3 Use procedure-level named constants
- A-4 Use a class-level variable
- A-5 Use a static variable
- A-6 Use a class-level named constant
- A-7 Professionalize your application's interface

A-1 Determine a Memory Location's Scope and Lifetime

Besides a name, a data type, and an initial value, every variable and named constant also has a scope and a lifetime. The **scope** indicates where the declared memory location can be used in an application's code, and the **lifetime** indicates how long the variable or named constant remains in the computer's main memory.

The scope and lifetime are determined by where you declare the memory location in your code. Memory locations declared in a procedure have **procedure scope** and are called **procedure-level variables** and **procedure-level named constants**. These variables and named constants can be used only within the procedure that contains their declaration statement, and only after their declaration statement. They are removed from the computer's main memory when the procedure ends. In other words, a procedure-level variable has the same lifetime as the procedure that declares it. In the Circle Area application from this chapter's Focus lesson, the dblRadius and dblArea variables are procedure-level variables because they are declared in the btnCalc_Click procedure (shown earlier in Figure 3-18). Likewise, the dblPI named constant declared in the procedure is a procedure-level named constant. Only the btnCalc_Click procedure can use both variables and the named constant, and the three memory locations are removed from main memory when the procedure ends.

Memory locations declared in a form class's declarations section, but outside of any procedures, have **class scope** and are referred to as **class-level variables** and **class-level named constants**. The **form class's declarations section** is the area between the form's Public Class and End Class clauses in the Code Editor window. However, class-level declaration statements typically appear immediately after the Public Class <*formname*> clause. (As you learned in Chapter 1, the Public Class frmMain clause declares a class named frmMain.) Class-level variables and named constants can be used by all of the procedures in the class that contains their declaration statement. In addition, they have the same lifetime as the application, which means they retain their values and remain in the computer's main memory until the application ends.

ChO3-Scope and Lifetime

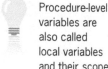

Procedure-level variables are also called local variables and their scope is often referred to as local scope.

Memory locations can also have namespace scope. Such memory locations can lead to unintentional errors in a program and should be avoided, if possible. For this reason, they are not covered in this book.

Mini-Quiz 3-7

1. Where are procedure-level variables declared?

2. Where are class-level named constants declared?

3. When are procedure-level named constants removed from the computer's main memory?

4. When are class-level variables removed from the computer's main memory?

3) when the procedure ends 4) when the application ends

1) in a procedure 2) immediately after the Public Class clause in a form class's declarations section

Because most of the memory locations declared in an application's code are procedure-level variables, we will begin with examples of those.

A-2 Use Procedure-Level Variables

Procedure-level variables are typically declared at the beginning of a procedure, and they can be used only after their declaration statement within the procedure. They remain in the computer's main memory only while the procedure is running, and they are removed from memory when the procedure ends. As mentioned earlier, most of the variables in your applications will be procedure-level variables. This is because fewer unintentional errors occur in applications when the variables are declared using the minimum scope needed, which usually is procedure scope.

In the *A-5 Use a Static Variable* section of this lesson, you will learn how to declare a procedure-level variable that remains in the computer's memory even when the procedure in which it is declared ends.

The Commission Calculator application illustrates the use of procedure-level variables. As the interface shown in Figure 3-19 indicates, the application displays the amount of a salesperson's commission. The commission is calculated by multiplying the salesperson's sales by the appropriate commission rate: either 8% or 10%.

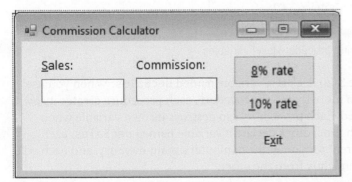

Figure 3-19   User interface for the Commission Calculator application

Figure 3-20 shows the Click event procedures for the 8% rate and 10% rate buttons. The comments in the figure indicate the purpose of each line of code. When each procedure ends, its procedure-level variables are removed from the computer's memory. The variables will be created again the next time the user clicks the button.

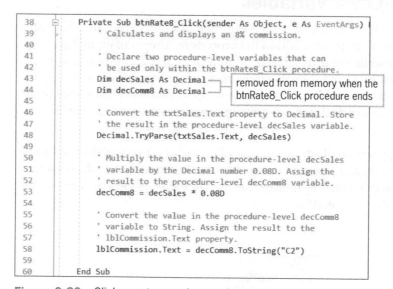

```
14   Private Sub btnRate10_Click(sender As Object, e As EventArgs)
15      ' Calculates and displays a 10% commission.
16
17      ' Declare two procedure-level variables that can
18      ' be used only within the btnRate10_Click procedure.
19      Dim decSales As Decimal          removed from memory when the
20      Dim decComm10 As Decimal         btnRate10_Click procedure ends
21
22      ' Convert the txtSales.Text property to Decimal. Store
23      ' the result in the procedure-level decSales variable.
24      Decimal.TryParse(txtSales.Text, decSales)
25
26      ' Multiply the value in the procedure-level decSales
27      ' variable by the Decimal number 0.1D. Assign the
28      ' result to the procedure-level decComm10 variable.
29      decComm10 = decSales * 0.1D
30
31      ' Convert the value in the procedure-level decComm10
32      ' variable to String. Assign the result to the
33      ' lblCommission.Text property.
34      lblCommission.Text = decComm10.ToString("C2")
35
36   End Sub

38   Private Sub btnRate8_Click(sender As Object, e As EventArgs)
39      ' Calculates and displays an 8% commission.
40
41      ' Declare two procedure-level variables that can
42      ' be used only within the btnRate8_Click procedure.
43      Dim decSales As Decimal          removed from memory when the
44      Dim decComm8 As Decimal          btnRate8_Click procedure ends
45
46      ' Convert the txtSales.Text property to Decimal. Store
47      ' the result in the procedure-level decSales variable.
48      Decimal.TryParse(txtSales.Text, decSales)
49
50      ' Multiply the value in the procedure-level decSales
51      ' variable by the Decimal number 0.08D. Assign the
52      ' result to the procedure-level decComm8 variable.
53      decComm8 = decSales * 0.08D
54
55      ' Convert the value in the procedure-level decComm8
56      ' variable to String. Assign the result to the
57      ' lblCommission.Text property.
58      lblCommission.Text = decComm8.ToString("C2")
59
60   End Sub
```

Figure 3-20   Click event procedures using procedure-level variables

Notice that both procedures in Figure 3-20 declare a variable named decSales. When you use the same name to declare a variable in more than one procedure, each procedure creates its own variable when the procedure is invoked. Each procedure also destroys its own variable when the procedure ends. So, although both procedures declare a variable named decSales, each decSales variable will refer to a different section in the computer's main memory, and each will be both created and destroyed independently from the other.

START HERE   **To code and then test the Commission Calculator application:**

1. Open the Commission Solution.sln file contained in the VB2017\Chap03\Commission Solution-Procedure-level folder. Open the Code Editor window. Notice that the three Option statements and the btnExit_Click procedure have already been entered in the Code Editor window.

2. Locate the btnRate10_Click procedure. Enter the two Dim statements, the TryParse method, and the two assignment statements shown in Figure 3-20. (The code appears on Lines 19, 20, 24, 29, and 34 in the figure.)

3. Next, locate the btnRate8_Click procedure. Enter the two Dim statements, the TryParse method, and the two assignment statements shown in Figure 3-20. (The code appears on Lines 43, 44, 48, 53, and 58 in the figure.)

4. Save the solution and then start the application. If necessary, press **Alt** to display the access keys in the interface.

   Note: The figures in this book usually show the interface's access keys. However, you can choose whether or not to display them on your screen.

5. First, calculate and display an 8% commission on $40,000. Type **40000** in the Sales box and then click the **8% rate** button. See Figure 3-21.

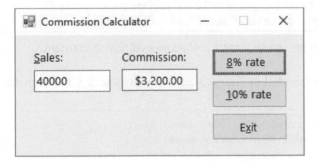

Figure 3-21   8% commission shown in the interface

6. Next, test the btnRate8_Click procedure using an invalid sales amount. Change the sales amount to the letter **a** and then click the **8% rate** button. The Commission box shows $0.00. (Recall that the TryParse method will store the number 0 in the decSales variable because the value in the txtSales.Text property cannot be converted to a number; 8% of 0 equals 0.)

7. Change the sales amount to **25000** and then click the **10% rate** button. The Commission box shows $2,500.00.

8. Now test the btnRate10_Click procedure using an invalid sales amount. Change the sales amount to **$900** (be sure to type the dollar sign) and then click the **10% rate** button. The Commission box shows $0.00. (Here too, the TryParse method will store the number 0 in the decSales variable because the value in the txtSales.Text property cannot be converted to a number; 10% of 0 equals 0.)

9. Click the **Exit** button.

A-3 Use Procedure-Level Named Constants

Like procedure-level variables, procedure-level named constants are declared at the beginning of a procedure, and they can be used only after their declaration statement within the procedure. Also like procedure-level variables, procedure-level named constants have the same lifetime as the procedure in which they are declared.

START HERE

To use procedure-level named constants in the Commission Calculator application:

1. Locate the btnRate10_Click procedure and then make the modifications shaded in Figure 3-22.

```
17        ' Declare a procedure-level named constant.
18        Const decRATE10 As Decimal = 0.1D
19        ' Declare two procedure-level variables that can
20        ' be used only within the btnRate10_Click procedure.
21        Dim decSales As Decimal
22        Dim decComm10 As Decimal
23
24        ' Convert the txtSales.Text property to Decimal. Store
25        ' the result in the procedure-level decSales variable.
26        Decimal.TryParse(txtSales.Text, decSales)
27
28        ' Multiply the value in the procedure-level decSales
29        ' variable by the Decimal named constant decRATE10. Assign the
30        ' result to the procedure-level decComm10 variable.
31        decComm10 = decSales * decRATE10
```

Figure 3-22   btnRate10_Click procedure using a procedure-level named constant

2. Now make the modifications shaded in Figure 3-23 to the btnRate8_Click procedure.

```
42
43        ' Declare a procedure-level named constant.
44        Const decRATE8 As Decimal = 0.08D
45        ' Declare two procedure-level variables that can
46        ' be used only within the btnRate8_Click procedure.
47        Dim decSales As Decimal
48        Dim decComm8 As Decimal
49
50        ' Convert the txtSales.Text property to Decimal. Store
51        ' the result in the procedure-level decSales variable.
52        Decimal.TryParse(txtSales.Text, decSales)
53
54        ' Multiply the value in the procedure-level decSales
55        ' variable by the Decimal named constant decRATE8. Assign the
56        ' result to the procedure-level decComm8 variable.
57        decComm8 = decSales * decRATE8
```

Figure 3-23   btnRate8_Click procedure using a procedure-level named constant

3. Save the solution and then start the application. Type **3000.75** in the Sales box and then click the **8% rate** button; the commission is $240.06. Now click the **10% rate** button; the commission is $300.08.

4. Click the **Exit** button. Close the Code Editor window and then close the solution.

A-4 Use a Class-Level Variable

Class-level variables are declared immediately after the Public Class clause in the Code Editor window, and they can be used by any of the procedures entered in the window. Class-level variables retain their values and remain in the computer's main memory until the application ends. Figure 3-24 shows the syntax and examples of declaring a class-level variable. As the figure indicates, class-level variables are declared using the **Private keyword**.

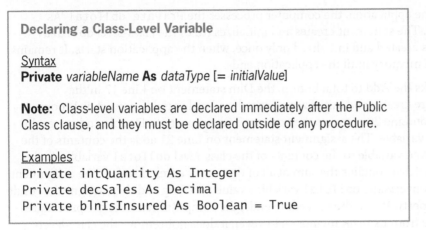

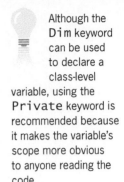

Declaring a Class-Level Variable

Syntax
Private *variableName* **As** *dataType* [= *initialValue*]

Note: Class-level variables are declared immediately after the Public Class clause, and they must be declared outside of any procedure.

Examples
```
Private intQuantity As Integer
Private decSales As Decimal
Private blnIsInsured As Boolean = True
```

Although the Dim keyword can be used to declare a class-level variable, using the Private keyword is recommended because it makes the variable's scope more obvious to anyone reading the code.

Figure 3-24 Syntax and examples of declaring class-level variables

You can use a class-level variable when two or more procedures in the same form need access to the same variable. You can observe this use of a class-level variable by completing Exercise 5 at the end of this lesson. You can also use a class-level variable when a procedure needs to retain a variable's value even after the procedure ends. This use of a class-level variable is illustrated in the Total Scores Accumulator application, which calculates and displays the total of the scores entered by the user. The application's interface is shown in Figure 3-25.

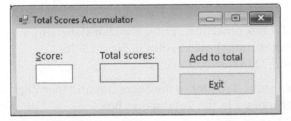

Figure 3-25 User interface for the Total Scores Accumulator application

Figure 3-26 shows most of the application's code, which uses a class-level variable named dblTotal to accumulate (add together) the scores entered by the user.

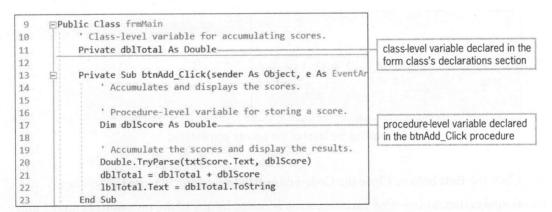

```
9   Public Class frmMain
10      ' Class-level variable for accumulating scores.
11      Private dblTotal As Double                          ← class-level variable declared in the
12                                                             form class's declarations section
13      Private Sub btnAdd_Click(sender As Object, e As EventAr
14          ' Accumulates and displays the scores.
15
16          ' Procedure-level variable for storing a score.
17          Dim dblScore As Double                          ← procedure-level variable declared
18                                                             in the btnAdd_Click procedure
19          ' Accumulate the scores and display the results.
20          Double.TryParse(txtScore.Text, dblScore)
21          dblTotal = dblTotal + dblScore
22          lblTotal.Text = dblTotal.ToString
23      End Sub
```

Figure 3-26 Most of the application's code using a class-level variable

When the user starts the application, the computer processes the `Private dblTotal As Double` statement first. The statement creates and initializes (to 0) the class-level `dblTotal` variable. The variable is created and initialized only once, when the application starts. It remains in the computer's main memory until the application ends.

Each time the user clicks the Add to total button, the Dim statement on Line 17 in the btnAdd_Click procedure creates and initializes a procedure-level variable named `dblScore`. The TryParse method on Line 20 converts the txtScore.Text property to Double and stores the result in the `dblScore` variable. The assignment statement on Line 21 adds the contents of the procedure-level `dblScore` variable to the contents of the class-level `dblTotal` variable. At this point, the `dblTotal` variable contains the sum of all of the scores entered so far. The assignment statement on Line 22 converts the `dblTotal` variable's value to String and then assigns the result to the lblTotal.Text property. When the procedure ends, the computer removes the procedure-level `dblScore` variable from its main memory. However, it does not remove the class-level `dblTotal` variable. The `dblTotal` variable is removed from the computer's memory only when the application ends.

START HERE

To code and then test the Total Scores Accumulator application:

1. Open the Total Scores Solution.sln file contained in the Total Scores Solution-Class-level folder. Open the Code Editor window. First, declare the class-level `dblTotal` variable in the form class's declarations section. Enter the following comment and declaration statement in the blank line below the Public Class clause:

   ```
   ' Class-level variable for accumulating scores.
   Private dblTotal As Double
   ```

2. Locate the code template for the btnAdd_Click procedure. Enter the Dim statement, TryParse method, and two assignment statements shown earlier in Figure 3-26. (The code appears on Lines 17, 20, 21, and 22 in the figure.)

3. Save the solution and then start the application. Type **89** in the Score box and then click the **Add to total** button. The number 89 appears in the Total scores box.

4. Change the score to **75** and then click the **Add to total** button. The number 164 appears in the Total scores box.

5. Change the score to **100** and then click the **Add to total** button. The number 264 appears in the Total scores box, as shown in Figure 3-27.

Figure 3-27 Interface showing the total of the scores you entered

6. Click the **Exit** button. Close the Code Editor window and then close the solution.

As mentioned earlier, a class-level variable can be accessed by any of the procedures entered in its Code Editor window. As a result, using class-level variables can lead to unexpected results when one of the procedures makes an inadvertent or incorrect change to the variable's value.

Tracking down the errors in an application's code becomes more complicated as the number of procedures having access to the same variable increases. Therefore, the use of class-level variables should be minimized. Always keep in mind that fewer unintentional errors occur when an application's variables are declared using the minimum scope needed, which usually is procedure scope. Rather than using a class-level variable to accumulate values, you can use a static variable.

A-5 Use a Static Variable

A **static variable** is a procedure-level variable that remains in memory and also retains its value even when its declaring procedure ends. Like a class-level variable, a static variable is not removed from the computer's main memory until the application ends. However, unlike a class-level variable, a static variable can be used only by the procedure in which it is declared. In other words, a static variable has a narrower (or more restrictive) scope than does a class-level variable. As mentioned earlier, many unintentional errors in your code can be avoided by simply declaring the variables using the minimum scope needed. Figure 3-28 shows the syntax and examples of declaring static variables. Keep in mind that the **Static keyword** can be used only in a procedure.

Declaring a Static Variable

<u>Syntax</u>
Static *variableName* **As** *dataType* [= *initialValue*]

Note: Static variables are declared in a procedure.

<u>Examples</u>
```
Static dblTotal As Double
Static intCount As Integer = 1
```

Figure 3-28 Syntax and examples of declaring static variables

The Total Scores Accumulator application from the previous section used a class-level variable to accumulate the scores entered by the user. Rather than using a class-level variable for that purpose, you can also use a static variable, as shown in the code in Figure 3-29.

```
9    Public Class frmMain
10       Private Sub btnAdd_Click(sender As Object, e As EventA
11           ' Accumulates and displays the scores.
12
13           ' Procedure-level variable for storing a score.
14           Dim dblScore As Double
15           ' Static variable for accumulating scores.
16           Static dblTotal As Double                          ──── static variable declared in the
17                                                                    btnAdd_Click procedure
18           ' Accumulate the scores and display the results.
19           Double.TryParse(txtScore.Text, dblScore)
20           dblTotal = dblTotal + dblScore
21           lblTotal.Text = dblTotal.ToString
22       End Sub
```

Figure 3-29 Most of the application's code using a static variable

The first time the user clicks the Add to total button, the button's Click event procedure creates and initializes (to 0) a procedure-level variable named dblScore and a static variable named dblTotal. The TryParse method on Line 19 converts the txtScore.Text property to Double and stores the result in the dblScore variable. The assignment statement on Line 20 adds the contents of the dblScore variable to the contents of the static dblTotal variable. The assignment statement on Line 21 converts the dblTotal variable's value to String and assigns the result to the lblTotal.Text property. When the procedure ends, the computer removes the variable declared using the Dim keyword (dblScore) from its main memory. But it does not remove the variable declared using the Static keyword (dblTotal).

Each subsequent time the user clicks the Add to total button, the computer recreates and reinitializes the dblScore variable. However, it does not recreate or reinitialize the static dblTotal variable because that variable, as well as its current value, is still in the computer's memory. After recreating and reinitializing the dblScore variable, the computer processes the remaining instructions contained in the button's Click event procedure. Here again, each time the procedure ends, the dblScore variable is removed from the computer's main memory. The dblTotal variable is removed only when the application ends.

START HERE

To use a static variable in the Total Scores Accumulator application:

1. Open the Total Scores Solution.sln file contained in the Total Scores Solution-Static folder. Open the Code Editor window. Delete the comment and the Private declaration statement entered in the form class's declarations section.

2. Locate the btnAdd_Click procedure and then click the **blank line** below the Dim statement. Enter the following comment and declaration statement:

   ```
   ' Static variable for accumulating scores.
   Static dblTotal As Double
   ```

3. Save the solution and then start the application.

4. Use the application to total the following three scores: **89**, **75**, and **100**. Be sure to click the **Add to total** button after typing each score. Also be sure to delete the previous score before entering the next score. When you are finished entering the scores, the number 264 appears in the Total scores box, as shown earlier in Figure 3-27.

5. Click the **Exit** button. Close the Code Editor window and then close the solution.

YOU DO IT 3!

Create an application named You Do It 3 and save it in the VB2017\Chap03 folder. Add a label and a button to the form. The button's Click event procedure should add the number 1 to the contents of a class-level Integer variable named intNumber and then display the variable's contents in the label. Code the application. Be sure to enter the three Option statements above the Public Class clause. Save the solution and then start and test the application. Next, change the class-level variable to a static variable. Save the solution and then start and test the application. Close the solution.

A-6 Use a Class-Level Named Constant

Earlier you learned that the use of class-level variables should be minimized because they can lead to errors that are difficult to locate in your code. Class-level named constants, however, do not have the same problem because their values cannot be changed during run time. Figure 3-30 shows the syntax and examples of declaring a class-level named constant. As the figure indicates, the declaration statement begins with the two keywords `Private Const`.

Declaring a Class-Level Named Constant

Syntax
Private Const constantName **As** dataType = expression

Note: Class-level named constants are declared immediately after the Public Class clause, and they must be declared outside of any procedure.

Examples
```
Private Const dblPI As Double = 3.14159
Private Const strCOMPANY As String = "ABC Inc."
Private Const decMinPay As Decimal = 15.65D
```

Figure 3-30   Syntax and examples of declaring class-level named constants

The Circle Area application that you coded in this chapter's Focus lesson declared a procedure-level named constant to represent the value of pi rounded to five decimal places. In the next set of steps, you will change the named constant to a class-level one.

To use a class-level named constant in the Circle Area application:

START HERE

1. Open the Circle Solution.sln file contained in the Circle Solution-Class-level folder. Open the Code Editor window and locate the btnCalc_Click procedure.

2. Highlight (select) the entire Const statement in the btnCalc_Click procedure and then press **Ctrl+x** to cut the statement from the procedure.

3. Click the **blank line** below the ` Class-level named constant.` comment and then press **Ctrl+v** to paste the Const statement in the form class's declarations section. Press **Enter**.

4. Insert the keyword `Private` at the beginning of the declaration statement, as shown in Figure 3-31.

```
 9    ⊟Public Class frmMain
10         ' Class-level named constant.
11         Private Const dblPI As Double = 3.14159 ─────────     insert the Private
12                                                                keyword at the beginning
13    ⊟    Private Sub btnCalc_Click(sender As Object, e As E     of the statement
14             ' Calculate and display the circle's area.
15
16             Dim dblRadius As Double
17             Dim dblArea As Double
18
19             Double.TryParse(txtRadius.Text, dblRadius)
20             dblArea = dblPI * dblRadius ^ 2
21             lblArea.Text = dblArea.ToString("N2")
22
23         End Sub
```

Figure 3-31   Class-level named constant entered in the form class's declarations section

5. Save the solution and then start the application. Type **15** in the Radius box and then click the **Calculate** button to display the circle's area, which is 706.86.

6. Click the **Exit** button to end the application. Close the Code Editor window and then close the solution.

Mini-Quiz 3-8

1. Write a statement that declares a procedure-level named constant whose value and name are 10.5 and decPAY, respectively.

2. Write a statement that declares a class-level variable named strName.

3. Write a statement that declares a procedure-level variable named dblNumber.

4. Write a statement that declares a procedure-level variable named dblSum. The variable should retain its value until the application ends.

3) Dim dblNumber As Double 4) Static dblSum As Double
1) Const decPAY As Decimal = 10.5D 2) Private strName As String

A-7 Professionalize Your Application's Interface

You can make your interfaces more professional-looking by coding each text box's TextChanged and Enter event procedures. In the next two sections, you will learn how to code both procedures using the Circle Area application from this chapter's Focus lesson.

START HERE

To open the Circle Area application:

1. Open the Circle Solution.sln file contained in the Circle Solution-TextChanged and Enter folder.

2. Start the application. Type **2** in the Radius box and then click the **Calculate** button. The Area box shows 12.57.

3. Now change the radius to **25**. Notice that the Area box still shows 12.57. The area will not be recalculated until you click the Calculate button again.

4. Click the **Exit** button.

Having the previously calculated area remain on the screen when a change is made to the radius could be misleading to the user. A better approach is to clear the Area box when the contents of the Radius text box changes. You can do this by coding the text box's TextChanged event procedure.

Coding the TextChanged Event Procedure

A control's **TextChanged event** occurs each time the value in its Text property changes. In the next set of steps, you will code the txtRadius_TextChanged procedure so that it clears the contents of the Area box when the event occurs. You can clear the contents of a control by assigning the value **String.Empty** to its Text property.

START HERE

To code the txtRadius_TextChanged event procedure:

1. Open the Code Editor window, and then open the code template for the txtRadius_TextChanged event procedure. Enter the comment and assignment statement shown in Figure 3-32.

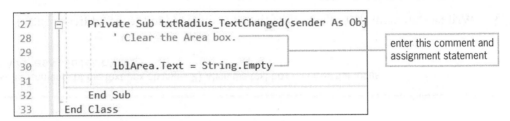

Figure 3-32   txtRadius_TextChanged event procedure

2. Save the solution and then start the application. Type **2** in the Radius box and then click the **Calculate** button. The Area box shows 12.57.

3. Change the radius to **25**. The txtRadius_TextChanged procedure clears the contents of the Area box. Click the **Calculate** button again. The Area box shows 1,963.49.

4. Now press the **Tab** key twice to send the focus to the Radius box. Notice that the insertion point appears at the end of the number 25. It is customary in Windows applications to have a text box's existing text selected (highlighted) when the text box receives the focus. You will learn how to select the existing text in the next section.

5. Click the **Exit** button.

Coding the Enter Event Procedure

A text box's **Enter event** occurs when the text box receives the focus. In the next set of steps, you will code the txtRadius_Enter procedure so that it selects (highlights) the contents of the text box when the event occurs. When the text is selected in a text box, the user can remove the text simply by pressing a key on the keyboard, such as the letter n; the pressed key—in this case, the letter n—replaces the selected text. You can select the existing text using the **SelectAll method**.

START HERE

To code the txtRadius_Enter event procedure:

1. Open the code template for the txtRadius_Enter event procedure. Enter the comment and SelectAll method shown in Figure 3-33.

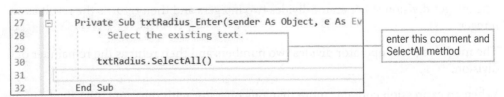

Figure 3-33   txtRadius_Enter event procedure

2. Save the solution and then start the application. Type **15** in the Radius box and then press the **Tab** key three times. The txtRadius_Enter event selects (highlights) the contents of the text box.

3. Click the **Exit** button. Close the Code Editor window and then close the solution.

Mini-Quiz 3-9

1. When does a text box's TextChanged event occur?

2. When does a text box's Enter event occur?

3. Write a statement that selects all of the text contained in the txtAddress control.

1) when the contents of the text box changes 2) when the text box receives the focus
3) txtAddress.SelectAll()

Summary

- Programmers use planning tools, such as flowcharts and pseudocode, when planning the steps a procedure needs to take to accomplish its goal.

- The ovals, rectangles, and parallelograms in a flowchart are called the start/stop, process, and input/output symbols, respectively.

- The main memory of a computer is called random access memory (RAM).

- Variables are memory locations used by programmers to store data during run time. The value stored in a variable can change while the application is running.

- User-provided items included in a calculation should be stored in variables. The results of calculations made by the application should also be stored in variables.

- In most procedures, the Dim statement is used to declare a variable.

- Each data type is a class from which a variable can be instantiated.

- The value stored in a control's Text property is always treated as a string.

- You can use the TryParse method to convert a string to a number.

- The arithmetic operators have an order of precedence. You can use parentheses to override the normal order of precedence.

- The integer division (\) operator divides two integers and then returns the result as an integer.

- The modulus (Mod) operator divides two numbers and then returns the remainder of the division.

- When an expression contains more than one operator with the same precedence number, those operators are evaluated from left to right.

- Arithmetic expressions should not contain dollar signs, commas, or percent signs.

- The data type of the expression assigned to a variable should match the variable's data type.

- You can use the literal type character D to convert a Double number to the Decimal data type.

- You can use the ToString method to convert a numeric value to a string. The method also allows you to specify the number of decimal places and the special characters to include in the string.

- To ensure that all of your variables have been declared, enter the `Option Explicit On` statement above the Public Class clause in the Code Editor window.

- To prevent the computer from inferring a variable's data type, enter the `Option Infer Off` statement above the Public Class clause in the Code Editor window.

- To prevent the computer from making implicit type conversions that may result in a loss of data, enter the `Option Strict On` statement above the Public Class clause in the Code Editor window.

- To use the Project Designer window to set Option Explicit, Option Strict, and Option Infer for an entire project, open the solution that contains the project. Right-click My Project in the Solution Explorer window and then click Open to open the Project Designer window. Click the Compile tab. Use the Option explicit, Option strict, and Option infer boxes to set the options. Save the solution and then close the Project Designer window.

- To use the Options dialog box to set Option Explicit, Option Strict, and Option Infer for all of the projects you create, click Tools on the Visual Studio menu bar and then click Options. When the Options dialog box opens, expand the Projects and Solutions node and then click VB Defaults. Use the Option Explicit, Option Strict, and Option Infer boxes to set the options. Click the OK button to close the Options dialog box.

- You use the Const statement to declare a named constant.

- A memory location's scope indicates where the variable or named constant can be used in an application's code.

- A memory location's lifetime indicates how long the variable or named constant remains in the computer's main memory.

- Variables and named constants declared in a procedure have procedure scope and can be used only after their declaration statement in the procedure.

- Variables and named constants declared in a form class's declarations section have class scope and can be used by all of the procedures in the class.

- Most of the memory locations declared in an application's code are procedure-level variables.

- A procedure does not have access to the memory locations declared in a different procedure.

- You should use the `Private` keyword to declare class-level memory locations (variables and named constants).

- You should limit the use of class-level variables because fewer unintentional errors occur when an application's variables are declared using the minimum scope needed, which usually is procedure scope.

- You can use the `Static` keyword to declare a procedure-level variable that retains its value even after the declaring procedure ends.

- A control's TextChanged event occurs each time the value in its Text property changes.

- A control's Enter event occurs when the control receives the focus.

- You can use the SelectAll method to select the text contained in a text box.

Key Terms

Arguments—items within parentheses after the name of a method; represents information that the method needs to perform its task(s)

Class scope—the scope of a class-level memory location (variable or named constant); refers to the fact that the memory location can be used by any procedure in the form class's declarations section

Class-level named constants—a named constant declared in a form class's declarations section; it has class scope and should be declared using the keywords `Private Const`

Class-level variables—a variable declared in a form class's declarations section; it has class scope and should be declared using the keyword `Private`

Const statement—the statement used to create a named constant

Declaring a memory location—reserving a location in the computer's main memory for use within an application's code

Demoted—the process of converting a value from one data type to another data type that can store only smaller numbers or numbers with less precision

Dim statement—the statement used to declare procedure-level variables

Enter event—occurs when a control receives the focus

Flowchart—a planning tool that uses standardized symbols to illustrate the steps a procedure must take to accomplish its purpose

Flowlines—the lines connecting the symbols in a flowchart

Form class's declarations section—the area located between the Public Class and End Class clauses in the Code Editor window; class-level memory locations are declared in this section

Format—specifying the number of decimal places and the special characters to display in a number treated as a string

Implicit type conversion—the process by which a value is automatically converted to fit the data type of the memory location to which it is assigned

Input/output symbol—the parallelogram in a flowchart

Integer division operator—represented by a backslash (\); divides two integers and then returns the quotient as an integer

Lifetime—indicates how long a variable or named constant remains in the computer's main memory

Literal type character—a character (such as the letter D) appended to a literal for the purpose of forcing the literal to assume a different data type (such as Decimal)

Modulus operator—represented by the keyword Mod; divides two numbers and then returns the remainder of the division

Named constant—a computer memory location where programmers can store data that cannot be changed during run time

Private keyword—used to declare class-level memory locations (variables and named constants)

Procedure scope—the scope of a procedure-level memory location (variable or named constant); refers to the fact that the memory location can be used only by the procedure that declares it

Procedure-level named constants—named constants declared in a procedure; the constants have procedure scope

Procedure-level variables—variables declared in a procedure; the variables have procedure scope

Process symbols—the rectangles in a flowchart

Promoted—the process of converting a value from one data type to another data type that can store either larger numbers or numbers with greater precision

Pseudocode—a planning tool that uses phrases to describe the steps a procedure must take to accomplish its purpose

RAM—random access memory

Random access memory—the main memory of a computer

Scope—indicates where a memory location (variable or named constant) can be used in an application's code

SelectAll method—used to select all of the text contained in a text box

Start/stop symbol—the ovals in a flowchart

Static keyword—used to declare a static variable

Static variable—a procedure-level variable that remains in main memory and also retains its value until the application (rather than its declaring procedure) ends

String—a sequence of characters (numbers, letters, special characters, and so on)

String.Empty—the value that represents the empty string in Visual Basic

TextChanged event—occurs each time the value in a control's Text property changes

ToString method—formats a copy of a number and returns the result as a string

TryParse method—used to convert a string to a specified numeric data type

Variable—a computer memory location where programmers can temporarily store data, as well as change the data, during run time

Review Questions

1. Which flowchart symbol represents a processing task?

    a. circle
    b. oval

    c. parallelogram
    d. rectangle

2. What is the result of the following expression: 96 \ 30?

    a. 3
    b. 3.2

    c. 6
    d. None of the above.

3. What is the result of the following expression: 96 Mod 30?

    a. 3
    b. 3.2

    c. 6
    d. None of the above.

4. Which of the following is an invalid name for a variable?

   a. `db18%Rate`   c. `strName`

   b. `decCost`   d. None of the above.

5. The expression `intNum * intNum * intNum` is equivalent to which of the following expressions?

   a. `intNum ^ 3`   c. `intNum ^ 2 * intNum`

   b. `intNum * 3`   d. Both a and c.

6. What is the result of the following expression: 3 * 5 \ 2 + 30 / 5?

   a. 7.5   c. 13.5

   b. 13   d. None of the above.

7. Which of the following is a computer memory location whose value does not change during run time?

   a. literal   c. static constant

   b. named constant   d. variable

8. Which of the following statements declares a procedure-level variable that remains in the computer's memory until the application ends?

   a. `Dim Static intScore As Integer`

   b. `Private Static intScore As Integer`

   c. `Static intScore As Integer`

   d. Both b and c.

9. Which of the following can be used to clear the text contained in the lblTax control?

   a. `lblTax = String.Empty`   c. `lblTax.ClearText`

   b. `lblTax.Text = String.Empty`   d. `lblTax.Text.Clear`

10. Which of the following statements declares a class-level variable?

   a. `Class intNum As Integer`

   b. `Private intNum As Integer`

   c. `Private Class intNum As Integer`

   d. `Private Dim intNum As Integer`

11. Which of the following declares a procedure-level String variable?

   a. `Dim String strCity`   c. `Private strCity As String`

   b. `Dim strCity As String`   d. Both b and c.

12. When entered in the txtName_Enter procedure, which of the following will select all of the text box's existing text?

   a. `txtName.SelectAll()`   c. `SelectAll().txtName`

   b. `txtName.SelectAllText()`   d. None of the above.

13. If Option Strict is set to On, which of the following statements will assign the contents of the txtSales control to a Double variable named dblSales?

    a. `dblSales = txtSales.Text`

    b. `dblSales = txtSales.Text.Convert.ToDouble`

    c. `Double.TryParse(txtSales.Text, dblSales)`

    d. `TryParse.Double(txtSales.Text, dblSales)`

14. Which of the following declares a named constant having the Double data type?

    a. `Const dblRATE As Double = 0.09`

    b. `Const dblRATE As Double`

    c. `Constant dblRATE = 0.09`

    d. Both a and b.

15. If Option Strict is set to On, which of the following statements assigns the sum of two Integer variables to the Text property of the lblTotal control?

    a. `lblTotal.Text = (intN1 + intN2).ToString`

    b. `lblTotal.Text = intN1.ToString + intN2.ToString`

    c. `lblTotal.Text = intN1 + intN2.ToString`

    d. `lblTotal.Text = ToString(intN1 + intN2)`

16. Which of the following statements prevents data loss due to implicit type conversions?

    a. `Option Convert Off`   c. `Option Implicit Off`

    b. `Option Explicit On`   d. `Option Strict On`

17. A static variable has the same _____ as a procedure-level variable but the same _____ as a class-level variable.

    a. lifetime, scope   b. scope, lifetime

18. If the **decPay** variable contains the number 1200.76, which of the following statements displays the number as 1,200.76?

    a. `lblPay.Text = decPay.ToString("N2")`

    b. `lblPay.Text = decPay.ToString("F2")`

    c. `lblPay.Text = decPay.ToString("D2")`

    d. `lblPay.Text = decPay.ToString("C2")`

19. Which of the following statements declares a procedure-level variable that is removed from the computer's memory when the procedure ends?

    a. `Const intCounter As Integer`   c. `Local intCounter As Integer`

    b. `Dim intCounter As Integer`   d. `Static intCounter As Integer`

20. Most of the memory locations declared in an application should be class-level variables.

    a. True   b. False

Exercises

INTRODUCTORY

1. In this exercise, you will complete the Restaurant Tip application from Chapter 2's Focus on the Concepts lesson. The application's Planning Chart is shown in Figure 3-34.

   a. Use either a flowchart or pseudocode to plan the btnCalc_Click procedure, which should calculate and display a server's tip.

   b. Open the Tip Solution.sln file contained in the VB2017\Chap03\Tip Solution folder. Enter the three Option statements in the Code Editor window. Use the comments as a guide when coding the btnCalc_Click procedure. Be sure to use variables in your code. Display the tip with a dollar sign and two decimal places. Save the solution and then start and test the application. (If the restaurant bill and tip percentage are 56 and 20, respectively, the tip is $11.20.)

   c. Now professionalize your interface by coding each text box's TextChanged and Enter event procedures. Save the solution and then start and test the application.

Planning Chart for the Restaurant Tip application	
Purpose: Calculate and display a server's tip.	
	How?
User-provided	
1. bill amount	user will enter in txtBill
2. tip percentage	user will enter in txtPercentage
Application-provided	
1. tip	btnCalc_Click will calculate and display in lblTip
2. button for ending the application	btnExit_Click will end the application

Figure 3-34 Planning Chart for Exercise 1

INTRODUCTORY

2. In this exercise, you will complete the Jacobson Furniture application from Chapter 2's Apply the Concepts lesson. The application's Planning Chart is shown in Figure 3-35.

   a. Use either a flowchart or pseudocode to plan the btnCalc_Click procedure, which should calculate and display both a 5% sales tax and the total due.

   b. Open the Jacobson Solution.sln file contained in the VB2017\Chap03\Jacobson Solution folder. Enter the three Option statements in the Code Editor window. Code the btnCalc_Click procedure using variables and a named constant. Display the sales tax with a comma (if necessary) and two decimal places. Display the total due with a comma (if necessary), a dollar sign and two decimal places. Save the solution and then start and test the application. (If the sales amount is 500, the sales tax and total due are 25.00 and $525.00, respectively.)

   c. Now professionalize your interface by coding the text box's TextChanged and Enter event procedures. Save the solution and then start and test the application.

Planning Chart for the Jacobson Furniture application

Purpose: Calculate and display the sales tax and total due amounts.

	How?
User-provided	
1. sales amount	user will enter in txtSales
Application-provided	
1. 5% sales tax	btnCalc_Click will calculate and display in lblTax
2. total due	btnCalc_Click will calculate and display in lblTotal
3. button for ending the application	btnExit_Click will end the application

Figure 3-35 Planning Chart for Exercise 2

3. In this exercise, you will complete the Moonbucks application that you created in Exercise 2 in Chapter 2.

INTRODUCTORY

a. Use Windows to copy the Moonbucks Solution folder from the VB2017\Chap02 folder to the VB2017\Chap03 folder. Open the Moonbucks Solution.sln file contained in the VB2017\Chap03\Moonbucks Solution folder. The application's Planning Chart is shown in Figure 3-36.

b. Use either a flowchart or pseudocode to plan the btnCalc_Click procedure. Enter the three Option statements in the Code Editor window. Code the procedure using variables and a named constant. Display the calculated amounts with a comma (if necessary) and two decimal places. Save the solution and then start and test the application. (If the current sales amount is 2300.75, the increase and projected sales amounts are 230.08 and 2,530.83, respectively.)

c. Now professionalize your interface by coding the text box's TextChanged and Enter event procedures. Save the solution and then start and test the application.

Planning Chart for the Moonbucks application

Purpose: Calculate and display the increase and projected sales amounts.

	How?
User-provided	
1. current sales amount	user will enter in txtCurrent
Application-provided	
1. 10% increase amount	btnCalc_Click will calculate and display in lblIncrease
2. projected sales amount	btnCalc_Click will calculate and display in lblProjected
3. button for ending the application	btnExit_Click will end the application

Figure 3-36 Planning Chart for Exercise 3

INTRODUCTORY

4. In this exercise, you will complete the Property Tax application that you created in Exercise 3 in Chapter 2.

    a. Use Windows to copy the Tax Solution folder from the VB2017\Chap02 folder to the VB2017\Chap03 folder. Open the Tax Solution.sln file contained in the VB2017\Chap03\Tax Solution folder. You created a Planning Chart for this application in Chapter 2. Enter the three Option statements in the Code Editor window. One of the buttons in the interface should calculate and display the property tax; use either a flowchart or pseudocode to plan the button's Click event procedure. Code the procedure using variables and a named constant. Display the tax with a comma (if necessary), a dollar sign and two decimal places. Save the solution and then start and test the application. (If the assessed value is 87650, the tax is $1,183.28.)

    b. Now professionalize your interface by coding the text box's TextChanged and Enter event procedures. Save the solution and then start and test the application.

INTERMEDIATE

5. Open the Orders Solution.sln file contained in the VB2017\Chap03\Orders Solution folder. The interface provides a button for adding the number ordered to the total ordered, and a button for subtracting the number ordered from the total ordered. Code the application using a class-level variable. Be sure to code the text box's TextChanged and Enter event procedures. Save the solution and then start the application. Test the application by adding any two numbers, then subtracting any three numbers, and then adding any four numbers. (If you add 7 and 5, and then subtract 2, 1, and 6, and then add 10, 7, 4, and 5, the total ordered will be 29.)

INTERMEDIATE

6. Open the Enrolled Solution.sln file contained in the VB2017\Chap03\Enrolled Solution folder. The application provides a text box and a button for updating the total number of enrollees. Code the application using a class-level variable. Be sure to code the text box's TextChanged and Enter event procedures. Save the solution and then start and test the application.

INTERMEDIATE

7. In this exercise, you modify the Enrollment application from Exercise 6. Use Windows to make a copy of the Enrolled Solution folder. Rename the folder Modified Enrolled Solution. Open the Enrolled Solution.sln file contained in the VB2017\Chap03\Modified Enrolled Solution folder. Code the application without using a class-level variable. Save the solution and then start and test the application.

INTERMEDIATE

8. In this exercise, you will complete the Rectangle Area application that you created in Exercise 4 in Chapter 2.

    a. Use Windows to copy the Area Solution folder from the VB2017\Chap02 folder to the VB2017\Chap03 folder. Open the Area Solution.sln file contained in the VB2017\Chap03\Area Solution folder. You created a Planning Chart for this application in Chapter 2. Enter the three Option statements in the Code Editor window. One of the buttons in the interface should calculate and display the rectangle's area in both square feet and square yards; use either a flowchart or pseudocode to plan the button's Click event procedure. Code the procedure using variables. Display the calculated amounts with a comma (if necessary) and one decimal place. Save the solution and then start and test the application.

    b. Now professionalize your interface by coding each text box's TextChanged and Enter event procedures. Save the solution and then start and test the application.

9. In this exercise, you will complete the Raises and New Salaries application that you created in Exercise 5 in Chapter 2.

INTERMEDIATE

   a. Use Windows to copy the Salary Solution folder from the VB2017\Chap02 folder to the VB2017\Chap03 folder. Open the Salary Solution.sln file contained in the VB2017\Chap03\Salary Solution folder. You created a Planning Chart for this application in Chapter 2.

   b. Enter the three Option statements in the Code Editor window. One of the buttons in the interface should calculate and display the two raises and the two new salaries; use either a flowchart or pseudocode to plan the button's Click event procedure. Code the procedure using variables and named constants. Display the calculated amounts with a comma (if necessary), a dollar sign and two decimal places.

   c. One of the buttons in the interface should clear the user input and calculated amounts from the screen. Code the button's Click event procedure appropriately.

   d. Code the text box's Enter and TextChanged event procedures.

   e. Save the solution and then start and test the application.

10. In this exercise, you will complete the Kramden Inc. application that you created in Exercise 6 in Chapter 2.

INTERMEDIATE

   a. Use Windows to copy the Kramden Solution folder from the VB2017\Chap02 folder to the VB2017\Chap03 folder. Open the Kramden Solution.sln file contained in the VB2017\Chap03\Kramden Solution folder. You created a Planning Chart for this application in Chapter 2. Enter the three Option statements in the Code Editor window. One of the buttons in the interface should calculate and display the total cost of the expense allowances; use either a flowchart or pseudocode to plan the button's Click event procedure. Code the procedure using variables. Display the total cost with a comma (if necessary), a dollar sign and two decimal places. Save the solution and then start and test the application.

   b. Now professionalize your interface by coding each text box's TextChanged and Enter event procedures. Save the solution and then start and test the application.

11. Create a Windows Forms application. Use the following names for the project and solution, respectively: Chopkins Project and Chopkins Solution. Save the application in the VB2017\Chap03 folder. Change the form file's name to Main Form.vb. Change the form's name to frmMain. Create the interface shown in Figure 3-37. The interface contains six labels, three text boxes, and two buttons. The application calculates and displays the total number of packs ordered and the total price of the order. The prices of a 12 pack, a 5 pack, and a 2 pack are $14.99, $6.99, and $2.50, respectively. Use variables and named constants in your code. Enter the three Option statements in the Code Editor window. The total sales amount should be displayed with a comma (if necessary), a dollar sign and two decimal places. Code each text box's TextChanged and Enter event procedures. Save the solution and then start and test the application.

INTERMEDIATE

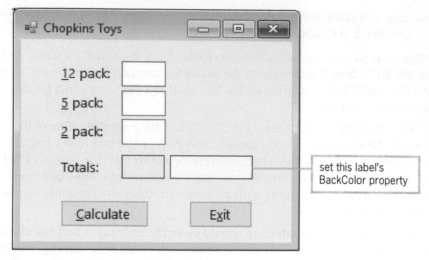

Figure 3-37 User interface for Exercise 11

ADVANCED ▶ 12. In this exercise, you modify the Chopkins Toys application from Exercise 11. Use Windows to make a copy of the Chopkins Solution folder. Rename the copy Modified Chopkins Solution. Open the Chopkins Solution.sln file contained in the Modified Chopkins Solution folder. Modify the interface as shown in Figure 3-38. The interface will now display the sale totals for each of the different packs. For example, if the customer purchased five 12 packs, the label that appears next to the associated text box should display 74.95 (5 * 14.99). Modify the btnCalc_Click procedure appropriately. The procedure should also allow the user to enter the shipping charge, which should be added to the total sale amount. Save the solution and then start and test the application.

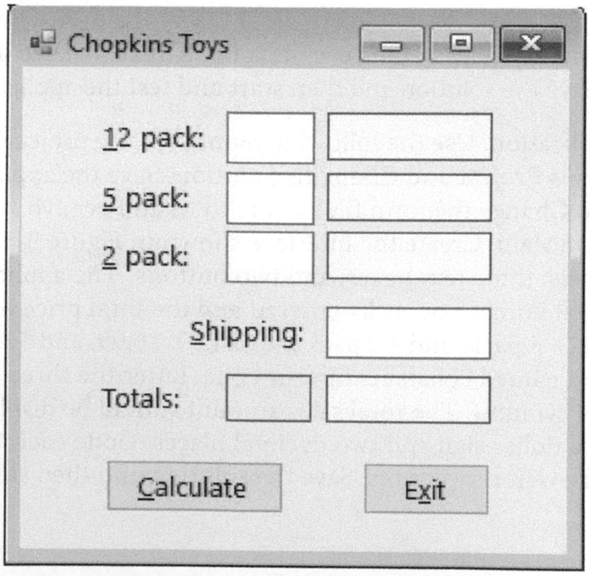

Figure 3-38 User interface for Exercise 12

13. In this exercise, you will complete the Grade Percentages application that you created in Exercise 7 in Chapter 2.

ADVANCED

a. Use Windows to copy the Grade Solution folder from the VB2017\Chap02 folder to the VB2017\Chap03 folder. Open the Grade Solution.sln file contained in the VB2017\Chap03\Grade Solution folder. You created a Planning Chart for this application in Chapter 2. Enter the three Option statements in the Code Editor window. One of the buttons in the interface should calculate and display the percentage of students receiving a grade of P (for Pass) and the percentage of students receiving a grade of F (for Fail). Code the button's Click event procedure using variables. Use Integer variables for the numbers of P and F grades. Use Double variables for the percentages. Display the percentages with a percent sign and one decimal place. Save the solution and then start and test the application. (When testing the application with invalid data, the percentages may display as NaN, which stands for Not a Number. The message is a result of dividing a number by 0. In Chapter 4, you will learn how to use a selection structure to prevent this error message.)

b. Now professionalize your interface by coding each text box's TextChanged and Enter event procedures. Save the solution and then start and test the application.

14. In this exercise, you will complete the Sales application that you created in Exercise 8 in Chapter 2.

ADVANCED

a. Use Windows to copy the Sales Solution folder from the VB2017\Chap02 folder to the VB2017\Chap03 folder. Open the Sales Solution.sln file contained in the VB2017\Chap03\Sales Solution folder. You created a Planning Chart for this application in Chapter 2. Enter the three Option statements in the Code Editor window. One of the buttons in the interface should calculate and display the percentage of the total sales made by each of the three salespeople. Code the button's Click event procedure using Double variables. Display the percentages with a percent sign and one decimal place. Save the solution and then start and test the application. (When testing the application with invalid data, the percentages may display as NaN, which stands for Not a Number. The message is a result of dividing a number by 0. In Chapter 4, you will learn how to use a selection structure to prevent this error message.)

b. Now professionalize your interface by coding each text box's TextChanged and Enter event procedures. Save the solution and then start and test the application.

15. Create a Windows Forms application. Use the following names for the project and solution, respectively: OnYourOwn Project and OnYourOwn Solution. Save the application in the VB2017\Chap03 folder. Plan and design an application of your choice. The only requirement is that you must follow the minimum guidelines listed in Figure 3-39. Before starting the application, be sure to verify the name of the startup form. Save the solution and then start and test the application.

ON YOUR OWN

1. The user interface must contain a minimum of two text boxes, four labels, and two buttons. One of the buttons must be an Exit button.
2. The interface can include a picture box, but this is not a requirement.
3. The interface must follow the GUI design guidelines summarized in Figure 2-20 in Chapter 2. The guidelines are also summarized in Appendix A.
4. Objects that are either coded or referred to in code should be named appropriately.
5. The Code Editor window must contain comments, the three Option statements, at least two variables, at least one named constant, at least two assignment statements, and the `Me.Close()` statement. The application must perform at least one calculation.
6. Each text box's TextChanged and Enter event procedures should be coded.

Figure 3-39   Guidelines for Exercise 15

FIX IT

16.   Open the VB2017\Chap03\FixIt Solution\FixIt Solution.sln file. The application should calculate and display the area of a rectangular floor (in square feet) and the total cost of tiling the floor. Open the Code Editor window and correct the errors in the code. Save the solution and then start and test the application.

CHAPTER 4

The Selection Structure

In this chapter's Focus on the Concepts lesson, you will learn how programmers direct the computer to make a decision before it selects the next instruction to process in a procedure. The Focus lesson also covers comparison and logical operators. In the Apply the Concepts lesson, you will learn how to add check boxes, group boxes, and radio buttons to an interface. You will use the concepts from the Focus lesson to code applications whose interfaces contain these controls.

FOCUS ON THE CONCEPTS LESSON

Concepts covered in this lesson:

- F-1 Selection structures
- F-2 If...Then...Else statement
- F-3 Comparison operators
- F-4 Logical operators
- F-5 Summary of operators
- F-6 String comparisons
- F-7 Nested selection structures
- F-8 Multiple-alternative selection structures
- F-9 Select Case statement

F-1 Selection Structures

Every procedure in an application is written using one or more of three basic control structures: sequence, selection, and repetition. They are called control structures because they control the order in which a procedure's instructions are processed. The procedures in the previous three chapters used the **sequence structure** only. When one of the procedures was invoked during run time, the computer processed its instructions in the order they appeared in the procedure—in other words, sequentially. Every procedure you write will contain the sequence structure.

Many times, however, a procedure will need to use the **selection structure**. This structure tells the computer that it needs to make a decision before it can select the next instruction to process. The decision is based on a condition specified at the beginning of the selection structure, and the next instruction to process is based on the result of that decision. Figure 4-1 shows examples of two different types of selection structures: single-alternative and dual-alternative. The examples are written in pseudocode, with each selection structure's condition shaded.

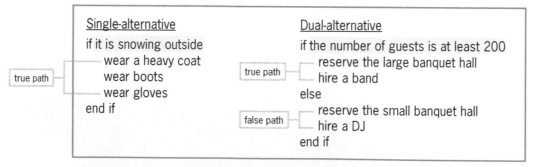

Figure 4-1   Examples of selection structures written in pseudocode

The **condition** in a selection structure must be phrased so that it evaluates to an answer of either true or false. A **single-alternative selection structure** requires one or more actions to be taken *only* when its condition evaluates to true. A **dual-alternative selection structure**, on the other hand, requires one set of instructions to be followed *only* when the condition is true and a different set of instructions *only* when it is false. The instructions to follow when the condition evaluates to true are called the **true path**. As Figure 4-1 indicates, the true path begins with the instruction immediately below the *if* and ends with either the *else* (if there is one) or the *end if*. The instructions to follow when the condition evaluates to false are called the **false path**. The false path begins with the instruction immediately below the *else* and ends with the *end if*. For clarity, the instructions in each path should be indented as shown in Figure 4-1.

As you learned in Chapter 3, many programmers use flowcharts (rather than pseudocode) when planning procedures. Figure 4-2 shows the flowcharts for the single-alternative and dual-alternative selection structures from Figure 4-1. The diamond in a flowchart is called the **decision symbol** because it is used to represent the selection structure's condition (decision). The condition in each flowchart is shaded in the figure.

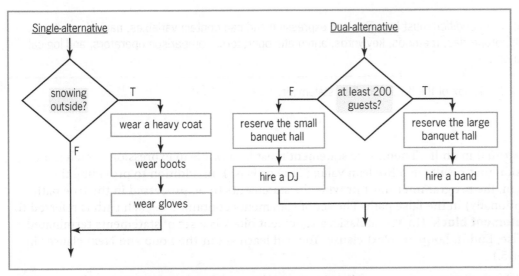

Figure 4-2 Examples of selection structures drawn in flowchart form

Notice that the conditions in both decision symbols evaluate to either true or false only. The flowline marked with a T points to the next instruction to be processed when the condition evaluates to true. Similarly, the flowline marked with an F points to the next instruction to be processed when the condition evaluates to false. You can also mark the flowlines leading out of a decision symbol with a Y and an N (for yes and no, respectively).

Mini-Quiz 4-1

1. Which type of selection structure provides instructions that are to be processed only when its condition evaluates to true?

2. Which type of selection structure provides one set of instructions to be processed *only* when its condition is true and a different set of instructions to be processed *only* when its condition is false?

3. What symbol is used in a flowchart to represent a selection structure's condition?

1) single-alternative 2) dual-alternative 3) diamond

F-2 If...Then...Else Statement

Visual Basic provides the **If...Then...Else statement** for coding single-alternative and dual-alternative selection structures. The statement's syntax is shown in Figure 4-3.

If...Then...Else Statement

Syntax
If *condition* **Then**
     statement block to be processed when the condition is true
[Else
     statement block to be processed when the condition is false]
End If

Note: The *condition* must be a Boolean expression and can contain variables, named constants, literals, properties, methods, keywords, arithmetic operators, comparison operators, and logical operators.

Figure 4-3   Syntax of the If...Then...Else statement

The *condition* in an If...Then...Else statement must be a Boolean expression, which is an expression that results in a Boolean value (True or False). In addition to providing the condition, the programmer must provide the statements to be processed in the true path and (optionally) in the false path. The set of statements contained in each path is referred to as a **statement block**. (In Visual Basic, a statement block is a set of statements terminated by an Else, End If, Loop, or Next clause. You will learn about the Loop and Next clauses in Chapter 5.)

An If...Then...Else statement's condition can contain variables, named constants, literals, properties, methods, keywords, arithmetic operators, comparison operators, and logical operators. You will learn about comparison operators and logical operators in this Focus lesson. We will begin with comparison operators.

F-3 Comparison Operators

Figure 4-4 lists the most commonly used **comparison operators** in Visual Basic. Comparison operators (also referred to as relational operators) are used to compare two values. When making comparisons, keep in mind that equal to (=) is the opposite of not equal to (<>), greater than (>) is the opposite of less than or equal to (<=), and less than (<) is the opposite of greater than or equal to (>=). Expressions containing a comparison operator always evaluate to a Boolean value: either True or False. Also included in Figure 4-4 are examples of using comparison operators in an If...Then...Else statement's condition.

Comparison Operators

Operator	Operation
=	equal to
>	greater than
>=	greater than or equal to
<	less than
<=	less than or equal to
<>	not equal to

Examples

```
If strState = "IL" Then
If decHours > 40 Then
If decMax >= 75.65D Then
If intOnHand < intOrdered Then
If dblTotal <= 999.99 Then
If strContinue <> "N" Then
If blnIsInsured = True Then
```

Note: In the last example shown above, the condition compares a Boolean variable's value to the Boolean value True. You can omit the = True and write the condition as simply `If blnIsInsured Then`.

Figure 4-4 List and examples of commonly used comparison operators

Unlike arithmetic operators, comparison operators in Visual Basic do not have an order of precedence. When an expression contains more than one comparison operator, the computer evaluates the comparison operators from left to right in the expression. Comparison operators, however, are evaluated after any arithmetic operators, as both examples in Figure 4-5 indicate.

Example 1
Expression: $14 / 2 < 15 - 2 * 3$

Division first	$14 / 2 < 15 - 2 * 3$
Multiplication next	$7 < 15 - 2 * 3$
Subtraction next	$7 < 15 - 6$
< comparison last	$7 < 9$
Answer:	True

Example 2
Expression: $6 * 2 + 3 >= 5 * 4$

Multiplication first	$6 * 2 + 3 >= 5 * 4$
Multiplication next	$12 + 3 >= 5 * 4$
Addition next	$12 + 3 >= 20$
>= comparison last	$15 >= 20$
Answer:	False

Figure 4-5 Evaluation steps for expressions containing arithmetic and comparison operators

Mini-Quiz 4-2

1. Evaluate the following expression: $4 + 3 * 2 > 2 * 10 - 11$.

2. Evaluate the following expression: $8 + 3 - 6 + 85 < 5 * 26$.

3. Evaluate the following expression: $10 / 5 + 3 - 6 * 2 > 0$.

4. Evaluate the following expression: $75 / 25 + 2 * 5 * 6 <= 8 * 8$.

5. What is the opposite of greater than?

1) True 2) True 3) False 4) True 5) less than or equal to

Comparison Operator Example: Total Due Application

The Total Due application displays the total amount a customer owes, which is based on the number of items purchased. Each item costs $8.50. However, the customer receives a 10% discount when the number of items purchased is at least 5.

START HERE

To code and then test the Total Due application:

1. Open the Total Due Solution.sln file contained in the VB2017\Chap04\Total Due Solution folder. If necessary, open the designer window.

2. Open the Code Editor window and locate the btnCalc_Click procedure. Enter the single-alternative selection structure shown in Figure 4-6. Notice that the Code Editor automatically indents the instructions in the true path for you. The two statements in the selection structure's true path will be processed only when the number purchased, which is stored in the **intPurchased** variable, is at least 5. ("At least" means "greater than or equal to.") The two instructions will be skipped over when the number purchased is less than 5.

 The opposite of >= (greater than or equal to) is < (less than).

enter this single-alternative selection structure

```
10      Private Sub btnCalc_Click(sender As Object, e As EventArgs) Handl
11          ' Calculate and display the total due.
12
13          Const dblUNIT_PRICE As Double = 8.5
14          Const dblDISCOUNT_RATE As Double = 0.1
15          Dim intPurchased As Integer
16          Dim dblTotalDue As Double
17          Dim dblDiscount As Double
18
19          Integer.TryParse(txtPurchased.Text, intPurchased)
20
21          dblTotalDue = intPurchased * dblUNIT_PRICE
22          ' If the number purchased is at least 5, give the discount.
23          If intPurchased >= 5 Then
24              dblDiscount = dblTotalDue * dblDISCOUNT_RATE
25              dblTotalDue = dblTotalDue - dblDiscount
26          End If
27
28          lblTotalDue.Text = dblTotalDue.ToString("C2")
29      End Sub
```

Figure 4-6   Single-alternative selection structure entered in the procedure

3. Save the solution and then start the application. Type **3** in the Number purchased box and then click the **Calculate** button. The total due is $25.50 (3 * 8.50). See Figure 4-7.

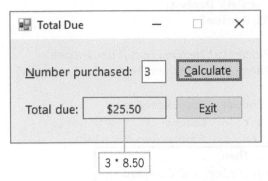

Figure 4-7 Interface showing the total due for 3 items

4. Change the number purchased to **7** and then click the **Calculate** button. The total due is $53.55 (7 * 8.50 minus the discount of 5.95 calculated by the instructions in the If statement's true path). See Figure 4-8.

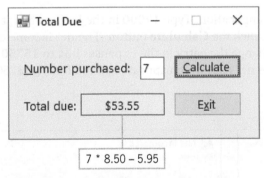

Figure 4-8 Interface showing the total due for 7 items

5. Click the **Exit** button. Close the Code Editor window and then close the solution.

Comparison Operator Example: Net Income/Loss Application

The Net Income/Loss application calculates either a company's net income or its net loss. It displays the net income using a black font and displays the net loss using a red font.

To code and then test the Net Income/Loss application:

START HERE

1. Open the Net Solution.sln file contained in the VB2017\Chap04\Net Solution folder.

2. Open the Code Editor window and locate the btnCalc_Click procedure. Enter the dual-alternative selection structure shown in Figure 4-9. Notice that the Code Editor automatically indents the instructions in both paths for you. The statement in the selection structure's true path will be processed only when the **decNet** variable's value is less than 0. Otherwise, which means the variable's value is greater than or equal to 0, the statement in the false path will be processed.

The opposite of < (less than) is >= (greater than or equal to).

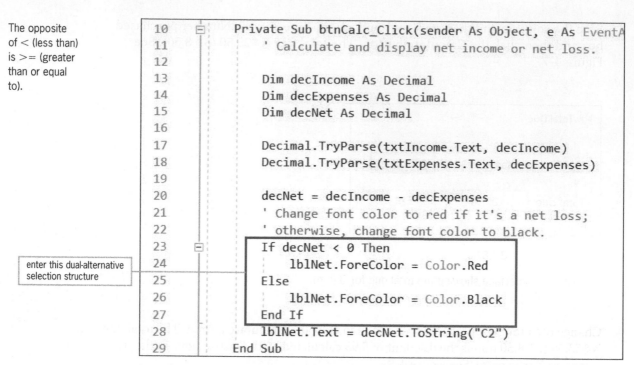

enter this dual-alternative selection structure

```
10    Private Sub btnCalc_Click(sender As Object, e As EventA
11        ' Calculate and display net income or net loss.
12
13        Dim decIncome As Decimal
14        Dim decExpenses As Decimal
15        Dim decNet As Decimal
16
17        Decimal.TryParse(txtIncome.Text, decIncome)
18        Decimal.TryParse(txtExpenses.Text, decExpenses)
19
20        decNet = decIncome - decExpenses
21        ' Change font color to red if it's a net loss;
22        ' otherwise, change font color to black.
23        If decNet < 0 Then
24            lblNet.ForeColor = Color.Red
25        Else
26            lblNet.ForeColor = Color.Black
27        End If
28        lblNet.Text = decNet.ToString("C2")
29    End Sub
```

Figure 4-9 Dual-alternative selection structure entered in the procedure

3. Save the solution and then start the application. Type **15000** in the Income box, type **9500** in the Expenses box, and then click the **Calculate** button. The net income of $5,500.00 appears in a black font. Change the entry in the Expenses box to **15750** and then click the **Calculate** button. The net loss, which appears in a red font, is ($750.00). See Figure 4-10.

Always be sure to use data that will test both paths in a selection structure.

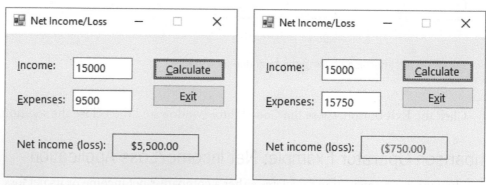

Figure 4-10 Interfaces showing the net income and net loss

4. Click the **Exit** button. Close the Code Editor window and then close the solution.

Mini-Quiz 4-3

1. Write an If clause that determines whether the value in the dblPay variable is at least 10.45.

2. Write an If clause that determines whether the value in the decSales variable is more than $1,500.99.

3. Write an If clause that determines whether the strFinished variable contains the letter Y.

4. Write an If clause that determines whether the blnIsInsured variable contains the keyword True.

1) If dblPay >= 10.45 Then 2) If decSales > 1500.99D Then 3) If strFinished = "Y" Then 4) If blnIsInsured = True Then or If blnIsInsured Then

YOU DO IT 1!

Create an application named You Do It 1 and save it in the VB2017\Chap04 folder. Add a text box, a label, and a button to the form. If the user enters a number that is greater than 100 in the text box, the button's Click event procedure should display the result of multiplying the number by 5; otherwise, it should display the result of dividing the number by 5. Code the procedure. Save the solution and then start and test the application. Close the solution.

YOU DO IT 2!

Create an application named You Do It 2 and save it in the VB2017\Chap04 folder. Add two text boxes, a label, and a button to the form. The button's Click event procedure should assign the contents of the text boxes to Double variables named dblNum1 and dblNum2. It then should divide the dblNum1 variable's value by the dblNum2 variable's value, assigning the result to a Double variable named dblAnswer. Display the answer in the label. Code the procedure. Save the solution and then start the application. Test the application using the numbers 6 and 2; the number 3 appears in the label control. Now test it using the numbers 6 and 0. The infinity symbol (∞) appears in the label control because the application is trying to divide a number by 0. Add a selection structure to the procedure. The selection structure should perform the division and display the quotient only if the value in the dblNum2 variable is not 0; otherwise, it should display N/A (for Not Available) in the label. Save the solution and then start and test the application. Close the solution.

F-4 Logical Operators

You can also include logical operators in an If...Then...Else statement's condition. Before learning about Visual Basic's logical operators, consider the two logical operators that you use on a daily basis: *and* and *or*. Examples of how you use these operators are shown in Figure 4-11; the operators are italicized in the examples.

If you finished your homework *and* you studied for tomorrow's exam, you can watch a movie.

If your cell phone rings *and* (it is your spouse calling *or* it is your child calling), answer your phone.

If you are driving your car *and* (it is raining *or* it is foggy *or* there is bug splatter on your windshield), turn your car's wipers on.

Figure 4-11   Examples of logical operators that you use on a daily basis

Figure 4-12 lists the logical operators available in Visual Basic and includes examples of using them in the If...Then...Else statement's condition. Logical operators have an order of precedence and are always evaluated after any arithmetic or comparison operators in an expression.

Logical Operators

Operator	Operation	Precedence number
Not	reverses the truth-value of the condition; True becomes False, and False becomes True	1
And	all subconditions must be true for the compound condition to evaluate to True	2
AndAlso	same as the And operator, except performs short-circuit evaluation	2
Or	only one of the subconditions needs to be true for the compound condition to evaluate to True	3
OrElse	same as the Or operator, except performs short-circuit evaluation	3
Xor	one and only one of the subconditions can be true for the compound condition to evaluate to True	4

Example 1
```
If Not blnSenior Then
```
The condition evaluates to True when the blnSenior variable contains the Boolean value False; otherwise, it evaluates to False. The clause could also be written more clearly as
```
If blnSenior = False Then.
```

Example 2
```
If dblRate > 0 AndAlso dblRate < 0.15 Then
```
The compound condition evaluates to True when the value in the dblRate variable is greater than 0 and, at the same time, less than 0.15; otherwise, it evaluates to False.

Example 3
```
If strCode = "1" AndAlso decSales > 4999.99D Then
```
The compound condition evaluates to True when the strCode variable contains the string "1" and, at the same time, the value in the decSales variable is greater than 4999.99; otherwise, it evaluates to False.

Figure 4-12   List and examples of logical operators *(continues)*

(continued)

Example 4
```
If strCode = "1" OrElse decSales > 4999.99D Then
```
The compound condition evaluates to True when the strCode variable contains the string "1" or when the value in the decSales variable is greater than 4999.99; otherwise, it evaluates to False.

Example 5
```
If strCoupon1 = "USE" Xor strCoupon2 = "USE" Then
```
The compound condition evaluates to True when only one of the variables contains the string "USE"; otherwise, it evaluates to False.

Figure 4-12   List and examples of logical operators

Except for the Not operator, all of the **logical operators** allow you to combine two or more conditions, called subconditions, into one compound condition. The compound condition will always evaluate to either True or False, which is why logical operators are often referred to as Boolean operators. Even though this book uses only the Not, AndAlso, and OrElse operators, you should familiarize yourself with the And, Or, and Xor operators because you may encounter them when modifying another programmer's code. The tables shown in Figure 4-13, called **truth tables**, summarize how the computer evaluates the logical operators in an expression.

Truth Tables for the Logical Operators Used in This Book

Not operator

value of condition	value of Not condition
True	False
False	True

AndAlso operator

subcondition1	subcondition2	subcondition1 AndAlso subcondition2
True	True	True
True	False	False
False	(not evaluated)	False

OrElse operator

subcondition1	subcondition2	subcondition1 OrElse subcondition2
True	(not evaluated)	True
False	True	True
False	False	False

Truth Tables for the Logical Operators Not Used in This Book

And operator

subcondition1	subcondition2	subcondition1 And subcondition2
True	True	True
True	False	False
False	True	False
False	False	False

Figure 4-13   Truth tables for the logical operators (continues)

(continued)

Or operator		
subcondition1	subcondition2	subcondition1 Or subcondition2
True	True	True
True	False	True
False	True	True
False	False	False

Xor operator		
subcondition1	subcondition2	subcondition1 Xor subcondition2
True	True	False
True	False	True
False	True	True
False	False	False

Figure 4-13   Truth tables for the logical operators

As the figure indicates, the **Not operator** reverses the truth-value of the *condition*. If the value of the *condition* is True, then the value of Not *condition* is False. Likewise, if the value of the *condition* is False, then the value of Not *condition* is True.

When you use either the **And operator** or the **AndAlso operator** to combine two subconditions, the resulting compound condition evaluates to True only when both subconditions are True. The difference between the operators is that the And operator always evaluates both subconditions, while the AndAlso operator performs a **short-circuit evaluation**, which means it does not bother evaluating subcondition2 when subcondition1 is False. This short-circuit evaluation makes the AndAlso operator more efficient than the And operator.

When you combine two subconditions using either the **Or operator** or the **OrElse operator**, the compound condition evaluates to True when either one or both of the subconditions is True. The compound condition evaluates to False only when both subconditions are False. The difference between the operators is that the Or operator always evaluates both subconditions, while the OrElse operator performs a short-circuit evaluation. The OrElse operator is more efficient than the Or operator because it does not bother evaluating subcondition2 when subcondition1 is True.

Finally, when you combine conditions using the **Xor operator**, the compound condition evaluates to True when only one of the subconditions is True. If both subconditions are True or both subconditions are False, then the compound condition evaluates to False.

Mini-Quiz 4-4

1. An online retailer offers free shipping on purchases over $100, but only when the customer has a free shipping code. If subcondition1 is dblPurchase > 100 and subcondition2 is strFreeShip = "Y", which logical operator should you use to combine both subconditions: AndAlso or OrElse? (Use the truth tables shown in Figure 4-13 as a guide.)

2.   Customers who belong to an online retailer's Free Ship club receive free shipping on all of their purchases. Customers who do not belong to the club must make a minimum purchase of $50 to receive free shipping. If subcondition1 is strClubMember = "Y" and subcondition2 is dblPurchase >= 50, which logical operator should you use to combine both subconditions: AndAlso or OrElse? (Use the truth tables shown in Figure 4-13 as a guide.)

3.   A movie theater charges $8 per ticket for children ages 2 through 12. The age information is stored in the intAge variable. Write an appropriate If clause.

1) AndAlso 2) OrElse 3) If intAge >= 2 AndAlso intAge <= 12 Then

Logical Operator Example: Gross Pay Calculator Application

The Gross Pay Calculator application calculates and displays an employee's weekly gross pay, given the number of hours worked and the hourly pay rate. The number of hours worked must be greater than 0 but less than or equal to 40. If the number of hours worked is not valid, the application should display N/A (for Not Available).

To code and then test the Gross Pay Calculator application:

START HERE

1.   Open the Gross Solution.sln file contained in the VB2017\Chap04\Gross Solution folder.

2.   Open the Code Editor window and locate the btnAndAlso_Click procedure. Click the **blank line** above the End Sub clause. Enter the dual-alternative selection structure shown in Figure 4-14. The statements in the selection structure's true path will be processed only when the value in the dblHours variable is greater than 0 and, at the same time, less than or equal to 40. The statement in the false path will be processed either when the value is less than or equal to 0 or when it is greater than 40.

```
10    Private Sub btnAndAlso_Click(sender As Object, e As E
11        ' Calculate and display weekly gross pay.
12
13        Dim dblHours As Double
14        Dim dblRate As Double
15        Dim dblGross As Double
16
17        Double.TryParse(txtHours.Text, dblHours)
18        Double.TryParse(txtRate.Text, dblRate)
19
20        If dblHours > 0 AndAlso dblHours <= 40 Then
21            dblGross = dblHours * dblRate
22            lblGross.Text = dblGross.ToString("C2")
23        Else
24            lblGross.Text = "N/A"
25        End If
26    End Sub
```

enter this dual-alternative selection structure

The opposite of > (greater than) is <= (less than or equal to) and vice versa.

Figure 4-14   Dual-alternative selection structure entered in the btnAndAlso procedure

3. Locate the btnOrElse_Click procedure and then click the **blank line** above the End Sub clause. Enter the dual-alternative selection structure shown in Figure 4-15. The statement in the selection structure's true path will be processed either when the value in the dblHours variable is less than or equal to 0 or when it is greater than 40. The statements in the false path will be processed only when the value is greater than 0 and, at the same time, less than or equal to 40.

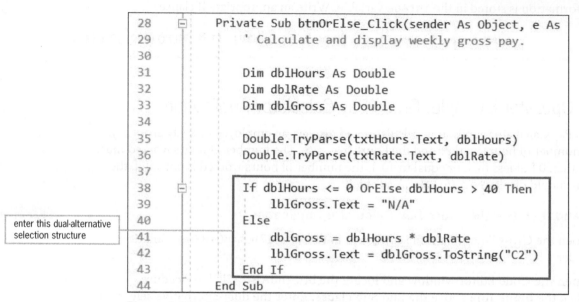

```
28    Private Sub btnOrElse_Click(sender As Object, e As
29        ' Calculate and display weekly gross pay.
30
31        Dim dblHours As Double
32        Dim dblRate As Double
33        Dim dblGross As Double
34
35        Double.TryParse(txtHours.Text, dblHours)
36        Double.TryParse(txtRate.Text, dblRate)
37
38        If dblHours <= 0 OrElse dblHours > 40 Then
39            lblGross.Text = "N/A"
40        Else
41            dblGross = dblHours * dblRate
42            lblGross.Text = dblGross.ToString("C2")
43        End If
44    End Sub
```

enter this dual-alternative selection structure

Figure 4-15 Dual-alternative selection structure entered in the btnOrElse procedure

4. Save the solution and then start the application. First, test the btnAndAlso_Click procedure using a valid number for the hours worked. Type **10** and **8** in the Hours worked and Hourly rate boxes, respectively. Click the **Calculate-AndAlso** button. See Figure 4-16.

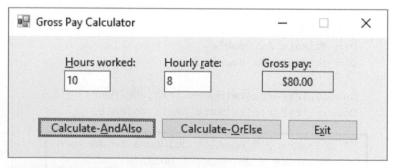

Figure 4-16 Sample run using a valid number of hours worked

5. Now test the btnAndAlso_Click procedure using an invalid number of hours worked. Change the number of hours worked to **43** and then click the **Calculate-AndAlso** button. See Figure 4-17.

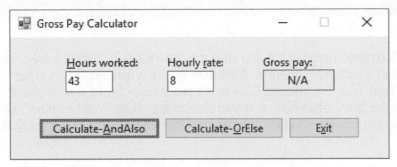

Figure 4-17   Sample run using an invalid number of hours worked

6. Change the number of hours worked to **10** and then click the **Calculate-OrElse** button. The gross pay is $80.00, as shown earlier in Figure 4-16. Change the number of hours worked to **43** and then click the **Calculate-OrElse** button. The N/A message appears in the Gross pay box, as shown earlier in Figure 4-17.

7. Click the **Exit** button. Close the Code Editor window and then close the solution.

If you are unsure whether to use AndAlso or OrElse in an If clause, test the selection structure using both operators because only the correct operator will give you the expected results. (If you want to try this with the Gross Pay Calculator application, complete You Do It 3!.)

YOU DO IT 3!

Use Windows to make a copy of the Gross Solution folder. Rename the copy You Do It 3 Solution. Open the Gross Solution.sln file contained in the You Do It 3 Solution folder and then open the Code Editor window.

1. In the btnAndAlso_Click procedure, change AndAlso to OrElse. Save the solution and then start the application. Type 10 and 8 in the Hours worked and Hourly rate boxes, respectively. Click the Calculate-AndAlso button. What appears in the Gross pay box? Is this value correct? Now, change the number of hours worked to 43 and then click the Calculate-AndAlso button. What appears in the Gross pay box? Is this value correct? Click the Exit button. Change OrElse in the btnAndAlso_Click procedure to AndAlso.

2. In the btnOrElse_Click procedure, change OrElse to AndAlso. Save the solution and then start the application. Type 10 and 8 in the Hours worked and Hourly rate boxes, respectively. Click the Calculate-OrElse button. What appears in the Gross pay box? Is this value correct? Now, change the number of hours worked to 43 and then click the Calculate-OrElse button. What appears in the Gross pay box? Is this value correct? Click the Exit button. Change AndAlso in the btnOrElse_Click procedure to OrElse. Save the solution. Close the Code Editor window and then close the solution.

YOU DO IT 4!

Create an application named You Do It 4 and save it in the VB2017\Chap04 folder. Add a text box, a label, and a button to the form. If the user enters a number that is either less than 0 or greater than 100, the button's Click event procedure should display the string "Invalid number" in the label; otherwise, it should display the string "Valid number". Code the procedure. Save the solution and then start and test the application. Close the solution.

F-5 Summary of Operators

Figure 4-18 shows the order of precedence for the arithmetic, comparison, and logical operators you have learned so far. Recall that when an expression contains more than one operator with the same precedence number, those operators are evaluated from left to right. The figure also shows the evaluation steps for an expression that contains two arithmetic operators, two comparison operators, and one logical operator. Notice that the arithmetic operators are evaluated first, followed by the comparison operators and then the logical operator. (Keep in mind that you can use parentheses to override the order of precedence.)

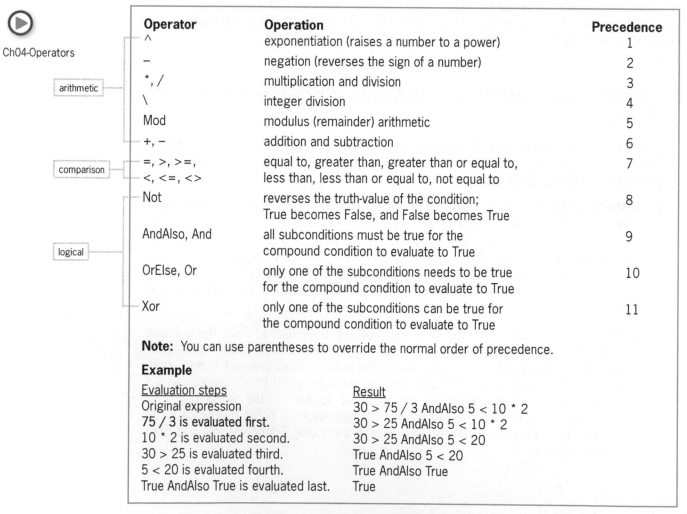

Operator	Operation	Precedence
^	exponentiation (raises a number to a power)	1
–	negation (reverses the sign of a number)	2
*, /	multiplication and division	3
\	integer division	4
Mod	modulus (remainder) arithmetic	5
+, –	addition and subtraction	6
=, >, >=, <, <=, <>	equal to, greater than, greater than or equal to, less than, less than or equal to, not equal to	7
Not	reverses the truth-value of the condition; True becomes False, and False becomes True	8
AndAlso, And	all subconditions must be true for the compound condition to evaluate to True	9
OrElse, Or	only one of the subconditions needs to be true for the compound condition to evaluate to True	10
Xor	only one of the subconditions can be true for the compound condition to evaluate to True	11

Note: You can use parentheses to override the normal order of precedence.

Example

Evaluation steps	Result
Original expression	30 > 75 / 3 AndAlso 5 < 10 * 2
75 / 3 is evaluated first.	30 > 25 AndAlso 5 < 10 * 2
10 * 2 is evaluated second.	30 > 25 AndAlso 5 < 20
30 > 25 is evaluated third.	True AndAlso 5 < 20
5 < 20 is evaluated fourth.	True AndAlso True
True AndAlso True is evaluated last.	True

Ch04-Operators

arithmetic

comparison

logical

Figure 4-18   List of arithmetic, comparison, and logical operators

Mini-Quiz 4-5

1. Evaluate the following expression: 6 / 2 + 7 − 5 > 4 AndAlso 7 > 3.

2. Evaluate the following expression: 8 < 12 / 2 OrElse 4 > 9 Mod 3 * 4.

3. Evaluate the following expression: 13 Mod 3 * 2 <= 1 AndAlso 9 \ 4 <= 2.

1) True 2) False 3) True

F-6 String Comparisons

String comparisons in Visual Basic are case sensitive, which means that the uppercase version of a letter and its lowercase counterpart are not interchangeable. So, although a human recognizes K and k as being the same letter, a computer does not; to a computer, a K is different from a k. The reason for this differentiation is that each character on the computer keyboard is stored using a different Unicode value in the computer's main memory. **Unicode** is the universal coding scheme for characters, and it assigns a unique value to each character used in the written languages of the world. For example, the Unicode value for the uppercase letter K is 004B, but the Unicode value for the lowercase letter k is 006B. Since both Unicode values are not the same, the condition "K" = "k" evaluates to False. Similarly, the condition strState = "Ky" will evaluate to True only when the strState variable contains the two letters Ky. It will evaluate to False when the variable contains anything other than Ky, such as KY, kY, ky, Ks, La, and so on.

 You can learn more about Unicode here: *unicode.org*.

String comparisons that involve user input can be problematic because the user might enter the string using any combination of uppercase and lowercase letters. You can avoid the comparison problem by using either the **ToUpper method** or the **ToLower method** to temporarily convert the string to either uppercase or lowercase, respectively, and then using the converted string in the comparison. Figure 4-19 shows the syntax of the ToUpper and ToLower methods and includes examples of using the methods.

ToUpper and ToLower Methods

<u>Syntax</u>
string.**ToUpper**
string.**ToLower**

<u>Example 1</u>
```
If strState.ToUpper = "KY" Then
```
Temporarily converts the contents of the strState variable to uppercase and then compares the result with the uppercase letters KY.

<u>Example 2</u>
```
If strName1.ToLower = strName2.ToLower Then
```
Temporarily converts the contents of the strName1 and strName2 variables to lowercase and then compares both results.

Figure 4-19 Syntax and examples of the ToUpper and ToLower methods *(continues)*

(continued)

Example 3
```
lblState.Text = strState.ToUpper
```
Temporarily converts the contents of the `strState` variable to uppercase and then assigns the result to the lblState.Text property.

Example 4
```
strName = strName.ToUpper
txtState.Text = txtState.Text.ToLower
```
Changes the contents of the `strName` variable to uppercase and changes the contents of the txtState.Text property to lowercase.

Figure 4-19 Syntax and examples of the ToUpper and ToLower methods

In each syntax, *string* is usually either the name of a String variable or the Text property of an object. Both methods copy the contents of the *string* to a temporary location in the computer's main memory. The methods convert the temporary string to the appropriate case (if necessary) and then return the temporary string. Keep in mind that the ToUpper and ToLower methods do not change the contents of the original *string*; they change only the copy stored in the temporary location. In addition, the ToUpper and ToLower methods affect only letters of the alphabet because they are the only characters that have uppercase and lowercase forms.

When using the ToUpper method in a comparison, be sure that everything you are comparing is uppercase, as shown in Example 1 in Figure 4-19; otherwise, the comparison will not evaluate correctly. Likewise, when using the ToLower method in a comparison, be sure that everything you are comparing is lowercase, as shown in Example 2. The statement in Example 3 temporarily converts the contents of the `strState` variable to uppercase and then assigns the result to the lblState.Text property. As Example 4 indicates, you can also use the ToUpper and ToLower methods to permanently convert the contents of either a String variable or a control's Text property to uppercase or lowercase, respectively.

When typing a value in a text box, users sometimes inadvertently include one or more space characters at either the beginning or the end of the entry. If the control's Text property is subsequently used in a string comparison, the extra spaces will cause the comparison to evaluate incorrectly. For example, if the txtState.Text property contains "La" followed by a space, the condition `txtState.Text.ToUpper = "LA"` will evaluate to False. You can fix this problem using the Trim method, like this: `txtState.Text.Trim.ToUpper = "LA"`. The **Trim method** removes any space characters from both the beginning and the end of a string. Figure 4-20 shows the method's syntax and includes examples of using it.

The Trim method can appear either before or after the ToUpper method.

Trim Method

Syntax
string.**Trim**

Example 1
```
If txtState.Text.Trim.ToUpper = "LA" Then
```
Copies the Text property's value to a temporary location in main memory, then removes any leading and trailing spaces from the copy, then converts the copy to uppercase, and then compares the result to the string "LA".

Figure 4-20 Syntax and examples of the Trim method *(continues)*

(continued)

Example 2
```
strCity = txtCity.Text.Trim.ToUpper
```
Copies the Text property's value to a temporary location in main memory, then removes any leading and trailing spaces from the copy, then converts the copy to uppercase, and then assigns the result to the `strCity` variable.

Example 3
```
txtName.Text = txtName.Text.Trim
```
Copies the Text property's value to a temporary location in main memory, then removes any leading and trailing spaces from the copy, and then assigns the result to the Text property.

Figure 4-20   Syntax and examples of the Trim method

In the syntax, *string* is usually either the name of a String variable or the Text property of an object. The Trim method copies the contents of the *string* to a temporary location in the computer's main memory. It then removes any leading and trailing spaces from the copy and returns a string with the appropriate characters removed. The Trim method does not remove any characters from the original *string*. To do that, you would need to use the assignment statement shown in Example 3 in Figure 4-20.

String Comparison Example: Shipping Application

A customer placing an order online can get free shipping by entering the FREESHIP code during checkout. Without the code, the shipping is $5. Figure 4-21 shows three ways of writing the If...Then...Else statement to accomplish this task.

Example 1—using the Trim and ToUpper methods in the condition
```
If txtCode.Text.Trim.ToUpper = "FREESHIP" Then
    intShipping = 0
Else
    intShipping = 5
End If
```

Example 2—assigning the results of the Trim and ToUpper methods to a variable
```
strCode = txtCode.Text.Trim.ToUpper
If strCode = "FREESHIP" Then
    intShipping = 0
Else
    intShipping = 5
End If
```

Example 3—using the Trim and ToLower methods in the condition
```
If txtCode.Text.Trim.ToLower = "freeship" Then
    intShipping = 0
Else
    intShipping = 5
End If
```

Figure 4-21   Free shipping If...Then...Else statements

START HERE **To code and then test the Shipping application:**

1. Open the Shipping Solution.sln file contained in the VB2017\Chap04\Shipping Solution folder.

2. Open the Code Editor window and locate the btnDisplay_Click procedure. Enter the dual-alternative selection structure shown in Figure 4-22.

enter this dual-alternative selection structure

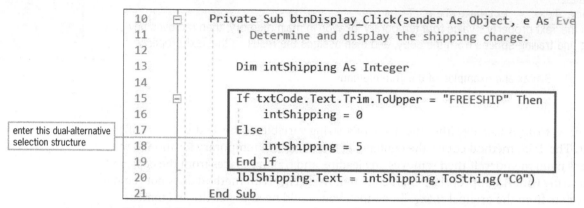

```
10      Private Sub btnDisplay_Click(sender As Object, e As Eve
11          ' Determine and display the shipping charge.
12
13          Dim intShipping As Integer
14
15          If txtCode.Text.Trim.ToUpper = "FREESHIP" Then
16              intShipping = 0
17          Else
18              intShipping = 5
19          End If
20          lblShipping.Text = intShipping.ToString("C0")
21      End Sub
```

Figure 4-22   Selection structure using the Trim and ToUpper methods

3. Save the solution and then start the application. Press the **Spacebar** twice, type **freeship** in the Code box, press the **Spacebar** three times, and then click the **Display shipping** button. The shipping charge is $0, as shown in Figure 4-23.

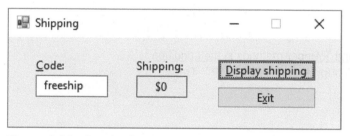

Figure 4-23   Result of entering the valid free shipping code

4. Change the contents of the Code text box to **ship4free** and then click the **Display shipping** button. The shipping charge is $5, as shown in Figure 4-24.

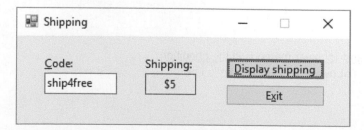

Figure 4-24   Result of entering an invalid code

5. Click the **Exit** button. Close the Code Editor window and then close the solution.

F-7 Nested Selection Structures

Both paths in a selection structure can include instructions that declare variables, perform calculations, and so on; both can also include other selection structures. When either a selection structure's true path or its false path contains another selection structure, the inner selection structure is referred to as a **nested selection structure** because it is contained (nested) entirely within the outer selection structure.

Figure 4-25 shows the pseudocode and flowchart for the btnDisplay_Click procedure in the Voter Eligibility application. The procedure contains an outer selection structure and a nested selection structure. The selection structures determine whether a person can vote and then display one of three messages. The appropriate message depends on the person's age and voter registration status. If the person is younger than 18 years old, the outer selection structure's false path displays the message "You are too young to vote." However, if the person is at least 18 years old, the nested selection structure displays one of two messages. The correct message to display is determined by the person's voter registration status. If the person is registered, then the appropriate message is "You can vote."; otherwise, it is "You must register before you can vote." After the appropriate message is displayed, the nested and outer selection structures end. Notice that the nested structure in Figure 4-25 is processed only when the outer structure's condition evaluates to True.

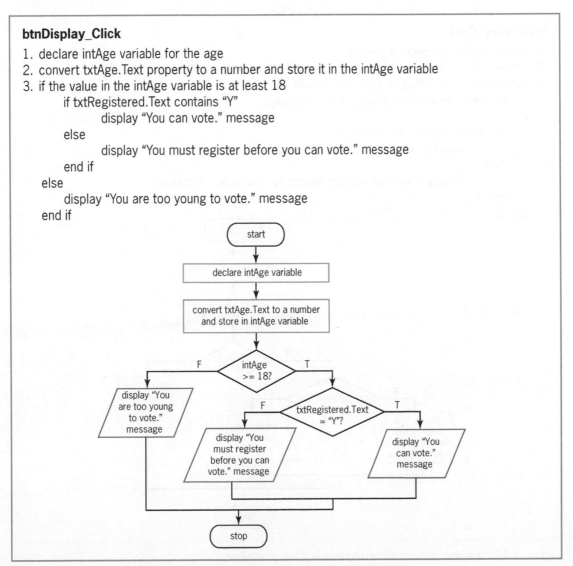

btnDisplay_Click
1. declare intAge variable for the age
2. convert txtAge.Text property to a number and store it in the intAge variable
3. if the value in the intAge variable is at least 18
    if txtRegistered.Text contains "Y"
        display "You can vote." message
    else
        display "You must register before you can vote." message
    end if
else
    display "You are too young to vote." message
end if

Figure 4-25   Pseudocode and flowchart for the btnDisplay_Click procedure

As the pseudocode and flowchart indicate, determining the person's voter registration status is important only *after* his or her age is determined. Because of this, the decision regarding the age is considered the primary decision, while the decision regarding the registration status is considered the secondary decision because whether it needs to be made depends on the result of the primary decision. A primary decision is always made by an outer selection structure, while a secondary decision is always made by a nested selection structure.

Even small procedures can be written in more than one way. Figure 4-26 shows another version of the btnDisplay_Click procedure. Like the procedure shown in Figure 4-25, the outer selection structure in this version of the procedure determines the age (the primary decision), and the nested selection structure determines the voter registration status (the secondary decision). In this version, however, the outer structure's condition is the opposite of the one in Figure 4-25: It checks whether the person's age is less than 18 rather than checking if it is greater than or equal to 18. (Recall that *less than* is the opposite of *greater than or equal to*.) In addition, the nested structure appears in the outer structure's false path in this version, which means it will be processed only when the outer structure's condition evaluates to False. The solutions in Figures 4-25 and 4-26 produce the same results. Neither version of the procedure is better than the other; each simply represents a different way of attaining the desired result.

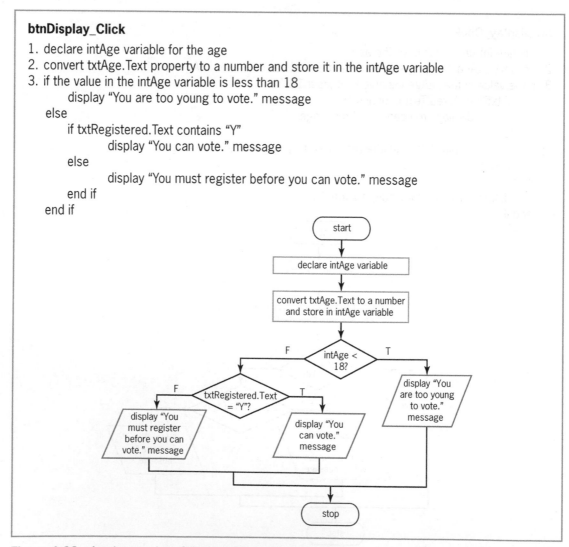

btnDisplay_Click
1. declare intAge variable for the age
2. convert txtAge.Text property to a number and store it in the intAge variable
3. if the value in the intAge variable is less than 18
        display "You are too young to vote." message
    else
        if txtRegistered.Text contains "Y"
                display "You can vote." message
        else
                display "You must register before you can vote." message
        end if
    end if

Figure 4-26   Another version of the btnDisplay_Click procedure

Figure 4-27 shows the code for the btnDisplay_Click procedures from Figures 4-25 and 4-26. The nested structures are shaded in the figure.

Code for the version shown in Figure 4-25

```
11    Private Sub btnDisplay_Click(sender As Object, e As EventArgs) Handl
12         ' Displays a message indicating whether a person can vote.
13
14         Dim intAge As Integer
15
16         Integer.TryParse(txtAge.Text, intAge)
17         ' Determine age.
18         If intAge >= 18 Then
19             ' Determine registration status.
20             If txtRegistered.Text.Trim.ToUpper = "Y" Then
21                 lblMsg.Text = "You can vote."
22             Else
23                 lblMsg.Text = "You must register before you can vote."
24             End If
25         Else
26             lblMsg.Text = "You are too young to vote."
27         End If
28     End Sub
```

nested in the outer selection structure's true path

Code for the version shown in Figure 4-26

```
11    Private Sub btnDisplay_Click(sender As Object, e As EventArgs) Handle
12         ' Displays a message indicating whether a person can vote.
13
14         Dim intAge As Integer
15
16         Integer.TryParse(txtAge.Text, intAge)
17         ' Determine age.
18         If intAge < 18 Then
19             lblMsg.Text = "You are too young to vote."
20         Else
21             ' Determine registration status.
22             If txtRegistered.Text.Trim.ToUpper = "Y" Then
23                 lblMsg.Text = "You can vote."
24             Else
25                 lblMsg.Text = "You must register before you can vote."
26             End If
27         End If
28     End Sub
```

nested in the outer selection structure's false path

Figure 4-27   Code for both versions of the btnDisplay_Click procedure

To code and then test the Voter Eligibility application:

START HERE

1. Open the Voter Solution.sln file contained in the VB2017\Chap04\Voter Solution folder.

2. Open the Code Editor window and locate the btnDisplay_Click procedure. Enter the selection structures shown in either of the examples in Figure 4-27.

3. Save the solution and then start the application. Type **27** in the Age box, type **y** in the Registered (Y/N) box, and then click the **Display** button. The "You can vote." message appears in the lblMsg control. See Figure 4-28.

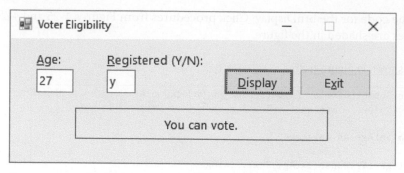

Figure 4-28   Correct message shown in the interface

4. Change the entry in the Registered (Y/N) box to **n** and then click the **Display** button. The "You must register before you can vote." message appears in the interface.

5. Change the age to **17** and then click the **Display** button. The "You are too young to vote." message appears in the interface.

6. Click the **Exit** button. Close the Code Editor window and then close the solution.

Mini-Quiz 4-6

1. Members of the Allen Golf Club pay a $100 green fee. Nonmembers golfing on Monday through Thursday pay $150. Nonmembers golfing on Friday through Sunday pay $200. What are the primary and secondary decisions?

2. Jake's Car Rental charges each customer a daily rental fee of $55. However, there is an additional charge for renting a luxury car. The additional charge is $10 if the customer has a Jake's Luxury coupon; otherwise, the additional charge is $30. What are the primary and secondary decisions?

1) The primary decision is the membership status, and the secondary decision is the day of the week.
2) The primary decision is the car's classification, and the secondary decision is the coupon status.

YOU DO IT 5!

Open the You Do It 5 Solution.sln file contained in the VB2017\Chap04\You Do It 5 Solution folder. Open the Code Editor window and locate the btnDisplay_Click procedure. The procedure should display the shipping charge, which is based on the information shown below. Complete the procedure by entering the appropriate outer and nested selection structures. Save the solution and then start and test the application. Close the solution.

Purchase amount at least $100: $4.99 shipping
Purchase amount less than $100: $10.99 shipping
FREESHIP shipping code: free shipping on any purchase amount

F-8 Multiple-Alternative Selection Structures

Some procedures require a selection structure that can choose from several different alternatives. Such selection structures are referred to as **multiple-alternative selection structures** or **extended selection structures**. Figure 4-29 shows the pseudocode and flowchart for a procedure that uses a multiple-alternative selection structure to display a message. The appropriate message to display is based on the warehouse designation entered by the user.

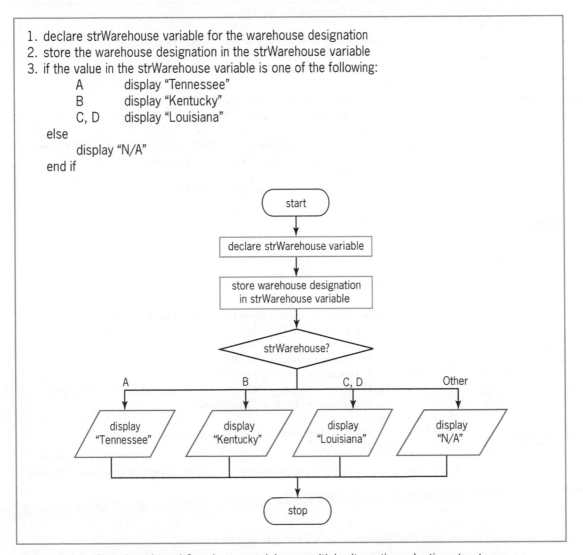

Figure 4-29 Pseudocode and flowchart containing a multiple-alternative selection structure

The diamond in the flowchart represents the condition in the multiple-alternative selection structure. Recall that the diamond is also used to represent the condition in both the single-alternative and dual-alternative selection structures. However, unlike the diamond in both of those selection structures, the diamond in a multiple-alternative selection structure has several flowlines (rather than only two flowlines) leading out of the symbol. Each flowline represents a possible path and must be marked appropriately, indicating the value or values necessary for the path to be chosen.

Figure 4-30 shows two versions of the code for the multiple-alternative selection structure from Figure 4-29; both versions use If...Then...Else statements. Although both versions produce the same result, Version 2 provides a more convenient way of using the If...Then...Else statement to code a multiple-alternative selection structure.

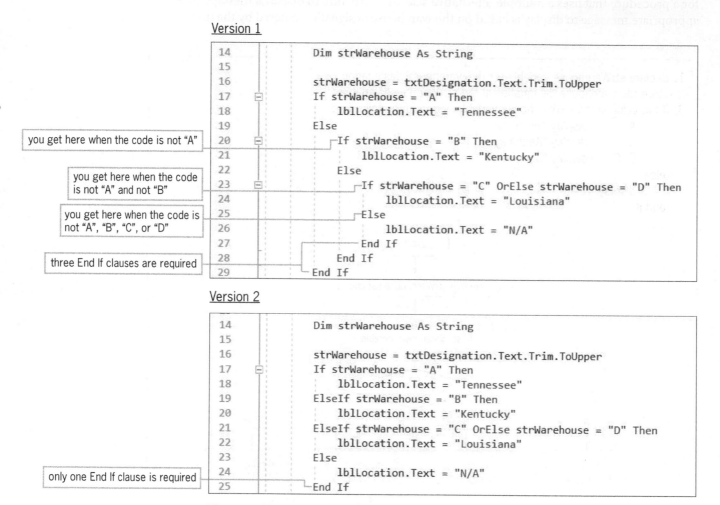

Version 1

```
14        Dim strWarehouse As String
15
16        strWarehouse = txtDesignation.Text.Trim.ToUpper
17        If strWarehouse = "A" Then
18            lblLocation.Text = "Tennessee"
19        Else
20            If strWarehouse = "B" Then
21                lblLocation.Text = "Kentucky"
22            Else
23                If strWarehouse = "C" OrElse strWarehouse = "D" Then
24                    lblLocation.Text = "Louisiana"
25                Else
26                    lblLocation.Text = "N/A"
27                End If
28            End If
29        End If
```

you get here when the code is not "A" → 20

you get here when the code is not "A" and not "B" → 23

you get here when the code is not "A", "B", "C", or "D" → 25

three End If clauses are required → 28

Version 2

```
14        Dim strWarehouse As String
15
16        strWarehouse = txtDesignation.Text.Trim.ToUpper
17        If strWarehouse = "A" Then
18            lblLocation.Text = "Tennessee"
19        ElseIf strWarehouse = "B" Then
20            lblLocation.Text = "Kentucky"
21        ElseIf strWarehouse = "C" OrElse strWarehouse = "D" Then
22            lblLocation.Text = "Louisiana"
23        Else
24            lblLocation.Text = "N/A"
25        End If
```

only one End If clause is required → 24

Figure 4-30 Two versions of the code containing a multiple-alternative selection structure

START HERE **To code and then test the Warehouse Location application:**

1. Open the Warehouse Solution.sln file contained in the VB2017\Chap04\Warehouse Solution-If folder.

2. Open the Code Editor window and locate the btnDisplay_Click procedure. Enter the multiple-alternative selection structure shown in Version 2 in Figure 4-30.

3. Save the solution and then start the application. Type **b** in the Warehouse designation box and then click the **Display** button. See Figure 4-31.

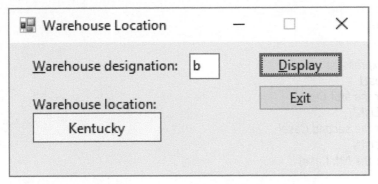

Figure 4-31 Kentucky message shown in the interface

4. On your own, test the application using the following warehouse designations: **a, d, k,** and **c**. When you are finished testing, click the **Exit** button. Close the Code Editor window and then close the solution.

YOU DO IT 6!

Create an application named You Do It 6 and save it in the VB2017\Chap04 folder. Add a text box, a label, and a button to the form. The button's Click event procedure should display (in the label) either the price of a concert ticket or the N/A message. The ticket price is based on the code entered in the text box, as shown below. Code the procedure. Save the solution and then start and test the application. Close the solution.

Code	Ticket price
1	$15
2	$15
3	$25
4	$35
5	$35
Other	N/A

F-9 Select Case Statement

When a multiple-alternative selection structure has many paths from which to choose, it is often simpler and clearer to code the selection structure using the **Select Case statement** rather than several If...Then...Else statements. The Select Case statement's syntax is shown in Figure 4-32. The figure also shows how you can use the statement to code the multiple-alternative selection structure shown earlier in Figure 4-30.

Ch04-Select Case

Select Case Statement

Syntax
Select Case *selectorExpression*
    Case *expressionList1*
        instructions for the first Case
    [Case *expressionList2*
        instructions for the second Case]
    [Case *expressionListN*
        instructions for the Nth Case]
    [Case Else
        instructions for when the selectorExpression does not match any of the expressionLists]
End Select

Select Case statement for the multiple-alternative structure from Figure 4-30

```
14          Dim strWarehouse As String
15
16          strWarehouse = txtDesignation.Text.Trim.ToUpper
17          Select Case strWarehouse
18              Case "A"
19                  lblLocation.Text = "Tennessee"
20              Case "B"
21                  lblLocation.Text = "Kentucky"
22              Case "C", "D"
23                  lblLocation.Text = "Louisiana"
24              Case Else
25                  lblLocation.Text = "N/A"
26          End Select
```

the *selectorExpression* needs to match only one of these values

Figure 4-32 Syntax and an example of the Select Case statement

The Select Case statement begins with the keywords `Select Case`, followed by a *selectorExpression*, which can contain any combination of variables, named constants, literals, keywords, functions, methods, operators, and properties. In the example in Figure 4-32, the selectorExpression is a String variable named `strWarehouse`.

The Select Case statement ends with the End Select clause. Between the Select Case and End Select clauses are the individual Case clauses. Each Case clause represents a different path that the computer can follow. It is customary to indent each Case clause and the instructions within each Case clause, as shown in Figure 4-32. You can have as many Case clauses as necessary in a Select Case statement. However, if the Select Case statement includes a Case Else clause, the Case Else clause must be the last clause in the statement.

Each of the individual Case clauses except the Case Else clause must contain an *expressionList*, which can include one or more expressions. To include more than one expression, you separate each expression with a comma, like this: `Case "C", "D"`. The selectorExpression needs to match only one of the expressions listed in an expressionList. The data type of the expressions must be compatible with the data type of the selectorExpression. If the selectorExpression is numeric, the expressions in the Case clauses should be numeric. Likewise, if the selectorExpression is a string, the expressions should be strings. In the example in Figure 4-32, the selectorExpression (`strWarehouse`) is a string, and so are the expressions "A", "B", "C", and "D".

The Select Case statement looks more complicated than it really is. When processing the statement, the computer simply compares the value of the selectorExpression with the value or values listed in each of the Case clauses, one Case clause at a time beginning with the first. If the selectorExpression matches at least one of the values listed in a Case clause, the computer processes only the instructions contained in that clause. After the clause's instructions are processed, the Select Case statement ends and the computer skips to the instruction following the End Select clause. For instance, if the `strWarehouse` variable in the example shown in Figure 4-32 contains the string "A", the computer will display the "Tennessee" message and then skip to the instruction following the End Select clause. Similarly, if the variable contains the string "D", the computer will display the "Louisiana" message and then skip to the instruction following the End Select clause. Keep in mind that if the selectorExpression matches a value in more than one Case clause, only the instructions in the first match's Case clause are processed.

If the selectorExpression does *not* match any of the values listed in any of the Case clauses, the next instruction processed depends on whether the Select Case statement contains a Case Else clause. If there is a Case Else clause, the computer processes the instructions in that clause and then skips to the instruction following the End Select clause. (Recall that the Case Else clause and its instructions immediately precede the End Select clause.) If the statement does not contain a Case Else clause, the computer just skips to the instruction following the End Select clause.

To use the Select Case statement in the Warehouse Location application:

START HERE

1. Open the Warehouse Solution.sln file contained in the VB2017\Chap04\Warehouse Solution-Select Case folder.

2. Open the Code Editor window and locate the btnDisplay_Click procedure. Enter the Select Case statement shown in Figure 4-32.

3. Save the solution and then start the application. Type **b** in the Warehouse designation box and then click the **Display** button. The Kentucky message appears in the interface.

4. On your own, test the application using the following warehouse designations: **a**, **d**, **k**, and **c**. When you are finished testing, click the **Exit** button. Close the Code Editor window and then close the solution.

Specifying a Range of Values in a Case Clause

In addition to specifying one or more discrete values in a Case clause, you can also specify a range of values, such as the values 1 through 4 or values greater than 10. You do this using either the keyword To or the keyword Is. You use the To keyword when you know both the upper and lower values in the range. The Is keyword is appropriate when you know only one end of the range (either the upper or lower end).

Figure 4-33 shows the syntax for using the Is and To keywords in a Case clause. It also contains an example of a Select Case statement that assigns a price based on the number of items ordered.

Specifying a Range of Values in a Case Clause

Syntax
Case *smallest value in the range* **To** *largest value in the range*
Case Is *comparisonOperator value*

Note: Be sure to test your code thoroughly because the computer will not display an error message when the value preceding To in a Case clause is greater than the value following To. Instead, the Select Case statement will not give the correct results.

Example
The ABC Corporation's price chart is shown here:

Quantity ordered	Price per item
1–5	$25
6–10	$23
More than 10	$20
Fewer than 1	$0

```
Select Case intQuantity
    Case 1 To 5
        intPrice = 25
    Case 6 To 10
        intPrice = 23
    Case Is > 10
        intPrice = 20
    Case Else
        intPrice = 0
End Select
```

Figure 4-33   Syntax and an example of specifying a range of values

According to the price chart shown in the figure, the price for 1 to 5 items is $25 each. Using discrete values, the first Case clause would look like this: `Case 1, 2, 3, 4, 5`. However, a more convenient way of writing that range of numbers is to use the To keyword, like this: `Case 1 To 5`. The expression `1 To 5` specifies the range of numbers from 1 to 5, inclusive. The expression `6 To 10` in the second Case clause in the example specifies the range of numbers from 6 through 10. Notice that both Case clauses state both the lower (1 and 6) and upper (5 and 10) values in each range.

The third Case clause, `Case Is > 10`, contains the `Is` keyword rather than the To keyword. Recall that you use the `Is` keyword when you know only one end of the range of values. In this case, you know only the lower end of the range, 10. The `Is` keyword is always used in combination with one of the following comparison operators: $=, <, <=, >, >=, <>$. The `Case Is > 10` clause specifies all numbers greater than the number 10. Because `intQuantity` is an Integer variable, you can also write this Case clause as `Case Is >= 11`. The Case Else clause in the example in Figure 4-33 is processed only when the `intQuantity` variable contains a value that is not included in any of the previous Case clauses.

To code and then test the ABC Corporation application:

1. Open the ABC Solution.sln file contained in the VB2017\Chap04\ABC Solution folder.

2. Open the Code Editor window and locate the btnDisplay_Click procedure. Enter the Select Case statement shown in Figure 4-34.

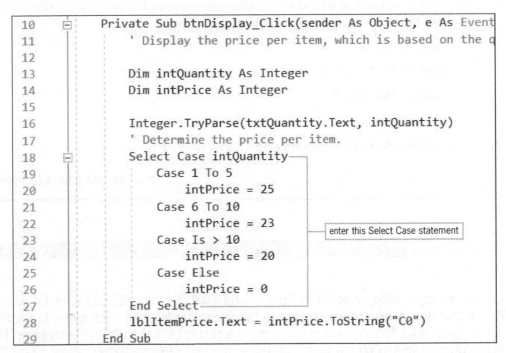

```
10      Private Sub btnDisplay_Click(sender As Object, e As Event
11          ' Display the price per item, which is based on the q
12
13          Dim intQuantity As Integer
14          Dim intPrice As Integer
15
16          Integer.TryParse(txtQuantity.Text, intQuantity)
17          ' Determine the price per item.
18          Select Case intQuantity
19              Case 1 To 5
20                  intPrice = 25
21              Case 6 To 10
22                  intPrice = 23
23              Case Is > 10
24                  intPrice = 20
25              Case Else
26                  intPrice = 0
27          End Select
28          lblItemPrice.Text = intPrice.ToString("C0")
29      End Sub
```
enter this Select Case statement

Figure 4-34   Select Case statement entered in the btnDisplay_Click procedure

3. Save the solution and then start the application. Type **9** in the Quantity ordered box and then click the **Display price** button. See Figure 4-35.

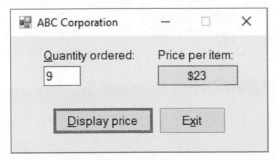

Figure 4-35   Price per item shown in the interface

4. On your own, test the application using **4**, **11**, and **0** as the quantity ordered. When you are finished testing, click the **Exit** button. Close the Code Editor window and then close the solution.

Mini-Quiz 4-7

1. Which flowchart symbol represents the condition in a multiple-alternative selection structure?

2. If the intCode variable is used as the selectorExpression in a Select Case statement, which of the following is a valid Case clause?

   a. Case 1, 2, 3

   b. Case "1", "2", "3"

   c. Case 1 Through 3

   d. All of the above.

3. Write a Case clause that specifies all numbers less than 0.

1) diamond 2) a. 3) Case Is < 0

YOU DO IT 7!

Create an application named You Do It 7 and save it in the VB2017\Chap04 folder. Add a text box, a label, and a button to the form. The button's Click event procedure should display (in the label) either the price of a concert ticket or the N/A message. The ticket price is based on the code entered in the text box, as shown below. Code the procedure using the Select Case statement. Save the solution and then start and test the application. Close the solution.

Code	Ticket price
1	$15
2	$15
3	$25
4	$35
5	$35
Other	N/A

APPLY THE CONCEPTS LESSON

After studying this lesson, you should be able to:

- A-1 Add a check box to a form
- A-2 Code an interface that contains check boxes
- A-3 Add a radio button to a form
- A-4 Code an interface that contains radio buttons
- A-5 Group objects using a group box control
- A-6 Professionalize your application's interface
- A-7 Professionalize your code using arithmetic assignment operators

A-1 Add a Check Box to a Form

You use the CheckBox tool in the toolbox to add a check box control to a form. A **check box** provides an option that the user can either choose to select or choose not to select. The check box's option should be entered using sentence capitalization in the control's Text property, and it should contain a unique access key. If an interface contains more than one check box, the option offered by each must be unique and unrelated to any of the other check box options. Figure 4-36 shows the most commonly used properties of a check box.

 The GUI design guidelines for check boxes are listed in Figure 4-52 and in Appendix A.

Name	Purpose
Checked	indicate whether the check box is selected or unselected
Font	specify the font to use for text
Name	give the check box a meaningful name (use chk as the ID)
Text	specify the text that appears inside the check box; the text should be entered using sentence capitalization and include a unique access key

Figure 4-36 Most commonly used properties of a check box

Because each check box in an interface is independent from any other check box, any number of them on a form can be selected at the same time. When a check box is selected, its Checked property contains the Boolean value True; otherwise, it contains the Boolean value False. You can use a selection structure to determine the value in a **check box's Checked property** and then take the appropriate action based on the result.

A-2 Code an Interface That Contains Check Boxes

Figure 4-37 shows the interface for the Seminars application, which uses check boxes to offer the user three different seminar options. Each seminar occurs on a different day, so the user can select one, two, or all three check boxes; or, he or she can leave all three check boxes unselected. When the user clicks the Calculate button, the button's Click event procedure will calculate and display the total amount due, which is based on which (if any) check boxes are selected.

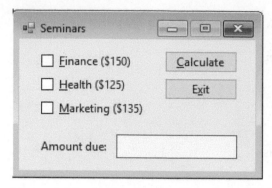

Figure 4-37   Seminars application using check boxes

START HERE **To complete the btnCalc_Click procedure:**

1. Open the Seminars Solution.sln file contained in the VB2017\Chap04\Seminars Solution-CheckBox folder.

2. Open the Code Editor window and locate the btnCalc_Click procedure. The procedure will use three single-alternative selection structures to determine which (if any) of the three check boxes are selected. If a selection structure's condition evaluates to True, the instruction in its true path will add the seminar's fee to the amount due. Enter the three selection structures shown in Figure 4-38.

> Because the Checked property contains a Boolean value, you can omit the = True from the three conditions. For example, you can use If chkFinance. Checked Then.

enter these three single-alternative selection structures

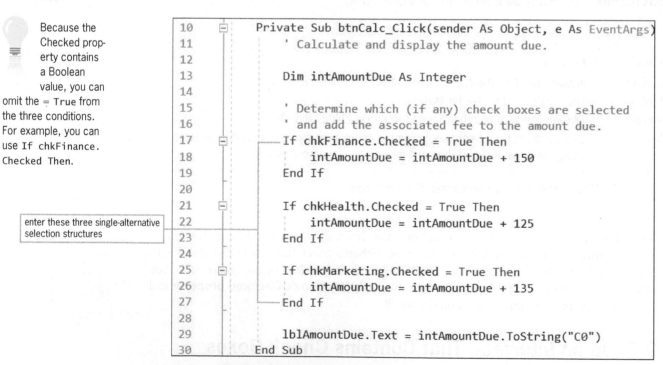

```
10    Private Sub btnCalc_Click(sender As Object, e As EventArgs)
11        ' Calculate and display the amount due.
12
13        Dim intAmountDue As Integer
14
15        ' Determine which (if any) check boxes are selected
16        ' and add the associated fee to the amount due.
17        If chkFinance.Checked = True Then
18            intAmountDue = intAmountDue + 150
19        End If
20
21        If chkHealth.Checked = True Then
22            intAmountDue = intAmountDue + 125
23        End If
24
25        If chkMarketing.Checked = True Then
26            intAmountDue = intAmountDue + 135
27        End If
28
29        lblAmountDue.Text = intAmountDue.ToString("C0")
30    End Sub
```

Figure 4-38   Selection structures entered in the btnCalc_Click procedure

3. Save the solution and then start the application. Click the **Calculate** button. No check boxes are selected, so $0 appears in the Amount due box.

4. Click the **Health ($125)** check box. (Notice that $0 still appears in the Amount due box, which could be misleading. You will fix this problem in the next section.) Click the **Calculate** button. The Amount due box shows $125, which is the price of the Health seminar.

5. Click the **Marketing ($135)** check box and then click the **Calculate** button. The Amount due box shows $260, which is the cost for the Health and Marketing seminars ($125 + $135).

6. Click the **Finance ($150)** check box and then click the **Calculate** button. The Amount due box shows $410, which is the cost for all three seminars.

7. Now, click the **Health ($125)** check box to deselect it and then click the **Calculate** button. The Amount due box shows $285, which is the cost for the Finance and Marketing seminars ($150 + $135).

8. Click the **Exit** button.

CheckBox's CheckedChanged Event

A **check box's CheckedChanged event** occurs when the value in its Checked property changes. For example, the event occurs when you select a check box because doing so changes the check box's Checked property from False to True. Deselecting a check box changes its Checked property from True to False, thereby invoking its CheckedChanged event. In the next set of steps, you will code each check box's CheckedChanged procedure to clear the contents of the Amount due box when the event occurs.

To code each check box's CheckedChanged procedure:

START HERE

1. Open the code template for the chkFinance_CheckedChanged procedure. Type **lblAmountDue.Text = String.Empty** and press **Enter**.

2. Now, enter the same assignment statement in the chkHealth_CheckedChanged and chkMarketing_CheckedChanged procedures, as shown in Figure 4-39.

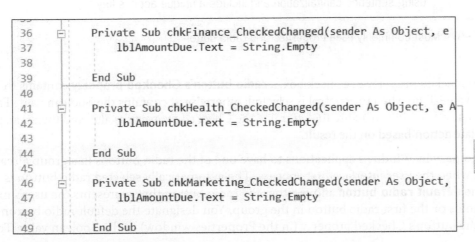

```
36        Private Sub chkFinance_CheckedChanged(sender As Object, e
37            lblAmountDue.Text = String.Empty
38
39        End Sub
40
41        Private Sub chkHealth_CheckedChanged(sender As Object, e A
42            lblAmountDue.Text = String.Empty
43
44        End Sub
45
46        Private Sub chkMarketing_CheckedChanged(sender As Object,
47            lblAmountDue.Text = String.Empty
48
49        End Sub
```

enter the assignment statement in these CheckedChanged procedures

Figure 4-39 Assignment statements entered in the CheckedChanged procedures

3. Save the solution and then start the application. Select all three check boxes and then click the **Calculate** button. The Amount due box shows $410.

4. Click the **Finance ($150)** check box to deselect it. The chkFinance_CheckedChanged procedure clears the contents of the Amount due box. Click the **Calculate** button. The Amount due box shows $260.

5. Click the **Health ($125)** check box to deselect it. The chkHealth_CheckedChanged procedure clears the contents of the Amount due box. Click the **Calculate** button. The Amount due box shows $135.

6. Click the **Marketing ($135)** check box to deselect it. The chkMarketing_CheckedChanged procedure clears the contents of the Amount due box. Click the **Calculate** button. The Amount due box shows $0.

7. Click the **Exit** button and then close the solution.

A-3 Add a Radio Button to a Form

The GUI design guidelines for radio buttons are listed in Figure 4-52 and in Appendix A.

You use the RadioButton tool in the toolbox to add a radio button control to a form. **Radio buttons** allow you to limit the user to only one choice from a group of two or more related but mutually exclusive options. Notice that the group must contain at least two radio buttons. This is because the only way to deselect a radio button is to select a different one.

Each radio button in an interface should be labeled so the user knows the choice it represents. You enter the label using sentence capitalization in the radio button's Text property. Each radio button should also have a unique access key that allows the user to select the button using the keyboard. Figure 4-40 shows the most commonly used properties of a radio button.

Name	Purpose
Checked	indicate whether the radio button is selected or unselected
Font	specify the font to use for text
Name	give the radio button a meaningful name (use rad as the ID)
Text	specify the text that appears inside the radio button; the text should be entered using sentence capitalization and include a unique access key

Figure 4-40   Most commonly used properties of a radio button

Like the Checked property of a check box, a **radio button's Checked property** contains the Boolean value True when the control is selected; otherwise, it contains the Boolean value False. You can use a selection structure to determine the Checked property's value and then take the appropriate action based on the result.

It is customary in Windows applications to have one of the radio buttons in a group already selected when the user interface first appears. The automatically selected radio button is called the **default radio button** and is either the radio button that represents the user's most likely choice or the first radio button in the group. You designate the default radio button by setting the button's Checked property (in the Properties window) to the Boolean value True.

A-4 Code an Interface That Contains Radio Buttons

In this section, you will code a different version of the Seminars application. This version uses radio buttons (rather than check boxes) to offer the user three different seminar options. Each seminar in this version occurs at the same time, so the user will be allowed to select only one of the options. When the user clicks the Calculate button, the button's Click event procedure will determine which radio button is selected and then assign and display the appropriate amount due.

To begin completing this version of the application:

START HERE

1. Open the Seminars Solution.sln file contained in the VB2017\Chap04\Seminars Solution-RadioButton-If folder. If necessary, open the designer window.

2. First, you will designate a default radio button. Click the **Finance ($150)** radio button and then set its Checked property to **True**. A colored dot appears inside the button's circle to indicate that the button is selected. See Figure 4-41.

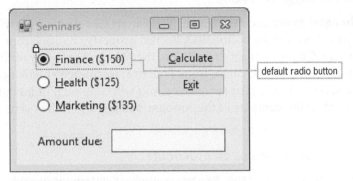

Figure 4-41   Default radio button in the group

3. Open the Code Editor window and locate the btnCalc_Click procedure. The procedure will use a multiple-alternative selection structure to determine which of the three radio buttons is selected. Enter the selection structure shown in Figure 4-42.

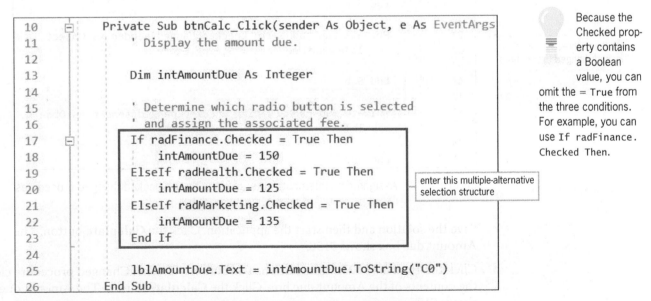

Figure 4-42   Selection structure entered in the btnCalc_Click procedure

Because the Checked property contains a Boolean value, you can omit the = True from the three conditions. For example, you can use If radFinance. Checked Then.

4. Save the solution and then start the application. The Finance ($150) radio button is already selected. Click the **Calculate** button. The Amount due box shows $150.

5. Click the **Health ($125)** radio button. The computer selects the Health ($125) radio button as it deselects the Finance ($150) radio button. This is because only one button in a group can be selected at any one time. (Do not worry about the $150 that appears in the Amount due box. You will fix this problem in the next section.)

6. Click the **Calculate** button. The Amount due box shows $125, which is the price of the Health seminar.

7. Click the **Marketing ($135)** radio button and then click the **Calculate** button. The Amount due box shows $135, which is the cost of the Marketing seminar.

8. Click the **Exit** button.

RadioButton's CheckedChanged Event

A **radio button's CheckedChanged event** occurs when the value in its Checked property changes. For example, when you select a radio button, its Checked property changes from False to True, invoking its CheckedChanged event. In addition, the Checked property of the previously selected radio button in the group changes from True to False, thereby invoking that radio button's CheckedChanged event. In the next set of steps, you will code each radio button's CheckedChanged procedure to clear the contents of the Amount due box when the event occurs.

START HERE **To code each radio button's CheckedChanged procedure:**

1. Enter the `lblAmountDue.Text = String.Empty` assignment statement in each radio button's CheckedChanged procedure, as shown in Figure 4-43.

code these three
CheckedChanged procedures

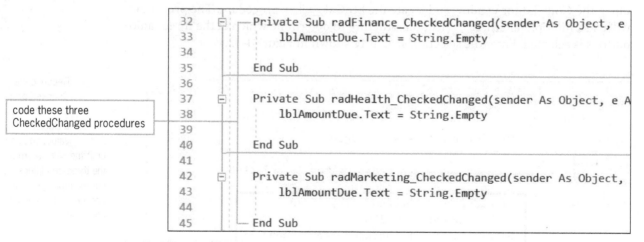

```
32      Private Sub radFinance_CheckedChanged(sender As Object, e
33          lblAmountDue.Text = String.Empty
34
35      End Sub
36
37      Private Sub radHealth_CheckedChanged(sender As Object, e A
38          lblAmountDue.Text = String.Empty
39
40      End Sub
41
42      Private Sub radMarketing_CheckedChanged(sender As Object,
43          lblAmountDue.Text = String.Empty
44
45      End Sub
```

Figure 4-43 Assignment statements entered in the three CheckedChanged procedures

2. Save the solution and then start the application. Click the **Calculate** button. The Amount due box shows $150.

3. Click the **Health ($125)** radio button. The button's CheckedChanged procedure clears the contents of the Amount due box. Click the **Calculate** button. The Amount due box shows $125.

4. Click the **Marketing ($135)** radio button. The button's CheckedChanged procedure clears the contents of the Amount due box. Click the **Calculate** button. The Amount due box shows $135.

5. Click the **Finance ($150)** radio button. The button's CheckedChanged procedure clears the contents of the Amount due box. Click the **Calculate** button. The Amount due box shows $150.

6. Click the **Exit** button and then close the solution.

Using the Select Case Statement with Radio Buttons

In the next set of steps, you will use the Select Case statement (rather than If...Then...Else statements) to code the btnCalc_Click procedure in the Seminars application.

To use the Select Case statement in the btnCalc_Click procedure:

START HERE

1. Open the Seminars Solution.sln file contained in the VB2017\Chap04\Seminars Solution-RadioButton-Select Case folder.

2. Open the Code Editor window and locate the btnCalc_Click procedure. Enter the Select Case statement shown in Figure 4-44.

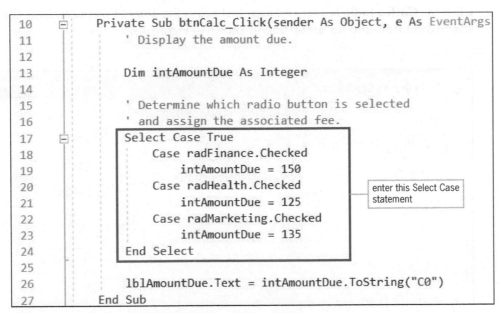

```vb
10      Private Sub btnCalc_Click(sender As Object, e As EventArgs
11          ' Display the amount due.
12
13          Dim intAmountDue As Integer
14
15          ' Determine which radio button is selected
16          ' and assign the associated fee.
17          Select Case True
18              Case radFinance.Checked
19                  intAmountDue = 150
20              Case radHealth.Checked
21                  intAmountDue = 125
22              Case radMarketing.Checked
23                  intAmountDue = 135
24          End Select
25
26          lblAmountDue.Text = intAmountDue.ToString("C0")
27      End Sub
```

enter this Select Case statement

Figure 4-44 Select Case statement entered in the btnCalc_Click procedure

3. Save the solution and then start and test the application.

4. Click the **Exit** button and then close the solution.

A-5 Group Objects Using a Group Box Control

You use the GroupBox tool, which is located in the Containers section of the toolbox, to add a group box to a form. A **group box** serves as a container for other controls and is typically used to visually separate related controls from other controls on the form. You can include an identifying label on a group box by setting the group box's Text property. Labeling a group box is optional; but if you do label it, the label should be entered using sentence capitalization. A group box and its controls are treated as one unit. Therefore, when you move or delete a group box, the controls inside the group box are also moved or deleted, respectively.

The GUI design guidelines for group boxes are listed in Figure 4-52 and in Appendix A.

The Seminars application that you completed in the previous section contained one group of radio buttons. If you need to include two groups of radio buttons in an interface, at least one of the groups must be placed within a container, such as a group box. Otherwise, the radio buttons are considered to be in the same group and only one can be selected at any one time.

Ch04-Radio Button Groups

START HERE **To use a group box to group radio buttons:**

1. Open the RadioButton Solution.sln file contained in the VB2017\Chap04\RadioButton Solution folder. If necessary, open the designer window. The interface contains two sets of radio buttons. The first set offers two choices: Coffee or Tea. The second set offers three choices: Small, Medium, or Large.

2. Start the application. Click **each radio button**. Notice that only one of the radio buttons on the form can be selected at any one time. Click the **Exit** button.

3. Expand the Containers node in the Toolbox window. Click the **GroupBox** tool and then drag the tool to the upper-left corner of the form. Release the mouse button. Set the group box's Text property to **Type**.

4. Click the **Coffee** radio button and then Ctrl+click the **Tea** radio button. Drag the selected controls into the group box, as shown in Figure 4-45.

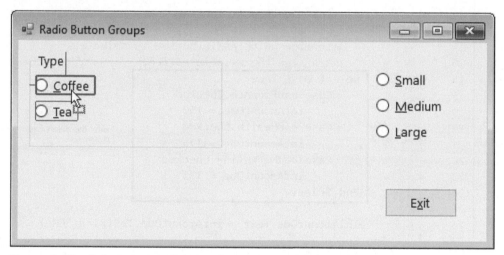

Figure 4-45　Selected controls being dragged into the Type group box

5. Release the mouse button. The interface now has two independent groups of radio buttons.

6. Click the **Type** group box and then drag its middle-right sizing handle to make it smaller.

7. Before starting and testing the application, you will specify the default button in each group. Use the Properties window to set the Coffee radio button's Checked property to **True**. Also set the Small radio button's Checked property to **True**.

8. Save the solution and then start the application. The two default radio buttons are automatically selected in the interface. Click the **Tea** radio button. Because only one of the radio buttons in the Type group can be selected at any one time, selecting the Tea radio button deselects the Coffee radio button. However, it has no effect on the Small radio button, which is part of a different group.

9. Click the **Medium** radio button and then click the **Large** radio button. Notice that only one of the radio buttons in this group can be selected at any one time. Also notice that making a selection in this group has no effect on the radio buttons in the Type group.

10. Click the **Exit** button.

11. On your own, add another group box to the form and then modify the interface as shown in Figure 4-46.

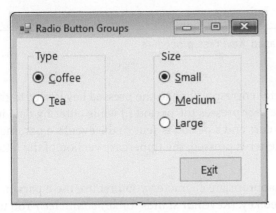

Figure 4-46   Modified interface

12. Lock the controls on the form. Save the solution and then start and test the application.

13. Click the **Exit** button and then close the solution.

Mini-Quiz 4-8

1. If a check box is not selected, what value is contained in its Checked property?

2. How do you specify the default radio button?

3. Radio button and check box controls have a CheckedChanged event that is invoked when a change is made to their Checked property. True or False?

4. A form contains six radio buttons. Three of the radio buttons are contained in a group box. How many of the radio buttons in the interface can be selected at the same time?

1) False 2) by setting its Checked property to True in the Properties window 3) True 4) two

A-6 Professionalize Your Application's Interface

In some applications, you can make the interface more professional-looking by coding a text box's KeyPress event procedure to prevent the control from accepting inappropriate characters. For example, if a text box requires a numeric entry, you can tell its KeyPress event procedure to accept only the numbers entered by the user, and to ignore all other characters.

Coding a Text Box's KeyPress Event Procedure

A text box's **KeyPress event** occurs each time the user presses a key while the text box has the focus. As indicated in Figure 4-47, the procedure associated with the KeyPress event has two parameters, which appear within the parentheses in the procedure header: sender and e. A **parameter** represents information that is passed to the procedure when the event occurs.

 Not every text box's KeyPress event procedure needs to be coded. You code the procedure only when you need to limit the user's entry to specific characters.

```
                              ┌──────────────────┐      ┌─────────────┐
                              │ sender parameter │      │ e parameter │
                              └────────┬─────────┘      └──────┬──────┘
 ┌──────────────────────────────────────────────────────────────────────────┐
 │ Private Sub txtPurchased_KeyPress(sender As Object, e As KeyPressEventArgs) Ha
 │
 │ End Sub
 └──────────────────────────────────────────────────────────────────────────┘
```

Figure 4-47 Code template for the txtPurchased_KeyPress procedure

When the KeyPress event occurs, a character corresponding to the pressed key is sent to the event's **e** parameter. For example, when the user presses the period (.) while entering data into a text box, the text box's KeyPress event occurs and a period is sent to the event's **e** parameter. Similarly, when the Shift key along with a letter is pressed, the uppercase version of the letter is sent to the **e** parameter.

To prevent a text box from accepting an inappropriate character, you first use the **e** parameter's **KeyChar property** to determine the pressed key. (*KeyChar* stands for *key character*.) You then use the **e** parameter's **Handled property** to cancel the key if it is an inappropriate one. You cancel the key by setting the Handled property to True, like this: `e.Handled = True`.

The KeyPress event automatically allows the use of the Delete key for editing.

Figure 4-48 shows examples of using the KeyChar and Handled properties in a text box's KeyPress event procedure. The condition in Example 1's selection structure compares the contents of the KeyChar property with a dollar sign. If the condition evaluates to True, the `e.Handled = True` instruction in the selection structure's true path cancels the $ key before it is entered in the txtSales control. You can use the selection structure in Example 2 to allow the txtAge control to accept only numbers and the Backspace key (which is used for editing). You refer to the Backspace key on your keyboard using Visual Basic's **ControlChars.Back constant**.

Controlling the Characters Accepted by a Text Box

Example 1

```
Private Sub txtSales_KeyPress(sender As Object, e As KeyPress
    ' Prevent the text box from accepting the dollar sign.

    If e.KeyChar = "$" Then
        e.Handled = True
    End If
End Sub
```

Example 2

```
Private Sub txtAge_KeyPress(sender As Object, e As KeyPress
    ' Accept only numbers and the Backspace key

    If (e.KeyChar < "0" OrElse e.KeyChar > "9") AndAlso
        e.KeyChar <> ControlChars.Back Then
        e.Handled = True
    End If
End Sub
```

Figure 4-48 Examples of using the KeyChar and Handled properties in the KeyPress event procedure

In the next set of steps, you will code the txtPurchased_KeyPress procedure, which is contained in the Total Due application from this chapter's Focus lesson.

To code the txtPurchased_KeyPress procedure:

START HERE

1. Open the Total Due Solution.sln file contained in the VB2017\Chap04\Total Due Solution-KeyPress folder.

2. Open the Code Editor window and then open the code template for the txtPurchased_KeyPress procedure. Enter the comment and selection structure shown in Figure 4-49.

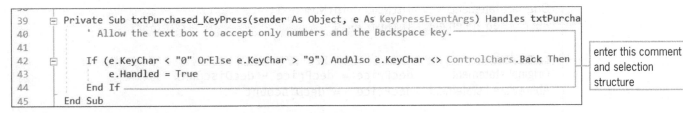

```
39   Private Sub txtPurchased_KeyPress(sender As Object, e As KeyPressEventArgs) Handles txtPurcha
40        ' Allow the text box to accept only numbers and the Backspace key.
41
42       If (e.KeyChar < "0" OrElse e.KeyChar > "9") AndAlso e.KeyChar <> ControlChars.Back Then
43            e.Handled = True
44       End If
45   End Sub
```
enter this comment and selection structure

Figure 4-49   Code entered in the txtPurchased_KeyPress procedure

3. Save the solution and then start the application. Try typing a letter, a period, and a $ in the Number purchased box. You will not be able to do so.

4. Type **12** in the Number purchased box and then click the **Calculate** button. The Total due box shows $91.80.

5. Click the **Exit** button.

A-7 Professionalize Your Code Using Arithmetic Assignment Operators

In addition to the standard arithmetic operators that you learned about in Chapter 3, Visual Basic provides several arithmetic assignment operators. You can use the **arithmetic assignment operators** to abbreviate an assignment statement that contains an arithmetic operator. However, the assignment statement must have the following format, in which *variableName* on both sides of the equal sign is the name of the same variable: *variableName = variableName arithmeticOperator value*. For example, you can use the addition assignment operator (+=) to abbreviate the statement `intNum = intNum + 1` as follows: `intNum += 1`. Both statements tell the computer to add the number 1 to the contents of the `intNum` variable and then store the result in the variable.

Figure 4-50 shows the syntax for using arithmetic assignment operators, and it includes examples of using them. Notice that each arithmetic assignment operator consists of an arithmetic operator followed immediately by the assignment operator (=). The arithmetic assignment operators do not contain a space. Including a space in an arithmetic assignment operator is a common syntax error. To abbreviate an assignment statement, you simply remove the variable name that appears on the left side of the assignment operator and then put the assignment operator immediately after the arithmetic operator.

Arithmetic Assignment Operators

Syntax
variableName arithmeticAssignmentOperator value

Operator	Purpose
+=	addition assignment
−=	subtraction assignment
*=	multiplication assignment
/=	division assignment

Example 1
Original statement: `intNum = intNum + 1`
Abbreviated statement: `intNum += 1`

Example 2
Original statement: `decPrice = decPrice - decDiscount`
Abbreviated statement: `decPrice -= decDiscount`

Example 3
Original statement: `dblPrice = dblPrice * 1.05`
Abbreviated statement: `dblPrice *= 1.05`

Example 4
Original statement: `dblNum = dblNum / 2`
Abbreviated statement: `dblNum /= 2`

Figure 4-50   Syntax and examples of using the arithmetic assignment operators

START HERE

To use an assignment operator in the btnCalc_Click procedure:

1. Locate the btnCalc_Click procedure. Modify the assignment statement that subtracts the discount from the total due as shown in Figure 4-51.

modify this statement to use an arithmetic assignment operator

```
23        If intPurchased >= 5 Then
24            dblDiscount = dblTotalDue * dblDISCOUNT_RATE
25            dblTotalDue -= dblDiscount
26        End If
```

Figure 4-51   Modified assignment statement in the btnCalc_Click procedure

2. Save the solution and then start the application. Type **10** in the Number purchased box and then click the **Calculate** button. The total due is $76.50.

3. Click the **Exit** button. Close the Code Editor window and then close the solution.

Mini-Quiz 4-9

1. Which property of the KeyPress procedure's **e** parameter is used to determine the key pressed by the user?

2. Which property of the KeyPress procedure's **e** parameter is used to cancel the key pressed by the user?

3. Every text box's KeyPress event procedure needs to be coded. True or False?

4. To cancel a key, you assign what value to the **e** parameter's Handled property?

5. Write a statement that uses an arithmetic assignment operator to add the number 1 to the `intAge` variable.

1) KeyChar 2) Handled 3) False 4) True 5) intAge += 1

Summary

- You can use the If...Then...Else statement to code single-alternative and dual-alternative selection structures. The statement's syntax is shown in Figure 4-3.

- You can use the comparison operators listed in Figure 4-4 to compare two values.

- To create a compound condition, use the logical operators and truth tables listed in Figures 4-12 and 4-13, respectively.

- When evaluating an expression that contains arithmetic, comparison, and logical operators, evaluate the arithmetic operators first, followed by the comparison operators and then the logical operators. The order of precedence for the operators is shown in Figure 4-18.

- To temporarily convert a string to either uppercase or lowercase, use the ToUpper and ToLower methods, respectively. The syntax of each method is shown in Figure 4-19.

- To remove leading and trailing spaces from a string, use the Trim method. The method's syntax is shown in Figure 4-20.

- To create a selection structure that evaluates both a primary and a secondary decision, place (nest) the secondary decision's selection structure entirely within either the true or false path of the primary decision's selection structure.

- You can use either If...Then...Else statements or the Select Case statement to code a multiple-alternative selection structure. Refer to the code shown in Figure 4-30 and the Select Case statement's syntax and example shown in Figure 4-32.

- To specify a range of values in a Select Case statement's Case clause, use the To keyword when you know both the upper and lower values in the range. Use the Is keyword when you know only one end of the range. The Is keyword is used in combination with one of the following comparison operators: =, <, <=, >, >=, <>. The syntax and an example of using both keywords are shown in Figure 4-33.

- To allow the user to select any number of choices from a group of one or more independent and nonexclusive options, use the CheckBox tool to add one or more check box controls to the form.

- To limit the user to only one choice in a group of two or more related but mutually exclusive options, use the RadioButton tool to add two or more radio buttons to the form. To include two groups of radio buttons on a form, at least one of the groups must be placed within a container, such as a group box.

- To determine whether a radio button or check box is selected or unselected, use the control's Checked property. The property will contain the Boolean value True if the control is selected; otherwise, it will contain the Boolean value False.

- To process code when the value in the Checked property of a radio button or check box changes, enter the code in the control's CheckedChanged event procedure.

- To group controls together using a group box, use the GroupBox tool to add a group box to the form. Drag controls from either the form or the toolbox into the group box. To include an optional identifying label on a group box, set the group box's Text property.

- To allow a text box to accept only certain keys, code the text box's KeyPress event procedure. The key the user pressed is stored in the e.KeyChar property. You use the `e.Handled = True` statement to cancel the key pressed by the user.

- You can abbreviate some assignment statements using the arithmetic assignment operators listed in Figure 4-50.

- Figure 4-52 lists the GUI design guidelines for check boxes, radio buttons, and group boxes. (The guidelines are also listed in Appendix A.)

GUI design guidelines for check boxes
- Use check boxes to allow the user to select any number of choices from a group of one or more independent and nonexclusive choices.
- The label in the check box's Text property should be entered using sentence capitalization.
- Assign a unique access key to each check box in an interface.

GUI design guidelines for radio buttons
- Use radio buttons to limit the user to one choice in a group of related but mutually exclusive choices.
- The minimum number of radio buttons in a group is two, and the recommended maximum number is seven.
- The label in the radio button's Text property should be entered using sentence capitalization.
- Assign a unique access key to each radio button in an interface.
- Use a container (such as a group box) to create separate groups of radio buttons. Only one button in each group can be selected at any one time.
- Designate a default radio button in each group of radio buttons.

GUI design guideline for group boxes
Use sentence capitalization for the optional identifying label, which is entered in the group box's Text property.

Figure 4-52 GUI design guidelines for check boxes, radio buttons, and group boxes

Key Terms

And operator—one of the logical operators; same as the AndAlso operator, but less efficient because it does not perform a short-circuit evaluation

AndAlso operator—one of the logical operators; when used to combine two subconditions, the resulting compound condition evaluates to True only when both subconditions are True, and it evaluates to False only when one or both of the subconditions are False; same as the And operator but more efficient because it performs a short-circuit evaluation

Arithmetic assignment operators—composed of an arithmetic operator followed by the assignment operator; used to abbreviate some assignment statements; see Figure 4-50 for the syntax and examples

Check box—used in an interface to offer the user one or more independent and nonexclusive choices

Check box's Checked property—contains a Boolean value that indicates whether the check box is selected (True) or not selected (False)

Check box's CheckedChanged event—occurs when the value in the check box's Checked property changes

Comparison operators—operators used to compare values in an expression; also called relational operators

Condition—specifies the decision that the computer needs to make; must be phrased so that it evaluates to an answer of either True or False

ControlChars.Back constant—the Visual Basic constant that represents the Backspace key on your keyboard

Decision symbol—the diamond in a flowchart; used to represent the condition in a selection structure

Default radio button—the radio button that is automatically selected when the application is started and the interface appears

Dual-alternative selection structure—a selection structure that requires one set of instructions to be followed only when the structure's condition evaluates to True and a different set of instructions to be followed only when the structure's condition evaluates to False

Extended selection structures—another name for multiple-alternative selection structures

False path—contains the instructions to be processed when a selection structure's condition evaluates to False

Group box—a control that is used to contain other controls; instantiated using the GroupBox tool, which is located in the Containers section of the toolbox

Handled property—a property of the KeyPress event procedure's e parameter; when assigned the value True, it cancels the key pressed by the user

If...Then...Else statement—used to code single-alternative, dual-alternative, and multiple-alternative selection structures in Visual Basic

KeyChar property—a property of the KeyPress event procedure's e parameter; stores the character associated with the key pressed by the user

KeyPress event—occurs each time the user presses a key while a control has the focus

Logical operators—operators used to combine two or more subconditions into one compound condition; also called Boolean operators

Multiple-alternative selection structures—selection structures that contain several alternatives; also called extended selection structures; can be coded using either If...Then...Else statements or the Select Case statement

Nested selection structure—a selection structure that is wholly contained (nested) within either the true or false path of another selection structure

Not operator—one of the logical operators; reverses the truth-value of a condition

Or operator—one of the logical operators; same as the OrElse operator but less efficient because it does not perform a short-circuit evaluation

OrElse operator—one of the logical operators; when used to combine two subconditions, the resulting compound condition evaluates to True when at least one of the subconditions is True and evaluates to False only when both subconditions are False; same as the Or operator but more efficient because it performs a short-circuit evaluation

Parameter—an item contained within parentheses in a procedure header; stores information passed to the procedure when the procedure is invoked

Radio buttons—controls used to limit the user to only one choice from a group of two or more related but mutually exclusive options

Radio button's CheckedChanged event—occurs when the value in the radio button's Checked property changes

Radio button's Checked property—contains a Boolean value that indicates whether the radio button is selected (True) or not selected (False)

Select Case statement—used to code a multiple-alternative selection structure in Visual Basic

Selection structure—one of the three basic control structures; tells the computer to make a decision based on some condition and then select the appropriate action

Sequence structure—one of the three basic control structures; directs the computer to process a procedure's instructions sequentially, which means in the order they appear in the procedure

Short-circuit evaluation—refers to the way the computer evaluates two subconditions connected by either the AndAlso or OrElse operator; when the AndAlso operator is used, the computer does not evaluate subcondition2 if subcondition1 is False; when the OrElse operator is used, the computer does not evaluate subcondition2 if subcondition1 is True

Single-alternative selection structure—a selection structure that requires a special set of actions to be performed only when the structure's condition evaluates to True

Statement block—in a selection structure, the set of statements terminated by an Else or End If clause

ToLower method—temporarily converts a string to lowercase

ToUpper method—temporarily converts a string to uppercase

Trim method—removes any leading or trailing spaces from a string

True path—contains the instructions to be processed when a selection structure's condition evaluates to True

Truth tables—tables that summarize how the computer evaluates the logical operators in an expression

Unicode—the universal coding scheme that assigns a unique numeric value to each character used in the written languages of the world

Xor operator—one of the logical operators; when used to combine two subconditions, the resulting compound condition evaluates to True when only one of the subconditions is True; it evaluates to False when either both subconditions are True or both subconditions are False

Review Questions

1. Which of the following compound conditions determines whether the value in the `intOrdered` variable is *outside* the range of 0 through 25?

   a. `intOrdered < 0 OrElse intOrdered > 25`

   b. `intOrdered > 0 AndAlso intOrdered < 25`

   c. `intOrdered <= 0 OrElse intOrdered >= 25`

   d. `intOrdered < 0 AndAlso intOrdered > 25`

2. Which of the following If clauses compares the string contained in the txtId control with the abbreviation for the state of Georgia?

   a. `If ToUpper(txtId.Text.Trim) = "GA" Then`

   b. `If txtId.Text.Trim.ToUpper = "GA" Then`

   c. `If txtId.Text.ToLower.Trim = "ga" Then`

   d. Both b and c.

3. Evaluate the following expression: `13 > 12 OrElse 6 < 5`.

   a. True   b. False

4. Evaluate the following expression: `6 + 3 > 7 AndAlso 11 < 2 * 5`.

   a. True   b. False

5. Evaluate the following expression: `8 <= 4 + 6 AndAlso 5 > 6 OrElse 4 < 7`.

   a. True   b. False

6. Evaluate the following expression: `7 + 3 * 2 > 6 * 3 AndAlso True`.

   a. True   b. False

7. Evaluate the following expression: `5 * 7 > 6 ^ 2`.

   a. True   b. False

8. Evaluate the following expression: `5 * 4 > 6 ^ 2 AndAlso True OrElse False`.

   a. True   b. False

Use the code shown in Figure 4-53 to answer Review Questions 9 through 12.

```
If intAge <= 5 Then
    intCost = 0
ElseIf intAge <= 12 Then
    intCost = 5
ElseIf intAge <= 55 Then
    intCost = 10
Else
    intCost = 8
End If
```

Figure 4-53 Code for Review Questions 9 through 12

9. What will the code in Figure 4-53 assign to the intCost variable when the intAge variable contains the number 65?

    a. 0   c. 8
    b. 5   d. 10

10. What will the code in Figure 4-53 assign to the intCost variable when the intAge variable contains the number 2?

    a. 0   c. 8
    b. 5   d. 10

11. What will the code in Figure 4-53 assign to the intCost variable when the intAge variable contains the number 12?

    a. 0   c. 8
    b. 5   d. 10

12. What will the code in Figure 4-53 assign to the intCost variable when the intAge variable contains the number 33?

    a. 0   c. 8
    b. 5   d. 10

Use the code shown in Figure 4-54 to answer Review Questions 13 through 16.

```
If strLevel = "1" OrElse strLevel = "2" Then
    lblStatus.Text = "Bronze"
ElseIf strLevel = "3" OrElse strLevel = "4" Then
    lblStatus.Text = "Silver"
ElseIf strLevel = "5" Then
    lblStatus.Text = "Gold"
Else
    lblStatus.Text = "Platinum"
End If
```

Figure 4-54 Code for Review Questions 13 through 16

13. What will the code in Figure 4-54 assign to the lblStatus control when the strLevel variable contains the string "2"?

   a. Bronze   c. Platinum

   b. Gold   d. Silver

14. What will the code in Figure 4-54 assign to the lblStatus control when the strLevel variable contains the string "5"?

   a. Bronze   c. Platinum

   b. Gold   d. Silver

15. What will the code in Figure 4-54 assign to the lblStatus control when the strLevel variable contains the string "10"?

   a. Bronze   c. Platinum

   b. Gold   d. Silver

16. What will the code in Figure 4-54 assign to the lblStatus control when the strLevel variable contains the string "3"?

   a. Bronze   c. Platinum

   b. Gold   d. Silver

17. Where can a nested selection structure appear?

   a. only in an outer selection structure's false path

   b. only in an outer selection structure's true path

   c. in either of an outer selection structure's paths

   d. only in another nested selection structure's true or false paths

18. Which of the following Case clauses is valid in a Select Case statement whose selectorExpression is an Integer variable named intAge?

   a. `Case Is > 21`   c. `Case 1 To 10`

   b. `Case 21, 65`   d. All of the above.

Use the code shown in Figure 4-55 to answer Review Questions 19 through 22.

```
Select Case intLevel
    Case 1, 2
        strStatus = "Bronze"
    Case 3 To 5
        strStatus = "Silver"
    Case 6, 7
        strStatus = "Gold"
    Case Else
        strStatus = "Platinum"
End Select
```

Figure 4-55 Code for Review Questions 19 through 22

19. What will the code in Figure 4-55 assign to the `strStatus` variable when the `intLevel` variable contains the number 4?

   a. Bronze

   b. Gold

   c. Platinum

   d. Silver

20. What will the code in Figure 4-55 assign to the `strStatus` variable when the `intLevel` variable contains the number 8?

   a. Bronze

   b. Gold

   c. Platinum

   d. Silver

21. What will the code in Figure 4-55 assign to the `strStatus` variable when the `intLevel` variable contains the number 7?

   a. Bronze

   b. Gold

   c. Platinum

   d. Silver

22. What will the code in Figure 4-55 assign to the `strStatus` variable when the `intLevel` variable contains the number 1?

   a. Bronze

   b. Gold

   c. Platinum

   d. Silver

23. What is the minimum number of radio buttons in a group?

   a. one

   b. two

   c. three

   d. There is no minimum number of radio buttons.

24. If a check box is not selected, what value is contained in its Checked property?

   a. True

   b. Unchecked

   c. False

   d. Unselected

25. Which capitalization should be used for the text appearing in check boxes and radio buttons?

   a. sentence capitalization

   b. book title capitalization

   c. either book title capitalization or sentence capitalization

   d. None of the above.

26. It is customary in Windows applications to designate a default check box.

   a. True

   b. False

27. A form contains six check boxes. Three of the check boxes are located in a group box. How many of the check boxes on the form can be selected at the same time?

   a. one

   b. two

   c. three

   d. six

28. If a radio button is selected, its _____ property contains the Boolean value True.

   a. Checked

   b. On

   c. Selected

   d. Selection

29. Which of the following If clauses will evaluate to True when the Bonus check box is selected?

   a. `If chkBonus.Check = True Then`

   b. `If chkBonus.Checked Then`

   c. `If chkBonus.Checked = True Then`

   d. Both b and c.

30. Which of the following events occurs when a check box is clicked?

   a. Changed

   b. Checked

   c. CheckedChanged

   d. None of the above.

31. When entering data in a text box, each key the user presses invokes the text box's _____ event.

   a. Focus

   b. Key

   c. KeyFocus

   d. KeyPress

32. When entered in the appropriate event procedure, which of the following statements cancels the key pressed by the user?

   a. `e.Handled = True`

   b. `e.Handled = False`

   c. `e.KeyCancel = True`

   d. `e.KeyCancel = False`

33. Which of the following If clauses determines whether the user pressed the Backspace key?

   a. `If e.KeyChar = ControlChars.Back Then`

   b. `If e.KeyChar = Backspace Then`

   c. `If e.KeyChar = ControlChars.Backspace Then`

   d. `If ControlChars.BackSpace = True Then`

34. Which of the following If clauses determines whether the user pressed the % key?

   a. `If ControlChars.PercentSign = True Then`

   b. `If e.KeyChar = "%" Then`

   c. `If e.KeyChar = Chars.PercentSign Then`

   d. `If e.KeyChar.ControlChars = "%" Then`

35. Which of the following statements is equivalent to the statement `dblTotal = dblRate * dblTotal`?

   a. `dblTotal =* dblRate`

   b. `dblTotal *= dblRate`

   c. `dblRate *= dblTotal`

   d. `dblRate =* dblTotal`

36. The six logical operators are listed below. Indicate their order of precedence by placing a number (1, 2, and so on) on the line to the left of the operator. If two or more operators have the same precedence, assign the same number to each.

_____ Xor

_____ And

_____ Not

_____ Or

_____ AndAlso

_____ OrElse

37. An expression can contain arithmetic, comparison, and logical operators. Indicate the order of precedence for the three types of operators by placing a number (1, 2, or 3) on the line to the left of the operator type.

_____ Arithmetic

_____ Logical

_____ Comparison

Exercises

INTRODUCTORY

1. Create a Windows Forms application. Use the following names for the project and solution, respectively: States Capitals Project and States Capitals Solution. Save the application in the VB2017\Chap04 folder. Change the form file's name to Main Form.vb. Change the form's name to frmMain. Add five radio buttons, two labels, and two buttons to the form. One of the buttons should be an Exit button; the other should be a Display button. Each radio button's Text property should contain the name of a different state; choose any five state names. The Display button should display (in one of the labels) the name of the capital associated with the selected state name. Code the button's Click event procedure using the If...Then...Else statement. Be sure to code each radio button's CheckedChanged procedure. Save the solution and then start and test the application.

INTRODUCTORY

2. Create a Windows Forms application. Use the following names for the project and solution, respectively: Hales Project and Hales Solution. Save the application in the VB2017\Chap04 folder. Change the form file's name to Main Form.vb. Change the form's name to frmMain. Create the interface shown in Figure 4-56. The interface contains a check box, a group box, four radio buttons, two labels, and two buttons. Be sure to set the tab order. The prices of the comforters sold at Hales Department Store, as well as the shipping fee, are included in Figure 4-56. The shipping fee is charged only when the customer is not taking advantage of the store pickup option. The Display cost button should determine the comforter's price and whether to charge a shipping fee. The button should display the cost of the comforter (which might include the shipping fee) with a dollar sign and two decimal places. Be sure to code the CheckedChanged procedures for the radio buttons and check box. Save the solution and then start and test the application. (The cost for a Queen comforter that will be picked up at the store is $49.99; if it is shipped, the cost is $54.99.)

Figure 4-56   Interface, prices, and shipping fee for Exercise 2

3. Create a Windows Forms application. Use the following names for the project
    and solution, respectively: Baxters Project and Baxters Solution. Save the applica-
    tion in the VB2017\Chap04 folder. Change the form file's name to Main Form.vb.
    Change the form's name to frmMain. Create the interface shown in Figure 4-57.
    The interface contains a text box, two check boxes, three labels, and two buttons.
    Be sure to set the tab order. Baxters (an online retailer) sells an 18-volt cordless
    drill for $25.99. Employees of Baxters receive a 10% discount on their total order,
    excluding shipping. The shipping fee is a flat rate of $9.99; however, if a customer
    has a shipping coupon, the shipping fee is $4.99. Code the application. Be sure to
    code the CheckedChanged procedures for the two check boxes. Also code the Enter,
    KeyPress, and TextChanged procedures for the text box. Save the solution and then
    start and test the application. (The total due for two drills with an employee discount
    and a $4.99 shipping coupon is $51.77.)

INTRODUCTORY

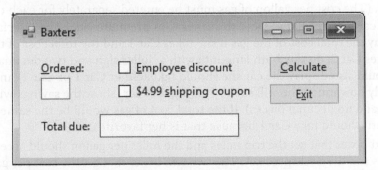

Figure 4-57   Interface for Exercise 3

INTERMEDIATE   4. In this exercise, you modify the application created in Exercise 2. Use Windows to make a copy of the Hales Solution folder. Rename the copy Hales Solution-Select Case. Open the Hales Solution.sln file contained in the Hales Solution-Select Case folder. Modify the Display cost button's Click event procedure to use the Select Case statement to determine the comforter's price. (Hint: You can use a Boolean value as the selectorExpression.) Save the solution and then start and test the application.

INTERMEDIATE   5. Lorenzo's is having a BoGoHo (Buy One, Get One Half Off) sale. The store manager wants an application that allows the salesclerk to enter the prices of two items. The half off should always be applied to the item that has the lowest price. The application should calculate and display the total amount the customer owes as well as the amount he or she saved. For example, if the two items cost $24.99 and $10.00, the half off is applied to the $10.00 item. The total owed is $29.99 and the savings is $5.00. Display the calculated amounts in label controls, and display them with a dollar sign and two decimal places.

   a. Create a Windows Forms application. Use the following names for the project and solution, respectively: Lorenzo Project and Lorenzo Solution. Save the application in the VB2017\Chap04 folder. Change the form file's name to Main Form.vb. Change the form's name to frmMain. Create an appropriate interface and then code the application.

   b. Save the solution and then start and test the application.

   c. Now professionalize your application's interface as follows: The calculated amounts should be removed from the interface when a change is made to the contents of a text box in the interface. The contents of each text box should be selected when the text box receives the focus. Each text box should accept only numbers, the period, and the Backspace key. Save the solution and then start and test the application.

INTERMEDIATE   6. Patti Garcia owns two cars, referred to as Car 1 and Car 2. She wants to drive one of the cars to her vacation destination, but she's not sure which one (if any) would cost her the least amount in gas. Create a Windows Forms application. Use the following names for the project and solution, respectively: Car Project and Car Solution. Save the application in the VB2017\Chap04 folder. Change the form file's name to Main Form.vb. Change the form's name to frmMain.

   a. The application's interface should provide text boxes for Patti to enter the following five items: the total miles she will drive, Car 1's miles per gallon (mpg), Car 2's miles per gallon (mpg), Car 1's cost per gallon of gas, and Car 2's cost per gallon of gas. (The cost per gallon of gas must be entered separately for each car because one car uses regular gas and the other uses premium gas.) The interface should display the total cost of the gas if she takes Car 1 and the total cost of the gas if she takes Car 2; display both amounts with a dollar sign and two decimal places. It should also display the car she should take (either Car 1 or Car 2) and approximately how much she will save by taking that car (show the savings with a dollar sign and no decimal places). If the total cost of gas would be the same for both cars, Patti should take Car 1 because that is her favorite car.

   b. The three text boxes that get the trip miles and the miles per gallon should accept only numbers and the Backspace key. The two text boxes that get the cost per gallon should accept only numbers, the period, and the Backspace key.

   c. When a text box receives the focus, its existing text should be selected.

d. The output should be cleared when a change is made to the contents of a text box in the interface.

e. Test the application using 1200, 28, 35, 1.97, and 2.09 as the trip miles, Car 1's mpg, Car 2's mpg, Car 1's cost per gallon, and Car 2's cost per gallon, respectively. (Hint: The total costs for Car 1 and Car 2 are $84.43 and $71.66, respectively. By taking Car 2, Patti will save approximately $13.)

f. Now, change Car 1's mpg to 35. Also, change Car 2's mpg to 28. Which car should Patti take, and how much (approximately) will she save?

g. Next, change Car 1's mpg and cost per gallon to 28 and 2.09, respectively. Which car should Patti take, and how much (approximately) will she save?

7. Open the Wedding Solution.sln file contained in the VB2017\Chap04\Wedding Solution folder. The application should display the number of round tables needed to seat only the guests at a wedding reception. (In other words, the bridal party does not need to be included in this calculation.) Each round table can accommodate a maximum of 8 guests. When the text box receives the focus, its existing text should be selected. The text box should accept only numbers and the Backspace key. The output should be cleared when a change is made to the contents of the text box. Code the application. Save the solution and then start and test the application. (If the number of guests is 235, the number of required tables is 30.)   **INTERMEDIATE**

8. In this exercise, you modify the application from Exercise 7. The modified application will display the number of rectangular tables needed to seat the bridal party as well as the number of round tables required for the guests. Each rectangular table can accommodate a maximum of 10 people. As in Exercise 7, a maximum of 8 guests can fit at each round table. Use Windows to make a copy of the Wedding Solution folder. Rename the copy Modified Wedding Solution. Open the Wedding Solution.sln file contained in the Modified Wedding Solution folder. In addition to entering the number of guests, the interface should now allow the user to also enter the number of people in the bridal party. Modify the interface by including three additional labels and a text box, and then reset the tab order. Make the appropriate modifications to the code. Be sure to code the new text box's Enter, KeyPress, and TextChanged procedures. Also, be sure to modify the txtGuests_TextChanged procedure. Save the solution and then start and test the application. (If the numbers of guests and bridal party members are 130 and 15, respectively, the numbers of required round and rectangular tables are 17 and 2, respectively.)   **INTERMEDIATE**

9. Software Haven sells a software package that is available in three editions. The application should display the price of the edition a customer wants to purchase. The retail prices for the Ultimate, Professional, and Student editions are $899.99, $599.99, and $99.99, respectively. Some customers may have a coupon worth 10% off the price of the Ultimate edition, while others may have a coupon worth 20% off the price of the Student edition. Create a Windows Forms application. Use the following names for the project and solution, respectively: Software Project and Software Solution. Save the application in the VB2017\Chap04 folder. Change the form file's name to Main Form.vb. Change the form's name to frmMain. Create the interface shown in Figure 4-58. The interface contains a group box, six radio buttons, two labels, and two buttons. Be sure to set the tab order. Code the application. Be sure to code each radio button's CheckedChanged procedure. Save the solution and then start and test the application.   **INTERMEDIATE**

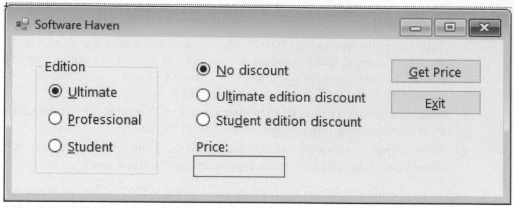

Figure 4-58   Interface for Exercise 9

INTERMEDIATE

10. Williams Cable Company wants an application that displays a customer's monthly cable bill, which is based on the information shown in Figure 4-59. Create a Windows Forms application. Use the following names for the project and solution, respectively: Williams Project and Williams Solution. Save the application in the VB2017\Chap04 folder. Change the form file's name to Main Form.vb. Change the form's name to frmMain. Create an appropriate interface using radio buttons for the different packages and check boxes for the additional features. Be sure to set the tab order. Code the application. Be sure to code the CheckedChanged procedures for the radio buttons and check boxes. Save the solution and then start and test the application.

Packages	Monthly charge ($)
Basic	24.99
Silver	42.99
Gold	84.99
Diamond	99.99

Additional features	Monthly charge ($)
Cinnematic movie channels	9.50
HBI movie channels	9.50
Showtimer movie channels	10.50
Local stations	6.00

Figure 4-59   Information for Exercise 10

ADVANCED

11. Each salesperson at Canton Inc. receives a commission based on the amount of his or her sales. The commission rates and additional payment amounts are shown in Figure 4-60. Create a Windows Forms application. Use the following names for the project and solution, respectively: Canton Project and Canton Solution. Save the application in the VB2017\Chap04 folder. Change the form file's name to Main Form.vb. Change the form's name to frmMain. Create the interface shown in Figure 4-60. The text box should accept only numbers, the period, and the Backspace key, and its text should be selected when it receives the focus. Calculate

the commission, any additional amount, and the total due only when the sales amount is greater than 0; otherwise, display $0.00 as the commission, additional amount, and total due. The calculated amounts should be cleared when a change is made to any of the input items. Save the solution and then start and test the application. (The total due for a salesperson who has been with the company for 11 years and whose sales are $13,000 is $2,010.00.)

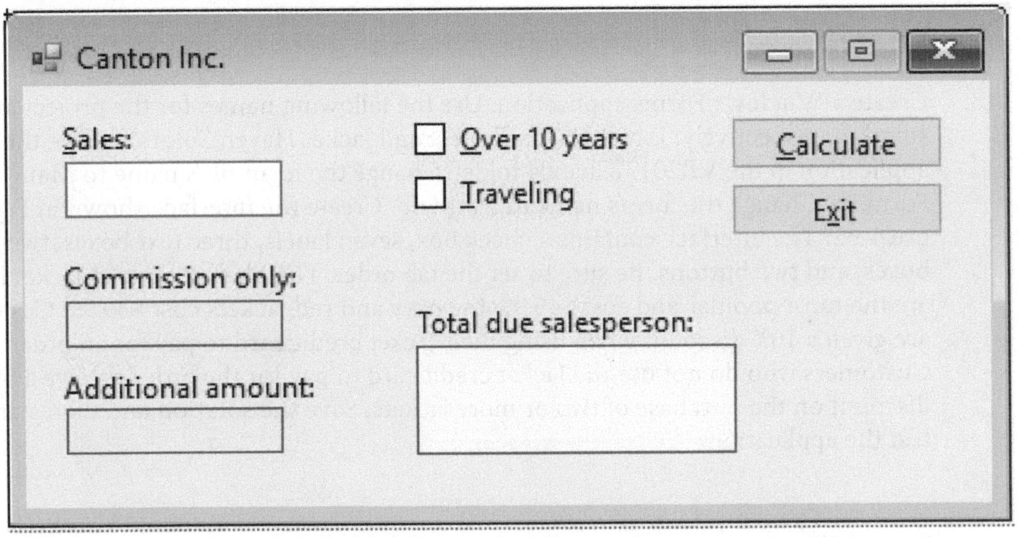

Sales ($)	Commission
1–5,999.99	10% of sales
6,000–29,999.99	$600 plus 13% of the sales over 6,000
30,000 and over	$3,720 plus 14% of the sales over 30,000

Additional
$500 if the salesperson has worked at the company for over 10 years and the sales amount is at least $10,000.
$700 if the salesperson travels.

Figure 4-60   Interface and commission information for Exercise 11

ADVANCED

12. In this exercise, you create an application for Genatone Inc. The application displays the price of an order based on the number of units ordered and the customer's status (either wholesaler or retailer). The price per unit is shown in Figure 4-61. Create a Windows Forms application. Use the following names for the project and solution, respectively: Genatone Project and Genatone Solution. Save the application in the VB2017\Chap04 folder. Change the form file's name to Main Form.vb. Change the form's name to frmMain. Create a suitable interface. Use radio buttons to determine the customer's status. Code the application. Save the solution and then start and test the application. (A wholesaler ordering 70 units will pay $910.00, while a retailer will pay $1,260.00.)

Wholesaler		Retailer	
Number of units	Price per unit ($)	Number of units	Price per unit ($)
1–50	15	1–25	22
51–150	13	Over 25	18
Over 150	10		

Figure 4-61   Pricing chart for Exercise 12

ADVANCED   13.   Create a Windows Forms application. Use the following names for the project and solution, respectively: Jacket Haven Project and Jacket Haven Solution. Save the application in the VB2017\Chap04 folder. Change the form file's name to Main Form.vb. Change the form's name to frmMain. Create the interface shown in Figure 4-62. The interface contains a check box, seven labels, three text boxes, two group boxes, and two buttons. Be sure to set the tab order. The black jackets at Jacket Haven are the most popular and cost $45.99; the navy and red jackets cost $39.99. Customers are given a 10% discount when using their Jacket credit card to pay for an order. Customers who do not use the Jacket credit card to pay for the order receive a 5% discount on the purchase of two or more jackets. Save the solution and then start and test the application.

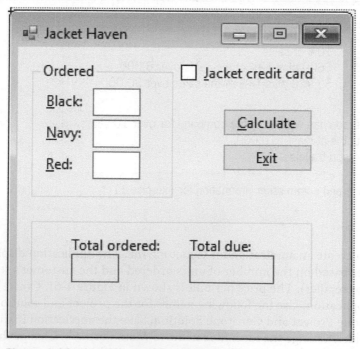

Figure 4-62   Interface for Exercise 13

14. In this exercise, you modify the Grade application from Exercise 13 in Chapter 3. Use Windows to copy the Grade Solution folder from the VB2017\Chap03 folder to the VB2017\Chap04 folder. Open the Grade Solution.sln file contained in the VB2017\Chap04\Grade Solution folder. Start the application and then click the Calculate button. The percentages display as NaN, which stands for Not a Number. The NaN message is a result of dividing a number by 0. Use a selection structure to display 0.0% rather than NaN as the percentages. Save the solution and then start and test the application. Now professionalize the interface by allowing the text boxes to accept only numbers and the Backspace key. Save the solution and then start and test the application.

▸ ADVANCED

15. In this exercise, you modify the Sales application from Exercise 14 in Chapter 3. Use Windows to copy the Sales Solution folder from the VB2017\Chap03 folder to the VB2017\Chap04 folder. Open the Sales Solution.sln file contained in the VB2017\Chap04\Sales Solution folder. Start the application and then click the Calculate button. The percentages display as NaN, which stands for Not a Number. The NaN message is a result of dividing a number by 0. Use a selection structure to display 0.0% rather than NaN as the percentages. Save the solution and then start and test the application. Now professionalize the interface by allowing the text boxes to accept only numbers, the period, and the Backspace key. Save the solution and then start and test the application.

▸ ADVANCED

16. Create a Windows Forms application. Use the following names for the project and solution, respectively: OnYourOwn Project and OnYourOwn Solution. Save the application in the VB2017\Chap04 folder. Plan and design an application of your choice. The only requirement is that you must follow the minimum guidelines listed in Figure 4-63. Before starting the application, be sure to verify the name of the startup form. Save the solution and then start and test the application.

▸ ON YOUR OWN

1. The user interface must contain a minimum of one text box, three labels, two radio buttons, one check box, and two buttons. One of the buttons must be an Exit button.
2. The interface can include a picture box, but this is not a requirement.
3. The interface must follow the GUI design guidelines summarized in Figure 2-20 in Chapter 2 and in Figure 4-52 in Chapter 4. (The guidelines are also listed in Appendix A.)
4. Objects that are either coded or referred to in code should be named appropriately.
5. The Code Editor window must contain comments, the three Option statements, at least two variables, at least two assignment statements, the Me.Close() statement, and at least one selection structure. The application must perform at least one calculation.
6. Every text box on the form should have its TextChanged and Enter event procedures coded. At least one of the text boxes should have its KeyPress event procedure coded.
7. Every radio button and check box should have its CheckedChanged event procedure coded.

Figure 4-63   Guidelines for Exercise 16

FIX IT 17. The purpose of this exercise is to demonstrate the importance of testing an application thoroughly. Open the FixIt Solution.sln file contained in the VB2017\Chap04\FixIt Solution folder. The application displays a shipping charge that is based on the total price entered by the user, as shown in Figure 4-64. Start the application and then test it by clicking the Display shipping button. Notice that the Shipping charge box contains $13, which is not correct. Now, test the application using the following total prices: 100, 501, 1500, 500.75, 30, 1000.33, and 2000. Here too, notice that the application does not always display the correct shipping charge. (More specifically, the shipping charge for two of the seven total prices is incorrect.) Open the Code Editor window and correct the errors in the code. Save the solution and then start and test the application.

Total price	Shipping
Less than $1	$ 0
At least $1 but less than $100	$13
At least $100 but less than $501	$10
At least $501 but less than $1,001	$ 7
At least $1,001	$ 5

Figure 4-64 Shipping charges for Exercise 17

CHAPTER 5

The Repetition Structure

In this chapter's Focus on the Concepts lesson, you will learn how programmers direct the computer to repeat one or more instructions a specified number of times or either while or until a condition evaluates to true. The Focus lesson also covers string concatenation as well as counters and accumulators, which are used to keep track of running totals.

In the Apply the Concepts lesson, you will learn how to use Visual Basic's Financial.Pmt method to calculate a periodic payment. You will also learn how to add a list box to an interface. You will use the concepts from the Focus lesson to code the applications in the Apply lesson.

▌FOCUS ON THE CONCEPTS LESSON

Concepts covered in this lesson:

- F-1 Repetition structures
- F-2 Do...Loop statement (pretest loop)
- F-3 String concatenation
- F-4 Infinite loops
- F-5 Do...Loop statement (posttest loop)
- F-6 Counters and accumulators
- F-7 For...Next statement

F-1 Repetition Structures

Programmers use the **repetition structure**, referred to more simply as a **loop**, when they need the computer to repeatedly process one or more program instructions. The loop contains a condition that controls whether the instructions are repeated. In many programming languages, the condition can be phrased in one of two ways: It can either specify the requirement for repeating the instructions or specify the requirement for *not* repeating them. The requirement for repeating the instructions is referred to as the **looping condition** because it indicates when the computer should continue "looping" through the instructions. The requirement for *not* repeating the instructions is referred to as the **loop exit condition** because it tells the computer when to exit (or stop) the loop. Every looping condition has an opposing loop exit condition; one is the opposite of the other. Figure 5-1 shows examples of both types of conditions that you use every day. The conditions are shaded in the figure.

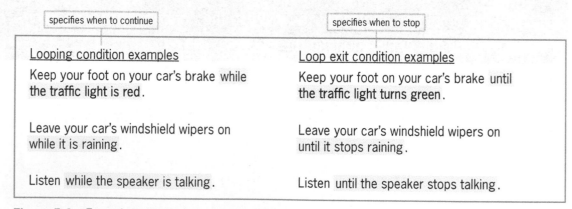

Figure 5-1   Examples of familiar looping conditions and loop exit conditions

The condition in a loop can appear at either the top or the bottom of the loop, as shown in the examples in Figure 5-2. The examples, which are written in pseudocode, display the numbers 1 through 5 in a label control. The condition in each example is shaded in the figure. Like the condition in a selection structure, the condition in a repetition structure must evaluate to either true or false. When the condition is at the top of the loop, the loop is referred to as a **pretest loop** because the condition is evaluated *before* the instructions within the loop are processed. When the condition is at the bottom of the loop, the loop is referred to as a **posttest loop** because the condition is evaluated *after* the instructions within the loop are processed.

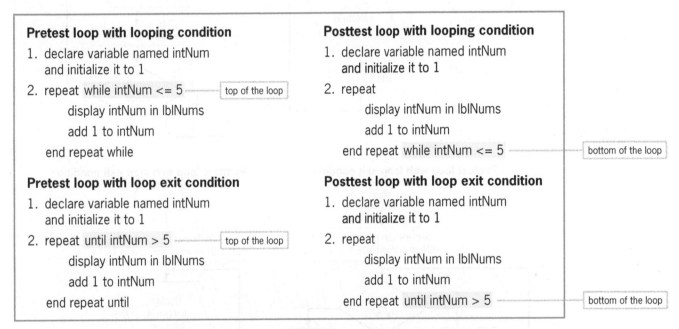

Figure 5-2 Examples of pretest and posttest loops written in pseudocode

The difference between a pretest loop and a posttest loop is that the instructions in a posttest loop will always be processed at least once, whereas the instructions in a pretest loop may never be processed. For example, if the intNum variable used in the examples in Figure 5-2 was initialized to 6 (rather than to 1), the conditions in both pretest loops would prevent the instructions in those loops from being processed. The instructions in both posttest loops, on the other hand, would be processed once before the conditions were evaluated the first time.

It is often easier to understand loops by viewing them in flowchart form. Figure 5-3 shows the flowcharts associated with the examples from Figure 5-2. Like the condition in a selection structure, the condition in a flowchart is represented by a diamond. As you learned in Chapter 4, the diamond is called the decision symbol. The condition is shaded in each decision symbol shown in Figure 5-3. Like the diamond in a selection structure, the diamond in a repetition structure has two flowlines leading out of the symbol. The flowlines are usually marked with a T (for True) and an F (for False); however, they can be marked with a Y and an N (for Yes and No).

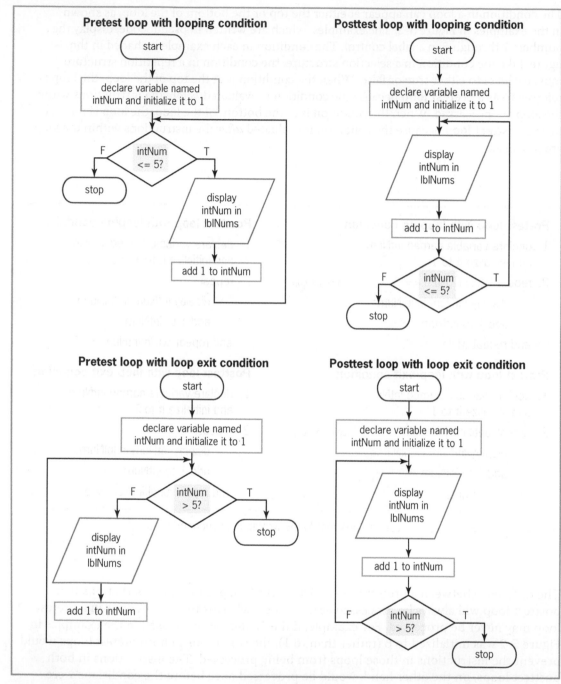

Figure 5-3 Flowcharts for the loop examples from Figure 5-2

The Visual Basic language provides three different statements for coding loops: Do...Loop, For...Next, and For Each...Next. The Do...Loop and For...Next statements are covered in this chapter. The For Each...Next statement is covered in Chapter 8.

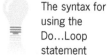

The syntax for using the Do...Loop statement to code a posttest loop is shown in Figure 5-6.

F-2 Do...Loop Statement (Pretest Loop)

Figure 5-4 shows the syntax for using the **Do...Loop statement** to code a pretest loop. The loop's *condition*, which must follow either the keyword `While` or the keyword `Until`, can be phrased as either a looping condition or a loop exit condition. You use the `While` keyword in a looping condition to specify that the loop body should be processed *while* (in other words, as long as) the condition is true. You use the `Until` keyword in a loop exit condition to specify that the loop body should be processed *until* the condition becomes true, at which time the loop should stop.

Like the condition in an If...Then...Else statement, the condition in a Do...Loop statement can contain variables, named constants, literals, properties, methods, keywords, and operators; it also must evaluate to a Boolean value. The condition is evaluated with each repetition of the loop and determines whether the computer processes the loop body. Figure 5-4 also includes examples of using the Do...Loop statement to code the pretest loops from Figures 5-2 and 5-3. The examples contain the concatenation operator (&), which you will learn about in the next section. In each example, the loop will stop when the value in `intNum` is 6.

Ch05-Pretest Do Loop

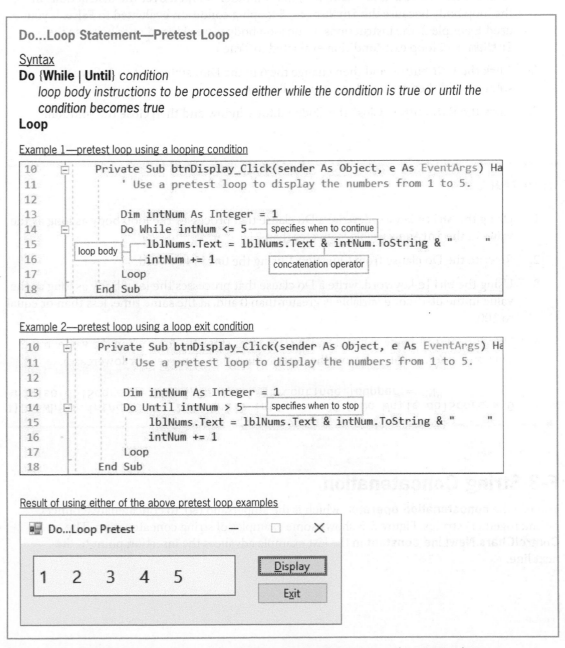

Figure 5-4   Syntax and examples of using the Do...Loop statement to code a pretest loop

START HERE   **To code and then test the Do...Loop Pretest application:**

1. Open the Do Loop Pretest Solution.sln file contained in the VB2017\Chap05\Do Loop Pretest Solution folder.

2. Open the Code Editor window and locate the btnDisplay_Click procedure. Enter the Do...Loop statement shown in either of the examples from Figure 5-4. (There are five space characters between the quotation marks in each example.)

3. Save the solution and then start the application. Click the **Display** button to display the numbers from 1 to 5 in the label control.

4. Click the **Exit** button. Now change the 1 in the Dim statement to **6**. Save the solution and then start the application. Click the **Display** button. No numbers appear in the label control. (If you used Example 1, the computer skipped over the instructions in the loop body because the intNum <= 5 looping condition evaluated to False. If you used Example 2, the instructions in the loop body were skipped over because the intNum > 5 loop exit condition evaluated to True.)

5. Click the **Exit** button and then change the 6 in the Dim statement to **1**. Save the solution and then start and test the application.

6. Click the **Exit** button. Close the Code Editor window and then close the solution.

Mini-Quiz 5-1

1. Using the While keyword, write a Do clause that processes the loop body as long as the value in the intAge variable is greater than 21.

2. Rewrite the Do clause from Question 1 using the Until keyword.

3. Using the While keyword, write a Do clause that processes the loop body as long as the value in the dblScore variable is greater than 0 and, at the same time, less than or equal to 100.

4. Using the Until keyword, write a Do clause that stops the loop when the value in the strContinue variable contains the letter N (in either uppercase or lowercase).

1) Do While intAge > 21 2) Do Until intAge <= 21 3) Do While dblScore > 0 AndAlso dblScore <= 100 4) Do Until strContinue.ToUpper = "N"

F-3 String Concatenation

You use the **concatenation operator**, which is the ampersand (**&**), to concatenate (connect or link together) strings. Figure 5-5 shows some examples of string concatenation. The **ControlChars.NewLine constant** in the last example advances the insertion point to the next line.

```
Concatenating Strings

Variables        Contents
strCity          Atlanta
strState         GA
intSalary        42500

Concatenated string                              Result
strCity & strState                               AtlantaGA
strCity & " " & strState                         Atlanta GA
strCity & ", " & strState                        Atlanta, GA
"She lives in " & strCity & "."                  She lives in Atlanta.
"Salary: " & intSalary.ToString("C0")            Salary: $42,500
strCity & ControlChars.NewLine & strState        Atlanta
                                                 GA
```

this constant advances the insertion point to the next line

Figure 5-5   Examples of string concatenation

YOU DO IT 1!

Create an application named You Do It 1 and save it in the VB2017\Chap05 folder. Add a label and a button to the form. The button should use a pretest loop and the concatenation operator to display the following numbers in the label: 1, 3, 5, and 7. Save the solution and then start and test the application. Close the solution.

F-4 Infinite Loops

A loop that has no way to end is called an **infinite loop** or an **endless loop**. An infinite loop is many times created when the loop body does not contain an instruction that will make either the looping condition evaluate to False or the loop exit condition evaluate to True. You can stop an infinite loop by clicking Debug on the menu bar and then clicking Stop Debugging. Or, you can click the Stop Debugging button (the red square) on the Standard toolbar.

To create and then stop an infinite loop:

START HERE

1. Open the Infinite Pretest Loop Solution.sln file contained in the VB2017\Chap05\ Infinite Pretest Loop Solution folder.

2. Open the Code Editor window and locate the btnDisplay_Click procedure. Turn the intNum += 1 assignment statement into a comment by inserting an apostrophe (') before it. Notice that the loop body no longer provides an instruction that can change the value stored in the intNum variable from its initial value of 1 to a value that can stop the loop—in this case, 6.

3. Save the solution and then start the application. Click the **Display** button. Wait a few seconds and then click the **Exit** button. Notice that the Exit button does not respond to its Click event. Click the **Display** button again. The Display button also does not respond to its Click event. Neither button responds because the Do…Loop statement is in an infinite loop. The loop has no way to stop because without the intNum += 1 statement, the intNum variable's value remains at 1.

4. Click the **Stop Debugging** button (the red square) on the Standard toolbar to stop the loop.

5. Remove the apostrophe from the assignment statement. Save the solution and then start and test the application.

6. Click the **Exit** button. Close the Code Editor window and then close the solution.

F-5 Do...Loop Statement (Posttest Loop)

The syntax for using the Do...Loop statement to code a pretest loop is shown in Figure 5-4.

Ch05-Posttest Do Loop

Figure 5-6 shows the syntax for using the Do...Loop statement to code a posttest loop. Except for the location of the keyword (While or Until) and the *condition*, the syntax is the same as the one shown earlier in Figure 5-4. The figure also shows how you can modify the Do...Loop statements from Figure 5-4 to use posttest loops rather than pretest ones. (The pseudocode and flowcharts for the posttest loops are shown earlier in Figures 5-2 and 5-3.) In each example, the loop will stop when the value in intNum is 6.

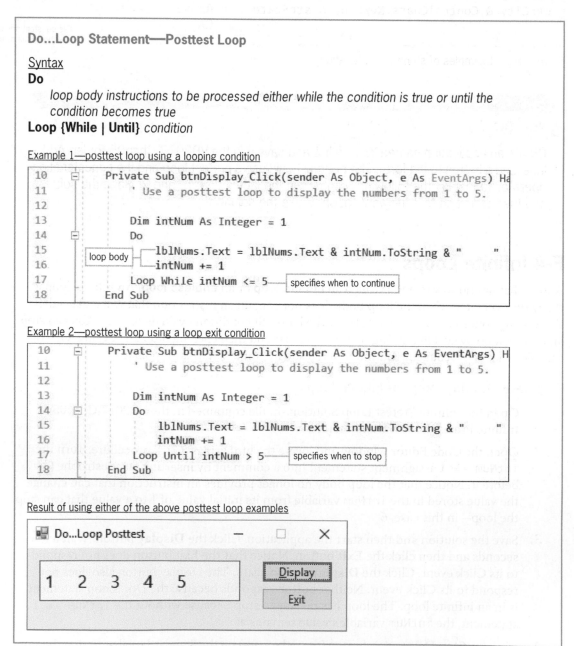

Figure 5-6 Syntax and examples of using the Do...Loop statement to code a posttest loop

To code and then test the Do...Loop Posttest application:

START HERE

1. Open the Do Loop Posttest Solution.sln file contained in the VB2017\Chap05\Do Loop Posttest Solution folder.

2. Open the Code Editor window and locate the btnDisplay_Click procedure. Enter the Do...Loop statement shown in either of the examples from Figure 5-6. (There are five space characters between the quotation marks in each example.)

3. Save the solution and then start the application. Click the **Display** button to display the numbers from 1 to 5 in the label control.

4. Click the **Exit** button. Now change the 1 in the Dim statement to **6**. Save the solution and then start the application. Click the **Display** button. Because the posttest loop's condition is not evaluated until after the instructions in the loop are processed the first time, the number 6 appears in the label control, as shown in Figure 5-7.

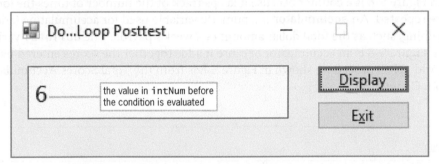

Figure 5-7   Result of the loop instructions being processed before the condition is evaluated

5. Click the **Exit** button and then change the 6 in the Dim statement to **1**. Save the solution and then start and test the application.

6. Click the **Exit** button. Close the Code Editor window and then close the solution.

Mini-Quiz 5-2

1. Using the `While` keyword, write a Loop clause that processes the loop body as long as the value in the `intAge` variable is greater than 21.

2. Rewrite the Loop clause from Question 1 using the `Until` keyword.

3. Using the `While` keyword, write a Loop clause that processes the loop body as long as the value in the `dblScore` variable is greater than 0 and, at the same time, less than or equal to 100.

4. Using the `Until` keyword, write a Loop clause that stops the loop when the value in the `strContinue` variable contains the letter N (in either uppercase or lowercase).

1) Loop While intAge > 21 2) Loop Until intAge <= 21 3) Loop While dblScore > 0 AndAlso dblScore <= 100 4) Loop Until strContinue.ToUpper = "N"

YOU DO IT 2!

Create an application named You Do It 2 and save it in the VB2017\Chap05 folder. Add a label and a button to the form. The button should use a posttest loop and the concatenation operator to display the following numbers in the label: 1, 3, 5, and 7. Save the solution and then start and test the application. Close the solution.

F-6 Counters and Accumulators

Some procedures require you to calculate a subtotal, a total, or an average. You make these calculations using a counter, an accumulator, or both. A **counter** is a numeric variable used for counting something, such as the number of employees paid in a week. The `intNum` variable in Example 1 in Figure 5-8 is a counter because it keeps track of the number of times the loop instructions are repeated. An **accumulator** is a numeric variable used for accumulating (adding together) something, such as the total dollar amount of a week's payroll. The `dblTotal` variable in Example 2 in Figure 5-8 is an accumulator because it adds together the scores entered by the user. (The btnAdd_Click procedure shown in Figure 5-8 is from the Total Scores Accumulator application from Chapter 3.)

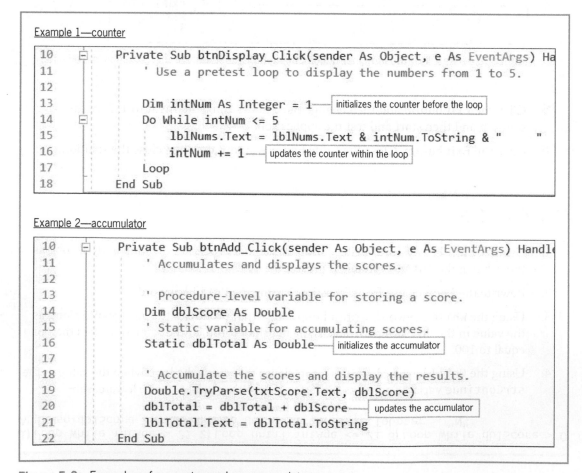

Figure 5-8   Examples of a counter and an accumulator

Counters and accumulators must be initialized and updated. In most cases, accumulators are initialized to 0. The Static statement in Example 2 in Figure 5-8, for instance, initializes the dblTotal accumulator variable to 0. Counters, on the other hand, are initialized to either 0 or 1, depending on the value required by the procedure's code. In Example 1, the Dim statement initializes the intNum counter variable to 1.

Counters and accumulators are updated by either adding a number to (called **incrementing**) or subtracting a number from (called **decrementing**) their value. The number can be either positive or negative, integer or non-integer. A counter is always updated by a constant amount—typically the number 1. The intNum += 1 statement in Example 1 in Figure 5-8 updates the intNum counter variable by 1. Unlike the intNum variable's initialization statement, which appears above the loop, its update statement is entered in the body of the loop. This is because the variable needs to be updated each time the loop instructions are processed. An accumulator, on the other hand, is usually updated by an amount that varies, and it is usually incremented rather than decremented. The dblTotal = dblTotal + dblScore statement in Example 2 updates the dblTotal accumulator variable by the current value stored in the dblScore variable.

Game programs make extensive use of counters and accumulators. The partial game program shown in Figure 5-9, for example, uses a counter to keep track of the number of smiley faces that Eddie (the character in the figure) destroys. After he destroys three smiley faces and then jumps through the manhole, he advances to the next level in the game, as shown in the figure.

 Ch05-Counter

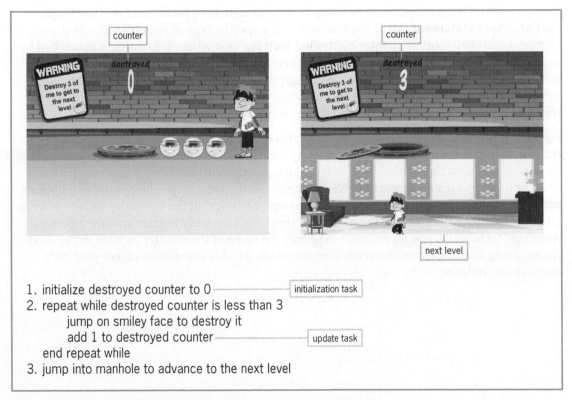

1. initialize destroyed counter to 0 ——————— initialization task
2. repeat while destroyed counter is less than 3
        jump on smiley face to destroy it
        add 1 to destroyed counter ——————— update task
   end repeat while
3. jump into manhole to advance to the next level

Figure 5-9   Example of a partial game program that uses a counter
Image by Diane Zak; created with Reallusion CrazyTalk Animator

Mini-Quiz 5-3

1. Write an assignment statement that increments the `intRegistered` counter variable by 2. Use an arithmetic assignment operator.

2. Write an assignment statement that decrements the `intNum` counter variable by 5. Use an arithmetic assignment operator.

3. Write an assignment statement that increments the `decTotal` variable by the value in the `decRegion` variable. Use an arithmetic assignment operator.

4. Which of the following is true?

   a. Counters and accumulators must be initialized.

   b. Counters and accumulators must be updated.

   c. Counters are usually updated by a constant amount.

   d. All of the above.

1) intRegistered += 2 2) intNum -= 5 or intNum += -5
3) decTotal += decRegion 4) d

F-7 For…Next Statement

Unlike the Do…Loop statement, which can be used to code both pretest and posttest loops, the **For…Next statement** can be used to code only a specific type of pretest loop, called a counter-controlled loop. A **counter-controlled loop** is a loop whose processing is controlled by a counter. You use a counter-controlled loop when you want the computer to process the loop instructions a precise number of times. Although you can also use the Do…Loop statement to code a counter-controlled loop, as shown earlier in Example 1 in Figure 5-8, the For…Next statement provides a more compact and convenient way of writing that type of loop.

Figure 5-10 shows the For…Next statement's syntax and includes examples of using the statement. It also shows the tasks performed by the computer when processing the statement. As Task 2 indicates, the loop's condition is evaluated *before* the loop body is processed. This is because the loop created by the For…Next statement is a pretest loop. The *counter* that appears in the For and Next clauses is the name of a numeric variable that the computer will use to keep track of (in other words, count) the number of times the loop body instructions are processed. Although, technically, you do not need to specify the name of the counter variable in the Next clause, doing so is highly recommended because such self-documentation makes your code easier to understand.

Ch05-For Next Loop

For...Next Statement

Syntax
For *counter* [**As** *dataType*] = *startValue* **To** *endValue* [**Step** *stepValue*]
    loop body instructions
Next *counter*

If the *stepValue* is a	The loop body is processed when the	The loop ends when the
positive number	*counter*'s value <= *endValue*	*counter*'s value > *endValue*
negative number	*counter*'s value >= *endValue*	*counter*'s value < *endValue*

Example 1
```
For intNum As Integer = 1 To 5
    lblNums.Text = lblNums.Text & intNum.ToString & "     "
Next intNum
```
displays the numbers from 1 to 5 in the lblNums control

Example 2
```
For intNum As Integer = 5 To 1 Step -1
    lblNums.Text = lblNums.Text & intNum.ToString & "     "
Next intNum
```
displays the numbers from 5 to 1 in the lblNums control

Example 3
```
Dim dblRate As Double
For dblRate = 0.05 To 0.1 Step 0.01
    lblRates.Text = lblRates.Text & dblRate.ToString("P0")
            & ControlChars.NewLine
Next dblRate
```
— advances the insertion point to the next line
displays 5 %, 6 %, 7 %, 8 %, 9 %, and 10 % on separate lines in the lblRates control

Processing tasks
1. If the *counter* is declared in the For clause, the variable is created and then initialized to the *startValue*; otherwise, it is just initialized to the *startValue*. The initialization task is done only once, at the beginning of the loop.
2. The *counter*'s value is compared with the *endValue* to determine whether the loop should end. If the *stepValue* is a positive number, the comparison is: *counter*'s value > *endValue*. If the *stepValue* is a negative number, the comparison is: *counter*'s value < *endValue*. Notice that the computer evaluates the loop condition before processing the instructions within the loop.
3. If the comparison from Task 2 evaluates to True, the loop ends and processing continues with the statement following the Next clause. If the comparison evaluates to False, the loop body instructions are processed and then Task 4 is performed.
4. Task 4 is performed only when the comparison from Task 2 evaluates to False. In this task, the *stepValue* is added to the *counter*'s value, and then Tasks 2, 3, and 4 are repeated until the loop condition evaluates to True.

Figure 5-10 For...Next statement's syntax, examples, and processing tasks

You can use the As *dataType* portion of the For clause to declare the counter variable, as shown in the first two examples in Figure 5-10. When you declare a variable in the For clause, the variable has **block scope** and can be used only within the For...Next loop. Alternatively, you can declare the counter variable in a Dim statement, as shown in Example 3. As you know, a variable declared in a Dim statement at the beginning of a procedure has procedure scope and can be used within the entire procedure.

When deciding where to declare the counter variable, keep in mind that if the variable is needed only by the For...Next loop, then it is a better programming practice to declare the variable in the For clause. As mentioned in Chapter 3, fewer unintentional errors occur in applications when the variables are declared using the minimum scope needed. Block-level variables have the smallest scope, followed by procedure-level variables and then class-level variables. You should declare the counter variable in a Dim statement only when its value is required by statements outside the For...Next loop in the procedure.

The *startValue*, *endValue*, and *stepValue* items in the For clause control the number of times the loop body is processed. The items must be numeric and can be either positive or negative, integer or non-integer. The startValue and endValue tell the computer where to begin and end counting, respectively. The stepValue tells the computer how much to count by—in other words, how much to add to the counter variable each time the loop body is processed. If you omit the stepValue, a stepValue of positive 1 is used. In Example 1 in Figure 5-10, the startValue is 1, the endValue is 5, and the stepValue (which is omitted) is 1. Those values tell the computer to start counting at 1 and, counting by 1s, stop at 5. The computer will process the instructions in Example 1's loop body five times. When the loop ends, the value in the `intNum` variable will be 6 because that is the first integer that is greater than the loop's endValue of 5.

As indicated in Figure 5-10, if the stepValue is a positive number, the loop ends when the counter's value is greater than the endValue. If the stepValue is a negative number, the loop ends when the counter's value is less than the endValue.

START HERE

To code and then test the For...Next application:

1. Open the For Next Solution.sln file contained in the VB2017\Chap05\For Next Solution folder.

2. Open the Code Editor window and locate the btnDisplay_Click procedure. Click the **blank line** above the End Sub clause and then enter the For...Next statement shown in Example 1 in Figure 5-10. Be sure to change the Next clause to `Next intNum`. (There are five space characters between the quotation marks.)

3. Save the solution and then start the application. Click the **Display** button to display the numbers from 1 to 5 in the label control. See Figure 5-11.

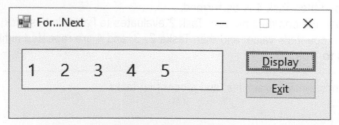

Figure 5-11 Output displayed by the For...Next statement

4. Click the **Exit** button. Now change the startValue in the For clause from 1 to **6**. Save the solution and then start the application. Click the **Display** button. Because the value in the For clause's counter variable (which is initialized to the startValue) is greater than the endValue, the pretest loop's condition evaluates to True and the computer does not process the instructions in the loop body. Therefore, no numbers appear in the label control.

5. Click the **Exit** button and then change the 6 in the For clause to **1**. Save the solution and then start and test the application.

6. Click the **Exit** button. Close the Code Editor window and then close the solution.

Comparing the For...Next and Do...Loop Statements

As mentioned earlier, you can code a counter-controlled loop by using either the For...Next statement or the Do...Loop statement. However, as Figure 5-12 indicates, the For...Next statement provides a more convenient way of coding that type of loop. When using the Do...Loop statement, you must include statements to declare, initialize, and update the counter variable, and you also must include the appropriate comparison in the Do clause. In a For...Next statement, the declaration, initialization, comparison, and update tasks are handled by the For clause.

For...Next Statement

```
For intNum As Integer = 1 To 5 ─── declares, initializes, compares, and updates the counter variable
    lblNums.Text = lblNums.Text & intNum.ToString & "        "
Next intNum
```

Do...Loop Statement

```
Dim intNum As Integer = 1 ─── declares and initializes the counter variable
Do While intNum <= 5 ─── compares the counter variable
    lblNums.Text = lblNums.Text & intNum.ToString & "        "
    intNum += 1 ─── updates the counter variable
Loop
```

Figure 5-12   Comparison of the For...Next and Do...Loop statements

Flowcharting a For...Next Loop

Figure 5-13 shows two ways of flowcharting a For...Next loop. In Example 1, the counter variable's initialization task is entered in a rectangle, its comparison task in a diamond, and its update task in another rectangle. In Example 2, a hexagon (a six-sided figure) is used to represent the tasks performed by the For clause. The counter variable's name and the stepValue are placed at the top and bottom, respectively, of the hexagon. The startValue and endValue are placed on the left and right side, respectively. Notice that a greater than sign (>) precedes the endValue in the hexagon. The > sign indicates that the loop will end when the counter variable's value is greater than 5.

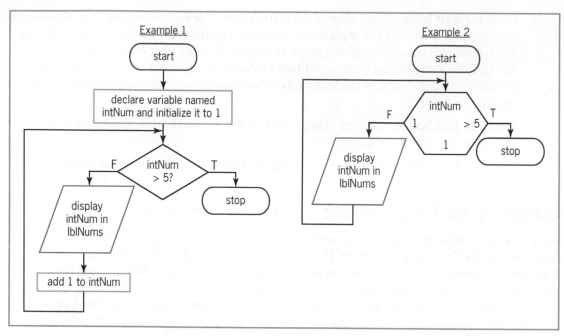

Figure 5-13 Flowcharts for a For...Next loop

Mini-Quiz 5-4

1. Write a For clause that repeats the loop body instructions 10 times. Use `intX` as the counter variable's name, and declare the variable in the For clause.

2. If the loop's For clause is `For intX = 2 To 8 Step 2`, how many times will the loop instructions be processed?

3. What value will be in the `intX` variable when the loop in Question 2 ends?

1) For intX As Integer = 1 To 10 2) 4 3) 10

YOU DO IT 3!

Create an application named You Do It 3 and save it in the VB2017\Chap05 folder. Add two labels and a button to the form. The button's Click event procedure should display the number of integers from 14 to 23 in one of the labels and the sum of those integers in the other label. Code the procedure using the For...Next statement. Save the solution and then start and test the application. (The procedure should display the numbers 10 and 185.) Close the solution.

APPLY THE CONCEPTS LESSON

After studying this lesson, you should be able to:

- A-1 Use a loop, a counter, and an accumulator

- A-2 Add a list box to a form

- A-3 Use the methods and a property of the Items collection

- A-4 Calculate a periodic payment

- A-5 Nest repetition structures

- A-6 Professionalize your application's interface

A-1 Use a Loop, a Counter, and an Accumulator

Figure 5-14 shows the interface for the Projected Sales application. Using the current sales amount entered by the user and a 3% annual growth rate, the application will calculate the number of years required for a company's projected sales to reach at least $150,000. It will also calculate the projected sales amount at that time. Both calculated amounts will be displayed in the lblProjSales control. Figure 5-14 also shows the pseudocode for the btnCalc_Click procedure.

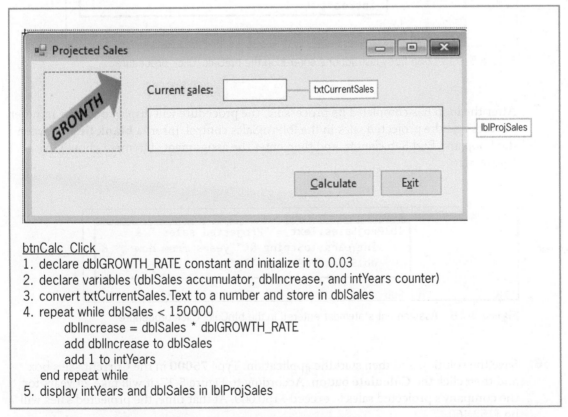

btnCalc_Click
1. declare dblGROWTH_RATE constant and initialize it to 0.03
2. declare variables (dblSales accumulator, dblIncrease, and intYears counter)
3. convert txtCurrentSales.Text to a number and store in dblSales
4. repeat while dblSales < 150000
     dblIncrease = dblSales * dblGROWTH_RATE
     add dblIncrease to dblSales
     add 1 to intYears
  end repeat while
5. display intYears and dblSales in lblProjSales

Figure 5-14 Interface and btnCalc_Click procedure's pseudocode

START HERE **To code and then test the Projected Sales application:**

1. Open the Projected Sales Solution.sln file contained in the VB2017\Chap05\Projected Sales Solution folder.

2. Open the Code Editor window and locate the btnCalc_Click procedure. The first three steps in the procedure's pseudocode have already been coded for you. The Dim statements that declare the accumulator and counter variables initialize both memory locations to 0.

3. Click the **blank line** above the End Sub clause. Step 4 in the pseudocode is a loop that repeats its instructions as long as (or while) the value in the dblSales variable is less than 150000. The loop will stop when the dblSales variable's value is greater than or equal to 150000. Type **Do While dblSales < 150000** and press **Enter**.

4. The first instruction in the loop calculates the sales increase for the current year. The second and third instructions update the accumulator and counter variables, respectively: The second instruction adds the sales increase to the dblSales variable, and the third instruction increments the intYears variable by 1. Enter the loop body instructions shown in Figure 5-15.

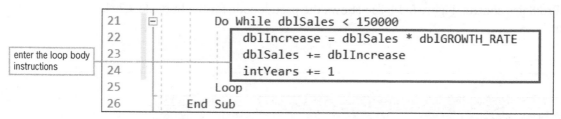

```
21          Do While dblSales < 150000
22              dblIncrease = dblSales * dblGROWTH_RATE
23              dblSales += dblIncrease
24              intYears += 1
25          Loop
26      End Sub
```

enter the loop body instructions

Figure 5-15 Loop body instructions entered in the btnCalc_Click procedure

5. After the loop has completed its processing, the procedure will display both the number of years and the projected sales in the lblProjSales control. Insert a **blank line** between the Loop and End Sub clauses, and then enter the assignment statement shown in Figure 5-16.

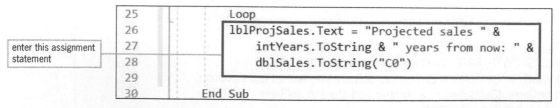

```
25          Loop
26          lblProjSales.Text = "Projected sales " &
27              intYears.ToString & " years from now: " &
28              dblSales.ToString("C0")
29
30      End Sub
```

enter this assignment statement

Figure 5-16 Assignment statement entered in the btnCalc_Click procedure

6. Save the solution and then start the application. Type **75000** in the Current sales box and then click the **Calculate** button. According to Figure 5-17, it will take 24 years for the company's projected sales to exceed $150,000. At that time, the projected sales will be $152,460.

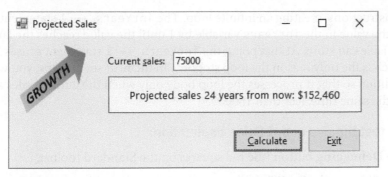

Figure 5-17 Sample run of the Projected Sales application

7. Delete the contents of the Current sales box and then click the **Calculate** button. After a short period of time, a run time error occurs and the error message box shown in Figure 5-18 appears on the screen. (It may take as long as 30 seconds for the error message box to appear.) Place your mouse pointer on `intYears`, as shown in the figure.

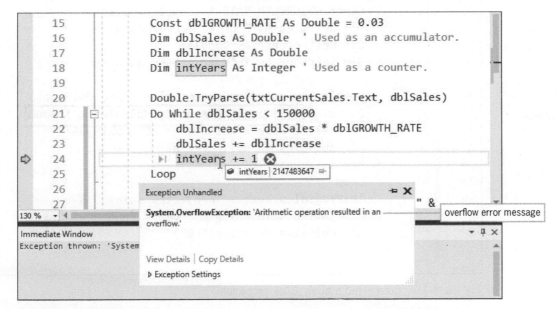

Figure 5-18 Screen showing the error message box

The error message informs you that an arithmetic operation—in this case, adding 1 to the `intYears` variable—resulted in an overflow. An **overflow error** occurs when the value assigned to a memory location is too large for the location's data type. (An overflow error is similar to trying to fill an 8-ounce glass with 10 ounces of water.) In this case, the `intYears` variable already contains the largest value that can be stored in an Integer variable (2,147,483,647 according to Figure 3-4 in Chapter 3). Therefore, when the `intYears += 1` statement attempts to increase the variable's value by 1, an overflow error occurs.

But why does the `intYears` variable contain 2,147,483,647? Because you didn't provide an initial value for the current sales amount, the `dblSales` variable contains the value assigned to it by the TryParse method: 0. The loop's condition (`dblSales < 150000`) evaluates to True the first time it is processed; therefore, the computer processes the loop's instructions. None of the instructions in the loop body change the value in the `dblSales` variable to anything other than 0. As a result, the loop's condition always evaluates to True and the computer continues to process the loop's instructions, creating an infinite loop. The `intYears += 1` statement continues to increase the value in the `intYears` variable by 1 until the value reaches the largest amount an Integer variable can store. At that point, the `intYears += 1` statement causes an overflow error, which is the only reason the loop stopped. In the next set of steps, you will modify the loop's condition so that it processes the loop body only when the current sales are greater than 0 and, at the same time, less than 150000.

START HERE

To modify and then test the Projected Sales application:

1. Click the **Stop Debugging** button (the red square) on the Standard toolbar.

2. Change the condition in the Do While clause to a compound condition, as indicated in Figure 5-19.

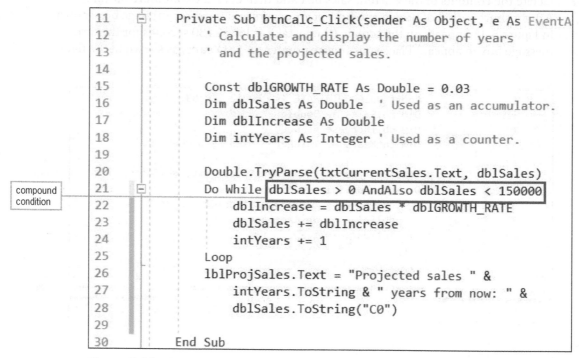

```
11        Private Sub btnCalc_Click(sender As Object, e As EventA
12            ' Calculate and display the number of years
13            ' and the projected sales.
14
15            Const dblGROWTH_RATE As Double = 0.03
16            Dim dblSales As Double   ' Used as an accumulator.
17            Dim dblIncrease As Double
18            Dim intYears As Integer ' Used as a counter.
19
20            Double.TryParse(txtCurrentSales.Text, dblSales)
21            Do While dblSales > 0 AndAlso dblSales < 150000
22                dblIncrease = dblSales * dblGROWTH_RATE
23                dblSales += dblIncrease
24                intYears += 1
25            Loop
26            lblProjSales.Text = "Projected sales " &
27                intYears.ToString & " years from now: " &
28                dblSales.ToString("C0")
29
30        End Sub
```

compound condition

Figure 5-19 Completed btnCalc_Click procedure

3. Save the solution and then start the application. Click the **Calculate** button. Notice that no overflow error occurs. Instead, the button's Click event procedure displays the "Projected sales 0 years from now: $0" message.

4. Type **75000** in the Current sales box and then click the **Calculate** button. The button's Click event procedure displays the message shown earlier in Figure 5-17.

5. On your own, test the application using different sales amounts. When you are finished testing, click the **Exit** button. Close the Code Editor window and then close the solution.

A Different Version of the Projected Sales Application

In this version of the Projected Sales application, the btnCalc_Click procedure will display the projected sales amount for each of four years, beginning with 2019. Figure 5-20 shows the modified interface and pseudocode.

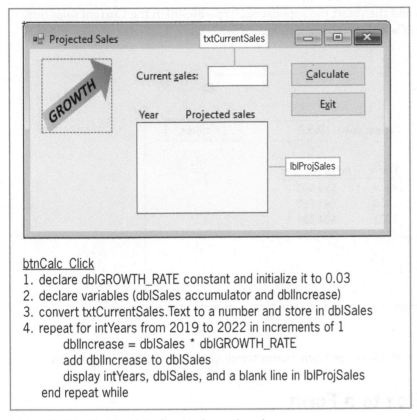

btnCalc_Click
1. declare dblGROWTH_RATE constant and initialize it to 0.03
2. declare variables (dblSales accumulator and dblIncrease)
3. convert txtCurrentSales.Text to a number and store in dblSales
4. repeat for intYears from 2019 to 2022 in increments of 1
        dblIncrease = dblSales * dblGROWTH_RATE
        add dblIncrease to dblSales
        display intYears, dblSales, and a blank line in lblProjSales
    end repeat while

Figure 5-20   Modified interface and pseudocode

START HERE

To code and then test this version of the application:

1. Open the Projected Sales Solution.sln file contained in the VB2017\Chap05\Projected Sales Solution-ForNext folder.

2. Open the Code Editor window and locate the btnCalc_Click procedure. The first three steps in the procedure's pseudocode have already been coded for you. The first Dim statement initializes the accumulator variable to 0.

3. Click the **blank line** above the End Sub clause and then enter the For...Next statement shown in Figure 5-21. Be sure to change the Next clause to `Next intYears`.

```
11      Private Sub btnCalc_Click(sender As Object, e As EventArgs)
12          ' Calculate and display the number of years
13          ' and the projected sales.
14
15          Const dblGROWTH_RATE As Double = 0.03
16          Dim dblSales As Double   ' Used as an accumulator.
17          Dim dblIncrease As Double
18
19          Double.TryParse(txtCurrentSales.Text, dblSales)
20          For intYears As Integer = 2019 To 2022
21              dblIncrease = dblSales * dblGROWTH_RATE
22              dblSales += dblIncrease
23              lblProjSales.Text = lblProjSales.Text &
24                  intYears.ToString & "          " &
25                  dblSales.ToString("C0") & ControlChars.NewLine
26          Next intYears
27      End Sub
```

enter this For...Next statement
(There are 10 space characters
between the quotation marks.)

Figure 5-21   For...Next statement entered in the btnCalc_Click procedure

4. Save the solution and then start the application. Type **86500** in the Current sales box and then click the **Calculate** button. See Figure 5-22.

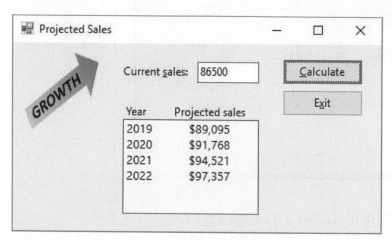

Figure 5-22   Interface showing the projected sales amounts for the four years

5. Click the **Exit** button. Close the Code Editor window and then close the solution.

A-2 Add a List Box to a Form

You use the ListBox tool to add a list box to an interface. A **list box** displays a list of items from which the user can select zero items, one item, or multiple items. The number of items that can be selected at any one time is determined by the list box's **SelectionMode property**, which is typically left at its default value: One. Figure 5-23 lists the most commonly used properties of a list box. Notice that the three-character ID for list box names is lst.

Name	Purpose
Font	specify the font to use for text
Name	give the list box a meaningful name (use lst as the ID)
SelectedIndex	get or set the index of the selected item
SelectedItem	get or set the value of the selected item
SelectionMode	indicate whether the user can select zero items, one item, or more than one item at a time; the default is one item
Sorted	specify whether the items in the list should appear in the order they are entered or in sorted order (When sorted, the items appear in dictionary order based on their leftmost characters. Dictionary order means that numbers appear before letters, and a lowercase letter appears before its uppercase equivalent.)

Figure 5-23   Most commonly used properties of a list box

Although you can make a list box any size you want, you should follow the Windows standard, which is to display at least three items but no more than eight items at a time. If you have more items than can fit into the list box, the control automatically displays a scroll bar for viewing the complete list of items. You should use a label control to provide keyboard access to the list box. For the access key to work correctly, you must set the label's TabIndex property to a value that is one number less than the list box's TabIndex value.

The GUI design guidelines for list boxes are listed in Figure 5-45 and in Appendix A.

Using the String Collection Editor to Add Items to a List Box

The items in a list box belong to a collection called the **Items collection**. A **collection** is a group of individual objects treated as one unit. Each item in the Items collection is identified by a unique number, called an index. The first item in the collection (which is also the first item in the list box) has an index of 0, the second item has an index of 1, and so on. The **String Collection Editor** provides an easy way to add items to the Items collection.

To use the String Collection Editor:

START HERE

1. Open the ListBox Solution.sln file contained in the VB2017\Chap05\ListBox Solution folder.

2. Click the **lstStates** list box and then click **Items** in the Properties window. Notice that (Collection) appears in the property's Settings box. Click the ... (ellipsis) button and then enter the four state IDs shown in Figure 5-24.

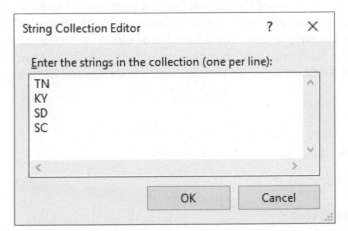

Figure 5-24 String Collection Editor

3. Click the **OK** button. Save the solution and then start the application. The four state IDs appear in the same order as they do in the String Collection Editor: TN, KY, SD, and SC.

4. Click the **Exit** button.

The Sorted Property

Typically, list box items are either arranged by use, with the most used entries appearing first in the list, or sorted in ascending order. You can use a list box's **Sorted property** to sort the items. Visual Basic sorts the items in **dictionary order**, which means that numbers are sorted before letters, and a lowercase letter is sorted before its uppercase equivalent. The items in a list box are sorted based on the leftmost characters in each item. This means that the state IDs shown in Figure 5-24 will appear in the following order when the Sorted property is set to True: KY, SC, SD, and TN. It also means that the numbers 1, 2, 3, and 10 will appear in the following order: 1, 10, 2, and 3.

START HERE

To sort the items in the lstStates control:

1. Set the lstStates control's Sorted property to **True**. Save the solution and then start the application. The state IDs are now sorted in ascending order.

2. Click the **Exit** button.

The SelectedItem and SelectedIndex Properties

As mentioned earlier, a list box's SelectionMode property determines the number of items the user can select at any one time. If a list box allows the user to make only one selection, it is customary in Windows applications to have one of the list box items already selected when the interface appears. The selected item, called the **default list box item**, should be either the item selected most frequently or the first item in the list. You can use either the **SelectedItem property** or the **SelectedIndex property** to select the default list box item from code, as shown in the examples in Figure 5-25. In most cases, you enter the appropriate code in the form's Load event procedure. A form's **Load event** occurs when the application is started and the form is displayed the first time.

Selecting the Default Item in a List Box

Example 1—SelectedItem property
```
lstStates.SelectedItem = "SD"
```
selects the SD item in the lstStates control

Example 2—SelectedIndex property
```
lstStates.SelectedIndex = 0
```
selects the first item in the lstStates control

Figure 5-25   Examples of selecting the default item in a list box

START HERE

To select the first item in the list box:

1. Open the Code Editor window. Click (**frmMain Events**) in the Object list box and then click **Load** in the Event list box.

2. Enter the comment and assignment statement shown in Figure 5-26.

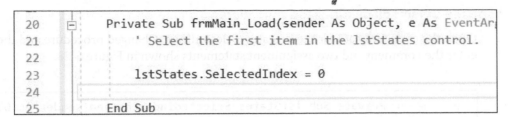

```
20  ⊟    Private Sub frmMain_Load(sender As Object, e As EventAr
21           ' Select the first item in the lstStates control.
22
23           lstStates.SelectedIndex = 0
24
25       End Sub
```

Figure 5-26 frmMain_Load procedure

3. Save the solution and then start the application. Notice that the first item in the list is selected (highlighted).

4. Click the **Exit** button.

You can also use either the SelectedItem property or the SelectedIndex property to determine which item (if any) is selected in a list box. If an item is selected, the SelectedItem and SelectedIndex properties contain the value of the selected item and the item's index, respectively. When no item is selected, the SelectedItem property contains the keyword Nothing and the SelectedIndex property contains the number −1 (negative 1). As you learned in Chapter 3, the Nothing keyword indicates that the property contains no data at all.

START HERE

To display the selected item and its index:

1. Locate the btnSelected_Click procedure. Click the **blank line** above the End Sub clause and then enter the assignment statements shown in Figure 5-27.

```
14  ⊟    Private Sub btnSelected_Click(sender As Object, e As Ev
15           ' Display the selected item and selected index.
16
17           lblItem.Text = lstStates.SelectedItem.ToString
18           lblIndex.Text = lstStates.SelectedIndex.ToString
19
20       End Sub
```

Figure 5-27 btnSelected_Click procedure

2. Save the solution and then start the application. Click the **Selected** button. KY and 0 appear in the Item and Index boxes, respectively.

3. Click **SD** in the list box. Do not be concerned that KY and 0 still appear in the interface; you will fix this problem in the next section. Click the **Selected** button. SD and 2 appear in the Item and Index boxes, respectively.

4. Click the **Exit** button.

The SelectedValueChanged and SelectedIndexChanged Events

Each time either the user or a statement selects an item in a list box, the list box's **SelectedValueChanged event** and its **SelectedIndexChanged event** occur. You can use the procedures associated with these events to perform one or more tasks when the selected item has changed. In the next set of steps, you will use the lstStates_SelectedIndexChanged procedure to clear the contents of the Item and Index boxes.

START HERE **To code the SelectedIndexChanged procedure:**

1. Open the code template for the lstStates_SelectedIndexChanged procedure and then enter the comment and two assignment statements shown in Figure 5-28.

```
29          Private Sub lstStates_SelectedIndexChanged(sender As Ob
30                  ' Clear the contents of the Item and Index boxes.
31
32              lblItem.Text = String.Empty
33              lblIndex.Text = String.Empty
34
35          End Sub
```

Figure 5-28　lstStates_SelectedIndexChanged procedure

2. Save the solution and then start the application. Click the **Selected** button. KY and 0 appear in the Item and Index boxes, respectively.

3. Click **SD** in the list box. The lstStates_SelectedIndexChanged procedure clears the contents of the Item and Index boxes. Click the **Selected** button. SD and 2 appear in the Item and Index boxes, respectively.

4. Click the **Exit** button. Close the Code Editor window and then close the solution.

Mini-Quiz 5-5

1. The items in a list box belong to which collection?

2. When a list box's Sorted property is set to True, in what order will the following items appear: Banana, Apple, Watermelon?

3. When a list box's Sorted property is set to True, in what order will the following items appear: 35, 40, 3, 4?

4. Which two properties can be used to select a default item in a list box?

1) Items 2) Apple, Banana, Watermelon 3) 3, 4, 35, 40 4) SelectedIndex and SelectedItem

A-3 Use the Methods and a Property of the Items Collection

At times, you might need to use the Items collection's **Add method** (rather than the String Collection Editor) to add items to a list box. For example, rather than typing the numbers 1 through 25 in the String Collection Editor, you can use the Add method along with a loop to add the numbers to the list box. Figure 5-29 shows the method's syntax along with examples of using it. In most cases, you enter the Add method in a form's Load event procedure because you typically want the list box to display its values when the form first appears on the screen.

Add Method (Items Collection)

<u>Syntax</u>
object.**Items.Add**(*item*)

<u>Example 1</u>
```
lstAnimals.Items.Add("Dog")
lstAnimals.Items.Add("Cat")
lstAnimals.Items.Add("Horse")
```
adds Dog, Cat, and Horse to the lstAnimals control

<u>Example 2</u>
```
For intCode As Integer = 100 To 105
    lstCodes.Items.Add(intCode)
Next intCode
```
adds 100, 101, 102, 103, 104, and 105 to the lstCodes control

<u>Example 3</u>
```
For decRate As Decimal = 0.1D To 0.3D Step 0.1D
    lstRates.Items.Add(decRate.ToString("P0"))
Next decRate
```
adds 10 %, 20 %, and 30 % to the lstRates control

Figure 5-29   Syntax and examples of the Items collection's Add method

To use the Add method:

START HERE

1. Open the ListBox Items Solution.sln file contained in the VB2017\Chap05\ListBox Items Solution folder.

2. Open the Code Editor window and locate the frmMain_Load procedure. Click the **blank line** above the End Sub clause and then enter the For...Next loop and assignment statement shown in Figure 5-30.

```
26    Private Sub frmMain_Load(sender As Object, e As EventArgs)
27        ' Add items to the list box and select the first item.
28
29        For intNum As Integer = 1 To 25
30            lstNums.Items.Add(intNum)
31        Next intNum
32        lstNums.SelectedIndex = 0
33
34    End Sub
```

Figure 5-30   Code entered in the frmMain_Load procedure

3. Save the solution and then start the application. The frmMain_Load procedure adds the numbers from 1 through 25 to the list box and then selects the first number (1). Use the scroll bar to view all of the numbers and then click the **Exit** button.

Count Property

The Items collection's **Count property** stores an integer that represents the number of list box items.

START HERE

To use the Count property:

1. Locate the btnCount_Click procedure. Click the **blank line** above the End Sub clause and then enter following assignment statement:

    ```
    lblItems.Text = lstNums.Items.Count.ToString
    ```

2. Save the solution and then start the application. Click the **Count** button. The number 25 appears in the Items box. Click the **Exit** button.

Clearing the Items from a List Box

The Items collection provides a **Clear method** for clearing (removing) the items from a list box. The method's syntax is *object*.**Items.Clear()**.

START HERE

To use the Clear method:

1. Locate the btnClear_Click procedure. Click the **blank line** above the End Sub clause and then enter the following two statements:

    ```
    lstNums.Items.Clear()
    lblItems.Text = String.Empty
    ```

2. Save the solution and then start the application. Click the **Count** button, which displays the number 25 in the Items box. Click the **Clear** button to clear the items from the list box, and then click the **Count** button. The number 0 appears in the Items box.

3. Click the **Exit** button. Close the Code Editor window and then close the solution.

Mini-Quiz 5-6

1. Write an Add method that adds the contents of the decPrice variable to the lstPrices control.

2. Write a statement that assigns the number of items in the lstPrices control to the intNumPrices variable.

3. Write a statement that removes the items from the lstPrices control.

1) lstPrices.Items.Add(decPrice) 2) intNumPrices = lstPrices.Items.Count
3) lstPrices.Items.Clear()

A-4 Calculate a Periodic Payment

Visual Basic's Financial class contains many methods that your applications can use to perform financial calculations. Figure 5-31 lists some of the more commonly used methods defined in the class. All of the methods return the result of their calculation as a Double number.

Method	Purpose
Financial.DDB	calculate the depreciation of an asset for a specific time period using the double-declining balance method
Financial.FV	calculate the future value of an annuity based on periodic fixed payments and a fixed interest rate
Financial.IPmt	calculate the interest payment for a given period of an annuity based on periodic fixed payments and a fixed interest rate
Financial.IRR	calculate the internal rate of return for a series of periodic cash flows (payments and receipts)
Financial.Pmt	calculate the payment for an annuity based on periodic fixed payments and a fixed interest rate
Financial.PPmt	calculate the principal payment for a given period of an annuity based on periodic fixed payments and a fixed interest rate
Financial.PV	calculate the present value of an annuity based on periodic fixed payments to be paid in the future and a fixed interest rate
Financial.SLN	calculate the straight-line depreciation of an asset for a single period
Financial.SYD	calculate the sum-of-the-years' digits depreciation of an asset for a specified period

Figure 5-31   Some of the methods defined in the Financial class

The Monthly Payment application, which you will code in the next section, uses the **Financial.Pmt method** to calculate a monthly mortgage payment. Figure 5-32 shows the method's syntax and lists the meaning of each argument. The *Rate* and *NPer* (number of periods) arguments must be expressed using the same units. If Rate is a monthly interest rate, then NPer must specify the number of monthly payments. Likewise, if Rate is an annual interest rate, then NPer must specify the number of annual payments. The figure also includes examples of using the method.

You can use the PMT function in Microsoft Excel to verify that the payments shown in Figure 5-32 are correct.

Financial.Pmt Method

Syntax
Financial.Pmt(*Rate*, *NPer*, *PV*)

Argument   Meaning
Rate   interest rate per period
NPer   total number of payment periods in the term
PV   present value of the loan (the principal)

Example 1
`Financial.Pmt(0.05, 3, 9000)`
Calculates the annual payment for a loan of $9,000 for 3 years with a 5% interest rate. *Rate* is 0.05, *NPer* is 3, and *PV* is 9000. The annual payment returned by the method (rounded to the nearest cent) is –3304.88.

Example 2
`-Financial.Pmt(0.03 / 12, 15 * 12, 125000)`
Calculates the monthly payment for a loan of $125,000 for 15 years with a 3% interest rate. *Rate* is 0.03 / 12, *NPer* is 15 * 12, and *PV* is 125000. The monthly payment returned by the method (rounded to the nearest cent and expressed as a positive number) is 863.23.

Figure 5-32   Syntax and examples of the Financial.Pmt method

Example 1 calculates the annual payment for a loan of $9,000 for 3 years with a 5% interest rate. As the example indicates, the annual payment returned by the method (rounded to the nearest cent) is –3304.88. This means that if you borrow $9,000 for 3 years at 5% interest, you will need to make three annual payments of $3,304.88 to pay off the loan. Notice that the Financial.Pmt method returns a negative number. You can change the negative number to a positive number by preceding the method with the negation operator, like this: –Financial.Pmt(.05, 3, 9000).

The Financial.Pmt method shown in Example 2 calculates the monthly payment for a loan of $125,000 for 15 years with a 3% interest rate. In this example, the *Rate* and *NPer* arguments are expressed in monthly terms rather than in annual terms. You change an annual rate to a monthly rate by dividing the annual rate by 12. You change the term from years to months by multiplying the number of years by 12. The monthly payment for the loan in Example 2, rounded to the nearest cent and expressed as a positive number, is 863.23.

Mini-Quiz 5-7

1. Write the Financial.Pmt method that calculates the monthly payment (expressed as a positive number) for a loan of $25,000 for 10 years with a 4% annual interest rate.

2. Write the Financial.Pmt method that calculates the monthly payment (expressed as a positive number) for a loan of $130,000 for 30 years with a 2% annual interest rate.

3. The Financial.Pmt method returns a number of which data type?

1) –Financial.Pmt(0.04 / 12, 10 * 12, 25000) 2) –Financial.Pmt(0.02 / 12, 30 * 12, 130000) 3) Double

YOU DO IT 4!

Create an application named You Do It 4 and save it in the VB2017\Chap05 folder. Add a label and a button to the form. The button's Click event procedure should calculate the monthly payment for a loan of $50,000 for three years with a 5% annual interest rate, and then display the result in the label. Display the monthly payment as a positive number with a dollar sign and two decimal places. Save the solution and then start and test the application. (The monthly payment is $1,498.54.) Close the solution.

ListBox, Loop, and Financial.Pmt Example: Monthly Payment Application

The Monthly Payment application will display the monthly payments on a mortgage loan, using terms of 15, 20, 25, and 30 years. The term is the number of years the borrower has to pay off the loan. The user will enter the loan amount, called the principal, in a text box. He or she will select the interest rate from a list box that contains rates ranging from 2.0% to 7.0% in increments of 0.5%.

START HERE

To code and then test the Monthly Payment application:

1. Open the Payment Solution.sln file contained in the VB2017\Chap05\Payment Solution folder. Figure 5-33 shows the application's interface.

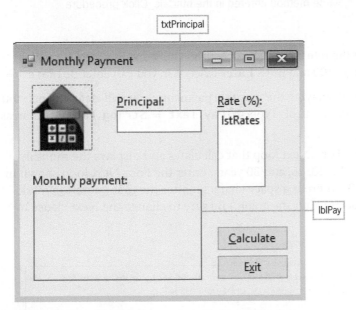

Figure 5-33   Monthly Payment application's interface

2. Open the Code Editor window, which already contains the code for many of the application's procedures. Locate the frmMain_Load procedure. Click the **blank line** above the End Sub clause and then enter the For...Next loop and assignment statement shown in Figure 5-34. Be sure to change the Next clause to `Next dblRates`.

```
11          Private Sub frmMain_Load(sender As Object, e As EventArgs)
12              ' Fill list box with rates and select 3.0 rate.
13
14          For dblRates As Double = 2 To 7 Step 0.5
15              lstRates.Items.Add(dblRates.ToString("N1"))
16          Next dblRates
17          lstRates.SelectedItem = "3.0"
18
19          End Sub
```

Figure 5-34   Completed frmMain_Load procedure

3. Save the solution and then start the application. Verify that the list box contains the appropriate rates and that the 3.0 rate is selected. Click the **Exit** button.

4. Locate the btnCalc_Click procedure. Click the **blank line** above the End Sub clause. First, you will enter a TryParse method that assigns the rate selected in the list box to the `dblRate` variable. Enter the TryParse method indicated in Figure 5-35.

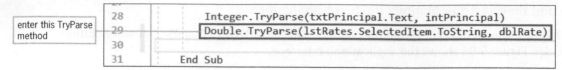

Figure 5-35 Double.TryParse method entered in the btnCalc_Click procedure

5. Next, you will convert the rate to its decimal equivalent by dividing it by 100. Type **dblRate = dblRate / 100** and press **Enter** twice. (Or, you can enter dblRate /= 100.)

6. Before calculating and displaying the monthly payments, you will clear any previous payments from the lblPay control. Type **lblPay.Text = String.Empty** and press **Enter**.

7. Finally, you will enter a For...Next loop that calculates and displays the monthly payments for terms of 15, 20, 25, and 30 years. Enter the For...Next loop shown in Figure 5-36. (In Line 37, there is a space character after the first quotation mark and three space characters after the colon.) Be sure to change the Next clause to Next intTerm.

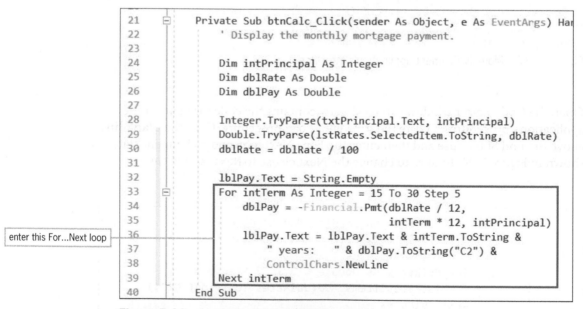

Figure 5-36 Completed btnCalc_Click procedure

8. Open the code template for the lstRates_SelectedIndexChanged procedure. You will have this procedure clear the contents of the lblPay control when a change is made to the rate selected in the lstRates control. Type **lblPay.Text = String.Empty** and press **Enter**.

9. Save the solution and then start the application. Type **125000** in the Principal box and then click the **Calculate** button. The monthly mortgage payments appear in the interface, as shown in Figure 5-37.

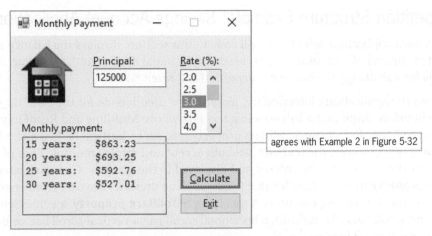

Figure 5-37   Monthly mortgage payments shown in the interface

10. On your own, test the application using different principals and rates. Also verify that the Monthly payment box is cleared when a change is made to either the principal or the rate.

11. When you are finished testing, click the **Exit** button. Close the Code Editor window and then close the solution.

A-5 Nest Repetition Structures

Like selection structures, repetition structures can be nested, which means you can place one loop (called the nested or inner loop) within another loop (called the outer loop). Both loops can be either pretest loops or posttest loops. Or, one can be a pretest loop and the other a posttest loop.

A clock uses nested loops to keep track of the time. For simplicity, consider a clock's minute and second hands only. The second hand on a clock moves one position, clockwise, for every second that has elapsed. After the second hand moves 60 positions, the minute hand moves one position, also clockwise. The second hand then begins its journey around the clock again.

Figure 5-38 shows the logic used by a clock's minute and second hands. As the figure indicates, an outer loop controls the minute hand, while the inner (nested) loop, which is shaded in the figure, controls the second hand. Notice that the entire nested loop is contained within the outer loop; this must be true for the loop to be nested and for it to work correctly. The next iteration of the outer loop (which controls the minute hand) occurs only after the nested loop (which controls the second hand) has finished processing.

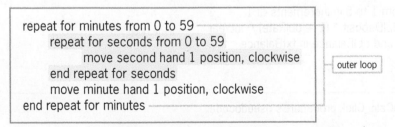

Figure 5-38   Logic used by a clock's minute and second hands

Nested Repetition Structure Example: Savings Account Application

The Savings Account application, which you will code in this section, displays the balance in a savings account at the end of each of five years, based on an initial deposit and rates from 3% to 7%. The formula for calculating the balance is $deposit * (1 + rate)^{year}$.

Figure 5-39 shows the application's interface and includes the pseudocode for the btnCalc_Click procedure. The interface displays the balances in a text box whose Multiline and ReadOnly properties are set to True, and whose ScrollBars property is to set to Vertical. When a text box's **Multiline property** is set to True, the text box can both accept and display multiple lines of text; otherwise, only one line of text can be entered and displayed in the text box. Changing a text box's **ReadOnly property** from its default value (False) to True prevents the user from changing the contents of the text box during run time. A text box's **ScrollBars property** specifies whether the text box has no scroll bars (the default), a horizontal scroll bar, a vertical scroll bar, or both horizontal and vertical scroll bars.

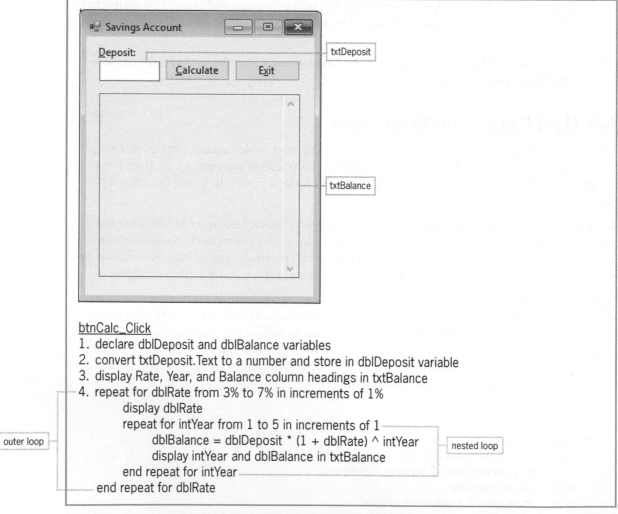

Figure 5-39   Interface and btnCalc_Click procedure's pseudocode

As the pseudocode in Figure 5-39 indicates, the btnCalc_Click procedure requires two loops, one nested within the other. The outer loop controls the rates, which range from 3% to 7% in increments of 1%. The inner loop controls the years, which range from 1 to 5 in increments of 1. When displaying the information in the txtBalance control, the procedure will use the **ControlChars.Tab constant**, which represents the Tab key, to align the information.

START HERE

To code and then test the btnCalc_Click procedure:

1. Open the Savings Solution.sln file contained in the VB2017\Chap05\Savings Solution folder.

2. Open the Code Editor window and locate the btnCalc_Click procedure. The first three steps in the pseudocode have already been coded for you.

3. Click the **blank line** above the End Sub clause and then enter the outer and nested loops shown in Figure 5-40.

```
12      Private Sub btnCalc_Click(sender As Object, e As EventArgs) Handles
13          ' Calculate account balances for each of five years
14          ' using rates from 3% to 7% in increments of 1%.
15
16          Dim dblDeposit As Double
17          Dim dblBalance As Double
18
19          Double.TryParse(txtDeposit.Text, dblDeposit)
20                                                              ┌─── Tab key
21          txtBalance.Text = "Rate" & ControlChars.Tab &
22              "Year" & ControlChars.Tab & "Balance" &
23              ControlChars.NewLine ──────────────────── Enter key
24
25          ' Calculate and display account balances.
26          For dblRate As Double = 0.03 To 0.07 Step 0.01
27              txtBalance.Text = txtBalance.Text &
28                  dblRate.ToString("P0") & ControlChars.NewLine
29              For intYear As Integer = 1 To 5
30                  dblBalance = dblDeposit * (1 + dblRate) ^ intYear
31                  txtBalance.Text = txtBalance.Text &
32                      ControlChars.Tab & intYear.ToString &
33                      ControlChars.Tab & dblBalance.ToString("C2") &
34                      ControlChars.NewLine
35              Next intYear
36          Next dblRate
37      End Sub
```

enter the outer and nested loops

Figure 5-40 Completed btnCalc_Click procedure

4. Save the solution and then start the application. Type **2500** in the Deposit box and then click the **Calculate** button. See Figure 5-41.

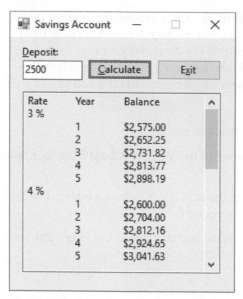

Figure 5-41   Account balances shown in the interface

5. Scroll the text box to verify that it contains the account balances for each of the five rates.

6. Click the **Exit** button. Close the Code Editor window and then close the solution.

A Caution About Real Numbers

Not all **real numbers**, which are numbers with a decimal place, can be stored precisely in the computer's main memory. Many can be stored only as an approximation, which may lead to unexpected results when two real numbers are compared with each other. For example, sometimes a Double number that is the result of a calculation does not compare precisely with the same number expressed as a literal. This is why it is so important to test your application's code thoroughly. In the next set of steps, you will observe how the comparison problem would affect the Savings Account application from the previous section.

START HERE

To modify the Savings Account application from the previous section:

1. Use Windows to make a copy of the Savings Solution folder and then rename the copy Savings Solution-Caution.

2. Open the Savings Solution.sln file contained in the Savings Solution-Caution folder.

3. Open the Code Editor window. You will modify the application so that it uses rates from 3% to 6% (rather than to 7%). In the fourth comment, change 7% to **6%**.

4. Locate the btnCalc_Click procedure. Change 7% in the second comment to **6%**. In the outer For clause, change 0.07 to **0.06**.

5. Save the solution and then start the application. Click the **Calculate** button and then scroll to the bottom of the txtBalance control. As shown in Figure 5-42, the information associated with the 6% rate is missing from the control.

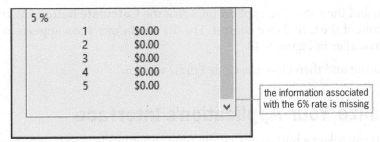

Figure 5-42 txtBalance control with the 6% rate information missing

6. Click the **Exit** button.

Consider why the loop that controls the rates failed to display the 6% rate information. Recall that the For clause in that loop tells the computer to stop processing the loop instructions when the value in the db1Rate variable is greater than 0.06. The fact that the 6% rate information did not display indicates that when the For clause compares the variable's value with the literal 0.06, the value is viewed as *greater* than the literal; this causes the loop to end prematurely. To fix this problem, you can either increase the literal's value slightly (e.g., you can use 0.0600001) or use the Decimal data type for the loop that controls the rates. You will try both methods in the next set of steps.

START HERE

To fix the comparison problem in the application:

1. First, you will increase the literal's value. Change 0.06 in the outer For clause to **0.0600001**. Save the solution and then start the application. Click the **Calculate** button and then scroll to the bottom of the txtBalance control. The control now includes the information pertaining to the 6% rate. See Figure 5-43.

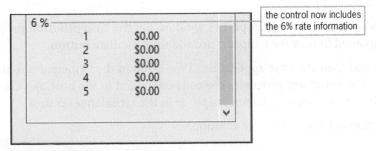

Figure 5-43 6% rate information shown in the txtBalance control

2. Click the **Exit** button. Next, you will try the second method of fixing the problem, which is to use the Decimal data type for the rates. Modify the code as indicated in Figure 5-44. The modifications are shaded in the figure.

```
25              ' Calculate and display account balances.
26              For decRate As Decimal = 0.03D To 0.06D Step 0.01D
27                  txtBalance.Text = txtBalance.Text &
28                      decRate.ToString("P0") & ControlChars.NewLine
29                  For intYear As Integer = 1 To 5
30                      dblBalance = dblDeposit * (1 + decRate) ^ intYear
31                      txtBalance.Text = txtBalance.Text &
32                          ControlChars.Tab & intYear.ToString &
33                          ControlChars.Tab & dblBalance.ToString("C2") &
34                          ControlChars.NewLine
35                  Next intYear
36              Next decRate
```

Figure 5-44 Modifications made to the code

3. Save the solution and then start the application. Click the **Calculate** button and then scroll to the bottom of the txtBalance control. The 6% rate information appears in the control, as shown earlier in Figure 5-43.

4. Click the **Exit** button and then close the Code Editor window.

A-6 Professionalize Your Application's Interface

The GUI design guidelines for default buttons are listed in Figure 5-45 and in Appendix A.

As you already know, you can select a button during run time either by clicking it or by pressing the Enter key when the button has the focus. If you make a button the **default button**, you can also select it by pressing the Enter key even when the button does not have the focus. When a button is selected, the computer processes the code contained in the button's Click event procedure.

An interface does not have to have a default button. However, if one is used, it should be the button that is most often selected by the user, except in cases where the tasks performed by the button are both destructive and irreversible. For example, a button that deletes information should not be designated as the default button unless the application provides a way for the information to be restored.

If you assign a default button in an interface, it typically is the first button on the left when the buttons are positioned horizontally but the first button on the top when they are stacked vertically. A form can have only one default button. You specify the default button (if any) by setting the form's **AcceptButton property** to the name of the button. Forms also have a **CancelButton property**, which allows the user to select a button by pressing the Esc key.

START HERE ▶

To designate a default button in the Savings Account application from the previous section:

1. Display the form's properties in the Properties window. Set the AcceptButton property to **btnCalc**. A darkened border now appears around the Calculate button.

2. Save the solution and then start the application. Type **5000** in the Principal box and then press **Enter**. The computer processes the code contained in the btnCalc_Click procedure, and the savings account balances appear in the txtBalance control.

3. Click the **Exit** button and then close the solution.

Mini-Quiz 5-8

1. Only the For...Next statement can be used to code a nested loop. True or False?

2. Which of a text box's properties determines whether the text box can accept either one or multiple lines of text?

3. Which constant is used to represent the Tab key?

4. Which of a form's properties specifies the default button (if any)?

1) False 2) Multiline 3) ControlChars.Tab 4) AcceptButton

Summary

- You use a repetition structure (loop) when you need the computer to repeatedly process one or more program instructions. The loop's condition can be phrased as either a looping condition or a loop exit condition. The condition must evaluate to either True or False.

- A looping condition indicates when the computer should continue processing the loop body. A loop exit condition indicates when the computer should stop processing the loop body.

- In a pretest loop, the condition is evaluated before the loop body is processed. In a posttest loop, the condition is evaluated after the loop body is processed.

- The loop body in a posttest loop will always be processed at least once. Depending on the result of the condition, the loop body in a pretest loop may never be processed.

- To use the Do...Loop statement to code a pretest loop: Refer to the syntax and examples shown in Figure 5-4.

- To use the Do...Loop statement to code a posttest loop: Refer to the syntax and examples shown in Figure 5-6.

- In a flowchart, you use the decision symbol (a diamond) to represent a loop's condition.

- To concatenate strings: Use the concatenation operator (&); refer to Figure 5-5 for examples.

- You can use the `ControlChars.NewLine` constant to advance the insertion point to the next line.

- You can stop an endless (infinite) loop by clicking Debug and then clicking Stop Debugging. Or, you click the Stop Debugging button (the red square) on the Standard toolbar.

- Counters and accumulators need to be initialized and updated. A counter is usually initialized to either 0 or 1; an accumulator is usually initialized to 0. A counter is updated by either incrementing or decrementing its value by a constant amount, which can be either positive or negative, integer or non-integer. An accumulator is typically updated by incrementing (rather than by decrementing) its value by an amount that varies. The amount can be either positive or negative, integer or non-integer.

- To use the For...Next statement to code a counter-controlled loop: Refer to Figure 5-10 for the statement's syntax, examples, and processing tasks. If the counter variable is declared in the For clause, it has block scope and can be used only within the For...Next loop.

- When using the For...Next statement, the number of iterations the loop will perform is controlled by the For clause's startValue, endValue, and stepValue. The startValue, endValue, and stepValue must be numeric and can be positive or negative, integer or non-integer. If you omit the stepValue, a stepValue of positive 1 is used.

- You can use either of the examples shown in Figure 5-13 to flowchart a For...Next loop.

- An overflow error occurs when the value assigned to a memory location is too large for the location's data type.

- A Do...Loop's body must contain an instruction that will stop the loop.

- You can use the ListBox tool in the toolbox to add a list box to a form.

- A list box's SelectionMode property determines whether the user can select zero items, one item, or multiple items.

- You can use either the String Collection Editor or the Items collection's Add method to add items to a list box. The Add method's syntax is shown in Figure 5-29.

- When a list box's Sorted property is set to True, the list box items appear in ascending order; otherwise, they appear in the order they are added to the list box.

- To determine the item selected in a list box or to select a list box item from code, use either the list box's SelectedItem property or its SelectedIndex property.

- When no item is selected in a list box, the SelectedItem property contains the keyword Nothing (which means it does not contain any data) and the SelectedIndex property contains −1 (negative one).

- If a list box allows the user to select only one item at a time, it is customary to specify a default list box item, which will be automatically selected when the application is started and the interface appears.

- To perform tasks when a different item is selected in a list box, enter the appropriate code in either the list box's SelectedValueChanged procedure or its SelectedIndexChanged procedure.

- The Items collection's Count property stores an integer that represents the number of list box items.

- To clear (remove) the items from a list box, use the Items collection's Clear method. The method's syntax is *object*.Items.Clear().

- To calculate a periodic payment on either a loan or an investment, use the Financial.Pmt method. The method's syntax is shown in Figure 5-32.

- Repetition structures (loops) can be nested, which means you can place one loop (called the nested loop) entirely within another loop (called the outer loop).

- To allow a text box to accept and display multiple lines of text, set its Multiline property to True.

- To prevent the user from changing the contents of a text box, set its ReadOnly property to True.

- To display scroll bars on a text box, set its ScrollBars property to Horizontal, Vertical, or Both.

- The ControlChars.Tab constant represents the Tab key.

- Not all real numbers can be stored precisely in the computer's main memory. Some are stored only as approximations.

- You designate a default button on a form by setting the form's AcceptButton property. The default button can be selected by pressing the Enter key even when it does not have the focus. Forms also have a CancelButton property that allows the user to select a button by pressing the Esc key.

- Figure 5-45 lists the GUI design guidelines for list boxes and default buttons.

GUI design guidelines for list boxes

- Use a list box only when you need to offer the user at least three different choices.
- Don't overwhelm the user with a lot of choices at the same time; instead, display from three to eight items and let the user employ the scroll bar to view the remaining ones.
- Use a label control to provide keyboard access to the list box. Set the label's TabIndex property to a value that is one number less than the list box's TabIndex value.
- List box items are either arranged by use, with the most used entries appearing first in the list, or sorted in ascending order.
- If a list box allows the user to make only one selection, a default item is typically selected when the interface first appears. The default item should be either the item selected most frequently or the first item in the list. However, if a list box allows more than one selection at a time, you do not select a default item.

GUI design guidelines for default buttons

- The default button should be the button that is most often selected by the user, except in cases where the tasks performed by the button are both destructive and irreversible.
- If a form contains a default button, it typically is the first button. A form can have only one default button.

Figure 5-45 GUI design guidelines for list boxes and default buttons

Key Terms

&—the concatenation operator in Visual Basic

AcceptButton property—a property of a form; used to designate the default button

Accumulator—a numeric variable used for accumulating (adding together) something

Add method—the Items collection's method used to add an item to a list box

Block scope—scope of the variable declared in a For...Next statement's For clause; indicates that the variable can be used only within the For...Next loop

CancelButton property—a property of a form; used to designate the button that can be selected by pressing the Esc key

Clear method—the Items collection's method used to clear (remove) items from a list box

Collection—a group of individual objects treated as one unit

Concatenation operator—the ampersand (&); used to concatenate strings

ControlChars.NewLine constant—advances the insertion point to the next line

ControlChars.Tab constant—represents the Tab key

Count property—stores an integer that represents the number of items in the Items collection

Counter—a numeric variable used for counting something

Counter-controlled loop—a loop whose processing is controlled by a counter; the loop body will be processed a precise number of times

Decrementing—decreasing a value

Default button—the button that can be selected by pressing the Enter key even when the button does not have the focus; designated by setting the form's AcceptButton property

Default list box item—the item automatically selected in a list box when the application is started and the interface appears

Dictionary order—numbers are sorted before letters, and a lowercase letter is sorted before its uppercase equivalent

Do...Loop statement—a Visual Basic statement that can be used to code both pretest loops and posttest loops

Endless loop—a loop whose instructions are processed indefinitely; also called an infinite loop

Financial.Pmt method—used to calculate the periodic payment on either a loan or an investment

For...Next statement—a Visual Basic statement that is used to code a specific type of pretest loop, called a counter-controlled loop

Incrementing—increasing a value

Infinite loop—another name for an endless loop

Items collection—the collection of items in a list box

List box—a control used to display a list of items from which the user can select zero items, one item, or multiple items

Load event—an event associated with a form; occurs when the application is started and the form is displayed the first time

Loop—another name for the repetition structure

Loop exit condition—the requirement that must be met for the computer to *stop* processing the loop body instructions

Looping condition—the requirement that must be met for the computer to *continue* processing the loop body instructions

Multiline property—a property of a text box; indicates whether the text box can accept and display either one or multiple lines of text

Overflow error—occurs when the value assigned to a memory location is too large for the location's data type

Posttest loop—a loop whose condition is evaluated *after* the instructions in its loop body are processed

Pretest loop—a loop whose condition is evaluated *before* the instructions in its loop body are processed

ReadOnly property—a property of a text box; specifies whether or not the user can change the contents of the text box

Real numbers—numbers with a decimal place

Repetition structure—the control structure used to repeatedly process one or more program instructions; also called a loop

ScrollBars property—a property of a text box; specifies whether the text box has no scroll bars, a horizontal scroll bar, a vertical scroll bar, or both horizontal and vertical scroll bars

SelectedIndex property—can be used to select an item in a list box and also to determine which item is selected; stores the index of the selected item

SelectedIndexChanged event—occurs when an item is selected in a list box

SelectedItem property—can be used to select an item in a list box and also to determine which item is selected; stores the value of the selected item

SelectedValueChanged event—occurs when an item is selected in a list box

SelectionMode property—determines the number of items that can be selected in a list box

Sorted property—specifies whether the list box items should appear in the order they are entered in the list box or in sorted order

String Collection Editor—provides an easy way to add items to a list box's Items collection

Review Questions

1. Which of the following clauses will stop the loop when the value in the `intPopulation` variable is less than the number 5000?

    a. `Do While intPopulation >= 5000`

    b. `Do Until intPopulation < 5000`

    c. `Loop While intPopulation >= 5000`

    d. All of the above.

2. Which of the following statements can be used to code a loop whose instructions you want processed 10 times?

    a. Do...Loop

    b. For...Next

    c. All of the above.

3. The instructions in a _____ loop might not be processed at all, whereas the instructions in a _____ loop are always processed at least once.

    a. posttest, pretest   b. pretest, posttest

4. How many times will the string literal "Hi" appear in the lblMsg control?

    ```
    Dim intCount As Integer
    Do While intCount > 4
        lblMsg.Text = lblMsg.Text &
            "Hi" & ControlChars.NewLine
        intCount += 1
    Loop
    ```

    a. zero   c. four

    b. one   d. five

5. How many times will the string literal "Hi" appear in the lblMsg control?

```
Dim intCount As Integer
Do
    lblMsg.Text = lblMsg.Text &
        "Hi" & ControlChars.NewLine
    intCount += 1
Loop While intCount > 4
```

   a. zero   c. four

   b. one   d. five

6. How many times will the string literal "Hi" appear in the lblMsg control?

```
For intCount As Integer = 6 To 13 Step 2
    lblMsg.Text = lblMsg.Text &
        "Hi" & ControlChars.NewLine
Next intCount
```

   a. three   c. five

   b. four   d. eight

7. The computer will stop processing the loop in Review Question 6 when the intCount variable contains the number _____.

   a. 11   c. 13

   b. 12   d. 14

Refer to Figure 5-46 to answer Review Questions 8 through 11.

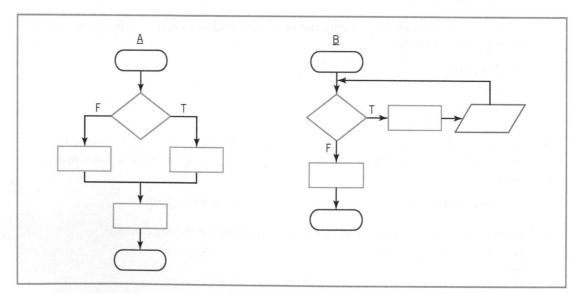

Figure 5-46 Flowcharts for Review Questions 8 through 11 *(continues)*

(continued)

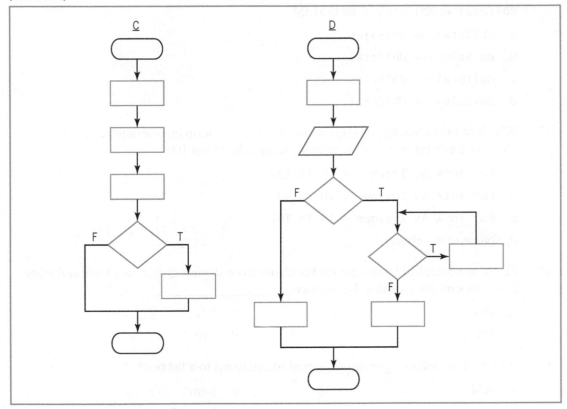

Figure 5-46 Flowcharts for Review Questions 8 through 11

8. In addition to the sequence structure, which of the following control structures is used in flowchart A in Figure 5-46?

   a. selection

   b. repetition

   c. Both a and b.

9. In addition to the sequence structure, which of the following control structures is used in flowchart B in Figure 5-46?

   a. selection

   b. repetition

   c. Both a and b.

10. In addition to the sequence structure, which of the following control structures is used in flowchart C in Figure 5-46?

    a. selection

    b. repetition

    c. Both a and b.

11. In addition to the sequence structure, which of the following control structures is used in flowchart D in Figure 5-46?

    a. selection

    b. repetition

    c. Both a and b.

12. Which of the following statements is equivalent to the statement
    `dblTotal = dblTotal + dblSales`?

    a. `dblTotal += dblSales`

    b. `dblSales += dblTotal`

    c. `dblTotal =+ dblSales`

    d. `dblSales =+ dblTotal`

13. Which of the following For clauses indicates that the loop instructions should be
    processed as long as the `intX` variable's value is less than 100?

    a. `For intX As Integer = 10 To 100`

    b. `For intX As Integer = 10 To 99`

    c. `For intX As Integer = 10 To 101`

    d. None of the above.

14. The loop controlled by the correct For clause from Review Question 13 will end when
    the `intX` variable contains the number _____.

    a. 100   c. 101

    b. 111   d. 110

15. Which of the following methods is used to add items to a list box?

    a. Add   c. Item

    b. AddList   d. ItemAdd

16. The items in a list box belong to which collection?

    a. Items   c. ListItems

    b. List   d. Values

17. Which of the following properties stores the index of the item selected in a list box?

    a. Index   c. Selection

    b. SelectedIndex   d. SelectionIndex

18. Which of the following statements selects the fourth item in the lstNames control?

    a. `lstNames.SelectIndex = 3`

    b. `lstNames.SelectIndex = 4`

    c. `lstNames.SelectedIndex = 3`

    d. `lstNames.SelectedItem = 4`

19. Which event occurs when the user selects a different item in a list box?

    a. SelectionChanged   c. SelectedValueChanged

    b. SelectedItemChanged   d. None of the above.

20. What will the following code display in the lblAsterisks control?

```
For intX As Integer = 1 To 2
  For intY As Integer = 1 To 3
    lblAsterisks.Text = lblAsterisks.Text &  "*"
  Next intY
  lblAsterisks.Text = lblAsterisks.Text & ControlChars.NewLine
Next intX
```

a. ***　　　　　　　　　　　　c. **
　　***　　　　　　　　　　　　　　　**
　　　　　　　　　　　　　　　　　　　**

b. ***
　　***　　　　　　　　　　　　d. ***
　　***　　　　　　　　　　　　　　***
　　　　　　　　　　　　　　　　　　***
　　　　　　　　　　　　　　　　　　***

21. What will the following code display in the lblSum control?

```
Dim intSum As Integer
Dim intY As Integer
Do While intY < 3
    For intX As Integer = 1 To 4
        intSum += intX
    Next intX
    intY += 1
Loop
lblSum.Text = intSum.ToString
```

a. 5　　　　　　　　　　　　　c. 15

b. 8　　　　　　　　　　　　　d. 30

22. Which of the following calculates the monthly payment (expressed as a positive number) for a loan of $10,000 for 2 years with a 3.5% annual interest rate?

a. -Financial.Pmt(0.035, 2, 10000)

b. -Financial.Pmt(0.035 / 12, 2 * 12, 10000)

c. -Financial.Pmt(2 * 12, 0.035 / 12, 10000)

d. -Financial.Pmt(10000, 0.035 / 12, 2 * 12)

23. To make the btnCalc control the default button, you need to set the _____ property.

a. btnCalc's AcceptButton　　　　　c. form's AcceptButton

b. btnCalc's DefaultButton　　　　　d. form's DefaultButton

24. If a list box's Sorted property is set to False, how will the numbers 4, 35, 3, 1, and 12 be displayed in the list box?

a. 4, 35, 3, 1, 12　　　　　　　　c. 1, 12, 3, 35, 4

b. 1, 3, 4, 12, 35　　　　　　　　d. 35, 12, 4, 3, 1

25. If a list box's Sorted property is set to True, how will the numbers 4, 35, 3, 1, and 12 be displayed in the list box?

   a. 4, 35, 3, 1, 12
   b. 1, 3, 4, 12, 35
   c. 1, 12, 3, 35, 4
   d. 35, 12, 4, 3, 1

Exercises

INTRODUCTORY

1. In this exercise, you modify the Monthly Payment application from this chapter's Apply lesson. Use Windows to make a copy of the Payment Solution folder. Rename the copy Payment Solution-DoLoop. Open the Payment.sln file contained in the Payment Solution-DoLoop folder. Change the For...Next statements in the frmMain_Load and btnCalc_Click procedures to Do...Loop statements. Save the solution and then start and test the application. (If you test the application using 125000 as the principal and 3.0 as the rate, the payments should be identical to those shown earlier in Figure 5-37.)

INTRODUCTORY

2. Create a Windows Form application. Use the following names for the project and solution, respectively: State Capital Project and State Capital Solution. Save the application in the VB2017\Chap05 folder. Add any five state names to a list box. When the user clicks a name in the list box, the list box's SelectedIndexChanged procedure should display the name of the state's capital in a label control. Save the solution and then start and test the application.

INTRODUCTORY

3. In this exercise, you modify the Savings Account application from this chapter's Apply lesson. Use Windows to make a copy of the Savings Solution folder. Rename the copy Modified Savings Solution. Open the Savings Solution.sln file contained in the Modified Savings Solution folder. In the btnCalc_Click procedure, change the For...Next statement that controls the years to a Do...Loop statement. Save the solution and then start and test the application. (If you test the application using 2500 as the deposit, the account balances should be identical to those shown earlier in Figure 5-41. Verify that the txtBalance control contains the 7% rate information.)

INTRODUCTORY

4. In this exercise, you modify one of the Projected Sales applications from this chapter's Apply lesson. Use Windows to make a copy of the Projected Sales Solution folder. Rename the copy Modified Projected Sales Solution. Open the Projected Sales Solution.sln file contained in the Modified Projected Sales Solution folder. Rather than using $150,000 as the sales goal, the user should be able to enter any sales goal. Modify the interface (using a text box for entering the sales goal) and code as needed. Be sure to reset the tab order. Also be sure to code the new text box's KeyPress, Enter, and TextChanged event procedures. Save the solution and then start and test the application. (If the current sales and sales goal are 50000 and 125000, respectively, it will take the company 31 years to reach $125,004 in sales.)

INTRODUCTORY

5. In this exercise, you modify one of the Projected Sales applications from this chapter's Apply lesson. Use Windows to make a copy of the Projected Sales Solution-ForNext folder. Rename the copy Projected Sales Solution-DoLoop. Open the Projected Sales

Solution.sln file contained in the Projected Sales Solution-DoLoop folder. Change the For...Next statement in the btnCalc_Click procedure to a Do...Loop statement. Save the solution and then start and test the application. (If the current sales amount is 86500, the projected sales amounts should be identical to those shown earlier in Figure 5-22.)

6. Open the Numbers Solution.sln file contained in the VB2017\Chap05\Numbers Solution folder. The application allows the user to display a list of numbers in a list box. The user will enter the start and end values for these numbers in the two text boxes.

   a. Open the Code Editor window. Locate the btnForNext_Click procedure and then click the blank line above its End Sub clause. Use the For...Next statement to display the range of numbers indicated by the user. For example, if the user enters the numbers 1 and 5 in the From and To boxes, respectively, the statement should display the numbers 1 through 5 in the list box. Display the numbers only when the value in the From box is less than the value in the To box; otherwise, leave the list box empty. Save the solution and then start and test the procedure.

   b. Now, locate the btnDoPretest_Click procedure and then click the blank line above its End Sub clause. Use a pretest Do...Loop statement to display the range of numbers indicated by the user. Display the numbers only when the value in the From box is less than the value in the To box; otherwise, leave the list box empty. Save the solution and then start and test the procedure.

   c. Finally, locate the btnDoPosttest_Click procedure and then click the blank line above its End Sub clause. Use a posttest Do...Loop statement to display the range of numbers indicated by the user. Display the numbers only when the value in the From box is less than the value in the To box; otherwise, leave the list box empty. Save the solution and then start and test the procedure.

7. In this exercise, you modify the Numbers application from Exercise 6. Use Windows to make a copy of the Numbers Solution folder. Rename the copy Modified Numbers Solution. Open the Numbers Solution.sln file contained in the Modified Numbers Solution folder.

   a. Open the Code Editor window. Modify the btnForNext_Click procedure to display only the even numbers within the range specified by the user. (If necessary, review the arithmetic operators listed in Figure 3-10 in Chapter 3.) Save the solution and then start and test the procedure. (If the From and To boxes contain 1 and 9, respectively, the procedure should display the numbers 2, 4, 6, and 8.)

   b. Now, modify the btnDoPretest_Click procedure to display only the odd numbers within the range specified by the user. Save the solution and then start and test the procedure. (If the From and To boxes contain 1 and 9, respectively, the procedure should display the numbers 1, 3, 5, 7, and 9.)

8. Open the Multiplication Solution.sln file contained in the VB2017\Chap05\Multiplication Solution folder. Code the application to display a multiplication table similar to the one shown in Figure 5-47. Use the For...Next statement in the btnForNext_Click procedure, and use the Do...Loop statement in the btnDoLoop_Click procedure. Save the solution and then start and test the application.

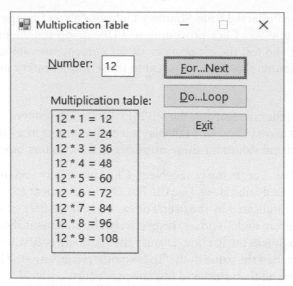

Figure 5-47 Sample multiplication table for Exercise 8

INTERMEDIATE

9. In this exercise, you create an application for Discount Warehouse. Create a Windows Forms application. Use the following names for the project and solution, respectively: Discount Project and Discount Solution. Save the application in the VB2017\Chap05 folder. The interface should allow the user to enter an item's original price and its discount rate. The discount rates should range from 10% through 40% in increments of 5%. Use a text box for entering the original price, and use a list box for entering the discount rates. The application should display the amount of the discount and also the discounted price. The button that calculates and displays the discount and discounted price should be the default button. Save the solution and then start and test the application.

INTERMEDIATE

10. In this exercise, you modify the Monthly Payment application from this chapter's Apply lesson. Use Windows to make a copy of the Payment Solution folder. Rename the copy Modified Payment Solution. Open the Payment Solution.sln file contained in the Modified Payment Solution folder. Modify the interface to allow the user to select the term (15, 20, 25 or 30) from a list box. Make any other modifications you deem necessary to the interface. Be sure to reset the tab order. Also be sure to select a default item in the new list box. The Calculate button should now display only the monthly payment corresponding to the selected term. Save the solution and then start and test the application. (If the principal, rate, and term are 125000, 3.0, and 30, respectively, the monthly payment is $527.01.)

ADVANCED

11. Create a Windows Forms application. Use the following names for the project and solution, respectively: Mills Project and Mills Solution. Save the application in the VB2017\Chap05 folder. Mills Skating Rink holds a weekly ice-skating competition. Competing skaters must perform a two-minute program in front of a panel of judges. The number of judges varies from week to week. At the end of a skater's program, each judge assigns a score of 0 through 10 to the skater. The manager of the ice rink wants you to create an application that allows him to enter each judge's score for a specific skater. The application should calculate and display the skater's average score. It should also display the skater's total score and the number of scores entered. Figure 5-48 shows a sample run of the application, assuming the manager entered

two scores: 10 and 8. (You enter a score by selecting it from the list box and then clicking the Record score button.) Code the application. Save the solution and then start and test the application.

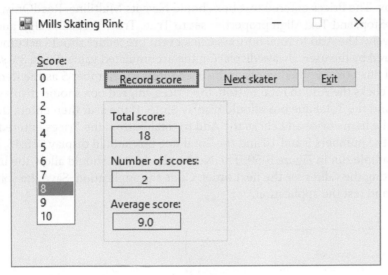

Figure 5-48 Interface for Exercise 11

12. In this exercise, you create an application that allows the user to enter the gender (either F or M) and GPA for any number of students. The application should calculate the average GPA for all students, the average GPA for male students, and the average GPA for female students. Create a Windows Forms application. Use the following names for the project and solution, respectively: GPA Project and GPA Solution. Save the application in the VB2017\Chap05 folder. The application's interface is shown in Figure 5-49. The list box should list GPAs from 1.0 through 4.0 in increments of 0.1 (e.g., 1.0, 1.1, 1.2, 1.3, etc.). Code the application. Save the solution and then start and test the application.

ADVANCED

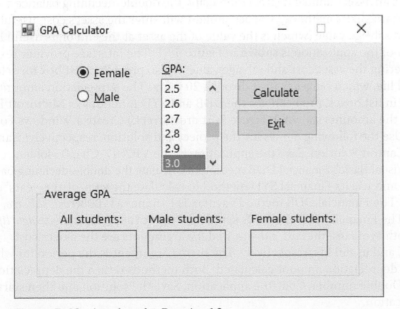

Figure 5-49 Interface for Exercise 12

ADVANCED 13. Create a Windows Forms application. Use the following names for the project and solution, respectively: General Project and General Solution. Save the application in the VB2017\Chap05 folder. A sample run of the application is shown in Figure 5-50. The interface allows the user to enter an item's price, which should be displayed in the Prices entered text box. The Prices entered text box should have its Multiline, ReadOnly, ScrollBars, TabStop, and TextAlign properties set to True, True, Vertical, False, and Right, respectively. The Add to total button's Click event procedure should accumulate the prices entered by the user, always displaying the accumulated value plus a 3% sales tax in the Total due box. In other words, if the user enters the number 5 as the item's price and then clicks the Add to total button, the Prices entered box should display the number 5 and the Total due box should display $5.15. If the user then enters the number 10 as the item's price and clicks the Add to total button, the Prices entered box should display the numbers 5 and 10 and the Total due box should display $15.45, as shown in the sample run in Figure 5-50. The Next order button should allow the user to start accumulating the values for the next order. Code the application. Save the solution and then start and test the application.

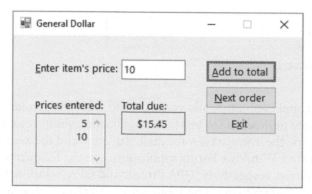

Figure 5-50 Sample run of the application for Exercise 13

ADVANCED 14. The accountant at Canton Manufacturing Company wants you to create an application that calculates an asset's annual depreciation using the double-declining balance and sum-of-the-years' digits methods. The accountant will enter the asset's cost, useful life (in years), and salvage value (which is the value of the asset at the end of its useful life). A sample run of the application is shown in Figure 5-51. The interface provides text boxes for entering the asset cost and salvage value. It also provides a list box for select-ing the useful life, which ranges from 3 through 20 years. The depreciation amounts are displayed in list boxes. (You can use the DDB and SYD functions in Microsoft Excel to verify that the amounts shown in Figure 5-51 are correct.) Create a Windows Forms application. Use the following names for the project and solution, respectively: Canton Project and Canton Solution. Save the application in the VB2017\Chap05 folder. You can use Visual Basic's Financial.DDB method to calculate the double-declining balance depreciation, and use its Financial.SYD method to calculate the sum-of-the-years' digits depreciation. The Financial.DDB method's syntax is `Financial.DDB`(*cost, salvage, life, period*). The Financial.SYD method's syntax is `Financial.SYD`(*cost, salvage, life, period*). In both syntaxes, the *cost*, *salvage*, and *life* arguments are the asset's cost, salvage value, and useful life, respectively. The *period* argument is the period for which you want the depreciation amount calculated. Both methods return the depreciation amount as a Double number. Code the application. Save the solution and then start and test the application.

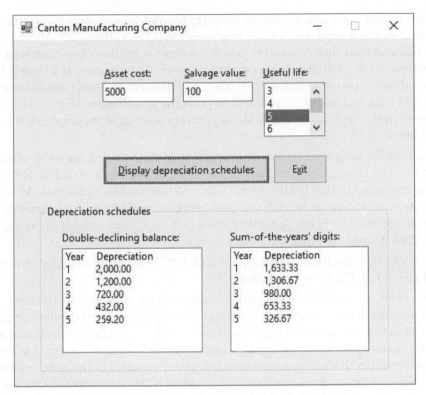

Figure 5-51 Sample run of the application for Exercise 14

15. Open the Fibonacci Solution.sln file contained in the VB2017\Chap05\Fibonacci Solution folder. The application should display the first 10 Fibonacci numbers: 1, 1, 2, 3, 5, 8, 13, 21, 34, and 55. Notice that beginning with the third number in the series, each Fibonacci number is the sum of the prior two numbers. For example, 2 is the sum of 1 plus 1, 3 is the sum of 1 plus 2, 5 is the sum of 2 plus 3, and so on. Display the numbers in the lblNumbers control. Code the btnDisplay_Click procedure. Save the solution and then start and test the application.

ADVANCED

16. In this exercise, you learn how to create a list box that allows the user to select more than one item at a time. Open the Multi Solution.sln file contained in the VB2017\Chap05\Multi Solution folder. The interface contains a list box named lstNames. The list box's Sorted and SelectionMode properties are set to True and One, respectively.

ADVANCED

   a. Open the Code Editor window. The frmMain_Load procedure adds five names to the lstNames control. Code the btnSingle_Click procedure so that it displays, in the lblResult control, the item selected in the list box. For example, if the user clicks Debbie in the list box and then clicks the Single selection button, the name Debbie should appear in the lblResult control.

   b. Save the solution and then start the application. Click Debbie in the list box, then click Ahmad, and then click Bill. Notice that when the list box's SelectionMode property is set to One, you can select only one item at a time in the list.

   c. Click the Single selection button. The name Bill appears in the lblResult control. Click the Exit button.

d. Change the list box's SelectionMode property to MultiSimple. Save the solution and then start the application. Click Debbie in the list box, then click Ahmad, then click Bill, and then click Ahmad. Notice that when the list box's SelectionMode property is set to MultiSimple, you can select more than one item at a time in the list. Also notice that you click to both select and deselect an item. (You also can use Ctrl+click and Shift+click, as well as press the spacebar, to select and deselect items when the list box's SelectionMode property is set to MultiSimple.) Click the Exit button.

e. Change the list box's SelectionMode property to MultiExtended. Save the solution and then start the application. Click Debbie in the list, and then click Jim. Notice that in this case, clicking Jim deselects Debbie. When a list box's SelectionMode property is set to MultiExtended, you use Ctrl+click to select multiple items in the list. You also use Ctrl+click to deselect items in the list. Click Debbie in the list, then Ctrl+click Ahmad, and then Ctrl+click Debbie.

f. Next, click Bill in the list, and then Shift+click Jim. This selects all of the names from Bill through Jim. Click the Exit button.

g. As you know, when a list box's SelectionMode property is set to One, the item selected in the list box is stored in the SelectedItem property, and the item's index is stored in the SelectedIndex property. However, when a list box's SelectionMode property is set to either MultiSimple or MultiExtended, the items selected in the list box are stored in the SelectedItems property, and the indices of the items are stored in the SelectedIndices property. Code the btnMulti_Click procedure so that it first clears the contents of the lblResult control. The procedure should then display the selected names (which are stored in the SelectedItems property) on separate lines in the lblResult control.

h. Save the solution and then start the application. Click Ahmad in the list box, and then Shift+click Jim. Click the Multi-selection button. The five names should appear on separate lines in the lblResult control. Click the Exit button.

ADVANCED ▶ 17. In this exercise, you learn how to use the Items collection's Insert, Remove, and RemoveAt methods. Open the Items Collection Solution.sln file contained in the VB2017\Chap05\Items Collection Solution folder.

a. The Items collection's Insert method allows you to add an item at a desired position in a list box during run time. The Insert method's syntax is *object*.Items.Insert(*position, item*), where *position* is the index of the item. Code the btnInsert_Click procedure so it adds your name as the fourth item in the list box. (Recall that the first item in a list box has an index of 0.)

b. The Items collection's Remove method allows you to remove an item from a list box during run time. The Remove method's syntax is *object*.Items.Remove(*item*), where *item* is the item's value. Code the btnRemove_Click procedure so it removes your name from the list box.

c. Like the Remove method, the Items collection's RemoveAt method also allows you to remove an item from a list box while an application is running. However, in the RemoveAt method, you specify the item's index rather than its value. The RemoveAt method's syntax is *object*.Items.RemoveAt(*index*), where *index* is the item's index. Code the btnRemoveAt_Click procedure so it removes the second name from the list box.

d. Save the solution and then start the application. Click the Insert button to add your name to the list box. Click the Remove button to remove your name from the list box. Click the RemoveAt button to remove the second name from the list box. Click the Exit button.

18. In this exercise, you modify the Savings Account application from this chapter's Apply lesson. Use Windows to make a copy of the Savings Solution folder. Rename the copy Savings Solution-Advanced. Open the Savings Solution.sln file contained in the Savings Solution-Advanced folder. The btnCalc_Click procedure should now display the account balances by rate within year (rather than by year within rate). Figure 5-52 shows a sample run of the application. Make the appropriate modifications to the code. Save the solution and then start and test the application.

ADVANCED

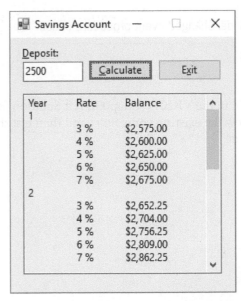

Figure 5-52   Sample run of the application for Exercise 18

19. Create a Windows Forms application. Use the following names for the project and solution, respectively: Salary Project and Salary Solution. Save the application in the VB2017\Chap05 folder. At the beginning of every year, you receive a raise on your previous year's salary. Create an application that displays the amount of your annual raises and also your new salaries for the next five years, using raise rates of 1.5%, 2%, 2.5%, and 3%. Create a suitable interface. Use a text box to enter your current salary. Code the application. Save the solution and then start and test the application.

ADVANCED

20. Create a Windows Forms application. Use the following names for the project and solution, respectively: OnYourOwn Project and OnYourOwn Solution. Save the application in the VB2017\Chap05 folder. Plan and design an application of your choice. The only requirement is that you must follow the minimum guidelines listed in Figure 5-53. Before starting the application, be sure to verify the name of the startup form. Save the solution and then start and test the application.

ON YOUR OWN

1. The user interface must contain a minimum of one text box, three labels, one list box, and two buttons. One of the buttons must be an Exit button.
2. The interface can include a picture box, but this is not a requirement.
3. The interface must follow the GUI design guidelines summarized in Figure 2-20 in Chapter 2, in Figure 4-52 in Chapter 4, and in Figure 5-45 in Chapter 5. The guidelines are also listed in Appendix A.
4. Objects that are either coded or referred to in code should be named appropriately.
5. The Code Editor window must contain comments, the three Option statements, at least two variables, at least two assignment statements, at least one loop, and the `Me.Close()` statement. The application must perform at least one calculation.
6. Every text box on the form should have its TextChanged and Enter event procedures coded. At least one of the text boxes should have its KeyPress event procedure coded.
7. The list box should have its SelectedIndexChanged event procedure coded.

Figure 5-53   Guidelines for Exercise 20

FIX IT

21.   Open the FixIt Solution.sln file contained in the VB2017\Chap05\FixIt Solution folder. Open the Code Editor window and review the existing code. Start and then test the application. Correct any errors in the code.

CHAPTER 6

Sub and Function Procedures

In this chapter's Focus on the Concepts lesson, you will learn how to connect multiple objects and events to the same procedure. Doing this tells the computer to process the procedure when any of the events occur. You will also learn how to create your own Sub and Function procedures, which will be processed only when your code invokes them. In addition, you will learn how to round numeric values to a specified number of decimal places.

In the Apply the Concepts lesson, you will learn how to add a combo box to an interface. You will also learn how to calculate an employee's weekly federal withholding tax. You will use the concepts from the Focus lesson to code the applications in the Apply lesson.

FOCUS ON THE CONCEPTS LESSON

Concepts covered in this lesson:

- F-1 Event-handling Sub procedures
- F-2 Independent Sub procedures
- F-3 Passing information to a procedure
- F-4 Rounding numbers
- F-5 Function procedures

F-1 Event-Handling Sub Procedures

Procedures that are processed only when a specific event occurs are called **event-handling Sub procedures** or, more simply, **event procedures**. All of the procedures that you coded in the previous chapters were event procedures. The Handles clause in an event procedure's header indicates the object and event associated with the procedure. The Handles clause in Figure 6-1 indicates that the procedure is associated with the Click event of the btnCalc control. As a result, the procedure will be processed when the control's Click event occurs.

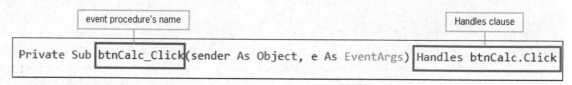

Figure 6-1 btnCalc_Click procedure header

By default, an event procedure's name is composed of the object's name followed by an underscore and the event's name. However, you can change the name to almost anything you like as long as the name follows the same rules for naming variables. Unlike variable names, however, procedure names are usually entered using **Pascal case**, which means you capitalize the first letter in the name and the first letter of each subsequent word in the name. It is a common practice to begin the name with a verb.

You can associate a procedure with more than one object and event as long as each event contains the same parameters in its procedure header. As you learned in Chapter 4, a parameter represents information that is passed to the event procedure when the event occurs. To associate multiple objects and events with a procedure, you list each object and event in the procedure's Handles clause. You separate the object and event with a period, like this: *object.event*. You use a comma to separate each *object.event* from the next *object.event*.

In the next set of steps, you will open the Monthly Payment application from Chapter 5. The application's code contains two event procedures that perform the same task. You will change one of the event procedure's names and then associate both events with that procedure. When doing this, the Handles clause will be rather long and, depending on the size of the font used in your Code Editor window, you might not be able to view the entire statement without scrolling the window. Fortunately, the Code Editor allows you to break a line of code into two or more physical lines as long as the break comes either before a closing parenthesis or after one of the following: a comma, an opening parenthesis, or an operator (arithmetic, assignment, comparison, logical, or concatenation). If you want to break a line of code anywhere else, you will need to use the **line continuation character**, which is an underscore (_) that is immediately preceded by a space; it must also appear at the end of a physical line of code.

To modify the Monthly Payment application:

START HERE

1. Open the Payment Solution.sln file contained in the VB2017\Chap06\Payment Solution folder.

2. Open the Code Editor window. Locate the txtPrincipal_TextChanged and lstRates_SelectedIndexChanged procedures. Notice that both procedures have the same parameters (**sender** and **e**) and both perform the same task of clearing the lblPay.Text property. Rather than having the same line of code in two procedures, you can create one procedure and associate the two events with it.

3. First, you will change the txtPrincipal_TextChanged procedure's name. In the procedure's header, change `txtPrincipal_TextChanged` to **ClearPay**.

4. Now, you will use the line continuation character to break the assignment statement before the Handles clause. Click **immediately before the letter H** in the keyword `Handles`. Type _ (an underscore). Be sure there is a space between the ending parenthesis and the underscore. Then press **Enter** to move the Handles clause to the next line in the procedure.

5. The ClearPay procedure is already associated with the TextChanged event, so you just need to associate it with the SelectedIndexChanged event. Modify the Handles clause as shown in Figure 6-2.

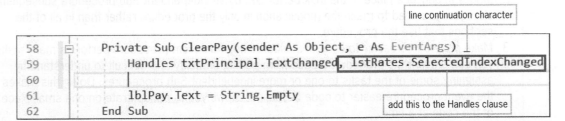

Figure 6-2 Completed Handles clause

6. Next, delete the lstRates_SelectedIndexChanged procedure from the Code Editor window.

7. Save the solution and then start the application. Click the **Calculate** button. The Monthly payment box shows $0.00 as the monthly payments. Type **3** in the Principal box. The ClearPay procedure, which is associated with the text box's TextChanged event, clears the Monthly payment box.

8. Click the **Calculate** button and then click **2.0** in the list box. The ClearPay procedure, which is associated with the list box's SelectedIndexChanged event, clears the Monthly payment box.

9. Click the **Exit** button. Close the Code Editor window and then close the solution.

Mini-Quiz 6-1

1. What is the line continuation character?

2. Without using the line continuation character, you can break a line of code immediately before a comma. True or False?

3. Write a Handles clause that associates a procedure with the TextChanged events for the txtFirst and txtSecond controls.

1) _ (an underscore) 2) False 3) Handles txtFirst.TextChanged, txtSecond.TextChanged

F-2 Independent Sub Procedures

Sub procedures that are not connected to any object and event are often referred to as **independent Sub procedures**. An independent Sub procedure is processed only when a statement in your code calls (or invokes) it. Figure 6-3 lists many of the reasons that programmers use independent Sub procedures.

---

1. *Avoid duplicating code:* When different sections of a program need to perform the same task, you can enter the code in a procedure and then have each section call the procedure to perform its task when needed.
2. *Modify in only one place:* If the task performed by an independent Sub procedure subsequently changes, you need to make the modification in only the procedure rather than in all of the sections that use the procedure.
3. *Make procedures easier to code and understand:* If an event procedure performs many tasks, you can prevent the procedure's code from getting unwieldy and difficult to understand by assigning some of the tasks to one or more independent Sub procedures. Doing this makes the event procedure easier to code because it allows you to concentrate on one small piece of the code at a time.
4. *Allow a team of programmers to code the application:* Independent Sub procedures are used extensively in large and complex applications, which typically are written by a team of programmers. The team will break up the application's code into small and manageable tasks, and then assign some of the tasks to different team members to be coded as independent Sub procedures. Doing this allows more than one programmer to work on the application at the same time, decreasing the time it takes to complete the application.

Figure 6-3 Reasons for using independent Sub procedures

Figure 6-4 shows the syntax of an independent Sub procedure along with the syntax for calling (invoking) the procedure. As the figure indicates, you invoke an independent Sub procedure using a stand-alone statement (referred to as the **calling statement**) that includes the Sub procedure's name followed by zero or more arguments that are separated by commas and enclosed in parentheses. The **arguments** represent information that the statement must pass to the Sub procedure in order for the procedure to perform its task. An argument can be a literal, a named constant, a keyword, or a variable; however, in most cases, the argument will be a variable.

Independent Sub Procedure and Calling Statement

Syntax of an independent Sub procedure
Private Sub *procedureName*(*[parameterList]*)
    statements
                    the received items are
End Sub   called parameters

Syntax of a calling statement
procedureName(*[argumentList]*)   the passed items are
                                called arguments

Figure 6-4 Syntax of an independent Sub procedure and its calling statement

---

An independent Sub procedure can be entered anywhere between the Public Class and End Class clauses in the Code Editor window, but it must be entered outside of any other procedure. In this book, the independent Sub procedures will be entered above the first event procedure.

Most times, an independent Sub procedure's header begins with the keyword `Private`, which indicates that the procedure can be used only within the class that defines it. The rules for naming an independent Sub procedure are the same as those for naming event-handling Sub procedures. The name is entered using Pascal case and typically begins with a verb. The name should indicate the task the procedure performs. For example, a good name for a Sub procedure that calculates an employee's net pay is CalcNet.

Following the procedure name in the procedure header is a set of parentheses that contains an optional *parameterList*, which lists the data type and name of one or more **parameters**. A parameter is simply a memory location; more specifically, it is a variable. Each parameter has procedure scope, which means it can be used only by the procedure in whose parameterList it appears. The variable will be removed from memory when the procedure ends.

Each parameter stores an item of data that it receives from the calling statement's *argumentList*. The number of arguments should agree with the number of parameters. If the parameterList does not contain any parameters, as shown in Example 1 in Figure 6-5, then an empty set of parentheses follows the procedure name in the calling statement. If the parameterList contains one parameter, as shown in Example 2, then the argumentList should have one argument. Similarly, a procedure header that contains three parameters, as shown in Example 3, requires three arguments in the calling statement. Do not be concerned if you do not understand everything in the figure right now. The Sub procedures and calling statements will be explained further in the following sections.

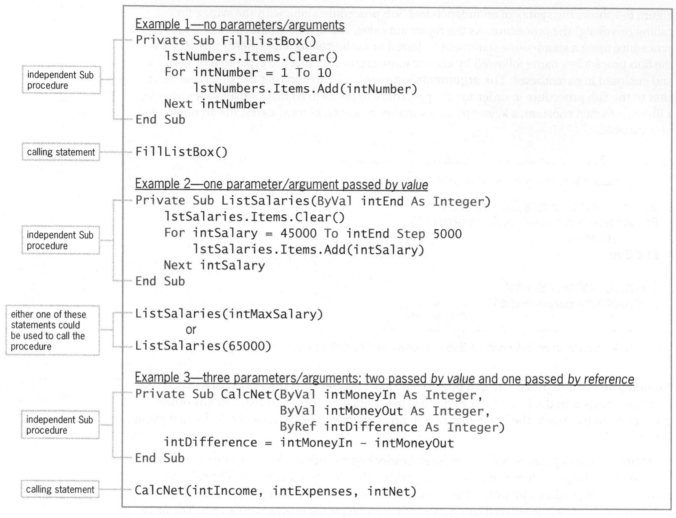

Figure 6-5   Examples of independent Sub procedures and calling statements

In addition to having the same number of arguments as parameters, the data type and order (or position) of each argument should agree with the data type and order (position) of its corresponding parameter. This is necessary because when the procedure is called, the computer associates the first argument with the first parameter, the second argument with the second parameter, and so on.

In the next section, you will code an application that creates and calls two independent Sub procedures. Neither of the procedures requires any parameters or arguments.

No Parameters/Arguments Example: History Grade Application

The History Grade application displays a student's grade for either a History 101 course or a History 201 course. The grade is based on the total points the student earned in the course. In the next set of steps, you will use two independent Sub procedures to display the appropriate grade.

START HERE   **To complete the History Grade application:**

1. Open the History Solution.sln file contained in the VB2017\Chap06\History Solution folder.

2. Open the Code Editor window. Locate the ClearGrade event-handling procedure. Notice that the procedure is associated with the text box's TextChanged event and also with the CheckedChanged events for the two radio buttons.

3. Scroll to the top of the Code Editor window, if necessary, and then click the **blank line** immediately below the ' Independent Sub procedures. comment. Enter the DisplayGrade101 procedure shown in Figure 6-6.

```
10          ' Independent Sub procedures.
11          Private Sub DisplayGrade101()
12              ' Display the grade for History 101.
13
14              Dim intPoints As Integer
15              Integer.TryParse(txtPoints.Text, intPoints)
16
17              Select Case intPoints
18                  Case Is >= 90
19                      lblGrade.Text = "A"
20                  Case Is >= 80
21                      lblGrade.Text = "B"
22                  Case Is >= 70
23                      lblGrade.Text = "C"
24                  Case Is >= 60
25                      lblGrade.Text = "D"
26                  Case Else
27                      lblGrade.Text = "F"
28              End Select
29          End Sub
```

enter this procedure

Figure 6-6   DisplayGrade101 procedure

4. Click the **blank line** immediately below the procedure's End Sub clause and then press **Enter**. Enter the DisplayGrade201 procedure shown in Figure 6-7. After entering the procedure, position the insertion point as shown in the figure.

```
31          Private Sub DisplayGrade201()
32              ' Display the grade for History 201.
33
34              Dim intPoints As Integer
35              Integer.TryParse(txtPoints.Text, intPoints)
36
37              If intPoints >= 75 Then
38                  lblGrade.Text = "P"
39              Else
40                  lblGrade.Text = "F"
41              End If
42          End Sub
43                  insertion point
44          Private Sub btnDisplay_Click(sender As Object, e As
```

enter this procedure

Figure 6-7   DisplayGrade201 procedure

5. Next, you will enter the code to call each procedure. Locate the btnDisplay_Click procedure and then click the **blank line** immediately above its End Sub clause. Enter the selection structure shown in Figure 6-8. (You can also use `radHis101.Checked = True` as the condition.)

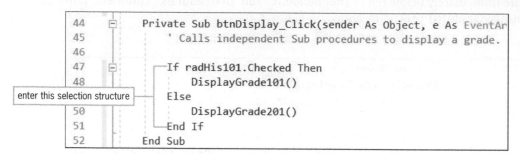

```
44        Private Sub btnDisplay_Click(sender As Object, e As EventAr
45            ' Calls independent Sub procedures to display a grade.
46
47            If radHis101.Checked Then
48                DisplayGrade101()
                Else
50                DisplayGrade201()
51            End If
52        End Sub
```

enter this selection structure

Figure 6-8   Completed btnDisplay_Click procedure

6. Save the solution and then start the application. The History 101 radio button is already selected. Type **83** in the Total points box and then click the **Display** button. The computer processes the btnDisplay_Click procedure, which contains a selection structure. The structure's condition evaluates to True, so the computer processes the `DisplayGrade101()` statement entered in the true path. At this point, the computer temporarily leaves the btnDisplay_Click procedure to process the code in the DisplayGrade101 procedure. That procedure displays the letter B in the Grade box, as shown in Figure 6-9. After the appropriate grade is displayed, the computer processes the DisplayGrade101 procedure's End Sub clause, which ends the procedure. The computer then returns to the btnDisplay_Click procedure to finish processing its code. In this case, the only code remaining to be processed is the btnDisplay_Click procedure's End Sub clause, which ends the procedure.

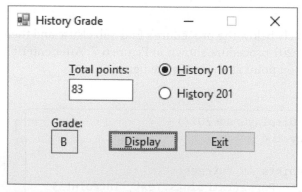

Figure 6-9   Grade displayed by the DisplayGrade101 procedure

7. Click the **History 201** radio button and then click the **Display** button. In this case, the selection structure's condition evaluates to False, so the computer processes the `DisplayGrade201()` statement entered in the false path. Here too, the computer temporarily leaves the btnDisplay_Click procedure, but this time to process the code in the DisplayGrade201 procedure. That procedure displays the letter P in the Grade box. After the appropriate grade is displayed, the computer processes the DisplayGrade201 procedure's End Sub clause, which ends the procedure. The computer then returns to the btnDisplay_Click procedure to finish processing its End Sub clause.

8. On your own, continue testing the application using various total points for each History course. When you are finished testing, click the **Exit** button. Close the Code Editor window and then close the solution.

Mini-Quiz 6-2

1. What is an item within parentheses in a procedure header called?

2. If the first parameter has the Integer data type and the second parameter has the Double data type, what data types should the first and second arguments have?

3. Write a statement that invokes the DisplayCompanyName procedure, which has no parameters.

1) a parameter 2) The first argument should have the Integer data type and the second argument should have the Double data type. 3) DisplayCompanyName()

F-3 Passing Information to a Procedure

As mentioned earlier, information is passed to a procedure through the calling statement's argumentList. An argument can be a literal, a named constant, a keyword, or a variable; however, in most cases, it will be a variable. Each variable has both a value and a unique address that represents its location in the computer's main memory. Visual Basic allows you to pass either a copy of the variable's value or the variable's address to the receiving procedure. Passing a copy of a variable's value is referred to as **passing by value**, whereas passing the variable's address is referred to as **passing by reference**. The method you choose—*by value* or *by reference*—depends on whether you want the receiving procedure to have access to the variable in memory. Keep in mind that when you give the receiving procedure access to the variable, it can change the variable's contents.

Passing Variables by Value Example: Gross Pay Application

To pass a variable *by value*, you include the keyword ByVal before the name of its corresponding parameter in the receiving procedure's parameterList. When you pass a variable *by value*, the computer passes a copy of the variable's contents to the receiving procedure. When only a copy of the contents is passed, the receiving procedure is not given access to the variable in memory; therefore, it cannot change the value stored inside the variable. You should pass a variable *by value* when the receiving procedure needs to *know* the variable's contents but does not need to *change* the contents.

In the next set of steps, you will complete the Gross Pay application, which uses two independent Sub procedures to display the gross pay for employees who are paid either weekly or twice per month. Employees who are paid weekly receive 52 paychecks per year. Employees who are paid twice per month receive 24 paychecks per year. Both procedures will contain one parameter in their parameterList, and the parameters will receive information that is passed *by value*. For the procedures to perform their assigned tasks, they will need their calling statements to pass them the employee's annual salary.

START HERE

To complete the Gross Pay application:

1. Open the Gross Solution.sln file contained in the VB2017\Chap06\Gross Solution folder.

2. Open the Code Editor window. Locate the ClearGross event-handling procedure. Notice that the procedure is associated with the text box's TextChanged event and also with the CheckedChanged events for the two radio buttons.

3. Scroll to the top of the Code Editor window, if necessary, and then click the **blank line** immediately below the ' Independent Sub procedures. comment. Enter the two procedures shown in Figure 6-10.

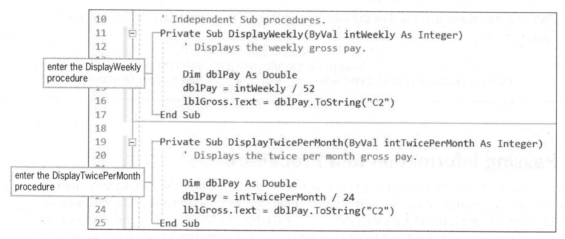

```
10        ' Independent Sub procedures.
11      ┌─Private Sub DisplayWeekly(ByVal intWeekly As Integer)
12            ' Displays the weekly gross pay.

          Dim dblPay As Double
          dblPay = intWeekly / 52
16            lblGross.Text = dblPay.ToString("C2")
17      └─End Sub
18
19      ┌─Private Sub DisplayTwicePerMonth(ByVal intTwicePerMonth As Integer)
20            ' Displays the twice per month gross pay.

          Dim dblPay As Double
          dblPay = intTwicePerMonth / 24
24            lblGross.Text = dblPay.ToString("C2")
25      └─End Sub
```

enter the DisplayWeekly procedure

enter the DisplayTwicePerMonth procedure

Figure 6-10   DisplayWeekly and DisplayTwicePerMonth procedures

4. Insert a **blank line** immediately below the DisplayTwicePerMonth procedure's End Sub clause.

5. Next, you will enter the code to call each procedure. Locate the btnCalc_Click procedure and then click the **blank line** immediately above its End Sub clause. Enter the code shown in Figure 6-11. (You can also use radWeekly.Checked = True as the condition.)

```
27      ┌─  Private Sub btnCalc_Click(sender As Object, e As Eve
28            ' Calls independent Sub procedures to calculate
29
30          ┌─Dim intSalary As Integer
31
32            Integer.TryParse(txtSalary.Text, intSalary)
33            If radWeekly.Checked Then
34                DisplayWeekly(intSalary)
35            Else
36                DisplayTwicePerMonth(intSalary)
37          └─End If
38        End Sub
```

enter this code

Figure 6-11   Completed btnCalc_Click procedure

F-3 Passing Information to a Procedure

6. Save the solution and then start the application. The Weekly radio button is already selected. Type **42500** in the Salary box and then click the **Calculate** button. The `DisplayWeekly(intSalary)` statement in the btnCalc_Click procedure invokes the DisplayWeekly procedure, passing it a copy of the value stored in the `intSalary` variable (42500). The DisplayWeekly procedure stores the value passed to it in its `intWeekly` parameter. The procedure then calculates and displays the weekly gross pay. See Figure 6-12.

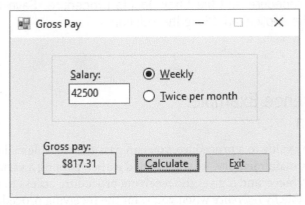

Figure 6-12   Weekly gross pay shown in the interface

7. Click the **Twice per month** radio button and then click the **Calculate** button. The `DisplayTwicePerMonth(intSalary)` statement in the btnCalc_Click procedure invokes the DisplayTwicePerMonth procedure, passing it a copy of the value stored in the `intSalary` variable (42500). The DisplayTwicePerMonth procedure stores the value passed to it in its `intTwicePerMonth` parameter. The procedure then calculates and displays the gross pay for an employee who is paid twice per month: $1,770.83.

8. Click the **Exit** button. Close the Code Editor window and then close the solution.

Figure 6-13 shows the two procedure headers and calling statements from the Gross Pay application. Notice that the data type of the argument in each calling statement matches the data type of its corresponding parameter in the procedure header. Also notice that the argument names do not need to be identical to the parameter names. In fact, to avoid confusion, you should use different names for an argument and its corresponding parameter. Finally, notice that the calling statement does not indicate whether a variable is being passed *by value* or *by reference*. To make that determination, you need to look at the receiving procedure's header.

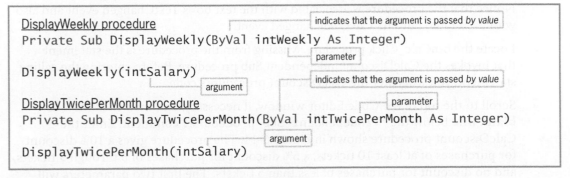

Figure 6-13   Procedure headers and calling statements

YOU DO IT 1!

Create an application named You Do It 1 and save it in the VB2017\Chap06 folder. Add a text box, a label, and a button to the form. The button's Click event procedure should assign the text box value to a Double variable and then pass a copy of the variable's value to an independent Sub procedure named ShowDouble. The ShowDouble procedure should multiply the value it receives by 2 and then display the result in the label control. Code the button's Click event procedure and the ShowDouble procedure. Save the solution and then start and test the application. Close the solution.

Passing Variables by Reference Example: Concert Tickets Application

Instead of passing a copy of a variable's value to a procedure, you can pass the variable's address, which is its location in the computer's main memory. As you learned earlier, passing a variable's address is referred to as passing *by reference*, and it gives the receiving procedure access to the variable being passed. You pass a variable *by reference* when you want the receiving procedure to change the contents of the variable.

To pass a variable *by reference* in Visual Basic, you include the keyword **ByRef** before the name of the corresponding parameter in the receiving procedure's header. The **ByRef** keyword tells the calling statement to pass the variable's address rather than a copy of its contents.

In this section, you will complete the Concert Tickets application, which uses an independent Sub procedure named CalcDiscount to calculate a customer's discount when purchasing specific numbers of tickets. In order to calculate the discount, the procedure will need to have its calling statement pass it two values: the number of tickets purchased and the cost of purchasing the tickets before any discount is applied. It will also need the calling statement to pass it the address of a memory location that it can use to store the discount. In order to accept the information passed to it, the procedure will need to have three parameters in its parameterList. The first two parameters will tell the calling statement to pass its first two arguments *by value*. The third parameter will tell the calling statement to pass its third argument *by reference*.

START HERE　**To complete the Concert Tickets application:**

1. Open the Concert Solution.sln file contained in the VB2017\Chap06\Concert Solution-Sub folder.

2. Open the Code Editor window. Locate the ClearLabels event-handling procedure. Notice that the procedure is associated with the text box's TextChanged event and also with each radio button's CheckedChanged event.

3. Locate the btnCalc_Click procedure. Missing from the procedure is the statement that invokes the CalcDiscount independent Sub procedure. Before entering the calling statement, you will enter the CalcDiscount procedure's code.

4. Scroll to the top of the Code Editor window, if necessary, and then click the **blank line** below the ' Independent Sub procedure. comment. Enter the CalcDiscount procedure shown in Figure 6-14. The procedure gives a 10% discount for purchases of at least 10 tickets, a 5% discount for purchases of 5 through 9 tickets, and no discount for purchases of less than 5 tickets. The first two parameters will

accept values that represent the number of tickets and the cost of the tickets before any discount. The third parameter will accept the address of a variable where the discount can be stored.

```
10          ' Independent Sub procedure.
11    ☐     Private Sub CalcDiscount(ByVal intNum As Integer,
12                              ByVal dblBeforeDiscount As Double,
13                              ByRef dblDisc As Double)
14    ☐         Select Case intNum
15                  Case Is >= 10
16                      dblDisc = dblBeforeDiscount * 0.1
17                  Case Is >= 5
18                      dblDisc = dblBeforeDiscount * 0.05
19                  Case Else
20                      dblDisc = 0
21              End Select
22          End Sub
```
— enter this procedure

Figure 6-14   CalcDiscount procedure

5. Now, click the **blank line** below the `' Use a procedure to calculate the discount.` comment in the btnCalc_Click procedure. The number of tickets is stored in the `intTickets` variable. The cost of the tickets before any discount is stored in the `dblSubtotal` variable. The btnCalc_Click procedure needs the CalcDiscount procedure to store the discount in the `dblDiscount` variable. Type the following calling statement and then press **Enter**:

```
CalcDiscount(intTickets, dblSubtotal, dblDiscount)
```

6. Save the solution and then start the application. Type **10** in the Tickets box and then click the **Calculate** button. See Figure 6-15.

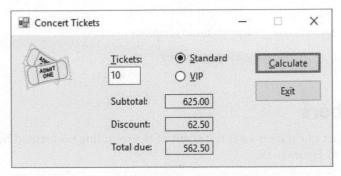

Figure 6-15   Calculated amounts shown in the interface

7. Change the number of tickets to **2**. Click the **VIP** radio button and then click the **Calculate** button. The subtotal, discount, and total due are 205.50, 0.00, and 205.50, respectively.

8. Change the number of tickets to **7**. Click the **Standard** radio button and then click the **Calculate** button. See Figure 6-16. Notice that the total due amount is off by one penny; it should be 415.62. You will learn how to fix this problem in the next section.

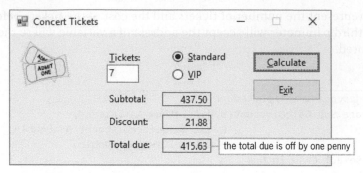

Figure 6-16   Interface showing the penny-off error

9. Click the **Exit** button.

Ch06-Sub Desk-Check

Figure 6-17 shows the procedure header and calling statement from the Concert Tickets application. Notice that the number, data type, and order (position) of the arguments in the calling statement match the number, data type, and order (position) of the parameters in the procedure header. Also notice that the names of the arguments are not identical to the names of their corresponding parameters. As mentioned earlier, it is best to use different names for an argument and its parameter. Here again, notice that the calling statement does not indicate whether a variable is being passed *by value* or *by reference*. To make that determination, you need to look at the receiving procedure's header.

indicates that the parameter is
receiving a copy of a value

```
Private Sub CalcDiscount(ByVal intNum As Integer,
                         ByVal dblBeforeDiscount As Double,
                         ByRef dblDisc As Double)

CalcDiscount(intTickets, dblSubtotal, dblDiscount)
```

indicates that the parameter is
receiving a variable's address

arguments passed *by value*   argument passed *by reference*

Figure 6-17   CalcDiscount procedure header and calling statement

F-4 Rounding Numbers

The penny-off error shown earlier in Figure 6-16 is the result of the rounding performed by the ToString method, as illustrated in Figure 6-18.

penny-off error occurs when these are
rounded by the ToString method

Calculation	Result stored in main memory	Displayed by the ToString method
Subtotal: 7 * 62.50	437.5	437.50
Discount: 437.5 * .05	21.875	21.88
Total due: 437.5 – 21.875	415.625	415.63

Figure 6-18   Penny-off error

To fix the penny-off error, you will use Visual Basic's **Math.Round method** to round the subtotal and discount amounts before they are used in the total due calculation. The method's syntax and examples are shown in Figure 6-19. In the syntax, *value* is a numeric expression and *digits* (which is optional) is an integer indicating how many places to the right of the decimal point are included in the rounding. If the *digits* argument is omitted, the Math.Round method returns an integer.

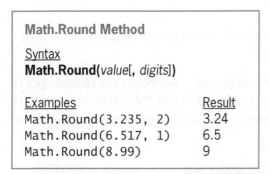

Math.Round Method

Syntax
Math.Round(value[, digits]**)**

Examples	Result
Math.Round(3.235, 2)	3.24
Math.Round(6.517, 1)	6.5
Math.Round(8.99)	9

Figure 6-19 Syntax and examples of the Math.Round method

To round the subtotal and discount amounts:

START HERE

1. In the btnCalc_Click procedure, enter the two assignment statements indicated in Figure 6-20. The Math.Round methods in the statements round the subtotal and discount amounts to two decimal places.

```
46          ' Calculate the total due.
47          dblSubtotal = Math.Round(dblSubtotal, 2)
48          dblDiscount = Math.Round(dblDiscount, 2)     enter these assignment statements
49          dblTotalDue = dblSubtotal - dblDiscount
```

Figure 6-20 Assignment statements containing the Math.Round method

2. Save the solution and then start the application. Type **7** in the Tickets box and then click the **Calculate** button. The Total due box shows the correct amount: 415.62. See Figure 6-21.

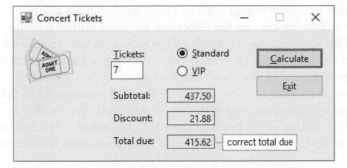

Figure 6-21 Correct total due shown in the interface

3. Click the **Exit** button. Close the Code Editor window and then close the solution.

Mini-Quiz 6-3

1. Write the parameterList for a procedure that receives a Decimal value followed by the address of a Decimal variable. Use decSales and decBonus as the parameter names.

2. Write a calling statement that invokes an independent Sub procedure named CalcBonus, passing it the value stored in the decFebSales variable and the address of the decFebBonus variable.

3. Write a statement that rounds the value stored in the dblRate variable to one decimal place and then assigns the result to the variable.

1) ByVal decSales As Decimal, ByRef decBonus As Decimal 2) CalcBonus(decFebSales, decFebBonus) 3) dblRate = Math.Round(dblRate, 1)

YOU DO IT 2!

Create an application named You Do It 2 and save it in the VB2017\Chap06 folder. Add a text box, a label, and a button to the form. The button's Click event procedure should assign the text box value to a Double variable. It should then invoke an independent Sub procedure named CalcDouble, passing the procedure the Double variable's address. The CalcDouble procedure should multiply the contents of the Double variable by 2. After the CalcDouble procedure ends, the button's Click event procedure should display the contents of the Double variable in the label. Code the button's Click event procedure and the CalcDouble procedure. Save the solution and then start and test the application. Close the solution.

F-5 Function Procedures

In addition to creating Sub procedures in Visual Basic, you can also create Function procedures. The difference between both types of procedures is that a **Function procedure** returns a value after performing its assigned task, whereas a Sub procedure does not return a value. Function procedures are referred to more simply as **functions**.

Figure 6-22 shows the syntax and examples of functions in Visual Basic. Unlike a Sub procedure, a function's header and footer contain the Function keyword rather than the Sub keyword. A function's header also includes the As *dataType* section, which specifies the data type of the value the function will return. The value is returned by the **Return statement**, which typically is the last statement within a function. The statement's syntax is Return *expression*, where *expression* represents the one and only value that will be returned to the statement that invoked the function. The data type of the *expression* must agree with the data type specified in the As *dataType* section of the header. Like a Sub procedure, a function can receive information passed to it either *by value* or *by reference*. The information it receives is listed in its parameterList.

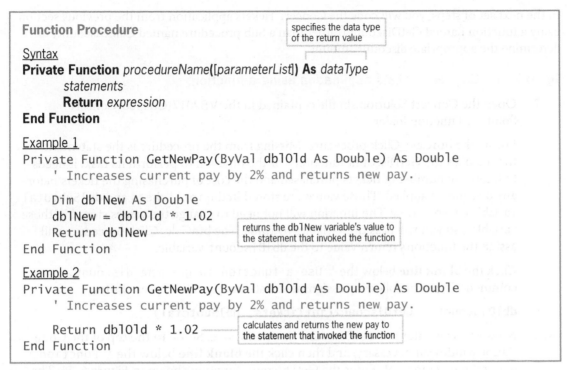

Figure 6-22   Syntax and examples of functions

As are Sub procedures, functions are entered between the Public Class and End Class clauses in the Code Editor window, and they must be entered outside of any other procedure. In this book, the functions will be entered above the first event procedure. Like Sub procedure names, function names are entered using Pascal case and typically begin with a verb. The name should indicate the task the function performs. The GetNewPay name used in the examples in Figure 6-22 indicates that each function returns a new pay amount.

You invoke a function by including the function's name and arguments (if any) in a statement. The number, data type, and position of the arguments should agree with the number, data type, and position of the function's parameters. In most cases, the statement that invokes a function assigns the function's return value to a variable. However, it also may use the return value in a calculation or simply display the return value. Figure 6-23 shows examples of invoking the GetNewPay function from Figure 6-22. The GetNewPay(dblPay) entry in each example invokes the function, passing it the value stored in the dblPay variable.

```
Invoking a Function

Example 1—assigns the return value to a variable
dblNewPay = GetNewPay(dblPay)
        or
dblPay = GetNewPay(dblPay)

Example 2—uses the return value in a calculation
dblNewWeekly = GetNewPay(dblPay) * 40

Example 3—displays the return value
lblNewPay.Text = GetNewPay(dblPay).ToString("C2")
```

Figure 6-23   Examples of invoking the GetNewPay function

Ch06-Function Desk-Check

In the next set of steps, you will code the Concert Tickets application from the previous section using a function named GetDiscount (rather than a Sub procedure named CalcDiscount) to determine the appropriate discount amount.

START HERE

To code the Concert Tickets application using a function:

1. Open the Concert Solution.sln file contained in the VB2017\Chap06\Concert Solution-Function folder.

2. Locate the btnCalc_Click procedure. Missing from the procedure is the statement that invokes the GetDiscount function. For the function to perform its task, it needs to know the number of tickets purchased and the cost of purchasing the tickets before any discount is applied. Those values are stored in the `intTickets` and `dblSubtotal` variables, respectively. The function will not need to change the values stored in those variables, so you will pass the variables *by value*. The btnCalc_Click procedure will assign the function's return value to the `dblDiscount` variable.

3. Click the **blank line** below the `' Use a function to get the discount.` comment. Type the following assignment statement and then press **Enter**:

```
dblDiscount = GetDiscount(intTickets, dblSubtotal)
```

4. Now, you will enter the GetDiscount function's code. Scroll to the top of the Code Editor window, if necessary, and then click the **blank line** below the `' Function procedure.` comment. Enter the GetDiscount function shown in Figure 6-24. The function's parameters will accept values that represent the number of tickets and the cost of the tickets before any discount. Notice that, unlike the CalcDiscount Sub procedure, the GetDiscount function does not need the calling statement to pass it the address of a variable in which to store the discount. This is because the function returns the discount to the statement that invoked it, which is the `dblDiscount = GetDiscount(intTickets, dblSubtotal)` assignment statement in the btnCalc_Click procedure. That assignment statement assigns the function's return value to the `dblDiscount` variable.

```
10        ' Function procedure.
11    ┌─Private Function GetDiscount(ByVal intNum As Integer,
12                                      ByVal dblBeforeDiscount As Double) As Double
13          Dim dblDisc As Double
14    ┌─     Select Case intNum
15              Case Is >= 10
16                  dblDisc = dblBeforeDiscount * 0.1
17              Case Is >= 5
18                  dblDisc = dblBeforeDiscount * 0.05
19              Case Else
20                  dblDisc = 0
21          End Select
22
23          Return dblDisc
24    └─End Function
```

enter this function

Figure 6-24 GetDiscount function

5. Save the solution and then start the application. Type **10** in the Tickets box and then click the **Calculate** button. The subtotal, discount, and total due are 625.00, 62.50, and 562.50, respectively.

6. Change the number of tickets to **2**. Click the **VIP** radio button and then click the **Calculate** button. The subtotal, discount, and total due are 205.50, 0.00, and 205.50, respectively.

7. Change the number of tickets to **7**. Click the **Standard** radio button and then click the **Calculate** button. The subtotal, discount, and total due are 437.50, 21.88, and 415.62, respectively.

8. Click the **Exit** button. Close the Code Editor window and then close the solution.

Mini-Quiz 6-4

1. A function named GetBonus receives a Double value and returns a Double value. Write the function header, using `dblSales` as the parameter name.

2. Write the Return statement for the GetBonus function from Question 1. The statement should return the value stored in its `dblBonus` variable.

3. Write a statement that invokes the GetBonus function from Question 1, passing it the value stored in the `dblFebSales` variable. The statement should assign the return value to the `dblFebBonus` variable.

1) Private Function GetBonus(ByVal dblSales As Double) As Double
2) Return dblBonus 3) dblFebBonus = GetBonus(dblFebSales)

YOU DO IT 3!

Create an application named You Do It 3 and save it in the VB2017\Chap06 folder. Add a text box, a label, and a button to the form. The button's Click event procedure should assign the text box value to a Double variable and then pass a copy of the variable's value to a function named GetDouble. The GetDouble function should multiply the value it receives by 2 and then return the result to the button's Click event procedure, which should assign the returned value to the Double variable and then display the contents of the Double variable in the label. Code the button's Click event procedure and the GetDouble function. Save the solution and then start and test the application. Close the solution.

APPLY THE CONCEPTS LESSON

After studying this lesson, you should be able to:

- A-1 Add a combo box to the form
- A-2 Add items to a combo box and select a default item
- A-3 Code a combo box's KeyPress event procedure
- A-4 Create an event-handling Sub procedure
- A-5 Calculate federal withholding tax
- A-6 Invoke an independent Sub procedure and a function
- A-7 Create an independent Sub procedure
- A-8 Create a function
- A-9 Validate an application's code
- A-10 Professionalize your application's interface

A-1 Add a Combo Box to the Form

In many interfaces, combo boxes are used in place of list boxes. You add a combo box to an interface using the ComboBox tool in the toolbox. A **combo box** is similar to a list box in that it offers the user a list of choices from which to select. However, unlike a list box, the full list of choices in a combo box can be hidden, allowing you to save space on the form. Also unlike a list box, a combo box contains a text field, which may or may not be editable by the user. Figure 6-25 lists the most commonly used properties of a combo box.

Name	Purpose
DropDownStyle	indicate the style of the combo box
Font	specify the font to use for text
SelectedIndex	get or set the index of the selected item
SelectedItem	get or set the value of the selected item
Sorted	specify whether the items in the list should appear in the order they are entered or in sorted order (When sorted, the items appear in dictionary order based on their leftmost characters.)
Name	give the combo box a meaningful name (use cbo as the ID)
Text	get or set the value that appears in the text portion

Figure 6-25 Most commonly used properties of a combo box

Three styles of combo boxes are available in Visual Basic. The style is controlled by the combo box's **DropDownStyle property**, which can be set to Simple, DropDown (the default), or DropDownList. Each style of combo box contains a text portion and a list portion. Figure 6-26 shows an example of each combo box style, and it indicates whether the text portion is editable as well as how to view the list portion.

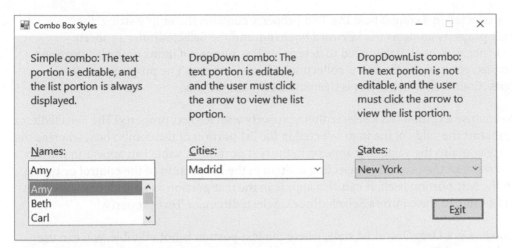

Figure 6-26 Examples of the combo box styles

To experiment with the combo boxes shown in Figure 6-26, open the application contained in the ComboBox Styles Solution folder.

You should use a label control to provide keyboard access to the combo box, as shown in the figure. For the access key to work correctly, you must set the label's TabIndex property to a value that is one number less than the combo box's TabIndex value.

Like the items in a list box, the items in the list portion of a combo box are either arranged by use, with the most used entries listed first, or sorted in ascending order. To sort the items in the list portion of a combo box, you set the combo box's Sorted property to True. Like the first item in a list box, the first item in a combo box has an index of 0.

The GUI design guidelines for combo boxes are listed in Figure 6-56 and in Appendix A.

As you can with a list box, you can use either the String Collection Editor or the Items collection's Add method to add an item to a combo box. Figure 6-27 shows the code used to fill the combo boxes in Figure 6-26 with values. It also shows how to select a default value, which will appear in the text portion of the combo box when the application is started. Notice that you can use any of the following properties to select the default value: SelectedIndex, SelectedItem, or Text.

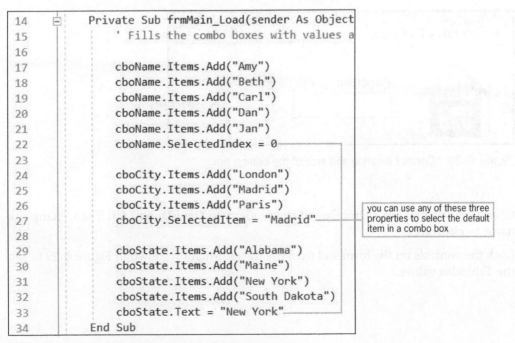

```
14    Private Sub frmMain_Load(sender As Object
15        ' Fills the combo boxes with values a
16
17        cboName.Items.Add("Amy")
18        cboName.Items.Add("Beth")
19        cboName.Items.Add("Carl")
20        cboName.Items.Add("Dan")
21        cboName.Items.Add("Jan")
22        cboName.SelectedIndex = 0
23
24        cboCity.Items.Add("London")
25        cboCity.Items.Add("Madrid")
26        cboCity.Items.Add("Paris")
27        cboCity.SelectedItem = "Madrid"
28
29        cboState.Items.Add("Alabama")
30        cboState.Items.Add("Maine")
31        cboState.Items.Add("New York")
32        cboState.Items.Add("South Dakota")
33        cboState.Text = "New York"
34    End Sub
```

you can use any of these three properties to select the default item in a combo box

Figure 6-27 Code for the combo boxes in Figure 6-26

If no item is selected in a combo box, the Text property contains the empty string, the SelectedItem property contains the keyword Nothing, and the SelectedIndex property contains −1 (negative one). If you need to determine the number of items in the list portion of a combo box, you can use the Items collection's Count property. The property's syntax is *object*.Items.Count, in which *object* is the name of the combo box.

It is easy to confuse a combo box's SelectedItem property with its Text property. The SelectedItem property contains the value of the item selected in the list portion of the combo box, whereas the Text property contains the value that appears in the text portion. A value can appear in the text portion as a result of the user either selecting an item in the list portion of the control or typing an entry in the text portion itself. It can also appear in the text portion as a result of a statement that assigns a value to the control's SelectedIndex, SelectedItem, or Text property.

If the combo box is a DropDownList style, where the text portion is not editable, you can use the SelectedItem and Text properties interchangeably. However, if the combo box is either a Simple or DropDown style, where the user can type an entry in the text portion, you should use the Text property because it contains the value either selected or entered by the user. When the value in the text portion of a combo box changes, the combo box's TextChanged event occurs. In the next set of steps, you will replace the list box in the Monthly Payment application with a combo box.

START HERE

To modify the Monthly Payment application:

1.　Open the Payment Solution.sln file contained in the VB2017\Chap06\Payment Solution-ComboBox folder.

2.　Unlock the controls on the form. Click the **lstRates** control and then press **Delete**. Click the **ComboBox** tool in the toolbox and then drag the mouse pointer to the form. Position the mouse pointer below the Rate (%): label and then release the mouse button. Size and position the combo box to match Figure 6-28.

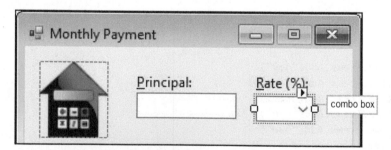

Figure 6-28　Correct location and size of the combo box

3.　Change the combo box's DropDownStyle property to **DropDownList**. Then, change its name to **cboRates**.

4.　Lock the controls on the form and then use the information shown in Figure 6-29 to set the TabIndex values.

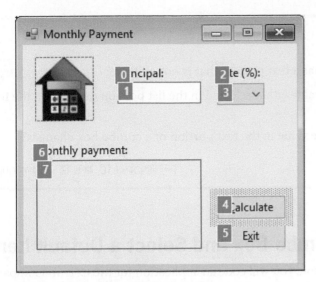

Figure 6-29 Correct TabIndex values

5. Press **Esc** to remove the TabIndex boxes from the form.

6. Open the Code Editor window and locate the frmMain_Load procedure. Change `list` in the comment to **combo**. Then change both occurrences of lstRates in the procedure's code to **cboRates**.

7. Locate the btnCalc_Click procedure. Replace `lstRates.SelectedItem.ToString` in the second TryParse method with **cboRates.Text**.

8. Locate the ClearPay procedure. Type **, cboRates.TextChanged** at the end of the Handles clause. (Be sure to type the comma.)

9. Save the solution and then start the application. Type **125000** in the Principal box. Click the **list arrow** in the combo box and then click **2.5** in the list. Click the **Calculate** button. See Figure 6-30.

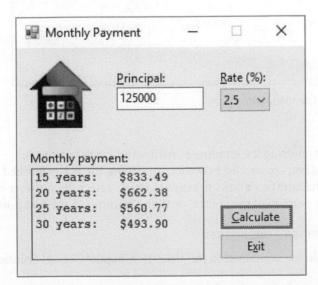

Figure 6-30 Monthly payments shown in the interface

10. Click the **Exit** button. Close the Code Editor window and then close the solution.

Mini-Quiz 6-5

1. Which style of combo box has a text portion that is not editable?

2. Which property stores the value either selected in the list portion or typed in the text portion of a combo box?

3. What event occurs when the value in the text portion of a combo box changes?

1) DropDownList 2) Text 3) TextChanged

A-2 Add Items to a Combo Box and Select a Default Item

In the remaining sections of this lesson, you will code an application for the Cerruti Company. The application will calculate an employee's weekly gross pay, federal withholding tax (FWT), Social Security and Medicare (FICA) tax, and net pay. The application's interface is shown in Figure 6-31.

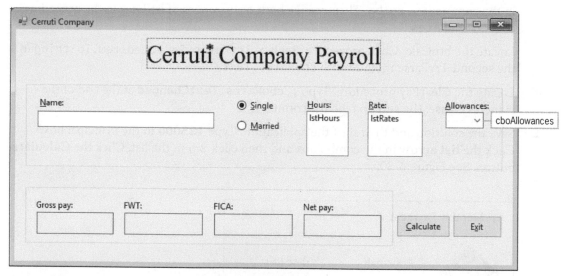

Figure 6-31   Interface for the Cerruti Company application

The interface provides a text box for entering the employee's name, and radio buttons for entering his or her marital status. It also provides list boxes for specifying the hours worked and rate of pay. The combo box in the interface allows the user to either select the number of withholding allowances from the list portion of the control or type a number in the text portion.

START HERE

To begin coding the Cerruti Company application:

1. Open the Cerruti Solution.sln file contained in the VB2017\Chap06\Cerruti Solution folder.

2. Open the Code Editor window and locate the frmMain_Load procedure. The procedure's code adds items to both list boxes and selects a default item in each one. Missing from the procedure is the code to add numbers from 0 through 10 to the

cboAllowances control and then select a default item. Click the **blank line** above the End Sub clause and then enter the For...Next loop and assignment statement shown in Figure 6-32. Be sure to change the Next clause to `Next intAllow`.

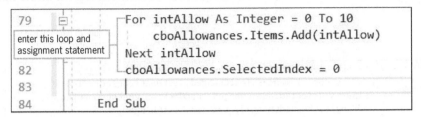

```
79          ┌For intAllow As Integer = 0 To 10
                   cboAllowances.Items.Add(intAllow)
            Next intAllow
82          └cboAllowances.SelectedIndex = 0
83          │
84          End Sub
```

enter this loop and assignment statement

Figure 6-32   Additional code entered in the frmMain_Load procedure

3. Save the solution and then start the application. Click the **list arrow** in the Allowances box. The list portion of the control displays the numbers from 0 through 10. Click the **list arrow** again to close the list and then click the **Exit** button.

A-3 Code a Combo Box's KeyPress Event Procedure

The cboAllowances control is a DropDown combo box, which means its text portion is editable. In the next set of steps, you will code the control's KeyPress procedure to accept only numbers and the Backspace key.

To code the combo box's KeyPress procedure:

START HERE

1. Open the code template for the cboAllowances_KeyPress procedure. Enter the comment and code shown in Figure 6-33.

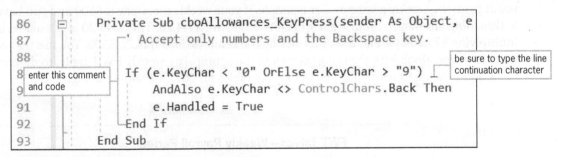

```
86      ⊟   Private Sub cboAllowances_KeyPress(sender As Object, e
87              ┌' Accept only numbers and the Backspace key.
88              │
89              │ If (e.KeyChar < "0" OrElse e.KeyChar > "9") ⌐
90              │     AndAlso e.KeyChar <> ControlChars.Back Then
91              │         e.Handled = True
92              └End If
93          End Sub
```

enter this comment and code

be sure to type the line continuation character

Figure 6-33   Completed cboAllowances_KeyPress procedure

2. Save the solution and then start the application. Click the **text portion of the Allowances** box and then verify that the text portion will accept only numbers and the Backspace key.

3. Click the **Exit** button.

A-4 Create an Event-Handling Sub Procedure

The calculated amounts (gross pay, FWT, FICA, and net pay) should be cleared from the interface when a change is made to the employee's name, marital status, hours worked, rate of pay, or number of withholding allowances. In the next set of steps, you will create an event-handling Sub procedure that will be processed when any of these changes occur.

START HERE

To create an event-handling Sub procedure:

1. Open the code template for the cboAllowances_TextChanged procedure. First, replace cboAllowances_TextChanged with **ClearOutput**. Then, modify the Handles clause as shown in Figure 6-34. Also, enter the four assignment statements shown in the figure.

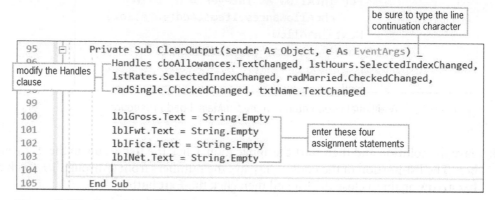

Figure 6-34   Completed ClearOutput procedure

2. Save the solution.

A-5 Calculate Federal Withholding Tax

The amount of FWT to deduct from an employee's weekly gross pay is based on his or her weekly taxable wages and filing status, which is either Single (including head of household) or Married. You calculate the weekly taxable wages by first multiplying the number of withholding allowances by $77.90 (the value of a withholding allowance in 2017) and then subtracting the result from the weekly gross pay. For example, if your weekly gross pay is $500 and you have two withholding allowances, your weekly taxable wages are $344.20. The $344.20 is calculated by multiplying $77.90 by 2 and then subtracting the result ($155.80) from $500. You use the weekly taxable wages, along with the filing status and the appropriate weekly FWT table, to determine the amount of tax to withhold. The weekly tax tables for 2017 are shown in Figure 6-35.

FWT Tables—Weekly Payroll Period

Single person (including head of household)
If the taxable
wages are: The amount of income tax to withhold is:

Over	But not over	Base amount	Percentage	Of excess over
	$ 44	0		
$ 44	$ 224	0	10%	$ 44
$ 224	$ 774	$ 18.00 plus	15%	$ 224
$ 774	$1,812	$ 100.50 plus	25%	$ 774
$1,812	$3,730	$ 360.00 plus	28%	$1,812
$3,730	$8,058	$ 897.04 plus	33%	$3,730
$8,058	$8,090	$2,325.28 plus	35%	$8,058
$8,090		$2,336.48 plus	39.6%	$8,090

Figure 6-35   Weekly FWT tables for the year 2017 (continues)

(continued)

Married person
If the taxable
wages are: The amount of income tax to withhold is:

Over	But not over	Base amount	Percentage	Of excess over
	$ 166	0		
$ 166	$ 525	0	10%	$ 166
$ 525	$1,626	$ 35.90 plus	15%	$ 525
$1,626	$3,111	$ 201.05 plus	25%	$1,626
$3,111	$4,654	$ 572.30 plus	28%	$3,111
$4,654	$8,180	$1,004.34 plus	33%	$4,654
$8,180	$9,218	$2,167.92 plus	35%	$8,180
$9,218		$2,531.22 plus	39.6%	$9,218

Figure 6-35   Weekly FWT tables for the year 2017

Each table in Figure 6-35 contains five columns of information. The first two columns list various ranges, also called brackets, of taxable wage amounts. The first column (Over) lists the amount that a taxable wage in that bracket must be over, and the second column (But not over) lists the maximum amount included in the bracket. The remaining three columns (Base amount, Percentage, and Of excess over) tell you how to calculate the tax for each range. For example, assume that your marital status is Single and your weekly taxable wages are $344.20. Before you can calculate the amount of your tax, you need to locate your taxable wages in the first two columns of the Single table. Taxable wages of $344.20 fall within the $224 through $774 bracket.

After locating the bracket that contains your taxable wages, you then use the remaining three columns in the table to calculate your tax. As the first example in Figure 6-36 indicates, you calculate the tax by first subtracting $224 (the amount shown in the Of excess over column) from your taxable wages of $344.20, giving $120.20. You then multiply $120.20 by 15% (the amount shown in the Percentage column), giving $18.03. You then add that amount to the amount shown in the Base amount column (in this case, $18.00), giving $36.03 as your tax. Figure 6-36 also shows how to calculate the FWT for a taxpayer whose marital status and weekly taxable wages are Married and $1,700.00, respectively; the FWT is $219.55.

Example 1—Single with weekly taxable wages of $344.20		Example 2—Married with weekly taxable wages of $1,700.00	
Taxable wages	$ 344.20	Taxable wages	$ 1,700.00
Of excess over	− 224.00	Of excess over	− 1,626.00
	120.20		74.00
Percentage	* 0.15	Percentage	* 0.25
	18.03		18.50
Base amount	+ 18.00	Base amount	+ 201.05
Tax	$ 36.03	Tax	$ 219.55

Figure 6-36   Examples of FWT calculations

A-6 Invoke an Independent Sub Procedure and a Function

To give you practice with creating both an independent Sub procedure and a function, the Cerutti Company application will use an independent Sub procedure to calculate the FWT for employees whose marital status is Single, but a function to calculate the FWT for employees whose marital status is Married. Before creating the Sub procedure and function, you will complete the btnCalc_Click procedure, which will use the Sub procedure and function to calculate the appropriate tax.

START HERE

To complete the btnCalc_Click procedure:

1. Locate the btnCalc_Click procedure. Most of the procedure's code has already been entered for you. The procedure declares two named constants and eight variables, as shown in Figure 6-37. The dblONE_ALLOWANCE constant is initialized to the value of a withholding allowance in 2017. The dblFICA_RATE constant is initialized to the FICA tax rate for 2017. (The number 0.0765 is the decimal equivalent of 7.65%.)

```
13          Private Sub btnCalc_Click(sender As Object, e As EventArgs) Handl
14              ' Calculates and displays gross pay, taxes, and net pay.
15
16              Const dblONE_ALLOWANCE As Double = 77.9
17              Const dblFICA_RATE As Double = 0.0765
18              Dim dblHours As Double
19              Dim dblPayRate As Double
20              Dim intAllowances As Integer
21              Dim dblGross As Double
22              Dim dblTaxable As Double
23              Dim dblFwt As Double
24              Dim dblFica As Double
25              Dim dblNet As Double
```

Figure 6-37 Named constants and variable declarations

2. The first two TryParse methods shown in Figure 6-38 store the selected list box items in variables. The third TryParse method stores (in a variable) the value contained in the combo box's Text property. Recall that the Text property contains the value either selected in the list portion or entered in the text portion.

```
27          Double.TryParse(lstHours.SelectedItem.ToString, dblHours)
28          Double.TryParse(lstRates.SelectedItem.ToString, dblPayRate)
29          Integer.TryParse(cboAllowances.Text, intAllowances)
```

Figure 6-38 TryParse methods in the btnCalc_Click procedure

3. The selection structure shown in Figure 6-39 calculates the employee's gross pay, giving time and a half for any hours worked over 40.

```
31          ' Calculate gross pay.
32          If dblHours <= 40 Then
33              dblGross = dblHours * dblPayRate
34          Else
35              dblGross = 40 * dblPayRate + (dblHours - 40) * dblPayRate * 1.5
36          End If
```

Figure 6-39 Selection structure in the btnCalc_Click procedure

4. The assignment statement shown in Figure 6-40 calculates the taxable wages by first multiplying the number of withholding allowances by the value of one withholding allowance, and then subtracting the result from the gross pay.

```
38            ' Calculate taxable wages.
39            dblTaxable = dblGross - (intAllowances * dblONE_ALLOWANCE)
```

Figure 6-40   Taxable wages calculation in the btnCalc_Click procedure

5. Click the **blank line** below the ' Determine the FWT. comment. Recall that the appropriate FWT table to use depends on the person's marital status, which the user specifies by selecting either the Single radio button or the Married radio button in the interface. Type the following If clause (you can also use radSingle.Checked = True as the condition) and then press **Enter**:

   If radSingle.Checked Then

6. If the Single radio button is selected, the selection structure's true path will call an independent Sub procedure named GetSingleFwt to calculate the appropriate tax. To make the calculation, the procedure will need to know the employee's taxable wages. It will also need the address of a variable where it can store the tax. Type the following calling statement and then press **Enter**:

   GetSingleFwt(dblTaxable, dblFwt)

7. Type **Else** and press **Enter**. If the Married radio button is selected, the selection structure's false path will invoke a function named GetMarriedFwt and assign its return value to the **dblFwt** variable. To calculate the FWT, the function will need to know the employee's taxable wages. Type the assignment statement shown in the selection structure's false path in Figure 6-41. (The red squiggles will disappear when you create the Sub procedure and function.)

```
41            ' Determine the FWT.
42            If radSingle.Checked Then
43                GetSingleFwt(dblTaxable, dblFwt)      ─── stand-alone statement uses an independent
                                                            Sub procedure to get the tax
44            Else
45                dblFwt = GetMarriedFwt(dblTaxable)    ─── type this assignment statement, which
                                                            uses a function to get the tax
46            End If
```

Figure 6-41   Completed selection structure

8. Below the selection structure is an assignment statement that calculates the FICA tax. As Figure 6-42 indicates, this tax is calculated by multiplying the employee's gross pay by the FICA tax rate.

```
48            ' Calculate FICA tax.
49            dblFica = dblGross * dblFICA_RATE
```

Figure 6-42   FICA tax calculation

9. Click the **blank line** below the ' Round gross pay, FWT, and FICA tax. comment and then enter the three assignment statements indicated in Figure 6-43. The statements round the gross pay, FWT, and FICA tax to two decimal places before using them in the net pay calculation, which is also shown in the figure.

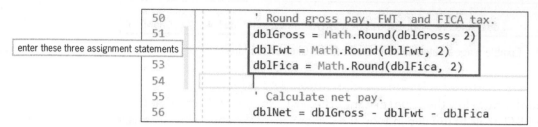

```
50          ' Round gross pay, FWT, and FICA tax.
51          dblGross = Math.Round(dblGross, 2)
            dblFwt = Math.Round(dblFwt, 2)
53          dblFica = Math.Round(dblFica, 2)
54
55          ' Calculate net pay.
56          dblNet = dblGross - dblFwt - dblFica
```

enter these three assignment statements

Figure 6-43　Rounding statements and net pay calculation

10. The last statements in the procedure are shown in Figure 6-44. These statements display the gross pay, FWT, FICA tax, and net pay in the interface.

```
58          ' Display calculated amounts.
59          lblGross.Text = dblGross.ToString("N2")
60          lblFwt.Text = dblFwt.ToString("N2")
61          lblFica.Text = dblFica.ToString("N2")
62          lblNet.Text = dblNet.ToString("N2")
```

Figure 6-44　Statements that display the calculated amounts

11. Save the solution.

A-7 Create an Independent Sub Procedure

In this section, you will code the GetSingleFwt Sub procedure, which will calculate the FWT for an employee whose marital status is Single. As indicated earlier, the procedure needs two items of information from its calling statement in the btnCalc_Click procedure: the employee's taxable wages and the address of a variable where the calculated tax can be stored.

START HERE

To create the GetSingleFwt Sub procedure:

1. Scroll to the top of the Code Editor window and then click the **blank line** below the ' Independent Sub procedure and function. comment. Enter the GetSingleFwt procedure header shown in Figure 6-45. The Code Editor will automatically enter the End Sub clause (the procedure footer) for you.

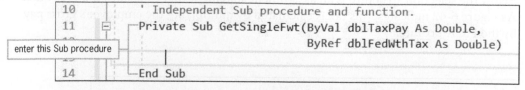

```
10          ' Independent Sub procedure and function.
11          Private Sub GetSingleFwt(ByVal dblTaxPay As Double,
                                     ByRef dblFedWthTax As Double)

14          End Sub
```

enter this Sub procedure

Figure 6-45　GetSingleFwt Sub procedure header and footer

2. For your convenience, you will find the code associated with the Single FWT table in the Single.txt file. Click **File** on the menu bar, point to **Open**, and then click **File**. If necessary, open the Cerruti Project folder. Click **Single.txt** in the list of filenames and then click the **Open** button. The Single.txt file appears in a separate window in the IDE. Click **Edit** on the menu bar and then click **Select All**. Press **Ctrl+c** to copy the selected text and then close the Single.txt window.

3. The insertion point should be in the blank line above the End Sub clause. Press **Ctrl+v** to paste the copied text into the GetSingleFwt procedure. See Figure 6-46.

```
11    Private Sub GetSingleFwt(ByVal dblTaxPay As Double,
12                             ByRef dblFedWthTax As Double)
13        Select Case dblTaxPay
14            Case Is <= 44
15                dblFedWthTax = 0
16            Case Is <= 224
17                dblFedWthTax = 0.1 * (dblTaxPay - 44)
18            Case Is <= 774
19                dblFedWthTax = 18 + 0.15 * (dblTaxPay - 224)
20            Case Is <= 1812
21                dblFedWthTax = 100.5 + 0.25 * (dblTaxPay - 774)
22            Case Is <= 3730
23                dblFedWthTax = 360 + 0.28 * (dblTaxPay - 1812)
24            Case Is <= 8058
25                dblFedWthTax = 897.04 + 0.33 * (dblTaxPay - 3730)
26            Case Is <= 8090
27                dblFedWthTax = 2325.28 + 0.35 * (dblTaxPay - 8058)
28            Case Else
29                dblFedWthTax = 2336.48 + 0.396 * (dblTaxPay - 8090)
30        End Select
31
32    End Sub
```

Figure 6-46   Completed GetSingleFwt Sub procedure

4. Save the solution.

A-8 Create a Function

In this section, you will code the GetMarriedFwt function, which will calculate the FWT for an employee whose marital status is Married. As indicated earlier, the procedure needs only one item of information from the statement that invokes it in the btnCalc_Click procedure: the employee's taxable wages. The function will return the calculated FWT to that statement, which will assign the returned value to the **dblFwt** variable.

To create the GetMarriedFwt function:

START HERE

1. Click the **blank line** below the GetSingleFwt procedure's End Sub clause and then press **Enter**. Enter the GetMarriedFwt function header shown in Figure 6-47. The Code Editor will automatically enter the End Function clause (the function footer) for you. (The green squiggle will disappear when you enter the Return statement.)

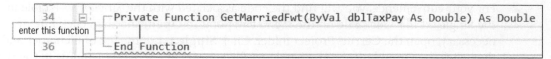

Figure 6-47   GetMarriedFwt function header and footer

2. First, you will declare a variable that will store the FWT after it has been calculated. Type the following Dim statement and then press **Enter** twice:

Dim dblFedWthTax As Double

3. You will find the code associated with the Married FWT table in the Married.txt file. Click **File** on the menu bar, point to **Open**, and then click **File**. If necessary, open the Cerruti Project folder. Click **Married.txt** in the list of filenames and then click the **Open** button. The Married.txt file appears in a separate window in the IDE. Click **Edit** on the menu bar and then click **Select All**. Press **Ctrl+c** to copy the selected text and then close the Married.txt window.

4. The insertion point should be in the blank line above the End Function clause. Press **Ctrl+v** to paste the copied text into the GetMarriedFwt procedure.

5. Finally, you will enter the Return statement that will return the calculated FWT to the statement that invoked the function in the btnCalc_Click procedure. Insert a blank line below the End Select clause and then type the Return statement shown in Figure 6-48.

```
34      Private Function GetMarriedFwt(ByVal dblTaxPay As Double) As Doub
35          Dim dblFedWthTax As Double
36
37          Select Case dblTaxPay
38              Case Is <= 166
39                  dblFedWthTax = 0
40              Case Is <= 525
41                  dblFedWthTax = 0.1 * (dblTaxPay - 166)
42              Case Is <= 1626
43                  dblFedWthTax = 35.9 + 0.15 * (dblTaxPay - 525)
44              Case Is <= 3111
45                  dblFedWthTax = 201.05 + 0.25 * (dblTaxPay - 1626)
46              Case Is <= 4654
47                  dblFedWthTax = 572.3 + 0.28 * (dblTaxPay - 3111)
48              Case Is <= 8180
49                  dblFedWthTax = 1004.34 + 0.33 * (dblTaxPay - 4654)
50              Case Is <= 9218
51                  dblFedWthTax = 2167.92 + 0.35 * (dblTaxPay - 8180)
52              Case Else
53                  dblFedWthTax = 2531.22 + 0.396 * (dblTaxPay - 9218)
54          End Select
55          Return dblFedWthTax      ┌ enter this Return statement
56      End Function
```

Figure 6-48   Completed GetMarriedFwt function

A-9 Validate an Application's Code

You will test the Cerruti Company application twice using the data shown in Figure 6-49. The figure also shows the correct amounts for the gross pay, taxes, and net pay; the amounts are shaded in the figure.

Test Data

<u>First test</u>

Carol Swanski, Single, 37.5 hours worked, $13.50 per hour, one allowance

Gross wages:	506.25
Allowance:	− 77.90
Taxable wages:	428.35
Of excess over:	−224.00
	204.35
Percentage:	* 0.15
	30.6525
Base amount:	+ 18.00
FWT:	48.65 (rounded to two decimal places)
FICA tax (506.25 * 0.0765):	38.73 (rounded to two decimal places)
Net pay (506.25 − 48.65 − 38.73):	418.87

<u>Second test</u>

Michael Williams, Married, 53.5 hours worked, $15 per hour, two allowances

Gross wages	903.75
Allowance deduction	− 155.80
Taxable wages	747.95
Of excess over	− 525.00
	222.95
Percentage	* 0.15
	33.4425
Base amount	+ 35.90
FWT tax	69.34 (rounded to two decimal places)
FICA tax (903.75 * 0.0765)	69.14 (rounded to two decimal places)
Net pay (903.75 − 69.34 − 69.14)	765.27

Figure 6-49   Test data for the Cerruti Company application

START HERE **To test the application:**

1. Save the solution and then start the application. Type **Carol Swanski** in the Name box. Click **37.5** in the Hours list box, **13.50** in the Rate list box, and **1** in the Allowances combo box. Click the **Calculate** button. See Figure 6-50. The gross pay, taxes, and net pay for this first test agree with the corresponding manual calculations shaded in Figure 6-49.

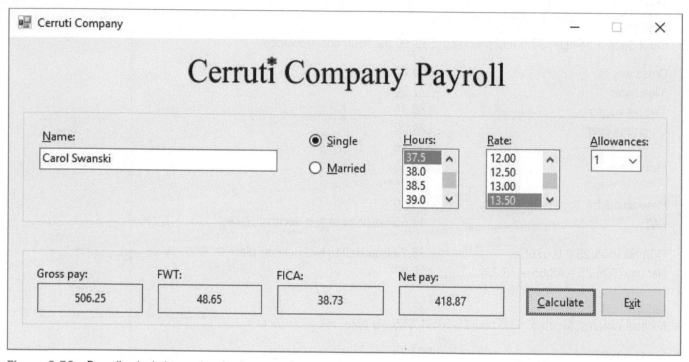

Figure 6-50 Payroll calculations using the first set of test data

2. Change the name entered in the Name box to **Michael Williams** and then click the **Married** radio button. Click **53.5** in the Hours list box and **15.00** in the Rate list box.

3. Press **Tab** to move the focus to the Allowances combo box. In addition to selecting the number of allowances in the list portion of the combo box, the user can also type the number in the text portion. Type **2** and then click the **Calculate** button. The gross pay, taxes, and net pay for this second test agree with the corresponding manual calculations shaded in Figure 6-49.

4. Click the **Exit** button.

A-10 Professionalize Your Application's Interface

At times, an application may need to communicate with the user during run time. You can accomplish this task by using Visual Basic's **MessageBox.Show method** to display a message box. The message box contains text, one or more buttons, and an icon. Figure 6-51 shows the method's syntax and lists the meaning of each argument. Figure 6-52 shows examples of using the method and includes the resulting message boxes.

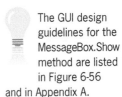

The GUI design guidelines for the MessageBox.Show method are listed in Figure 6-56 and in Appendix A.

MessageBox.Show Method

Syntax
MessageBox.Show(text, *caption, buttons, icon*[, *defaultButton*]**)**

Argument	Meaning
text	text to display in the message box; use sentence capitalization
caption	text to display in the message box's title bar; use book title capitalization
buttons	buttons to display in the message box; can be one of the following constants:
	`MessageBoxButtons.AbortRetryIgnore`
	`MessageBoxButtons.OK` (default setting)
	`MessageBoxButtons.OKCancel`
	`MessageBoxButtons.RetryCancel`
	`MessageBoxButtons.YesNo`
	`MessageBoxButtons.YesNoCancel`
icon	icon to display in the message box; typically, one of the following constants:
	`MessageBoxIcon.Exclamation` ⚠
	`MessageBoxIcon.Information` ⓘ
	`MessageBoxIcon.Stop` ⊗
defaultButton	button automatically selected when the user presses Enter; can be one of the following constants:
	`MessageBoxDefaultButton.Button1` (default setting)
	`MessageBoxDefaultButton.Button2`
	`MessageBoxDefaultButton.Button3`

Figure 6-51 Syntax of the MessageBox.Show method

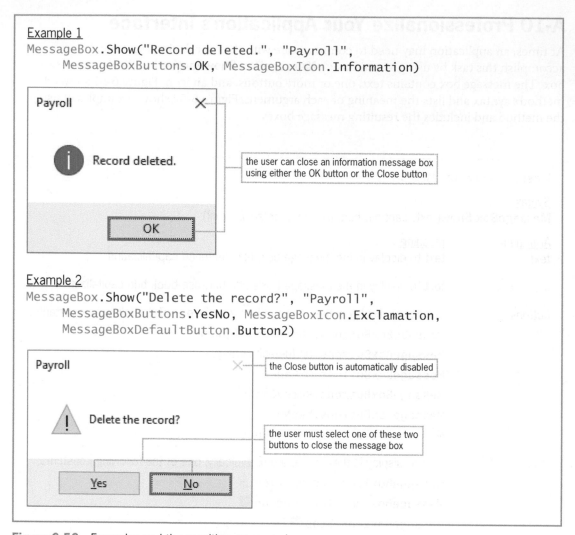

Figure 6-52 Examples and the resulting message boxes

After displaying the message box, the MessageBox.Show method waits for the user to choose one of the buttons. It then closes the message box and returns an integer indicating the button chosen by the user. Sometimes you are not interested in the value returned by the MessageBox.Show method. This is the case when the message box is for informational purposes only, such as the message box shown in Example 1 in Figure 6-52. Many times, however, the button selected by the user determines the next task performed by the application. Selecting the Yes button in the message box shown in Example 2 tells the application to delete the record; selecting the No button tells it *not* to delete the record.

Figure 6-53 lists the integer values returned by the MessageBox.Show method. Each value is associated with a button that can appear in a message box. The figure also lists the DialogResult values assigned to each integer as well as the meaning of the integers and values. As the figure indicates, the MessageBox.Show method returns the integer 6 when the user selects the Yes button. The integer 6 is represented by the DialogResult value `DialogResult.Yes`. When referring to the method's return value in code, you should use the DialogResult values rather than the integers because the values make the code more self-documenting and easier to understand. Figure 6-53 also shows two examples of using the MessageBox.Show method's return value.

MessageBox.Show Method's Return Values

Integer	DialogResult value	Meaning
1	`DialogResult.OK`	user chose the OK button
2	`DialogResult.Cancel`	user chose the Cancel button
3	`DialogResult.Abort`	user chose the Abort button
4	`DialogResult.Retry`	user chose the Retry button
5	`DialogResult.Ignore`	user chose the Ignore button
6	`DialogResult.Yes`	user chose the Yes button
7	`DialogResult.No`	user chose the No button

Example 1
```
Dim dlgButton As DialogResult
dlgButton =
    MessageBox.Show("Delete the record?", "Payroll",
    MessageBoxButtons.YesNo, MessageBoxIcon.Exclamation,
    MessageBoxDefaultButton.Button2)
If dlgButton = DialogResult.Yes Then
    instructions to delete the record
End If
```

Example 2
```
If MessageBox.Show("Play another game?", "Math Monster",
    MessageBoxButtons.YesNo,
    MessageBoxIcon.Exclamation) = DialogResult.Yes Then
    instructions to start another game
Else ' No button is selected.
    instructions to close the game application
End If
```

Figure 6-53   Values returned by the MessageBox.Show method

In the first example in Figure 6-53, the MessageBox.Show method's return value is assigned to a DialogResult variable named `dlgButton`. The selection structure in the example compares the contents of the variable with the `DialogResult.Yes` value. In the second example, the method's return value is not stored in a variable. Instead, the method appears in the selection structure's condition, where its return value is compared with the `DialogResult.Yes` value. The selection structure in Example 2 performs one set of tasks when the user selects the Yes button in the message box, and it performs a different set of tasks when the user selects the No button. Many programmers document the Else portion of the selection structure as shown in Example 2 because it clearly states that the Else portion is processed only when the user selects the No button.

A common use for the MessageBox.Show method is to verify that the user wants to exit an application when he or she clicks the Exit button. The method is typically entered in the form's FormClosing event procedure. The **FormClosing event** occurs when a form is about to be closed. In most cases, this happens when the computer processes the `Me.Close()` statement in the application's code. However, it also occurs when the user clicks the Close button on the form's title bar. You prevent the computer from closing a form by setting the **Cancel property** of the FormClosing event's e parameter to True, like this: `e.Cancel = True`. In the next set of steps, you will include the MessageBox.Show method in the Cerruti Company application's FormClosing event procedure.

START HERE

To code the frmMain_FormClosing procedure:

1. Open the code template for the frmMain_FormClosing procedure. (Be sure to open the FormClosing template and not the FormClosed template.) Enter the comments and code shown in Figure 6-54.

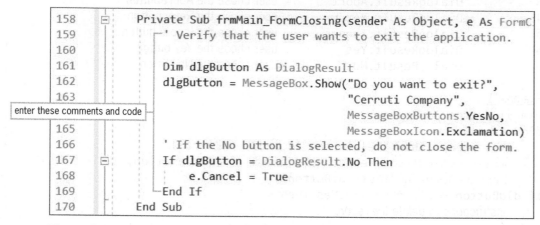

```
158     ⊟        Private Sub frmMain_FormClosing(sender As Object, e As FormC
159               ' Verify that the user wants to exit the application.
160
161               Dim dlgButton As DialogResult
162               dlgButton = MessageBox.Show("Do you want to exit?",
163                                "Cerruti Company",
                                 MessageBoxButtons.YesNo,
165                                MessageBoxIcon.Exclamation)
166               ' If the No button is selected, do not close the form.
167     ⊟         If dlgButton = DialogResult.No Then
168                   e.Cancel = True
169               End If
170           End Sub
```

enter these comments and code

Figure 6-54 Completed frmMain_FormClosing procedure

2. Save the solution and then start the application. Click the **Exit** button. The message box shown in Figure 6-55 appears on the screen.

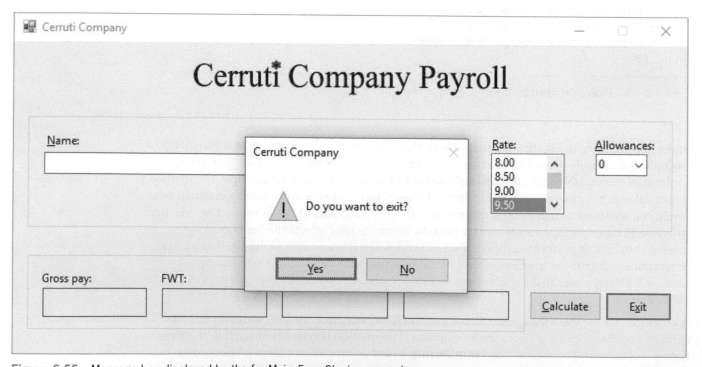

Figure 6-55 Message box displayed by the frmMain_FormClosing procedure

3. Click the **No** button. The form remains on the screen. Now, click the **Close** button on the form's title bar. This time, click the **Yes** button to end the application.

4. Close the Code Editor window and then close the solution.

Mini-Quiz 6-6

1. What constant is associated with the Information icon in the MessageBox.Show method?

2. If the user clicks the Cancel button in a message box, the MessageBox.Show method returns the integer 2, which is represented by which DialogResult value?

3. When entered in a form's FormClosing procedure, what statement prevents the computer from closing the form?

1) MessageBoxIcon.Information 2) DialogResult.Cancel 3) e.Cancel = True

Summary

- To create an independent Sub procedure, use the syntax shown in Figure 6-4.

- You call (invoke) an independent Sub procedure using a stand-alone statement, referred to as the calling statement. The statement's syntax is shown in Figure 6-4.

- You pass information to a Sub or Function procedure by including the information in the calling statement's argumentList. In the parameterList in the receiving procedure's header, you include the names of variables that will store the information passed to the procedure. The number, data type, and order (position) of the arguments in the argumentList should agree with the number, data type, and order (position) of the parameters in the parameterList.

- You can pass a variable *by value* to a procedure. You do this by including the ByVal keyword before the parameter name in the receiving procedure's parameterList. Because only a copy of the variable's value is passed, the receiving procedure cannot access the variable.

- You can pass a variable *by reference* to a procedure. You do this by including the ByRef keyword before the parameter name in the receiving procedure's parameterList. Because the variable's address is passed, the receiving procedure can change the contents of the variable.

- You can use the Math.Round method to round a number to a specified number of decimal places. The syntax and examples are shown in Figure 6-19.

- To create a Function procedure, use the syntax shown in Figure 6-22.

- You invoke a function using a statement that assigns the function's return value to a variable, uses the return value in a calculation, or displays the return value. Examples of statements that invoke a function are shown in Figure 6-23.

- You use the ComboBox tool in the toolbox to add a combo box to a form. The combo box's style is specified in its DropDownStyle property. The different styles are shown in Figure 6-26.

- You can use either the String Collection Editor or the Items collection's Add method to add items to a combo box. The Add method's syntax is *object*.Items.Add(*item*). In the syntax, *object* is the name of the combo box and *item* is the text you want added to the list portion of the control.

- To automatically sort the items in the list portion of a combo box, set the combo box's Sorted property to True.

- To determine the number of items in the list portion of a combo box, use the Items collection's Count property. Its syntax is *object*.`Items.Count`, in which *object* is the name of the combo box.

- You can use any of the following properties to select a combo box item from code: SelectedIndex, SelectedItem, or Text.

- To determine the item either selected in the list portion of a combo box or entered in the text portion, use the combo box's Text property. However, if the combo box is a DropDownList style, you can also use the SelectedIndex or SelectedItem property.

- To process code when the value in a combo box's Text property changes, enter the code in the combo box's TextChanged event procedure.

- You can use the MessageBox.Show method to display a message box that contains text, one or more buttons, and an icon. The method's syntax is shown in Figure 6-51, and its return values are explained in Figure 6-53.

- To process code when a form is about to be closed, enter the code in the form's FormClosing event procedure. The FormClosing event occurs when the user clicks the Close button on a form's title bar or when the computer processes the `Me.Close()` statement.

- To prevent a form from being closed, set the Cancel property of the FormClosing event procedure's **e** parameter to True.

- Figure 6-56 lists the GUI design guidelines for combo boxes and the MessageBox.Show method.

GUI design guidelines for combo boxes

- Use a label control to provide keyboard access to the combo box. Set the label's TabIndex property to a value that is one number less than the combo box's TabIndex value.
- Combo box items are either arranged by use, with the most used entries appearing first in the list, or sorted in ascending order.

GUI design guidelines for the MessageBox.Show method

- Use sentence capitalization for the *text* argument, but use book title capitalization for the *caption* argument.
- Display the Exclamation icon to alert the user that he or she must make a decision before the application can continue. You can phrase the message as a question. Message boxes that contain the Exclamation icon typically contain more than one button.
- Display the Information icon along with an OK button in a message box that displays an informational message.
- Display the Stop icon to alert the user of a serious problem that must be corrected before the application can continue.
- The default button in the message box should represent the user's most likely action as long as that action is not destructive.

Figure 6-56   GUI design guidelines for combo boxes and the MessageBox.Show method

Key Terms

Arguments—the items of information in a calling statement; items passed to a Sub procedure, function, or method

Calling statement—a statement that invokes (calls) an independent Sub procedure or function

Cancel property—a property of the e parameter in the form's FormClosing event procedure; when set to True, it prevents the form from closing

Combo box—a control that offers the user a list of choices and also has a text field that may or may not be editable

DropDownStyle property—determines the style of a combo box

Event procedures—Sub procedures that are processed only when a specific event occurs; also called event-handling Sub procedures

Event-handling Sub procedures—procedures that are processed only when a specific event occurs; also called event procedures

FormClosing event—occurs when a form is about to be closed, which can happen as a result of the computer processing the Me.Close() statement or the user clicking the Close button on the form's title bar

Function procedure—a procedure that returns a value after performing its assigned task; also referred to more simply as a function

Functions—another name for Function procedures

Independent Sub procedures—procedures that are not connected to any object and event; the procedure is processed only when called (invoked) from code

Line continuation character—an underscore that is immediately preceded by a space and located at the end of a physical line of code in the Code Editor window; used to split a long instruction into two or more physical lines

Math.Round method—rounds a numeric value to a specific number of decimal places

MessageBox.Show method—displays a message box that contains text, one or more buttons, and an icon; allows an application to communicate with the user while the application is running

Parameters—memory locations (variables) declared in a procedure header; accepts the information passed to the procedure

Pascal case—used when naming Sub procedures and functions; the practice of capitalizing the first letter in the name and the first letter of each subsequent word in the name

Passing by reference—refers to the process of passing a variable's address to a procedure so that the value in the variable can be changed

Passing by value—refers to the process of passing a copy of a variable's value to a procedure

Return statement—the Visual Basic statement that returns a function's value to the statement that invoked the function

Review Questions

1. Which of the following is false?

   a. A function returns only one value to the statement that invoked it.

   b. A Sub procedure can accept only one item of data passed to it.

   c. The parameterList in a procedure header is optional.

   d. None of the above.

2. What are the items that appear within parentheses in a calling statement called?

   a. arguments   c. passers

   b. parameters   d. None of the above.

3. What are the items that appear within parentheses in a procedure header called?

   a. arguments   c. passers

   b. parameters   d. None of the above.

4. Which of the following indicates whether a variable is being passed *by value* or *by reference*?

   a. the calling statement

   b. the receiving procedure's header

   c. the statements entered within the receiving procedure

   d. All of the above.

5. Which of the following statements invokes the GetArea Sub procedure, passing it two variables *by value*?

   a. `GetArea(dblLength, dblWidth) As Double`

   b. `GetArea(ByVal dblLength, ByVal dblWidth)`

   c. `GetArea ByVal(dblLength, dblWidth)`

   d. `GetArea(dblLength, dblWidth)`

6. Which of the following is a valid header for a procedure that receives a copy of the value stored in a String variable?

   a. `Private Sub DisplayName(ByCopy strName As String)`

   b. `Private Sub DisplayName ByVal(strName As String)`

   c. `Private Sub DisplayName(ByVal strName As String)`

   d. None of the above.

7. Which of the following is a valid header for a procedure that receives an integer followed by a number with a decimal place?

   a. `Private Sub GetFee(intBase As Value, decRate As Value)`

   b. `Private Sub GetFee(ByRef intBase As Integer, ByRef decRate As Decimal)`

   c. `Private Sub GetFee(ByVal intBase As Integer, ByVal decRate As Decimal)`

   d. None of the above.

8. Which of the following is false?

   a. The order of the arguments listed in the calling statement should agree with the order of the parameters listed in the receiving procedure's header.

   b. The data type of each argument in the calling statement should match the data type of its corresponding parameter in the procedure header.

   c. When you pass an item to a procedure *by value*, the procedure stores the item's value in a separate memory location.

   d. The name of each argument in the calling statement should be identical to the name of its corresponding parameter in the procedure header.

9. Which of the following instructs a function to return the value stored in the `dblBonus` variable?

   a. `Return dblBonus`   c. `Send dblBonus`

   b. `Return ByVal dblBonus`   d. `SendBack dblBonus`

10. Which of the following is a valid header for a procedure that receives the address of a Decimal variable followed by an integer?

    a. `Private Sub GetFee(ByVal decX As Decimal, ByAdd intY As Integer)`

    b. `Private Sub GetFee(decX As Decimal, intY As Integer)`

    c. `Private Sub GetFee(ByRef decX As Decimal, ByVal intY As Integer)`

    d. None of the above.

11. Which of the following is a valid header for a procedure that is passed the number 15?

    a. `Private Function GetTax(ByVal intRate As Integer) As Decimal`

    b. `Private Function GetTax(ByAdd intRate As Integer) As Decimal`

    c. `Private Sub CalcTax(ByVal intRate As Integer)`

    d. Both a and c.

12. If a statement passes a variable's address, the variable is said to be passed

    _____.

    a. *by address*   c. *by reference*

    b. *by content*   d. *by value*

13. Which of the following is false?

    a. When you pass a variable *by reference*, the receiving procedure can change its contents.

    b. To pass a variable *by reference*, you include the `ByRef` keyword before the variable's name in the calling statement.

    c. When you pass a variable *by value*, the receiving procedure creates a procedure-level variable to store the value passed to it.

    d. When you pass a variable *by value*, the receiving procedure cannot change its contents.

14. A Sub procedure named GetEndInv is passed four Integer variables from its calling statement. The first three variables store the following three values: beginning inventory, number sold, and number purchased. The procedure should use these values to calculate the ending inventory, and then store the result in the fourth variable. Which of the following procedure headers is correct?

   a. `Private Sub GetEndInv(ByVal intB As Integer, ByVal intS As Integer, ByVal intP As Integer, ByRef intFinal As Integer)`

   b. `Private Sub GetEndInv(ByVal intB As Integer, ByVal intS As Integer, ByVal intP As Integer, ByVal intFinal As Integer)`

   c. `Private Sub GetEndInv(ByRef intB As Integer, ByRef intS As Integer, ByRef intP As Integer, ByVal intFinal As Integer)`

   d. `Private Sub GetEndInv(ByRef intB As Integer, ByRef intS As Integer, ByRef intP As Integer, ByRef intFinal As Integer)`

15. The memory locations listed in a procedure header's parameterList have procedure scope and are removed from the computer's main memory when the procedure ends.

   a. True   b. False

16. Which of the following statements invokes the GetDiscount function, passing it the contents of two Decimal variables named `decSales` and `decRate`? The statement should assign the function's return value to the `decDiscount` variable.

   a. `decDiscount = GetDiscount(ByVal decSales, ByVal decRate)`

   b. `GetDiscount(decSales, decRate, decDiscount)`

   c. `decDiscount = GetDiscount(decSales, decRate)`

   d. None of the above.

17. Which property is used to specify a combo box's style?

   a. ComboBoxStyle   c. DropStyle

   b. DropDownStyle   d. Style

18. The items in a combo box belong to which collection?

   a. Items   c. ListBox

   b. List   d. Values

19. Which of the following selects the Cat item, which appears third in the cboAnimal control?

   a. `cboAnimal.SelectedIndex = 2`

   b. `cboAnimal.SelectedItem = "Cat"`

   c. `cboAnimal.Text = "Cat"`

   d. All of the above.

20. The item that appears in the text portion of a combo box is stored in which property?

   a. SelectedText   c. Text

   b. SelectedValue   d. TextItem

21. Which event occurs when the user either types a value in the text portion of a combo box or selects a different item in the list portion?

   a. ChangedItem
   b. ChangedValue
   c. SelectedItemChanged
   d. TextChanged

22. Which of a form's events is triggered when you click the Close button on its title bar?

   a. FormClose
   b. FormClosing
   c. FormExit
   d. None of the above.

23. Which of the following rounds the contents of the `dblSales` variable to two decimal places?

   a. `dblSales = Math.Round(dblSales, 2)`
   b. `dblSales = Math.Round(2, dblSales)`
   c. `dblSales = Round.Math(dblSales, 2)`
   d. `dblSales = Round.Math(2, dblSales)`

24. Which event is triggered when the computer processes the `Me.Close()` statement entered in the btnExit_Click procedure?

   a. the form's Closing event
   b. the form's FormClosing event
   c. the btnExit control's Closing event
   d. the btnExit control's FormClosing event

25. Which of the following statements prevents a form from being closed?

   a. `e.Cancel = False`
   b. `e.Cancel = True`
   c. `e.Close = False`
   d. `e.sender.Close = False`

26. Which constant displays the Exclamation icon in a message box?

   a. `MessageBox.Exclamation`
   b. `MessageBox.IconExclamation`
   c. `MessageBoxIcon.Exclamation`
   d. `MessageBox.WarningIcon`

27. If a message is for informational purposes only and does not require the user to make a decision, the message box should display which of the following?

   a. an OK button and the Information icon
   b. an OK button and the Exclamation icon
   c. a Yes button and the Stop icon
   d. a No button and the Stop icon

28. Explain the difference between a Sub procedure and a Function procedure.

29. Explain the difference between passing a variable *by value* and passing it *by reference*.

30. Explain the difference between invoking a Sub procedure and invoking a function.

Exercises

INTRODUCTORY 1. In this exercise, you modify the History Grade application from this chapter's Focus lesson. Use Windows to make a copy of the History Solution folder. Rename the copy History Solution-Functions. Open the History Solution.sln file contained in the History Solution-Functions folder. Modify the btnDisplay_Click procedure so that it uses two functions named GetGrade101 and GetGrade201 to get the appropriate grade; the procedure should then display the grade in the lblGrade control. Change the two independent Sub procedures to functions that return the appropriate grade to the statements that invoke them in the btnDisplay_Click procedure. Each function should contain a parameter that accepts the total points passed to it. Save the solution and then start and test the application.

INTRODUCTORY 2. In this exercise, you modify the Gross Pay application from this chapter's Focus lesson. Use Windows to make a copy of the Gross Solution folder. Rename the copy Modified Gross Solution. Open the Gross Solution.sln file contained in the Modified Gross Solution folder. Change the names of the two independent Sub procedures to CalcWeekly and CalcTwicePerMonth. Modify the code so that the btnCalc_Click procedure (rather than the two independent Sub procedures) displays the gross pay in the lblGross control. Save the solution and then start and test the application.

INTRODUCTORY 3. In this exercise, you modify the Gross Pay application from this chapter's Focus lesson. Use Windows to make a copy of the Gross Solution folder. Rename the copy Gross Solution-Functions. Open the Gross Solution.sln file contained in the Gross Solution-Functions folder. Change the two independent Sub procedures to functions named GetWeekly and GetTwicePerMonth. Modify the code so that the btnCalc_Click procedure (rather than the two functions) displays the gross pay in the lblGross control. Save the solution and then start and test the application.

INTRODUCTORY 4. In this exercise, you modify the Cerruti Company application from this chapter's Apply lesson. Use Windows to make a copy of the Cerruti Solution folder. Rename the copy Modified Cerruti Solution. Open the Cerruti Solution.sln file contained in the Modified Cerruti Solution folder. Change the GetSingleFwt Sub procedure to a function. Then, change the GetMarriedFwt function to a Sub procedure. Make the necessary modifications to the btnCalc_Click procedure. Save the solution and then start and test the application.

INTRODUCTORY 5. In this exercise, you modify one of the Seminars applications from Chapter 4's Apply lesson. Open the Seminars Solution.sln file contained in the Seminars Solution-CheckBox folder. Create an event-handling Sub procedure named ClearAmountDue and associate it with each check box's CheckChanged event. Then, create a function that determines which (if any) check boxes are selected and then adds the associated fee to the total due. The function should return the total due to the statement that invoked it. Also, make the necessary modifications to the btnCalc_Click procedure's code. Save the solution and then start and test the application.

INTRODUCTORY 6. In this exercise, you modify one of the Seminars applications from Chapter 4's Apply lesson. Open the Seminars Solution.sln file contained in the Seminars Solution-RadioButton folder. Create an event-handling Sub procedure named ClearDue and associate it with each radio button's CheckedChanged event. Then, create a Sub procedure that determines the appropriate fee, which is based on the selected radio button. Also, make the necessary modifications to the btnCalc_Click procedure's code. Save the solution and then start and test the application.

INTERMEDIATE 7. The Donut Shoppe sells four varieties of doughnuts: Glazed ($1.05), Sugar ($1.05), Chocolate ($1.25), and Filled ($1.50). It also sells regular coffee ($1.50) and cappuccino ($2.75). The store manager wants you to create an application that displays a customer's subtotal, 6% sales tax, and total due. Create a Windows Forms application. Use the following names for the project and solution, respectively: Donut Project and Donut Solution. Save the application in the VB2017\Chap06 folder. Create the interface shown in Figure 6-57. When coding the application, use one independent Sub procedure to determine the subtotal, which is the total cost without the sales tax. Use a function to determine the sales tax. Use an event-handling Sub procedure to clear the output. Save the solution and then start and test the application.

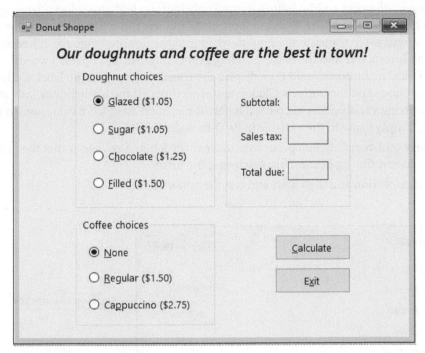

Figure 6-57 Interface for Exercise 7

8. Mats-R-Us sells three different types of mats: Standard ($99), Deluxe ($129), and Premium ($179). All of the mats are available in blue, red ($10 extra), and pink ($15 extra). There is also an extra $25 charge if the customer wants the mat to be foldable. Create a Windows Forms application. Use the following names for the project and solution, respectively: Mats Project and Mats Solution. Save the application in the VB2017\Chap06 folder. Create the interface shown in Figure 6-58. Use a function to determine the price of the mat before any additional charges. Use a Sub procedure to calculate the total additional charge (if any). Use an event-handling Sub procedure to clear the price. Also, verify that the user wants to exit the application before closing the form. Save the solution and then start and test the application appropriately.

INTERMEDIATE

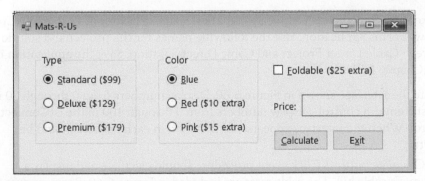

Figure 6-58 Interface for Exercise 8

INTERMEDIATE

9. Create a Windows Forms application. Use the following names for the project and solution, respectively: Translator Project and Translator Solution. Save the application in the VB2017\Chap06 folder.

a. Create the interface shown in Figure 6-59. The combo box should display the following words: French, Italian, and Spanish. When the interface appears, the first item in the combo box should be selected.

b. The user will select a radio button in the English group and also select a language from the combo box. The Translate button should use three functions (one for each language) to translate the English word into the desired language. If necessary, use the Internet to find the corresponding French, Italian, and Spanish words. The Translate button should then display the translated word in the label. Code the functions and the button's Click event procedure. (If the Code Editor indicates that a String variable is being passed before it has been assigned a value, assign the String.Empty value to the variable in its Dim statement.)

c. Use an event-handling Sub procedure to clear the label. Also, verify that the user wants to exit the application before closing the form.

d. Save the solution and then start and test the application.

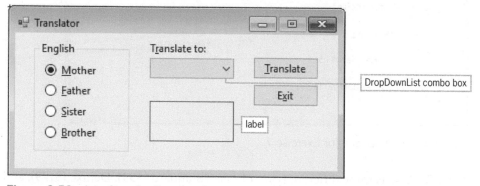

Figure 6-59   Interface for Exercise 9

INTERMEDIATE

10. In this exercise, you modify the application created in Exercise 9. Use Windows to make a copy of the Translator Solution folder. Rename the copy Translator Solution-Sub. Open the Translator Solution.sln file contained in the Translator Solution-Sub folder. Change the three functions to Sub procedures. (If the Code Editor indicates that a String variable is being passed before it has been assigned a value, assign the String.Empty value to the variable in its Dim statement.) Save the solution and then start and test the application appropriately.

ADVANCED

11. In this exercise, you create an application that calculates a customer's cable bill. Create a Windows Forms application. Use the following names for the project and solution, respectively: Cable Direct Project and Cable Direct Solution. Save the application in the VB2017\Chap06 folder.

a. Create the interface shown in Figure 6-60. Display numbers from 0 through 20 in the lstPremium control. Display numbers from 0 through 100 in the lstConnections control. When the interface appears, the first item in each list box should be selected.

b. The Calculate button's Click event procedure should calculate and display a customer's cable bill. The cable rates are included in Figure 6-60. Business customers must have at least one connection. Use two functions: one to calculate and return the total due for business customers, and one to calculate and return the total due for residential customers.

c. The form's FormClosing event procedure should verify that the user wants to close the application.

d. The total due should be cleared when a change is made to a radio button or list box.

e. Save the solution and then start and test the application. (The total due for a business customer with 3 premium channels and 12 connections is $254.50. The total due for a residential customer with 3 premium channels is $49.50.)

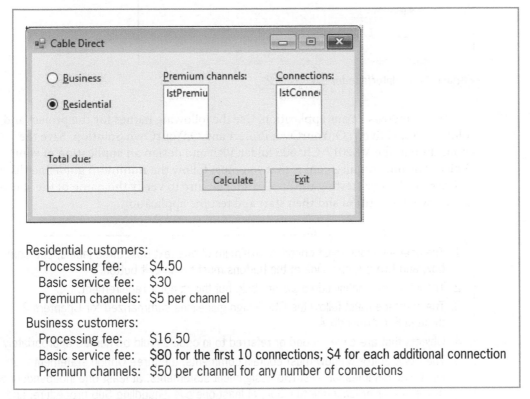

Residential customers:
    Processing fee: $4.50
    Basic service fee: $30
    Premium channels: $5 per channel

Business customers:
    Processing fee: $16.50
    Basic service fee: $80 for the first 10 connections; $4 for each additional connection
    Premium channels: $50 per channel for any number of connections

Figure 6-60   Interface for Exercise 11

12. In this exercise, you create an application that calculates the number of single rolls of wallpaper required to cover a room. Create a Windows Forms application. Use the following names for the project and solution, respectively: Wallpaper Project and Wallpaper Solution. Save the application in the VB2017\Chap06 folder.

ADVANCED

a. Create the interface shown in Figure 6-61. The four combo boxes have the DropDown style. Display numbers from 8 through 30 in the combo boxes that get the room's length, width, and height. Display numbers from 30 through 40, in increments of 0.5, in the combo box that gets the roll coverage. When the interface appears, the numbers 10, 10, 8, and 37 should be selected in the Length, Width, Height, and Roll coverage combo boxes, respectively.

b. The Calculate button's Click event procedure should calculate and display the number of single rolls of wallpaper required to cover a room. Use a Sub procedure to make the calculation. The number of single rolls should be displayed as an integer. (If the number of single rolls contains a decimal place, it should be rounded to the next highest integer. For example, 8.2 rolls should be rounded up to 9.)

    c. The number of rolls should be cleared when a change is made to a combo box.

    d. Save the solution and then start and test the application. (If the roll coverage is 38.5 square feet and the room's length, width, and height are 14, 20, and 8, respectively, the number of single rolls is 15.)

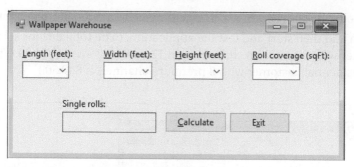

Figure 6-61   Interface for Exercise 12

ON YOUR OWN

13. Create a Windows Forms application. Use the following names for the project and solution, respectively: OnYourOwn Project and OnYourOwn Solution. Save the application in the VB2017\Chap06 folder. Plan and design an application of your choice. The only requirement is that you must follow the minimum guidelines listed in Figure 6-62. Before starting the application, be sure to verify the name of the startup form. Save the solution and then start and test the application.

1. The user interface must contain a minimum of one text box, three labels, one combo box, and two buttons. One of the buttons must be an Exit button.
2. The interface can include a picture box, but this is not a requirement.
3. The interface must follow the GUI design guidelines summarized for Chapters 2 through 6 in Appendix A.
4. Objects that are either coded or referred to in code should be named appropriately.
5. The Code Editor window must contain comments, the three Option statements, at least two variables, at least two assignment statements, at least one independent Sub procedure or at least one function, at least one event-handling Sub procedure, and the Me.Close() statement. The application must perform at least one calculation.
6. Every text box on the form should have its TextChanged and Enter event procedures coded. At least one of the text boxes should have its KeyPress event procedure coded.
7. The combo box should have its TextChanged event procedure coded.
8. The form's FormClosing procedure should verify that the user wants to end the application.

Figure 6-62   Guidelines for Exercise 13

FIX IT

14. Open the VB2017\Chap06\FixIt Solution\FixIt Solution.sln file. Start the application. Click 20 in the Length combo box and then click 30 in the Width combo box. Click the Calculate area button, which should display the area of a rectangle having a length of 20 feet and a width of 30 feet. Notice that the application does not display the correct area. Stop the application. Correct the application's code.

CHAPTER 7

String Manipulation

In many cases, an application's code will need to manipulate (process) string data in some way. For example, it may need to look at the first character in an inventory part number to determine the part's location in the warehouse. Or, it may need to search an address to determine the street name. Or, it may need to verify that the input entered by the user is in the expected format. In this chapter's Focus on the Concepts lesson, you will learn several ways of manipulating strings in Visual Basic.

In the Apply the Concepts lesson, you will learn how to code applications that create check digits and passwords. You will also learn how to generate random numbers. You will use the concepts from the Focus lesson to code the applications in the Apply lesson.

▌FOCUS ON THE CONCEPTS LESSON

Concepts covered in this lesson:

- F-1 Length property
- F-2 Insert method
- F-3 PadLeft and PadRight methods
- F-4 Contains and IndexOf methods
- F-5 Substring method
- F-6 Character array
- F-7 Remove method
- F-8 Trim, TrimStart, and TrimEnd methods
- F-9 Replace method
- F-10 Like operator

F-1 Length Property

If an application expects the user to enter a seven-digit phone number or a five-digit ZIP code, you should verify that the user's input contains the required number of characters. The number of characters contained in a string is stored as an integer in the string's **Length property**. Figure 7-1 shows the property's syntax and includes examples of using it. In the syntax, *string* can be a String variable, a String named constant, or the Text property of a control.

Length Property

<u>Syntax</u>
string.**Length**

<u>Example 1</u>
```
strCountry = "Mexico"
intNumChars = strCountry.Length
```
assigns the number 6 to the `intNumChars` variable

<u>Example 2</u>
```
intChars = txtName.Text.Trim.Length
```
assigns the number of characters in the txtName.Text property, excluding any leading or trailing space characters, to the `intChars` variable

---

Figure 7-1   Syntax and examples of the Length property

The Product ID Application

You will use the Length property in the Product ID application, which displays a listing of the product IDs entered by the user. Each product ID must contain exactly five characters.

START HERE

To code the Product ID application:

1. Open the Product Solution.sln file contained in the VB2017\Chap07\Product Solution folder. Open the Code Editor window and locate the btnAdd_Click procedure. (You learned about the ToUpper and Trim methods in Chapter 4.) Modify the If clause as shown in Figure 7-2.

```
18  □    Private Sub btnAdd_Click(sender As Object, e As EventArgs) Han
19            ' Add a product ID to a list box.
20
21          Dim strId As String
22                                              add this condition to the If clause
23          strId = txtId.Text.ToUpper.Trim
24  □       If strId.Length = 5 Then
25              lstIds.Items.Add(strId)
26          Else
27            MessageBox.Show("The ID must contain 5 characters.",
28                    "Product ID", MessageBoxButtons.OK,
29                    MessageBoxIcon.Information)
30          End If
31       End Sub
```

Figure 7-2 Completed btnAdd_Click procedure

2. Save the solution and then start the application. Type **abcd** as the ID and then click the **Add to list** button. A message box opens and displays the message "The ID must contain 5 characters." Close the message box.

3. Change the ID to **abcd4** and then click the **Add to list** button. The button's Click event procedure adds the ABCD4 ID to the list box. See Figure 7-3.

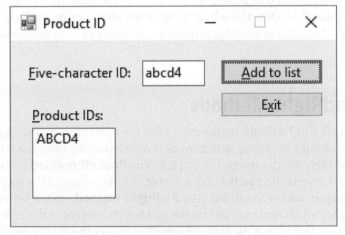

Figure 7-3 Product ID added to the list box

4. On your own, test the application using an ID that contains nine characters. Also test it using an ID that contains both leading and trailing spaces. When you are finished testing the application, click the **Exit** button. Close the Code Editor window and then close the solution.

F-2 Insert Method

Visual Basic's **Insert method** allows you to insert characters anywhere in a string. It then returns a string with the appropriate characters inserted. The method's syntax is shown in Figure 7-4 along with examples of using it. In the syntax, *string* can be a String variable, a String named constant, or the Text property of a control. When processing the Insert method, the computer first stores a temporary copy of the *string* in its main memory. It then performs the specified insertion on the copy only; the Insert method does not affect the original *string*.

Insert Method

Syntax
string.**Insert**(*startIndex*, *value*)

Example 1
strPhone = "111-2222"   ┌─ space character
txtPhone.Text = strPhone.Insert(0, "(877) ")
assigns the string "(877) 111-2222" to the txtPhone.Text property

Example 2
strName = "Jess Gonzales"   ┌─ space character
strName = strName.Insert(5, "M. ")
assigns the string "Jess M. Gonzales" to the strName variable

---

Figure 7-4 Syntax and examples of the Insert method

The Insert method's *startIndex* argument is an integer that specifies where in the string's copy you want the *value* inserted. The integer represents the character's index—in other words, its position in the string. The first character in a string has an index of 0; the second character has an index of 1, and so on. The Insert method in Example 1 in Figure 7-4 inserts the string, which is the area code followed by a space character, at the beginning of the phone number. To insert a value beginning with the sixth character in a string, you use a startIndex of 5, as shown in Example 2.

F-3 PadLeft and PadRight Methods

You can use Visual Basic's PadLeft and PadRight methods to align the characters in a string. The methods do this by inserting (padding) the string with zero or more characters until the string is a specified length; each method then returns the padded string. The **PadLeft method** pads the string on the left, which means it inserts the padded characters at the beginning of the string, thereby right-aligning the characters within the string. The **PadRight method**, on the other hand, pads the string on the right, which means it inserts the padded characters at the end of the string and left-aligns the characters within the string. Figure 7-5 shows the syntax of both methods and includes examples of using them. In each syntax, *string* can be a String variable, a String named constant, or the Text property of a control.

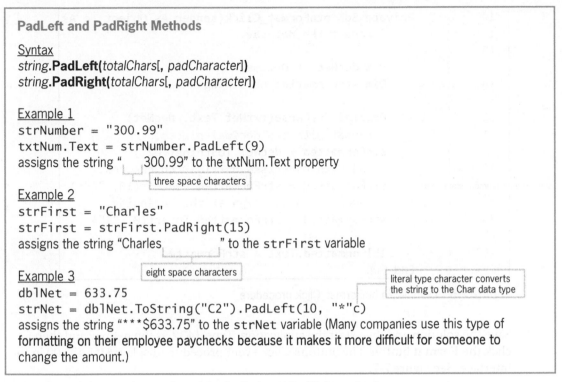

Figure 7-5 Syntax and examples of the PadLeft and PadRight methods

When processing the PadLeft and PadRight methods, the computer first makes a temporary copy of the *string* in memory; it then pads the copy only. The *totalChars* argument is an integer that represents the total number of characters you want the string's copy to contain. The optional *padCharacter* argument is the character that is used to pad the string until the desired number of characters is reached. If the *padCharacter* argument is omitted, the default padding character is the space character.

Notice the letter c that appears at the end of the *padCharacter* argument in Example 3. The letter c is one of the literal type characters in Visual Basic. As you learned in Chapter 3, a literal type character forces a literal constant to assume a data type other than the one its form indicates. In this case, the letter c forces the "*" string to assume the Char (character) data type. (Recall that the literal type character D forces a Double number to assume the Decimal data type.)

The Net Pay Application

The Net Pay application will use the Insert and PadLeft methods to display an employee's net pay with a leading dollar sign, asterisks, and two decimal places.

To code the Net Pay application:

START HERE

1. Open the Net Pay Solution.sln file contained in the VB2017\Chap07\Net Pay Solution folder. Open the Code Editor window and locate the btnFormat_Click procedure. First, the procedure will format the net pay to include two decimal places. Then, it will pad the net pay with asterisks (if necessary) until the net pay contains 10 characters. Finally, it will insert a dollar sign at the beginning of the formatted net pay. Type the three assignment statements indicated in Figure 7-6.

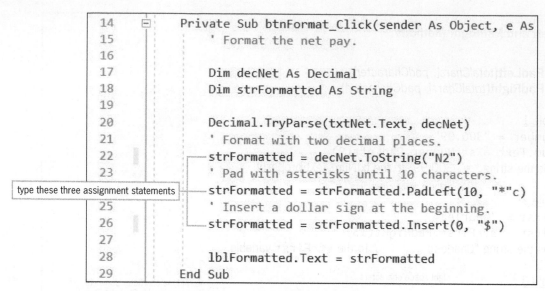

```
14    ⊟         Private Sub btnFormat_Click(sender As Object, e As
15                  ' Format the net pay.
16
17              Dim decNet As Decimal
18              Dim strFormatted As String
19
20              Decimal.TryParse(txtNet.Text, decNet)
21                  ' Format with two decimal places.
22              strFormatted = decNet.ToString("N2")
23                  ' Pad with asterisks until 10 characters.
24              strFormatted = strFormatted.PadLeft(10, "*"c)
25                  ' Insert a dollar sign at the beginning.
26              strFormatted = strFormatted.Insert(0, "$")
27
28              lblFormatted.Text = strFormatted
29         End Sub
```

type these three assignment statements

Figure 7-6   Completed btnFormat_Click procedure

2. Save the solution and then start the application. Type **1432** as the net pay and then click the **Format** button. The button's Click event procedure displays $**1,432.00 in the interface. See Figure 7-7.

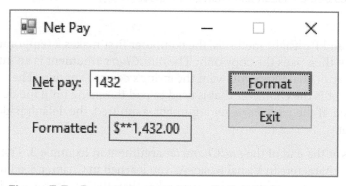

Figure 7-7   Formatted net pay shown in the interface

3. Click the **Exit** button. Close the Code Editor window and then close the solution.

Mini-Quiz 7-1

1. Write a statement that assigns the number of characters in the strZip variable to the intNum variable.

2. Write a statement that uses the Insert method to change the contents of the strState variable from "Ky" to "Kentucky".

3. Write a statement that uses the PadRight method to change the contents of the strBonus variable from "100" to "100$$$".

1) intNum = strZip.Length 2) strState = strState.Insert(1, "entuck") 3) strBonus = strBonus.PadRight(6, "$"c)

YOU DO IT 1!

Create an application named You Do It 1 and save it in the VB2017\Chap07 folder. Add a text box, a label, and a button to the form. The button's Click event procedure should assign the contents of the text box, excluding any leading or trailing space characters, to a String variable. If the variable contains at least two characters but less than seven characters, the procedure should insert a number sign (#) as the second character and then pad the variable's value (on the right) with asterisks until the variable contains 10 characters. Finally, the procedure should display the variable's contents in the label. Code the procedure. Save the solution and then start and test the application. (If you enter 1234567, the label will display 1234567. If you enter 123456, the label will display 1#23456***.) Close the solution.

F-4 Contains and IndexOf Methods

You can use either the **Contains method** or the **IndexOf method** to determine whether a string contains a specific sequence of characters. Figure 7-8 shows the syntax of both methods. In each syntax, *string* can be a String variable, a String named constant, or the Text property of a control. The *subString* argument represents the sequence of characters for which you are searching. Both methods perform a case-sensitive search, which means the case of the subString must match the case of the string in order for both to be considered equal.

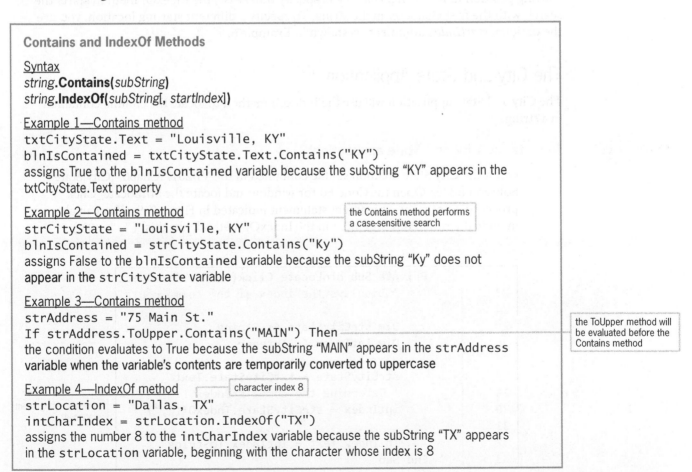

Contains and IndexOf Methods

Syntax
string.**Contains**(*subString*)
string.**IndexOf**(*subString*[, *startIndex*])

Example 1—Contains method
txtCityState.Text = "Louisville, KY"
blnIsContained = txtCityState.Text.Contains("KY")
assigns True to the blnIsContained variable because the subString "KY" appears in the txtCityState.Text property

Example 2—Contains method
strCityState = "Louisville, KY"
blnIsContained = strCityState.Contains("Ky")   the Contains method performs a case-sensitive search
assigns False to the blnIsContained variable because the subString "Ky" does not appear in the strCityState variable

Example 3—Contains method
strAddress = "75 Main St."
If strAddress.ToUpper.Contains("MAIN") Then   the ToUpper method will be evaluated before the Contains method
the condition evaluates to True because the subString "MAIN" appears in the strAddress variable when the variable's contents are temporarily converted to uppercase

Example 4—IndexOf method   character index 8
strLocation = "Dallas, TX"
intCharIndex = strLocation.IndexOf("TX")
assigns the number 8 to the intCharIndex variable because the subString "TX" appears in the strLocation variable, beginning with the character whose index is 8

Figure 7-8 Syntax and examples of the Contains and IndexOf methods (continues)

(continued)

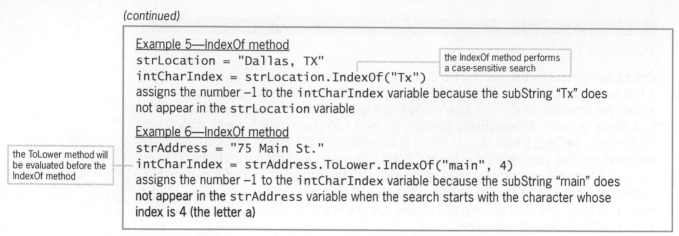

Example 5—IndexOf method
```
strLocation = "Dallas, TX"
intCharIndex = strLocation.IndexOf("Tx")
```
the IndexOf method performs a case-sensitive search

assigns the number −1 to the intCharIndex variable because the subString "Tx" does not appear in the strLocation variable

Example 6—IndexOf method
```
strAddress = "75 Main St."
intCharIndex = strAddress.ToLower.IndexOf("main", 4)
```
the ToLower method will be evaluated before the IndexOf method

assigns the number −1 to the intCharIndex variable because the subString "main" does not appear in the strAddress variable when the search starts with the character whose index is 4 (the letter a)

Figure 7-8   Syntax and examples of the Contains and IndexOf methods

The Contains method, which appears in Examples 1 through 3, returns the Boolean value True when the subString is contained anywhere in the string; otherwise, it returns the Boolean value False. The Contains method always begins the search with the first character in the string.

The IndexOf method, which appears in Examples 4 through 6, returns an integer: either −1 or a number that is greater than or equal to 0. The −1 indicates that the subString is not contained in the string. A number other than −1 is the character index of the subString's starting position in the string. Unless you specify otherwise, the IndexOf method starts the search with the first character in the string. To specify a different starting location, you use the optional *startIndex* argument, as shown in Example 6.

The City and State Application

The City and State application will use the IndexOf method to locate the comma contained in a string.

START HERE

To code the City and State application:

1. Open the City State Solution.sln file contained in the VB2017\Chap07\City State Solution folder. Open the Code Editor window and locate the btnLocate_Click procedure. Enter the assignment statement indicated in Figure 7-9. (You can also include the *startIndex* argument in the IndexOf method, like this: (",", 0).)

```
22      Private Sub btnLocate_Click(sender As Object
23          ' Displays the index of the comma contai
24
25          Dim strCityState As String
26          Dim intIndex As Integer
27
28          strCityState = txtCityState.Text
29          ' Determine the comma's index.
30          intIndex = strCityState.IndexOf(",")
31
32          lblIndex.Text = intIndex.ToString
33      End Sub
```
enter this assignment statement

Figure 7-9   Completed btnLocate_Click procedure

2. Save the solution and then start the application. Type **Minot, ND** in the text box and then click the **Locate the comma** button. The comma has an index of 5. See Figure 7-10.

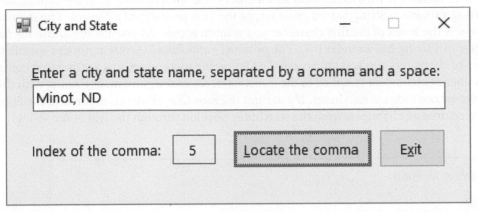

Figure 7-10 Interface showing the comma's index

3. Next, type **New York** in the text box and then click the **Locate the comma** button. The −1 that appears in the label indicates that the text box does not contain a comma. Click the **Exit** button. Close the Code Editor window and then close the solution.

Mini-Quiz 7-2

1. Write a statement that uses the Contains method to determine whether the strAddress variable contains the string "Elm St." (in uppercase, lowercase, or a combination of uppercase and lowercase). Assign the return value to the blnIsContained variable.

2. Write a statement that uses the IndexOf method to determine whether the strAddress variable contains the string "Elm St." (in uppercase, lowercase, or a combination of uppercase and lowercase). Assign the return value to the intIndex variable.

3. What does the IndexOf method return when the string does not contain the subString?

4. What does the Contains method return when the string does not contain the subString?

1) blnIsContained = strAddress.ToUpper.Contains("ELM ST.") 2) intIndex = strAddress.ToUpper.IndexOf("ELM ST.") 3) −1 4) False

F-5 Substring Method

Visual Basic provides the **Substring method** for accessing any number of characters in a string. Figure 7-11 shows the method's syntax and includes examples of using it. In the syntax, *string* can be a String variable, a String named constant, or the Text property of a control. The *startIndex* argument is the index of the first character you want to access. As you already know, the first character in a string has an index of 0. The optional *numCharsToAccess* argument specifies the number of characters you want to access. The Substring method returns a string that contains the number of characters specified in the *numCharsToAccess* argument, beginning with the character whose index is startIndex. If you omit the *numCharsToAccess* argument, the Substring method returns all characters from the startIndex position through the end of the string.

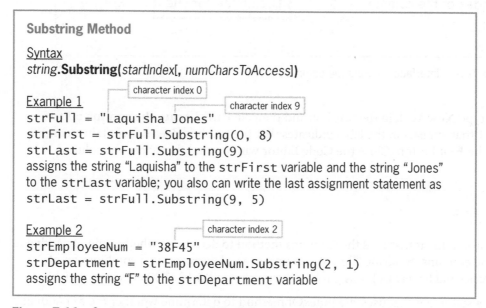

Figure 7-11 Syntax and examples of the Substring method

The Rearrange Name Application

Ch07-Rearranging a Name

You will use the Substring method in the Rearrange Name application. The application's interface provides a text box for entering a person's first name followed by a space and the person's last name. The application rearranges the name so that the last name comes first, followed by a comma, a space, and the first name.

START HERE

To code the Rearrange Name application:

1. Open the Rearrange Solution.sln file contained in the VB2017\Chap07\Rearrange Solution folder. Open the Code Editor window and locate the btnRearrange_Click procedure. The procedure assigns the name entered by the user, excluding any leading or trailing spaces, to the **strName** variable.

2. Before you can rearrange the name stored in the variable, you need to separate the first name from the last name. To do this, you first search for the space character that appears between the names. Click the **blank line** below the ' Search for the space in the name. comment. Type the following assignment statement, being sure to include a space character between the quotation marks, and then press **Enter**:

   ```
   intIndex = strName.IndexOf(" ")
   ```

3. If the value in the `intIndex` variable is not −1, it means that the IndexOf method found a space character in the variable. In that case, the selection structure's true path should continue rearranging the name; otherwise, its false path should display an appropriate message. Notice that the statement to display the message is already entered in the selection structure's false path. Change the If clause in the procedure to the following:

```
If intIndex <> -1 Then
```

4. Now you can use the value stored in the `intIndex` variable to separate the first name from the last name. Click the **blank line** below the `' Separate the first and last names.` comment. All of the characters to the left of the space character represent the first name, and all of the characters to the right of the space character represent the last name. Enter the following assignment statements:

```
strFirstName = strName.Substring(0, intIndex)
strLastName = strName.Substring(intIndex + 1)
```

5. Finally, you will display the rearranged name in the interface. Click the **blank line** above the Else clause and then enter the additional assignment statement indicated in Figure 7-12. Be sure to include a space character after the comma.

```
14    Private Sub btnRearrange_Click(sender As Object, e As EventArgs) H
15        ' Rearranges and then displays a name.
16
17        Dim strName As String
18        Dim strFirstName As String
19        Dim strLastName As String
20        Dim intIndex As Integer
21
22        strName = txtName.Text.Trim
23        ' Search for the space in the name.
24        intIndex = strName.IndexOf(" ")
25
26        If intIndex <> -1 Then
27            ' Separate the first and last names.
28            strFirstName = strName.Substring(0, intIndex)
29            strLastName = strName.Substring(intIndex + 1)
30
31            ' Display last name, comma, space, and first name.
32            lblRearranged.Text = strLastName & ", " & strFirstName       ← enter this assignment statement
33
34        Else
35            MessageBox.Show("The name does not contain a space.",
36                "Rearrange Name", MessageBoxButtons.OK,
37                MessageBoxIcon.Information)
38        End If
39    End Sub
```

Figure 7-12   Completed btnRearrange_Click procedure

6. Save the solution and then start the application. Type **Jack Carlson** as the name and then click the **Rearrange the name** button. The rearranged name appears in the interface. See Figure 7-13.

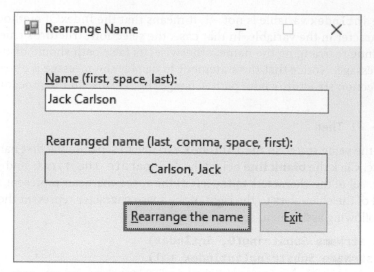

Figure 7-13　Rearranged name shown in the interface

7. Change the name to **Pam** and then click the **Rearrange the name** button. The message "The name does not contain a space." appears in a message box. Click the **OK** button.

8. Click the **Exit** button. Close the Code Editor window and then close the solution.

YOU DO IT 3!

Create an application named You Do It 3 and save it in the VB2017\Chap07 folder. Add a label and a button to the form. The button's Click event procedure should declare a String variable named strAlphabet and initialize it to the 26 uppercase letters of the alphabet. It then should use the Substring method to display only the letters O, P, Q, R, and S in the label. Code the procedure. Save the solution and then start and test the application. Close the solution.

F-6 Character Array

A string is simply a group of related characters and is commonly referred to as an **array of characters** or a **character array**. Each character in a character array, or string, has a unique index that represents its position in the string; this is illustrated in Figure 7-14. The first character has an index of 0; the second character has an index of 1, and so on. Because each character has a unique index, you can use the index to refer to an individual character in the string. You do this by using the name of the location (variable, named constant, or Text property) where the string is stored followed by the character's index enclosed in parentheses. As Example 1 in Figure 7-14 shows, you use strName(0) to refer to the first character in the string stored in the strName variable. Using strName(0) is equivalent to using strName.Substring(0, 1). Similarly, you use strName(4) to refer to the last character, as shown in Example 2; strName(4) is equivalent to strName.Substring(4, 1).

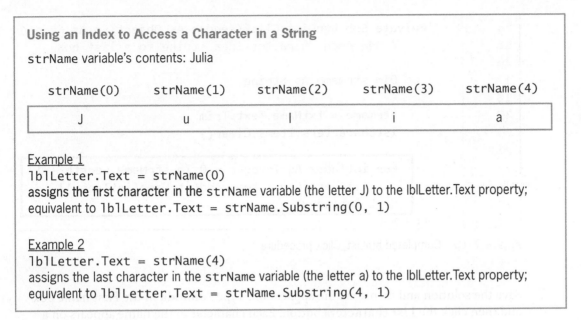

Using an Index to Access a Character in a String

strName variable's contents: Julia

strName(0)	strName(1)	strName(2)	strName(3)	strName(4)
J	u	l	i	a

Example 1
lblLetter.Text = strName(0)
assigns the first character in the strName **variable (the letter J) to the** lblLetter.Text **property;**
equivalent to lblLetter.Text = strName.Substring(0, 1)

Example 2
lblLetter.Text = strName(4)
assigns the last character in the strName **variable (the letter a) to the** lblLetter.Text **property;**
equivalent to lblLetter.Text = strName.Substring(4, 1)

Figure 7-14 Illustration and examples of using a character's index

Although the character's index can typically be used in place of the Substring method to refer to one character, there is a difference between both: the character's index (for example, strName(0)) returns a value that has the Char (character) data type, whereas the Substring method returns a value that has the String data type. This is important because you cannot use a String method, such as ToUpper, on the value returned by using the character's index. You would first need to use the ToString method to convert the Char value to the String data type, like this: strName(3).ToString.ToUpper.

The First Name Application

The First Name application's interface provides a text box for entering a person's first name. The List characters button in the interface uses the index of each character in the name to add the individual characters to a list box.

To code the First Name application:

START HERE

1. Open the Name Solution.sln file contained in the VB2017\Chap07\Name Solution folder. Open the Code Editor window and locate the btnList_Click procedure. The procedure assigns the name entered by the user, excluding any leading or trailing spaces, to the strName variable. It then clears the contents of the lstCharacters list box.

2. Click the **blank line** above the End Sub clause and then enter the For...Next loop shown in Figure 7-15.

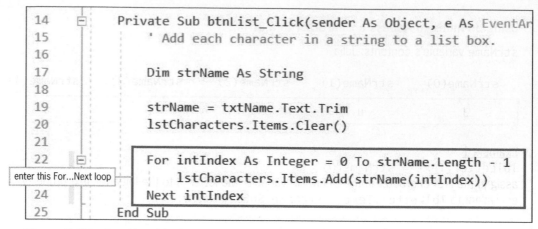

```
14  ⊟        Private Sub btnList_Click(sender As Object, e As EventAr
15             ' Add each character in a string to a list box.
16
17             Dim strName As String
18
19             strName = txtName.Text.Trim
20             lstCharacters.Items.Clear()
21
22  ⊟         For intIndex As Integer = 0 To strName.Length - 1
                   lstCharacters.Items.Add(strName(intIndex))
24             Next intIndex
25             End Sub
```

enter this For...Next loop

Figure 7-15 Completed btnList_Click procedure

3. Save the solution and then start the application. Type **Amanda** in the First name box and then click the **List characters** button. Each character in the name appears on a separate line in the list box. See Figure 7-16.

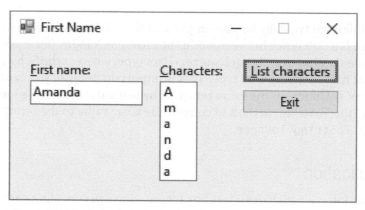

Figure 7-16 Individual characters added to the list box

4. Click the **Exit** button. Close the Code Editor window and then close the solution.

Mini-Quiz 7-3

1. The `strItem` variable contains the string "XMredBQ". Write a statement that uses the Substring method to assign the string "red" to the `strColor` variable.

2. The `strName` variable contains the string "Jane H. Doe". Write a statement that uses the Substring method to assign the string "H" to the `strInitial` variable.

3. Rewrite the statement from Question 2 using the H character's index.

3) strInitial = strName(5)
1) strColor = strItem.Substring(2, 3) 2) strInitial = strName.Substring(5, 1)

YOU DO IT 4!

Create an application named You Do It 4 and save it in the VB2017\Chap07 folder. Add two labels and two buttons to the form. Create a class-level variable named `strLetters` and initialize it to the first 10 uppercase letters of the alphabet (the letters A through J). The first button's Click event procedure should use the appropriate character's index to display the fifth letter from the `strLetters` variable (the letter E) in the first label. The second button should use a loop and the appropriate indexes to display the letters CDEF in the second label. Code the procedures. Save the solution and then start and test the application. Close the solution.

F-7 Remove Method

You can use Visual Basic's **Remove method** to remove a specified number of characters located anywhere in a string. The method returns a string with the appropriate characters removed. Figure 7-17 shows the method's syntax and includes examples of using it. In the syntax, *string* can be a String variable, a String named constant, or the Text property of a control. When processing the method, the computer first stores a temporary copy of the *string* in its main memory. It then performs the specified removal on the copy only; it does not remove any characters from the original *string*.

Remove Method

Syntax
string.**Remove**(*startIndex*[, *numCharsToRemove*])

Example 1
```
strCityState = "Atlanta, GA"
txtState.Text = strCityState.Remove(0, 9)
```
assigns the string "GA" to the txtState.Text property

Example 2
```
strCityState = "Atlanta, GA"
txtCity.Text = strCityState.Remove(7)
```
assigns the string "Atlanta" to the txtCity.Text property. (You can also write the assignment statement as `txtCity.Text = strCityState.Remove(7, 4)`.)

Example 3
```
strFirst = "John"
strFirst = strFirst.Remove(2, 1)
```
assigns the string "Jon" to the `strFirst` variable.

Figure 7-17 Syntax and examples of the Remove method

The method's *startIndex* argument is the index of the first character you want removed from the copy of the *string*. The optional *numCharsToRemove* argument is the number of characters you want removed. To remove only the first character from a string, you use 0 as the startIndex and

1 as the numCharsToRemove. To remove the fourth through eighth characters, you use 3 as the startIndex and 5 as the numCharsToRemove. If the *numCharsToRemove* argument is omitted, the method removes all of the characters from the startIndex position through the end of the string, as shown in Example 2 in Figure 7-17.

F-8 Trim, TrimStart, and TrimEnd Methods

In Chapter 4, you learned how to use the **Trim method** to remove space characters from both the beginning and end of a string. You can also use the Trim method to remove other characters, such as the dollar sign or percent sign. If you need to remove characters from only the beginning of a string, you use the **TrimStart method**. Similarly, to remove characters from only the end of a string, you use the **TrimEnd method**. Figure 7-18 shows the syntax of these methods along with examples of using them. In each syntax, *string* can be a String variable, a String named constant, or the Text property of a control. The optional *trimChars* argument is a comma-separated list of characters that you want removed (trimmed). The default value for the *trimChars* argument is the space character (" "c). When processing the methods, the computer makes a temporary copy of the *string* in memory; it then removes the characters from the copy only.

Trim, TrimStart, and TrimEnd Methods

Syntax
string.**Trim**[(*trimChars*)]
string.**TrimStart**[(*trimChars*)]
string.**TrimEnd**[(*trimChars*)]

Example 1
```
txtPrice.Text = "$$$34$$"
strPrice = txtPrice.Text.Trim("$"c)
```
assigns the string "34" to the strPrice variable

Example 2
```
txtSales.Text = " $456.25   "
strSales = txtSales.Text.Trim("$"c, " "c )
```
assigns the string "456.25" to the strSales variable

— a space character

Example 3
```
strNetPay = "$****340.56"
strNetPay = strNetPay.TrimStart("$"c, "*"c)
```
assigns the string "340.56" to the strNetPay variable.

Example 4
```
strRate = "10%"
lblRate.Text = strRate.TrimEnd("%"c)
```
assigns the string "10" to the lblRate.Text property

Figure 7-18 Syntax and examples of the Trim, TrimStart, and TrimEnd methods

The Trim("$"c) method in Example 1 makes a temporary copy of the value stored in the txtPrice.Text property and then removes any leading or trailing dollar signs from the copy. As you learned earlier, the letter c is the literal type character that forces a string to assume the Char (character) data type. The Trim("$"c, " "c) method in Example 2 copies the value stored in the txtSales.Text property and then removes any leading or trailing dollar signs and space characters from the copy. In Example 3, the TrimStart("$"c, "*"c) method copies the value stored in the **strNetPay** variable and then removes any leading dollar signs and asterisks from the copy. In Example 4, the TrimEnd("%"c) method removes any trailing percent signs from a copy of the value stored in the **strRate** variable.

The Tax Calculator Application

You will use the TrimEnd method in the Tax Calculator application, which calculates the amount of sales tax to charge a customer.

To code the Tax Calculator application:

START HERE

1. Open the Tax Solution.sln file contained in the VB2017\Chap07\Tax Solution folder.

2. Open the Code Editor window and locate the frmMain_Load procedure. The procedure adds three tax rates to the lstRates control, formatting each with a percent sign and no decimal places. It then selects the first rate in the list.

3. Start the application. Type **100** in the Sales box and then click the **Calculate** button. The Sales tax box shows $0.00, which is incorrect. Click the **Exit** button.

4. Locate the btnCalc_Click procedure. The assignment statement on Line 20 assigns the item selected in the lstRates control to the **strRate** variable, and the TryParse method on Line 21 tries to convert the variable's contents to the Double data type. However, as you learned in Chapter 3, the TryParse method cannot convert a string that contains a percent sign. You can use the TrimEnd method to fix this problem.

5. Type the comment and TrimEnd method indicated in Figure 7-19.

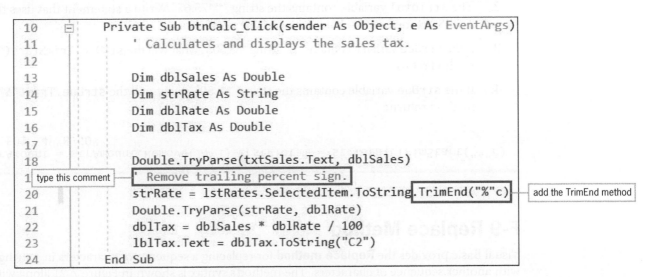

```
10    Private Sub btnCalc_Click(sender As Object, e As EventArgs)
11        ' Calculates and displays the sales tax.
12
13        Dim dblSales As Double
14        Dim strRate As String
15        Dim dblRate As Double
16        Dim dblTax As Double
17
18        Double.TryParse(txtSales.Text, dblSales)
19        ' Remove trailing percent sign.          ← type this comment
20        strRate = lstRates.SelectedItem.ToString.TrimEnd("%"c)   ← add the TrimEnd method
21        Double.TryParse(strRate, dblRate)
22        dblTax = dblSales * dblRate / 100
23        lblTax.Text = dblTax.ToString("C2")
24    End Sub
```

Figure 7-19 Comment and TrimEnd method entered in the procedure

6. Save the solution and then start the application. Type **100** in the Sales box and then click the **Calculate** button. The correct sales tax appears in the Sales tax box. See Figure 7-20.

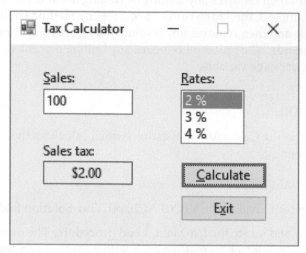

Figure 7-20   Interface showing the correct sales tax

7. Click the **Exit** button. Close the Code Editor window and then close the solution.

Mini-Quiz 7-4

1. The `strAmount` variable contains the string "1,234". Write a statement that uses the Remove method to change the variable's contents to "1234".

2. The `strTotal` variable contains the string "***75.67". Write a statement that uses the TrimStart method to change the variable's contents to "75.67".

3. If the `strDue` variable contains the string "8.50", what will the `strDue.TrimStart("$"c)` method return?

4. If the `strDue` variable contains the string "8.50", what will the `strDue.Trim("$"c)` method return?

3) "8.50$" 4) "8.50"
1) strAmount = strAmount.Remove(1, 1) 2) strTotal = strTotal.TrimStart("*"c)

F-9 Replace Method

Visual Basic provides the **Replace method** for replacing a sequence of characters in a string with another sequence of characters. The method's syntax is shown in Figure 7-21 along with examples of using it. In the syntax, *string* can be a String variable, a String named constant, or the Text property of a control. When processing the method, the computer makes a temporary copy of the *string* in memory and then replaces the characters in the copy only. The method returns a string with all occurrences of *oldValue* replaced with *newValue*.

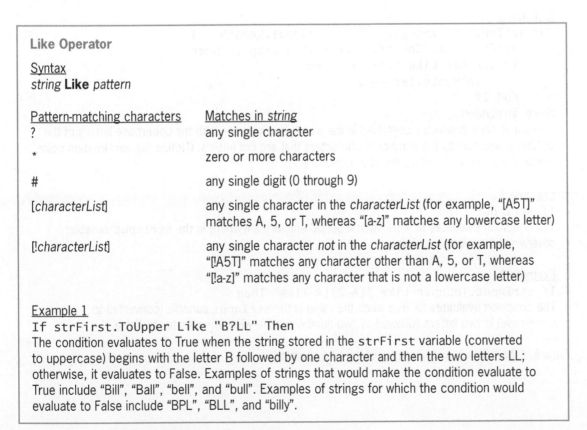

Replace Method

Syntax
string.**Replace**(*oldValue*, *newValue*)

Example 1
strQuote = "To Be Or Not To Be" [space character]
strQuote = strQuote.Replace("To ", "2")
assigns the string "2Be Or Not 2Be" to the strQuote variable

Example 2
txtCode.Text = "45-6-789"
strCode = txtCode.Text.Replace("-","")
assigns the string "456789" to the strCode variable

Figure 7-21   Syntax and examples of the Replace method

F-10 Like Operator

The **Like operator** allows you to use pattern-matching characters to determine whether one string is equal to another string. Figure 7-22 shows the operator's syntax and includes examples of using it. In the syntax, *string* can be a String variable, a String named constant, or the Text property of a control. *Pattern* is a String expression containing one or more of the pattern-matching characters listed in the figure.

Like Operator

Syntax
string **Like** *pattern*

Pattern-matching characters	Matches in *string*
?	any single character
*	zero or more characters
#	any single digit (0 through 9)
[*characterList*]	any single character in the *characterList* (for example, "[A5T]" matches A, 5, or T, whereas "[a-z]" matches any lowercase letter)
[!*characterList*]	any single character *not* in the *characterList* (for example, "[!A5T]" matches any character other than A, 5, or T, whereas "[!a-z]" matches any character that is not a lowercase letter)

Example 1
If strFirst.ToUpper Like "B?LL" Then
The condition evaluates to True when the string stored in the strFirst variable (converted to uppercase) begins with the letter B followed by one character and then the two letters LL; otherwise, it evaluates to False. Examples of strings that would make the condition evaluate to True include "Bill", "Ball", "bell", and "bull". Examples of strings for which the condition would evaluate to False include "BPL", "BLL", and "billy".

Figure 7-22   Syntax and examples of the Like operator (continues)

(continued)

Example 2

```
If txtState.Text Like "K*" Then
```

The condition evaluates to True when the value in the txtState control's Text property begins with the letter K followed by zero or more characters; otherwise, it evaluates to False. Examples of strings that would make the condition evaluate to True include "KANSAS", "Ky", and "Kentucky". Examples of strings for which the condition would evaluate to False include "kansas" and "ky".

Example 3

```
Do While strId Like "###*"
```

The condition evaluates to True when the string stored in the strId variable begins with three digits followed by zero or more characters; otherwise, it evaluates to False. Examples of strings that would make the condition evaluate to True include "178" and "983Ab". Examples of strings for which the condition would evaluate to False include "X34" and "34Z5".

Example 4

```
If strFirst.ToUpper Like "T[OI]M" Then
```

The condition evaluates to True when the string stored in the strFirst variable (converted to uppercase) is either "TOM" or "TIM". When the variable (converted to uppercase) does not contain "TOM" or "TIM"—for example, when it contains "TAM" or "TOMMY"—the condition evaluates to False.

Example 5

```
If strLetter Like "[a-z]" Then
```

The condition evaluates to True when the string stored in the strLetter variable is one lowercase letter; otherwise, it evaluates to False.

Example 6

```
For intIndex As Integer = 0 To strInput.Length - 1
    strChar = strInput(intIndex).ToString.ToUpper
    If strChar Like "[!A-Z]" Then
        intNonLetter += 1
    End If
Next intIndex
```

Compares each character contained in the strInput variable with the uppercase letters of the alphabet, and counts the number of characters that are not letters. (Notice the exclamation point, which stands for *not*, before the *characterList*.)

Example 7

```
If strInput Like "*.*" Then
```

The condition evaluates to True when a period appears anywhere in the strInput variable; otherwise, it evaluates to False.

Example 8

```
If strInput.ToUpper Like "[A-Z][A-Z]##" Then
```

The condition evaluates to True when the value in the strInput variable (converted to uppercase) is two letters followed by two numbers; otherwise, it evaluates to False.

Figure 7-22   Syntax and examples of the Like operator

As Figure 7-22 indicates, the question mark (?) character in a pattern represents one character only, whereas the asterisk (*) character represents zero or more characters. To represent a single digit in a pattern, you use the number sign (#) character. The last two pattern-matching characters listed in the figure contain a *characterList*, which is simply a listing of characters. "[K9M]" is a characterList that contains three characters: K, 9, and M. You can also include a range of values in a characterList. You do this using a hyphen to separate the lowest value in the range from the highest value in the range. For example, to include all lowercase letters in a characterList, you use "[a-z]". To include both lowercase and uppercase letters in a characterList, you use "[a-zA-Z]".

The Like operator performs a case-sensitive comparison of the *string* to the *pattern*. If the string matches the pattern, the Like operator returns the Boolean value True; otherwise, it returns the Boolean value False.

Inventory Application

The Inventory application will use the Like operator to verify that the inventory number entered by the user consists of three letters followed by two numbers.

To code the Inventory application:

START HERE

1. Open the Inventory Solution.sln file contained in the VB2017\Chap07\Inventory Solution folder. Open the Code Editor window and locate the btnAdd_Click procedure. Modify the If clause as shown in Figure 7-23.

```
18    Private Sub btnAdd_Click(sender As Object, e As EventArgs) H
19        ' Add an inventory number to a list box.
20
21        Dim strNumber As String
22
23        strNumber = txtNumber.Text.ToUpper.Trim
24        If strNumber Like "[A-Z][A-Z][A-Z]##" Then      add this condition to the If clause
25            lstNumbers.Items.Add(strNumber)
26        Else
27            MessageBox.Show("Incorrect inventory number.",
28                            "Inventory", MessageBoxButtons.OK,
29                            MessageBoxIcon.Information)
30        End If
31    End Sub
```

Figure 7-23 Completed btnAdd_Click procedure

2. Save the solution and then start the application. First, test the application using an invalid inventory number. Type **abc2f** as the inventory number and then click the **Add to list** button. The "Incorrect inventory number." message appears in a message box. Close the message box.

3. Next, test the application using a valid inventory number. Change the inventory number to **abc23** and then click the **Add to list** button. ABC23 appears in the Inventory list box. See Figure 7-24.

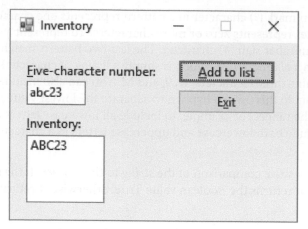

Figure 7-24 Inventory number added to the list box

4. On your own, test the application using different valid and invalid inventory numbers. When you are finished testing the application, click the **Exit** button. Close the Code Editor window and then close the solution.

Mini-Quiz 7-5

1. The `strTotal` variable contains the string "***75.67". Write a statement that uses the Replace method to change the variable's contents to "75.67".

2. Write an If clause that determines whether the `strInput` variable contains two numbers followed by an uppercase letter.

3. Write an If clause that determines whether the `strInput` variable contains a dollar sign followed by a number and a letter (in uppercase or lowercase).

3) If strInput Like "[$]#[a-zA-Z]" Then
1) strTotal = strTotal.Replace("*","") 2) If strInput Like "##[A-Z]" Then

YOU DO IT 5!

Create an application named You Do It 5 and save it in the VB2017\Chap07 folder. Add a text box, a label, and a button to the form. The button's Click event procedure should display the message "OK" when the text box contains two numbers followed by zero or more characters; otherwise, it should display the message "Not OK". Display the message in the label control. Code the procedure. Save the solution and then start and test the application. Close the solution.

APPLY THE CONCEPTS LESSON

After studying this lesson, you should be able to:

- A-1 Code the Check Digit application
- A-2 Code the Password application
- A-3 Generate random integers
- A-4 Code the Guess a Letter application
- A-5 Code the Guess the Word Game application

A-1 Code the Check Digit Application

A **check digit** is a digit that is added to either the beginning or the end (but typically the end) of a number for the purpose of validating the number's authenticity. A check digit is used on a credit card number, a bank account number, a product's UPC (Universal Product Code), and a book's ISBN (International Standard Book Number). Many algorithms for creating a check digit have been developed, including the one shown in Figure 7-25, which is used for 13-character ISBNs.

Algorithm

1. Starting with the second digit, multiply every other digit by 3, and then total the results. In other words, multiply the second, fourth, sixth, eighth, tenth, and twelfth digits by 3, and then add together all of the products.
2. Add together each of the digits skipped in Step 1. These will be the first, third, fifth, seventh, ninth, and eleventh digits.
3. Add the sum from Step 1 to the sum from Step 2.
4. Divide the sum from Step 3 by 10 and find the remainder.
5. If the remainder from Step 4 is 0, then the check digit is 0. Otherwise, subtract the remainder from 10, giving the check digit.

<u>Example</u>
ISBN without check digit: 978-1-337-10212
ISBN with check digit: 978-1-337-10212-4 (calculated as shown here)

Step 1:	9	7 *3 21	8	1 *3 3	3	3 *3 9	7	1 *3 3	0	2 *3 6	1	2 *3 6	48
Step 2:	9		8		3		7		0		1		28
Step 3:													48 + 28 = 76
Step 4:													76 Mod 10 = 6
Step 5:													10 − 6 = 4	⟶ check digit

Figure 7-25   Check digit algorithm for 13-character ISBNs

Figure 7-26 shows the interface for the Check Digit application. The interface provides a text box for the user to enter a book's ISBN without the check digit and without any hyphens. The Assign check digit button will calculate the appropriate check digit and then display the final ISBN in the interface.

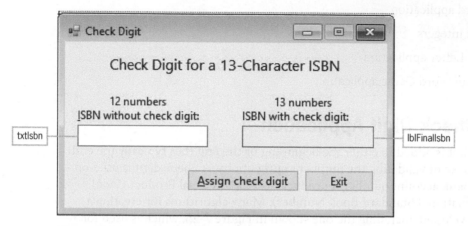

Figure 7-26　Check Digit application's interface

START HERE

To code the Check Digit application:

1. Open the Check Digit Solution.sln file contained in the VB2017\Chap07\Check Digit Solution folder.

2. Open the Code Editor window and locate the txtIsbn_KeyPress procedure. The procedure allows the text box to accept only numbers and the Backspace key.

3. Locate the btnAssign_Click procedure. The procedure declares seven variables. The strIsbn variable will store the 12 characters entered in the text box. The intDigit variable will be used by a TryParse method that converts each character stored in the strIsbn variable to an integer. The intTotalOdd, intTotalEven, and intGrandTotal variables will store the sums from Steps 1, 2, and 3 in the check digit algorithm. The intRemainder variable will store the remainder calculated in the algorithm's Step 4, and the intCheckDigit variable will store the check digit.

4. Before coding the check digit algorithm, you need to verify that the user entered exactly 12 characters in the txtIsbn control. Modify the selection structure's If clause as indicated in Figure 7-27, and then position the insertion point as shown in the figure.

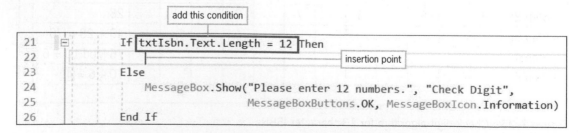

Figure 7-27　Condition added to the If clause

5. If the control does not contain exactly 12 characters, the selection structure will display an appropriate message. Notice that the code to display the message has already been entered in the structure's false path. On the other hand, if the control contains the correct number of characters, the selection structure's true path will assign the characters to the `strIsbn` variable. Type the following assignment statement and then press **Enter**:

```
strIsbn = txtIsbn.Text
```

6. Now you can start coding the check digit algorithm. The first step in the algorithm multiplies every other digit (starting with the second digit) by 3 and then totals the results. As mentioned earlier in Figure 7-25, these are the second, fourth, sixth, eighth, tenth, and twelfth digits in the ISBN. In the `strIsbn` variable, however, these digits will have indexes of 1, 3, 5, 7, 9, and 11. You can use a For...Next loop and either the Substring method or the character's index to access the individual characters. Enter the For...Next loop shown in Figure 7-28, and then position the insertion point as shown in the figure. (The parentheses in the assignment statement are not necessary because multiplication has a higher precedence than addition; however, they serve to make the statement easier to understand. In the TryParse method, you can use `strIsbn.Substring(intOdd, 1)` instead of `strIsbn(intOdd)`.)

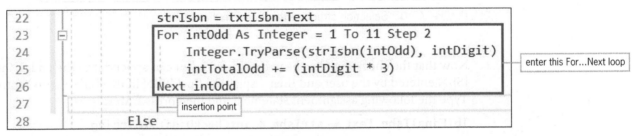

Figure 7-28 For...Next loop for Step 1 in the algorithm

7. The second step in the algorithm adds together each of the digits skipped in the algorithm's first step. These are the first, third, fifth, seventh, ninth, and eleventh digits in the ISBN. In the `strIsbn` variable, these digits will have indexes of 0, 2, 4, 6, 8, and 10. Here too, you can use a For...Next loop and either the Substring method or the character's index to access the characters. Enter the For...Next loop shown in Figure 7-29, and then position the insertion point as shown in the figure. (In the TryParse method, you can use `strIsbn.Substring(intEven, 1)` instead of `strIsbn(intEven)`.)

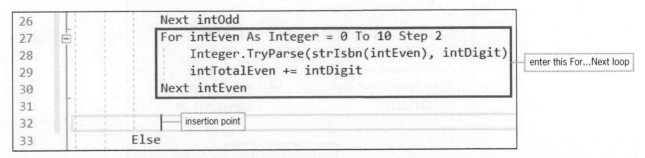

Figure 7-29 For...Next loop for Step 2 in the algorithm

8. The third step in the algorithm adds together the sums from the first two steps in the algorithm. Type the following assignment statement and then press **Enter**:

`intGrandTotal = intTotalOdd + intTotalEven`

9. The fourth step in the algorithm finds the remainder after dividing the total sum by 10. Type the following assignment statement and then press **Enter** twice:

`intRemainder = intGrandTotal Mod 10`

10. The last step in the check digit algorithm uses the remainder calculated in the previous step to determine the check digit. As indicated earlier in Figure 7-25, if the remainder is 0, then the check digit is 0. If the remainder is not 0, then the check digit is calculated by subtracting the remainder from the number 10. Enter the selection structure shown in Figure 7-30, and then position the insertion point as shown in the figure.

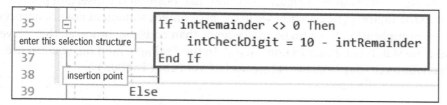

Figure 7-30 Selection structure for Step 5 in the algorithm

11. Now that the check digit has been determined, you can append it to the end of the ISBN entered by the user and then display the final ISBN in the lblFinalIsbn control. Type the following assignment statement and then press **Enter**:

`lblFinalIsbn.Text = strIsbn & intCheckDigit.ToString`

12. Save the solution and then start the application. First, you will enter an invalid number of characters. Type **9781** and then click the **Assign check digit** button. The "Please enter 12 numbers." message appears in a message box. Close the message box.

13. Change the text box entry to **978133710212** and then click the **Assign check digit** button. The button's Click event procedure calculates the appropriate check digit (4), appends it to the ISBN entered by the user, and then displays the final ISBN in the interface. See Figure 7-31.

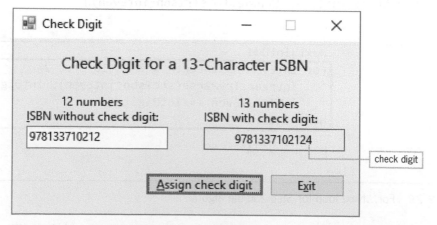

Figure 7-31 Final ISBN shown in the interface

14. On your own, display the final ISBNs for the following books: 978-1-285-86026, 978-1-285-86019, 978-1-285-85691, and 978-1-305-87001. (The check digits should be 8, 0, 9, and 7, respectively.)

15. When you are finished testing the application, click the **Exit** button. Close the Code Editor window and then close the solution. The completed btnAssign_Click procedure is shown in Figure 7-32.

```
Private Sub btnAssign_Click(sender As Object, e As EventArgs) Handles
btnAssign.Click
    ' Assign a check digit to an ISBN.

    Dim strIsbn As String
    Dim intDigit As Integer
    Dim intTotalOdd As Integer
    Dim intTotalEven As Integer
    Dim intGrandTotal As Integer
    Dim intRemainder As Integer
    Dim intCheckDigit As Integer

    If txtIsbn.Text.Length = 12 Then
        strIsbn = txtIsbn.Text
        For intOdd As Integer = 1 To 11 Step 2
            Integer.TryParse(strIsbn(intOdd), intDigit)
            intTotalOdd += (intDigit * 3)
        Next intOdd
        For intEven As Integer = 0 To 10 Step 2
            Integer.TryParse(strIsbn(intEven), intDigit)
            intTotalEven += intDigit
        Next intEven

        intGrandTotal = intTotalOdd + intTotalEven
        intRemainder = intGrandTotal Mod 10

        If intRemainder <> 0 Then
            intCheckDigit = 10 - intRemainder
        End If
        lblFinalIsbn.Text = strIsbn & intCheckDigit.ToString

    Else
        MessageBox.Show("Please enter 12 numbers.", "Check Digit",
                    MessageBoxButtons.OK, MessageBoxIcon.Information)

    End If
End Sub
```

Figure 7-32   Completed btnAssign_Click procedure

A-2 Code the Password Application

Figure 7-33 shows the interface for the Password application. The interface provides a text box for the user to enter one or more words. The Create password button will create a password using the first letter from each of the words. It will then insert a number immediately after the first character. The number will represent the length of the password before the number is inserted.

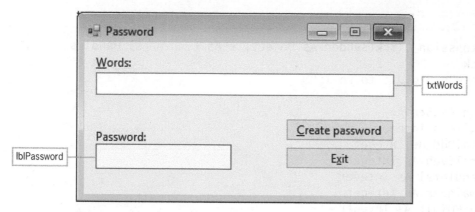

Figure 7-33   Password application's interface

START HERE

To code the Password application:

1. Open the Password Solution.sln file contained in the VB2017\Chap07\Password Solution folder.

2. Open the Code Editor window and locate the btnCreate_Click procedure. The procedure will use the `strWords` variable to store the user's input, and use the `strPassword` variable to store the password. It will use the `intSpaceIndex` variable to store the indexes of the space characters that separate each word entered by the user.

3. First, you will assign the contents of the txtWords.Text property, excluding any leading or trailing spaces, to the `strWords` variable. Click the **blank line** above the If clause. Type the following assignment statement and then press **Enter**:

   ```
   strWords = txtWords.Text.Trim
   ```

4. Next, you will verify that the `strWords` variable is not empty. Change the If clause as follows:

   ```
   If strWords <> String.Empty Then
   ```

5. Click the **blank line** below the first comment in the selection structure's true path. The first character in the password should be the first character entered by the user. You can access the first character using either `strWords.Substring(0, 1)` or `strWords(0)`. Type the following assignment statement and then press **Enter**:

   ```
   strPassword = strWords(0)
   ```

6. Now that the first character from the first word has been assigned to the password, you can move on to the next word in the `strWords` variable. You do this by searching for the space character that separates the first word from the second word. Click the **blank line** above the Do Until clause. Type the following assignment statement (be sure to include a space character between the quotation marks) and then press **Enter**:

   ```
   intSpaceIndex = strWords.IndexOf(" ")
   ```

7. If the strWords variable contains only one word, the IndexOf method will return −1 because it did not locate a space character; the search can stop at that point. However, if it does not contain −1, the search for spaces should continue until it does. Change the Do Until clause as follows:

Do Until intSpaceIndex = -1

8. If the intSpaceIndex variable contains a value other than −1, it means that a space was located. In that case, you will concatenate the character that appears immediately after the space to the contents of the strPassword variable. Click the **blank line** below the **'** the space to the password. comment and then type the assignment statement shown in Figure 7-34.

```
26      Do Until intSpaceIndex = -1
27          ' Concatenate the character that follows
28          ' the space to the password.
29          strPassword = strPassword & strWords(intSpaceIndex + 1)      type this assignment
30          ' Search for the next space.                                  statement
```

Figure 7-34   Concatenation assignment statement entered in the procedure

9. Now you can search for the next space character in the strWords variable. Click the **blank line** above the Loop clause. Type the assignment statement shown in Figure 7-35.

```
30          ' Search for the next space.
31          intSpaceIndex = strWords.IndexOf(" ", intSpaceIndex + 1)      type this assignment
32      Loop                                                              statement
```

Figure 7-35   Search assignment statement entered in the procedure

10. When the loop ends, the strPassword variable will contain the first letter from each of the words entered by the user. To create the final password, you just need to insert a number after the first character in the variable. The number represents the length of the password before the number is inserted. After inserting the number, the procedure can display the final password in the lblPassword control. Type the two additional assignment statements indicated in Figure 7-36.

```
34          ' Insert the number after the first character.
35          strPassword = strPassword.Insert(1, strPassword.Length.ToString)   type these two assignment
36          ' Display the final password.                                       statements
37          lblPassword.Text = strPassword
38      End If
```

Figure 7-36   Additional assignment statements entered in the procedure

11. Save the solution and then start the application. Type **May the Force be with you** and then click the **Create password** button. The btnCreate_Click procedure displays the password shown in Figure 7-37. (The number 6 is the length of the password without the number.)

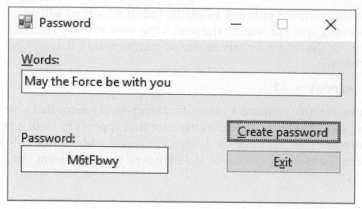

Figure 7-37   Password created by the btnCreate_Click procedure

12. On your own, test the application using different words. When you are finished testing, click the **Exit** button. Close the Code Editor window and then close the solution. The completed btnCreate_Click procedure is shown in Figure 7-38.

```
Private Sub btnCreate_Click(sender As Object, e As EventArgs) Handles
btnCreate.Click
    ' Create a password.

    Dim strWords As String
    Dim strPassword As String
    Dim intSpaceIndex As Integer

    strWords = txtWords.Text.Trim

    If strWords <> String.Empty Then
        ' Assign the first character as the password.
        strPassword = strWords(0)

        ' Search for the first space in the input.
        intSpaceIndex = strWords.IndexOf(" ")

        Do Until intSpaceIndex = -1
            ' Concatenate the character that follows
            ' the space to the password.
            strPassword = strPassword & strWords(intSpaceIndex + 1)
            ' Search for the next space.
            intSpaceIndex = strWords.IndexOf(" ", intSpaceIndex + 1)
        Loop

        ' Insert the number after the first character.
        strPassword = strPassword.Insert(1, strPassword.Length.ToString)
        ' Display the final password.
        lblPassword.Text = strPassword
    End If
End Sub
```

Figure 7-38   Completed btnCreate_Click procedure

A-3 Generate Random Integers

Random numbers are used in many computer game programs. The numbers can be integers or real numbers, which are numbers with a decimal place. In this lesson, you will learn how to generate random integers.

Most programming languages provide a **pseudo-random number generator**, which is a mathematical algorithm that produces a sequence of numbers. Although the numbers are not completely random, they are sufficiently random for practical purposes. The pseudo-random number generator in Visual Basic is represented by an object whose data type is Random.

Figure 7-39 shows the syntax and examples of generating random integers in Visual Basic. As the figure indicates, you first create a **Random object** to represent the pseudo-random number generator in your application's code. You create the object by declaring it in a Dim statement, which you enter in the procedure that will use the generator. After the Random object is created, you can use the object's **Random.Next method** to generate random integers. In the method's syntax, *randomObject* is the name of the Random object. The *minValue* and *maxValue* arguments must be integers, and minValue must be less than maxValue. The Random.Next method returns an integer that is greater than or equal to minValue but less than maxValue.

Generating Random Integers

Syntax
Dim *randomObject* **As New Random**
randomObject.**Next(***minValue, maxValue***)**

Example 1
```
Dim randGen As New Random
intNum = randGen.Next(1, 51)
```
The Dim statement creates a Random object named randGen. The randGen.Next(1, 51) expression generates a random integer from 1 through 50. The assignment statement assigns the random integer to the intNum variable.

Example 2
```
Dim randGen As New Random
intNum = randGen.Next(-10, 20)
```
The Dim statement creates a Random object named randGen. The randGen.Next(-10, 20) expression generates a random integer from –10 through 19. The assignment statement assigns the random integer to the intNum variable.

Figure 7-39   Syntax and examples of generating random integers

---

Mini-Quiz 7-6

1. Write a Dim statement that creates a Random object named randGen.

2. Using the Random object created in Question 1, write a statement that assigns a random integer from 25 to 100 (including 100) to the intNum variable.

3. Using the Random object created in Question 1, write a statement that assigns a random integer from 2 to 25 (excluding 25) to the intNum variable.

3) intNum = randGen.Next(2, 25)
1) Dim randGen As New Random 2) intNum = randGen.Next(25, 101)

A-4 Code the Guess a Letter Application

You will use random numbers in the Guess a Letter application, which you will code in this section. The application's interface and pseudocode are shown in Figure 7-40.

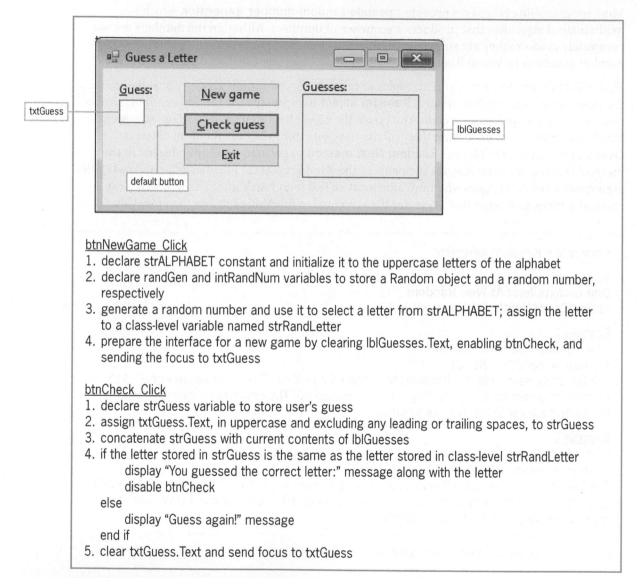

btnNewGame_Click
1. declare strALPHABET constant and initialize it to the uppercase letters of the alphabet
2. declare randGen and intRandNum variables to store a Random object and a random number, respectively
3. generate a random number and use it to select a letter from strALPHABET; assign the letter to a class-level variable named strRandLetter
4. prepare the interface for a new game by clearing lblGuesses.Text, enabling btnCheck, and sending the focus to txtGuess

btnCheck_Click
1. declare strGuess variable to store user's guess
2. assign txtGuess.Text, in uppercase and excluding any leading or trailing spaces, to strGuess
3. concatenate strGuess with current contents of lblGuesses
4. if the letter stored in strGuess is the same as the letter stored in class-level strRandLetter
      display "You guessed the correct letter:" message along with the letter
      disable btnCheck
else
      display "Guess again!" message
end if
5. clear txtGuess.Text and send focus to txtGuess

Figure 7-40 Guess a Letter application's interface and pseudocode

The btnNewGame_Click procedure generates a random number and then uses the number to select a letter from the strALPHABET constant, which contains the uppercase letters of the alphabet. The user enters his or her guess in the txtGuess control and then clicks the Check guess button. The btnCheck_Click procedure records the guess in the lblGuesses control; doing this allows the user to view his or her previous guesses. The procedure then displays a message indicating whether or not the user's guess is correct.

To begin coding the Guess a Letter application: START HERE

1. Open the Letter Guess Solution.sln file contained in the VB2017\Chap07\Letter Guess Solution folder. The Check guess button is the default button in the interface.

2. Open the Code Editor window. First, you will create a class-level variable to store the random letter. A class-level variable is appropriate in this case because the variable will need to be used by two procedures: btnNewGame_Click and btnCheck_Click. Click the **blank line** below the ' Class-level variable. comment. Type the following declaration statement and then press **Enter**:

   ```
   Private strRandLetter As String
   ```

3. Locate the btnNewGame_Click procedure. The procedure declares a String constant named strALPHABET and initializes it to the 26 uppercase letters of the alphabet. The procedure will also need two variables: one to store a Random object and the second to store a random number. Click the **blank line** below the Const statement and then enter the following two Dim statements:

   ```
   Dim randGen As New Random
   Dim intRandNum As Integer
   ```

4. Now the procedure can generate the random number and then use it to select a letter from the strALPHABET constant. The letters contained in the constant have indexes of 0 through 25, so you will need to use 0 and 26 as the minValue and maxValue, respectively, in the Random.Next method. (Recall that the method returns a value that is greater than or equal to the minValue but less than the maxValue.) Click the **blank line** below the second comment in the procedure and then enter the following two assignment statements:

   ```
   intRandNum = randGen.Next(0, 26)
   strRandLetter = strALPHABET(intRandNum)
   ```

5. Before finishing the procedure's code, you will observe how the code you entered so far works. Type the following statement but do not press Enter:

   ```
   MessageBox.Show(strRandLetter)
   ```

6. Save the solution and then start the application. The Check guess button appears dimmed (grayed out) because its Enabled property is set to False in the Properties window. You will learn about the Enabled property in the next section.

7. Click the **New game** button. The random letter selected by the btnNewGame_Click procedure appears in a message box. Close the message box and then click the **New game** button again. A different letter appears in the message box. (If the same letter appears, close the message box and then click the New game button again.) Close the message box and then click the **Exit** button.

8. Delete the **MessageBox.Show(strRandLetter)** statement from the procedure and then save the solution.

Use the Enabled Property and Focus Method

A control's **Enabled property**, which can be set to either True or False, determines whether the control will respond to the user. When the property is set to False, the control appears dimmed (grayed out) during run time, indicating that it is not available for use. You can set the Enabled property either in the Properties window or in a procedure's code.

You can use the **Focus method** to move the focus to a control during run time. The method's syntax is *object*.Focus(), in which *object* is the name of the object to which you want the focus sent. For example, to send the focus to the txtGuess control, you use txtGuess.Focus().

START HERE

To finish coding the btnNewGame_Click procedure:

1. Click the **blank line** above the procedure's End Sub clause and then enter the additional statements shown in Figure 7-41.

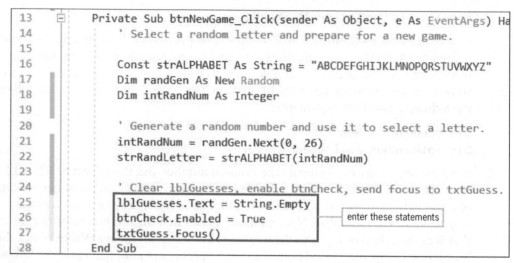

```
13      Private Sub btnNewGame_Click(sender As Object, e As EventArgs) Ha
14          ' Select a random letter and prepare for a new game.
15
16          Const strALPHABET As String = "ABCDEFGHIJKLMNOPQRSTUVWXYZ"
17          Dim randGen As New Random
18          Dim intRandNum As Integer
19
20          ' Generate a random number and use it to select a letter.
21          intRandNum = randGen.Next(0, 26)
22          strRandLetter = strALPHABET(intRandNum)
23
24          ' Clear lblGuesses, enable btnCheck, send focus to txtGuess.
25          lblGuesses.Text = String.Empty          enter these statements
26          btnCheck.Enabled = True
27          txtGuess.Focus()
28      End Sub
```

Figure 7-41   Completed btnNewGame_Click procedure

2. Save the solution.

In the next set of steps, you will code the btnCheck_Click procedure. The procedure's pseudocode is shown earlier in Figure 7-40.

START HERE

To code the btnCheck_Click procedure:

1. Locate the btnCheck_Click procedure. The first two steps in the pseudocode have already been coded: The procedure declares a String variable named strGuess and then assigns the txtGuess.Text property (in uppercase and without any leading or trailing spaces) to the variable.

2. The third step in the pseudocode concatenates the user's guess with the current contents of the lblGuesses control. Click the **blank line** below the ' Display guess in lblGuesses. comment and then enter the assignment statement shown in Figure 7-42. Be sure to type a space character between the quotation marks.

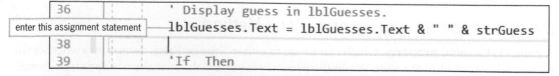

```
36              ' Display guess in lblGuesses.
    enter this assignment statement ——— lblGuesses.Text = lblGuesses.Text & " " & strGuess
38              |
39              'If  Then
```

Figure 7-42   Concatenation assignment statement entered in the procedure

3. The fourth step in the pseudocode is a selection structure whose condition determines whether the user guessed the random letter. Both paths in the structure then display an appropriate message. The code to display the messages has already been entered in the procedure. First, delete the ' (apostrophe) that appears before the If, Else, and End If clauses. Then, change the If clause as follows:

```
If strGuess = strRandLetter Then
```

4. After displaying the appropriate message, the selection structure's true path should disable the btnCheck control because there is no reason to continue checking when the user guessed the random letter. Click the **blank line** above the Else clause. Type the following assignment statement and then press **Enter**:

```
btnCheck.Enabled = False
```

5. The last step in the pseudocode clears the txtGuess.Text property and then sends the focus to the txtGuess control. Click the **blank line** above the End Sub clause and then enter the two additional statements shown in Figure 7-43.

```
30    Private Sub btnCheck_Click(sender As Object, e As EventArgs) Handles btnCh
31        ' Determine whether the user guessed the random letter.
32
33        Dim strGuess As String
34
35        strGuess = txtGuess.Text.Trim.ToUpper
36        ' Display guess in lblGuesses.
37        lblGuesses.Text = lblGuesses.Text & " " & strGuess
38
39        If strGuess = strRandLetter Then
40            MessageBox.Show("You guessed the correct letter: " & strGuess,
41                            "Guess a Letter", MessageBoxButtons.OK,
42                            MessageBoxIcon.Information)
43            btnCheck.Enabled = False
44
45        Else
46            MessageBox.Show("Guess again!", "Guess a Letter",
47                            MessageBoxButtons.OK, MessageBoxIcon.Information)
48        End If
49        txtGuess.Text = String.Empty      ⟵ enter these statements
50        txtGuess.Focus()
51    End Sub
```

Figure 7-43   Completed btnCheck_Click procedure

6. Save the solution and then start the application. Click the **New game** button. Type a letter in the Guess box and then press **Enter**. (Recall that the Check guess button is the default button.) The btnCheck_Click procedure displays an appropriate message. Close the message box. The letter you guessed appears in the lblGuesses control.

7. If you did not guess the correct letter, keep guessing until you do. A sample run of the application is shown in Figure 7-44. Notice that the Check guess button is dimmed when the user's guess is correct.

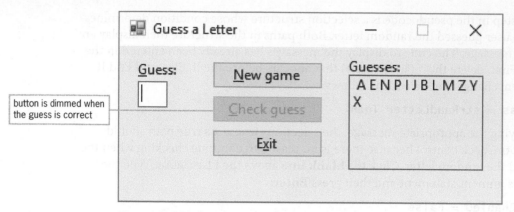

button is dimmed when the guess is correct

Figure 7-44 Sample run of the Guess a Letter application

8. Click the **Exit** button. Close the Code Editor window and then close the solution.

Mini-Quiz 7-7

1. Write a statement that prevents the btnCalc control from responding to the user.

2. Write a statement that reverses the statement from Question 1.

3. Write a statement that moves the insertion point to the txtName control.

1) btnCalc.Enabled = False 2) btnCalc.Enabled = True 3) txtName.Focus()

A-5 Code the Guess the Word Game Application

In this section, you will use many of the concepts you learned in the Focus lesson to code the Guess the Word Game application. The application's interface is shown in Figure 7-45.

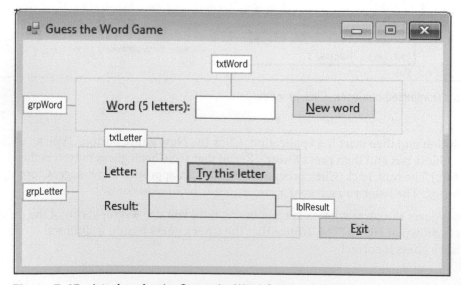

Figure 7-45 Interface for the Guess the Word Game application

The game requires two players. First, player 1 will enter a five-letter word in the txtWord control and then click the New word button. The btnNewWord_Click procedure will display five hyphens in the lblResult control; each hyphen represents a letter in the word. Next, player 2 will enter a letter in the txtLetter control and then click the Try this letter button. The btnTryLetter_Click procedure will determine whether the letter appears in player 1's word. If it does, the procedure will replace the hyphen in the lblResult control with the letter. When all of the hyphens have been replaced, it means that the user guessed the word. At that point, the btnTryLetter_Click procedure will display an appropriate message.

In the next set of steps, you will set the grpLetter control's Enabled property to False; doing this will disable all of the controls contained in the group box during run time. You will also set each text box's **MaxLength property**, which specifies the maximum number of characters the text box will accept. Finally, you will set the txtWord control's **PasswordChar property**, which is typically used for text boxes that contain passwords. The PasswordChar property hides the user's entry by displaying a replacement character (such as an asterisk) in place of the character the user entered. In this case, you will use the property to hide player 1's word from player 2.

To set some properties in the Guess the Word Game application: START HERE

1. Open the Word Guess Solution.sln file contained in the VB2017\Chap07\Word Guess Solution folder. The Try this letter button is the default button in the interface.

2. Click the **grpLetter** control and then set its Enabled property to **False**.

3. Click the **txtLetter** control and then set its MaxLength property to **1**.

4. Click the **txtWord** control and then set its MaxLength property to **5**. Also set its PasswordChar property to * (an asterisk).

5. Save the solution.

Coding the btnNewWord_Click Procedure

The pseudocode for the btnNewWord_Click procedure is shown in Figure 7-46.

```
btnNewWord_Click
if txtWord.Text contains five letters
        disable grpWord
        enable grpLetter
        display five hyphens in lblResult
        send focus to txtLetter
else
        display "Please enter 5 letters." message
end if
```

Figure 7-46   Pseudocode for the btnNewWord_Click procedure

To code the btnNewWord_Click procedure: START HERE

1. Open the Code Editor window and locate the btnNewWord_Click procedure. According to its pseudocode, the procedure will use a selection structure to verify that the txtWord.Text property contains five letters. If it does contain five letters, the structure's true path will perform four tasks; otherwise, its false path will display an appropriate message. The false path has already been coded for you. Change the If clause as shown in Figure 7-47, and also enter the four statements in the true path.

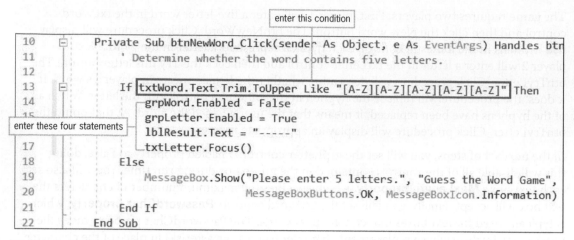

Figure 7-47 Completed btnNewWord_Click procedure

2. Save the solution and then start the application. Type **b** in the Word (5 letters) box. Notice that the letter b is replaced by an asterisk. Click the **New word** button. The btnNewWord_Click procedure displays the "Please enter 5 letters." message. Close the message box.

3. Change the entry in the Word (5 letters) box to **basic** and then click the **New word** button. The btnNewWord_Click procedure performs the four tasks listed in the selection structure's true path. See Figure 7-48.

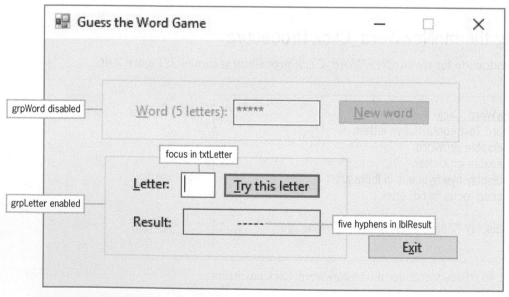

Figure 7-48 Interface showing the tasks performed by the btnNewWord_Click procedure

4. Click the **Exit** button.

Coding the btnTryLetter_Click Procedure

The pseudocode for the btnTryLetter_Click procedure is shown in Figure 7-49.

btnTryLetter_Click
1. declare strWord, strLetter, and strResult variables
2. assign txtWord.Text, in uppercase and excluding any leading or trailing spaces, to strWord
3. assign txtLetter.Text, in uppercase and excluding any leading or trailing spaces, to strLetter
4. assign lblResult.Text to strResult
5. if strWord contains the letter stored in strLetter
    repeat the following for each letter in strWord
        if the current letter in strWord is the same as the letter in strLetter
          remove the hyphen from strResult
          insert the letter in strResult
        end if
    end repeat

    display the contents of strResult in lblResult

    if strResult does not contain any hyphens
        display "You guessed it:" message along with strWord
        enable grpWord
        disable grpLetter
        clear lblResult.Text
        send focus to txtWord
    end if
  else
    display "Try again!" message
  end if
6. clear txtLetter.Text

Figure 7-49 Pseudocode for the btnTryLetter_Click procedure

START HERE

To code the btnTryLetter_Click procedure:

1. Locate the btnTryLetter_Click procedure. The first four steps in the pseudocode have already been coded for you. The **strWord** variable contains the word entered by player 1, and the **strLetter** variable contains the letter entered by player 2. The **strResult** variable contains the current contents of the lblResult.Text property. The first time the procedure is processed, the **strResult** variable will contain the five hyphens assigned to the lblResult control by the btnNewWord_Click procedure.

2. Delete the ' (apostrophe) from the beginning of the If, Else, and End If clauses.

3. According to Step 5 in the pseudocode, the procedure will use a selection structure to determine whether player 1's word contains player 2's letter. Change the If clause as follows:

```
If strWord.Contains(strLetter) Then
```

4. If the letter is not in the word, the selection structure's false path will display the "Try again!" message. The code to display the message is already entered in the procedure. On the other hand, if the letter appears in the word, the selection structure's true path will use a loop to look at each character in the word. Click the **blank line** below the ' Replace the hyphen(s) in strResult. comment. Type the following For clause and then press **Enter**:

```
For intIndex As Integer = 0 To strWord.Length - 1
```

5. Change the Next clause to **Next intIndex** and then click the **blank line** above the clause.

6. The loop body will use a selection structure to determine whether the current character in the word matches player 2's letter. If it does, the structure's true path will remove the hyphen from the strResult variable and then insert the letter in its place. Enter the nested selection structure shown in Figure 7-50.

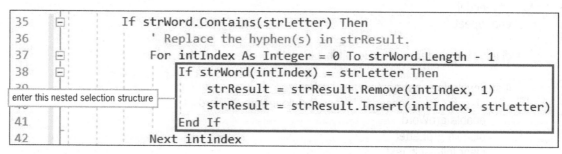

```
35    ⊟        If strWord.Contains(strLetter) Then
36                 ' Replace the hyphen(s) in strResult.
37    ⊟             For intIndex As Integer = 0 To strWord.Length - 1
38    ⊟             If strWord(intIndex) = strLetter Then
39                      strResult = strResult.Remove(intIndex, 1)
40                      strResult = strResult.Insert(intIndex, strLetter)
41                  End If
42             Next intindex
```

enter this nested selection structure

Figure 7-50   Nested selection structure entered in the procedure

7. After the loop has finished processing, the outer selection structure's true path will display the contents of the strResult variable in the lblResult control. Click the **blank line** below the ' Display the contents of strResult. comment. Type the following assignment statement and then press **Enter**:

```
lblResult.Text = strResult
```

8. Next, the outer selection structure's true path needs to determine whether the strResult variable contains any hyphens. Click the **blank line** above the Else clause. Type the following nested If clause and then press **Enter**:

```
If strResult.Contains("-") = False Then
```

9. If there are no more hyphens in the variable, it means that player 2 guessed all of the letters in player 1's word. In that case, the nested selection structure should display the "You guessed it:" message along with the word. It should also enable the grpWord control, disable the grpLetter control, clear the lblResult.Text property, and send the focus to the txtWord control. Enter the five statements indicated in Figure 7-51.

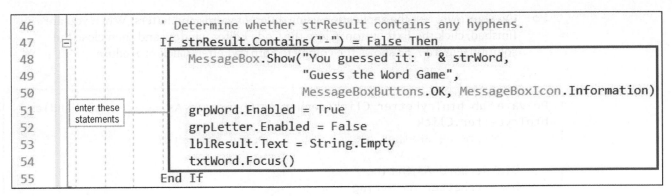

```
46              ' Determine whether strResult contains any hyphens.
47        ⊟      If strResult.Contains("-") = False Then
48                  MessageBox.Show("You guessed it: " & strWord,
49                              "Guess the Word Game",
50                              MessageBoxButtons.OK, MessageBoxIcon.Information)
51   enter these   grpWord.Enabled = True
52   statements    grpLetter.Enabled = False
53                  lblResult.Text = String.Empty
54                  txtWord.Focus()
55              End If
```

Figure 7-51   Nested selection structure's true path

10. The last step in the pseudocode clears the txtLetter.Text property. The code for this step has already been entered above the procedure's End Sub clause. Save the solution and then start the application. Type **apple** and then click the **New word** button.

11. Type **e** and then press **Enter**. (Recall that the Try this letter button is the default button.) The letter E appears after the four hyphens in the Result box.

12. Type **k** and press **Enter**. The "Try again!" message appears. Close the message box.

13. Type **p** and press **Enter**. The Result box now shows a hyphen followed by the letters PP, another hyphen, and the letter E. See Figure 7-52.

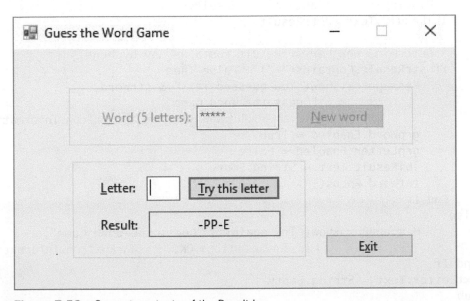

Figure 7-52   Current contents of the Result box

14. Type **a** and press **Enter**, then type **l** (the letter l) and press **Enter**. The "You guessed it: APPLE" message appears. Close the message box.

15. On your own, test the application using different words and letters. When you are finished, click the **Exit** button. Close the Code Editor window and then close the solution. Figure 7-53 shows the completed btnTryLetter_Click procedure.

```
Private Sub btnTryLetter_Click(sender As Object, e As EventArgs) Handles
btnTryLetter.Click
    ' Determine whether player 2 has guessed the word.

    Dim strWord As String
    Dim strLetter As String
    Dim strResult As String

    strWord = txtWord.Text.Trim.ToUpper
    strLetter = txtLetter.Text.Trim.ToUpper
    strResult = lblResult.Text

    If strWord.Contains(strLetter) Then
        ' Replace the hyphen(s) in strResult.
        For intIndex As Integer = 0 To strWord.Length - 1
            If strWord(intIndex) = strLetter Then
                strResult = strResult.Remove(intIndex, 1)
                strResult = strResult.Insert(intIndex, strLetter)
            End If
        Next intIndex
        ' Display the contents of strResult.
        lblResult.Text = strResult

        ' Determine whether strResult contains any hyphens.
        If strResult.Contains("-") = False Then
            MessageBox.Show("You guessed it: " & strWord,
                        "Guess the Word Game",
                        MessageBoxButtons.OK, MessageBoxIcon.Information)
            grpWord.Enabled = True
            grpLetter.Enabled = False
            lblResult.Text = String.Empty
            txtWord.Focus()
        End If
    Else
            MessageBox.Show("Try again!", "Guess the Word Game",
                        MessageBoxButtons.OK, MessageBoxIcon.Information)
    End If
    txtLetter.Text = String.Empty
End Sub
```

Figure 7-53   Completed btnTryLetter_Click procedure

Summary

- Check digits are used for validating numbers, such as credit card numbers, bank account numbers, product UPCs, and book ISBNs.

- To generate random integers, you first create a Random object to represent the pseudo-random number generator. You then use the object's Random.Next method to generate a random integer. The method returns a number that is greater than or equal to its *minValue* argument but less than its *maxValue* argument. Refer to the syntax and examples shown earlier in Figure 7-39.

- You disable a control by setting its Enabled property to False either in the Properties window or in a procedure's code. You enable it by setting its Enabled property to True.

- You can send the focus to a control using the control's Focus method.

- A text box's MaxLength property specifies the maximum number of characters that the text box will accept.

- A text box's PasswordChar property specifies the character to use in place of each character entered in the text box.

- Figure 7-54 contains a summary of the concepts covered in this chapter's Focus lesson.

Concept	Syntax	Purpose
Character array	*string*(index)	accesses an individual character in a string
Contains method	*string*.**Contains(**subString**)**	determines whether a string contains a specific sequence of characters; returns a Boolean value
IndexOf method	*string*.**IndexOf(**subString[, startIndex]**)**	determines whether a string contains a specific sequence of characters; returns either −1 or an integer that indicates the starting position of the characters in the string
Insert method	*string*.**Insert(**startIndex, value**)**	inserts characters in a string
Length property	*string*.**Length**	stores an integer that represents the number of characters contained in a string
Like operator	*string* **Like** pattern	uses pattern matching to compare strings
PadLeft method	*string*.**PadLeft(**totalChars[, padCharacter]**)**	pads the beginning of a string with a character until the string has the specified number of characters; right-aligns the string

Figure 7-54 Summary of the concepts covered in the Focus lesson (continues)

(continued)

Concept	Syntax	Purpose
PadRight method	*string*.**PadRight(***totalChars*[, *padCharacter*]**)**	pads the end of a string with a character until the string has the specified number of characters; left-aligns the string
Remove method	*string*.**Remove(***startIndex*[, *numCharsToRemove*]**)**	removes characters from a string
Replace method	*string*.**Replace(***oldValue*, *newValue***)**	replaces all occurrences of *oldValue* in a string with *newValue*
Substring method	*string*.**Substring(***startIndex*[, *numCharsToAccess*]**)**	accesses one or more characters in a string
Trim method	*string*.**Trim**[(*trimChars*)]	removes all *trimChars* from both the beginning and the end of a string
TrimEnd method	*string*.**TrimEnd**[(*trimChars*)]	removes all *trimChars* from the end of a string
TrimStart method	*string*.**TrimStart**[(*trimChars*)]	removes all *trimChars* from the beginning of a string

Figure 7-54 Summary of the concepts covered in the Focus lesson

Key Terms

Array of characters—a string; also called a character array

Character array—a string; a group (or array) of related characters

Check digit—a digit that is added to either the beginning or end (but typically the end) of a number for the purpose of validating the number's authenticity

Contains method—performs a case-sensitive search to determine whether a string contains a specific sequence of characters; returns a Boolean value (True or False)

Enabled property—used to enable (True) or disable (False) a control during run time

Focus method—moves the focus to a specified control during run time

IndexOf method—performs a case-sensitive search to determine whether a string contains a specific sequence of characters; returns either −1 (if the string does not contain the sequence of characters) or an integer that represents the starting position of the sequence of characters

Insert method—inserts characters anywhere in a string

Length property—stores an integer that represents the number of characters contained in a string

Like operator—uses pattern-matching characters to determine whether one string is equal to another string; performs a case-sensitive comparison

MaxLength property—a property of a text box control; specifies the maximum number of characters the control will accept

PadLeft method—right-aligns a string by inserting characters at the beginning of the string

PadRight method—left-aligns a string by inserting characters at the end of the string

PasswordChar property—specifies the character used to hide the user's input

Pseudo-random number generator—a mathematical algorithm that produces a sequence of random numbers; in Visual Basic, the pseudo-random generator is represented by an object whose data type is Random

Random object—represents the pseudo-random number generator in Visual Basic

Random.Next method—used to generate a random integer that is greater than or equal to a minimum value but less than a maximum value

Remove method—removes a specified number of characters located anywhere in a string

Replace method—replaces a sequence of characters in a string with another sequence of characters

Substring method—used to access any number of characters contained in a string

Trim method—removes characters from both the beginning and the end of a string

TrimEnd method—removes characters from the end of a string

TrimStart method—removes characters from the beginning of a string

Review Questions

1. Which of the following assigns the number of characters in the `strAddress` variable to the `intNum` variable?

   a. `intNum = strAddress.Length`

   b. `intNum = strAddress.LengthOf`

   c. `intNum = Length(strAddress)`

   d. `intNum = LengthOf(strAddress)`

2. Which of the following statements changes the contents of the `strWord` variable from "led" to "lead"?

   a. `strWord = strWord.AddTo(2, "a")`

   b. `strWord = strWord.Insert(2, "a")`

   c. `strWord = strWord.Insert(3, "a")`

   d. `strWord = strWord.Into(3, "a"c)`

3. The `strAmount` variable contains the string "678.95". Which of the following statements changes the contents of the variable to the string "678.95!!!"?

   a. `strAmount = strAmount.PadRight(9, "!")`

   b. `strAmount = strAmount.PadRight(9, "!"c)`

   c. `strAmount = strAmount.PadRight(3, "!"c)`

   d. None of the above.

4. Which of the following methods can be used to determine whether the `strRate` variable contains the percent sign?

    a. `blnResult = strRate.Contains("%")`

    b. `intResult = strRate.IndexOf("%")`

    c. `intResult = strRate.IndexOf("%", 0)`

    d. All of the above.

5. If the `strPresident` variable contains the string "Abraham Lincoln", what value will the `strPresident.IndexOf("ham")` method return?

    a. True

    b. −1

    c. 4

    d. 5

6. If the `strName` variable contains the string "Sharon Kelper", which of the following changes the contents of the variable to the string "Sharon P. Kelper"?

    a. `strName = strName.Insert(6, " P.")`

    b. `strName = strName.Insert(7, " P.")`

    c. `strName = strName.Insert(8, "P. ")`

    d. None of the above.

7. If the `strMsg` variable contains the string "Her birthday is Friday!", which of the following assigns the number 16 to the `intNum` variable?

    a. `intNum = strMsg.Substring(0, "F")`

    b. `intNum = strMsg.Contains("F")`

    c. `intNum = strMsg.IndexOf("F")`

    d. `intNum = strMsg.IndexOf(0, "F")`

8. If the `strAddress` variable contains the string "41 Main Street", what will the `strAddress.IndexOf("Main")` method return?

    a. −1

    b. 3

    c. 4

    d. True

9. If the `strAddress` variable contains the string "15 Palm Ave.", what will the `strAddress.IndexOf("Palm", 5)` method return?

    a. −1

    b. 5

    c. 6

    d. False

10. Which of the following statements assigns the first four characters in the `strItem` variable to the `strWarehouse` variable?

    a. `strWarehouse = strItem.Assign(0, 4)`

    b. `strWarehouse = strItem.Assign(1, 4)`

    c. `strWarehouse = strItem.Substring(0, 4)`

    d. `strWarehouse = strItem.Substring(1, 4)`

11. The `strName` variable contains the string "Doe Jane". Which of the following changes the variable's contents to the string "Doe, Jane"?

    a. `strName = strName.Insert(3, ",")`

    b. `strName = strName.Insert(4, ",")`

    c. `strName = strName.AddTo(3, ",")`

    d. None of the above.

12. If the `strWord` variable contains the string "crispy", which of the following statements assigns the letter s to the `strLetter` variable?

    a. `strLetter = strWord.Substring(3)`

    b. `strLetter = strWord.Substring(3, 1)`

    c. `strLetter = strWord.Substring(4, 1)`

    d. None of the above.

13. The `strDue` variable contains the string "$****75". Which of the following statements removes the dollar sign and asterisks from the variable?

    a. `strDue = strDue.Trim("$"c, "*"c)`

    b. `strDue = strDue.TrimStart("*"c, "$"c)`

    c. `strDue = strDue.TrimStart("$"c, "*"c)`

    d. All of the above.

14. The `strName` variable contains the string "Jeffers". Which of the following statements changes the contents of the variable to the string "Jeff"?

    a. `strName = strName.Remove(4)`

    b. `strName = strName.Remove(5)`

    c. `strName = strName.Remove(5, 3)`

    d. `strName = strName.Remove(3, 5)`

15. Which of the following statements changes the contents of the `strZip` variable from 60521 to 60461?

    a. `strZip = strZip.Insert(2, "46")`
       `strZip = strZip.Remove(4, 2)`

    b. `strZip = strZip.Remove(2)`
       `strZip = strZip.Insert(2, "461")`

    c. `strZip = strZip.Remove(2, 2)`
       `strZip = strZip.Insert(2, "46")`

    d. All of the above.

16. If the `strWord` variable contains the string "spring", which of the following statements assigns the letter r to the `strLetter` variable?

    a. `strLetter = strWord.Substring(2)`

    b. `strLetter = strWord(2)`

    c. `strLetter = strWord(2, 1)`

    d. All of the above.

17. Which of the following statements changes the contents of the `strSocSec` variable from "000-11-2222" to "000112222"?

    a. `strSocSec = strSocSec.Remove("-")`

    b. `strSocSec = strSocSec.RemoveAll("-")`

    c. `strSocSec = strSocSec.Replace("-","")`

    d. `strSocSec = strSocSec.ReplaceAll("-")`

18. Which of the following expressions evaluates to True when the `strItem` variable contains the string "1234Y5"?

    a. `strItem Like "####[A-Z]#"`

    c. `strItem Like "######"`

    b. `strItem Like "9999[A-Z]9"`

    d. None of the above.

19. Which of the following statements declares an object to represent the pseudo-random number generator in a procedure?

    a. `Dim randGen As New RandomNumber`

    b. `Dim randGen As New Generator`

    c. `Dim randGen As New Random`

    d. `Dim randGen As New RandomObject`

20. Which of the following statements generates a random integer from 1 to 25 (including 25)?

    a. `intNum = randGen.Next(1, 25)`

    b. `intNum = randGen.Next(1, 26)`

    c. `intNum = randGen(1, 25)`

    d. `intNum = randGen.NextNumber(1, 26)`

21. Which of the following statements sends the focus to the btnClear control?

    a. `btnClear.Focus()`

    c. `btnClear.SendFocus()`

    b. `btnClear.Focus() = True`

    d. `btnClear.SetFocus()`

22. Which of the following statements enables the btnClear control?

    a. `btnClear.Enabled()`

    c. `btnClear.Enabled = True`

    b. `btnClear.Enabled = Yes`

    d. `btnClear.Enable = True`

23. Which property specifies the number of characters that a text box will accept?

    a. Length

    c. LengthMax

    b. MaxLength

    d. Maximum

24. Which property allows you to specify a specific character that will always be displayed in a text box, no matter what character the user types?

    a. Char

    c. Password

    b. CharPassword

    d. PasswordChar

25. Which method right-aligns a string?

    a. PadLeft

    c. LeftAlign

    b. PadRight

    d. RightAlign

Exercises

1. In this exercise, you modify the Check Digit application from this chapter's Apply lesson. Use Windows to make a copy of the Check Digit Solution folder. Rename the copy Check Digit Solution-Hyphens. Open the Check Digit Solution.sln file contained in the Check Digit Solution-Hyphens folder.

   INTRODUCTORY

   a. Modify the txtIsbn_KeyPress procedure to allow the user to also enter hyphens.

   b. Before verifying the length of the ISBN entered by the user, the btnAssign_Click procedure should assign the ISBN (without any hyphens) to the **strIsbn** variable. Make the appropriate modifications to the procedure.

   c. When displaying the ISBN in the lblFinalIsbn control, the btnAssign_Click procedure should insert a hyphen after the third number, the fourth number, the seventh number, and the twelfth number (for example, 978-1-337-10212-4). Make the appropriate modifications to the procedure.

   d. Save the solution and then start and test the application. (If the user enters 978-1-285-86026, with or without the hyphens, the btnAssign_Click procedure should display 978-1-285-86026-8.)

2. In this exercise, you modify the Password application from this chapter's Apply lesson. Use Windows to make a copy of the Password Solution folder. Rename the copy Modified Password Solution. Open the Password Solution.sln file contained in the Modified Password Solution folder. The btnCreate_Click procedure inserts a number immediately after the first character in the password. The number represents the length of the string before the number is inserted. Modify the procedure so that the number always contains two characters. For example, if the length of the string is 6, insert "06" (a zero and the number 6). Save the solution and then start and test the application. (If the user enters "May the Force be with you", the Create password button should display M06tFbwy.)

   INTRODUCTORY

3. Open the Validate ISBN Solution.sln file contained in the VB2017\Chap07\Validate ISBN Solution folder. The interface provides a text box for entering a 13-character ISBN. The btnValidate_Click procedure should use the ISBN's check digit, which is the last digit in the number, to determine whether the ISBN is valid. (The check digit algorithm is shown earlier in Figure 7-25.) If the ISBN is valid, the procedure should display the "Valid" message in the lblStatus control; otherwise, it should display the "Not valid" message. Code the procedure. Save the solution and then start and test the application. (If the user enters 9781285860268, the btnValidate_Click procedure should display the "Valid" message.)

   INTRODUCTORY

4. In this exercise, you modify the Password application from this chapter's Apply lesson. Use Windows to make a copy of the Password Solution folder. Rename the copy Password Solution-Spaces. Open the Password Solution.sln file contained in the Password Solution-Spaces folder.

   INTRODUCTORY

   a. Start the application. Type the following three words, using two spaces (rather than one space) to separate each word: programming is fun. Click the Create password button. The Password box displays p5 followed by a space, the letter i, a space and the letter f. Click the Exit button.

   b. Open the Code Editor window and locate the btnCreate_Click procedure. The first instruction in the loop concatenates the character that follows the space. Modify the loop's code so that it performs the concatenation only when the character is not a space. Save the solution and then start the application. Use the information in Step a to test the application. This time, the Password box should display p3if.

INTRODUCTORY

5. Open the Color Solution.sln file contained in the VB2017\Chap07\Color Solution folder. The btnDisplay_Click procedure should display the color of the item whose item number is entered by the user. All item numbers contain exactly five characters. All items are available in four colors: blue, green, red, and white. The third character in the item number indicates the item's color, as follows: B or b indicates Blue, G or g indicates Green, R or r indicates Red, and W or w indicates White. The procedure should display an appropriate error message if the item number does not contain exactly five characters. It should also display an appropriate message if the third character is not one of the valid color characters. Before ending, the procedure should send the focus to the txtItem control. Code the procedure. Save the solution and then start the application. Test the application using the following invalid item numbers: 123, 12345, 123456, and 12Y45. Then, test it using the following valid item numbers: 12b34, abr73, n6gtn, and 12w87.

INTERMEDIATE

6. Open the Proper Case Solution.sln file contained in the VB2017\Chap07\Proper Case Solution folder. The interface provides a text box for entering a person's first and last names. The btnProper_Click procedure should display the first and last names in the proper case. In other words, the first and last names should begin with an uppercase letter and the remaining letters in each name should be lowercase. If the user enters only one name, display the name in proper case. Be sure the btnProper_Click procedure works correctly if the user inadvertently enters more than one space between the first and last names. After displaying the name, the procedure should send the focus to the txtName control. Code the procedure. Save the solution and then start and test the application. (If the user enters "john smith" as the name, the application should display "John Smith". If the user enters "carol" followed by three spaces and then "jones", the application should display "Carol Jones". If the user enters three spaces followed by "jack" and another three spaces, the application should display "Jack".)

INTERMEDIATE

7. Open the Zip Solution.sln file contained in the VB2017\Chap07\Zip Solution folder file. The btnDisplay_Click procedure should validate the ZIP code entered by the user. To be valid, the first four digits in the ZIP code must be 4210, and the last digit must be 2, 3, or 4. Use one selection structure along with the Like operator to validate the ZIP code. Display the "Valid" message if the ZIP code is valid; otherwise, display the "Not valid" message. After displaying the message, the procedure should send the focus to the txtZip control. Code the procedure. Save the solution and then start and test the application.

INTERMEDIATE

8. In this exercise, you modify the Check Digit application from this chapter's Apply lesson. Use Windows to make a copy of the Check Digit Solution folder. Rename the copy Check Digit Solution-ForNext. Open the Check Digit Solution.sln file contained in the Check Digit Solution-ForNext folder. Delete the `intGrandTotal = intTotalOdd + intTotalEven` statement from the btnAssign_Click procedure. Also delete the two Dim statements that declare the `intTotalOdd` and `intTotalEven` variables. Modify the procedure to use one For...Next loop (rather than two For...Next loops) to calculate the grand total. Save the solution and then start and test the application. (If the user enters 978128586026, the btnAssign_Click procedure should display 9781285860268.)

INTERMEDIATE

9. In this exercise, you modify the Password application from this chapter's Apply lesson. Use Windows to make a copy of the Password Solution folder. Rename the copy Password Solution-Index. Open the Password Solution.sln file contained in the Password Solution-Index folder. In the btnCreate_Click procedure, declare a constant

named strALPHABET and initialize it to the 26 uppercase letters of the alphabet. Then, rather than inserting the length of the password, the procedure should insert a number that represents the position of the password's first character in the alphabet. For example, if the first character in the password is the letter A, the procedure should insert the number 1. Similarly, if the first character is the letter Z, the procedure should insert the number 26. Insert the number after the last character in the password (rather than after the first character). Save the solution and then start and test the application. (If the user enters "show me the money", the Create password button should display smtm19.)

10. Open the Shipping Solution.sln file contained in the VB2017\Chap07\Shipping Solution folder. The interface provides a text box for entering a shipping code, which should consist of two numbers followed by either one or two letters. The letter(s) represent the delivery method, as follows: MS represents Mail – Standard, MP represents Mail – Priority, FS represents FedEx – Standard, FO represents FedEx – Overnight, and U represents UPS. The btnDelivery_Click procedure should use the Like operator to determine the delivery method to select in the list box. For example, if the shipping code is 73mp, the procedure should select the Mail – Priority item in the list box. The procedure should display an appropriate message when the shipping code is not valid. Code the procedure. Save the solution and then start the application. Test the application using the following valid codes: 73mp, 34fs, 88FO, 12u, and 34ms. Then, test it using the following invalid codes: 9fo and 78hs.   **INTERMEDIATE**

11. In this exercise, you modify the Password application from this chapter's Apply lesson. Use Windows to make a copy of the Password Solution folder. Rename the copy Password Solution-Advanced. Open the Password Solution.sln file contained in the Password Solution-Advanced folder. Before inserting the number, the btnCreate_Click procedure should alternate the case of each letter in the password. If the first character is lowercase, the procedure should change it to uppercase; it should then change the second letter to lowercase, the third letter to uppercase, and so on. For example, if the password is abcd, the procedure should change it to AbCd. On the other hand, if the first character is uppercase, the procedure should change it to lowercase and then alternate the case of the following letters. For example, if the password is Abcd, the procedure should change it to aBcD. Modify the procedure's code. Save the solution and then start and test the application. (If the user enters "May the Force be with you", the procedure should display m6TfBwY. If the user enters "may the Force be with you", the procedure should display M6tFbWy.)   **ADVANCED**

12. In this exercise, you modify the Proper Case application from Exercise 6. If necessary, complete Exercise 6. Then, use Windows to make a copy of the Proper Case Solution folder. Rename the copy Proper Case Solution-Middle. Open the Proper Case Solution.sln file contained in the Proper Case Solution-Middle folder. Modify the application to allow the user to also enter his or her middle name or middle initial. The btnProper_Click procedure should display the full name, which might include a middle name or middle initial, in proper case. Save the solution and then start and test the application. (If the user enters "john smith" as the name, the application should display "John Smith". If the user enters "john thomas smith", the application should display "John Thomas Smith". If the user enters "carol g. jones", the application should display "Carol G. Jones". If the user enters two spaces, "pam", two spaces, "grace", three spaces, "darwin", and two spaces, the application should display "Pam Grace Darwin".)   **ADVANCED**

ADVANCED   13. In this exercise, you modify the Proper Case application from Exercise 6. If necessary, complete Exercise 6. Then, use Windows to make a copy of the Proper Case Solution folder. Rename the copy Proper Case Solution-Hyphenated. Open the Proper Case Solution.sln file contained in the Proper Case Solution-Hyphenated folder. Start the application. Type "carol mason-smith" (without the quotes) as the name and then click the Proper case button. The btnProper_Click procedure displays "Carol Mason-smith". Click the Exit button. Modify the procedure to display hyphenated names in proper case; for example, the procedure should display "Carol Mason-Smith". Save the solution and then start and test the application. Be sure the application works correctly if the user inadvertently enters "carol mason-" (notice the hyphen at the end of the entry).

ADVANCED   14. Each salesperson at Rembrandt Auto-Mart is assigned an ID number that consists of five characters. The first three characters are numbers. The fourth character is a letter: either the letter N if the salesperson sells new cars or the letter U if the salesperson sells used cars. The fifth character is also a letter: either the letter F if the salesperson is a full-time employee or the letter P if the salesperson is a part-time employee. Create a Windows Forms application. Use the following names for the project and solution, respectively: Rembrandt Project and Rembrandt Solution. Save the application in the VB2017\Chap07 folder. Create the interface shown in Figure 7-55. Make the Calculate button the default button. The application should allow the sales manager to enter the ID and the number of cars sold for as many salespeople as needed. The btnCalc_Click procedure should display the total number of cars sold by each of the following four categories of employees: full-time employees, part-time employees, employees selling new cars, and employees selling used cars. Code the application. Save the solution and then start and test the application.

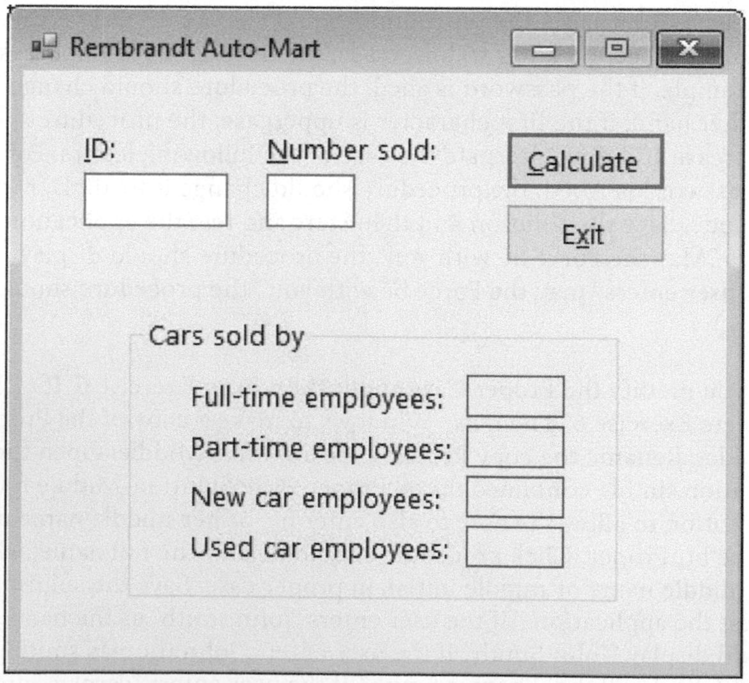

Figure 7-55   Interface for Exercise 14

15. Open the Addition Solution.sln file contained in the VB2017\Chap07\Addition Solution folder. The btnNew_Click procedure is responsible for generating two random integers from 0 to 10 (including 10) and displaying them in the lblNum1 and lblNum2 controls. The btnCheck_Click procedure is responsible for determining whether the user's answer, which is entered in the txtAnswer control, is correct. If the answer is correct, the procedure should display an appropriate message and then clear the problem and answer from the interface. If the answer is not correct, the procedure should display an appropriate message and then allow the user to answer the addition problem again. Code both procedures. Include any other code that will professionalize the interface. Save the solution and then start and test the application.

ADVANCED

16. Open the Validate Number Solution.sln file contained in the VB2017\Chap07\Validate Number Solution folder. The interface provides a text box for entering a 9-digit number. The btnValidate_Click procedure should use the algorithm and example shown in Figure 7-56 to validate the user's entry. The procedure should display a message indicating whether the entry is or is not valid. Code the procedure. Include any other code that will professionalize the interface. Save the solution and then start and test the application.

ADVANCED

Algorithm

1. Starting with the second digit, multiply every other digit by 2. (These will be the second, fourth, sixth, and eighth digits.)
2. If a product from Step 1 is greater than 9, sum the two digits in the product. For example, if the product is 12, add the 1 to the 2, giving 3.
3. Add together the results from Steps 1 and 2 and each of the digits skipped in Step 1. (The skipped digits will be the first, third, fifth, seventh, and ninth digits.)
4. Divide the sum from Step 3 by 10 and find the remainder. If the remainder is 0, then the number is valid.

Number: 631620176

Step 1:	6	3 $*$ 2 / 6	1	6 $*$ 2 / 12	2	0 $*$ 2 / 0	1	7 $*$ 2 / 14	6	
Step 2:				1 + 2 = 3				1 + 4 = 5		
Step 3:	6	6	1	3	2	0	1	5	6	30
Step 4:										30 Mod 10 = 0

the 0 indicates that the number is valid

Figure 7-56 Algorithm and example for Exercise 16

17. Create a Windows Forms application. Use the following names for the project and solution, respectively: OnYourOwn Project and OnYourOwn Solution. Save the application in the VB2017\Chap07 folder. Plan and design an application of your choice. The only requirement is that you must follow the minimum guidelines listed in Figure 7-57. Before starting the application, be sure to verify the name of the startup form. Save the solution and then start and test the application.

ON YOUR OWN

1. The user interface must contain a minimum of one text box, three labels, and two buttons. One of the buttons must be an Exit button.
2. The interface can include a picture box, but this is not a requirement.
3. The interface must follow the GUI design guidelines summarized for Chapters 2 through 6 in Appendix A.
4. Objects that are either coded or referred to in code should be named appropriately.
5. The Code Editor window must contain comments, the three Option statements, at least two variables, at least two assignment statements, at least two of the concepts covered in the Focus lesson, and the Me.Close() statement.
6. Every text box on the form should have its TextChanged and Enter event procedures coded. At least one of the text boxes should have its KeyPress event procedure coded.

Figure 7-57 Guidelines for Exercise 17

FIX IT

18. Open the VB2017\Chap07\FixIt Solution\FixIt Solution.sln file. The interface provides a text box for the user to enter one or more words. The btnReverse_Click procedure should display the characters in reverse order. In other words, if the user enters the words "Show me the money", the procedure should display "yenom eht em wohS". Start and test the application. Notice that the application is not working properly. Correct the application's code.

CHAPTER 8

Arrays

In Chapter 7, you learned that a string is simply a group of related characters, commonly referred to as an array of characters or a character array. In this chapter's Focus on the Concepts lesson, you will learn how to create an array of variables, which is a group of related variables. Programmers refer to an array of variables as simply an array. You will use arrays in all of the applications coded in this chapter's Apply the Concepts lesson.

■ FOCUS ON THE CONCEPTS LESSON

Concepts covered in this lesson:

- F-1 Arrays
- F-2 Declaring one-dimensional arrays
- F-3 For Each...Next statement
- F-4 Calculating the average array value
- F-5 Finding the highest array value
- F-6 Sorting a one-dimensional array
- F-7 Two-dimensional arrays

F-1 Arrays

All of the variables you have used so far have been simple variables. A **simple variable**, also called a **scalar variable**, is one that is unrelated to any other variable in memory. At times, however, you will encounter applications in which some of the variables *are* related to each other. In those applications, it is easier and more efficient to treat the related variables as a group.

A group of related variables is referred to as an array of variables or, more simply, an **array**. You might use an array of 50 variables to store the population of each U.S. state. Or, you might use an array of eight variables to store the sales made in each of your company's eight sales regions.

After your application enters the data into an array, it can use the data as many times as necessary without having to enter the data again. Your company's sales application, for example, can use the sales amounts stored in an array to calculate the total company sales and the percentage that each region contributed to the total sales. It can also use the sales amounts in the array either to calculate the average sales amount or to simply display the sales made in a specific region.

As you will learn in this lesson, the variables in an array can be used just like any other variables. You can assign values to them, use them in calculations, display their contents, and so on. The most commonly used arrays in business applications are one-dimensional and two-dimensional. You will learn about one-dimensional arrays first.

F-2 Declaring One-Dimensional Arrays

The variables in an array are stored in consecutive locations in the computer's main memory. Each variable in an array has the same name and data type. You distinguish one variable in a **one-dimensional array** from another variable in the same array by using a unique number, called a **subscript**. The subscript, which is always an integer, indicates the variable's position in the array and is assigned by the computer when the array is created in main memory. The first variable in a one-dimensional array is assigned a subscript of 0, the second a subscript of 1, and so on.

Figure 8-1 illustrates a one-dimensional array named `intSales` that contains four variables. The variables are related in that each stores the annual sales made by one of a company's four salespeople.

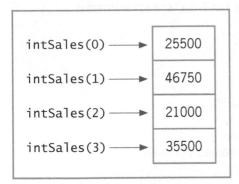

Figure 8-1   Illustration of the one-dimensional `intSales` array

You refer to each variable in an array by the array's name and the variable's subscript, which is specified in a set of parentheses immediately following the array name. For example, you use `intSales(0)`—read "`intSales` sub zero"—to refer to the first variable in the `intSales` array, and use `intSales(3)` to refer to the last variable. Because array subscripts in Visual Basic (and in many other programming languages) start at 0, the last subscript in an array is always one number less than the number of variables in the array.

You declare (create) an array using one of the two syntax versions shown in Figure 8-2. The `{Dim | Private | Static}` portion in each version indicates that you can select only one of the keywords appearing within the braces. The appropriate keyword depends on whether you are creating a procedure-level array or a class-level array. *DataType* is the type of data the array variables, referred to as **elements**, will store.

In syntax Version 1, *highestSubscript* is an integer that specifies the highest subscript in the array. Because the first element in a one-dimensional array has a subscript of 0, the array will contain one element more than the number specified in the *highestSubscript* argument. In other words, an array whose highest subscript is 2 will contain three elements. In syntax Version 2, *initialValues* is a comma-separated list of values you want assigned to the array elements. Also included in Figure 8-2 are examples of using both versions of the syntax.

Like class-level variables, class-level arrays are declared in the form class's declarations section.

Declaring a One-Dimensional Array

Syntax–Version 1
{Dim | Private | Static} *arrayName*(*highestSubscript*) **As** *dataType*

Syntax–Version 2
{Dim | Private | Static} *arrayName*() **As** *dataType* = {*initialValues*}

Example 1
```
Dim strWarehouse(2) As String
```
declares a three-element procedure-level array named `strWarehouse`; each element is automatically initialized using the keyword `Nothing`

Figure 8-2   Syntax versions and examples of declaring a one-dimensional array *(continues)*

(continued)

```
Example 2
Static intTotals(4) As Integer
declares a static, five-element procedure-level array named intTotals; each element is
automatically initialized to 0


Example 3
Dim strNames() As String = {"Harry Potter",
                            "Ron Weasley",
                            "Hermione Granger",
                            "Lord Voldemort",
                            "Albus Dumbledore"}
declares and initializes a five-element procedure-level array named strNames


Example 4
Private intSales() As Integer = {25500, 46750, 21000, 35500}
declares and initializes a four-element class-level array named intSales
```

Figure 8-2   Syntax versions and examples of declaring a one-dimensional array

When you use syntax Version 1, the computer automatically initializes each array element when the array is created. This is similar to the way it automatically initializes the scalar variables you have been declaring since Chapter 3. If the array's data type is String, each element is initialized using the keyword Nothing. As you learned in Chapter 3, variables initialized to Nothing do not actually contain the word *Nothing*; rather, they contain no data at all. Elements in a numeric array are initialized to the number 0, and elements in a Boolean array are initialized using the Boolean keyword False.

Rather than having the computer use a default value to initialize each array element, you can use syntax Version 2 to specify each element's initial value when the array is declared. Assigning initial values to an array is often referred to as **populating the array**. You list the initial values in the initialValues section of the syntax, using commas to separate the values, and you enclose the list of values in braces ({}).

Notice that syntax Version 2 does not include the *highestSubscript* argument; instead, an empty set of parentheses follows the array name. The computer automatically calculates the highest subscript based on the number of values listed in the initialValues section. Because the first subscript in a one-dimensional array is the number 0, the highest subscript is always one number less than the number of values listed in the initialValues section. The Dim statement in Example 3 in Figure 8-2, for instance, creates a five-element array with subscripts of 0, 1, 2, 3, and 4. It initializes the array using the names of five of the characters from the Harry Potter books. Similarly, the Private statement in Example 4 creates and initializes the four-element array shown earlier in Figure 8-1; the array has subscripts of 0, 1, 2, and 3.

Storing Data in a One-Dimensional Array

After an array is declared, you can use another statement to store a different value in an array element. Examples of such statements include assignment statements and statements that contain the TryParse method. Figure 8-3 shows examples of both types of statements.

Storing Data in a One-Dimensional Array

Example 1
```
Dim strCity(5) As String
strCity(0) = "Nashville"
```
assigns the string "Nashville" to the first element in the strCity array

Example 2
```
Dim intNumbers(4) As Integer
For intX As Integer = 1 To 5
    intNumbers(intX - 1) = intX ^ 2
Next intX
```
assigns the squares of the numbers from 1 through 5 to the intNumbers array

Example 3
```
Dim intNumbers(4) As Integer
Dim intSub As Integer
Do While intSub < 5
    intNumbers(intSub) = 100
    intSub += 1
Loop
```
assigns the number 100 to each element in the intNumbers array

Example 4
```
Dim dblPrice() As Double = {45.25, 56.99, 33.75}
dblPrice(1) *= 1.25
```
multiplies the contents of the second element in the dblPrice array by 1.25 and then assigns the result to the element; you also can write this statement as dblPrice(1) = dblPrice(1) * 1.25

Example 5
```
Dim dblRates(9) As Double
Double.TryParse(txtRate.Text, dblRates(2))
```
assigns either the value entered in the txtRate control (converted to Double) or the number 0 to the third element in the dblRates array

---

Figure 8-3   Examples of statements used to store data in a one-dimensional array

Determining the Number of Elements in a One-Dimensional Array

The number of elements in a one-dimensional array is stored as an integer in the array's **Length property**. Figure 8-4 shows the property's syntax and includes an example of using the property. Notice that the value in the Length property is one number more than the highest subscript.

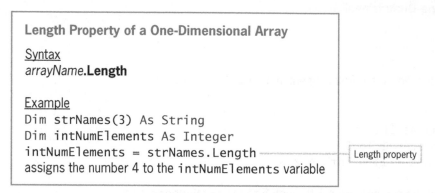

Figure 8-4   Syntax and an example of a one-dimensional array's Length property

Determining the Highest Subscript in a One-Dimensional Array

The highest subscript in a one-dimensional array is always one number less than the number of array elements. Therefore, one way to determine the highest subscript is by subtracting the number 1 from the array's Length property. However, you also can use the array's GetUpperBound method, as shown in Figure 8-5. The **GetUpperBound method** returns an integer that represents the highest subscript in the specified dimension of the array. When used with a one-dimensional array, the specified dimension, which appears between the parentheses after the method's name, is always 0.

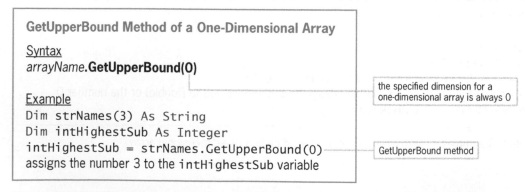

Figure 8-5   Syntax and an example of a one-dimensional array's GetUpperBound method

Mini-Quiz 8-1

1. Write a statement that declares a procedure-level one-dimensional array named intOrders. The array should contain 15 elements.

2. Write a statement that assigns the number 150 to the third element in the intOrders array.

3. Write a statement that assigns the number of elements in the intOrders array to the intNum variable.

4. Write a statement that assigns the highest subscript in the intOrders array to the intLastSub variable.

intOrders.GetUpperBound(0) or intLastSub = intOrders.Length - 1

intOrders.Length or intNum = intOrders.GetUpperBound(0) + 1 **4)** intLastSub =

= intNum **3)** 150 = (2)intOrders **2)** Integer As intOrders(14) Dim **1)**

YOU DO IT 1!

Create an application named You Do It 1 and save it in the VB2017\Chap08 folder. Add two labels and a button to the form. The button's Click event procedure should declare and initialize an Integer array named intNums. Use the following numbers to initialize the array: 2, 4, 6, 8, 10, and 12. The procedure should display the number of array elements in both label controls. Use the Length property for one of the labels and use the GetUpperBound method for the other label. Code the procedure. Save the solution and then start and test the application. Close the solution.

Traversing a One-Dimensional Array

At times, you may need to traverse an array, which means to look at each array element, one by one, beginning with the first element and ending with the last element. You traverse an array using a loop. Figure 8-6 shows two examples of loops that traverse the strNames array declared in Figure 8-2. The loop instructions display each element's value in the lstNames control.

Traversing a One-Dimensional Array

Example 1—For...Next
```
Dim intHighSub As Integer = strNames.GetUpperBound(0)
For intSub As Integer = 0 To intHighSub
    lstNames.Items.Add(strNames(intSub))
Next intSub
```

Example 2—Do...Loop
```
Dim intHighSub As Integer = strNames.Length - 1
Dim intSub As Integer
Do While intSub <= intHighSub
    lstNames.Items.Add(strNames(intSub))
    intSub += 1
Loop
```

Figure 8-6 Examples of loops used to traverse a one-dimensional array

START HERE **To code the Harry Potter Characters application:**

1. Open the Potter Solution.sln file contained in the VB2017\Chap08\Potter Solution folder. The interface contains a list box, three labels, and a button.

2. Open the Code Editor window and locate the lstNames_SelectedIndexChanged procedure. The procedure assigns the item selected in the list box to the lblSelection.Text property.

3. Locate the frmMain_Load procedure. Click the **blank line** above the End Sub clause. Enter the array declaration statement shown in Figure 8-7, and then position the insertion point as shown in the figure.

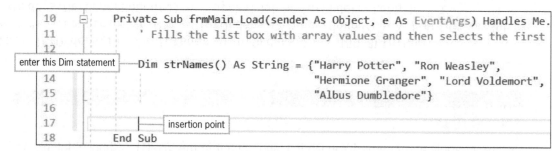

```
10  ⊟        Private Sub frmMain_Load(sender As Object, e As EventArgs) Handles Me.
11                  ' Fills the list box with array values and then selects the first
12
   enter this Dim statement ──Dim strNames() As String = {"Harry Potter", "Ron Weasley",
14                                           "Hermione Granger", "Lord Voldemort",
15                                           "Albus Dumbledore"}
16
17                  ──insertion point
18           End Sub
```

Figure 8-7   Array declaration statement entered in the frmMain_Load procedure

4. The procedure will fill the list box with the values stored in the array. Enter the lines of code shown in either of the examples from Figure 8-6.

5. Finally, the procedure will select the first item in the list box. Insert a **blank line** above the End Sub clause and then enter the following assignment statement:

lstNames.SelectedIndex = 0

6. Save the solution and then start the application. The frmMain_Load procedure creates and initializes the **strNames** array. The loop then adds the contents of each array element to the lstNames control. The loop stops when the **intSub** variable contains the number 5, which is one number more than the highest subscript in the array. The last statement in the frmMain_Load procedure invokes the list box's SelectedIndexChanged event, whose procedure displays the selected item in the You selected box. See Figure 8-8.

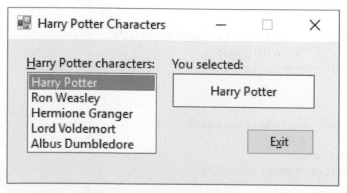

Figure 8-8   Sample run of the Harry Potter Characters application

7. Click **each name** in the list box, one at a time, to verify that the application works correctly.

8. Click the **Exit** button. Close the Code Editor window and then close the solution.

F-3 For Each...Next Statement

In addition to using the Do...Loop and For...Next statements to code a loop, you can also use the For Each...Next statement. The **For Each...Next statement** provides a convenient way of coding a loop whose instructions you want processed for each element in a group, such as for each variable in an array. An advantage of using the For Each...Next statement to process an array is that your code does not need to keep track of the array subscripts or even know the number of array elements. However, unlike the loop instructions in a Do...Loop or For...Next statement, the instructions in a For Each...Next statement can only read the array values; they cannot permanently modify the values.

Figure 8-9 shows the For Each...Next statement's syntax. The *elementVariable* that appears in the For Each and Next clauses is the name of a variable that the computer can use to keep track of each element in the *group*. The variable's data type is specified in the As *dataType* portion of the For Each clause and must be the same as the group's data type. A variable declared in the For Each clause has block scope (which you learned about in Chapter 5) and is recognized only by the instructions within the For Each...Next loop. The example in Figure 8-9 shows how to write the loops from Figure 8-6 using the For Each...Next statement.

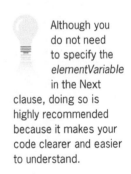 Although you do not need to specify the *elementVariable* in the Next clause, doing so is highly recommended because it makes your code clearer and easier to understand.

For Each...Next Statement

Syntax
For Each *elementVariable* **As** *dataType* **In** *group*
    loop body instructions
Next *elementVariable*

Example
```
For Each strElement As String In strNames
     lstNames.Items.Add(strElement)
Next strElement
```

Figure 8-9   Syntax and an example of the For Each...Next statement

To use the For Each...Next statement in the Harry Potter Characters application: START HERE

1. Open the Potter Solution.sln file contained in the VB2017\Chap08\Potter Solution-ForEachNext folder.

2. Open the Code Editor window and locate the frmMain_Load procedure. Click the **blank line** above the assignment statement and then enter the code shown in Figure 8-9. Be sure to change the Next clause to Next strElement.

3. Save the solution and then start the application. The five array values appear in the list box. Click **each name** in the list box, one at a time, to verify that the application works correctly.

4. Click the **Exit** button. Close the Code Editor window and then close the solution.

YOU DO IT 2!

Create an application named You Do It 2 and save it in the VB2017\Chap08 folder. Add a button and three list boxes to the form. The button's Click event procedure should declare and initialize a one-dimensional String array. Use any four names to initialize the array. The procedure should use the For Each...Next statement to display the contents of the array in the first list box. It should use the Do...Loop statement to display the contents of the array in the second list box, and use the For...Next statement to display the contents of the array in the third list box. Code the procedure. Save the solution and then start and test the application. Close the solution.

F-4 Calculating the Average Array Value

To calculate the average of the values stored in an array, you first total the values and then divide the total by the number of array elements. In the next set of steps, you will code an application that calculates the average price of a company's stock.

START HERE

To begin coding the Waterson Company application:

1. Open the Waterson Solution.sln file contained in the VB2017\Chap08\Waterson Solution-Average folder.

2. Open the Code Editor window. The Private statement in the form class's declarations section stores the company's 10-day stock prices in a class-level array named dblPrices. A class-level array is appropriate in this case because two procedures (frmMain_Load and btnCalc_Click) will need access to the array.

3. Locate the frmMain_Load procedure. The procedure will use the For Each...Next statement to fill the list box with the prices stored in the array. Click the **blank line** above the End Sub clause and then enter the loop shown in Figure 8-10.

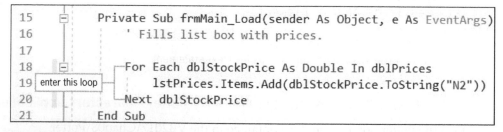

```
15      Private Sub frmMain_Load(sender As Object, e As EventArgs)
16          ' Fills list box with prices.
17
18          For Each dblStockPrice As Double In dblPrices
19  enter this loop    lstPrices.Items.Add(dblStockPrice.ToString("N2"))
20          Next dblStockPrice
21      End Sub
```

Figure 8-10   Completed frmMain_Load procedure

4. Locate the btnCalc_Click procedure. The procedure declares two variables named dblTotal and dblAvg. The dblTotal variable will be used to accumulate the prices stored in the array. The dblAvg variable will store the average price.

Figure 8-11 shows three examples of code for accumulating the values stored in the array. Each example uses a loop to add each array element's value to the `dblTotal` variable. Notice that you need to specify the highest array subscript in the Do...Loop and For...Next statements, but not in the For Each...Next statement. The Do...Loop and For...Next statements must also keep track of the array subscripts; this task is not necessary in the For Each...Next statement. When each loop has finished processing, the `dblTotal` variable contains the sum of the 10 stock prices stored in the array.

Ch08-Accumulating
Array Values

```
Example 1—Do...Loop statement
Dim intHighSub As Integer = dblPrices.GetUpperBound(0)
Dim intSub As Integer
' Accumulate stock prices.
Do While intSub <= intHighSub
    dblTotal += dblPrices(intSub)
    intSub += 1
Loop

Example 2—For...Next statement
Dim intHighSub As Integer = dblPrices.GetUpperBound(0)
' Accumulate stock prices.
For intSub As Integer = 0 To intHighSub
    dblTotal += dblPrices(intSub)
Next intSub

Example 3—For Each...Next statement
' Accumulate stock prices.
For Each dblDay As Double In dblPrices
    dblTotal += dblDay
Next dblDay
```

Figure 8-11   Examples of accumulating the array values

To complete the Waterson Company application:

START HERE

1. Click the **blank line** above the End Sub clause in the btnCalc_Click procedure. Enter the comment and code shown in any of the three examples from Figure 8-11.

2. Next, the procedure will calculate the average price by dividing the value stored in the `dblTotal` variable by the number of array elements. It then will display the average price. If necessary, insert a **blank line** above the End Sub clause. Enter the following comment and assignment statements:

```
' Calculate and display the average.
dblAvg = dblTotal / dblPrices.Length
lblAvg.Text = dblAvg.ToString("C2")
```

3. Save the solution and then start the application. Click the **Calculate** button. See Figure 8-12.

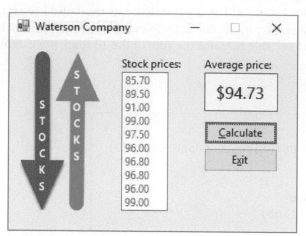

Figure 8-12 Average stock price shown in the interface

4. Click the **Exit** button. Close the Code Editor window and then close the solution.

Mini-Quiz 8-2

1. In order to access each element in an array, the Do...Loop statement needs to know the highest subscript in the array. True or False?

2. In order to access each element in an array, the For...Next statement needs to know the highest subscript in the array. True or False?

3. In order to access each element in an array, the For Each...Next statement needs to know the highest subscript in the array. True or False?

4. When traversing an array, which of the following statements does not need to keep track of the individual array subscripts: Do...Loop, For...Next, or For Each...Next?

1) True 2) True 3) False 4) For Each...Next

YOU DO IT 3!

Create an application named You Do It 3 and save it in the VB2017\Chap08 folder. Add three labels and a button to the form. The button's Click event procedure should declare and initialize a one-dimensional Integer array. Use any five integers to initialize the array. The procedure should total the five integers and then display the result in the labels. Use the Do...Loop statement to calculate the total to display in the first label. Use the For Each...Next statement to calculate the total to display in the second label. Use the For...Next statement to calculate the total to display in the third label. Code the procedure. Save the solution and then start and test the application. Close the solution.

F-5 Finding the Highest Array Value

In this section, you will code a different application for the Waterson Company. Rather than displaying the average stock price, this application displays the highest stock price and the number of days the stock closed at that price. Figure 8-13 shows the pseudocode for the btnDisplay_Click procedure.

---

btnDisplay_Click

1. declare intLastSub variable and initialize it to last array subscript
2. declare dblHighest variable and initialize it to the price stored in the first array element
3. declare intDays counter variable and initialize it to 1
4. repeat for each element in the dblPrices array, starting with the second element
      if the current element's price is equal to the price stored in dblHighest
          add 1 to the intDays counter variable
      else
          if the current element's price is greater than the price stored in dblHighest
             assign the current element's price to dblHighest
             assign 1 to the intDays counter variable
          end if
      end if
   end repeat
5. display the highest price (dblHighest) and number of days (intDays) in lblHighest and lblDays

---

Figure 8-13 Pseudocode for the btnDisplay_Click procedure

To code this version of the Waterson Company application:

START HERE

1. Open the Waterson Solution.sln file contained in the VB2017\Chap08\Waterson Solution-Highest folder.

2. Open the Code Editor window. The Private statement in the form class's declarations section creates and initializes the class-level `dblPrices` array. A class-level array is appropriate in this case because two procedures (frmMain_Load and btnDisplay_Click) will need access to the array.

3. Locate the frmMain_Load procedure. The procedure fills the list box with the array values.

4. Locate the btnDisplay_Click procedure. The procedure contains the code for the last step in the pseudocode, which is to display the highest price and the number of days.

5. Click the **blank line** below the ` Declare variables.` comment. The first step in the pseudocode declares a variable named `intLastSub` and initializes it to the last subscript in the array. Type the following declaration statement and then press **Enter**:

   ```
   Dim intLastSub As Integer = dblPrices.GetUpperBound(0)
   ```

6. The next step in the pseudocode declares a variable named `dblHighest` and initializes it to the first price stored in the array. When searching an array for the highest (or lowest) value, it is a common programming practice to initialize the variable to the value stored in the first array element. Type the following declaration statement and then press **Enter**:

   ```
   Dim dblHighest As Double = dblPrices(0)
   ```

7. Next, the procedure will declare and initialize a counter variable named `intDays`. The variable will keep track of the number of elements (days) whose stock price matches the value stored in the `dblHighest` variable. The procedure will initialize the variable

to 1 because, at this point, only one element (the first one) contains the price currently stored in the dblHighest variable. Type the following Dim statement and then press **Enter** twice:

```
Dim intDays As Integer = 1
```

8. Next, the procedure will use the For...Next statement to traverse the second through the last elements in the array. Each element's value will be compared, one at a time, to the value stored in the dblHighest variable. You do not need to look at the first element because its value is already contained in the dblHighest variable. Enter the following For clause:

```
For intSub As Integer = 1 To intLastSub
```

9. Change the Next clause to **Next intSub** and then click the **blank line** below the For clause.

10. The loop contains a selection structure whose condition determines whether the price stored in the current array element is equal to the price stored in the dblHighest variable. If both prices are equal, the selection structure's true path adds 1 to the intDays counter variable. Enter the following If clause and assignment statement:

```
If dblPrices(intSub) = dblHighest Then
    intDays += 1
```

11. If both prices are not equal, the selection structure's false path determines whether the price stored in the current array element is greater than the price stored in the dblHighest variable. Enter the following ElseIf clause:

```
ElseIf dblPrices(intSub) > dblHighest Then
```

12. If the price in the current array element is greater than the price in the dblHighest variable, the selection structure should assign the higher value to the dblHighest variable. It should also reset the number of days counter to 1 because, at this point, only one element (the current one) contains that price. Enter the additional assignment statements indicated in Figure 8-14.

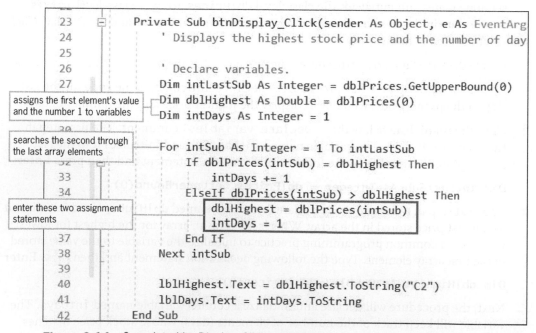

Figure 8-14 Completed btnDisplay_Click procedure

13. Save the solution and then start the application. Click the **Display** button. The highest stock price ($99.00) and the number of days the stock closed at that price (2) appear in the interface. See Figure 8-15.

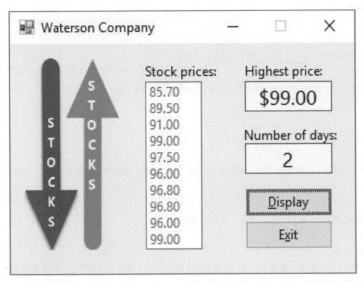

Figure 8-15 Highest price and number of days shown in the interface

14. Click the **Exit** button. Close the Code Editor window and then close the solution.

YOU DO IT 4!

Create an application named You Do It 4 and save it in the VB2017\Chap08 folder. Add a label and a button to the form. The button's Click event procedure should declare and initialize a one-dimensional Double array. Use any six numbers to initialize the array. The procedure should display (in the label) the lowest value stored in the array. Code the procedure using the For...Next statement. Save the solution and then start and test the application. Close the solution.

F-6 Sorting a One-Dimensional Array

You can use the **Array.Sort method** to sort the values in a one-dimensional array in ascending order. To sort the values in descending order, you first use the Array.Sort method to sort the values in ascending order; you then use the **Array.Reverse method** to reverse the sorted values. Figure 8-16 shows the syntax of both methods. In each syntax, *arrayName* is the name of a one-dimensional array.

Array.Sort and Array.Reverse Methods of a One-Dimensional Array

Syntax
Array.Sort(arrayName**)**
Array.Reverse(arrayName**)**

Example 1
```
Dim intScores() As Integer = {78, 90, 75, 83}
Array.Sort(intScores)
```
sorts the contents of the array in ascending order, as follows: 75, 78, 83, and 90

Example 2
```
Dim intScores() As Integer = {78, 90, 75, 83}
Array.Reverse(intScores)
```
reverses the contents of the array, placing the values in the following order: 83, 75, 90, and 78

Example 3
```
Dim intScores() As Integer = {78, 90, 75, 83}
Array.Sort(intScores)
Array.Reverse(intScores)
```
sorts the contents of the array in ascending order and then reverses the contents, placing the values in descending order as follows: 90, 83, 78, and 75

Figure 8-16 Syntax and examples of the Array.Sort and Array.Reverse methods

You will use the Array.Sort and Array.Reverse methods in the Continents application, which you finish coding in the next set of steps. The application stores the names of the seven continents in a one-dimensional array named `strContinents`. It then allows the user to display the names in a list box, in either ascending or descending order.

START HERE

To finish coding the Continents application:

1. Open the Continents Solution.sln file contained in the VB2017\Chap08\Continents Solution folder.

2. Open the Code Editor window. The form class's declarations section contains two Private statements. The first statement declares the `strContinents` array and initializes it to the names of the seven continents. The second statement declares the `intLastSub` variable and initializes it to the last subscript in the array. The array and variable were declared as class-level memory locations because both need to be accessed by two procedures (btnAscending_Click and btnDescending_Click).

3. Locate the btnAscending_Click and btnDescending_Click procedures. Both procedures contain the `lstContinents.Items.Clear()` statement, which clears the contents of the list box. Both procedures also contain a loop that displays the array contents in the list box. Enter the three statements indicated in Figure 8-17.

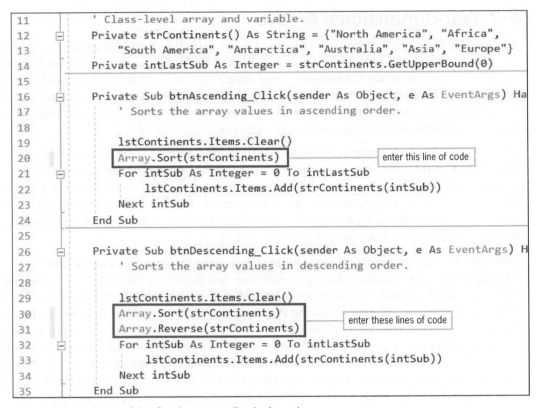

```
11          ' Class-level array and variable.
12          Private strContinents() As String = {"North America", "Africa",
13              "South America", "Antarctica", "Australia", "Asia", "Europe"}
14          Private intLastSub As Integer = strContinents.GetUpperBound(0)
15
16          Private Sub btnAscending_Click(sender As Object, e As EventArgs) Ha
17              ' Sorts the array values in ascending order.
18
19              lstContinents.Items.Clear()
20              Array.Sort(strContinents)                    enter this line of code
21              For intSub As Integer = 0 To intLastSub
22                  lstContinents.Items.Add(strContinents(intSub))
23              Next intSub
24          End Sub
25
26          Private Sub btnDescending_Click(sender As Object, e As EventArgs) H
27              ' Sorts the array values in descending order.
28
29              lstContinents.Items.Clear()
30              Array.Sort(strContinents)                    enter these lines of code
31              Array.Reverse(strContinents)
32              For intSub As Integer = 0 To intLastSub
33                  lstContinents.Items.Add(strContinents(intSub))
34              Next intSub
35          End Sub
```

Figure 8-17   Most of the Continents application's code

4. Save the solution and then start the application. Click the **Ascending order** button to display the names in ascending order. See Figure 8-18.

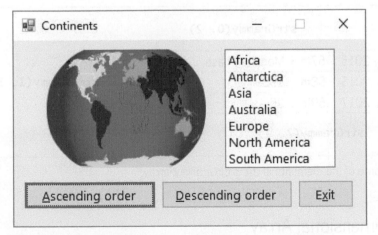

Figure 8-18   Continent names displayed in ascending order

5. Click the **Descending order** button to display the names in descending order.

6. Click the **Exit** button. Close the Code Editor window and then close the solution.

F-7 Two-Dimensional Arrays

As mentioned earlier, the most commonly used arrays in business applications are one-dimensional and two-dimensional. Unlike a one-dimensional array, which you can visualize as a column of variables in memory, a **two-dimensional array** resembles a table in that the variables (elements) are in rows and columns. You can determine the number of elements in a two-dimensional array by multiplying the number of its rows by the number of its columns. An array that has four rows and three columns, for example, contains 12 elements.

Each element in a two-dimensional array is identified by a unique combination of two subscripts that the computer assigns to the element when the array is created. The subscripts specify the element's row and column positions in the array. All of the elements in the first row have a row subscript of 0, elements in the second row have a row subscript of 1, and so on. Similarly, all of the elements in the first column have a column subscript of 0, elements in the second column have a column subscript of 1, and so on.

You refer to each element in a two-dimensional array by the array's name and the element's row and column subscripts, with the row subscript listed first and the column subscript listed second. The subscripts are separated by a comma and specified in a set of parentheses immediately following the array name. For example, to refer to the element located in the first row, first column in a two-dimensional array named strGrammy, you use strGrammy(0, 0)—read "strGrammy sub zero comma zero." Similarly, to refer to the element located in the second row, fourth column, you use strGrammy(1, 3). Notice that the subscripts are one number less than the row and column in which the element is located. This is because the row and column subscripts start at 0 rather than at 1. You will find that the last row subscript in an array is always one number less than the number of rows, and the last column subscript is always one number less than the number of columns. Figure 8-19 illustrates the elements contained in the two-dimensional strGrammy array.

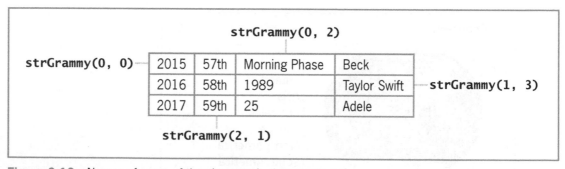

Figure 8-19   Names of some of the elements in the strGrammy array

Declaring a Two-Dimensional Array

Figure 8-20 shows two versions of the syntax for declaring a two-dimensional array in Visual Basic. The figure also includes examples of using both syntax versions. In each version, *dataType* is the type of data the array variables will store.

Declaring a Two-Dimensional Array

Syntax – Version 1
{**Dim** | **Private** | **Static**} *arrayName*(*highestRowSub*, *highestColumnSub*) **As** *dataType*

Syntax – Version 2
{**Dim** | **Private** | **Static**} *arrayName*(**,**) **As** *dataType* = {{*initialValues*},...{*initialValues*}}

Example 1
```
Dim strStateCapitals(49, 1) As String
```
declares a 50-row, two-column procedure-level array named `strStateCapitals`; each element
is automatically initialized using the keyword `Nothing`

Example 2
```
Static intNumSold(5, 4) As Integer
```
declares a static, six-row, five-column procedure-level array named `intNumSold`; each element
is automatically initialized to 0

Example 3
```
Private strGrammy(,) As String =
        {{"2015", "57th", "Morning Phase", "Beck"},
         {"2016", "58th", "1989", "Taylor Swift"},
         {"2017", "59th", "25", "Adele"}}
```
declares and initializes a three-row, four-column class-level array named `strGrammy` (the array
is illustrated in Figure 8-19)

Example 4
```
Private dblSales(,) As Double = {{75.33, 9.65},
                                 {23.55, 6.89},
                                 {4.5, 89.3},
                                 {100.67, 38.92}}
```
declares and initializes a four-row, two-column class-level array named `dblSales`

Figure 8-20 Syntax versions and examples of declaring a two-dimensional array

In Version 1's syntax, *highestRowSub* and *highestColumnSub* are integers that specify the
highest row and column subscripts, respectively, in the array. When the array is created, it
will contain one row more than the number specified in the *highestRowSub* argument and one
column more than the number specified in the *highestColumnSub* argument. This is because
the first row and column subscripts in a two-dimensional array are 0. When you declare a
two-dimensional array using Version 1's syntax, the computer automatically initializes each
element in the array when the array is created.

You would use Version 2's syntax when you want to specify each variable's initial value. You do
this by including a separate *initialValues* section, enclosed in braces, for each row in the array. If
the array has two rows, then the statement that declares and initializes the array should have two
initialValues sections. If the array has five rows, then the declaration statement should have five
initialValues sections.

Within the individual initialValues sections, you enter one or more values separated by
commas. The number of values to enter corresponds to the number of columns in the array.
If the array contains 10 columns, then each individual initialValues section should contain
10 values. In addition to the set of braces enclosing each individual initialValues section,
Version 2's syntax also requires all of the initialValues sections to be enclosed in a set
of braces.

When using Version 2's syntax, be sure to include a comma within the parentheses that follow the array's name. The comma indicates that the array is a two-dimensional array. (Recall that a comma is used to separate the row subscript from the column subscript in a two-dimensional array.)

Storing Data in a Two-Dimensional Array

After an array is declared, you can use another statement to store a different value in an array element. Examples of such statements include assignment statements and statements that contain the TryParse method. Figure 8-21 shows examples of both types of statements, using three of the arrays declared in Figure 8-20.

Storing Data in a Two-Dimensional Array

Example 1
```
strStateCapitals(0, 0) = "AL"
strStateCapitals(0, 1) = "Montgomery"
```
assigns the strings "AL" and "Montgomery" to the elements located in the first row in the strStateCapitals array; "AL" is assigned to the first column, and "Montgomery" is assigned to the second column

Example 2
```
For intRow As Integer = 0 To 5
    For intColumn As Integer = 0 To 4
        intNumSold(intRow, intColumn) += 1
    Next intColumn
Next intRow
```
adds the number 1 to the contents of each element in the intNumSold array

Example 3
```
Dim intRow As Integer
Dim intCol As Integer
Do While intRow <= 3
    intCol = 0
    Do While intCol <= 1
        dblSales(intRow, intCol) *= 1.1
        intCol += 1
    Loop
    intRow += 1
Loop
```
multiplies each element in the dblSales array by 1.1 and stores the result in the element

Example 4
```
dblSales(2, 1) *= 0.07
```
multiplies the value contained in the third row, second column in the dblSales array by 0.07 and then assigns the result to the element; you can also write this statement as dblSales(2, 1) = dblSales(2, 1) * 0.07

Example 5
```
Double.TryParse(txtSales.Text, dblSales(0, 0))
```
assigns either the value entered in the txtSales control (converted to Double) or the number 0 to the element located in the first row, first column in the dblSales array

---

Figure 8-21   Examples of statements used to store data in a two-dimensional array

Determining the Highest Subscript in a Two-Dimensional Array

Earlier in this lesson, you learned how to use the GetUpperBound method to determine the highest subscript in a one-dimensional array. You can also use the GetUpperBound method to determine the highest row and column subscripts in a two-dimensional array, as shown in Figure 8-22.

GetUpperBound Method of a Two-Dimensional Array

Syntax to determine the highest row subscript
arrayName.**GetUpperBound(0)**

the row dimension is always 0

Syntax to determine the highest column subscript
arrayName.**GetUpperBound(1)**

the column dimension is always 1

Example
```
Dim strOrders(10, 3) As String
Dim intHighestRowSub As Integer
Dim intHighestColumnSub As Integer
intHighestRowSub = strOrders.GetUpperBound(0)
intHighestColumnSub = strOrders.GetUpperBound(1)
```
GetUpperBound method

assigns the numbers 10 and 3 to the intHighestRowSub and intHighestColumnSub variables, respectively

---

Figure 8-22   Syntax and an example of a two-dimensional array's GetUpperBound method

---

Mini-Quiz 8-3

1. Write a statement that declares a class-level two-dimensional array named intOrders. The array should contain five rows and three columns.

2. Write a statement that assigns the number 150 to the element located in the fourth row, third column in the intOrders array.

3. Write a statement that assigns the number of rows in the intOrders array to the intRows variable.

4. Write a statement that assigns the highest column subscript in the intOrders array to the intLastColSub variable.

1) Private intOrders(4, 2) As Integer 2) intOrders(3, 2) = 150 3) intRows = intOrders.GetUpperBound(0) + 1 4) intLastColSub = intOrders.GetUpperBound(1)

Traversing a Two-Dimensional Array

Recall that you use a loop to traverse a one-dimensional array. To traverse a two-dimensional array, you typically use two loops: an outer loop and a nested loop. One of the loops keeps track of the row subscript, and the other keeps track of the column subscript. You can code the loops using either the For...Next statement or the Do...Loop statement. Rather than using two loops to traverse a two-dimensional array, you can also use one For Each...Next loop. However, recall that the instructions in a For Each...Next loop can only read the array values; they cannot permanently modify the values.

Figure 8-23 shows examples of loops that traverse the strMonths array, displaying each element's value in the lstMonths control. Both loops in Example 1 are coded using the For...Next statement. However, either one of the loops could be coded using the Do...Loop statement instead. You could also code both loops using only the Do...Loop statement, as shown in Example 2. The loop in Example 3 is coded using the For Each...Next statement.

Traversing a Two-Dimensional Array

```
Dim strMonths(,) As String = {{"Jan", "31"},
                              {"Feb", "28 or 29"},
                              {"Mar", "31"},
                              {"Apr", "30"}}
```

Example 1
```
Dim intHighRow As Integer = strMonths.GetUpperBound(0)
Dim intHighCol As Integer = strMonths.GetUpperBound(1)
For intRow As Integer = 0 To intHighRow
    For intCol As Integer = 0 To intHighCol
        lstMonths.Items.Add(strMonths(intRow, intCol))
    Next intCol
Next intRow
```
displays the contents of the strMonths array in the lstMonths control; the array values are displayed row by row, as follows: Jan, 31, Feb, 28 or 29, Mar, 31, Apr, and 30

Example 2
```
Dim intHighRow As Integer = strMonths.GetUpperBound(0)
Dim intHighCol As Integer = strMonths.GetUpperBound(1)
Dim intRow As Integer
Dim intCow As Integer
Do While intCol <= intHighCol
    intRow = 0
    Do While intRow <= intHighRow
        lstMonths.Items.Add(strMonths(intRow, intCol))
        intRow += 1
    Loop
    intCol += 1
Loop
```
displays the contents of the strMonths array in the lstMonths control; the array values are displayed column by column, as follows: Jan, Feb, Mar, Apr, 31, 28 or 29, 31, and 30

Example 3
```
For Each strElement As String In strMonths
    lstMonths.Items.Add(strElement)
Next strElement
```
displays the contents of the strMonths array in the lstMonths control; the array values are displayed as follows: Jan, 31, Feb, 28 or 29, Mar, 31, Apr, and 30

Figure 8-23   Examples of loops used to traverse a two-dimensional array

START HERE

To open and then finish coding the Months application:

1. Open the Months Solution.sln file contained in the VB2017\Chap08\Months Solution folder.

2. Open the Code Editor window and locate the btnDisplay_Click procedure. Click the **blank line** above the End Sub clause and then enter one of the three examples shown in Figure 8-23.

3. Save the solution and then start the application. Click the **Display** button. See Figure 8-24.

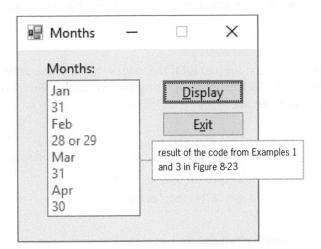

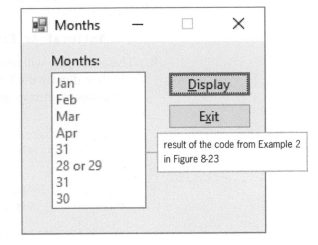

Figure 8-24   Months array displayed in the list box

4. Click the **Exit** button. Close the Code Editor window and then close the solution.

Totaling the Values Stored in a Two-Dimensional Array

In this section, you will finish coding the Jenko Booksellers application, which displays the total sales made in the company's three stores. The sales amounts are stored in a two-dimensional array that has three rows and two columns. Each row contains the sales amounts for one of the three stores, with the first column for the sales of paperback books and the second column for the sales of hardcover books.

START HERE

To finish coding the Jenko Booksellers application:

1. Open the Jenko Solution.sln file contained in the VB2017\Chap08\Jenko Solution folder.

2. Open the Code Editor window and locate the btnCalc_Click procedure. First, the procedure will declare and initialize a two-dimensional array to store the sales amounts. Click the **blank line** above the End Sub clause, and then enter the array declaration statement shown in Figure 8-25.

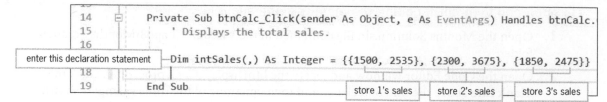

```
14    ⊟          Private Sub btnCalc_Click(sender As Object, e As EventArgs) Handles btnCalc.
15                   ' Displays the total sales.
16
                  ─Dim intSales(,) As Integer = {{1500, 2535}, {2300, 3675}, {1850, 2475}}
18
19               End Sub
```

enter this declaration statement

store 1's sales · store 2's sales · store 3's sales

Figure 8-25 Array declaration statement entered in the btnCalc_Click procedure

3. The procedure will also declare a variable that it can use to accumulate the sales amounts stored in the array. Type the following declaration statement and then press **Enter** twice:

```
Dim intTotal As Integer
```

4. The procedure will use a For Each...Next loop to total the values stored in the array. It will then display the total sales in the lblTotal control. Enter the For Each...Next loop and assignment statement shown in Figure 8-26.

```
14    ⊟          Private Sub btnCalc_Click(sender As Object, e As EventArgs) Handles btnCalc.
15                   ' Displays the total sales.
16
17                   Dim intSales(,) As Integer = {{1500, 2535}, {2300, 3675}, {1850, 2475}}
18                   Dim intTotal As Integer
19
20    ⊟           ┌For Each intElement As Integer In intSales
                  │    intTotal += intElement
                  │Next intElement
23                └lblTotal.Text = intTotal.ToString("C0")
24               End Sub
```

enter these lines of code

Figure 8-26 Completed btnCalc_Click procedure

5. Save the solution and then start the application. Click the **Calculate** button. The total sales amount is $14,335. See Figure 8-27.

Figure 8-27 Total sales amount displayed in the interface

6. Click the **Exit** button. Close the Code Editor window and then close the solution.

YOU DO IT 5!

Create an application named You Do It 5 and save it in the VB2017\Chap08 folder. Add a button and three labels to the form. The button's Click event procedure should declare and initialize a two-dimensional Integer array that contains three rows and two columns. Use any six integers to initialize the array. The procedure should use the For Each...Next statement to total the array values and then display the total in the first label. It should use the Do...Loop statement to total the array values and then display the total in the second label, and use the For...Next statement to total the array values and then display the total in the third label. Code the procedure. Save the solution and then start and test the application. Close the solution.

Mini-Quiz 8-4

1. The code to traverse a two-dimensional array using the Do...Loop statement requires two loops. True or False?

2. The code to traverse a two-dimensional array using the For...Next statement requires two loops. True or False?

3. The code to traverse a two-dimensional array using the For Each...Next statement requires two loops. True or False?

4. When using two loops to traverse an array, you can use the For...Next statement to code the outer loop and use the For Each...Next statement to code the nested loop. True or False?

1) True 2) True 3) False 4) False

APPLY THE CONCEPTS LESSON

After studying this lesson, you should be able to:

- A-1 Associate an array with a collection
- A-2 Create accumulator and counter arrays
- A-3 Create parallel one-dimensional arrays
- A-4 Search a two-dimensional array

A-1 Associate an Array with a Collection

It is not uncommon for programmers to associate the items in a list box with the values stored in an array. This is because the items in a list box belong to a collection (namely, the Items collection), and collections and arrays have several things in common. First, each is a group of individual objects treated as one unit. Second, each individual object in the group is identified by a unique number, which is called an index when referring to a collection, but a subscript when referring to an array. Third, both the first index in a collection and the first subscript in an array are 0. These commonalities allow you to associate the list box items and array elements by their positions within their respective groups.

To associate a list box with an array, you first add the appropriate items to the list box. You then store each item's related value in its corresponding position in the array. Figure 8-28 illustrates the relationship between the items in the lstPresidents control and the elements in a one-dimensional array named **strVPs**.

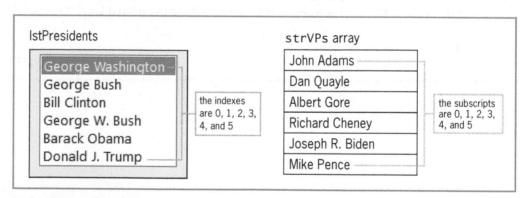

Figure 8-28 Illustration of the list box and array

START HERE

To finish coding the Presidents and Vice Presidents application:

1. Open the Presidents Solution.sln file contained in the VB2017\Chap08\Presidents Solution folder.

2. Open the Code Editor window. The form class's declarations section contains a Private statement that declares and initializes the **strVPs** array illustrated in Figure 8-28. The frmMain_Load procedure adds the names from the array to the lstPresidents control and then selects the first name in the list.

3. Locate the lstPresidents_SelectedIndexChanged procedure. When the user selects a president's name in the list box, the procedure should display the appropriate vice president's name in the Vice President box. You can use the index of the selected item to access the appropriate name from the **strVPs** array. Click the **blank line** above the End Sub clause. Type the assignment statement shown in Figure 8-29.

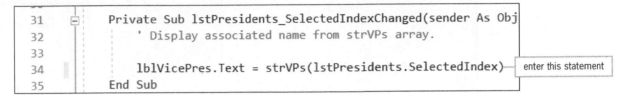

```
31    Private Sub lstPresidents_SelectedIndexChanged(sender As Obj
32        ' Display associated name from strVPs array.
33
34        lblVicePres.Text = strVPs(lstPresidents.SelectedIndex)──  enter this statement
35    End Sub
```

Figure 8-29   Assignment statement to display the vice president's name

4. Save the solution and then start the application. The first item in the list box (George Washington) is already selected, and the name of his vice president (John Adams) appears in the Vice President box. See Figure 8-30.

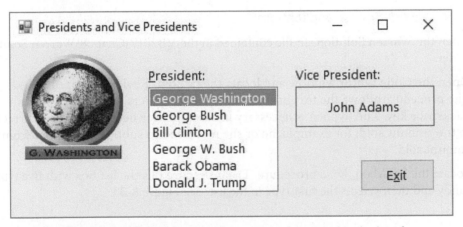

Figure 8-30   Name of the associated vice president displayed in the interface

5. On your own, verify that the application displays the appropriate vice president's name for the remaining list box items.

6. Click the **Exit** button. Close the Code Editor window and then close the solution.

A-2 Create Accumulator and Counter Arrays

One-dimensional arrays are often used to either accumulate or count related values; these arrays are commonly referred to as **accumulator arrays** and **counter arrays**, respectively. The Warren School application, which you code next, uses an accumulator array to keep track of the number of candy bars sold by each student. The application's interface is shown in Figure 8-31. The interface provides a list box for selecting the candy type, and provides a text box for entering the number sold by a student. The Add to total button will accumulate the numbers sold and then display the totals, by candy type, in the interface.

Figure 8-31 Interface for the Warren School application

START HERE **To code the Warren School application:**

1. Open the Warren Solution.sln file contained in the VB2017\Chap08\Warren Solution folder.

2. Open the Code Editor window and locate the txtSold_KeyPress procedure. The procedure allows the text box to accept only numbers, the hyphen, and the Backspace key. The hyphen is necessary in case the user needs to make a correction to the amount sold; for example, he or she may need to subtract a number from the amount sold.

3. Locate the frmMain_Load procedure. The procedure fills the list box with five types of candy and then selects the first type in the list. See Figure 8-32.

```
10      Private Sub frmMain_Load(sender As Object, e As
11          ' Fills the list box with values and then s
12
13          lstCandy.Items.Add("Choco Bar")
14          lstCandy.Items.Add("Choco Bar-Peanuts")
15          lstCandy.Items.Add("Kit Kat")
16          lstCandy.Items.Add("Peanut Butter Cups")
17          lstCandy.Items.Add("Take 5 Bar")
18          lstCandy.SelectedIndex = 0
19      End Sub
```

Figure 8-32 frmMain_Load procedure

4. Locate the btnAdd_Click procedure. The procedure will declare a one-dimensional accumulator array named intCandy. The array will have five elements, with each corresponding to a candy type listed in the list box. Each array element will be used to accumulate the sales of its corresponding list box item.

5. Click the **blank line** below the ' Declare array and variable. comment. The intCandy array will need to retain its values until the application ends. You can accomplish this by declaring the array either in the form class's declarations section (using the Private keyword to make it a class-level array) or in the btnAdd_Click procedure (using the Static keyword to make it a static procedure-level array); you will use the latter approach. Like static variables, which you learned about in Chapter 3, static arrays remain in memory and retain their values until the application ends. Type the following declaration statement and then press **Enter**:

```
Static intCandy(4) As Integer
```

6. In addition to the array, the procedure will use an Integer variable to store the amount sold. Type the following Dim statement and then press **Enter** twice:

```
Dim intSold As Integer
```

7. Next, the procedure needs to convert the txtSold.Text property to Integer and store the result in the intSold variable. Type the following TryParse method and then press **Enter**:

```
Integer.TryParse(txtSold.Text, intSold)
```

8. The procedure will use the index of the item selected in the list box to update the appropriate array element. Click the **blank line** below the ' Update array value. comment. Type the following assignment statement and then press **Enter**:

```
intCandy(lstCandy.SelectedIndex) += intSold
```

9. Finally, the procedure will display the array values in the interface. Click the **blank line** below the ' Display array values. comment and then enter the five assignment statements indicated in Figure 8-33.

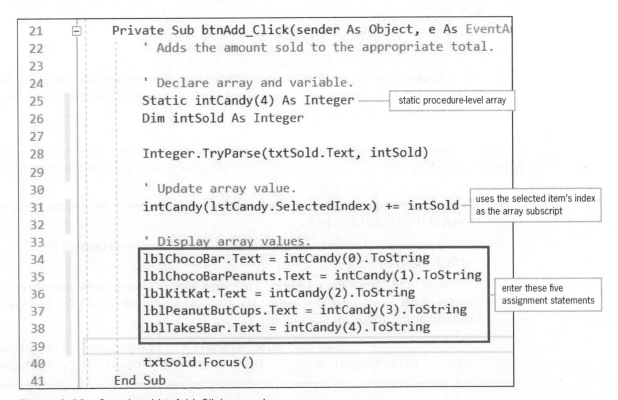

```
21      Private Sub btnAdd_Click(sender As Object, e As EventA
22          ' Adds the amount sold to the appropriate total.
23
24          ' Declare array and variable.
25          Static intCandy(4) As Integer          static procedure-level array
26          Dim intSold As Integer
27
28          Integer.TryParse(txtSold.Text, intSold)
29
30          ' Update array value.
31          intCandy(lstCandy.SelectedIndex) += intSold    uses the selected item's index
32                                                          as the array subscript
33          ' Display array values.
34          lblChocoBar.Text = intCandy(0).ToString
35          lblChocoBarPeanuts.Text = intCandy(1).ToString
36          lblKitKat.Text = intCandy(2).ToString          enter these five
37          lblPeanutButCups.Text = intCandy(3).ToString   assignment statements
38          lblTake5Bar.Text = intCandy(4).ToString
39
40          txtSold.Focus()
41      End Sub
```

Figure 8-33   Completed btnAdd_Click procedure

10. Save the solution and then start the application. Type **100** in the Sold box and then click the **Add to total** button. The number 100 appears in the Choco Bar box.

11. Click **Kit Kat** in the Candy box. Change the 100 in the Sold box to **45** and then press **Enter** to select the Add to total button, which is the default button in the interface.

12. Now, change the 45 in the Sold box to **-6** (a negative number 6) and then press **Enter**.

13. Next, change the -6 in the Sold box to **36**, click **Peanut Butter Cups**, and then press **Enter**.

14. On your own, record the following two candy sales: **10** of the **Take 5 Bar** and **2** of the **Choco Bar-Peanuts**. See Figure 8-34.

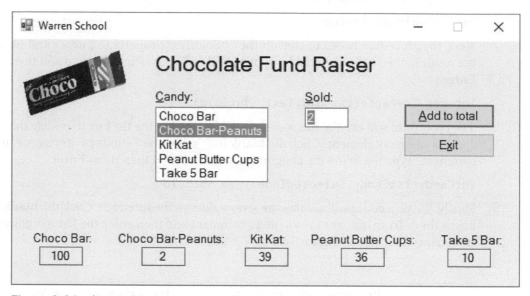

Figure 8-34 Accumulated array values shown in the interface

15. On your own, test the application using different candy types and sales amounts. When you are finished testing the application, click the **Exit** button. Close the Code Editor window and then close the solution.

Mini-Quiz 8-5

1. Write a statement that updates the second element in the intOrders array by the value stored in the intSold variable.

2. Write a statement that subtracts the number 10 from the first element in the intOrders array.

3. The items in the intOrders array are associated with the items listed in the lstProducts control. Write a statement that assigns the array value associated with the selected list box item to the intQuantity variable.

1) intOrders(1) += intSold 2) intOrders(0) -= 10 or intOrders(0) += -10
3) intQuantity = intOrders(lstProducts.SelectedIndex)

YOU DO IT 6!

Create an application named You Do It 6 and save it in the VB2017\Chap08 folder. Add two list boxes and a button to the form. The button's Click event procedure should declare and initialize a one-dimensional Integer array. Use any 10 integers to initialize the array. The procedure should use the For Each...Next statement to display the contents of the array in the first list box. The procedure should then use the For...Next statement to increase each array element's value by 2. Finally, it should use the Do...Loop statement to display the updated results in the second list box. Code the procedure. Save the solution and then start and test the application. Close the solution.

A-3 Create Parallel One-Dimensional Arrays

All of the variables in an array must have the same data type. So how can you store a price list, which is composed of a string (the product ID) and a number (the product's price), in an array? One solution is to use two **parallel one-dimensional arrays**, as illustrated in Figure 8-35: a String array to store the IDs and a Double array to store the prices. The arrays are parallel because each element in the strIds array corresponds to the element located in the same position in the dblPrices array. For example, the price of item A45G [strIds(0)] is 8.99 [dblPrices(0)]. Likewise, the price of item J63Y [strIds(1)] is 12.99 [dblPrices(1)]. The same relationship is true for the remaining elements in both arrays. To determine an item's price, you locate the item's ID in the strIds array and then view its corresponding element in the dblPrices array.

strIds(0)	A45G		8.99	dblPrices(0)
strIds(1)	J63Y		12.99	dblPrices(1)
strIds(2)	M93K		5.99	dblPrices(2)
strIds(3)	C20P		13.5	dblPrices(3)
strIds(4)	F77T		7.25	dblPrices(4)

Figure 8-35   Illustration of two parallel one-dimensional arrays

You will use the two parallel arrays from Figure 8-35 in the Paper Warehouse application, which you code in the next set of steps. The application will search the strIds array for the product ID entered by the user and then display the corresponding price from the dblPrices array. Figure 8-36 shows the pseudocode for the btnGet_Click procedure in the application.

1. declare strSearchId variable to store the ID entered in the txtId.Text property
2. declare intSub variable to keep track of array subscripts
3. assign txtId.Text property to strSearchId
4. repeat until all of the elements in the strIds array have been searched or the search ID is located in the array
　　add 1 to intSub so the loop can search the next element in the strIds array
　end repeat
5. if the search ID was located in the strIds array
　　display the price, which is contained in the same location in the dblPrices array, in lblPrice
　else
　　display "ID not found." message in a message box
　end if

Figure 8-36　Pseudocode for the btnGet_Click procedure using parallel arrays

START HERE

To code the Paper Warehouse application using parallel arrays:

1. Open the Paper Solution.sln file contained in the VB2017\Chap08\Paper Solution-Parallel folder. Open the Code Editor window. The code to declare the parallel arrays is already entered in the form class's declarations section. See Figure 8-37.

```
9     ☐Public Class frmMain
10           ' Declare parallel arrays.
11           Private strIds() As String = {"A45G", "J63Y", "M93K", "C20P", "F77T"}
12           Private dblPrices() As Double = {8.99, 12.99, 5.99, 13.5, 7.25}
```

Figure 8-37　Array declaration statements

2. Locate the btnGet_Click procedure. The procedure contains the code for the first three steps in the pseudocode.

3. The fourth step in the pseudocode is a loop that searches each element in the `strIds` array, stopping either when the end of the array is reached or when the ID is located in the array. Click the **blank line** above the End Sub clause. Enter the loop shown in Figure 8-38 and then position the insertion point as shown in the figure.

```
22            ' Search the strIds array until the
23            ' end of the array or the ID Is found.
24          ┌─Do Until intSub = strIds.Length OrElse strIds(intSub) = strSearchId
  enter this loop ┤    intSub += 1
26          └─Loop
27                        insertion point
28          End Sub
```

Figure 8-38　Loop entered in the btnGet_Click procedure

4. The last step in the pseudocode is a selection structure whose condition determines why the loop ended. You can make this determination by looking at the value in the `intSub` variable. If the loop ended because it reached the end of the `strIds` array without locating the ID, the `intSub` variable's value will be equal to the array's length. (Recall that an array's length is always one number more than its last subscript.) On the

other hand, if the loop ended because it located the ID in the `strIds` array, the `intSub` variable's value will be less than the array's length. Type the following If clause and then press **Enter**:

```
If intSub < strIds.Length Then
```

5. If the selection structure's condition evaluates to True, it means that the ID was located in the `strIds` array. In that case, the structure's true path should display (in the lblPrice control) the price located in the same position in the `dblPrices` array. Otherwise, its false path should display the "ID not found." message. Enter the additional code indicated in Figure 8-39.

```
14    Private Sub btnGet_Click(sender As Object, e As EventArgs) Handles btnGet.
15        ' Displays an item's price.
16
17        Dim strSearchId As String
18        Dim intSub As Integer
19
20        strSearchId = txtId.Text.Trim.ToUpper
21
22        ' Search the strIds array until the
23        ' end of the array or the ID Is found.
24        Do Until intSub = strIds.Length OrElse strIds(intSub) = strSearchId    ── searches for the ID in
25            intSub += 1                                                           the strIds array
26        Loop
27        If intSub < strIds.Length Then
28            lblPrice.Text = dblPrices(intSub).ToString("C2")    ── displays the corresponding
29        Else                                                       price from the dblPrices array
30            MessageBox.Show("ID not found.", "Paper Warehouse",
31                            MessageBoxButtons.OK, MessageBoxIcon.Information)    ── enter these lines of code
32        End If
33    End Sub
```

Figure 8-39 Completed btnGet_Click procedure

6. Save the solution and then start the application. Type **m93k** in the ID box and then click the **Get price** button. $5.99 appears in the Price box. See Figure 8-40.

Figure 8-40 Interface showing the price for item M93K

7. Type **a45h** in the ID box and then click the **Get price** button. The "ID not found." message appears in a message box. Close the message box.

8. On your own, test the application using other valid and invalid IDs. When you are finished testing the application, click the **Exit** button. Close the Code Editor window and then close the solution.

A-4 Search a Two-Dimensional Array

In the previous section, you used two parallel one-dimensional arrays to code the Paper Warehouse application: a String array for the item IDs and a Double array for the corresponding prices. Instead of storing the price list in two parallel one-dimensional arrays, you can store it in a two-dimensional array, with the first column storing the IDs and the second column storing the prices. However, you will need to treat the prices as strings because all of the data in an array must have the same data type. The strItems array is illustrated in Figure 8-41.

Figure 8-41 Illustration of the two-dimensional strItems array

Figure 8-42 shows the pseudocode for the btnGet_Click procedure using a two-dimensional array.

1. declare strSearchId variable to store the ID entered in the txtId.Text property
2. declare intRow variable to keep track of the array's row subscripts
3. assign txtId.Text property to strSearchId
4. repeat until all of the elements (rows) in the strItems array's first column have been searched or the search ID is located in the first column
     add 1 to intRow so the loop can search the next row in the array's first column
   end repeat
5. if the search ID was located in the array's first column
     display the price, which is contained in the same row as the ID, but in the second column; display the price in lblPrice
   else
     display "ID not found." message in a message box
   end if

Figure 8-42 Pseudocode for the btnGet_Click procedure using a two-dimensional array

To code the Paper Warehouse application using a two-dimensional array:

START HERE

1. Open the Paper Solution.sln file contained in the VB2017\Chap08\Paper Solution-TwoDim folder. Open the Code Editor window. The code to declare the two-dimensional array illustrated in Figure 8-41 is already entered in the form class's declarations section. See Figure 8-43.

```
9    ☐Public Class frmMain
10          ' Declare two-dimensional array.
11   ☐      Private strItems(,) As String = {{"A45G", "8.99"},
12                                            {"J63Y", "12.99"},
13                                            {"M93K", "5.99"},
14                                            {"C20P", "13.50"},
15                                            {"F77T", "7.25"}}
```

the 0 allows you to display the price without having to format it

Figure 8-43   Array declaration statement

2. Locate the btnGet_Click procedure. The procedure contains the code for the first three steps in the pseudocode.

3. The fourth step in the pseudocode is a loop that searches each element (row) in the first column in the **strItems** array, stopping either when all of the elements (rows) in the first column have been searched or when the ID is located in the first column. Click the **blank line** above the End Sub clause. Enter the loop shown in Figure 8-44 and then position the insertion point as shown in the figure.

```
25          ' Search the first column for the ID. Continue searching
26          ' until the end of the first column or the ID is found.
27   ☐    ┌Do Until intRow > strItems.GetUpperBound(0) OrElse
28         │            strItems(intRow, 0) = strSearchId
   enter this loop
29         │        intRow += 1
30         └Loop
31                    insertion point
32          End Sub
```

Figure 8-44   Loop entered in the btnGet_Click procedure

4. The last step in the pseudocode is a selection structure whose condition determines why the loop ended. You can make this determination by looking at the value in the **intRow** variable. If the loop ended because it reached the end of the array's first column without locating the ID, the **intRow** variable's value will be greater than the highest row subscript. On the other hand, if the loop ended because it located the ID in the first column, the **intRow** variable's value will be less than or equal to the highest row subscript. Type the following If clause and then press **Enter**:

If intRow <= strItems.GetUpperBound(0) Then

5. If the selection structure's condition evaluates to True, it means that the ID was located in the first column of the array. In that case, the structure's true path should display (in the lblPrice control) the price contained in the same row as the ID, but in the second column in the array. Otherwise, its false path should display the "ID not found." message. Enter the additional code indicated in Figure 8-45.

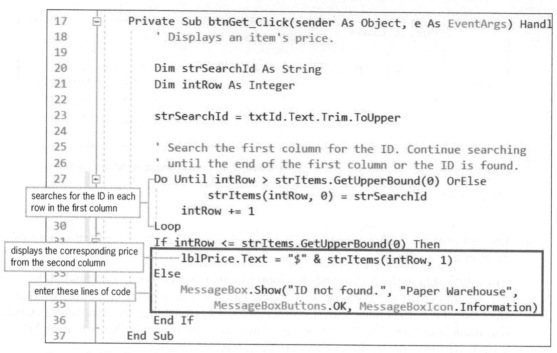

```
17  ⊟     Private Sub btnGet_Click(sender As Object, e As EventArgs) Handl
18            ' Displays an item's price.
19
20            Dim strSearchId As String
21            Dim intRow As Integer
22
23            strSearchId = txtId.Text.Trim.ToUpper
24
25            ' Search the first column for the ID. Continue searching
26            ' until the end of the first column or the ID is found.
27  ⊟         Do Until intRow > strItems.GetUpperBound(0) OrElse
                      strItems(intRow, 0) = strSearchId
                 intRow += 1
30            Loop
31            If intRow <= strItems.GetUpperBound(0) Then
                 lblPrice.Text = "$" & strItems(intRow, 1)
33            Else
                 MessageBox.Show("ID not found.", "Paper Warehouse",
35                    MessageBoxButtons.OK, MessageBoxIcon.Information)
36            End If
37         End Sub
```

searches for the ID in each row in the first column

displays the corresponding price from the second column

enter these lines of code

Figure 8-45   Completed btnGet_Click procedure

6. Save the solution and then start the application. Type **c20p** in the ID box and then click the **Get price** button. $13.50 appears in the Price box. See Figure 8-46.

Figure 8-46   Interface showing the price for item C20P

7. Type **a45h** in the ID box and then click the **Get price** button. The "ID not found." message appears in a message box. Close the message box.

8. On your own, test the application using other valid and invalid IDs. When you are finished testing the application, click the **Exit** button. Close the Code Editor window and then close the solution.

Summary

- You refer to an element in a one-dimensional array using the array's name followed by the element's subscript. The subscript is specified in a set of parentheses immediately following the array name.

- You declare a one-dimensional array using either of the syntax versions shown in Figure 8-2. The *highestSubscript* argument in Version 1 is an integer that specifies the highest subscript in the array. Using Version 1's syntax, the computer automatically initializes the array elements. The *initialValues* section in Version 2 is a list of values separated by commas and enclosed in braces. The values are used to initialize each element in the array.

- Examples of statements that you can use to store data in a one-dimensional array include an assignment statement and the TryParse method. Examples are shown in Figure 8-3.

- You can use a one-dimensional array's Length property to determine the number of elements in the array. Or, you can add the number 1 to the value returned by the array's GetUpperBound method.

- To determine the highest subscript in a one-dimensional array, use the array's GetUpperBound method with the number 0 as the specified dimension. Or, you can subtract the number 1 from the value stored in the array's Length property.

- You use a loop to traverse (or look at) each element in a one-dimensional array. You can code the loop using one of the following statements: Do...Loop, For...Next, or For Each...Next.

- The For Each...Next statement provides a convenient way to process one or more instructions for each element in a group. The statement's syntax is shown in Figure 8-9.

- The Array.Sort method sorts a one-dimensional array's values in ascending order. The method's syntax is shown in Figure 8-16.

- The Array.Reverse method reverses the order of the values stored in a one-dimensional array. The method's syntax is shown in Figure 8-16.

- To sort the values in a one-dimensional array in descending order, you first use the Array.Sort method to sort the values in ascending order and then use the Array.Reverse method to reverse the methods.

- To declare a two-dimensional array, use either of the syntax versions shown in Figure 8-20. In Version 1, the *highestRowSub* and *highestColumnSub* arguments are integers that specify the highest row and column subscripts, respectively, in the array. Using Version 1's syntax, the computer automatically initializes the array elements. In Version 2, the *initialValues* section is a list of values separated by commas and enclosed in braces. You include a separate initialValues section for each row in the array. Each initialValues section should contain the same number of values as there are columns in the array.

- Examples of statements that you can use to store data in a two-dimensional array include an assignment statement and the TryParse method. Examples are shown in Figure 8-21.

- You refer to an element in a two-dimensional array using the array's name followed by a set of parentheses that contains the element's row subscript, a comma, and its column subscript.

- To determine the highest row subscript in a two-dimensional array, use the array's GetUpperBound method with the number 0 as the specified dimension.

- To determine the highest column subscript in a two-dimensional array, use the array's GetUpperBound method with the number 1 as the specified dimension.

- You traverse (or look at) each element in a two-dimensional array using either one or two loops. One loop is all that is required when using the For Each...Next statement. Two loops are required when using the Do...Loop or For...Next statements.

- To associate the items in a list box (in other words, the Items collection) with the elements in an array, add the appropriate items to the list box and then store each item's related value in its corresponding position in the array. Each item's index in the list box should be the same as its subscript in the array.

- One-dimensional arrays are often used to either accumulate or count related values.

- To create parallel one-dimensional arrays, create two or more one-dimensional arrays. When assigning values to the arrays, be sure that the value stored in each element in the first array corresponds to the values stored in the same elements in the other arrays.

Key Terms

Accumulator arrays—arrays whose elements are used to accumulate (add together) values

Array.Reverse method—reverses the order of the values stored in a one-dimensional array

Array.Sort method—sorts the values stored in a one-dimensional array in ascending order

Array—a group of related variables that have the same name and data type and are stored in consecutive locations in the computer's main memory

Counter arrays—arrays whose elements are used for counting something

Elements—the variables in an array

For Each...Next statement—used to code a loop whose instructions should be processed for each element in a group

GetUpperBound method—returns an integer that represents the highest subscript in a specified dimension of an array; when used with a one-dimensional array, the dimension is 0; when used with a two-dimensional array, the dimension is 0 for the row subscript and 1 for the column subscript

Length property—one of the properties of a one-dimensional array; stores an integer that represents the number of array elements

One-dimensional array—an array whose elements are identified by a unique subscript

Parallel one-dimensional arrays—two or more one-dimensional arrays whose elements are related by their subscripts (positions) in the arrays

Populating the array—refers to the process of initializing the elements in an array

Scalar variable—another name for a simple variable

Simple variable—a variable that is unrelated to any other variable in the computer's main memory; also called a scalar variable

Subscript—a unique integer that identifies the position of an element in an array

Two-dimensional array—an array made up of rows and columns; each element has the same name and data type and is identified by a unique combination of two subscripts: a row subscript and a column subscript

Review Questions

1. Which of the following declares a five-element one-dimensional array?

   a. `Dim intSold(4) As Integer`

   b. `Dim intSold(5) As Integer = {4, 78, 65, 23, 2}`

   c. `Dim intSold() As Integer = {4, 78, 65, 23, 2}`

   d. Both a and c.

2. The `strItems` array is declared as follows: `Dim strItems(20) As String`. The `intSub` variable keeps track of the array subscripts and is initialized to 0. Which of the following Do clauses will process the loop instructions for each element in the array?

   a. `Do While intSub > 20`

   b. `Do While intSub < 20`

   c. `Do While intSub >= 20`

   d. `Do While intSub <= 20`

3. The `intSales` array is declared as follows: `Dim intSales() As Integer = {10000, 12000, 900, 500, 20000}`. The statement `intSales(2) += 10` will _____.

   a. replace the 900 amount with 10

   b. replace the 900 amount with 910

   c. replace the 12000 amount with 10

   d. replace the 12000 amount with 12010

4. The `intSales` array is declared as follows: `Dim intSales() As Integer = {10000, 12000, 900, 500, 20000}`. Which of the following loops will correctly multiply each element by 2? The `intSub` variable contains the number 0 before the loop is processed.

   a. ```
      Do While intSub <= 4
          intSub *= 2
      Loop
      ```

   b. ```
      Do While intSub <= 4
          intSales *= 2
          intSub += 1
      Loop
      ```

   c. ```
      Do While intSub < 5
          intSales(intSub) *= 2
          intSub += 1
      Loop
      ```

   d. None of the above.
      ```

5. The `intNums` array is declared as follows: `Dim intNums() As Integer = {10, 5, 7, 2}`. Which of the following blocks of code correctly calculates the average value stored in the array? The `intTotal`, `intSub`, and `dblAvg` variables contain the number 0 before the loop is processed.

a.
```
Do While intSub < 4
    intNums(intSub) = intTotal + intTotal
    intSub += 1
Loop
dblAvg = intTotal / intSub
```

b.
```
Do While intSub < 4
    intTotal += intNums(intSub)
    intSub = intSub + 1
Loop
dblAvg = intTotal / intSub
```

c.
```
Do While intSub < 4
    intTotal += intNums(intSub)
    intSub += 1
Loop
dblAvg = intTotal / intSub - 1
```

d.
```
Do While intSub < 4
    intTotal = intTotal + intNums(intSub)
    intSub = intSub + 1
Loop
dblAvg = intTotal / (intSub - 1)
```

6. Which of the following statements sorts the `intQuantities` array in ascending order?

a. `Array.Sort(intQuantities)`   c. `Sort(intQuantities)`

b. `intQuantities.Sort`   d. `SortArray(intQuantities)`

7. If the `intNums` array contains six elements, which of the following statements assigns the number 6 to the `intElements` variable?

a. `intElements = Len(intNums)`

b. `intElements = Length(intNums)`

c. `intElements = intNums.Len`

d. `intElements = intNums.Length`

8. Which of the following assigns the string "Rover" to the fifth element in a one-dimensional array named `strPetNames`?

a. `strPetNames(4) = "Rover"`

b. `strPetNames[4] = "Rover"`

c. `strPetNames(5) = "Rover"`

d. `strPetNames.Items.Add(5) = "Rover"`

9. The `intCounters` array contains five elements. Which of the following assigns the number 1 to each element?

a. ```
For intSub As Integer = 0 To 4
    intCounters(intSub) = 1
Next intSub
```

b. ```
Dim intSub As Integer
Do While intSub < 5
    intCounters(intSub) = 1
    intSub += 1
Loop
```

c. ```
For intSub As Integer = 1 To 5
    intCounters(intSub - 1) = 1
Next intSub
```

d. All of the above.

10. The `intNums` array is declared as follows: `Dim intNums() As Integer = {10, 5, 7, 2}`. Which of the following blocks of code correctly calculates the average value stored in the array? The `intTotal` variable contains the number 0 before the loop is processed.

a. ```
For Each intX As Integer In intNums
    intTotal += intX
Next intX
dblAvg = intTotal / intNums.Length
```

b. ```
For Each intX As Integer In intNums
    intTotal += intNums(intX)
Next intX
dblAvg = intTotal / intX
```

c. ```
For Each intX As Integer In intNums
    intTotal += intNums(intX)
    intX += 1
Next intX
dblAvg = intTotal / intX
```

d. None of the above.

11. The `strNames` array contains 100 elements. Which of the following statements assigns the number 99 to the `intLastSub` variable?

a. `intLastSub = strNames.Length`

b. `intLastSub = strNames.GetUpperBound(0) + 1`

c. `intLastSub = strNames.GetUpperBound(0)`

d. Both a and b.

12. The `intSales` array is declared as follows: `Dim intSales() As Integer = {10000, 12000, 900, 500, 20000}`. Which of the following If clauses determines whether the `intSub` variable contains a valid subscript for the array?

a. `If intSub >= 0 AndAlso intSub <= 4 Then`

b. `If intSub >= 0 AndAlso intSub < 4 Then`

c. `If intSub >= 0 AndAlso intSub <= 5 Then`

d. `If intSub > 0 AndAlso intSub < 5 Then`

13. If the elements in two arrays are related by their subscripts, the arrays are called
    _____ arrays.

    a. associated

    b. coupled

    c. matching

    d. parallel

14. The `strStates` and `strCapitals` arrays are parallel arrays. If Illinois is stored in the second element in the `strStates` array, where is its capital (Springfield) stored?

    a. `strCapitals(1)`

    b. `strCapitals(2)`

15. The `dblNums` array is a six-element Double array. Which of the following If clauses determines whether the entire array has been searched?

    a. `If intSub = dblNums.Length Then`

    b. `If intSub <= dblNums.Length Then`

    c. `If intSub > dblNums.GetUpperBound(0) Then`

    d. Both a and c.

16. Which of the following declares a two-dimensional array that has four rows and three columns?

    a. `Dim decNums(2, 3) As Decimal`

    b. `Dim decNums(3, 4) As Decimal`

    c. `Dim decNums(3, 2) As Decimal`

    d. `Dim decNums(4, 3) As Decimal`

17. The `intNum` array is declared as follows: `Dim intNum(,) As Integer = {{6, 12, 9, 5, 2}, {35, 60, 17, 8, 10}}`. The `intNum(1, 4) = intNum(1, 2) - 5` statement will _____.

    a. replace the 10 amount with 12

    b. replace the 5 amount with 7

    c. replace the 2 amount with 4

    d. None of the above.

18. The `intNum` array is declared as follows: `Dim intNum(,) As Integer = {{6, 12, 9, 5, 2}, {35, 60, 17, 8, 10}}`. Which of the following If clauses determines whether the `intRow` and `intCol` variables contain valid row and column subscripts, respectively, for the array?

    a. `If intNum(intRow, intCol) >= 0 AndAlso`
       `      intNum(intRow, intCol) < 5 Then`

    b. `If intNum(intRow, intCol) >= 0 AndAlso`
       `      intNum(intRow, intCol) <= 5 Then`

    c. `If intRow >= 0 AndAlso intRow < 3 AndAlso`
       `      intCol >= 0 AndAlso intCol < 6 Then`

    d. `If intRow >= 0 AndAlso intRow < 2 AndAlso`
       `      intCol >= 0 AndAlso intCol < 5 Then`

19. Which of the following statements assigns the string "California" to the element located in the fourth column, sixth row in the two-dimensional `strStates` array?

    a. `strStates(3, 5) = "California"`

    b. `strStates(5, 3) = "California"`

    c. `strStates(6, 3) = "California"`

    d. `strStates(3, 6) = "California"`

20. Which of the following assigns the number 0 to each element in a two-row, four-column Integer array named `intSums`?

    a.
```
For intRow As Integer = 0 To 1
    For intCol As Integer = 0 To 3
        intSums(intRow, intCol) = 0
    Next intCol
Next intRow
```

    b.
```
Dim intRow As Integer
Dim intCol As Integer
Do While intRow < 2
    intCol = 0
    Do While intCol < 4
        intSums(intRow, intCol) = 0
        intCol += 1
    Loop
    intRow += 1
Loop
```

    c.
```
For intX As Integer = 1 To 2
    For intY As Integer = 1 To 4
        intSums(intX - 1, intY - 1) = 0
    Next intY
Next intX
```

    d. All of the above.

21. Which of the following returns the highest column subscript in a two-dimensional array named `decPays`?

    a. `decPays.GetUpperBound(1)`

    b. `decPays.GetUpperBound(0)`

    c. `decPays.GetUpperSubscript(0)`

    d. `decPays.GetHighestColumn(0)`

Exercises

1. In this exercise, you modify one of the Waterson Company applications from this chapter's Apply lesson. Use Windows to make a copy of the Waterson Solution-Highest folder. Rename the copy Waterson Solution-Highest-DoLoop. Open the Waterson Solution.sln file contained in the Waterson Solution-Highest-DoLoop folder. Change the For...Next statement in the btnDisplay_Click procedure to the Do...Loop statement. Save the solution and then start and test the application.

INTRODUCTORY

INTRODUCTORY   2.   Open the Electricity Solution.sln file contained in the VB2017\Chap08\Electricity Solution folder. Open the Code Editor window and locate the btnCalc_Click procedure. Each of the 12 numbers in the array declaration statement represents the cost of electricity for a month. The procedure should use the For Each...Next statement to calculate the average monthly cost for electricity. Display the average with a dollar sign and two decimal places in the lblAvg control. Code the procedure. Save the solution and then start and test the application. (The average is $119.81.)

INTRODUCTORY   3.   Open the Gross Pay Solution.sln file contained in the VB2017\Chap08\Gross Pay Solution folder. The interface provides a text box for entering the number of hours an employee worked. It also provides a list box for selecting the employee's pay code. The btnCalc_Click procedure should display the gross pay, using the number of hours worked and the pay rate corresponding to the selected code. The pay codes and rates are listed in Figure 8-47. Employees working more than 40 hours receive time and a half for the hours worked over 40. Code the application. Use a class-level array to store the pay rates. Save the solution and then start and test the application.

Pay code	Pay rate
P23	10.50
P56	12.50
F45	14.25
F68	15.75
F96	17.65

Figure 8-47   Pay codes and rates for Exercise 3

INTRODUCTORY   4.   Open the CityState Solution.sln file contained in the VB2017\Chap08\CityState Solution folder. Open the Code Editor window. Locate the btnDisplay_Click procedure. The procedure should declare and initialize two parallel one-dimensional arrays named strStates and strCities. Use the names of any five states to initialize the strStates array. Initialize the strCities array with the capital of its corresponding state in the strStates array. The procedure should display the contents of the arrays in the list box, using the following format: the city name followed by a comma, a space, and the state name. (Be sure to clear the list box before displaying the names.) Save the solution and then start and test the application.

INTERMEDIATE   5.   Open the Professor Juarez Solution.sln file contained in the VB2017\Chap08\Professor Juarez Solution folder.

a.   Open the Code Editor window and locate the btnDisplay_Click procedure. The procedure declares and initializes two parallel one-dimensional arrays named strNames and strGrades. Code the procedure to display the names of students who have earned the grade selected in the lstGrades control. It should also display the number of students who have earned that grade.

b.   The first item in the lstGrades control should be selected when the interface appears. Code the appropriate procedure.

c.   The contents of the lstNames and lblNumber controls should be cleared when a different grade is selected in the lstGrades control. Code the appropriate procedure.

d.   Save the solution and then start and test the application.

6. In this exercise, you modify one of the Waterson Company applications from this chapter's Apply lesson. Use Windows to make a copy of the Waterson Solution-Highest folder. Rename the copy Waterson Solution-Lowest. Open the Waterson Solution.sln file contained in the Waterson Solution-Lowest folder. The application should now display the lowest price and the number of days the stock closed at that price. Make the appropriate modifications to the interface as well as to the comments and code in the Code Editor window. Save the solution and then start and test the application.

INTERMEDIATE

7. In this exercise, you modify the Professor Juarez application from Exercise 5. Use Windows to make a copy of the Professor Juarez Solution folder. Rename the copy Professor Juarez Solution-TwoDim. Open the Professor Juarez Solution.sln file contained in the Professor Juarez Solution-TwoDim folder. Change the two parallel arrays to a two-dimensional array named strStudents, and then make the appropriate modifications to the btnDisplay_Click procedure's code. Save the solution and then start and test the application.

INTERMEDIATE

8. Open the Calories Solution.sln file contained in the VB2017\Chap08\Calories Solution folder. Open the Code Editor window and locate the btnDisplay_Click procedure. The procedure declares and initializes a one-dimensional array named intCalories. The array stores the numbers of daily calories consumed. The procedure should calculate and display the average number of calories consumed; use the Math.Round method to round the average to an integer. (You learned about the Math.Round method in Chapter 6.) The procedure should also display the number of days in which the daily calories were greater than the average, the number of days in which the daily calories were the same as the average, and the number of days in which the daily calories were less than the average. Code the procedure. Save the solution and then start and test the application.

INTERMEDIATE

9. Open the Computer Solution.sln file contained in the VB2017\Chap08\Computer Solution folder. The interface allows the user to enter the number of either new or refurbished computers sold. Open the Code Editor window and locate the btnAdd_Click procedure. The procedure should use an array to accumulate the numbers sold by type. It also should display (in the labels) the total number sold for each type. Before the procedure ends, it should send the focus to the txtSold control and also select the control's existing text. Code the procedure. Save the solution and then start and test the application.

INTERMEDIATE

10. In this exercise, you code the Professor Schneider application, which displays a grade based on the number of points entered by the user. The number of points should always be less than or equal to 500. The grading scale is shown in Figure 8-48. Open the Schneider Solution.sln file contained in the VB2017\Chap08\Schneider Solution folder. Store the minimum points and grades in two parallel one-dimensional arrays named intMins and strGrades. The btnDisplay_Click procedure should use the number of points entered by the user to search the intMins array and then display the corresponding grade from the strGrades array. If the user enters a number that is greater than 500, the procedure should display an appropriate message and then display N/A as the grade. Code the application. Save the solution and then start and test the application.

ADVANCED

Minimum points	Maximum points	Grade
0	299	F
300	349	D
350	414	C
415	464	B
465	500	A

Figure 8-48 Grading scale for Exercise 10

ADVANCED   11. In this exercise, you modify the Professor Schneider application from Exercise 10. Use Windows to make a copy of the Schneider Solution folder. Rename the copy Schneider Solution-TwoDim. Open the Schneider Solution.sln file contained in the Schneider Solution-TwoDim folder. Change the two parallel arrays to a two-dimensional array named strGradeInfo, and then make the appropriate modifications to the btnDisplay_Click procedure's code. Save the solution and then start and test the application.

ADVANCED   12. Open the Kraston Solution.sln file contained in the VB2017\Chap08\Kraston Solution folder. The btnDisplay_Click procedure should display a shipping charge that is based on the number of items a customer orders. The order amounts and shipping charges are listed in Figure 8-49. Store the minimum order amounts and shipping charges in a class-level two-dimensional array. Display the appropriate shipping charge with a dollar sign and two decimal places. Code the btnDisplay_Click procedure. Save the solution and then start and test the application.

Minimum order	Maximum order	Shipping charge
0	0	N/A
1	5	10.99
6	10	7.99
11	20	3.99
21	No maximum	0

Figure 8-49 Order amounts and shipping charges for Exercise 12

ADVANCED   13. Create a Windows Forms application. Use the following names for the project and solution, respectively: Shipping Depot Project and Shipping Depot Solution. Save the application in the VB2017\Chap08 folder. The Shipping Depot store ships packages by FedEx, UPS, and USPS. Create the interface shown in Figure 8-50; the interface contains a group box, 11 labels, and two buttons. The Display button's Click event procedure should declare a two-dimensional array that contains four rows (one for each week) and three columns (one for each shipper). Initialize the array using the data shown in Figure 8-50. The procedure should display the total number of packages shipped, the total shipped by FedEx, the total shipped by UPS, and the total shipped by USPS. It should also display the percentage of the total number shipped by each of the different shippers. Display the percentages with a percent sign and no decimal places. Code the application. Save the solution and then start and test the application.

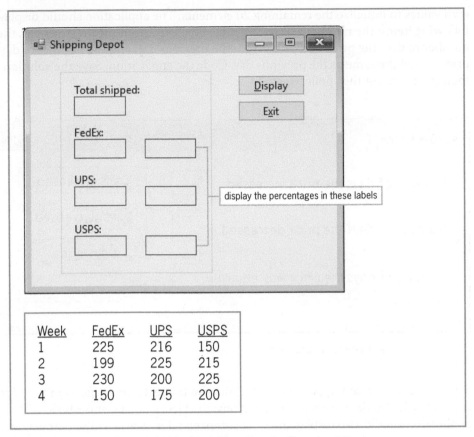

Figure 8-50 Interface and shipping information for Exercise 13

14. In this exercise, you modify the Shipping Depot application from Exercise 13. Use Windows to make a copy of the Shipping Depot Solution folder. Rename the copy Modified Shipping Depot Solution. Open the Shipping Depot Solution.sln file contained in the Modified Shipping Depot Solution folder. Open the Code Editor window and locate the Display button's Click event procedure. Change the four-row, three-column array to a three-row (one for each shipper), four-column (one for each week) array. Make the necessary modifications to the procedure's code.

    ADVANCED

15. In this exercise, you code an application that generates and displays six unique random numbers for a lottery game. Each lottery number can range from 1 through 54 only. Open the Lottery Solution.sln file contained in the VB2017\Chap08\Lottery Solution folder. The btnDisplay_Click procedure should display six unique random numbers in the interface. Code the application. Save the solution and then start and test the application.

    ADVANCED

16. Create a Windows Forms application. Use the following names for the project and solution, respectively: Gas Prices Project and Gas Prices Solution. Save the application in the VB2017\Chap08 folder. Create the interface shown in Figure 8-51. The application should declare a class-level Double array that contains 30 elements. Each element will store the daily price of a gallon of gas. Initialize the first 10 elements using the following values: 2.25, 2.25, 2.24, 2.15, 2.05, 1.97, 2.25, 2.87, 2.5, and 2.4. Use your

    ADVANCED

own values to initialize the remaining 20 elements. The application should display the following items: the number of days the price increased from the previous day, the number of days the price decreased from the previous day, and the number of days the price stayed the same as the previous day. Code the application. Save the solution and then start and test the application.

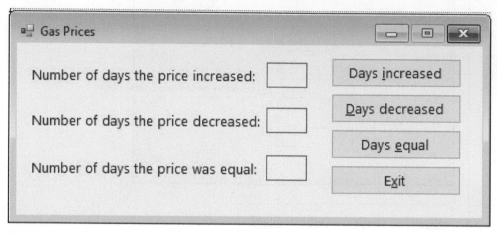

Figure 8-51 Interface for Exercise 16

ADVANCED 17. The sales manager at Organic Market wants you to create an application that displays the total sales made in each of three regions: the U.S., Canada, and Mexico. The application should also display the total company sales as well as the percentage that each region contributed to the total sales. Display the sales amounts with a dollar sign and no decimal places. Display the percentages with a percent sign and no decimal places. The sales amounts for six months are shown in Figure 8-52. Create a Windows Forms application. Use the following names for the project and solution, respectively: Organic Project and Organic Solution. Save the application in the VB2017\Chap08 folder. Create a suitable interface and then code the application. Store the sales amounts in a two-dimensional array. Save the solution and then start and test the application.

Month	U.S. sales ($)	Canada sales ($)	Mexico sales ($)
1	120,000	90,000	65,000
2	190,000	85,000	64,000
3	175,000	80,000	71,000
4	188,000	83,000	67,000
5	125,000	87,000	65,000
6	163,000	80,000	64,000

Figure 8-52 Sales amounts for Exercise 17

ADVANCED 18. Create a Windows Forms application. Use the following names for the project and solution, respectively: Bindy Project and Bindy Solution. Save the application in the VB2017\Chap08 folder. Bindy Enterprises sells the 10 items listed in Figure 8-53. The figure also contains the major tasks that the application needs to perform. Create a suitable interface and then code the application. Save the solution and then start and test the application.

```
ID       Color      Price
101      Blue        4.99
102      Red         4.99
103      Blue       10.49
104      Red        10.49
105      White       6.79
106      Red         6.79
107      Blue        6.79
108      Black      21.99
109      White      21.99
110      Blue       21.99
```

Tasks

1). When the user selects the ID from a list box, the application should display the ID's color and price.

2). When the user selects the color from a list box, the application should display the IDs and prices of all items available in that color.

3). When the user enters a price in a text box, the application should display the IDs, colors, and prices of items selling at or below that price.

Figure 8-53   Information for Exercise 18

19. Create a Windows Forms application. Use the following names for the project and solution, respectively: Adaline Project and Adaline Solution. Save the application in the VB2017\Chap08 folder. Create the interface shown in Figure 8-54. The figure also contains the major tasks that the application needs to perform. Code the application. Save the solution and then start and test the application.

ADVANCED

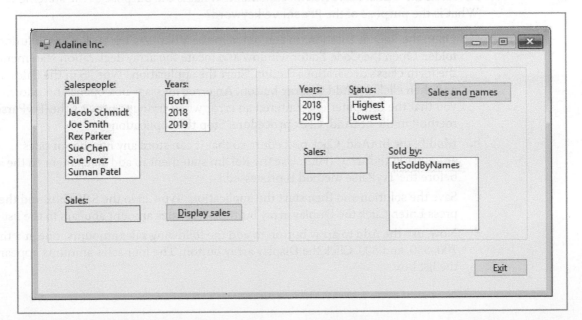

Figure 8-54   Interface and information for Exercise 19 *(continues)*

(continued)

Tasks

1). Declare a class-level Integer array to store the sales amounts for the following salespeople. You can create either a two-row, six-column array or a six-row, two-column array.

Salespeople	2018 Sales ($)	2019 Sales ($)
Jacob Schmidt	4000	7200
Joe Smith	4000	5000
Rex Parker	2500	6500
Sue Chen	4000	7200
Sue Perez	3900	6000
Suman Patel	3600	7000

2). Regarding the controls in the first group box: The Display sales button should display the sales amount associated with the items selected in the Salespeople and Years list boxes. For example, if All and Both are selected, the button should display the total of all the sales stored in the array ($60,900). If All and 2019 are selected, the button should display only the sales amounts for the year 2019 ($38,900). If Sue Chen and Both are selected, the button should display the total sales made by Sue Chen for both years ($11,200). If Sue Chen and 2018 are selected, the button should display only the amount Sue Chen sold in 2018 ($4,000).

3). Regarding the controls in the second group box: The Sales and names button should display the sales amount and names associated with the items selected in the Years and Status list boxes. For example, if 2018 and Highest are selected, the button should display the highest sales amount made in 2018 ($4,000) and the name(s) of each salesperson who made that sales amount (Jacob Schmidt, Joe Smith, and Sue Chen).

Figure 8-54   Interface and information for Exercise 19

ADVANCED

20. Research the Visual Basic ReDim statement. What is the purpose of the statement? What is the purpose of the **Preserve** keyword?

a. Open the ReDim Solution.sln contained in the VB2017\Chap08\ReDim Solution folder. Open the Code Editor window and locate the array declaration statement in the form class's declarations section. Start the application. Type 25 in the Sales box and then click the Add to array button. An error message box opens and informs you that the computer encountered an error when trying to process the TryParse method in the btnAdd_Click procedure. Stop the application.

b. Modify the btnAdd_Click procedure so that it can store any number of sales amounts in the array. (Hint: Use the ReDim statement to add an element to the array before the TryParse method is processed.)

c. Save the solution and then start the application. Type 25 in the Sales box and then press Enter. Click the Display array button . The sales amount appears in the list box.

d. Now, use the Add to array button to add the following sales amounts, one at a time: 700, 550, and 800. Click the Display array button. The four sales amounts appear in the list box.

21. Create a Windows Forms application. Use the following names for the project and solution, respectively: OnYourOwn Project and OnYourOwn Solution. Save the application in the VB2017\Chap08 folder. Plan and design an application of your choice. The only requirement is that you must follow the minimum guidelines listed in Figure 8-55. Before starting the application, be sure to verify the name of the startup form. Save the solution and then start and test the application.

ON YOUR OWN

1. The user interface must contain a minimum of one text box, three labels, and two buttons. One of the buttons must be an Exit button.
2. The interface can include a picture box, but this is not a requirement.
3. The interface must follow the GUI design guidelines summarized for Chapters 2 through 8 in Appendix A.
4. Objects that are either coded or referred to in code should be named appropriately.
5. The Code Editor window must contain comments, the three Option statements, at least two variables, at least two assignment statements, at least two of the concepts covered in the Focus lesson, and the Me.Close() statement.
6. Every text box on the form should have its TextChanged and Enter event procedures coded.

Figure 8-55 Guidelines for Exercise 21

22. Open the VB2017\Chap08\FixIt Solution\FixIt Solution.sln file. Open the Code Editor window and locate the btnDisplay_Click procedure. The first column in the array contains first names, and the second column contains last names. The procedure should add each person's first and last names, separated by a space character, to the list box. Correct the syntax error(s) in the existing code. Save the solution and then start the application. Click the Display button. If the btnDisplay_Click procedure is not working correctly, stop the application and correct the procedure's code.

FIX IT

Sequential Access Files and Menus

In addition to getting data from the keyboard and sending data to the computer screen, an application can also read data from and write data to a file on a disk. In this chapter's Focus on the Concepts lesson, you will learn how to create and use a special type of file, called a sequential access file. You will use sequential access files in the applications coded in this chapter's Apply the Concepts lesson. The Apply lesson also covers the creation and coding of menus.

FOCUS ON THE CONCEPTS LESSON

Concepts covered in this lesson:

- F-1 Sequential access files
- F-2 Sequential access output files
- F-3 Sequential access input files

F-1 Sequential Access Files

At times, an application may need to read data from and write data to a file on a disk. The data is composed of a sequence of characters, which programmers refer to as a **stream of characters** or a **character stream**. Files to which data is written are called **output files** because the files store the output produced by an application. Files that are read by the computer are called **input files** because an application uses the data in these files as input.

The characters in most input and output files are both read and written in consecutive order, one character at a time, beginning with the first character and ending with the last character. Such files are referred to as **sequential access files** because of the manner in which the characters are accessed. They are also called **text files** because they can be opened and modified by a text editor, such as Notepad. Examples of text stored in sequential access files include an employee list, a memo, and a sales report.

F-2 Sequential Access Output Files

Figure 9-1 lists the steps for creating and using an output file. The figure also includes the syntax for performing each step, as well as examples of using each syntax. The IO that appears in the syntaxes and examples in the first two steps stands for Input/Output.

Creating and Using an Output File

1. Use the StreamWriter class to declare a StreamWriter variable.

   Syntax
   {Dim | Private} *streamWriterVariable* **As IO.StreamWriter**

   Examples
   ```
   Dim outFile As IO.StreamWriter
   Private outFile As IO.StreamWriter
   ```

2. Use either the CreateText method or the AppendText method to open the file. Assign the StreamWriter object created by either method to the StreamWriter variable from Step 1.

   Syntax
   IO.File.CreateText(*fileName***)**
   IO.File.AppendText(*fileName***)**

   > the computer will search for the employee.txt file in the project's bin\Debug folder

   Examples
   ```
   outFile = IO.File.CreateText("employee.txt")
   outFile = IO.File.AppendText("F:\Chap09\report.txt")
   ```

Figure 9-1 Steps, syntaxes, and examples for creating and using an output file *(continues)*

(continued)

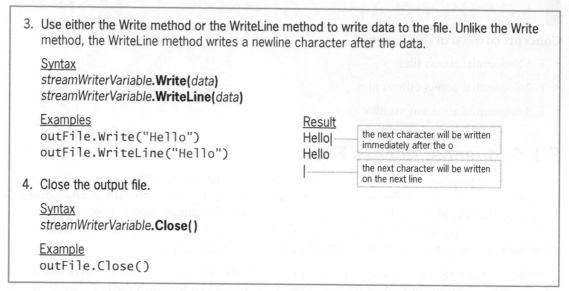

3. Use either the Write method or the WriteLine method to write data to the file. Unlike the Write method, the WriteLine method writes a newline character after the data.

Syntax
streamWriterVariable.**Write**(*data*)
streamWriterVariable.**WriteLine**(*data*)

Examples   Result
outFile.Write("Hello")   Hello| ⎯ the next character will be written immediately after the o
outFile.WriteLine("Hello")   Hello
                                                      | ⎯ the next character will be written on the next line

4. Close the output file.

Syntax
streamWriterVariable.**Close**()

Example
outFile.Close()

Figure 9-1   Steps, syntaxes, and examples for creating and using an output file

Step 1 in Figure 9-1 uses the **StreamWriter class** to declare a **StreamWriter variable**. Although it is not necessary to start the variable's name with the three letters out, using this naming convention helps to distinguish variables that represent output files from those that represent input files. As you will learn later in this lesson, the names of variables that represent input files begin with the two letters in. The StreamWriter variable will store the **StreamWriter object** created by the methods in Step 2, and it will be used to refer to the file in your application's code.

The second step in Figure 9-1 opens the sequential access file. You use the **CreateText method** to open the file for output and use the **AppendText method** to open it for append. When a file is opened for output, the computer creates a new, empty file to which data can be written. If the file already exists, the computer erases the contents of the file before writing any data to it. When a file is opened for append, on the other hand, new data is written after any existing data in the file. If the file does not exist, the computer creates the file for you. The CreateText and AppendText methods automatically create a StreamWriter object to represent the file in the application. As noted in Step 2, you assign the object to the StreamWriter variable declared in Step 1.

Notice that only the second example in Step 2 contains a folder path (F:\Chap09\) in the *filename* argument. If the folder path is omitted, the computer will search for the file in the default folder, which is the current project's bin\Debug folder. When deciding whether to include the folder path in the *fileName* argument, keep in mind that a USB drive may have a different letter designation on another computer. Therefore, you should specify the folder path only when you are sure that it will not change.

After opening the file for either output or append, you can begin writing data to it. As Step 3 in Figure 9-1 indicates, you can use either the **Write method** or the **WriteLine method** to write the data. The difference between these methods is that the WriteLine method writes a newline character after the data. Notice that the file's name is not required in either method's syntax. This is because both methods write the data to the file associated with the StreamWriter variable.

You should always use the **Close method**, which is shown in Step 4 in Figure 9-1, to close an output file as soon as you are finished using it. This ensures that the data is saved, and it makes the file available for use elsewhere in the application. A run time error will occur if a program statement attempts to open a file that is already open. Here too, you use the StreamWriter variable to refer to the file you want to close.

Output File Example: Game Show Application

The Game Show application writes the names of contestants to a sequential access file named contestants.txt. The application's interface is shown in Figure 9-2. You will code the Write to file button in the next set of steps.

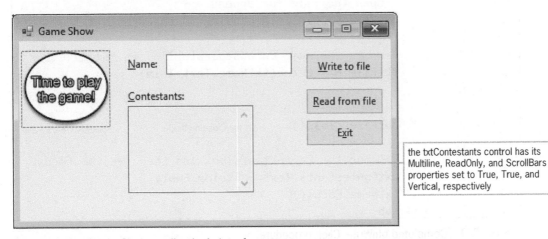

Figure 9-2   Game Show application's interface

To code the btnWrite_Click procedure:

START HERE

1. Open the Game Show Solution.sln file contained in the VB2017\Chap09\Game Show Solution-TextBox folder.

2. Open the Code Editor window and locate the btnWrite_Click procedure. Recall that the first step listed in Figure 9-1 is to declare a StreamWriter variable. Click the **blank line** below the ' Declare a StreamWriter variable. comment. Type the following declaration statement and then press **Enter**:

    ```
    Dim outFile As IO.StreamWriter
    ```

3. The btnWrite_Click procedure should add the name entered in the text box to the end of the existing names in the file. Therefore, you will need to open the file for append. A descriptive name for a file that stores the names of contestants is contestants.txt. Although it is not a requirement, the "txt" (short for "text") filename extension is commonly used when naming sequential access files. Click the **blank line** below the ' Open the file for append. comment. Type the following assignment statement and then press **Enter**:

    ```
    outFile = IO.File.AppendText("contestants.txt")
    ```

4. Each contestant's name should appear on a separate line in the file, so you will use the WriteLine method to write each name to the file. Click the **blank line** below the ' Write the name on a separate line in the file. comment. Type the following statement and then press **Enter**:

    ```
    outFile.WriteLine(txtName.Text.Trim)
    ```

5. The last step listed earlier in Figure 9-1 is to close the file. Click the **blank line** below the ' Close the file. comment and then enter the Close method shown in Figure 9-3.

```
10    Private Sub btnWrite_Click(sender As Object, e As EventAr
11         ' Writes a name to a sequential access file.
12
13         ' Declare a StreamWriter variable.
14         Dim outFile As IO.StreamWriter
15
16         ' Open the file for append.
17         outFile = IO.File.AppendText("contestants.txt")
18
19         ' Write the name on a separate line in the file.
20         outFile.WriteLine(txtName.Text.Trim)
21
22         ' Close the file.
23         outFile.Close()───[ enter the Close method ]
24
25         ' Clear the Contestants box and then set the focus.
26         txtContestants.Text = String.Empty
27         txtName.Focus()
28    End Sub
```

Figure 9-3   Completed btnWrite_Click procedure

6. Save the solution and then start the application. Type **Jess Svarni** in the Name box and then click the **Write to file** button. Use the application to write the following four names to the file: **Harry Chou, Patti Munez, Sam Sportenski,** and **Judy Johanson**.

7. Click the **Exit** button. Now, you will open the contestants.txt file to verify its contents. Click **File** on the menu bar, point to **Open**, and then click **File**. Open the project's bin\Debug folder. Click **contestants.txt** in the list of filenames and then click the **Open** button. The contestants.txt window opens and shows the five names contained in the file. See Figure 9-4.

```
contestants.txt  ⇱ ✕  Main Form.vb        Main Form.vb [Design]
    1    Jess Svarni
    2    Harry Chou
    3    Patti Munez
    4    Sam Sportenski
    5    Judy Johanson
    6
```

Figure 9-4   Contents of the contestants.txt file

8. Close the contestants.txt window.

Mini-Quiz 9-1

1. Write a declaration statement for a procedure-level variable named `outInventory`. The variable will store a StreamWriter object.

2. Using the variable from Question 1, write a statement to open a sequential access file named inventory.txt for output.

3. Using the variable from Question 1, write a statement that writes the contents of the `strId` variable on a separate line in the file.

4. Write a statement to close the file associated with the variable from Question 1.

3) outInventory.WriteLine(strId) 4) outInventory.Close()
2) outInventory = IO.File.CreateText("inventory.txt")
1) Dim outInventory As IO.StreamWriter

F-3 Sequential Access Input Files

Figure 9-5 lists the steps for creating and using an input file. The figure also includes the syntax for performing each step, as well as examples of using each syntax.

Creating and Using an Input File

1. Use the StreamReader class to declare a StreamReader variable.

Syntax
{**Dim | Private**} *streamReaderVariable* **As IO.StreamReader**

Examples
```
Dim inFile As IO.StreamReader
Private inFile As IO.StreamReader
```

2. Use the Exists method to determine whether the input file exists.

Syntax
IO.File.Exists(fileName**)**

Example
```
If IO.File.Exists("employee.txt") Then
```

3. If the Exists method determines that the file exists, use the OpenText method to open the file for input. Assign the StreamReader object created by the method to the StreamReader variable from Step 1.

Syntax
IO.File.OpenText(fileName**)**

Example
```
inFile = IO.File.OpenText("employee.txt")
```

Figure 9-5 Steps, syntaxes, and examples for creating and using an input file *(continues)*

(continued)

> 4. To read the file, line by line, use the Peek and ReadLine methods along with a loop. To read the entire file all at once, use the ReadToEnd method.
>
> <u>Syntax</u>
> *streamReaderVariable*.**Peek**
> *streamReaderVariable*.**ReadLine**
> *streamReaderVariable*.**ReadToEnd**
>
> <u>Example of reading the file, line by line</u>
> ```
> Dim strLineOfText As String
> Do Until inFile.Peek = -1
>     strLineOfText = inFile.ReadLine
>     [instructions]
> Loop
> ```
>
> <u>Example of reading the entire file all at once</u>
> ```
> txtReport.Text = inFile.ReadToEnd
> ```
>
> 5. Close the input file.
>
> <u>Syntax</u>
> *streamReaderVariable*.**Close()**
>
> <u>Example</u>
> ```
> inFile.Close()
> ```

Figure 9-5 Steps, syntaxes, and examples for creating and using an input file

Step 1 in Figure 9-5 uses the **StreamReader class** to declare a **StreamReader variable**. The variable will store the **StreamReader object** created by the OpenText method in Step 3, and it will be used to refer to the file in your application's code. It is not necessary to start the variable's name with the two letters in; however, doing this helps to distinguish an application's input files from its output files, which begin with the three letters out.

The second step in Figure 9-5 uses the **Exists method** to determine whether the input file that you want to open exists. It is important to make this determination because a run time error will occur if your code attempts to open an input file that the computer cannot locate. The Exists method returns the Boolean value True if the file exists; otherwise, it returns the Boolean value False. If the method's *fileName* argument does not include a folder path, the computer searches for the file in the current project's bin\Debug folder.

If the Exists method determines that the file exists, you can use the **OpenText method** to open the file for input; this is Step 3 in Figure 9-5. When a file is opened for input, the computer can read the characters stored in the file. The OpenText method automatically creates a StreamReader object to represent the file in the application. You assign the object to the StreamReader variable declared in Step 1. Here too, if you do not include a folder path in the method's *fileName* argument, the computer searches for the input file in the default folder, which is the current project's bin\Debug folder.

The fourth step in Figure 9-5 reads the file, either line by line or all at once. To read the file, line by line, you use a loop along with the Peek and ReadLine methods, as shown in the first example in Step 4. The **Peek method** "peeks" into the file to determine whether the file contains another character to read. If the file contains another character, the Peek method returns the character; otherwise, it returns the number −1 (a negative 1). The Do Until inFile.Peek = −1 clause in the first example tells the computer to process the loop instructions until the Peek method returns the number −1. In other words, the clause tells the computer to process the loop instructions until the end of the file is reached.

If the Peek method does not return the number −1, you can use the **ReadLine method** to read the next line of text in the file. A **line** is defined as a sequence (stream) of characters followed by the newline character. The ReadLine method returns a string that contains only the sequence of characters in the current line. The returned string does not include the newline character at the end of the line. The ReadLine method does not require you to provide the file's name because it uses the file associated with the StreamReader variable.

Rather than reading a file, line by line, an application may need to read the entire file all at once. In those cases, you can use the **ReadToEnd method**, as shown in the second example in Step 4. This method also uses the StreamReader variable to refer to the file you want to read.

As you do with an output file, you should use the Close method, which is shown in Step 5 in Figure 9-5, to close an input sequential access file as soon as you are finished using it. Doing this makes the file available for use elsewhere in the application. If you do not close the file, a run time error will occur if a program statement attempts to open the file. Here too, you use the StreamReader variable to refer to the file you want to close.

ReadToEnd Method Example: Game Show Application

The Read from file button in the Game Show application reads the names from the contestants.txt file and displays them in the txtContestants control.

To code the btnRead_Click procedure: START HERE

1. Locate the btnRead_Click procedure. Recall that the first step listed in Figure 9-5 declares a StreamReader variable. Click the **blank line** below the ' Declare variable. comment. Type the following declaration statement and then press **Enter**:

   ```
   Dim inFile As IO.StreamReader
   ```

2. The second step in Figure 9-5 uses the Exists method to determine whether the input file (in this case, the contestants.txt file) exists. Click the **blank line** above the End Sub clause and then enter the partial selection structure shown in Figure 9-6. The structure's false path displays an appropriate message if the file does not exist.

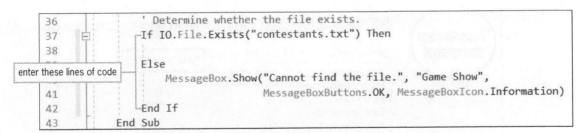

```
36          ' Determine whether the file exists.
37          If IO.File.Exists("contestants.txt") Then
38
            Else
enter these lines of code
                MessageBox.Show("Cannot find the file.", "Game Show",
41                              MessageBoxButtons.OK, MessageBoxIcon.Information)
42          End If
43      End Sub
```

Figure 9-6   Partial selection structure entered in the btnRead_Click procedure

3. If the contestants.txt file exists, the selection structure's true path will use the OpenText method to open the file for input. (This is Step 3 in Figure 9-5.) Click the **blank line** above the Else clause and then enter the following comment and assignment statement:

   ```
   ' Open the file for input.
   inFile = IO.File.OpenText("contestants.txt")
   ```

4. Next, the selection structure's true path will use the ReadToEnd method to read the entire input file, all at once. (This is Step 4 in Figure 9-5.) It will display the file's contents in the txtContestants control. Enter the following comment and statement:

```
' Read the file and assign to Contestants box.
txtContestants.Text = inFile.ReadToEnd
```

5. The last step listed in Figure 9-5 is to close the file. Type the Close method shown in Figure 9-7.

```
30          Private Sub btnRead_Click(sender As Object, e As EventArgs) Handles btnRea
31              ' Reads names from a sequential access file and displays them in the i
32
33              ' Declare variable.
34              Dim inFile As IO.StreamReader
35
36              ' Determine whether the file exists.
37              If IO.File.Exists("contestants.txt") Then
38                  ' Open the file for input.
39                  inFile = IO.File.OpenText("contestants.txt")
40                  ' Read the file and assign to Contestants box.
41                  txtContestants.Text = inFile.ReadToEnd
42                  inFile.Close()————| enter the Close method |
43              Else
44                  MessageBox.Show("Cannot find the file.", "Game Show",
45                      MessageBoxButtons.OK, MessageBoxIcon.Information)
46              End If
47          End Sub
```

Figure 9-7 Completed btnRead_Click procedure using the ReadToEnd method

6. Save the solution and then start the application. Click the **Read from file** button. The five names contained in the contestants.txt file appear in the Contestants box. See Figure 9-8.

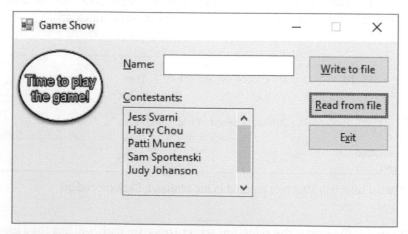

Figure 9-8 Five names displayed in the Contestants text box

7. Add the following four names to the file: **Dusty Jones, Grace Peters, Andrew Chen**, and **Karen York**.

8. Click the **Read from file** button to display the nine names in the Contestants box. See Figure 9-9.

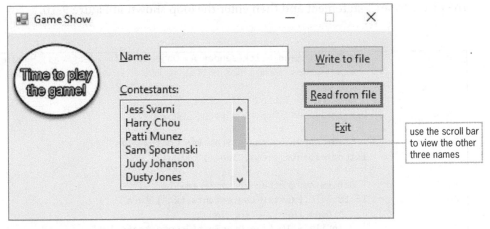

Figure 9-9   Nine names displayed in the Contestants text box

9. Click the **Exit** button.

As you learned in Chapter 4, you should always test both paths in a selection structure. In the next set of steps, you will change the filename in the If clause from contestants.txt to contestant.txt. Doing this will allow you to test the code entered in the selection structure's false path.

To test the selection structure's false path: START HERE

1. In the selection structure's If clause, change `contestants.txt` to **`contestant.txt`**.

2. Save the solution and then start the application. Click the **Read from file** button. Because the contestant.txt file does not exist, the Exists method returns the Boolean value False. As a result, the instruction in the selection structure's false path displays the "Cannot find the file." message in a message box. Close the message box and then click the **Exit** button.

3. In the If clause, change `contestant.txt` to **`contestants.txt`**. Save the solution and then start the application. Click the **Read from file** button, which displays the nine names in the list box.

4. Click the **Exit** button. Close the Code Editor window and then close the solution.

ReadLine Method Example: Game Show Application

In this section, you will code a slightly different version of the Game Show application. This version also reads the names from the contestants.txt file, but it displays them in a list box rather than in a text box.

To code the btnRead_Click procedure in this version of the application: START HERE

1. Open the Game Show Solution.sln file contained in the VB2017\Chap09\Game Show Solution-ListBox folder.

2. Open the Code Editor window. Most of the application has already been coded for you.

3. Locate the btnRead_Click procedure. In order to add each name contained in the contestants.txt file to the list box, the procedure will need to read the file, line by line. As indicated earlier in Figure 9-5, the procedure can accomplish this task by using a loop along with the Peek and ReadLine methods. Click the **blank line** above the `inFile.Close()` statement and then enter the loop shown in Figure 9-10.

```
30      Private Sub btnRead_Click(sender As Object, e As EventArgs) Handles btnRea
31          ' Reads names from a sequential access file and displays them in the i
32
33          ' Declare variable.
34          Dim inFile As IO.StreamReader
35
36          ' Clear previous names from the Contestants box.
37          lstContestants.Items.Clear()
38
39          ' Determine whether the file exists.
40          If IO.File.Exists("contestants.txt") Then
41              ' Open the file for input.
42              inFile = IO.File.OpenText("contestants.txt")
43              ' Process loop instructions until end of file.
44              Do Until inFile.Peek = -1
45                  lstContestants.Items.Add(inFile.ReadLine)
46              Loop
47              inFile.Close()
48          Else
49              MessageBox.Show("Cannot find the file.", "Game Show",
50                              MessageBoxButtons.OK, MessageBoxIcon.Information)
51          End If
52      End Sub
```

enter these lines of code → (lines 44–46)

Figure 9-10   Loop entered in the completed btnRead_Click procedure

4. Save the solution and then start the application. Click the **Read from file** button. The btnRead_Click procedure adds the nine names contained in the contestants.txt file to the Contestants list box. See Figure 9-11.

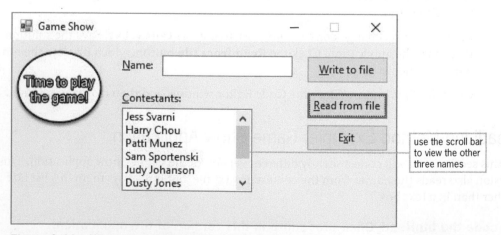

Figure 9-11   Nine names displayed in the Contestants list box

5. Click the **Exit** button. Close the Code Editor window and then close the solution.

Mini-Quiz 9-2

1. Write a declaration statement for a procedure-level variable named `inInventory`. The variable will be used to read data from a sequential access file.

2. Write an If clause that determines whether the inventory.txt file exists.

3. Using the variable from Question 1, write a statement to open a sequential access file named inventory.txt for input.

4. Write a statement that reads a line of text from the file associated with the variable from Question 1. Assign the line of text to the `strProduct` variable.

5. Write a Do clause that processes the loop instructions until the end of the file is reached. The file is associated with the variable from Question 1.

6. Write a statement to close the file associated with the variable from Question 1.

7. Write a statement that reads the entire file associated with the `inFile` variable and assigns the file's contents to the txtDocument control.

1) Dim inInventory As IO.StreamReader 2) If IO.File.Exists("inventory.txt") Then 3) inInventory = IO.File.OpenText("inventory.txt") 4) strProduct = inInventory.ReadLine 5) Do Until inInventory.Peek = -1 or Do While inInventory.Peek <> -1 6) inInventory.Close() 7) txtDocument.Text = inFile.ReadToEnd

YOU DO IT 1!

Create an application named You Do It 1 and save it in the VB2017\Chap09 folder. Add three text boxes and three buttons to the form. Set the second and third text boxes' Multiline, ReadOnly, and ScrollBars properties to True, True, and Vertical, respectively. The user will enter a number in the first text box and then click the first button. The first button's Click event procedure should write the number on a separate line in a sequential access file. The second button's Click event procedure should read the entire sequential access file all at once, and display the file's contents in the second text box. The third button's Click event procedure should read the sequential access file, line by line, and display the file's contents in the third text box; display each number on a separate line. Code the procedures. Save the solution and then start the application. Use the first button to write any six numbers to the file. Then, use the second and third buttons to display the contents of the file in their respective text boxes. Close the solution.

▊ APPLY THE CONCEPTS LESSON

After studying this lesson, you should be able to:

- A-1 Add a menu to a form
- A-2 Code the items on a menu
- A-3 Modify a menu
- A-4 Accumulate the values stored in a file
- A-5 Sort the data contained in a file
- A-6 Professionalize your application's interface

A-1 Add a Menu to a Form

The Menus and Toolbars section of the toolbox contains a MenuStrip tool for instantiating a **menu strip control**. The control allows you to add one or more menus to a Windows form. Each menu contains a menu title, which appears on the menu bar at the top of the form.

When you click a menu title, its corresponding menu opens and displays a list of options, called menu items. The menu items can be commands (such as Open or Exit), separator bars, or submenu titles. The purpose of a separator bar is to visually group together related items on a menu or submenu.

As in all Windows applications, clicking a command on a menu executes the command, and clicking a submenu title opens an additional menu of options. Each of the options on a submenu is referred to as a submenu item. Although you can create many levels of submenus, it is best to use only one level in your application because including too many layers of submenus can confuse the user. Figure 9-12 identifies the location of the various menu elements.

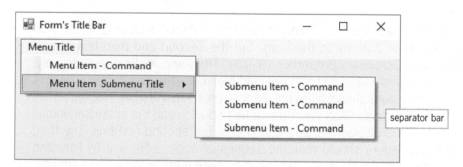

Figure 9-12   Location of menu elements

Each menu element is considered an object, and each has a set of properties associated with it. The most commonly used properties for a menu element are the Name and Text properties. The programmer uses the Name property to refer to the menu element in code. The Text property stores the menu element's caption, which is the text that the user sees when he or she is working with the menu. The caption indicates the purpose of the menu element. Examples of familiar captions for menu elements include Edit, Save As, Copy, and Exit.

GUI Guidelines for Menus

The GUI design guidelines for menus are listed in Figure 9-35 and in Appendix A.

Menu title captions should be one word, with only the first letter capitalized. Each menu title should have a unique access key. The access key allows the user to open the menu by pressing the Alt key in combination with the access key. Unlike the captions for menu titles, the captions for menu items typically consist of one to three words and are entered using book title capitalization. Each menu item should have an access key that is unique within its menu. The access key allows the user to select the item by pressing the access key when the menu is open.

The menus included in your application should follow the standard Windows conventions. For example, if your application uses a File menu, it should be the first menu on the menu bar. File menus typically contain commands for opening, saving, and printing files, as well as exiting the application. Commonly used menu items should be assigned shortcut keys. The **shortcut keys** appear to the right of a menu item and allow the user to select the item without opening the menu. Examples of familiar shortcut keys are Ctrl+s (for the Save command on a File menu) and Ctrl+c (for the Copy command on an Edit menu).

Menu Example: Continents Application

As you may remember, the Continents application that you coded in Chapter 8's Focus lesson stored the names of the seven continents in an array. The application's interface provided two buttons for adding the names to a list box, in either ascending or descending order. It also provided a button for exiting the application. In this section, you will code a different version of the application. Instead of initializing the array in its declaration statement, as you did in Chapter 8, the array in this chapter's application will get its values from a sequential access file named continents.txt. Sequential access files are often used to fill arrays with values. In addition, the interface in this chapter will use menus rather than buttons.

Instead of using a StreamWriter object and the WriteLine method to create the continents.txt file, you can use the New File option on the File menu.

To create the continents.txt file:

START HERE

1. Open the Continents Solution.sln file contained in the VB2017\Chap09\Continents Solution folder. Click **File**, click **New File**, click **Text File**, and then click **Open**. An empty file appears in the TextFile1.txt window.

2. Click **File** and then click **Save TextFile1.txt As**. Open the Continents Project's **bin\Debug** folder. Change the name in the File name box to **continents** and then click the **Save** button. The file will be saved as continents.txt.

3. Enter the seven continent names shown in Figure 9-13.

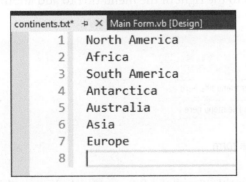

Figure 9-13   Seven names entered in the continents.txt file

4. Save the solution and then close the continents.txt window.

In the next set of steps, you will add two menus to the form: File and Sort. The File menu will contain an Exit option. The Sort menu will contain two options: Ascending and Descending.

START HERE **To add two menus to the form:**

1. If necessary, display the toolbox. Expand the **Menus & Toolbars** node. Click the **MenuStrip** tool and then drag your mouse pointer to the form. (Do not worry about the exact location.) Release the mouse button. The MenuStrip1 control appears in the component tray at the bottom of the IDE, and the words "Type Here" appear in a box below the form's title bar. See Figure 9-14.

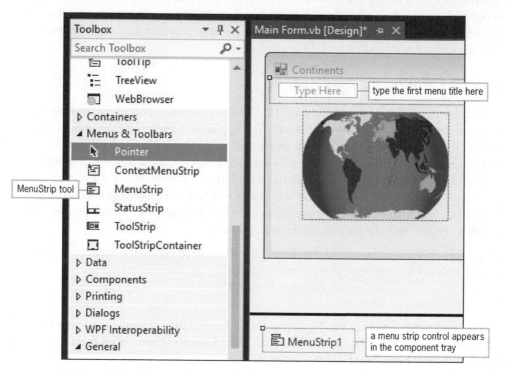

Figure 9-14 Menu strip control added to the form

2. Auto-hide the toolbox. If necessary, display the Properties window. Click the **Type Here** box on the menu bar and then type **&File**. See Figure 9-15. You use the Type Here box that appears below the menu title to add a menu item to the File menu. You use the Type Here box that appears to the right of the menu title to add another menu title to the menu bar.

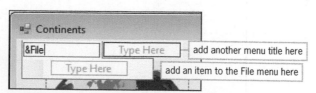

Figure 9-15 File menu title included on the form

3. Press **Enter** and then click the **File** menu title. Scroll the Properties window until you see the Text property, which contains &File. Now, scroll to the top of the Properties window and then click (**Name**). The three character ID for menus is mnu. Type **mnuFile** and then press **Enter**.

4. Click the **Type Here** box that appears below the File menu title. Type **E&xit** and then press **Enter**. Click the **Exit** menu item and then change its name to **mnuFileExit**.

5. Next, you will add a Sort menu to the form. Click the **Type Here** box that appears to the right of the File menu title. Type **&Sort** and then press **Enter**. Click the **Sort** menu title and then change its name to **mnuSort**.

6. The Sort menu will have two options: Ascending and Descending. In addition to their access keys, these options will also have shortcut keys. Click the **Type Here** box that appears below the Sort menu title. Type **&Ascending** and then press **Enter**. Click the **Ascending** menu item and then change its name to **mnuSortAscending**.

7. Click **ShortcutKeys** in the Properties list and then click the **list arrow** in the Settings box. A box opens and allows you to specify a modifier and a key. In this case, the modifier and key will be Ctrl and A, respectively. Click the **Ctrl** check box to select it, and then click the **list arrow** that appears in the Key combo box. An alphabetical list of keys appears. Click **A** in the list. See Figure 9-16.

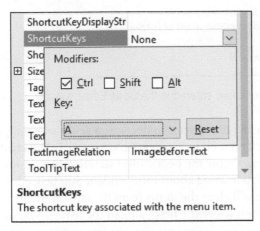

Figure 9-16　Shortcut keys specified in the ShortcutKeys box

8. Press **Enter**. Ctrl+A appears in the ShortcutKeys property and also to the right of the Ascending menu item.

9. On your own, add the Descending menu item to the Sort menu. Use the letter **D** as the access key and use **Ctrl+D** as the shortcut keys. Also, name the menu item **mnuSortDescending**.

10. Auto-hide the Properties window and then click the **form's title bar** to close the menu. Save the solution and then start the application. Click **File** on the menu bar. The menu opens and offers an Exit option. Place your mouse pointer on the Sort menu title, which displays two options: Ascending and Descending. (If the Sort menu does not open, click Sort.) Both open menus are shown in Figure 9-17.

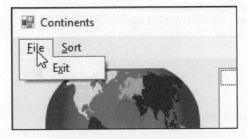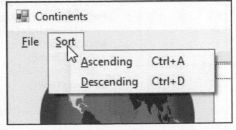

Figure 9-17　Open File and Sort menus

11. Click the form's **Close** button to end the application.

A-2 Code the Items on a Menu

Now that you have completed the interface for the Continents application, you can begin coding it. Figure 9-18 shows the code that has already been entered in the Code Editor window for you. You will complete the application's code in the next set of steps.

```
 9      ⊟Public Class frmMain
10      ⌐' Class-level array and variable.
11       │ Private strContinents(6) As String
12       │ Private intLastSub As Integer = strContinents.GetUpperBound(0)
13       │
14     ⊟ │ Private Sub AddToListBox()
15       │    ' Add array values to list box and select first value.
17       │    lstContinents.Items.Clear()
18     ⊟ │    For intSub As Integer = 0 To intLastSub
19       │        lstContinents.Items.Add(strContinents(intSub))
20       │    Next intSub
21       │    lstContinents.SelectedIndex = 0
22      └─End Sub
```

form class's declarations section

Figure 9-18   Declaration statements and Sub procedure entered in the Code Editor window

As indicated in Figure 9-18, the form class's declarations section declares a seven-element, class-level array named strContinents. It also declares a class-level variable named intLastSub and initializes it to the highest subscript in the array. Below the declaration statements is an independent Sub procedure named AddToListBox. (You learned about independent Sub procedures in Chapter 6.) When it is invoked, the procedure will clear the items from the lstContinents control, add each array value to the control, and then select the first value in the list.

START HERE

To complete the application's code:

1. Open the Code Editor window and locate the frmMain_Load procedure. The procedure will fill the array with the values stored in the continents.txt file that you created earlier. It will then call the AddToListBox procedure to add the names to the lstContinents control. Enter the additional comment and lines of code indicated in Figure 9-19.

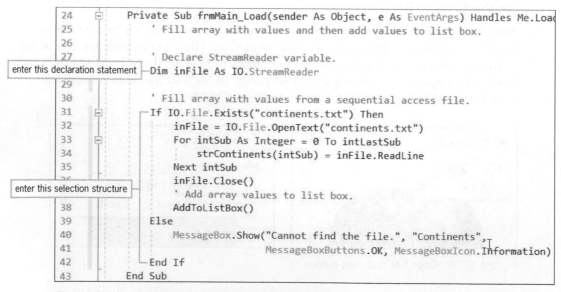

```
24     ⊟      Private Sub frmMain_Load(sender As Object, e As EventArgs) Handles Me.Load
25            ' Fill array with values and then add values to list box.
26
27            ' Declare StreamReader variable.
              Dim inFile As IO.StreamReader
29
30            ' Fill array with values from a sequential access file.
31     ⊟      If IO.File.Exists("continents.txt") Then
32                inFile = IO.File.OpenText("continents.txt")
33     ⊟          For intSub As Integer = 0 To intLastSub
34                    strContinents(intSub) = inFile.ReadLine
35                Next intSub
                  inFile.Close()
                  ' Add array values to list box.
38                AddToListBox()
39            Else
40                MessageBox.Show("Cannot find the file.", "Continents",
41                          MessageBoxButtons.OK, MessageBoxIcon.Information)
42     └      End If
43            End Sub
```

enter this declaration statement

enter this selection structure

Figure 9-19   Completed frmMain_Load procedure

2. Save the solution and then start the application. The frmMain_Load procedure adds the seven names to the list box. Notice that the names appear in the same order as they do in both the file and the array. See Figure 9-20.

Figure 9-20 Names added to the list box

3. Click the form's **Close** button to end the application. Next, you will code the Exit option on the File menu. Open the code template for the mnuFileExit_Click procedure. Type **Me.Close()** and press **Enter**. Save the solution and then start the application. Click **File** on the application's menu bar and then click **Exit** to end the application.

4. Open the code template for the mnuSortAscending_Click procedure. The procedure will sort the array values in ascending order and then call the AddToListBox procedure to add the values to the lstContinents control. Enter the comment and code shown in Figure 9-21.

```
50    Private Sub mnuSortAscending_Click(sender As Object, e As EventA
51        ' Adds the array values in ascending order to the list box.
52
53        Array.Sort(strContinents)
54        AddToListBox()
55    End Sub
```
enter this comment and code

Figure 9-21 Completed mnuSortAscending_Click procedure

5. Open the code template for the mnuSortDescending_Click procedure. The procedure will sort the array values in ascending order, reverse the values, and then call the AddToListBox procedure to add the values to the lstContinents control. Enter the comment and code shown in Figure 9-22.

```
57    Private Sub mnuSortDescending_Click(sender As Object, e As EventA
58        ' Adds the array values in descending order to the list box.
59
60        Array.Sort(strContinents)
61        Array.Reverse(strContinents)
62        AddToListBox()
63    End Sub
```
enter this comment and code

Figure 9-22 Completed mnuSortDescending_Click procedure

6. Save the solution and then start the application. Click **Sort** on the menu bar and then click **Descending**. The continent names appear in descending order. Click **Sort** and then click **Ascending** to display the names in ascending order. Notice that once you select an option from the Sort menu, the interface does not provide a way to return the names to their original order. You will fix this in the next section.

7. Now, you will verify that the shortcut keys work correctly. Press **Ctrl+d** to sort the names in descending order. Then, press **Ctrl+a** to sort them in ascending order.

8. Press **Alt+f** to open the File menu and then tap the letter **x** to select the Exit option, which ends the application.

A-3 Modify a Menu

In this section, you will add another option to the Sort menu. The option will allow the user to display the continent names in their original order, which is the order they were entered in the sequential access file.

START HERE

To modify the Sort menu:

1. Click the **Main Form.vb [Design]** tab to return to the designer window. Click **Sort**, place your mouse pointer on the Type Here box below the Descending option, and then click the **list arrow** in the box. See Figure 9-23.

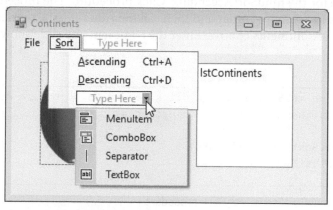

Figure 9-23 Drop-down list

2. Click **Separator** to add a separator bar (horizontal line) below the Descending option.

3. Click the **Type Here** box below the separator bar. Type **&Original Order** and press **Enter**. Click the **Original Order** menu item. Change the item's Name and ShortcutKeys properties to **mnuSortOriginal** and **Ctrl+O**, respectively. (Be sure to use the letter O and not the number 0.)

4. Click the **form's title bar** to close the menu.

5. Click the **Main Form.vb** tab to return to the Code Editor window. The mnuSortOriginal_Click procedure will need to perform the same tasks as the frmMain_Load procedure performs. Rather than having the same code in both procedures, you will enter the code in an independent Sub procedure that both procedures can invoke when needed.

6. Click the **blank line** above the `Private Sub AddToListBox()` procedure header and then press **Enter**. Type the following procedure header and then press **Enter**:

`Private Sub FillArrayAndListBox()`

7. Insert a **blank line** below the procedure's End Sub clause.

8. Locate the frmMain_Load procedure. Highlight (select) all of the lines between the procedure header and procedure footer. (Do not select the header or footer.) Press **Ctrl+x** to cut the lines from the procedure.

9. Click the **blank line** below the FillArrayAndListBox procedure header. Press **Ctrl+v** to paste the lines in the procedure. See Figure 9-24.

```
14    Private Sub FillArrayAndListBox()
15        ' Fill array with values and then add values to list box.
16
17        ' Declare StreamReader variable.
18        Dim inFile As IO.StreamReader
19
20        ' Fill array with values from a sequential access file.
21        If IO.File.Exists("continents.txt") Then
22            inFile = IO.File.OpenText("continents.txt")
23            For intSub As Integer = 0 To intLastSub
24                strContinents(intSub) = inFile.ReadLine
25            Next intSub
26            inFile.Close()
27            ' Add array values to list box.
28            AddToListBox()
29        Else
30            MessageBox.Show("Cannot find the file.", "Continents",
31                            MessageBoxButtons.OK, MessageBoxIcon.Information)
32        End If
33    End Sub
```

Figure 9-24   FillArrayAndListBox procedure

10. Now, click the **blank line** below the frmMain_Load procedure header. Enter the comment and statement shown in Figure 9-25.

```
45    Private Sub frmMain_Load(sender As Object, e As EventAr
46        ' Use a Sub procedure to fill array and list box.
47
48        FillArrayAndListBox()
49    End Sub
```
enter this comment and statement

Figure 9-25   frmMain_Load procedure

11. Open the code template for the mnuSortOriginal_Click procedure. Enter the comment and statement shown in Figure 9-26.

```
71    Private Sub mnuSortOriginal_Click(sender As Object, e As EventArgs)
72        ' Adds the array values in the original order to the list box.
73
74        FillArrayAndListBox()
75    End Sub
```
enter this comment and statement

Figure 9-26   mnuSortOriginal_Click procedure

12. Save the solution and then start the application. Click **Sort** and then click **Descending**. The continent names appear in descending order. Click **Sort** and then click **Original Order** to display the names in their original order. Click **Sort** and then click **Ascending** to display the names in ascending order. Press **Ctrl+o** to display the names in their original order.

13. Click **File** and then click **Exit**. Close the Code Editor window and then close the solution.

A-4 Accumulate the Values Stored in a File

Harkins Company stores its annual sales information in a sequential access file named sales.txt. The current year's sales.txt file is shown in Figure 9-27. The file contains the current year's sales for each of five different product categories: Beverage, Food, Packaged coffee, Packaged tea, and Other. Notice that each category and its corresponding sales amount appear on separate lines in the file.

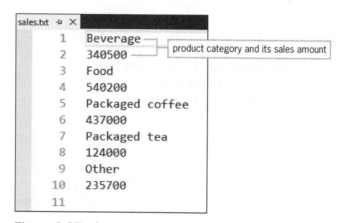

Figure 9-27   Current year's sales.txt file

The Harkins Company application, which you code in the next set of steps, accumulates the annual sales amounts stored in the file and then displays the total annual sales in a label.

START HERE

To finish coding the Harkins Company application:

1. Open the Harkins Solution.sln file contained in the VB2017\Chap09\Harkins Solution folder.

2. Open the Code Editor window and locate the btnCalc_Click procedure. The procedure declares four variables. The `inFile` variable will store the StreamReader object that represents the sales.txt file. The `strCategory` and `intSales` variables will store the product categories and sales amounts, respectively, read from the file. The procedure will use the `intAnnualSales` variable to accumulate the sales amounts.

3. First, the procedure needs to determine whether the sales.txt file exists in the project's bin\Debug folder. Modify the If clause as follows:

```
If IO.File.Exists("sales.txt") Then
```

4. If the file exists, the selection structure's true path should open the file for input. Click the **blank line** below the If clause. Type the following assignment statement and then press **Enter**:

```
inFile = IO.File.OpenText("sales.txt")
```

5. The procedure needs to read the file line by line, stopping only when the end of the file is reached. Type the following Do clause and then press **Enter**:

```
Do Until inFile.Peek = -1
```

6. The first instruction in the loop will use the ReadLine method to read the product category and then store it in the `strCategory` variable. Enter the following comment and assignment statement:

```
' Read product category.
strCategory = inFile.ReadLine
```

7. The next instruction in the loop will use the ReadLine method to read the sales amount from the file, and then use the Integer.TryParse method to convert the amount to the Integer data type. (Recall that the ReadLine method returns a string.) Enter the following comment and statement:

```
' Read sales amount and convert to Integer.
Integer.TryParse(inFile.ReadLine, intSales)
```

8. The last instruction in the loop will add the sales amount to the accumulator variable. Enter the following comment and statement:

```
' Add sales amount to accumulator.
intAnnualSales += intSales
```

9. If necessary, delete the **blank line** above the Loop clause.

10. After the loop has finished processing, the procedure needs to close the file and then display the annual sales in the lblAnnualSales control. Insert a **blank line** below the Loop clause and then enter the additional statements indicated in Figure 9-28.

```
14  Private Sub btnCalc_Click(sender As Object, e As EventArgs) Handles btnCal
15          ' Calculate and display the annual sales amount.
16
17          ' Declare variables.
18          Dim inFile As IO.StreamReader
19          Dim strCategory As String
20          Dim intSales As Integer
21          Dim intAnnualSales As Integer
22
23          If IO.File.Exists("sales.txt") Then
24              inFile = IO.File.OpenText("sales.txt")
25              Do Until inFile.Peek = -1
26                  ' Read product category.
27                  strCategory = inFile.ReadLine
28                  ' Read sales amount and convert to Integer.
29                  Integer.TryParse(inFile.ReadLine, intSales)
30                  ' Add sales amount to accumulator.
31                  intAnnualSales += intSales
32              Loop
33              inFile.Close()                                          ┐ enter these
34              lblAnnualSales.Text = intAnnualSales.ToString("C0")     ┘ two statements
35          Else
36              MessageBox.Show("Cannot find the file.", "Company Sales",
37                              MessageBoxButtons.OK, MessageBoxIcon.Information)
38              lblAnnualSales.Text = "N/A"
39          End If
40      End Sub
```

Figure 9-28   Completed btnCalc_Click procedure

11. Save the solution and then start the application. Click the **Calculate** button. The company's annual sales amount is $1,677,400. See Figure 9-29.

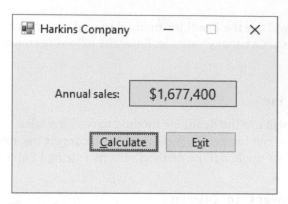

Figure 9-29   Annual sales amount displayed in the interface

12. Click the **Exit** button. Close the Code Editor window and then close the solution.

A-5 Sort the Data Contained in a File

In this section, you will learn an easy way to sort the data contained in a sequential access file. You first read the unsorted data from the file, storing it in a list box whose Sorted property is set to True. You then write the sorted contents of the list box either to the same file or to a different file.

START HERE

To sort the data contained in a sequential access file:

1. Open the States Solution.sln file contained in the VB2017\Chap09\States Solution folder. The lstStates control in the interface has its Sorted property set to True.

2. Click **File**, point to **Open**, and then click **File**. Open the States Project's bin\Debug folder. Click **states.txt** and then click **Open**. The file contains the names of the 50 states; Figure 9-30 shows only the first 10 names. Notice that the names are not in alphabetical order.

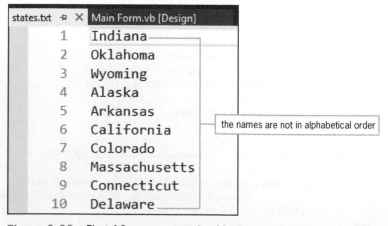

Figure 9-30   First 10 names contained in the unsorted states.txt file

3. Close the states.txt window. Open the Code Editor window and locate the frmMain_Load procedure, which is shown in Figure 9-31. The procedure reads the names from the states.txt file and adds each name to the lstStates control.

```
14      Private Sub frmMain_Load(sender As Object, e As EventArgs) Handles Me.Load
15          ' Add file's contents to a list box.
16
17          Dim inFile As IO.StreamReader
18
19          If IO.File.Exists("states.txt") Then
20              inFile = IO.File.OpenText("states.txt")
21              Do Until inFile.Peek = -1
22                  lstStates.Items.Add(inFile.ReadLine)
23              Loop
24              inFile.Close()
25          Else
26              MessageBox.Show("Cannot find the file.", "States",
27                              MessageBoxButtons.OK, MessageBoxIcon.Information)
28          End If
29      End Sub
```

Figure 9-31   frmMain_Load procedure

4. Start the application. The lstStates control's Sorted property is set to True, so the state names appear in ascending order. Click the **Exit** button.

5. Locate the btnWrite_Click procedure. The procedure will write the sorted contents of the list box to the states.txt file. Click the **blank line** above the End Sub clause and then enter the code shown in Figure 9-32.

```
31      Private Sub btnWrite_Click(sender As Object, e As EventArgs) Handles b
32          ' Write the sorted contents of the list box to a file.
33
34          Dim outFile As IO.StreamWriter
35
36          outFile = IO.File.CreateText("states.txt")
37          For intIndex As Integer = 0 To lstStates.Items.Count - 1
38              outFile.WriteLine(lstStates.Items(intIndex))
39          Next intIndex
40          outFile.Close()
41          MessageBox.Show("File written successfully.", "States",
42                          MessageBoxButtons.OK, MessageBoxIcon.Information)
43      End Sub
```
← enter these lines of code

Figure 9-32   Completed btnWrite_Click procedure

6. Save the solution and then start the application. Click the **Write to file** button. The btnWrite_Click procedure writes the contents of the list box to the states.txt file and displays the "File written successfully." message. Click the **OK** button to close the message box and then click the **Exit** button.

7. Open the states.txt file. Verify that the 50 names are now in alphabetical order. The first 10 names are shown in Figure 9-33.

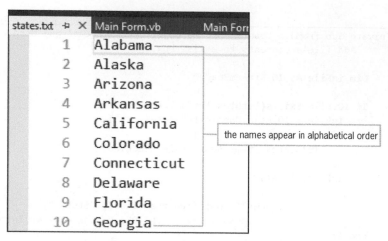

Figure 9-33   First 10 names contained in the sorted states.txt file

8. Close the states.txt window, the Code Editor window, and the solution.

A-6 Professionalize Your Application's Interface

In this section, you will professionalize the interface for one of the Game Show applications from this chapter's Focus lesson. More specifically, you will have the application display a message each time the user clicks the Write to file button. The message will confirm that the contestant's name was written to the contestants.txt file. You can display the message in either a message box or a label on the form. You will use a label so that the user will not need to close the message box each time a record is written to the file.

START HERE

To professionalize the application's interface:

1. Open the Game Show Solution.sln file contained in the VB2017\Chap09\Game Show Solution-Professionalize folder.

2. Add a label to the form. Position it in the lower-left corner. Change its Name, Text, and Visible properties to **lblMessage**, **Name written to file.**, and **False**, respectively.

3. Open the Code Editor window and locate the btnWrite_Click procedure. Insert a **blank line** above the End Sub clause. Type **lblMessage.Visible = True** and then press **Enter**.

4. Open the code template for the txtName_TextChanged procedure. Type **lblMessage.Visible = False** and then press **Enter**.

5. Save the solution and then start the application. Type **Avery Jones** in the Name box and then click the **Write to file** button. The btnWrite_Click procedure changes the lblMessage control's Visible property to True. As a result, the "Name written to file." message appears in the lower-left corner of the interface. See Figure 9-34.

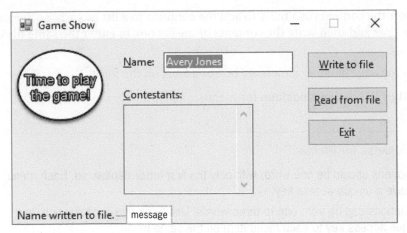

Figure 9-34   Interface showing the "Name written to file." message.

6. Type **Casey Marion** in the Name box. The message disappears because the txtName_TextChanged procedure changes the lblMessage control's Visible property to False. Click the **Write to file** button. The message appears once again.

7. Click the **Exit** button. Close the Code Editor window and then close the solution.

Summary

- Sequential access files can be used for an application's input or for its output.

- Sequential access files are composed of streams of characters that are both read and written in consecutive order.

- Sequential access files are also called text files.

- To create and use an output sequential access file, use the steps and syntaxes shown in Figure 9-1.

- To create and use an input sequential access file, use the steps and syntaxes shown in Figure 9-5.

- The ReadLine and ReadToEnd methods return strings.

- You use the MenuStrip tool, which is located in the Menus & Toolbars section of the toolbox, to add a menu strip control to a form.

- You create a menu by replacing the words "Type Here" with the menu element's caption. You should assign a meaningful name and a unique access key to each menu element, with the exception of separator bars.

- To include a separator bar on a menu, place your mouse pointer on a Type Here box, click the list arrow that appears inside the box, and then click Separator on the list.

- You use a menu item's ShortcutKeys property to assign shortcut keys to the item.

- You use a menu item's access key to select the item when the menu is open. You use its shortcut keys to select it when the menu is closed.

- An easy way to sort the contents of a file is to add the contents to a list box whose Sorted property is set to True and then write the contents of the list box to either the same file or a different file.

- You can display a message in either a message box or a label on the form.

- Figure 9-35 lists the GUI design guidelines for menus.

GUI design guidelines for menus

- Menu title captions should be one word, with only the first letter capitalized. Each menu title should have a unique access key.

- Menu item captions can be from one to three words. Use book title capitalization, and assign a unique access key to each menu item on the same menu.

- Assign unique shortcut keys to commonly used menu items.

- If a menu item requires additional information from the user, place an ellipsis (...) at the end of the item's caption, which is entered in the item's Text property.

- Follow the Windows standards for the placement of menu titles and items.

- Use a separator bar to separate groups of related menu items.

Figure 9-35   GUI design guidelines for menus

Key Terms

AppendText method—used with a StreamWriter variable to open a sequential access file for append

Character stream—a sequence (stream) of characters

Close method—used with either a StreamWriter variable or a StreamReader variable to close a sequential access file

CreateText method—used with a StreamWriter variable to open a sequential access file for output

Exists method—used to determine whether a file exists

Input files—files from which an application reads data

Line—a sequence (stream) of characters followed by the newline character

Menu strip control—used to include one or more menus on a form; instantiated using the MenuStrip tool located in the Menus & Toolbars section of the toolbox

OpenText method—used with a StreamReader variable to open a sequential access file for input

Output files—files to which an application writes data

Peek method—used with a StreamReader variable to determine whether a file contains another character to read

ReadLine method—used with a StreamReader variable to read a line of text from a sequential access file

ReadToEnd method—used with a StreamReader variable to read a sequential access file, all at once

Sequential access files —files composed of characters that are both read and written sequentially; also called text files

Shortcut keys—appear to the right of a menu item and allow the user to select the item without opening the menu

Stream of characters—a sequence of characters; also called a character stream

StreamReader class—the Visual Basic class used to create StreamReader objects

StreamReader object—used to read a sequence (stream) of characters from a sequential access file

StreamReader variable—a variable that stores a StreamReader object; used to refer to a sequential access input file in code

StreamWriter class—the Visual Basic class used to create StreamWriter objects

StreamWriter object—used to write a sequence (stream) of characters to a sequential access file

StreamWriter variable—a variable that stores a StreamWriter object; used to refer to a sequential access output file in code

Text files—another name for sequential access files

Write method—used with a StreamWriter variable to write data to a sequential access file; differs from the WriteLine method in that it does not write a newline character after the data

WriteLine method—used with a StreamWriter variable to write data to a sequential access file; differs from the Write method in that it writes a newline character after the data

Review Questions

1. Which of the following opens the employ.txt file and allows the computer to write new data to the end of the file's existing data?

    a. `outFile = IO.File.AddText("employ.txt")`

    b. `outFile = IO.File.AppendText("employ.txt")`

    c. `outFile = IO.File.InsertText("employ.txt")`

    d. `outFile = IO.File.WriteText("employ.txt")`

2. If the file to be opened exists, which method erases the file's contents?

    a. AppendText   c. InsertText

    b. CreateText   d. OpenText

3. Which of the following reads a line of text from a sequential access file and assigns the line (excluding the newline character) to the **strText** variable?

    a. `inFile.Read(strText)`   c. `strText = inFile.ReadLine`

    b. `inFile.ReadLine(strText)`   d. `strText = inFile.Read(line)`

4. What does the Peek method return when the end of the file is reached?

    a. −1   c. the last character in the file

    b. 0   d. the newline character

5. Which of the following can be used to determine whether the employ.txt file exists?

    a. `If IO.File.Exists("employ.txt") Then`

    b. `If IO.File("employ.txt").Exists Then`

    c. `If IO.Exists("employ.txt") = True Then`

    d. `If IO.Exists.File("employ.txt") = True Then`

6. What type of object is created by the OpenText method?

    a. File

    b. SequenceReader

    c. StreamWriter

    d. None of the above.

7. What type of object is created by the AppendText method?

    a. File

    b. SequenceReader

    c. StreamWriter

    d. None of the above.

8. The horizontal line in a menu is called _____.

    a. a menu bar

    b. a separator bar

    c. an item separator

    d. None of the above.

9. The underlined letter in a menu element's caption is called _____.

    a. an access key

    b. a menu key

    c. a shortcut key

    d. None of the above.

10. Which of the following allows the user to access a menu item without opening the menu?

    a. an access key

    b. a menu key

    c. shortcut keys

    d. None of the above.

11. Which of the following is false?

    a. Menu titles should be one word only.

    b. Each menu title should have a unique access key.

    c. You should assign shortcut keys to commonly used menu titles.

    d. Menu items should be entered using book title capitalization.

Exercises

INTRODUCTORY

1. Open the Electricity Solution.sln file contained in the VB2017\Chap09\Electricity Solution folder. Open the monthlyBills.txt file. Each of the 12 numbers in the file represents the cost of electricity for a month. Close the monthlyBills.txt window. The btnCalc_Click procedure should display the average monthly cost for electricity. Display the average with a dollar sign and two decimal places. Code the procedure. Save the solution and then start and test the application. (The average is $119.81. If you need to recreate the file, the project's bin\Debug folder contains a copy of the original file.)

INTRODUCTORY

2. Open the Workers Solution.sln file contained in the VB2017\Chap09\Workers Solution folder. The user will enter a name in the txtName control and then click the Add to list button, which should add the name to the lstWorkers control. When the user is finished entering names, the frmMain_FormClosing procedure should write the contents of the list box to a new sequential access file named workers.txt. Code the procedure. Save the solution and then start the application. Test the application by entering the following two names: Henry Kaplan and Mario Brown. Stop the application and verify that the workers.txt file contains both names. Now, start the application and enter the following three names: Jose Juarez, Maya Harris, and Savannah Carlisle. Stop the application and verify that the workers.txt file contains only three names.

INTRODUCTORY

3. Create a Windows Forms application. Use the following names for the project and solution, respectively: Customer Project and Customer Solution. Save the application in the VB2017\Chap09 folder.

    a. Create the interface shown in Figure 9-36. The File menu should have an Exit option. Change the lblMessage control's Visible property to False.

    b. Code the File menu's Exit option.

    c. The lblMessage control should disappear when a change is made to any of the text boxes. Create one event-handling Sub procedure to handle this task.

    d. Code each text box's Enter event procedure.

    e. The Save button should save the customer information to a sequential access file named customers.txt. Before saving the information, be sure to verify that all of the text boxes contain data; display an appropriate message if at least one text box is empty. Use the following format when saving the information: Save the customer's first name and last name, separated by a space character, on the same line. Then, on the next line, save the customer's address, followed by a comma, a space character, the city name, a comma, a space character, and the ZIP code. A blank line should separate each customer's information from the next customer's information. Figure 9-36 shows a sample of the sequential access file.

    f. Save the solution and then start and test the application. Stop the application and verify the contents of the customers.txt file.

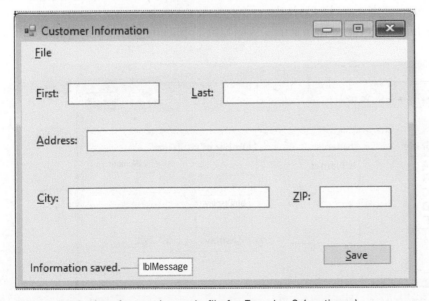

Figure 9-36 Interface and sample file for Exercise 3 (continues)

(continued)

customers.txt	⊞ ✕	Main Form.vb	Main Form.vb [Design]
1	Thomas Young		
2	1155 W. Main Street, Nashville, 37011		
3			
4	Susan Rogers		
5	56 Main Street, Bowling Green, 42101		
6			
7			

Figure 9-36   Interface and sample file for Exercise 3

INTERMEDIATE

4. Create a Windows Forms application. Use the following names for the project and solution, respectively: Potter Project and Potter Solution. Save the application in the VB2017\Chap09 folder.

a. The application will display the names of students who have earned the grade selected in a list box. The student names and grades are stored in the NamesAndGrades.txt file. Copy the file from the VB2017\Chap09 folder to the Potter Project's bin\Debug folder. Now, open the NamesAndGrades.txt file. The file contains 15 names and 15 grades. Close the NamesAndGrades.txt window.

b. Create the interface shown in Figure 9-37. Use the String Collection Editor to enter the five grades in the lstGrades control. Change the lstNames control's SelectionMode and Sorted properties to None and True, respectively.

c. Code the Exit button's Click event procedure.

d. The first item in the lstGrades control should be selected when the interface appears. Code the appropriate procedure.

e. The contents of the lstNames and lblNumber controls should be cleared when a different grade is selected in the lstGrades control. Code the appropriate procedure.

f. The Display button should display the names of students who have earned the grade selected in the lstGrades control. It should also display the number of students who have earned that grade. Code the appropriate procedure.

g. Save the solution and then start and test the application.

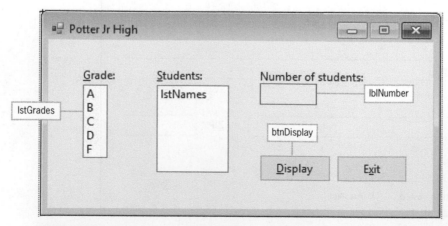

Figure 9-37   Interface for Exercise 4

5. Create a Windows Forms application. Use the following names for the project and solution, respectively: Cookies Project and Cookies Solution. Save the application in the VB2017\Chap09 folder.

INTERMEDIATE

   a. Copy the cookieSales.txt file from the VB2017\Chap09 folder to the Cookies Project's bin\Debug folder. Open the cookieSales.txt file. The file contains the numbers of boxes sold for four different cookie types. Close the cookieSales.txt window.

   b. Create the interface shown in Figure 9-38. Code the Exit button's Click event procedure.

   c. The Display totals button should calculate and display the total number of boxes of each cookie type sold. Use a one-dimensional array to accumulate the numbers of boxes sold by cookie type. Then, display the array values in the label controls in the interface.

   d. Save the solution and then start and test the application. (The total number of boxes of chocolate chip cookies sold is 30.)

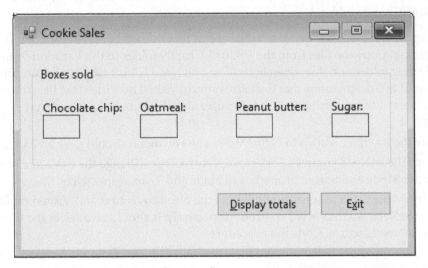

Figure 9-38   Interface for Exercise 5

6. In this exercise, you will modify the Warren School application from Chapter 8's Apply the Concepts lesson.

INTERMEDIATE

   a. Open the Warren Solution.sln file contained in the VB2017\Chap09\Warren Solution folder.

   b. The frmMain_FormClosing procedure should save the sales amounts stored in the intCandy array to a sequential access file named candySales.txt. Code the procedure.

   c. The frmMain_Load procedure should fill the array with the sales amounts from the candySales.txt file. (*Hint:* If the file does not exist, you do not need to display a message to the user.)

   d. The frmMain_Load procedure should also display the array amounts in the appropriate label controls. Create an independent Sub procedure named DisplayArray to handle this task. Then, modify the btnAdd_Click procedure so it uses the DisplayArray procedure.

   e. Save the solution and then start the application. Type 7 in the Sold box and then click the Add to total button. The number 7 appears in the Choco Bar box. Now, click Kit Kat in the Candy list box, type 10 in the Sold box, and then click the Add to total button. The number 10 appears in the Kit Kat box. Click the Exit button.

f. Open the candySales.txt file. The file contains the numbers 7, 0, 10, 0, and 0. Close the candySales.txt file.

g. Start the application again. The candy boxes on the form reflect the amounts stored in the file: 7, 0, 10, 0, and 0.

h. Click Kit Kat in the Candy box, type 20 in the Sold box, and then click the Add to total button. The number 30 appears in the Kit Kat box. Click the Exit button.

i. Open the candySales.txt file. The file now contains the numbers 7, 0, 30, 0, and 0. Close the candySales.txt file.

j. Start the application again. The candy boxes on the form reflect the amounts stored in the file: 7, 0, 30, 0, and 0. On your own, continue testing the application. When you are finished testing, click the Exit button.

ADVANCED   7. Create a Windows Forms application. Use the following names for the project and solution, respectively: Vacation Project and Vacation Solution. Save the application in the VB2017\Chap09 folder.

a. The application will use two sequential access files named NeedToVisit.txt and Visited.txt. Copy the files from the VB2017\Chap09 folder to the Vacation Project's bin\Debug folder and then open both files. The NeedToVisit.txt file contains the names of five destinations that the user wants to visit. The Visited.txt file contains the names of three destinations that the user already visited. Close both .txt windows.

b. Create the interface shown in Figure 9-39. The File menu should have an Exit option.

c. Change the lstNeed control's Sorted property to True. Change the lstVisited control's SelectionMode and Sorted properties to None and True, respectively.

d. The frmMain_Load procedure should use the NeedToVisit.txt and Visited.txt files to fill the lstNeed and lstVisited controls, respectively. It should also select the first item in the lstNeed control. Code the procedure.

e. The Move to visited button should move the selected item from the lstNeed control to the lstVisited control. Code the appropriate procedure.

f. If at least one change was made to the list boxes, the frmMain_FormClosing procedure should use a message box to ask the user whether he or she wants to save the change(s). If the user clicks the Yes button, the procedure should save the items in both list boxes to the appropriate files before the form closes.

g. Save the solution and then start and test the application.

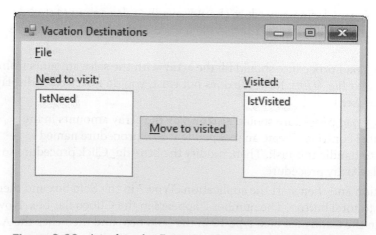

Figure 9-39   Interface for Exercise 7

ADVANCED

8. In this exercise, you modify the application from Exercise 2. Use Windows to make a copy of the Workers Solution folder. Rename the copy Workers Solution-Filename.

   a. Open the Workers Solution.sln file contained in the Workers Solution-Filename folder. Add a label and a text box to the form. Position both above the existing controls. (You will need to unlock the controls and then reposition the existing ones.) Change the new label's Text property to &Filename:. Change the new text box's name to txtFilename. Lock the controls and then reset the tab order.

   b. Open the Code Editor window. Code the txtFilename_KeyPress procedure to accept only numbers, letters (uppercase and lowercase), and the Backspace key.

   c. Modify the frmMain_FormClosing procedure using the rules shown in Figure 9-40.

   d. Save the solution and then start and test the application.

---

1. If the user does not provide a filename in the txtFilename control, the procedure should use a message box to display the "Please provide a filename." message along with an OK button and the Information icon; it should then prevent the form from being closed.

2. The procedure should append the .txt extension to the filename and then determine whether the file already exists. If the file does not exist, the procedure should write the list box information to the file. Use an independent Sub procedure to write the information to the file.

3. If the file exists, the procedure should use a message box to display the "Replace existing file before exiting?" message along with Yes, No, and Cancel buttons and the Exclamation icon.

4. If the user selects the Cancel button, the procedure should prevent the form from being closed. If the user selects the Yes button, the procedure should replace the file before the form is closed; use the independent Sub procedure from Step 2 to write the information to the file. If the user selects the No button, the procedure should close the form without saving the information.

Figure 9-40 Rules for Exercise 8

ADVANCED

9. Create a Windows Forms application. Use the following names for the project and solution, respectively: Wedding Project and Wedding Solution. Save the application in the VB2017\Chap09 folder.

   a. Create a sequential access file named invited.txt and save it in the Wedding Project's bin\Debug folder. Enter the names of 20 guests in the file. Each guest's name should be entered on the same line in this format: last, first (the last name followed by a comma, a space character, and the first name). Close the invited.txt window.

   b. Create a second sequential access file named accepted.txt and save it in the Wedding Project's bin\Debug folder. Enter the following two names in the file: Nitzki, Akanna and Jefferson, Josephine. Close the accepted.txt file.

   c. Create a third sequential access file named rejected.txt and save it in the Wedding Project's bin\Debug folder. Enter the following name in the file: Kellog, Zelda. Close the rejected.txt file.

   d. The application's interface should contain three list boxes named lstInvited, lstAccepted, and lstRejected. Each list box's Sorted property should be set to True. The lstAccepted and lstRejected controls should have their SelectionMode property set to None. When the interface appears, the contents of the invited.txt, accepted.txt, and rejected.txt files should appear in the appropriate list boxes.

e. The interface should also contain three buttons with the following captions: Accepted, Rejected, and Exit. The Accepted button should move the name selected in the lstInvited control to the lstAccepted control. The Rejected button should move the name selected in the lstInvited control to the lstRejected control.

f. Before the form is closed, its FormClosing procedure should save the contents of each list box in the appropriate file.

g. Save the solution and then start and test the application.

ON YOUR OWN   10. Create a Windows Forms application. Use the following names for the project and solution, respectively: OnYourOwn Project and OnYourOwn Solution. Save the application in the VB2017\Chap09 folder. Plan and design an application of your choice. The only requirement is that you must follow the minimum guidelines listed in Figure 9-41. Before starting the application, be sure to verify the name of the startup form. Save the solution and then start and test the application.

---

1. The user interface must contain a minimum of three labels and one button. It must also contain a File menu with an Exit option. You can include other menus and/or options as well.

2. The interface can include a picture box, but this is not a requirement.

3. The interface must follow the GUI design guidelines summarized for Chapters 2 through 9 in Appendix A.

4. Objects that are either coded or referred to in code should be named appropriately.

5. The application must use at least one input sequential access file and one output sequential access file.

6. The Code Editor window must contain comments, the three Option statements, at least two variables, at least two assignment statements, and the Me.Close() statement.

Figure 9-41   Guidelines for Exercise 10

FIX IT   11. Open the VB2017\Chap09\FixIt Solution\FixIt Solution.sln file. Open the Code Editor window and study the existing code. Start the application. Enter Sue and 1000 and then click the Calculate and save button. Now, enter Pete and 5000 and then click the Calculate and save button. A run time error occurs. Read the error message. Click Debug on the menu bar and then click Stop Debugging. Open the bonus.txt file contained in the project's bin\Debug folder. Notice that the file is empty. Close the bonus.txt window. Locate and correct the error(s) in the code. Save the solution and then start and test the application again. Verify that the bonus.txt file contains the two names and bonus amounts.

Classes and Objects

You already are familiar with classes and objects because you have been using them since Chapter 1. For example, you used Visual Basic's Button class to create a button object and used its String class to create a String variable. In this chapter's Focus on the Concepts lesson, you will learn how to define your own classes and then use them to instantiate objects in an application. The Apply the Concepts lesson expands on the topics covered in the Focus lesson.

▌ FOCUS ON THE CONCEPTS LESSON

Concepts covered in this lesson:

- F-1 Object-oriented programming
- F-2 Creating a class
- F-3 Instantiating an object
- F-4 Attributes section of a class
- F-5 Behaviors section of a class
- F-6 Adding a parameterized constructor to a class
- F-7 Reusing a class

F-1 Object-Oriented Programming

As you learned in Chapter 1, Visual Basic is an **object-oriented programming language**, which is a language that allows the programmer to use objects in an application's interface and also in its code. In object-oriented programming, or **OOP**, an **object** is anything that can be seen, touched, or used. In other words, an object is nearly any *thing*.

The objects used in an object-oriented program can take on many different forms. The text boxes, list boxes, and buttons that appear in an application's interface are objects. The variables and named constants declared in an application's code are also objects. An object can also represent something found in real life, such as a file on a disk.

Every object in an object-oriented program is created from a **class**, which is a pattern that the computer uses to create the object. The class contains the instructions that tell the computer how the object should look and behave.

An object created from a class is called an **instance** of the class and is said to be **instantiated** from the class. A button control, for example, is an instance of the Button class and is instantiated when you drag the Button tool from the toolbox to the form. A String variable, on the other hand, is an instance of the String class and is instantiated the first time you refer to the variable in code. Keep in mind that the class itself is not an object; only an instance of a class is an object.

Every object has a set of **attributes**, which are the characteristics that describe the object. Attributes are also called properties. Included in the attributes of buttons and text boxes are the Name and Text properties. String variables, on the other hand, have a Length property.

Every object also has a set of **behaviors**, which include both methods and events. **Methods** are the operations (actions) that the object is capable of performing. For example, a button can use its Focus method to send the focus to itself. Similarly, a String variable can use its ToUpper method to temporarily convert its contents to uppercase. **Events**, on the other hand, are the actions to which an object can respond. A button's Click event, for instance, allows the button to respond to a mouse click.

A class contains—or, in OOP terms, it **encapsulates**—all of the attributes and behaviors of the object it instantiates. The term *encapsulate* means to enclose in a capsule. In the context of OOP, the "capsule" is a class.

Mini-Quiz 10-1

1. A class is an object. True or False?

2. An object is an instance of a class. True or False?

3. An object's attributes indicate the tasks that the object can perform. True or False?

4. What is a class?

1) False 2) True 3) False 4) A class is a pattern that the computer uses to create an object.

F-2 Creating a Class

In previous chapters, you instantiated objects using classes that are built into Visual Basic, such as the TextBox and Label classes. You used the instantiated objects in a variety of ways in many different applications. For example, in some applications you used a text box to enter a name, while in others you used it to enter a sales tax rate. Similarly, you used label controls to identify text boxes and also to display the result of calculations. The ability to use an object for more than one purpose saves programming time and money—an advantage that contributes to the popularity of object-oriented programming.

You can also define your own classes in Visual Basic and then create instances (objects) from those classes. Creating a class whose objects can be used in a variety of ways by many different applications requires a lot of planning. However, the time and effort spent planning the class will pay off in the long run.

You define a class using the **Class statement**, which you enter in a class file. Figure 10-1 shows the statement's syntax and lists the steps for adding a class file to an open project. It also includes an example of a class file named TimeCard.vb. The three Option statements in the TimeCard.vb file have the same meaning as they have in a form file.

Class Statement

Syntax
Public Class className
    attributes section
    behaviors section
End Class

Adding a class file to an open project
1. Click Project on the menu bar and then click Add Class. The Add New Item dialog box opens with Class selected in the middle column of the dialog box.
2. Type the name of the class, followed by a period and the letters vb, in the Name box.
3. Click the Add button.

Figure 10-1   Class statement syntax, steps, and example *(continues)*

(continued)

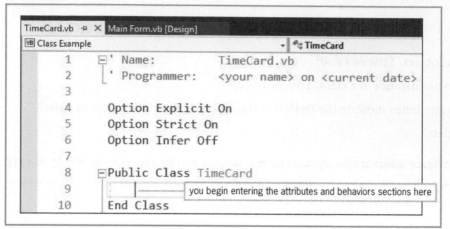

Figure 10-1 Class statement syntax, steps, and example

Although it is not a requirement, the convention is to use Pascal case for the class name. The names of Visual Basic classes (for example, String and TextBox) also follow this naming convention. Within the Class statement, you define the attributes and behaviors of the objects the class will create. In most cases, the attributes are represented by Private variables and Public property procedures. The behaviors are represented by methods, which are usually Sub procedures or functions. (You can also include Event procedures in a Class statement. However, that topic is beyond the scope of this book.) Before learning how to complete the attributes and behaviors sections of a class, you will learn how to use the class to instantiate an object.

F-3 Instantiating an Object

After you define a class, you can use either of the syntax versions in Figure 10-2 to instantiate one or more objects. In both versions, *variable* is the name of a variable that will represent the object. The difference between the versions relates to when the object is actually created. The computer creates the object only when it processes the statement containing the New keyword, which you will learn more about later in this lesson. Also included in Figure 10-2 is an example of using each version of the syntax.

Instantiating an Object

Syntax—Version 1
{**Dim** | **Private**} *variable* **As** *className*
variable = **New** *className*

Syntax—Version 2
{**Dim** | **Private**} *variable* **As New** *className*

Example 1 (using syntax version 1)
```
Private hoursInfo As TimeCard
hoursInfo = New TimeCard
```
The Private instruction creates a TimeCard variable named hoursInfo. The assignment statement then instantiates a TimeCard object and assigns it to the hoursInfo variable.

Example 2 (using syntax version 2)
```
Dim hoursInfo As New TimeCard
```
The Dim instruction creates a TimeCard variable named hoursInfo and also instantiates a TimeCard object, which it assigns to the hoursInfo variable.

Figure 10-2 Syntax and examples of instantiating an object

The Private instruction in Example 1 creates a class-level variable that can represent a TimeCard object; however, it does not create the object. The object isn't created (instantiated) until the computer processes the `hoursInfo = New TimeCard` statement. The Dim statement in Example 2, on the other hand, not only creates a procedure-level variable named `hoursInfo`, but it also instantiates a TimeCard object and then assigns the object to the variable.

Mini-Quiz 10-2

1. Write a statement that declares a procedure-level Employee variable named `manager`.

2. Write a statement that instantiates an Employee object and assigns it to the `manager` variable from Question 1.

3. Write a statement that declares a procedure-level Employee variable named `hourly`. The statement should also instantiate an Employee object, storing it in the `hourly` variable.

1) Dim manager As Employee 2) manager = New Employee 3) Dim hourly As New Employee

F-4 Attributes Section of a Class

The attributes section of a Class statement typically contains the declaration statements for one or more variables, referred to as **member variables**. Each member variable represents an attribute of the object that the class will create. Most of the member variables are declared using the keyword `Private`. When an application uses the class to instantiate an object, the Private member variables will not be visible to the application; using OOP terminology, they will be **hidden** from it. For an application to assign data to or retrieve data from a Private member variable, it must use a Public property. This is because only items declared using the keyword `Public` will be visible to the application; or, using OOP terminology, **exposed** to it. In other words, an application cannot directly refer to a Private member in a class. Instead, it must refer to the member, indirectly, through the use of a Public member. Figure 10-3 shows the syntax for a **Public property procedure**, which allows an application to refer to a Private member variable in a class.

Public Property Procedures

Syntax
Public [ReadOnly | WriteOnly] Property *propertyName*[(*parameterList*)] **As** *dataType*
   Get
      [*instructions*]
      Return *privateVariable*
   End Get
   Set(value As *dataType*)
      [*instructions*]
      privateVariable = {**value** | *defaultValue*}
   End Set
End Property

Figure 10-3   Syntax and examples of Public property procedures *(continues)*

(continued)

Example 1—an application can both retrieve and set the Side property's value

```
Private intSide As Integer

Public Property Side As Integer
    Get
        Return intSide
    End Get
    Set(value As Integer)
        If value > 0 Then
            intSide = value
        Else
            intSide = 0
        End If
    End Set
End Property
```

Example 2—an application can only retrieve the Bonus property's value

```
Private dblBonus As Double

Public ReadOnly Property Bonus As Double
    Get
        Return dblBonus
    End Get
End Property
```

Example 3—an application can only set the AnnualSales property's value

```
Private decAnnualSales As Decimal

Public WriteOnly Property AnnualSales As Decimal
    Set(value As Decimal)
        decAnnualSales = value
    End Set
End Property
```

Figure 10-3 Syntax and examples of Public property procedures

> The Length property of a one-dimensional array is an example of a ReadOnly property.

In most cases, a Property procedure header begins with the keywords `Public Property`. However, as the syntax indicates, the header can also include one of the following keywords: `ReadOnly` or `WriteOnly`. The **ReadOnly keyword** indicates that the property's value can be retrieved (read) by an application, but the application cannot set (write to) the property. The property would get its value from the class itself rather than from the application. The **WriteOnly keyword** indicates that an application can set the property's value, but it cannot retrieve the value. In this case, the value would be set by the application for use within the class.

As Figure 10-3 shows, the name of the property follows the `Property` keyword in the header. You should use nouns and adjectives for a property's name and enter it using Pascal case, as in Side, Bonus, and AnnualSales. Following the property name is an optional *parameterList* enclosed in parentheses, the keyword `As`, and the property's *dataType*. The dataType must match the data type of the Private variable associated with the Property procedure.

Between a Property procedure's header and footer, you include a Get block of code, a Set block of code, or both Get and Set blocks of code. The appropriate block or blocks of code to include depends on the keywords contained in the procedure header. If the header contains the ReadOnly keyword, you include only a Get block of code in the Property procedure. The code contained in the **Get block** returns the contents of the Private variable associated with the property and stores the returned value in the property itself. In the Property procedure shown in Example 2 in Figure 10-3, the ReadOnly keyword indicates that an application can retrieve the contents of the Bonus property, but it cannot set the property's value. The value can be set only by a procedure within the class.

If the header contains the WriteOnly keyword, on the other hand, you include only a Set block of code in the procedure. The code in the **Set block** assigns the value received from an application to the Private variable associated with the property. In the Property procedure shown in Example 3 in Figure 10-3, the WriteOnly keyword indicates that an application can set the AnnualSales property's value, but it cannot retrieve the value. Only a procedure within the class can retrieve the value.

If the Property procedure header does not contain the ReadOnly or WriteOnly keywords, you include both a Get block of code and a Set block of code in the procedure, as shown in Example 1 in Figure 10-3. In this case, an application can both retrieve and set the Side property's value.

The Get block in a Property procedure contains the **Get statement**, which begins with the Get clause and ends with the End Get clause. Most times, you will enter only the Return *privateVariable* instruction within the Get statement. The instruction returns the contents of the Private variable associated with the property. In Example 1 in Figure 10-3, the Return intSide statement in the Side property's Get statement returns the contents of the intSide variable, which is the Private variable associated with the Side property. Similarly, the Return dblBonus statement in Example 2 returns the contents of the dblBonus variable, which is the Private variable associated with the Bonus property. Example 3 does not contain a Get statement because the AnnualSales property is designated as a WriteOnly property.

The Set block contains the **Set statement**, which begins with the Set clause and ends with the End Set clause. The Set clause's value parameter temporarily stores the value that is passed to the property by the application. The value parameter's *dataType* must match the data type of the Private variable associated with the Property procedure. You can enter one or more instructions between the Set and End Set clauses. One of the instructions should assign the contents of the value parameter to the Private variable associated with the property. In Example 3 in Figure 10-3, the decAnnualSales = value statement in the Set statement assigns the contents of the AnnualSales property's value parameter to the Private decAnnualSales variable.

In the Set statement, you often will include instructions to validate the value received from the application before assigning it to the Private variable. The Set statement in Example 1 in Figure 10-3 includes a selection structure that determines whether the side measurement received from the application is greater than 0. If it is, the intSide = value instruction assigns the integer stored in the value parameter to the Private intSide variable. Otherwise, the intSide = 0 instruction assigns a default value (in this case, 0) to the variable. The Property procedure in Example 2 in Figure 10-3 does not contain a Set statement because the Bonus property is designated as a ReadOnly property.

Attributes Section Example: Franklin Decks Application

In this section, you will begin defining the Rectangle class, which the Franklin Decks application will use to instantiate a Rectangle object that represents a rectangular deck. The application will display the number of square feet of building material required for the deck as well as the total cost of the deck.

START HERE

To begin creating the Rectangle class:

1. Open the Franklin Solution.sln file contained in the VB2017\Chap10\Franklin Solution folder. If necessary, open the designer window.

2. Click **Project** on the menu bar and then click **Add Class**. The Add New Item dialog box opens with Class selected in the middle column. Type **Rectangle.vb** in the Name box. As you learned in Chapter 1, the .vb at the end of a filename indicates that the file contains Visual Basic code.

3. Click the **Add** button. The computer adds the Rectangle.vb file to the project. It also opens the file, which contains the Class statement, in a separate window. Temporarily display the Solution Explorer window (if necessary) to verify that the class file's name appears in the list of project items.

4. Insert a **blank line** above the Class statement and then enter the comments and Option statements shown in Figure 10-4. Replace <your name> and <current date> with your name and the current date, respectively. Also, position the insertion point as shown in the figure.

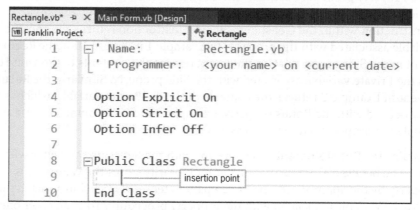

Figure 10-4 Comments and Option statements entered in the class file

5. A rectangle has two attributes: length and width. You will use two Private variables to represent these attributes. Enter the following two Private statements. Press **Enter** twice after typing the second statement.

```
Private intLength As Integer
Private intWidth As Integer
```

6. Next, you need to create a Public property for each of the two Private variables. As you learned earlier, an application needs to use a Public property to access a Private variable in a class. Enter the following Property procedure header and Get clause. When you press Enter after typing the Get clause, the Code Editor automatically enters the End Get clause, the Set statement, and the End Property clause.

```
Public Property Length As Integer
Get
```

7. Recall that in most cases, the Get statement simply returns the contents of the Private variable associated with the Property procedure. Type the following statement after the Get clause, but don't press Enter:

```
Return intLength
```

8. The Set statement should assign either the contents of its `value` parameter or a default value to the Private variable associated with the Property procedure. In this case, you will assign the integer stored in the `value` parameter only when it is greater than 0; otherwise, you will assign the number 0. Enter the selection structure shown in Figure 10-5.

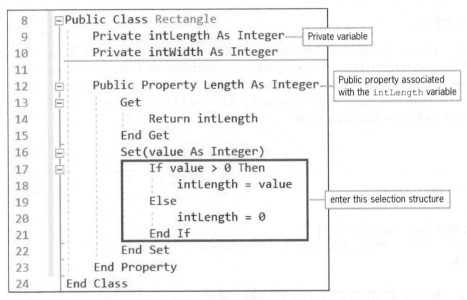

```
8    Public Class Rectangle
9        Private intLength As Integer        Private variable
10       Private intWidth As Integer
11
12       Public Property Length As Integer    Public property associated
                                              with the intLength variable
13           Get
14               Return intLength
15           End Get
16           Set(value As Integer)
17               If value > 0 Then
18                   intLength = value
19               Else                         enter this selection structure
20                   intLength = 0
21               End If
22           End Set
23       End Property
24   End Class
```

Figure 10-5   Length Property procedure entered in the class

9. Insert **two blank lines** below the End Property clause. On your own, enter a similar Property procedure for the `intWidth` variable. Use **Width** as the property's name. (If you need help, you can look ahead to Figure 10-12.)

10. Save the solution.

When the class is used to instantiate an object, each object will have its own copy of the Private variables and Public properties defined in the class's attributes section.

Mini-Quiz 10-3

1. An application must use a Public member of a class to access the class's Private members. True or False?

2. Which keyword indicates that a property's value can be displayed but not changed by an application?

3. In a Property procedure, validation code is typically entered in which statement: Get or Set?

1) True 2) ReadOnly 3) Set

F-5 Behaviors Section of a Class

Now that you have completed the attributes section, you can begin coding the behaviors section. As mentioned earlier, the behaviors section of a Class statement contains methods—either Sub procedures or functions. The methods allow the class's objects to perform tasks. Here too, any object instantiated from the class will have its own copy of the methods defined in the behaviors section of the class. The first method you will learn about is called a constructor.

Constructors

Most classes contain at least one constructor. A **constructor** is a class method that is always named New. The sole purpose of a constructor is to initialize the Private variables declared in the class. Constructors never return a value, so they are always Sub procedures rather than functions. The syntax for creating a constructor is shown in Figure 10-6 along with examples of constructors for the Rectangle class.

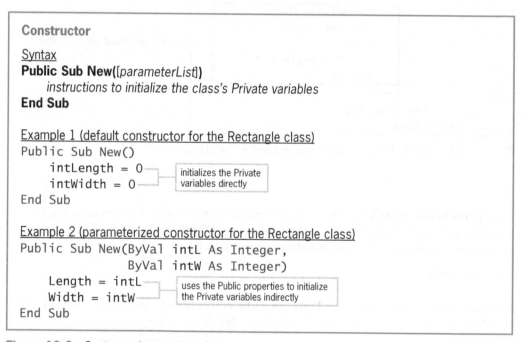

Figure 10-6   Syntax and examples of a constructor

Notice that a constructor's *parameterList* is optional. A constructor that has no parameters, like the constructor in Example 1, is called the **default constructor**. A class can have only one default constructor. A constructor that contains one or more parameters, like the constructor in Example 2, is called a **parameterized constructor**. A class can have as many parameterized constructors as needed. However, the parameterList in each parameterized constructor must be unique within the class. The method name (in this case, New) combined with its optional parameterList is called the method's **signature**.

A default constructor is allowed to initialize an object's Private variables directly, as indicated in Example 1 in Figure 10-6. Parameterized constructors, on the other hand, should use the class's Public properties to access the Private variables indirectly. This is because the values passed to a parameterized constructor come from the application rather than from the class itself. Using a Public property to access a Private variable ensures that the Property procedure's Set block, which typically contains validation code, is processed. The parameterized constructor shown in Example 2 in Figure 10-6 uses the class's Public properties to initialize its Private variables, thereby invoking each property's validation code.

When an object is instantiated, the computer uses one of the class's constructors to initialize the object's Private variables. If a class contains more than one constructor, the computer determines the appropriate constructor by matching the number, data type, and position of the arguments in the statement that instantiates the object with the number, data type, and position of the parameters listed in each constructor's parameterList. The statements in Examples 1 and 2 in Figure 10-7 will invoke the Rectangle class's default constructor because neither statement contains any arguments. The statements in Examples 3 and 4 will invoke the class's parameterized constructor because both statements contain two arguments whose data type is Integer.

Invoking a Constructor

Example 1 (invokes the default constructor)
```
Dim deck As New Rectangle
```

Example 2 (invokes the default constructor)
```
deck = New Rectangle
```

Example 3 (invokes the parameterized constructor)
```
Dim deck As New Rectangle(16, 14)
```

Example 4 (invokes the parameterized constructor)
```
deck = New Rectangle(intDeckLen, intDeckWid)
```

Figure 10-7 Statements that invoke the constructors shown in Figure 10-6

The `Dim randGen As New Random` statement from Chapter 7 instantiates a Random object and invokes the object's default constructor.

Methods Other than Constructors

Except for constructors, which must be Sub procedures, the other methods in a class can be either Sub procedures or functions. As you learned in Chapter 6, the difference between a Sub procedure and a function is that a function returns a value after performing its assigned task, whereas a Sub procedure does not return a value.

Figure 10-8 shows the syntax for a method that is not a constructor. Like property names, method names should be entered using Pascal case. However, unlike property names, the first word in a method name should be a verb, and any subsequent words should be nouns and adjectives. (Visual Basic's SelectAll and TryParse methods follow this naming convention.)

Figure 10-8 also includes two examples of a method that allows a Rectangle object to calculate its area. Notice that you can write the method as either a function or a Sub procedure. You will use the GetArea method in the Franklin Decks application to calculate the deck's area. Calculating the area will give you the number of square feet of material required for the deck.

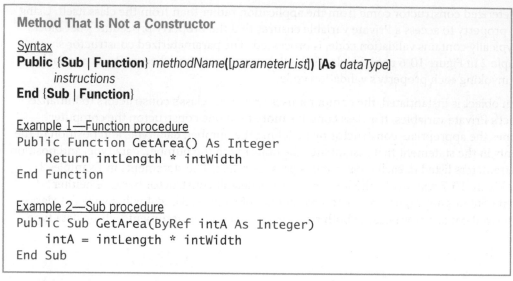

Method That Is Not a Constructor

Syntax
Public {Sub | Function} methodName([parameterList]) [**As** dataType]
    instructions
End {Sub | Function}

Example 1—Function procedure
Public Function GetArea() As Integer
    Return intLength * intWidth
End Function

Example 2—Sub procedure
Public Sub GetArea(ByRef intA As Integer)
    intA = intLength * intWidth
End Sub

Figure 10-8   Syntax and examples of a method that is not a constructor

Behaviors Section Example: Franklin Decks Application

In this section, you will complete the Rectangle class by adding a constructor and the GetArea method to its behaviors section.

START HERE

To complete the Rectangle class:

1. Insert **two blank lines** below the Width property's End Property clause. Enter the default constructor and GetArea method shown in Figure 10-9.

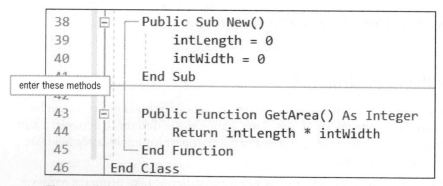

```
38    ┌─ Public Sub New()
39    │      intLength = 0
40    │      intWidth = 0
41    │   End Sub
42
43    ┌─ Public Function GetArea() As Integer
44    │      Return intLength * intWidth
45    └─ End Function
46    End Class
```

enter these methods

Figure 10-9   Code entered in the behaviors section of the class

2. Save the solution.

Using the Rectangle Class: Franklin Decks Application

Now that you have defined the Rectangle class, you can use it to instantiate a Rectangle object in the Franklin Decks application. The application's interface and pseudocode are shown in Figure 10-10.

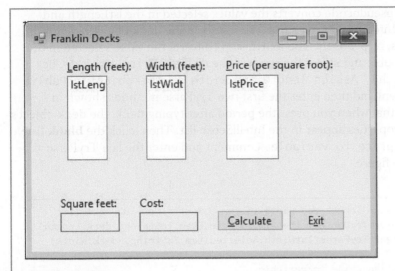

btnCalc Click
1. declare a Rectangle variable named deck; instantiate a Rectangle object and store it in the deck variable
2. declare dblSqFtPrice, intSqFt, and dblCost variables to store the price per square foot of material, the required number of square feet of material, and the cost of the deck
3. convert the items selected in the lstLength and lstWidth controls to Integer and then store the results in the deck object's Length and Width properties
4. convert the item selected in the lstPrice control to Double and store it in the dblSqFtPrice variable
5. calculate the required number of square feet of material by finding the deck's area; use the deck object's GetArea method; assign the method's return value to the intSqFt variable
6. calculate the cost of the deck by multiplying the required number of square feet of material (intSqFt) by the price per square foot of material (dblSqFtPrice); assign the result to the dblCost variable
7. display the required number of square feet of material (intSqFt) and the cost of the deck (dblCost) in lblSqFt and lblCost

Figure 10-10 Franklin Decks interface and pseudocode

To use the Rectangle class in the Franklin Decks application:

START HERE

1. Click the **Main Form.vb [Design]** tab. Open the Code Editor window and locate the btnCalc_Click procedure.

2. The first step in the pseudocode declares a Rectangle variable named **deck**. It also instantiates a Rectangle object and then stores the object (which represents the deck) in the Rectangle variable. Click the **blank line** below the `' Instantiate a Rectangle object.` comment. Type the following Dim statement and then press **Enter**:

   ```
   Dim deck As New Rectangle
   ```

3. Next, the procedure will declare variables to store the price of a square foot of material, the number of square feet needed, and the cost of the deck. Click the **blank line** below the `' Declare variables.` comment and then enter the following three Dim statements:

   ```
   Dim dblSqFtPrice As Double
   Dim intSqFt As Integer
   Dim dblCost As Double
   ```

4. The third step in the pseudocode converts the values selected in the lstLength and lstWidth controls to Integer and then stores the results in the deck object's Length and Width properties, respectively. The fourth step converts the value selected in the lstPrice control to Double and stores the result in the dblSqFtPrice variable. Click the **blank line** below the ' Assign length and width to the object's Public properties. comment and then enter the first two TryParse methods shown in Figure 10-11. Notice that when you press the period after typing deck, the deck object's Length and Width properties appear in the IntelliSense list. Then, click the **blank line** below the ' Assign price to variable. comment and enter the last TryParse method shown in the figure.

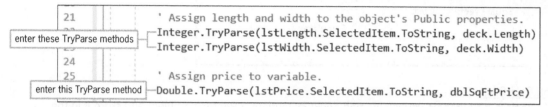

```
21              ' Assign length and width to the object's Public properties.
                Integer.TryParse(lstLength.SelectedItem.ToString, deck.Length)
                Integer.TryParse(lstWidth.SelectedItem.ToString, deck.Width)
24
25              ' Assign price to variable.
                Double.TryParse(lstPrice.SelectedItem.ToString, dblSqFtPrice)
```

enter these TryParse methods

enter this TryParse method

Figure 10-11   TryParse methods entered in the procedure

5. The fifth step in the pseudocode uses the deck object's GetArea method to calculate the required number of square feet of material. It assigns the method's return value to the intSqFt variable. Click the **blank line** below the ' Calculate area in square feet. comment and then enter the following assignment statement. Here again, notice that when you press the period after typing deck, the deck object's GetArea method appears in the IntelliSense list.

intSqFt = deck.GetArea

6. The sixth step in the pseudocode calculates the cost of the deck by multiplying the number of square feet by the price per square foot. Click the **blank line** below the ' Calculate cost of deck. comment and then enter the following assignment statement:

dblCost = intSqFt * dblSqFtPrice

7. The last step in the pseudocode displays the required number of square feet and the cost of the deck. The code for this step has already been entered for you.

8. Save the solution.

Figure 10-12 shows the Rectangle class definition entered in the Rectangle.vb file. It also shows the btnCalc_Click procedure entered in the Main Form.vb file.

```
Class statement entered in the Rectangle.vb file
1 ' Name:          Rectangle.vb
2 ' Programmer:    <your name> on <current date>
3
4 Option Explicit On
5 Option Strict On
6 Option Infer Off
7
```

Figure 10-12   Rectangle class definition and btnCalc_Click procedure (*continues*)

(continued)

```
 8 Public Class Rectangle
 9     Private intLength As Integer
10     Private intWidth As Integer
11
12     Public Property Length As Integer
13         Get
14             Return intLength
15         End Get
16         Set(value As Integer)
17             If value > 0 Then
18                 intLength = value
19             Else
20                 intLength = 0
21             End If
22         End Set
23     End Property
24
25     Public Property Width As Integer
26         Get
27             Return intWidth
28         End Get
29         Set(value As Integer)
30             If value > 0 Then
31                 intWidth = value
32             Else
33                 intWidth = 0
34             End If
35         End Set
36     End Property
37
38     Public Sub New()
39         intLength = 0
40         intWidth = 0
41     End Sub
42
43     Public Function GetArea() As Integer
44         Return intLength * intWidth
45     End Function
46 End Class
```

btnCalc_Click procedure entered in the Main Form.vb file
```
10 Private Sub btnCalc_Click(sender As Object, e As EventArgs) Handles
   btnCalc.Click
11     ' Displays square feet and deck cost.
12
13     ' Instantiate a Rectangle object.
14     Dim deck As New Rectangle          ┌─ instantiates a Rectangle object and initializes
15                                        └─ it using the default constructor
16     ' Declare variables.
17     Dim dblSqFtPrice As Double
18     Dim intSqFt As Integer
19     Dim dblCost As Double
```

Figure 10-12 Rectangle class definition and btnCalc_Click procedure *(continues)*

(continued)

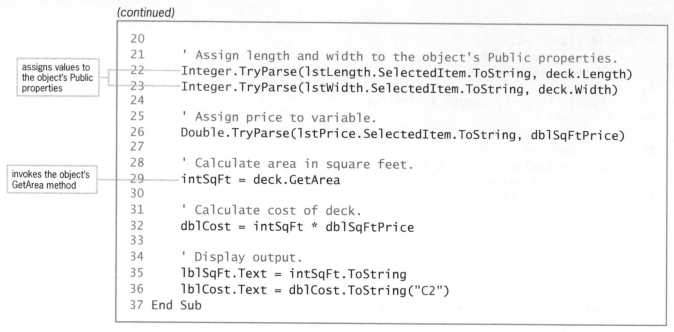

assigns values to the object's Public properties

invokes the object's GetArea method

```
20
21      ' Assign length and width to the object's Public properties.
22      Integer.TryParse(lstLength.SelectedItem.ToString, deck.Length)
23      Integer.TryParse(lstWidth.SelectedItem.ToString, deck.Width)
24
25      ' Assign price to variable.
26      Double.TryParse(lstPrice.SelectedItem.ToString, dblSqFtPrice)
27
28      ' Calculate area in square feet.
29      intSqFt = deck.GetArea
30
31      ' Calculate cost of deck.
32      dblCost = intSqFt * dblSqFtPrice
33
34      ' Display output.
35      lblSqFt.Text = intSqFt.ToString
36      lblCost.Text = dblCost.ToString("C2")
37 End Sub
```

Figure 10-12 Rectangle class definition and btnCalc_Click procedure

START HERE

To test the Franklin Decks application:

1. Start the application. Click **16** and **14** in the Length (feet) and Width (feet) boxes, respectively. Click **9.50** in the Price (per square foot) box and then click the **Calculate** button. The btnCalc_Click procedure displays both the required number of square feet and the cost of the deck. See Figure 10-13.

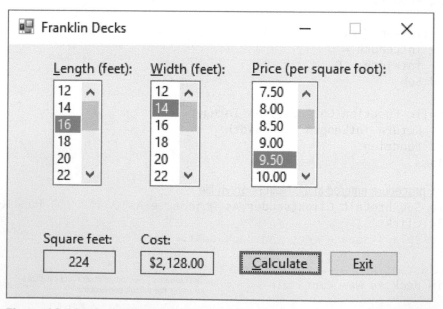

Figure 10-13 Square feet and cost displayed in the interface

2. On your own, test the application using different lengths, widths, and prices. When you are finished, click the **Exit** button. Close the Code Editor and Rectangle.vb windows and then close the solution.

YOU DO IT 1!

Create an application named You Do It 1 and save it in the VB2017\Chap10 folder. Add a text box, a label, and a button to the form. Add a class file named Circle.vb to the project. Define a class named Circle that contains one attribute: the circle's radius. It should also contain a default constructor and a method that calculates and returns the circle's area. Use the following formula to calculate the area: 3.141592 * *radius*^{2}. Open the form's Code Editor window. Code the button's Click event procedure so that it instantiates a Circle object and then uses the radius entered by the user to calculate the object's area. Display the area in the label control. Save the solution and then start and test the application. Close the solution.

F-6 Adding a Parameterized Constructor to a Class

In this section, you will add a parameterized constructor to the Rectangle class. You will then modify the Franklin Decks application to use the parameterized constructor rather than the default constructor. Recall that a parameterized constructor is simply a constructor that has parameters.

To modify the Rectangle class: START HERE

1. Use Windows to make a copy of the Franklin Solution folder. Rename the copy **Franklin Solution-Parameterized**. Open the Franklin Solution.sln file contained in the Franklin Solution-Parameterized folder, and then open the designer window.

2. Right-click **Rectangle.vb** in the Solution Explorer window and then click **View Code**.

3. Click the **blank line** below the default constructor's End Sub clause and then press **Enter**. Enter the parameterized constructor shown in Figure 10-14 and then insert a **blank line** below its End Sub clause.

4. Save the solution and then close the Rectangle.vb window.

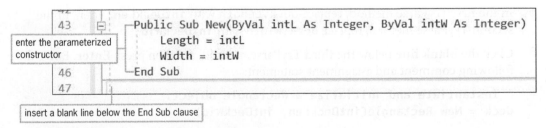

```
43    ⊟   ┌Public Sub New(ByVal intL As Integer, ByVal intW As Integer)
              │   Length = intL
              │   Width = intW
46            └End Sub
47
```

enter the parameterized constructor

insert a blank line below the End Sub clause

Figure 10-14 Parameterized constructor entered in the class

Figure 10-15 shows the Rectangle class's default and parameterized constructors. Unlike the default constructor, which automatically initializes the Private variables to 0 when a Rectangle object is created, the parameterized constructor allows an application to specify the object's initial values. In this case, the initial values must have the Integer data type because the constructor's parameterList contains two Integer variables. You include the initial values, enclosed in a set of parentheses, in the statement that instantiates the object. In other words, you include them in the statement that contains the New keyword, such as the `Dim deck As New Rectangle(16, 14)` statement or the `deck = New Rectangle(intDeckLen, intDeckWid)` statement.

```
Default constructor
Public Sub New()
    intLength = 0 ─┐      ┌─────────────────────────┐
    intWidth = 0 ──┴──────│ accesses the Private     │
                          │ variables directly       │
End Sub                   └─────────────────────────┘
                          ┌──────────────────────────────────┐
                          │ these values come from the application │
                          │ that instantiates a Rectangle object   │
Parameterized constructor └──────────────────────────────────┘
Public Sub New(ByVal intL As Integer, ByVal intW As Integer)
    Length = intL ─┐      ┌────────────────────────────┐
    Width = intW ──┴──────│ uses the Public properties to │
                          │ access the Private variables   │
End Sub                   └────────────────────────────┘
```

Figure 10-15   Default and parameterized constructors

START HERE

To use the parameterized constructor in the btnCalc_Click procedure:

1. Open the form's Code Editor window and locate the btnCalc_Click procedure. Replace the word `Instantiate` in the second comment with the words **Declare a variable for**.

2. Delete the New keyword from the first Dim statement. The statement should now say `Dim deck As Rectangle`.

3. Click the **blank line** below the last Dim statement and then enter the following two declaration statements:

    Dim intDeckLen As Integer
    Dim intDeckWid As Integer

4. In the comment above the first TryParse method, replace the words `the object's Public properties` with the word **variables**.

5. In the first TryParse method, replace `deck.Length` with **intDeckLen**. Then, in the second TryParse method, replace `deck.Width` with **intDeckWid**.

6. Click the **blank line** below the third TryParse method and then press **Enter**. Enter the following comment and assignment statement:

    ' Instantiate and initialize a Rectangle object.
    deck = New Rectangle(intDeckLen, intDeckWid)

7. Save the solution.

The modifications made to the class's behaviors section and to the btnCalc_Click procedure are shaded in Figure 10-16. (The original code is shown earlier in Figure 10-12.)

Partial Rectangle class entered in the Rectangle.vb file

```vb
 8 Public Class Rectangle
 9     Private intLength As Integer
10     Private intWidth As Integer
11
12     Public Property Length As Integer
13         Get
14             Return intLength
15         End Get
16         Set(value As Integer)
17             If value > 0 Then
18                 intLength = value
19             Else
20                 intLength = 0
21             End If
22         End Set
23     End Property
24
25     Public Property Width As Integer
26         Get
27             Return intWidth
28         End Get
29         Set(value As Integer)
30             If value > 0 Then
31                 intWidth = value
32             Else
33                 intWidth = 0
34             End If
35         End Set
36     End Property
37
38     Public Sub New()
39         intLength = 0
40         intWidth = 0
41     End Sub
42
43     Public Sub New(ByVal intL As Integer, ByVal intW As Integer) ─┐
44         Length = intL                                              │ parameterized
45         Width = intW                                               │ constructor
46     End Sub ──────────────────────────────────────────────────────┘
46
48     Public Function GetArea() As Integer
49         Return intLength * intWidth
50     End Function
51 End Class
```

Figure 10-16   Modified class and procedure (continues)

(continued)

btnCalc_Click procedure entered in the Main Form.vb file

```
10 Private Sub btnCalc_Click(sender As Object, e As EventArgs) Handles
   btnCalc.Click
11     ' Displays square feet and deck cost.
12
13     ' Declare a variable for a Rectangle object.
14     Dim deck As Rectangle
15
16     ' Declare variables.
17     Dim dblSqFtPrice As Double
18     Dim intSqFt As Integer
19     Dim dblCost As Double
20     Dim intDeckLen As Integer
21     Dim intDeckWid As Integer
22
23     ' Assign length and width to variables.
24     Integer.TryParse(lstLength.SelectedItem.ToString, intDeckLen)
25     Integer.TryParse(lstWidth.SelectedItem.ToString, intDeckWid)
26
27     ' Assign price to variable.
28     Double.TryParse(lstPrice.SelectedItem.ToString, dblSqFtPrice)
29
30     ' Instantiate and initialize a Rectangle object.
31     deck = New Rectangle(intDeckLen, intDeckWid)
32
33     ' Calculate area in square feet.
34     intSqFt = deck.GetArea
35
36     ' Calculate cost of deck.
37     dblCost = intSqFt * dblSqFtPrice
38
39     ' Display output.
40     lblSqFt.Text = intSqFt.ToString
41     lblCost.Text = dblCost.ToString("C2")
42 End Sub
```

declares a variable that can store a Rectangle object → (line 14)

instantiates a Rectangle object and initializes it using the parameterized constructor → (line 31)

Figure 10-16 Modified class and procedure

When the user clicks the Calculate button, the `Dim deck As Rectangle` instruction creates a variable that can store a Rectangle object, but it does not create the object. The remaining Dim statements create and initialize five variables. The TryParse methods assign the input values to the `intDeckLen`, `intDeckWid`, and `dblSqFtPrice` variables.

The next statement in the procedure, `deck = New Rectangle(intDeckLen, intDeckWid)`, instantiates a Rectangle object named `deck`. The two Integer arguments in the statement tell the computer to use the parameterized constructor to initialize the object's Private variables. The computer passes the two arguments (*by value*) to the constructor, which stores them in its `intL` and `intW` parameters. The assignment statements in the constructor then assign the parameter values to the object's Public Length and Width properties.

When you assign a value to a property, the computer passes the value to the property's Set statement, where it is stored in the Set statement's `value` parameter. In this case, the selection structure in the Length property's Set statement compares the value stored in the `value` parameter with the number 0. If the value is greater than 0, the selection structure's true path assigns the value to the Private `intLength` variable; otherwise, its false path assigns the number 0 to the variable. The selection structure in the Width property's Set statement works the same way, except it assigns the appropriate number to the Private `intWidth` variable.

Notice that a parameterized constructor uses the class's Public properties to access the Private variables indirectly. This is because the values passed to a parameterized constructor come from the application rather than from the class itself. As mentioned earlier, values that originate outside of the class should always be assigned to the Private variables indirectly through the Public properties. Doing this ensures that the Property procedure's Set block, which typically contains validation code, is processed.

After the Rectangle object is instantiated and its Private variables are initialized, the btnCalc_Click procedure uses the object's GetArea method to calculate and return the area of the deck. The area represents the required number of square feet of building material. Finally, the procedure calculates the cost of the deck and then displays both the required number of square feet and the cost.

To test the modified application:

START HERE

1. Start the application. Click **16** and **14** in the Length (feet) and Width (feet) boxes, respectively. Click **9.50** in the Price (per square foot) box and then click the **Calculate** button. The btnCalc_Click procedure displays both the required number of square feet (224) and the cost of the deck ($2,128.00), as shown earlier in Figure 10-13.

2. On your own, test the application using different lengths, widths, and prices. When you are finished, click the **Exit** button. Close the Code Editor window and then close the solution.

YOU DO IT 2!

Create an application named You Do It 2 and save it in the VB2017\Chap10 folder. Add a text box, a label, and a button to the form. Add a class file named Circle.vb to the project. Define a class named Circle that contains one attribute: the circle's radius. It should also contain a default constructor, a parameterized constructor, and a method that calculates and returns the circle's area. Use the following formula to calculate the area: $3.141592 * radius^2$. Open the form's Code Editor window. Code the button's Click event procedure so that it instantiates a Circle object, using the radius entered by the user to initialize the object's radius. The procedure should calculate the object's area and then display the area in the label control. Save the solution and then start and test the application. Close the solution.

F-7 Reusing a Class

A good class is one that can be used in a variety of ways in many different applications. In this section, you will use the Rectangle class that you created for the Franklin Decks application in the Pete's Pizzeria application. In this case, the Rectangle object will represent a square pizza rather than a rectangular deck. (A square is simply a rectangle that has four equal sides.) The application will calculate the number of square pizza slices that can be cut from the entire pizza.

To add the Rectangle.vb file to the Pete's Pizzeria application:

1. Use Windows to copy the Rectangle.vb file from the Franklin Solution-Parameterized\ Franklin Project folder to the VB2017\Chap10\Pizzeria Solution\Pizzeria Project folder. (If you did not complete the modified Franklin Decks application from the previous section, you can copy the Rectangle.vb file contained in the VB2017\Chap10 folder.)

2. Open the Pizzeria Solution.sln file contained in the Pizzeria Solution folder and then open the designer window. The interface provides text boxes for entering the side measurements of both the entire pizza and a pizza slice. The application will use these measurements to calculate the number of pizza slices.

3. Click **Project** on the menu bar and then click **Add Existing Item**. Open the Pizzeria Project folder (if necessary) and then click **Rectangle.vb** in the list of filenames. Click the **Add** button. Temporarily display the Solution Explorer window (if necessary) to verify that the Rectangle.vb file was added to the project.

Figure 10-17 shows the pseudocode for the Calculate button's Click event procedure.

btnCalc Click
1. declare Rectangle variables named entirePizza and pizzaSlice
2. declare intEntireSide, intSliceSide, intEntireArea, intSliceArea, and dblSlices variables to store the side measurement of the entire pizza, the side measurement of a pizza slice, the area of the entire pizza, the area of a pizza slice, and the number of slices
3. convert the side measurement of entire pizza to Integer and store it in the intEntireSide variable
4. convert the side measurement of a pizza slice to Integer and store it in the intSliceSide variable
5. if the side measurements of the entire pizza (intEntireSide) and a pizza slice (intSliceSide) are greater than 0

    instantiate a Rectangle object and store it in the entirePizza variable; use the value in the intEntireSide variable as the object's length and width parameters

    instantiate a Rectangle object and store it in the pizzaSlice variable; use the value in the intSliceSide variable as the object's length and width parameters

    use the entirePizza object's GetArea method to calculate the area of the entire pizza; assign the method's return value to the intEntireArea variable

    use the pizzaSlice object's GetArea method to calculate the area of a pizza slice; assign the method's return value to the intSliceArea variable

    calculate the number of pizza slices by dividing the area of the entire pizza by the area of a pizza slice; assign the result to the dblSlices variable

    end if
6. display the number of pizza slices (dblSlices) in lblSlices

Figure 10-17 Pseudocode for the btnCalc_Click procedure

START HERE

To code the btnCalc_Click procedure:

1. Open the form's Code Editor window and locate the btnCalc_Click procedure. The first step in the pseudocode declares two Rectangle variables named `entirePizza` and `pizzaSlice`. The variables will store objects that represent the entire pizza and a pizza slice, both of which are squares. Click the **blank line** below the ' Declare variables. comment and then enter the following two Dim statements:

   ```
   Dim entirePizza As Rectangle
   Dim pizzaSlice As Rectangle
   ```

2. Next, the procedure will declare variables to store the side measurement of the entire pizza, the side measurement of a pizza slice, the area of the entire pizza, the area of a pizza slice, and the number of slices. Enter the following five Dim statements. Press **Enter** twice after typing the last Dim statement.

   ```
   Dim intEntireSide As Integer
   Dim intSliceSide As Integer
   Dim intEntireArea As Integer
   Dim intSliceArea As Integer
   Dim dblSlices As Double
   ```

3. The third step in the pseudocode converts the side measurement of the entire pizza to Integer and then stores the result in the `intEntireSide` variable. Similarly, the fourth step converts the side measurement of a pizza slice to Integer and stores the result in the `intSliceSide` variable. Enter the following two TryParse methods:

   ```
   Integer.TryParse(txtEntireSide.Text, intEntireSide)
   Integer.TryParse(txtSliceSide.Text, intSliceSide)
   ```

4. The fifth step in the pseudocode is a selection structure that determines whether the side measurements entered by the user are greater than 0. Enter the following If clause:

   ```
   If intEntireSide > 0 AndAlso intSliceSide > 0 Then
   ```

5. If both side measurements are greater than 0, the selection structure's true path performs five tasks. The first two tasks instantiate and initialize two Rectangle objects and store the objects in the `entirePizza` and `pizzaSlice` variables. Each object's length and width attributes are initialized using the side measurements entered by the user. Enter the comment and assignment statements indicated in Figure 10-18.

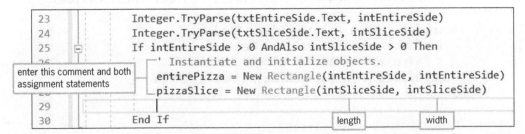

Figure 10-18 Comment and assignment statements entered in the btnCalc_Click procedure

6. The next two tasks in the true path use each object's GetArea method to calculate the object's area. The values returned by the entirePizza.GetArea and pizzaSlice.GetArea methods are assigned to the `intEntireArea` and `intSliceArea` variables, respectively.

Enter the following comment and assignment statements. Notice that when you press the period after typing either entirePizza or pizzaSlice, the object's GetArea method appears in the IntelliSense list.

```
' Calculate areas.
intEntireArea = entirePizza.GetArea
intSliceArea = pizzaSlice.GetArea
```

7. The last task in the true path calculates the number of pizza slices by dividing the area of the entire pizza by the area of a pizza slice. Enter the following comment and assignment statement:

```
' Calculate number of slices.
dblSlices = intEntireArea / intSliceArea
```

8. If necessary, delete the **blank line** above the End If clause.

9. The last step in the pseudocode displays the number of pizza slices. The code for this step has already been entered for you. Save the solution.

The btnCalc_Click procedure is shown in Figure 10-19.

```
11 Private Sub btnCalc_Click(sender As Object, e As EventArgs) Handles
   btnCalc.Click
12      ' Displays the number of square pizza slices.
13
14      ' Declare variables.
15      Dim entirePizza As Rectangle
16      Dim pizzaSlice As Rectangle
17      Dim intEntireSide As Integer
18      Dim intSliceSide As Integer
19      Dim intEntireArea As Integer
20      Dim intSliceArea As Integer
21      Dim dblSlices As Double
22
23      Integer.TryParse(txtEntireSide.Text, intEntireSide)
24      Integer.TryParse(txtSliceSide.Text, intSliceSide)
25      If intEntireSide > 0 AndAlso intSliceSide > 0 Then
26          ' Instantiate and initialize objects.
27          entirePizza = New Rectangle(intEntireSide, intEntireSide)
28          pizzaSlice = New Rectangle(intSliceSide, intSliceSide)
29          ' Calculate areas.
30          intEntireArea = entirePizza.GetArea
31          intSliceArea = pizzaSlice.GetArea
32          ' Calculate number of slices.
33          dblSlices = intEntireArea / intSliceArea
34      End If
35
36      ' Display number of slices.
37      lblSlices.Text = dblSlices.ToString("N1")
38 End Sub
```

instantiates two Rectangle objects and uses the parameterized constructor to initialize the object's length and width measurements

invokes each object's GetArea method

Figure 10-19 Completed btnCalc_Click procedure

To test the application's code:

1. Start the application. First, determine the number of 4-inch slices that can be cut from a 12-inch pizza. Type **12** in the Entire square pizza box and then type **4** in the Square pizza slice box. Click the **Calculate** button. As Figure 10-20 indicates, the pizza can be cut into nine slices.

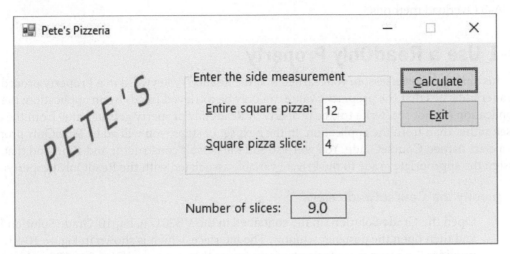

Figure 10-20 Number of pizza slices shown in the interface

2. On your own, test the application using different side measurements. When you are finished, click the **Exit** button. Close the Code Editor window and then close the solution.

APPLY THE CONCEPTS LESSON

After studying this lesson, you should be able to:

- A-1 Use a ReadOnly property
- A-2 Create auto-implemented properties
- A-3 Overload methods

A-1 Use a ReadOnly Property

In this chapter's Focus lesson, you learned that the `ReadOnly` keyword in a Property procedure's header indicates that the property's value can only be retrieved (read) by an application; the application cannot set (write to) the property. A ReadOnly property gets its value from the class itself rather than from the application. In the next set of steps, you will add a ReadOnly property to a class named CourseGrade. You will also add the default constructor and a method that will assign the appropriate grade to the Private variable associated with the ReadOnly property.

START HERE ▶   **To modify the CourseGrade class:**

1. Open the Grade Solution.sln file contained in the VB2017\Chap10\Grade Solution folder and then open the designer window. The interface, which is shown in Figure 10-21, provides list boxes for entering two test scores that can range from 0 to 100 points each.

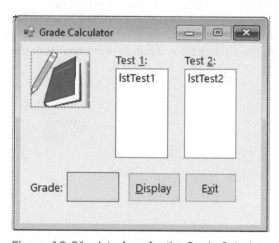

Figure 10-21   Interface for the Grade Calculator application

2. Right-click **CourseGrade.vb** in the Solution Explorer window and then click **View Code**.

3. The CourseGrade class should contain three attributes: two test scores and a letter grade. The Private variable for the letter grade is missing from the code. Click the **blank line** below the `Private intScore2 As Integer` statement and then enter the following Private statement:

   Private strGrade As String

4. Next, you will create a Public property for the Private `strGrade` variable. You will make the property ReadOnly so that the class (rather than the Grade Calculator application) determines the appropriate grade. By making the property ReadOnly, the application will only be able to retrieve the grade; it will not be able to change the grade. Click the **blank line** immediately above the End Class clause and then enter the following Property procedure header and Get clause. When you press Enter after

typing the Get clause, the Code Editor automatically includes the End Get and End Property clauses in the procedure. It does not enter the Set block of code because the header contains the ReadOnly keyword.

```
Public ReadOnly Property Grade As String
    Get
```

5. Type the following Return statement in the blank line below the Get clause, but don't press Enter:

```
Return strGrade
```

6. Next, you will enter the default constructor in the class. The default constructor will initialize the Private variables when a CourseGrade object is instantiated. Insert two **blank lines** above the End Class clause and then enter the following default constructor:

```
Public Sub New()
    intScore1 = 0
    intScore2 = 0
    strGrade = String.Empty
End Sub
```

7. Finally, you will enter the DetermineGrade method, which will assign the appropriate letter grade to the strGrade variable. The method will be a Sub procedure because it will not need to return a value to the application that invokes it. Insert two **blank lines** above the End Class clause and then enter the code shown in Figure 10-22.

```
43    Public Sub DetermineGrade()
44        Select Case intScore1 + intScore2
45            Case Is >= 180
46                strGrade = "A"
47            Case Is >= 160
48                strGrade = "B"
49            Case Is >= 140
50                strGrade = "C"      ← enter these lines of code
51            Case Is >= 120
52                strGrade = "D"
53            Case Else
54                strGrade = "F"
55        End Select
56    End Sub
```

Figure 10-22   DetermineGrade method

8. Save the solution.

Now that you have finished defining the class, you can use the class to instantiate a CourseGrade object in the Grade Calculator application, which displays a grade based on two test scores entered by the user.

To complete the Grade Calculator application:

START HERE

1. Click the **Main Form.vb [Design]** tab. Open the form's Code Editor window and locate the btnDisplay_Click procedure. First, the procedure will instantiate a CourseGrade object. Click the **blank line** above the second comment. Type the following Dim statement and then press **Enter**:

```
Dim studentGrade As New CourseGrade
```

2. Now the procedure will assign the test scores selected in the list boxes to the object's properties. Click the **blank line** below the second comment and then enter the TryParse methods shown in Figure 10-23.

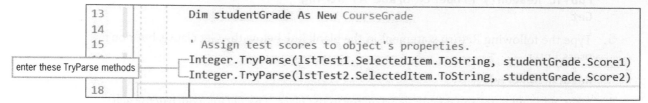

```
13          Dim studentGrade As New CourseGrade
14
15          ' Assign test scores to object's properties.
            Integer.TryParse(lstTest1.SelectedItem.ToString, studentGrade.Score1)
            Integer.TryParse(lstTest2.SelectedItem.ToString, studentGrade.Score2)
18
```

enter these TryParse methods

Figure 10-23   TryParse methods entered in the btnDisplay_Click procedure

3. Next, the procedure will use the object's DetermineGrade method to determine the appropriate grade. Click the **blank line** below the third comment and then enter the following statement:

studentGrade.DetermineGrade()

4. Finally, the procedure will display the grade stored in the object's ReadOnly Grade property. Click the **blank line** above the End Sub clause. Type the following code (including the period at the end), but don't press Enter:

lblGrade.Text = studentGrade.

5. Click **Grade** in the IntelliSense list. See Figure 10-24. The message that appears next to the IntelliSense list indicates that the Grade property is ReadOnly.

```
22              ' Display grade stored in object's ReadOnly property.
23              lblGrade.Text = studentGrade.
24          End Sub                         ⊕ DetermineGrade
25                                          ⊕ Equals
26          Private Sub frmMain_Load(sender A ⊕ GetHashCode    EventArgs) Handles Me.Load
27              ' Fills the list boxes with v ⊕ GetType        ts default values
28                                          🔧 Grade          ReadOnly Property CourseGrade.Grade As String
29              For intScore As Integer = 0 T 🔧 Score1
30                  lstTest1.Items.Add(intSco 🔧 Score2         the message indicates that the
31                  lstTest2.Items.Add(intSco ⊕ ToString       Grade property is ReadOnly
                                             🔧 ⊕
```

Figure 10-24   ReadOnly property message

6. Press **Tab** to include the Grade property in the assignment statement and then save the solution.

Figure 10-25 shows the CourseGrade class definition and the btnDisplay_Click procedure.

```
Class statement entered in the CourseGrade.vb file
1 ' Name:          CourseGrade.vb
2 ' Programmer:    <your name> on <current date>
3
4 Option Explicit On
5 Option Strict On
6 Option Infer Off
```

Figure 10-25   CourseGrade class definition and btnDisplay_Click procedure *(continues)*

(continued)

```
7
8 Public Class CourseGrade
9      Private intScore1 As Integer
10     Private intScore2 As Integer
11     Private strGrade As String
12
13     Public Property Score1 As Integer
14         Get
15             Return intScore1
16         End Get
17         Set(value As Integer)
18             intScore1 = value
19         End Set
20     End Property
21
22     Public Property Score2 As Integer
23         Get
24             Return intScore2
25         End Get
26         Set(value As Integer)
27             intScore2 = value
28         End Set
29     End Property
30
31     Public ReadOnly Property Grade As String
32         Get
33             Return strGrade
34         End Get
35     End Property
36
37     Public Sub New()
38         intScore1 = 0
39         intScore2 = 0
40         strGrade = String.Empty
41     End Sub
42
43     Public Sub DetermineGrade()
44         Select Case intScore1 + intScore2
45             Case Is >= 180
46                 strGrade = "A"
47             Case Is >= 160
48                 strGrade = "B"
49             Case Is >= 140
50                 strGrade = "C"
51             Case Is >= 120
52                 strGrade = "D"
53             Case Else
54                 strGrade = "F"
55         End Select
56     End Sub
57 End Class
```

Figure 10-25 CourseGrade class definition and btnDisplay_Click procedure *(continues)*

(continued)

```
btnDisplay_Click procedure entered in the Main Form.vb file
10 Private Sub btnDisplay_Click(sender As Object, e As EventArgs)
   Handles btnDisplay.Click
11      ' Calculates and displays a letter grade.
12
13      Dim studentGrade As New CourseGrade
14
15      ' Assign test scores to object's properties.
16      Integer.TryParse(lstTest1.SelectedItem.ToString, studentGrade.Score1)
17      Integer.TryParse(lstTest2.SelectedItem.ToString, studentGrade.Score2)
18
19      ' Calculate grade using object's DetermineGrade method.
20      studentGrade.DetermineGrade()      invokes the object's DetermineGrade method
21
22      ' Display grade stored in object's ReadOnly property.
23      lblGrade.Text = studentGrade.Grade      refers to the object's ReadOnly Grade property
24 End Sub
```

Figure 10-25 CourseGrade class definition and btnDisplay_Click procedure

START HERE

To test the Grade Calculator application:

1. Start the application. Click **72** and **88** in the Test 1 and Test 2 boxes, respectively, and then click the **Display** button. The letter B appears in the Grade box, as shown in Figure 10-26.

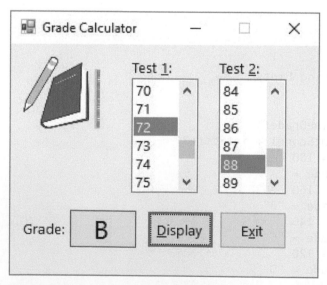

Figure 10-26 Grade shown in the interface

2. On your own, test the application using different test scores. When you are finished, click the **Exit** button. Close the Code Editor and CourseGrade.vb windows and then close the solution.

A-2 Create Auto-Implemented Properties

The **auto-implemented properties** feature in Visual Basic enables you to specify the property of a class in one line of code, as shown in Figure 10-27. When you enter the line of code in the Code Editor window, Visual Basic automatically creates a hidden Private variable that it associates with the property. It also automatically creates hidden Get and Set blocks. The Private variable's name will be the same as the property's name, but it will be preceded by an underscore. For example, if you create an auto-implemented property named City, Visual Basic will create a hidden Private variable named _City. Although the auto-implemented properties feature provides a shorter syntax for you to use when creating a class, keep in mind that you will need to use the standard syntax if you want to add validation code to the Set block, or if you want the property to be either ReadOnly or WriteOnly.

Auto-Implemented Property

Syntax
Public Property propertyName **As** dataType

Example 1
```
Public Property City As Integer
```
creates a Public property named City, a hidden Private variable
named _City, and hidden Get and Set blocks

Example 2
```
Public Property Sales As Integer
```
creates a Public property named Sales, a hidden Private variable
named _Sales, and hidden Get and Set blocks

Figure 10-27   Syntax and examples of creating an auto-implemented property

You can use the auto-implemented properties feature to create the Score1 and Score2 properties in the CourseGrade class from the previous section. This is because neither of those properties is either ReadOnly or WriteOnly, and neither contains any validation code in its Set block. You cannot use the auto-implemented properties feature for the class's Grade property because that property is ReadOnly.

To use the auto-implemented properties feature in the CourseGrade class: `START HERE`

1. Use Windows to make a copy of the Grade Solution folder. Rename the copy Grade Solution-Auto. Open the Grade Solution.sln file contained in the Grade Solution-Auto folder. Open the designer window.

2. Right-click **CourseGrade.vb** in the Solution Explorer window and then click **View Code**. Replace the first two Private declaration statements with the following statements:

   ```
   Public Property Score1 As Integer
   Public Property Score2 As Integer
   ```

3. Next, delete the Score1 and Score2 Property procedures. (Do not delete the Grade property procedure.)

4. Recall that the name of the Private variable associated with an auto-implemented property is the property's name preceded by an underscore. In both the default constructor and the DetermineGrade method, change intScore1 and intScore2 to **_Score1** and **_Score2**, respectively.

Figure 10-28 shows the modified class definition. The code pertaining to the two auto-implemented properties (Score1 and Score2) is shaded in the figure.

```
 8 Public Class CourseGrade
 9     Public Property Score1 As Integer ──┐
10     Public Property Score2 As Integer ──┤ ─── auto-implemented properties
11     Private strGrade As String
12
13     Public ReadOnly Property Grade As String ── a ReadOnly property cannot be
14         Get                                      an auto-implemented property
15             Return strGrade
16         End Get
17     End Property
18
19     Public Sub New()
20         _Score1 = 0
21         _Score2 = 0
22         strGrade = String.Empty
23     End Sub
24
25     Public Sub DetermineGrade()
26         Select Case _Score1 + _Score2
27             Case Is >= 180
28                 strGrade = "A"
29             Case Is >= 160
30                 strGrade = "B"
31             Case Is >= 140
32                 strGrade = "C"
33             Case Is >= 120
34                 strGrade = "D"
35             Case Else
36                 strGrade = "F"
36         End Select
38     End Sub
39 End Class
```

Figure 10-28   Modified CourseGrade class definition

START HERE

To test the modified Grade Calculator application:

1. Save the solution and then start the application. Click **95** and **85** in the Test 1 and Test 2 boxes, respectively, and then click the **Display** button. The letter A appears in the Grade box.

2. On your own, test the application using different test scores. When you are finished, click the **Exit** button. Close the CourseGrade.vb window and then close the solution.

YOU DO IT 3!

Create an application named You Do It 3 and save it in the VB2017\Chap10 folder. Add a text box, a label, and a button to the form. Add a class file named Square.vb to the project. The Square class should contain an auto-implemented property that will store the side measurement of a square. It should also contain a default constructor and a method that calculates and returns the square's perimeter. Use the following formula to calculate the perimeter: 4 * *side*. Code the Square class. Next, open the form's Code Editor window. Code the button's Click event procedure so that it instantiates a Square object. The procedure should calculate the square's perimeter, using the side measurement entered by the user, and then display the perimeter in the label control. Save the solution and then start and test the application. Close the solution.

A-3 Overload Methods

In this section, you will use a class named Employee to instantiate an object. Employee objects have the attributes and behaviors listed in Figure 10-29.

Attributes of an Employee object
employee number
employee name

Behaviors of an Employee object
1. An employee object can initialize its attributes using values provided by the class.
2. An employee object can initialize its attributes using values provided by the application in which it is instantiated.
3. An employee object can calculate and return the gross pay for salaried employees, who are paid twice per month. The gross pay is calculated by dividing the salaried employee's annual salary by 24.
4. An employee object can calculate and return the gross pay for hourly employees, who are paid weekly. The gross pay is calculated by multiplying the number of hours the employee worked during the week by his or her pay rate.

Figure 10-29   Attributes and behaviors of an Employee object

Figure 10-30 shows the Employee class defined in the Employee.vb file. The class contains two auto-implemented properties and four methods. The two New methods are the class's default and parameterized constructors. Notice that the default constructor initializes the class's Private variables directly, while the parameterized constructor uses the class's Public properties to initialize the Private variables indirectly. As you learned in this chapter's Focus lesson, using a Public property in this manner ensures that the computer processes any validation code associated with the property. Even though the Number and EmpName properties in Figure 10-30 do not have any validation code, you should use the properties in the parameterized constructor in case validation code is added to the class in the future.

```
 1 ' Name:         Employee.vb
 2 ' Programmer:   <your name> on <current date>
 3
 4 Option Explicit On
 5 Option Strict On
 6 Option Infer Off
 7
 8 Public Class Employee
 9         Public Property Number As String
10         Public Property EmpName As String
11
12         Public Sub New()
13             _Number = String.Empty
14             _EmpName = String.Empty
15         End Sub
16
17         Public Sub New(ByVal strNum As String, ByVal strName As String)
18             Number = strNum
19             EmpName = strName
20         End Sub
21
22         Public Function GetGross(ByVal dblSalary As Double) As Double
23             ' Calculates the gross pay for salaried
24             ' employees, who are paid twice per month.
25
26             Return dblSalary / 24
27         End Function
28
29         Public Function GetGross(ByVal dblHours As Double,
30                                  ByVal dblRate As Double) As Double
31             ' Calculates the weekly gross pay for hourly employees.
32
33             Return dblHours * dblRate
34         End Function
35 End Class
```

auto-implemented properties

overloaded constructors

initializes the Private variables directly

uses the Public properties to initialize the Private variables

overloaded GetGross methods

Figure 10-30   Employee class definition

When two or more methods have the same name but different parameters, the methods are referred to as **overloaded methods**. The two constructors in Figure 10-30 are considered overloaded methods because each is named New and each has a different parameterList. You can overload any of the methods contained in a class, not just constructors. The two GetGross methods in the figure are also overloaded methods because they have the same name but a different parameterList.

In previous chapters, you used several of the overloaded methods built into Visual Basic, such as the ToString, TryParse, and MessageBox.Show methods. When you enter the name of an overloaded method in the Code Editor window, the Code Editor's IntelliSense feature displays a box that allows you to view the method's signatures, one signature at a time. Recall that a method's signature includes its name and an optional parameterList. The box shown in Figure 10-31 displays the first of the MessageBox.Show method's 21 signatures. You use the up and down arrows in the box to display the other signatures. If a class you create contains overloaded methods, the signatures of those methods will also be displayed in the IntelliSense box.

```
MessageBox.Show()
▲ 1 of 21 ▼ MessageBox.Show(text As String) As DialogResult
Displays a message box with specified text.
text: The text to display in the message box.
```

Figure 10-31 First of the MessageBox.Show method's signatures

Overloading is useful when two or more methods require different parameters to perform essentially the same task. Both overloaded constructors in the Employee class, for example, initialize the class's Private variables. However, the default constructor does not need to be passed any information to perform the task, whereas the parameterized constructor requires two items of information (the employee number and name). Similarly, both GetGross methods calculate and return a gross pay amount. However, the first GetGross method performs its task for salaried employees and requires an application to pass it one item of information: the employee's annual salary. The second GetGross method performs its task for hourly employees and requires two items of information: the number of hours the employee worked and his or her rate of pay. Rather than using two overloaded GetGross methods, you could have used two methods having different names, such as GetSalariedGross and GetHourlyGross. An advantage of overloading the GetGross method is that you need to remember the name of only one method.

You will use the Employee class when coding the Woods Manufacturing application, which displays the gross pay for salaried and hourly employees. Salaried employees are paid twice per month. Therefore, each salaried employee's gross pay is calculated by dividing his or her annual salary by 24. Hourly employees are paid weekly. The gross pay for an hourly employee is calculated by multiplying the number of hours the employee worked during the week by his or her hourly pay rate. The application also displays a report showing each employee's number, name, and gross pay. Figure 10-32 shows the pseudocode for the btnCalc_Click procedure in the application.

```
btnCalc Click
1. declare an Employee variable named ourEmployee
2. declare dblAnnualSalary, dblHours, dblHourRate, and dblGross variables to store the annual
   salary, hours worked, hourly pay rate, and gross pay
3. instantiate an Employee object to represent an employee; initialize the object's variables using
   the number and name entered in the text boxes
4. if the Hourly employee radio button is selected
       assign the hours worked and the hourly pay rate to the dblHours and dblHourRate variables
       use the Employee object's GetGross method to calculate the gross pay
   else
       assign the annual salary to the dblAnnualSalary variable
       use the Employee object's GetGross method to calculate the gross pay
   end if
5. display the gross pay and the report
6. send the focus to the txtNum control
```

Figure 10-32 Pseudocode for the btnCalc_Click procedure

START HERE **To code the Woods Manufacturing application:**

1. Open the Woods Solution.sln file contained in the VB2017\Chap10\Woods Solution folder. If necessary, open the designer window. See Figure 10-33.

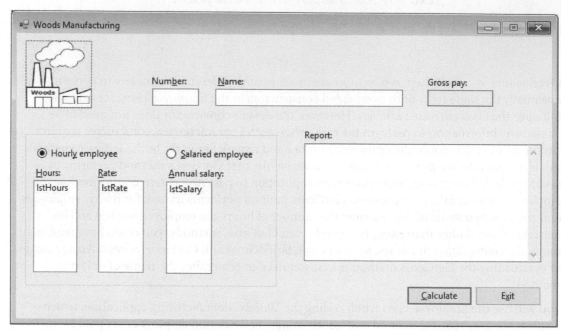

Figure 10-33 Interface for the Woods Manufacturing application

2. Right-click **Employee.vb** in the Solution Explorer window and then click **View Code**. The class definition from Figure 10-30 appears in the Employee.vb window. Close the Employee.vb window.

3. Open the form's Code Editor window and locate the btnCalc_Click procedure. First, the procedure will declare the necessary variables. Click the **blank line** below the `' Declare variables.` comment and then enter the following five Dim statements:

```
Dim ourEmployee As Employee
Dim dblAnnualSalary As Double
Dim dblHours As Double
Dim dblHourRate As Double
Dim dblGross As Double
```

4. Next, the procedure will instantiate an Employee object, using the text box values to initialize the object's variables. Click the **blank line** below the `' Instantiate and initialize an Employee object.` comment and then enter the assignment statement shown in Figure 10-34.

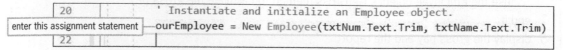

```
20          ' Instantiate and initialize an Employee object.
enter this assignment statement    ourEmployee = New Employee(txtNum.Text.Trim, txtName.Text.Trim)
22
```

Figure 10-34 Assignment statement entered in the btnCalc_Click procedure

5. The fourth step in the pseudocode is a selection structure that determines the selected radio button and then takes the appropriate action. Click the **blank line** below the ` Determine the selected radio button.` comment and then enter the following If clause:

```
If radHourly.Checked Then
```

6. If the Hourly employee radio button is selected, the selection structure's true path should use the Employee object's GetGross method to calculate the gross pay for an hourly employee. Otherwise, its false path should use the method to calculate the gross pay for a salaried employee. Enter the comments and code indicated in Figure 10-35.

```
23              ' Determine the selected radio button.
24         ⊟    If radHourly.Checked Then
25                  ' Calculate the gross pay for an hourly employee.
26                  Double.TryParse(lstHours.SelectedItem.ToString, dblHours)
27                  Double.TryParse(lstRate.SelectedItem.ToString, dblHourRate)
[enter these comments    dblGross = ourEmployee.GetGross(dblHours, dblHourRate)
and lines of code]  Else
30                  ' Calculate the gross pay for a salaried employee.
31                  Double.TryParse(lstSalary.SelectedItem.ToString, dblAnnualSalary)
32                  dblGross = ourEmployee.GetGross(dblAnnualSalary)
33              End If
```

Figure 10-35   Selection structure's true and false paths entered in the btnCalc_Click procedure

7. Next, the procedure needs to display both the gross pay and the report and then send the focus to the txtNum control. Click the **blank line** above the End Sub clause and then enter the lines of code indicated in Figure 10-36. (You learned about the PadLeft and PadRight methods in Chapter 7.)

```
35              ' Display the gross pay and report.
36              lblGross.Text = dblGross.ToString("C2")
37              txtReport.Text = txtReport.Text & ourEmployee.Number.PadRight(6) &
[enter these lines of code]  ourEmployee.EmpName.PadRight(25) &
39                  dblGross.ToString("N2").PadLeft(9) & ControlChars.NewLine
40              txtNum.Focus()
41          End Sub
```

Figure 10-36   Additional lines of code entered in the procedure

Figure 10-37 shows the completed btnCalc_Click procedure.

```
10 Private Sub btnCalc_Click(sender As Object, e As EventArgs)
   Handles btnCalc.Click
11      ' Displays the gross pay and a report.
12
13      ' Declare variables.
14      Dim ourEmployee As Employee        [declares a variable to store
15      Dim dblAnnualSalary As Double       an Employee object]
16      Dim dblHours As Double
17      Dim dblHourRate As Double
18      Dim dblGross As Double
19
```

Figure 10-37   Completed btnCalc_Click procedure *(continues)*

(continued)

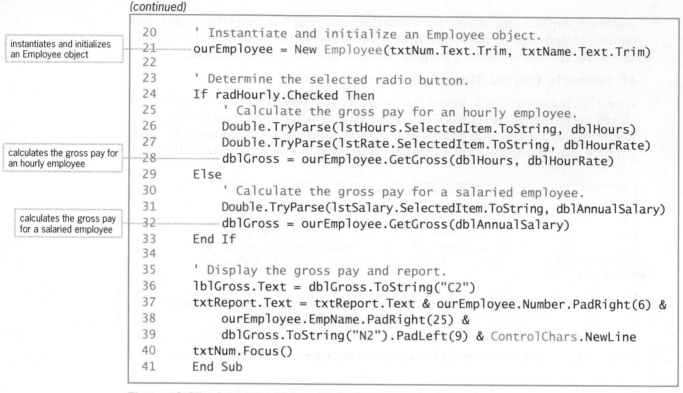

instantiates and initializes an Employee object

calculates the gross pay for an hourly employee

calculates the gross pay for a salaried employee

```
20      ' Instantiate and initialize an Employee object.
21      ourEmployee = New Employee(txtNum.Text.Trim, txtName.Text.Trim)
22
23      ' Determine the selected radio button.
24      If radHourly.Checked Then
25          ' Calculate the gross pay for an hourly employee.
26          Double.TryParse(lstHours.SelectedItem.ToString, dblHours)
27          Double.TryParse(lstRate.SelectedItem.ToString, dblHourRate)
28          dblGross = ourEmployee.GetGross(dblHours, dblHourRate)
29      Else
30          ' Calculate the gross pay for a salaried employee.
31          Double.TryParse(lstSalary.SelectedItem.ToString, dblAnnualSalary)
32          dblGross = ourEmployee.GetGross(dblAnnualSalary)
33      End If
34
35      ' Display the gross pay and report.
36      lblGross.Text = dblGross.ToString("C2")
37      txtReport.Text = txtReport.Text & ourEmployee.Number.PadRight(6) &
38          ourEmployee.EmpName.PadRight(25) &
39          dblGross.ToString("N2").PadLeft(9) & ControlChars.NewLine
40      txtNum.Focus()
41  End Sub
```

Figure 10-37   Completed btnCalc_Click procedure

START HERE

To test the application:

1. Save the solution and then start the application. Type **0487** and **Shaun Jones** in the Number and Name boxes, respectively. Click **14.50** in the Rate box and then click the **Calculate** button. $580.00 appears in the Gross pay box, and Shaun's information appears in the Report box. See Figure 10-38.

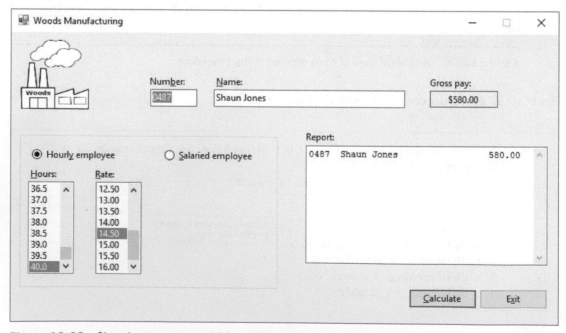

Figure 10-38   Shaun's gross pay and information shown in the interface

2. Type **1245** and **Jackie Kason** in the Number and Name boxes, respectively. Click the **Salaried employee** radio button and then click **31000** in the Annual salary box. Click the **Calculate** button. $1,291.67 appears in the Gross pay box, and Jackie's information appears in the Report box. See Figure 10-39.

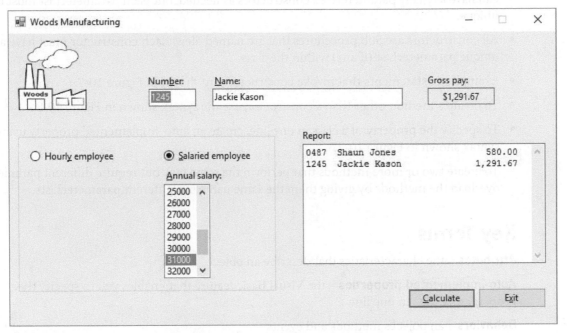

Figure 10-39 Jackie's gross pay and information shown in the interface

3. Click the **Exit** button. Close the Code Editor window and then close the solution.

Summary

- You use the Class statement to create your own classes in Visual Basic. The statement's syntax is shown in Figure 10-1.

- To add a new class file to a project, click Project on the menu bar and then click Add Class. In the Name box, type the name of the class followed by a period and the letters vb, and then click the Add button.

- To instantiate (create) an object from a class, use either of the syntax versions shown in Figure 10-2.

- To create a Property procedure, use the syntax shown in Figure 10-3. The Get block allows an application to retrieve the contents of the Private variable associated with the Property procedure. The Set block allows an application to assign a value to the Private variable associated with the Property procedure.

- To create a property whose value an application can only retrieve, include the ReadOnly keyword in the Property procedure's header.

- To create a property whose value an application can only set, include the WriteOnly keyword in the Property procedure's header.

- To create a constructor, use the syntax shown in Figure 10-6.

- A constructor that has no parameters is called the default constructor. A class can have only one default constructor.

- A constructor that has one or more parameters is called a parameterized constructor. A class can have as many parameterized constructors as needed, but each parameterList must be unique.

- All constructors are Sub procedures that are named New. Each constructor must have a unique parameterList (if any) within the class.

- Examples of statements that invoke constructors are shown in Figure 10-7.

- To create a method other than a constructor, use the syntax shown in Figure 10-8.

- To specify the property of a class in one line, create an auto-implemented property using the syntax shown in Figure 10-27.

- To create two or more methods that perform the same task but require different parameters, overload the methods by giving them the same name but different parameterLists.

Key Terms

Attributes—the characteristics that describe an object

Auto-implemented properties—the Visual Basic feature that enables you to specify the property of a class in one line

Behaviors—an object's methods and events

Class—a pattern that the computer follows when instantiating (creating) an object

Class statement—the statement used to define a class in Visual Basic

Constructor—a method whose instructions are automatically processed each time the class is used to instantiate an object; used to initialize the class's Private variables; always a Sub procedure named New

Default constructor—a constructor that has no parameters; a class can have only one default constructor

Encapsulates—an OOP term that means "contains" in a class

Events—the actions to which an object can respond

Exposed—in OOP, this term refers to the fact that an object's Public members are visible to an application

Get block—the section of a Property procedure that contains the Get statement

Get statement—appears in a Get block in a Property procedure; contains the code that allows an application to retrieve the contents of the Private variable associated with the property

Hidden—in OOP, this term refers to the fact that an object's Private members are not visible to an application

Instance—an object created from a class

Instantiated—the process of creating an object from a class

Member variables—the variables declared in the attributes section of a class

Methods—the actions that an object is capable of performing

Object—anything that can be seen, touched, or used

Object-oriented programming language—a programming language that allows the use of objects in an application's interface and code

OOP—the acronym for object-oriented programming

Overloaded methods—two or more class methods that have the same name but different parameterLists

Parameterized constructor—a constructor that contains one or more parameters

Public property procedure—creates a Public property that an application can use to access a Private variable in a class

ReadOnly keyword—used when defining a Property procedure; indicates that the property's value can only be retrieved (read) by an application

Set block—the section of a Property procedure that contains the Set statement

Set statement—appears in a Set block in a Property procedure; contains the code that allows an application to assign a value to the Private variable associated with the property; may also contain validation code

Signature—a method's name combined with its optional parameterList

WriteOnly keyword—used when defining a Property procedure; indicates that an application can only set (write to) the property's value

Review Questions

1. The name of a class file ends with which of the following filename extensions?

   a. .cla

   b. .cls

   c. .vb

   d. None of the above.

2. A constructor is _____.

   a. a function

   b. a Property procedure

   c. a Sub procedure

   d. either a function or a Sub procedure

3. The Inventory class contains a Private variable named `strId`. The variable is associated with the Public ItemId property. An application instantiates an Inventory object and assigns it to a variable named `onHand`. Which of the following can be used by the application to assign the string "XG45" to the `strId` variable?

   a. `onHand.ItemId = "XG45"`

   b. `ItemId.strId = "XG45"`

   c. `onHand.strId = "XG45"`

   d. `ItemId.strId = "XG45"`

4. The Item class contains a Public method named GetDiscount. The method is a function. An application instantiates an Item object and assigns it to a variable named `cellPhone`. Which of the following can be used by the application to invoke the GetDiscount method?

   a. `dblDiscount = Item.GetDiscount`

   b. `dblDiscount = cellPhone.GetDiscount`

   c. `dblDiscount = GetDiscount.cellPhone`

   d. `cellPhone.GetDiscount`

5. Which of the following statements is false?

    a. A class can contain only one constructor.

    b. An example of a behavior is the SetTime method in a Time class.

    c. An object created from a class is referred to as an instance of the class.

    d. An instance of a class is considered an object.

6. A Private variable in a class can be accessed directly by a Public method in the same class.

    a. True   b. False

7. How can an application access the Private variables in a class?

    a. directly

    b. using properties created by Public Property procedures

    c. through Private procedures contained in the class

    d. None of the above.

8. To hide one of a class's members, you declare the member using which of the following keywords?

    a. `Hide`   c. `Private`

    b. `Invisible`   d. `ReadOnly`

9. Which of the following is the name of the Inventory class's default constructor?

    a. Inventory   c. Default

    b. InventoryConstructor   d. New

10. Which of the following instantiates an Inventory object and assigns it to the `chair` variable?

    a. `Dim chair As Inventory`   c. `Dim chair = New Inventory`

    b. `Dim chair As New Inventory`   d. `Dim New chair As Inventory`

11. If you need to validate a value before assigning it to a Private variable, you enter the validation code in which block in a Property procedure?

    a. Assign   c. Set

    b. Get   d. Validate

12. The Return statement is entered in which statement in a Property procedure?

    a. Get   b. Set

13. A class contains a Private variable named `strState`. The variable is associated with a Public property named State. Which of the following is the best way for a parameterized constructor to assign the value stored in its `strName` parameter to the variable?

    a. `strState = strName`   c. `strState = State.strName`

    b. `State = strState`   d. `State = strName`

14. Two or more methods that have the same name but different parameterLists are referred to as what type of methods?

    a. loaded

    b. overloaded

    c. parallel

    d. signature

15. The method name combined with the method's optional parameterList is called the method's _____.

    a. autograph

    b. inscription

    c. signature

    d. statement

16. A class contains an auto-implemented property named Title. Which of the following is the correct way for the default constructor to assign the string "Unknown" to the variable associated with the property?

    a. `_Title = "Unknown"`

    b. `_Title.strTitle = "Unknown"`

    c. `Title = "Unknown"`

    d. None of the above.

17. A WriteOnly property can be an auto-implemented property.

    a. True

    b. False

18. The Purchase class contains a ReadOnly property named Tax. The property is associated with the Private `dblTax` variable. A button's Click event procedure instantiates a Purchase object and assigns it to the `currentSale` variable. Which of the following is valid in the Click event procedure?

    a. `lblTax.Text = currentSale.Tax.ToString("C2")`

    b. `currentSale.Tax = 15`

    c. `currentSale.Tax = dblPrice * 0.05`

    d. None of the above.

Exercises

1. In this exercise, you modify the Pete's Pizzeria application from this chapter's Focus lesson. Use Windows to make a copy of the Pizzeria Solution folder. Rename the copy Pizzeria Solution-Default. Open the Pizzeria Solution.sln file contained in the Pizzeria Solution-Default folder. Open the Code Editor window and locate the btnCalc_Click procedure. Modify the procedure so it uses the Rectangle class's default constructor (rather than its parameterized constructor) when instantiating the `entirePizza` and `pizzaSlice` objects. Save the solution and then start and test the application.

   INTRODUCTORY

2. Open the Palace Solution.sln file contained in the VB2017\Chap10\Palace Solution folder.

   INTRODUCTORY

   a. Use Windows to copy the Rectangle.vb file from the VB2017\Chap10 folder to the Palace Project folder. Then, use the Add Existing Item option on the Project menu to add the file to the project.

   b. Modify the Rectangle class to use Double variables rather than Integer variables.

   c. Change the name of the GetArea method to GetAreaSqFt.

d. Add another method to the class. Use GetAreaSqYds as the method's name. The method should calculate and return the area of a rectangle in square yards.

e. The application's Calculate button should calculate and display the number of square yards of carpeting needed to carpet a rectangular floor. Code the btnCalc_Click procedure. Display the number of yards with one decimal place. Save the solution and then start and test the application.

INTERMEDIATE

3. In this exercise, you create an application that can be used to estimate the cost of laying sod on a rectangular piece of property. Create a Windows Forms application. Use the following names for the project and solution, respectively: Sod Project and Sod Solution. Save the application in the VB2017\Chap10 folder. Use Windows to copy the Rectangle.vb file from the VB2017\Chap10 folder to the Sod Project folder. Then, use the Project menu to add the file to the project. Create the interface shown in Figure 10-40 and then code the application using the Integer data type for the length and width measurements. Display the total price with a dollar sign and two decimal places. Save the solution and then start and test the application.

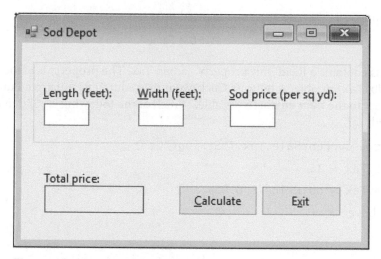

Figure 10-40 Interface for Exercise 3

INTERMEDIATE

4. In this exercise, you create an application that can be used to calculate the cost of installing a fence around a rectangular area. Create a Windows Forms application. Use the following names for the project and solution, respectively: Fence Project and Fence Solution. Save the application in the VB2017\Chap10 folder.

a. Use Windows to copy the Rectangle.vb file from the VB2017\Chap10 folder to the Fence Project folder. Then, use the Project menu to add the file to the project.

b. Modify the Rectangle class to use Double (rather than Integer) variables.

c. Add a method named GetPerimeter to the Rectangle class. The method should calculate and return the perimeter of a rectangle. To calculate the perimeter, the method will need to add together the length and width measurements and then multiply the sum by 2.

d. Create the interface shown in Figure 10-41 and then code the application. Save the solution and then start and test the application.

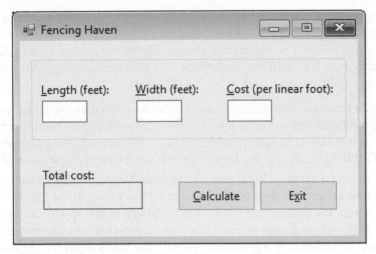

Figure 10-41   Interface for Exercise 4

5. In this exercise, you modify the Grade Calculator application from this chapter's Apply lesson. Use Windows to make a copy of the Grade Solution folder. Rename the copy Grade Solution-Intermediate. Open the Grade Solution.sln file contained in the Grade Solution-Intermediate folder.

   INTERMEDIATE

   a. Open the CourseGrade.vb file. The DetermineGrade method should accept an integer that represents the total number of points that can be earned in the course. (Currently, the total number of points is 200: 100 points per test.) For an A grade, the student must earn at least 90% of the total points. For a B, C, and D grade, the student must earn at least 80%, 70%, and 60%, respectively. If the student earns less than 60% of the total points, the grade is F. Make the appropriate modifications to the DetermineGrade method and then save the solution.

   b. Unlock the controls on the form. Add a label control and a text box to the form. Change the label control's Text property to "&Maximum points:" (without the quotation marks). Change the text box's name to txtMax. Lock the controls and then reset the tab order.

   c. Open the form's Code Editor window. The txtMax control should accept only numbers and the Backspace key. Code the appropriate procedure.

   d. The grade should be cleared when the user makes a change to the contents of the txtMax control. Code the appropriate procedure.

   e. Modify the frmMain_Load procedure so that each list box displays numbers from 0 through 200.

   f. Locate the btnDisplay_Click procedure. If the txtMax control does not contain a value, display an appropriate message. The maximum number allowed in the txtMax control should be 400; if the control contains a number that is more than 400, display an appropriate message. The statement that calculates the grade should pass the maximum number of points to the studentGrade object's DetermineGrade method. Make the necessary modifications to the procedure.

   g. Save the solution and then start and test the application.

ADVANCED

6. Create a Windows Forms application. Use the following names for the project and solution, respectively: Playground Project and Playground Solution. Save the application in the VB2017\Chap10 folder. The application should display the area of a triangular playground in square feet. It should also display the cost of covering the playground with artificial grass.

a. Create a suitable interface. Provide list boxes for the user to enter the playground's base and height dimensions in yards. Both list boxes should display numbers from 20 to 50 in increments of 0.5. Also, provide a list box for entering the price per square foot. This list box should display numbers from 1 to 6 in increments of 0.5.

b. Create a class named Triangle. The Triangle class should verify that the base and height dimensions are greater than 0 before assigning the values to the Private variables. (Although the dimensions come from list boxes in this application, the Triangle class might subsequently be used in an application whose dimensions come from text boxes. Therefore, it is a good idea to verify the user's input.) The class should also include a default constructor, a parameterized constructor, and a method to calculate and return the area of a triangle.

c. Code the application. Save the solution and then start and test the application.

ADVANCED

7. Create a Windows Forms application. Use the following names for the project and solution, respectively: Fire Project and Fire Solution. Save the application in the VB2017\Chap10 folder. The application should display the capacity (volume) of a water tank on a fire engine in both cubic feet and gallons, given the tank's length, width, and height measurements. Create a suitable interface. Code the application by using a class to instantiate a water tank object. Display the output with one decimal place. Save the solution and then start and test the application. (Hint: There are 7.48 gallons in one cubic foot.)

ADVANCED

8. Create a Windows Forms application. Use the following names for the project and solution, respectively: Parking Project and Parking Solution. Save the application in the VB2017\Chap10 folder. The application should display the total cost of paving the parking lot illustrated in Figure 10-42. (The parking lot's shape is a parallelogram.) Create a suitable interface. The user will enter the dimensions in feet and the cost per square yard. Code the application by using a class to instantiate a parking lot object. Save the solution and then start and test the application.

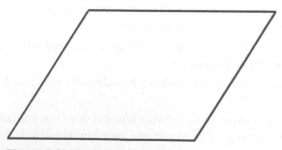

Figure 10-42 Parking lot illustration for Exercise 8

ADVANCED

9. Create a Windows Forms application. Use the following names for the project and solution, respectively: Glasgow Project and Glasgow Solution. Save the application in the VB2017\Chap10 folder. Create the interface shown in Figure 10-43. Each member of Glasgow Health Club must pay monthly dues that consist of a basic fee and one or more optional charges. The basic monthly fee for a single membership is $50; for a family membership, it is $90. If the member has a single membership, the additional monthly charges are $25 for golf, $30 for tennis, and $20 for racquetball. If the member

has a family membership, the additional monthly charges are $35 for golf, $50 for tennis, and $30 for racquetball. The application should display the member's basic fee, additional charges, and monthly dues. Create a class named Dues that contains two auto-implemented properties for the basic and additional charges. The class should also contain a default constructor, a parameterized constructor, and a method that calculates and returns the total monthly dues. Use the class to code the application. Save the solution and then start and test the application.

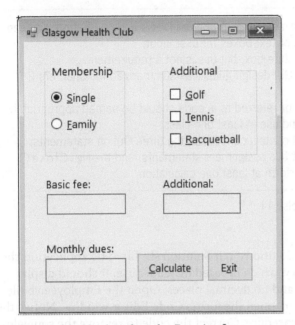

Figure 10-43   Interface for Exercise 9

10. Create a Windows Forms application. Use the following names for the project and solution, respectively: Serenity Project and Serenity Solution. Save the application in the VB2017\Chap10 folder. Create the interface shown in Figure 10-44. The manager of the Accounts Payable department at Serenity Photos wants you to create an application that keeps track of the checks written by her department. More specifically, she wants to record (in a sequential access file) the check number, date, payee, and amount of each check. Create a class that can instantiate a check object. The class should contain a default constructor, a parameterized constructor, and a method that saves the check information to a sequential access file. Use the class to code the application. Save the solution and then start and test the application.

ADVANCED

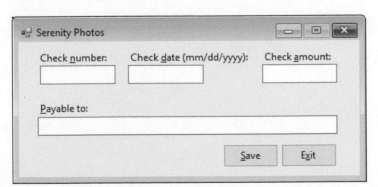

Figure 10-44   Interface for Exercise 10

ON YOUR OWN

11. Create a Windows Forms application. Use the following names for the project and solution, respectively: OnYourOwn Project and OnYourOwn Solution. Save the application in the VB2017\Chap10 folder. Plan and design an application of your choice. The only requirement is that you must follow the minimum guidelines listed in Figure 10-45. Before starting the application, be sure to verify the name of the startup form. Save the solution and then start and test the application.

1. The user interface must contain a minimum of three labels and one button. You can use list boxes, combo boxes, or text boxes for user input.
2. The interface can include a picture box, but this is not a requirement.
3. The interface must follow the GUI design guidelines summarized for Chapters 2 through 10 in Appendix A.
4. Objects that are either coded or referred to in code should be named appropriately.
5. The application must define and use at least one class.
6. The Code Editor window must contain comments, the three Option statements, at least two variables, at least two assignment statements, and the Me.Close() statement. The code must perform at least one calculation.

Figure 10-45 Guidelines for Exercise 11

FIX IT

12. Open the VB2017\Chap10\FixIt Solution\FixIt Solution.sln file. The application should calculate an employee's new salary, which is based on a 5% raise. It should display the new salary with a dollar sign and no decimal places. Open the Employee.vb file and review the existing code. Then, open the form's Code Editor window. Notice the squiggles in the btnCalc_Click procedure. Correct the code to remove the squiggles. Save the solution and then start and test the application. (If the current salary is 12000, the new salary is $12,600.)

SQL Server Databases

Most businesses need to keep track of vast amounts of information pertaining to their customers, employees, and inventory. Although a business could store the information in sequential access files, which you learned about in Chapter 9, it is much easier to manipulate the information when it is stored in computer databases. In this chapter's Focus on the Concepts lesson, you will learn how to create computer databases and then use them in applications. The Apply the Concepts lesson expands on the topics covered in the Focus lesson.

FOCUS ON THE CONCEPTS LESSON

Concepts covered in this lesson:

- F-1 Basic database terminology
- F-2 Creating a SQL Server database
- F-3 Adding a table to a database
- F-4 Adding records to a table
- F-5 Data Source Configuration Wizard
- F-6 Binding the objects in a dataset
- F-7 DataGridView control
- F-8 Copy to Output Directory property
- F-9 Try...Catch statement
- F-10 Two-table databases

F-1 Basic Database Terminology

In order to maintain accurate records, most businesses store their employee, customer, and inventory information in computer databases. A **computer database** is an electronic file that contains an organized collection of related information. Most databases are created and manipulated using relational database management systems (or RDBMSs). The databases are called **relational databases** because the information in them can be related in different ways. Some of the most popular RDBMSs are Microsoft SQL Server, Oracle, and IBM DB2; in this chapter, you will use Microsoft SQL Server.

The information in a relational database is stored in one or more tables. Each table is composed of columns and rows, similar to the format used in a spreadsheet. Figure 11-1 shows an example of a table named Courses that keeps track of a student's college courses.

ID	Code	Title	Hours	Grade
1	ACCOU110	Accounting Procedures	3	A
2	ENG101	English Composition	3	W
3	CIS110	Introduction to Programming	3	A
4	BIO111	Environmental Biology	3	C
5	ENG101	English Composition	3	B
6	CIS112	The Internet	2	A

Figure 11-1   Courses table

Each column in the Courses table represents a field, and each row represents a record. A **field** is a single item of information about a person, place, or thing. The five fields in the Courses table, for example, contain information related to each college course. The combination of related fields creates a **record**. The Courses table contains six records, each composed of five fields. Just as a record is a group of related fields, a **table** is a group of related records.

Most tables have a **primary key**, which is a field that uniquely identifies each record. In the table shown in Figure 11-1, the ID field is the primary key.

As mentioned earlier, a relational database can contain multiple tables. Figure 11-2 shows an example of a two-table database. The Salesperson table contains each salesperson's ID, first name, and last name. It also contains a numeric code (1, 2, or 3) that represents the country in which the salesperson is located. The meaning of each code can be found in the Location table: 1 for the United States, 2 for Canada, and 3 for Mexico. Storing the country codes in a separate table has the following advantages: It allows the input clerk to enter a number, rather than the country name, in each record in the Salesperson table, resulting in less chance of a typing error. Also, the Salesperson table will require less of the computer's main memory to store a number in each record rather than storing the country name.

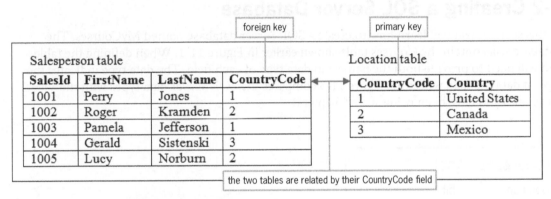

Figure 11-2 Example of a two-table relational database

Recall that a primary key is a field that uniquely identifies each record in a table. The SalesId field is the primary key in the Salesperson table, and the CountryCode field is the primary key in the Location table. Notice that the Salesperson table also has a CountryCode field. The CountryCode field in the Salesperson table is called a **foreign key**, which is a field that typically refers to a primary key in another table. However, it can also refer to any other key that uniquely identifies each row in another table. In this case, the CountryCode (foreign) key in the Salesperson table refers to the CountryCode (primary) key in the Location table; both keys create a relationship between the two tables. The table that contains the foreign key is often called the **child table**, while the table that contains the matching primary key is called the **parent table**. The relationship between both tables is referred to as a one-to-many relationship because each country code can appear only once in the Location (parent) table, but it can appear many times in the Salesperson (child) table.

Storing data in a relational database offers many advantages. The computer can retrieve data stored in a relational format both quickly and easily, and the data can be displayed in any order. The information in the two-table database shown in Figure 11-2, for example, can be arranged by the salesperson's ID, first name, last name, or country. You also can control the amount of information you want to view from a relational database. You can view all of the information in the database, only the information pertaining to a certain salesperson, or only the names of the salespeople located in a specific country.

Mini-Quiz 11-1

1. What is a field?

2. What is a group of related fields called?

3. What is a group of related records called?

4. What is a primary key?

1) A field is a single item of information about a person, place, or thing. 2) record 3) table
4) A primary key is a field that uniquely identifies each record in a table.

F-2 Creating a SQL Server Database

In this section, you will learn how to create a SQL Server database named MyCourses. The database will contain the Courses table shown earlier in Figure 11-1. When defining the table, you will need to provide both the name and data type of each field. The data type indicates the type of data the field will store. Figure 11-3 compares the SQL Server data types with the Visual Basic ones you have been using since Chapter 3.

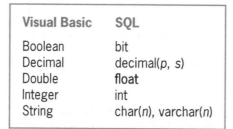

Visual Basic	SQL
Boolean	bit
Decimal	decimal(p, s)
Double	**float**
Integer	int
String	char(n), varchar(n)

Figure 11-3   Comparison of Visual Basic and SQL Server data types

Notice that Visual Basic's String data type is associated with two SQL Server data types: char(*n*) and varchar(*n*). The *n* argument in each type is an integer that represents the maximum number of characters the field will store. You use the char(*n*) type to store fixed-length strings and use the varchar(*n*) type to store variable-length strings. (The *var* stands for *variable-length*.)

In the SQL decimal data type shown in Figure 11-3, the *p* and *s* arguments stand for *precision* and *scale*, respectively. The *p* argument is an integer that represents the total number of digits that will be stored. The *s* argument is an integer that represents the total number of digits that will be stored to the right of the decimal point. For example, the decimal(5, 2) data type will store a number with five digits: three digits to the left of the decimal point and two digits to the right of the decimal point.

START HERE

To create a SQL Server database and add a table to it:

1. Open the Course Info Solution.sln file contained in the VB2017\Chap11\Course Info Solution folder. Open the designer window.

2. If necessary, auto-hide the Toolbox, Properties, and Solution Explorer windows.

3. Click **Project** on the menu bar and then click **Add New Item**. If necessary, expand the **Installed** node and then expand the **Common Items** node. Click **Data**. Click **Service-based Database** in the middle column of the Add New Item dialog box. Change the name in the Name box to **MyCourses.mdf**. (The mdf filename extension is commonly used when naming SQL Server databases; mdf stands for *master database file*.) See Figure 11-4.

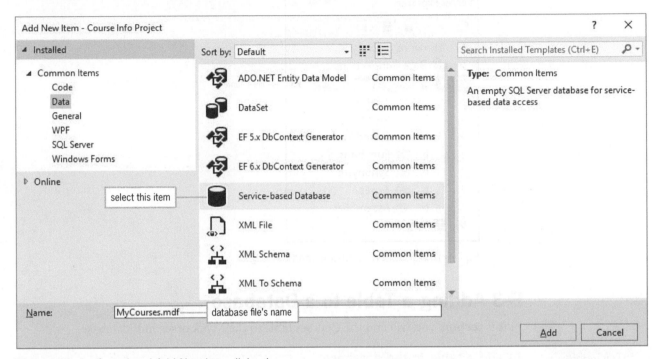

Figure 11-4 Completed Add New Item dialog box

4. Click the **Add** button. If a message box appears alerting you that some packages are missing, click the **OK** button and then click the **Yes** button to allow changes to your device. If necessary, exit Visual Studio. Then, click the **Install** button in the Visual Studio Community 2017 window to install the Data sources for SQL Server support component. Finally, repeat Steps 1 through 4.

5. Temporarily display the Solution Explorer window. The MyCourses.mdf database file is saved in the Course Info Project folder. See Figure 11-5.

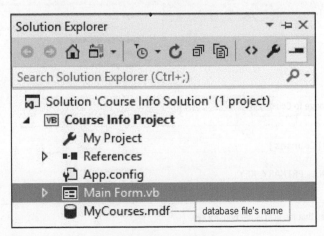

Figure 11-5 Solution Explorer window

6. Right-click **MyCourses.mdf** in the Solution Explorer window and then click **Open** to open the Server Explorer window. Permanently display the Server Explorer window, expand the **Data Connections** node, and then expand the **MyCourses.mdf** node. See Figure 11-6. (Do not be concerned if you are not connected to Azure.)

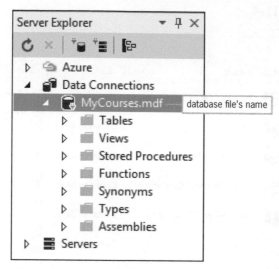

Figure 11-6   Server Explorer window

F-3 Adding a Table to a Database

In this section, you will add the Courses table to the MyCourses.mdf database.

START HERE

To add a table to the database:

1. Right-click **Tables** in the Server Explorer window and then click **Add New Table**. The database table designer window opens. When the design surface has finished loading, change [Table] in the T-SQL pane to [Courses]. The key that appears next to Id in the Name column indicates that the Id field is the primary key. The keywords PRIMARY KEY also appear in the T-SQL pane. See Figure 11-7.

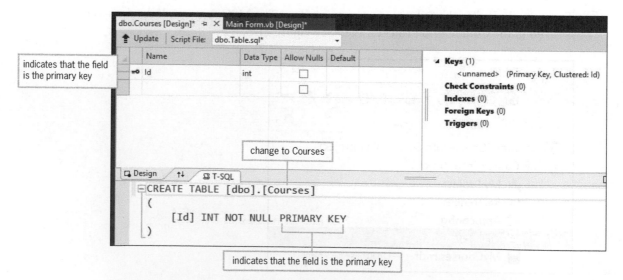

Figure 11-7   Database table designer window

2. You will change the field name to ID and then have the database automatically number the field whenever a new record is added to the table. Change Id in the Name column to **ID**.

3. Temporarily display the Properties window. Expand the **Identity Specification** property, click **(Is Identity)** and then change the setting to **True**. The keyword IDENTITY now appears in the T-SQL pane, as shown in Figure 11-8. The Identity Seed property in the Properties window indicates the starting number for the first record's ID; in this case, the starting number will be 1. The Identity Increment property indicates the number by which each subsequent ID will be increased. In this case, each subsequent ID will be one number more than the previous ID.

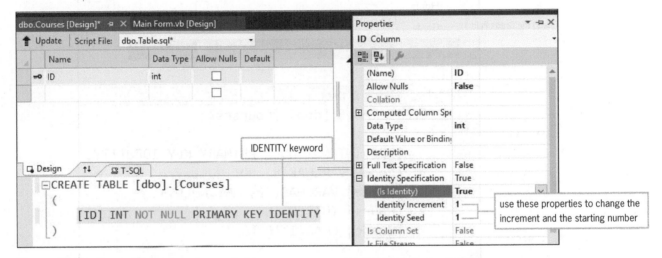

Figure 11-8   Properties and designer windows

4. The ID field will contain integers, so its data type should be left at the default value, int. A field that is a primary key should never be empty; therefore, you will leave the Allow Nulls check box unselected for this field.

5. Next, you will add the Code field to the table. Click the **blank line** below ID in the designer window. Type **Code** and then press **Tab**. The course codes will contain from six to eight characters. Click the **list arrow**, scroll down the list and then click **varchar(50)** in the list. Change 50 in the data type to **8**. Each record should always have a course code, so uncheck the **Allow Nulls** check box for this field.

6. The Title field will contain strings of variable lengths, so you will use varchar(40) as the data type. This data type will allow the field to store up to 40 characters, which should be more than enough for a course title. Click the **blank line** below Code. Type **Title**, press **Tab**, click the **list arrow**, and then click **varchar(50)** in the list. Change 50 in the data type to **40**. The course title should always be completed in each record, so uncheck the **Allow Nulls** check box for this field.

7. The Hours field will contain an integer and should never contain a null value. Click the **blank line** below Title. Type **Hours**, press **Tab**, click the **list arrow**, click **int** in the list, and then uncheck the **Allow Nulls** check box for this field.

8. The Grade field is last. This field will contain one character, so you will use char(1) as its data type. You will allow nulls in this field in case the student wants to add the

course to the table before receiving his or her grade. Use Figure 11-9 as a guide when adding the Grade field to the table. (You will need to select the char(10) data type, then change 10 to 1, and then press Enter.)

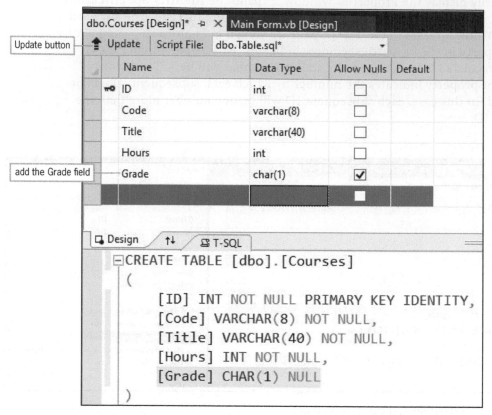

Figure 11-9   Completed table definition

9. Click the **Update** button, which appears below the dbo.Courses [Design] tab. The Preview Database Updates dialog box opens. See Figure 11-10.

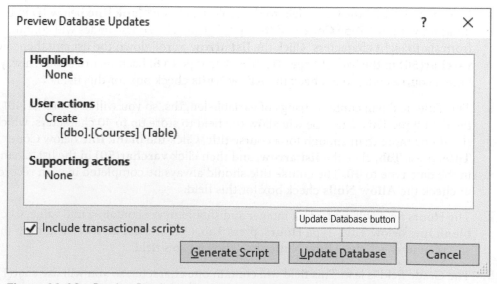

Figure 11-10   Preview Database Updates dialog box

10. Click the **Update Database** button. The "Update completed successfully" message appears in the Data Tools Operations window. See Figure 11-11.

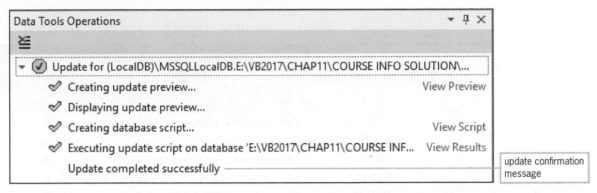

Figure 11-11 Data Tools Operations window

11. Close the Data Tools Operations window.

F-4 Adding Records to a Table

Now that you have finished defining the Courses table, you can add records to it.

To add records to the Courses table:

START HERE

1. Expand the **Tables** node in the Server Explorer window and then expand the **Courses** node. (If the Courses node does not appear below the Tables node, click the Server Explorer window's Refresh button.) See Figure 11-12.

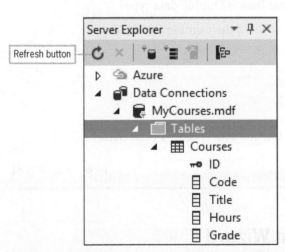

Figure 11-12 Courses table in the Server Explorer window

2. Right-click **Courses** in the Server Explorer window and then click **Show Table Data**. Auto-hide the Server Explorer window.

3. The first record you will add is for the Accounting Procedures course. You do not need to enter the course's ID because the database will automatically enter it each time a record is added to the table. Click **NULL** in the Code field, type **ACCOU110** and then press **Tab**. (The circle with the exclamation point inside will disappear when you press Tab after completing the record.) Type **Accounting Procedures**, press **Tab**, type **3**, press **Tab**, type **A**, and press **Tab**. Notice that the number 1 now appears in this record's ID field.

4. Use Figure 11-13 as a guide when entering the additional five records. (You can use the vertical lines in the column headers to adjust a column's width.)

you can use the vertical line to adjust the Title column's width

dbo.Courses [Data]	⊟ ×	dbo.Courses [Design]	Main Form.vb [Design]		

■ ♻ ▼₀ ▼ | ▶ | Max Rows: 1000 ▾ | ⎁ ⎀

ID	Code	Title	Hours	Grade
1	ACCOU110	Accounting Procedures	3	A
2	ENG101	English Composition	3	W
3	CIS110	Introduction to Programming	3	A
4	BIO111	Environmental Biology	3	C
5	ENG101	English Composition	3	B
6	CIS112	The Internet	2	A
▶* NULL	NULL	NULL	NULL	NULL

Figure 11-13   Records entered in the table

5. Save the solution and then close the dbo.Courses [Data] and dbo.Courses [Design] windows.

Mini-Quiz 11-2

1. What SQL data type is equivalent to Visual Basic's Double data type?

2. Which of the following SQL data types can store the number 2316.26?

    a. decimal(2, 4)

    b. decimal(2, 6)

    c. decimal(4, 2)

    d. decimal(6, 2)

3. What SQL data type is equivalent to the Integer data type in Visual Basic?

1) float 2) d. 3) int

F-5 Data Source Configuration Wizard

Although the MyCourses.mdf file is contained in the Course Info Project folder, you still need to tell the application to use the file as a data source—in other words, as a source for data. You can do this by using the Data Source Configuration Wizard to connect the application to the file. The wizard allows you to specify the data you want to access from the file. The computer makes a copy of the specified data and stores the copy in its main memory. The copy of the data you want to access is called a **dataset**.

START HERE ▶   **To create a dataset and then view its contents:**

1. Click **View** on the menu bar, point to **Other Windows**, and then click **Data Sources**. If necessary, permanently display the Data Sources window.

2. Click **Add New Data Source** in the Data Sources window to start the Data Source Configuration Wizard. If necessary, click **Database** on the Choose a Data Source Type screen. See Figure 11-14.

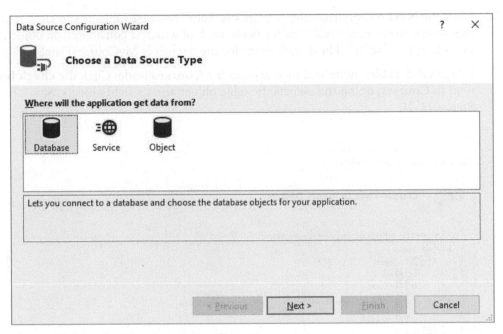

Figure 11-14   Choose a Data Source Type screen

3. Click the **Next** button to display the Choose a Database Model screen. If necessary, click **Dataset**.

4. Click the **Next** button to display the Choose Your Data Connection screen. MyCourses.mdf appears as the data connection. See Figure 11-15.

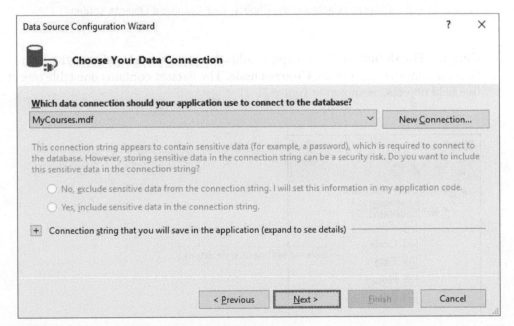

Figure 11-15   Choose Your Data Connection screen

5. Click the **Next** button. The Save the Connection String to the Application Configuration File screen appears and displays the name of the connection string, MyCoursesConnectionString. Verify that the "Yes, save the connection as" check box is selected.

6. Click the **Next** button to display the Choose Your Database Objects screen. You use this screen to select the table and/or fields, each of which is considered an object, to include in the dataset. The default name for the dataset is MyCoursesDataSet.

7. Expand the **Tables** node and then expand the **Courses** node. Click the **check box** next to Courses; doing this selects the table object and its field objects. See Figure 11-16.

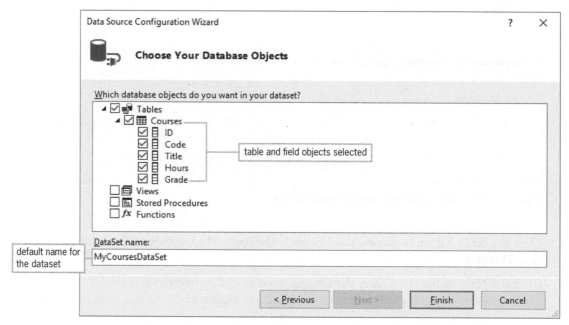

Figure 11-16   Objects selected in the Choose Your Database Objects screen

8. Click the **Finish** button. The computer adds the MyCoursesDataSet to the Data Sources window. Expand the **Courses** node. The dataset contains one table object and five field objects, as shown in Figure 11-17.

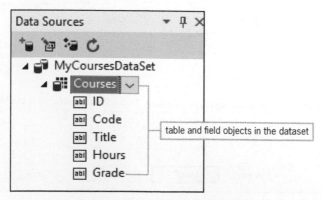

Figure 11-17   Result of running the Data Source Configuration Wizard

9. Right-click **MyCoursesDataSet** in the Data Sources window, click **Preview Data**, and then click the **Preview** button. The dataset contains six records (rows), each having five fields (columns). See Figure 11-18. Notice the information that appears in the "Select an object to preview" box. MyCoursesDataSet is the name of the dataset in the application, and Courses is the name of the table included in the dataset. Fill and GetData are methods. The Fill method populates an existing table with data, while the GetData method creates a new table and populates it with data.

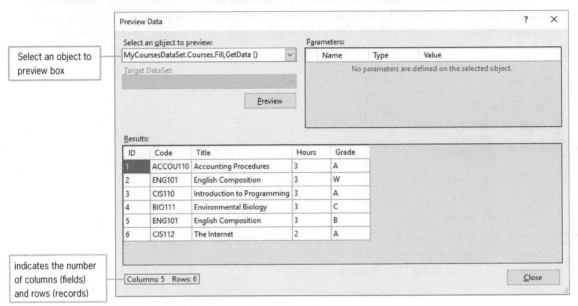

Figure 11-18   Data displayed in the Preview Data dialog box

10. Click the **Close** button to close the Preview Data dialog box.

F-6 Binding the Objects in a Dataset

For the user to view the contents of a dataset while an application is running, you need to connect one or more objects in the dataset to one or more controls in the interface. Connecting an object to a control is called **binding**, and the connected controls are called **bound controls**. As indicated in Figure 11-19, you can bind the object either to a control that the computer creates for you or to an existing control in the interface. In this lesson, you will let the computer create the controls for you. (Binding objects to existing controls is covered in the Apply lesson.)

> **Binding an Object in a Dataset to a Control**
>
> *To have the computer create a control and then bind an object to it:*
> In the Data Sources window, click the object you want to bind. If necessary, use the object's list arrow to change the control type. Drag the object to an empty area on the form, and then release the mouse button.
>
> *To bind an object to an existing control:*
> In the Data Sources window, click the object you want to bind. Drag the object to the control on the form and then release the mouse button. Alternatively, you can click the control on the form and then use the Properties window to set the appropriate property or properties. (Refer to the *A-2 Bind Field Objects to Existing Controls* section in this chapter's Apply the Concepts lesson.)

Figure 11-19   Ways to bind an object in a dataset to a control

Having the Computer Create a Bound Control

When you drag an object from a dataset to an empty area on the form, the computer creates a control and automatically binds the object to it. The icon that appears before the object's name in the Data Sources window indicates the type of control the computer will create. The icon next to Courses in Figure 11-20 indicates that a DataGridView control will be created when you drag the Courses table object to the form. A DataGridView control displays the table data in a row and column format, similar to a spreadsheet. You will learn more about the DataGridView control in the next section. The icon next to each of the four field objects, on the other hand, indicates that the computer creates a text box when a field object is dragged to the form.

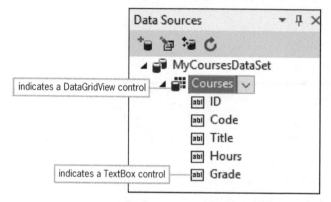

Figure 11-20   Icons in the Data Sources window

When an object is selected in the Data Sources window, you can use the list arrow that appears next to the object's name to change the type of control the computer creates. For example, to display the table data in separate text boxes rather than in a DataGridView control, you click Courses in the Data Sources window and then click the Courses list arrow, as shown in Figure 11-21. Clicking Details in the list tells the computer to create a separate control for each field in the table. Similarly, to display the Grade field's data in a label control rather than in a text box, you first click Grade in the Data Sources window. You then click the field's list arrow, as shown in Figure 11-21, and then click Label in the list.

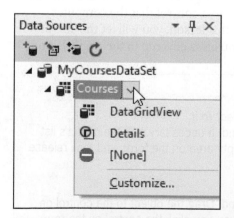
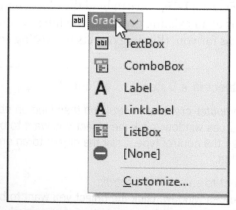

Figure 11-21   Result of clicking the Courses and Grade list arrows

In the following set of steps, you will drag the Courses object from the Data Sources window to the form, using the default control type for a table.

START HERE

To bind the Courses object to a DataGridView control:

1. Click **Courses** in the Data Sources window (if necessary) to select the Courses object.

2. Drag the object from the Data Sources window to the middle of the form and then release the mouse button. The computer adds a DataGridView control to the form, and it binds the Courses object to the control. See Figure 11-22.

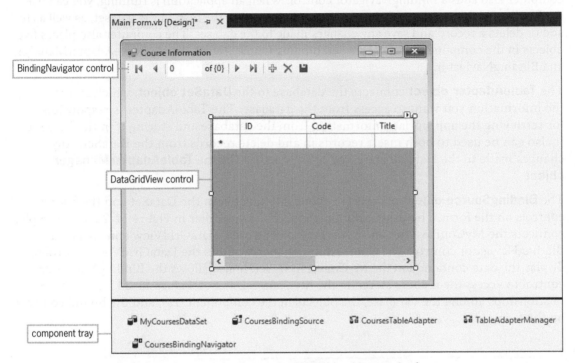

Figure 11-22 Result of dragging the table object to the form

3. Save the solution and then start the application. The six records appear in the DataGridView control. See Figure 11-23. Use the scroll bar to view the remaining fields. (You will improve the appearance of the control in the next section.)

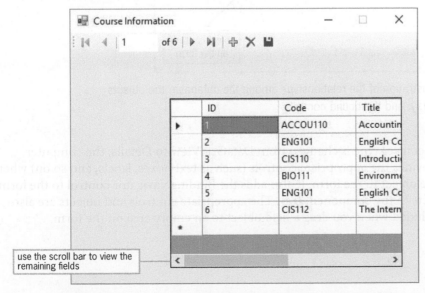

Figure 11-23 Dataset displayed in the DataGridView control

4. Click the **Code** header to display the records in ascending order by the Code field. Then, click the **Code** header again to display the records in descending order by the Code field.

5. Close the application by clicking the **Close** button on the form's title bar.

As shown earlier in Figure 11-22, besides adding a DataGridView control to the form, the computer also adds a BindingNavigator control. When an application is running, you can use the **BindingNavigator control** to move from one record to the next in the dataset, as well as to add or delete a record and save any changes made to the dataset. The computer also places five objects in the component tray: a DataSet, BindingSource, TableAdapter, TableAdapterManager, and BindingNavigator.

The **TableAdapter object** connects the database to the **DataSet object**, which stores the information you want to access from the database. The TableAdapter is responsible for retrieving the appropriate information from the database and storing it in the DataSet. It also can be used to both insert records in and delete records from the DataSet. Any changes made to the DataSet are saved to the database by the **TableAdapterManager object**.

The **BindingSource object** provides the connection between the DataSet and the bound controls on the form. The CoursesBindingSource shown earlier in Figure 11-22, for example, connects the MyCoursesDataSet to two bound controls: a DataGridView control and a BindingNavigator control. The CoursesBindingSource allows the DataGridView control to display the data contained in the MyCoursesDataSet. It also allows the BindingNavigator control to access the records stored in the MyCoursesDataSet. Figure 11-24 illustrates the relationships among the database, the objects in the component tray, and the bound controls on the form.

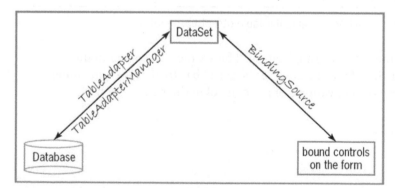

Figure 11-24 Illustration of the relationships among the database, the objects in the component tray, and the bound controls

If a table object's control type is changed from DataGridView to Details, the computer automatically provides the appropriate controls (such as text boxes, labels, and so on) when you drag the table object to the form. It also adds the BindingNavigator control to the form and the five objects to the component tray. The appropriate controls and objects are also automatically included when you drag a field object to an empty area on the form.

F-7 DataGridView Control

The **DataGridView control** is one of the most popular controls for displaying table data because it allows you to view a great deal of information at the same time. The control displays the data in a row and column format, similar to a spreadsheet. Each row represents a record, and each column represents a field. The intersection of a row and a column in a DataGridView control is called a **cell**.

The control's **AutoSizeColumnsMode property**, which has seven different settings, determines the way the column widths are sized in the control. The Fill setting automatically adjusts the column widths so that all of the columns exactly fill the display area of the control. The ColumnHeader setting, on the other hand, adjusts the column widths based on the header text.

Like the PictureBox control, the DataGridView control has a task list. The task list is shown in Figure 11-25 along with a description of each task.

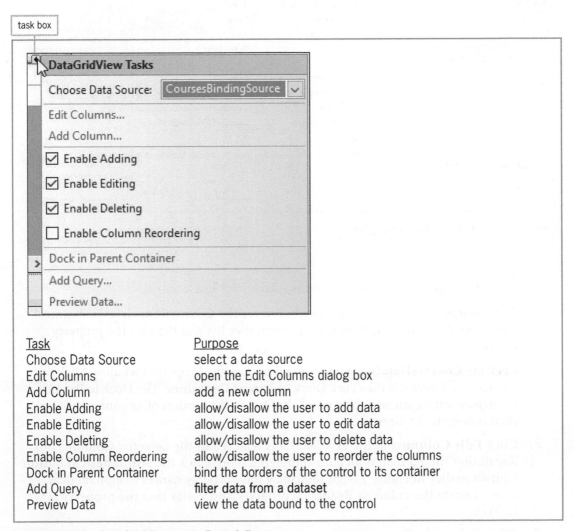

Task	Purpose
Choose Data Source	select a data source
Edit Columns	open the Edit Columns dialog box
Add Column	add a new column
Enable Adding	allow/disallow the user to add data
Enable Editing	allow/disallow the user to edit data
Enable Deleting	allow/disallow the user to delete data
Enable Column Reordering	allow/disallow the user to reorder the columns
Dock in Parent Container	bind the borders of the control to its container
Add Query	filter data from a dataset
Preview Data	view the data bound to the control

Figure 11-25 DataGridView control's task list

Figure 11-26 shows the Edit Columns dialog box that opens when you click Edit Columns on the DataGridView control's task list. You can use the Edit Columns dialog box during design time to add columns to the control, remove columns from the control, and reorder the columns. You also can use it to set the properties of the bound columns. For example, you can use a column's DefaultCellStyle property to format the column's data as well as to change the column's width and alignment. You can use a column's HeaderText property to change a column's heading.

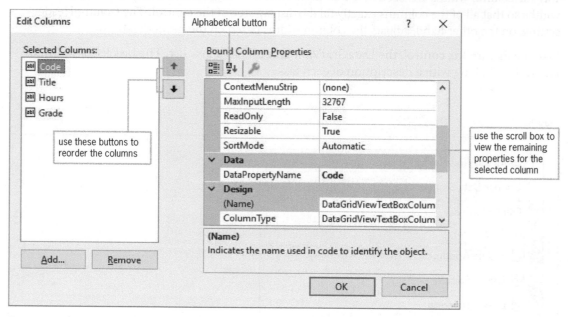

Figure 11-26 Edit Columns dialog box

START HERE

To improve the appearance of the CoursesDataGridView control:

1. Temporarily display the Properties window for the CoursesDataGridView control. Click **AutoSizeColumnsMode** in the Properties list and then set the property to **Fill**.

2. Click the **CoursesDataGridView control** to close the Properties window. Click the control's **task box** and then click **Dock in Parent Container**. The Dock in Parent Container setting anchors the control's borders to the borders of its container, which (in this case) is the form.

3. Click **Edit Columns** in the task list. ID is selected in the Selected Columns box. Recall that the ID field is an auto-numbered field. Click the **Alphabetical** button (shown earlier in Figure 11-26) to display the property names in alphabetical order. Locate the column's ReadOnly property and verify that the property is set to True.

4. Click **Code** in the Selected Columns box. Change the column's AutoSizeMode property to **AllCells**.

5. Click **Title** in the Selected Columns box and then change its AutoSizeMode property to **AllCells**.

6. Click **Hours** in the Selected Columns box. Click **DefaultCellStyle**, and then click the **...** (ellipsis) button to open the CellStyle Builder dialog box. You can use this dialog box to format a column's numbers and also to specify its alignment. See Figure 11-27.

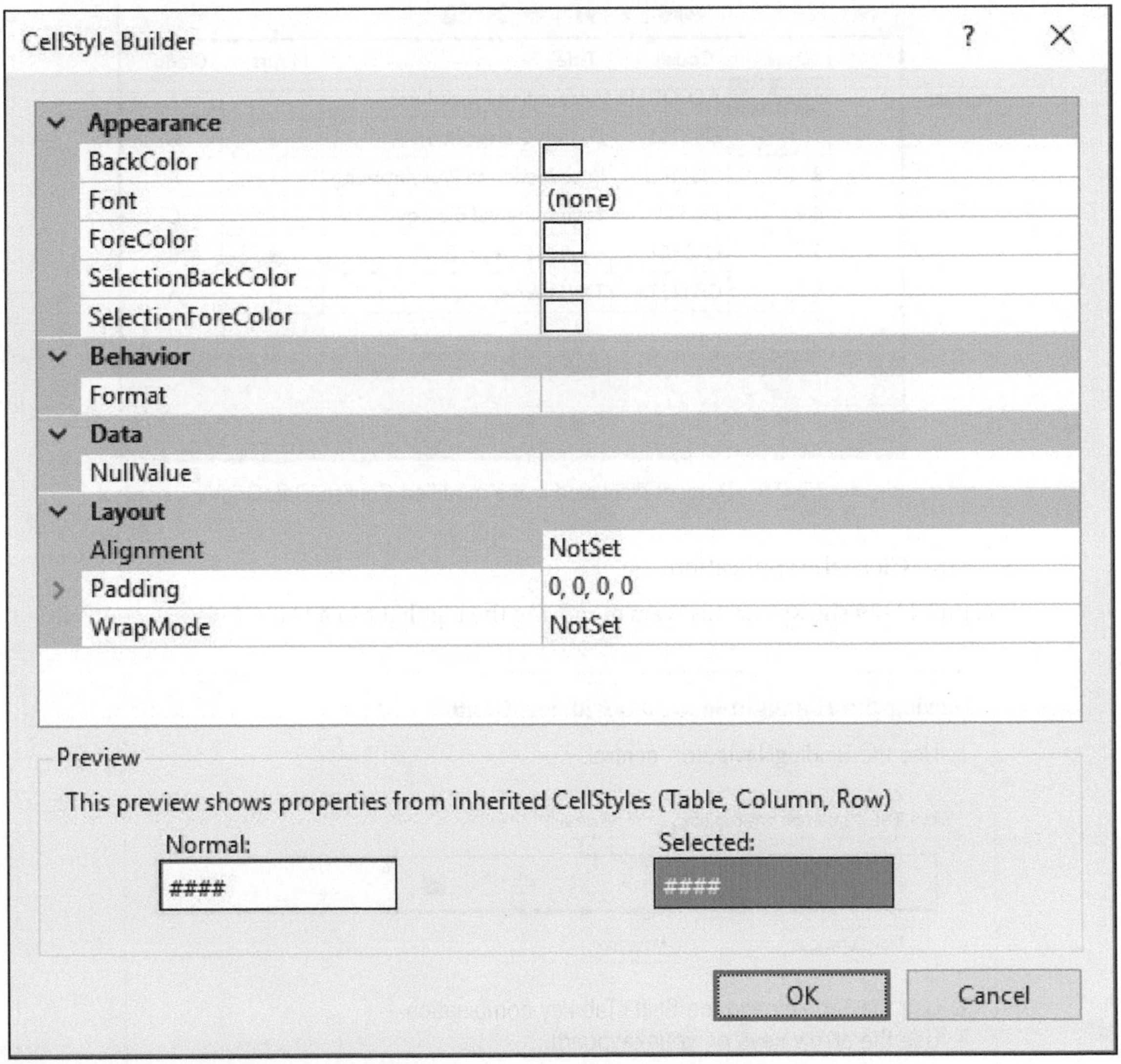

CellStyle Builder

Appearance	
BackColor	☐
Font	(none)
ForeColor	☐
SelectionBackColor	☐
SelectionForeColor	☐
Behavior	
Format	
Data	
NullValue	
Layout	
Alignment	NotSet
Padding	0, 0, 0, 0
WrapMode	NotSet

Preview

This preview shows properties from inherited CellStyles (Table, Column, Row)

Normal: `####`   Selected: `####`

OK   Cancel

Figure 11-27   CellStyle Builder dialog box

7. Click **Alignment**, click the **list arrow**, click **MiddleCenter**, and then click the **OK** button.

8. Click **Grade** in the Selected Columns box, click **DefaultCellStyle**, and then click the **...** (ellipsis) button. Use the CellStyle Builder dialog box to change the Grade field's Alignment property to **MiddleCenter**.

9. Click the **OK** button to close the CellStyle Builder dialog box, and then click the **OK** button to close the Edit Columns dialog box.

10. Click the **CoursesDataGridView** control to close its task list. Auto-hide the Data Sources window.

11. Save the solution and then start the application. The six records in the dataset appear in the CoursesDataGridView control, with the first record's ID highlighted. See Figure 11-28.

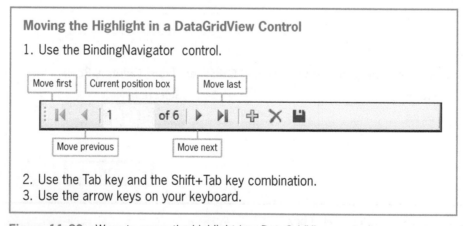

Figure 11-28   Dataset displayed in the modified CoursesDataGridView control

12. Close the application.

Figure 11-29 shows various ways of moving the highlight in a DataGridView control.

Moving the Highlight in a DataGridView Control

1. Use the BindingNavigator control.

| Move first | Current position box | | Move last |

[BindingNavigator control image]

| Move previous | | Move next |

2. Use the Tab key and the Shift+Tab key combination.
3. Use the arrow keys on your keyboard.

Figure 11-29   Ways to move the highlight in a DataGridView control

---

Mini-Quiz 11-3

1. Connecting a field object from a dataset to a control is called _____.

2. Which object connects a dataset to a text box?

3. Which control contains buttons for adding, deleting, and saving records?

4. The intersection of a column and a row in a DataGridView control is called _____.

F-8 Copy to Output Directory Property

A database file contained in a project—like the MyCourses.mdf file contained in the Course Info Project—is referred to as a local database file. The way Visual Basic saves the changes made to a local database file is determined by the file's **Copy to Output Directory property**. Figure 11-30 lists the values that can be assigned to the property.

Copy to Output Directory Property

Property setting	Meaning
Do not copy	The file in the project folder is not copied to the bin\Debug folder when the application is started.
Copy always	The file in the project folder is copied to the bin\Debug folder each time the application is started.
Copy if newer	When an application is started, the computer compares the date on the file in the project folder with the date on the file in the bin\Debug folder. The file from the project folder is copied to the bin\Debug folder only when its date is newer.

Figure 11-30   Settings for the Copy to Output Directory property

When a file's Copy to Output Directory property is set to its default setting, Copy always, the file is copied from the project folder to the project folder's bin\Debug folder each time you start the application. In this case, the MyCourses.mdf file is copied from the Course Info Project folder to the Course Info Project\bin\Debug folder. As a result, the file will appear in two different folders in the solution.

When you click the Save Data button (the disk) on the BindingNavigator control, any changes made in the DataGridView control are recorded only in the file stored in the bin\Debug folder; the file stored in the project folder is not changed. The next time you start the application, the file in the project folder is copied to the bin\Debug folder, overwriting the file that contains the changes. You can modify this behavior by setting the database file's Copy to Output Directory property to "Copy if newer". The "Copy if newer" setting tells the computer to compare the dates on both files to determine which file has the newer (i.e., more current) date. If the database file in the project folder has a newer date, the computer should copy it to the bin\Debug folder; otherwise, it should not copy it.

To change the MyCourses.mdf file's Copy to Output Directory property:

START HERE

1. Temporarily display the Solution Explorer window. Right-click **MyCourses.mdf** and then click **Properties**. Change the file's Copy to Output Directory property to **Copy if newer**.

2. Save the solution and then start the application. Click the **empty cell** below CIS112. Do not be concerned about the −1 (negative 1) that appears in the ID column. Type **PSYCH100**, press **Tab**, type **General Psychology**, press **Tab**, and then type **3**. The student has not completed the course yet, so you will leave the Grade field empty. Click the **Save Data** button (the disk) on the BindingNavigator control to save the new record to the dataset. Notice that the −1 in the ID column changes to the number 7.

3. Now, enter the following record below the PSYCH100 record: **ART100, Ceramics, 2, B**.

4. Click the **Save Data** button. Close the application by clicking the **Close** button on the form's title bar. Then, start the application again. The new records appear in the DataGridView control. See Figure 11-31.

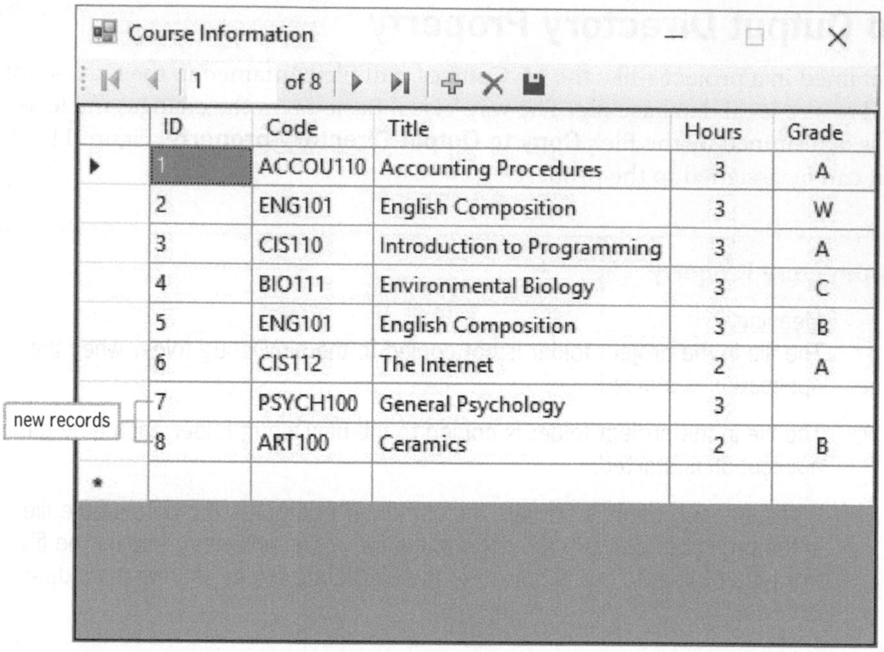

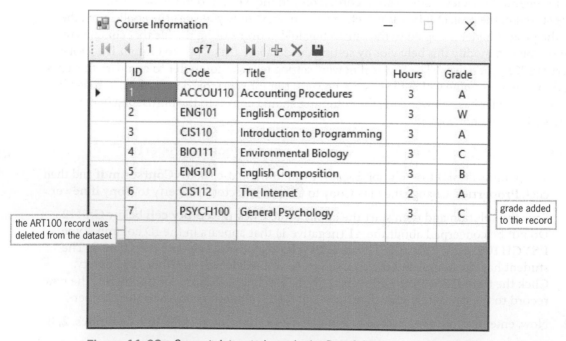

Figure 11-31 New records shown in the DataGridView control

5. Type **C** in the PSYCH100 course's Grade field. Click **ART100** in the Code column and then click the **Delete** button (the red *X*) on the BindingNavigator control. Click the **Save Data** button to save the changes.

6. Close the application and then start it again to verify that the changes you made were saved. The PSYCH100 grade (C) appears in the course's Grade field, and the ART100 record was removed from the dataset. See Figure 11-32.

Figure 11-32 Current dataset shown in the DataGridView control

7. Close the application.

F-9 Try...Catch Statement

In addition to adding the appropriate controls and objects to the application when a table or field object is dragged to the form, Visual Basic also enters some code in the Code Editor window.

To view the code automatically entered in the Code Editor window:

START HERE

1. Open the Code Editor window. The two procedures shown in Figure 11-33 were automatically entered when you dragged the Courses table object to the form. (Recall that the keyword Me refers to the current form. Although the keyword is included in the statements, it is optional.)

```
 9  Public Class frmMain
10      Private Sub CoursesBindingNavigatorSaveItem_Click(sender As Object, e As
            EventArgs) Handles CoursesBindingNavigatorSaveItem.Click
11          Me.Validate()
12          Me.CoursesBindingSource.EndEdit()
13          Me.TableAdapterManager.UpdateAll(Me.MyCoursesDataSet)
14
15      End Sub
16
17      Private Sub frmMain_Load(sender As Object, e As EventArgs) Handles MyBase.Load
18          'TODO: This line of code loads data into the 'MyCoursesDataSet.Courses'
                table. You can move, or remove it, as needed.
19          Me.CoursesTableAdapter.Fill(Me.MyCoursesDataSet.Courses)
20
21      End Sub
22  End Class
```

Figure 11-33   Code automatically entered in the Code Editor window

The form's Load event procedure uses the TableAdapter object's Fill method to retrieve the data from the database and store it in the DataSet object. In most applications, the code to fill a dataset belongs in this procedure. However, as the comments in the procedure indicate, you can either move or delete the code.

The CoursesBindingNavigatorSaveItem_Click procedure is processed when you click the Save Data button on the BindingNavigator control. The procedure's code validates the changes made to the data before saving the data to the database. Two methods are involved in the save operation: the BindingSource object's EndEdit method and the TableAdapterManager's UpdateAll method. The EndEdit method applies any pending changes (such as new records, deleted records, and changed records) to the dataset, and the UpdateAll method commits the changes to the database.

Because it is possible for an error to occur when saving data to a database, you should add error-handling code to the Save Data button's Click event procedure. An error that occurs while an application is running is called an **exception**. If your code does not contain specific instructions for handling the exceptions that may occur, Visual Basic handles them for you. Typically, it does this by displaying an error message and then abruptly terminating the application. You can prevent your application from behaving in such an unfriendly manner by taking control of the exception handling in your code; you can do this by using the **Try...Catch statement**. Figure 11-34 shows the statement's basic syntax and includes examples of using it.

 When an error occurs in a procedure's code during run time, programmers say that the procedure "threw an exception."

The Try...Catch statement can also include a Finally block, whose code is processed whether or not an exception is thrown within the Try block.

Try...Catch Statement

<u>Basic syntax</u>
Try
    one or more statements that might generate an exception
Catch ex As Exception
    one or more statements to execute when an exception occurs
End Try

<u>Example 1</u>
```
Private Sub CoursesBindingNavigatorSaveItem_Click _
        (sender As Object, e As EventArgs) _
        Handles CoursesBindingNavigatorSaveItem.Click
    Try
        Me.Validate()
        Me.CoursesBindingSource.EndEdit()
        Me.TableAdapterManager.UpdateAll(Me.MyCoursesDataSet)
    Catch ex As Exception
        MessageBox.Show(ex.Message, "Course Information",
            MessageBoxButtons.OK, MessageBoxIcon.Information)
    End Try
End Sub
```

<u>Example 2</u>
```
Private Sub btnDisplay_Click(sender As Object, e As EventArgs) _
        Handles btnDisplay.Click
    Dim inFile As IO.StreamReader

    Try
        inFile = IO.File.OpenText("names.txt")
        Do Until inFile.Peek = -1
            lstNames.Items.Add(inFile.ReadLine)
        Loop
        inFile.Close()
    Catch ex As Exception
        MessageBox.Show("Sequential file error.", "JK's",
                    MessageBoxButtons.OK,
                    MessageBoxIcon.Information)
    End Try
End Sub
```

Figure 11-34 Basic syntax and examples of the Try...Catch statement

The basic syntax of the statement contains only a Try block and a Catch block. Within the Try block, you place the code that could possibly generate an exception. When an exception occurs in the Try block's code, the computer processes the code contained in the Catch block and then skips to the code following the End Try clause. A description of the exception that occurred is stored in the **Message property** of the Catch block's **ex** parameter. You can access the description using the code **ex.Message**, as shown in Example 1 in the figure. Or, you can display your own message, as shown in Example 2.

To include a Try...Catch statement in the Save Data button's Click event procedure:

START HERE

1. Insert a **blank line** above the Me.Validate() statement in the CoursesBindingNavigatorSaveItem_Click procedure. Type **Try** and press **Enter**. The Code Editor automatically enters the Catch ex As Exception and End Try clauses for you.

2. Move the three statements that appear below the End Try clause, as well as the blank line below the statements, into the Try block.

3. If the three statements in the Try block do not produce (throw) an exception, the Try block should display the "Changes saved." message; otherwise, the Catch block should display a description of the exception. Enter the two MessageBox.Show methods indicated in Figure 11-35, and then delete the **blank line** below the End Try clause.

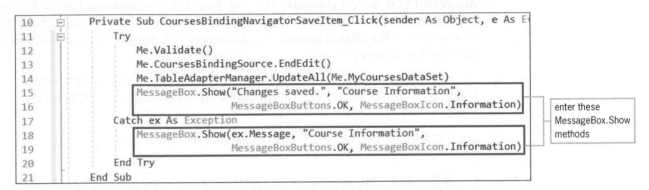

```
10      Private Sub CoursesBindingNavigatorSaveItem_Click(sender As Object, e As E
11          Try
12              Me.Validate()
13              Me.CoursesBindingSource.EndEdit()
14              Me.TableAdapterManager.UpdateAll(Me.MyCoursesDataSet)
15              MessageBox.Show("Changes saved.", "Course Information",
16                      MessageBoxButtons.OK, MessageBoxIcon.Information)
17          Catch ex As Exception
18              MessageBox.Show(ex.Message, "Course Information",
19                      MessageBoxButtons.OK, MessageBoxIcon.Information)
20          End Try
21      End Sub
```

enter these MessageBox.Show methods

Figure 11-35 Completed Click event procedure for the Save Data button

4. Save the solution and then start the application. The statement in the frmMain_Load procedure (shown earlier in Figure 11-33) retrieves the appropriate data from the MyCourses.mdf database file and loads the data into the MyCoursesDataSet. The data is displayed in the DataGridView control, which is bound to the Courses table contained in the dataset.

5. Delete the PSYCH100 record and then click the **Save Data** button. The "Changes saved." message appears in a message box. Close the message box.

6. Stop the application and then start it again to verify that the PSYCH100 record is no longer in the dataset.

7. Stop the application. Close the Code Editor window and then close the solution.

F-10 Two-Table Databases

Earlier, in Figure 11-2, you viewed a database that contains two tables named Salesperson and Location. In the remainder of this lesson, you will learn how to relate the tables by their CountryCode field and then display the dataset information in a DataGridView control. First, however, you need to open the Charleston Sales application and connect it to the Charleston.mdf database file.

START HERE **To open the Charleston Sales application and connect it to the Charleston.mdf database file:**

1. Open the Charleston Sales Solution.sln file contained in the VB2017\Chap11\ Charleston Sales Solution folder. Open the designer window.

2. If necessary, permanently display the Data Sources window. (If the window is not open, click View on the menu bar, point to Other Windows, and then click Data Sources.)

3. Click **Add New Data Source** in the Data Sources window to start the Data Source Configuration Wizard. If necessary, click **Database** on the Choose a Data Source Type screen.

4. Click the **Next** button to display the Choose a Database Model screen. If necessary, click **Dataset**.

5. Click the **Next** button to display the Choose Your Data Connection screen. Click the **New Connection** button. Either the Choose Data Source dialog box or the Add Connection dialog box will open. If the Choose Data Source dialog box opens, click **Microsoft SQL Server Database File** and then click the **Continue** button. Verify that Microsoft SQL Server Database File (SqlClient) appears in the Data source box. (If it does not, click the Change button, click Microsoft SQL Server Database File, and then click the OK button.)

6. Click the **Browse** button in the Add Connection dialog box. Open the VB2017\ Chap11\Databases folder, click **Charleston.mdf**, and then click the **Open** button. See Figure 11-36.

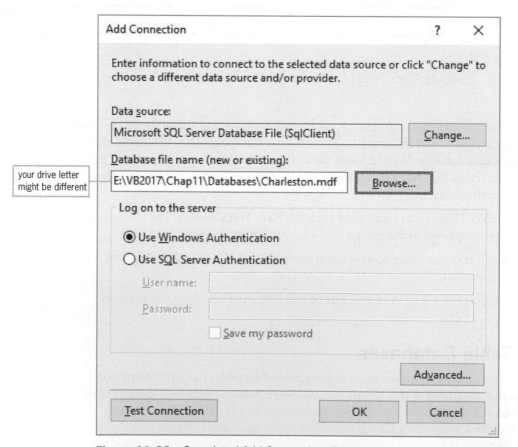

Figure 11-36 Completed Add Connection dialog box

7. Click the **Test Connection** button. The "Test connection succeeded." message appears in a message box. Close the message box.

8. Click the **OK** button in the Add Connection dialog box. Charleston.mdf appears next to the New Connection button. Click the **Next** button. The message box shown in Figure 11-37 opens. The message asks whether you want to include the database file in the current project. By including the file in the current project, you can more easily copy the application and its database to another computer.

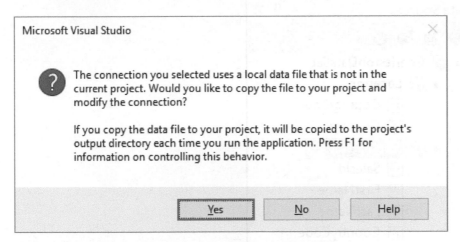

Microsoft Visual Studio   ×

? The connection you selected uses a local data file that is not in the current project. Would you like to copy the file to your project and modify the connection?

If you copy the data file to your project, it will be copied to the project's output directory each time you run the application. Press F1 for information on controlling this behavior.

<u>Y</u>es   <u>N</u>o   Help

Figure 11-37 Message regarding copying the database file

9. Click the **Yes** button to add the Charleston.mdf file to the application's project folder. The Save the Connection String to the Application Configuration File screen appears next and displays the name of the connection string, CharlestonConnectionString. Verify that the "Yes, save the connection as" check box is selected.

10. Click the **Next** button to display the Choose Your Database Objects screen. As you learned earlier, you use this screen to select the table and/or field objects to include in the dataset. The default name for the dataset is CharlestonDataSet.

11. Expand the **Tables** node and then expand the **Location** and **Salesperson** nodes. Click the **check box** next to Tables. See Figure 11-38.

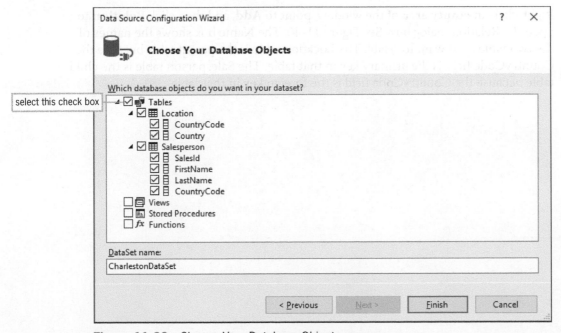

Data Source Configuration Wizard   ?   ×

Choose Your Database Objects

Which database objects do you want in your dataset?

select this check box ─── Tables
    Location
        CountryCode
        Country
    Salesperson
        SalesId
        FirstName
        LastName
        CountryCode
    Views
    Stored Procedures
    Functions

<u>D</u>ataSet name:

CharlestonDataSet

< <u>P</u>revious   Next >   <u>F</u>inish   Cancel

Figure 11-38 Choose Your Database Objects screen

12. Click the **Finish** button. The computer adds the CharlestonDataSet to the Data Sources window. The dataset contains two table objects. Expand the **Location** and **Salesperson** nodes in the Data Sources window. See Figure 11-39.

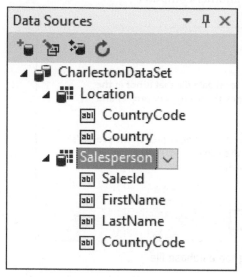

Figure 11-39 Data Sources window

Relating the Tables

Now that both tables are in the dataset, you can tell the computer to relate them by their common field: CountryCode.

START HERE **To relate both tables by their CountryCode field:**

1. Right-click **CharlestonDataSet** in the Data Sources window and then click **Edit DataSet with Designer**. The DataSet Designer window opens.

2. Right-click an **empty area** of the window, point to **Add**, and then click **Relation** to open the Relation dialog box. See Figure 11-40. The Name box shows the names of the two tables you want to relate. The Location table is the parent table because the CountryCode field is the primary key in that table. The Salesperson table is the child table because the CountryCode field is the foreign key in that table.

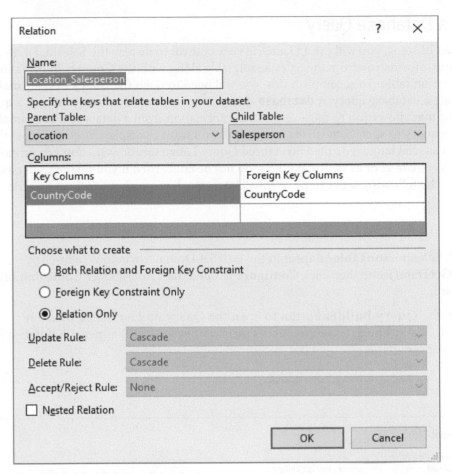

Figure 11-40　Relation dialog box

3. Click the **OK** button. The line between both tables in the DataSet Designer window indicates that a one-to-many relationship exists between the tables. See Figure 11-41.

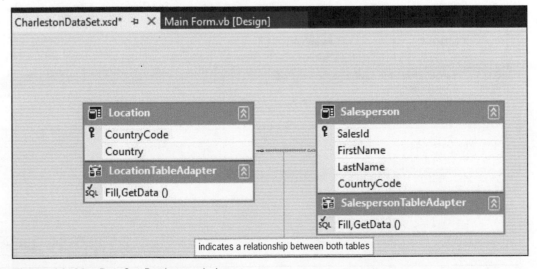

Figure 11-41　DataSet Designer window

4. Save the solution.

Creating a Database Query

In the next set of steps, you will use a DataGridView control to display the SalesId, FirstName, and LastName information from the Salesperson table along with the Country information from the Location table. To accomplish this, you will need to open the **Query Builder dialog box** and create a database query. A **database query**, often referred to more simply as a **query**, is a statement that allows you to retrieve specific information from a database. For example, you can use a query to specify the fields and records you want to display. You will create the query using a special language called Structured Query Language, or SQL. You can pronounce SQL either as *ess-cue-el* or as *sequel*. For now, do not be concerned if you do not understand everything in the following set of steps. You will learn much more about SQL and queries in Chapter 12.

START HERE

To create a query:

1. Click **SalespersonTableAdapter** in the DataSet Designer window, right-click **Fill,GetData()**, and then click **Configure** to open the TableAdapter Configuration Wizard.

2. Click the **Query Builder** button to open the Query Builder dialog box. See Figure 11-42. The Salesperson table's primary key (SalesId) appears boldfaced in the Diagram pane.

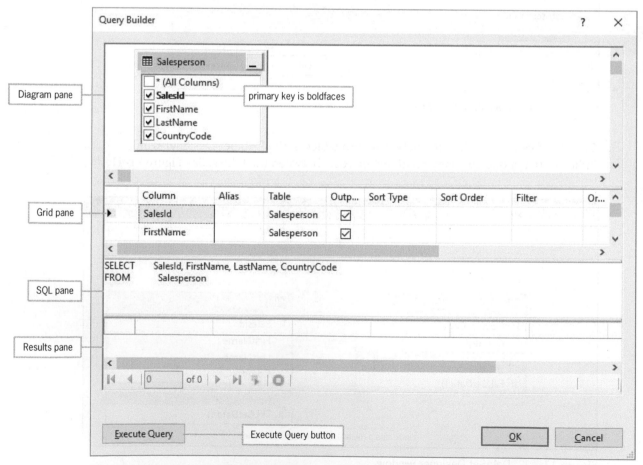

Figure 11-42 Query Builder dialog box

3. Right-click an **empty area** in the Diagram pane and then click **Add Table** to open the Add Table dialog box. The Location table is selected on the Tables tab. Click the **Add** button and then click the **Close** button. The Location table appears next to the Salesperson table in the Diagram pane. Notice that its primary key (CountryCode) appears boldfaced.

4. In the Location table, click the **Country** check box to select the Country field. Then, in the Salesperson table, click the **CountryCode** check box to deselect the CountryCode field.

5. Click the **Execute Query** button. The Results pane displays the SalesId, FirstName, and LastName fields for each record in the Salesperson table, as well as each record's corresponding Country field from the Location table. See Figure 11-43. Scroll the Results pane to view the remaining records.

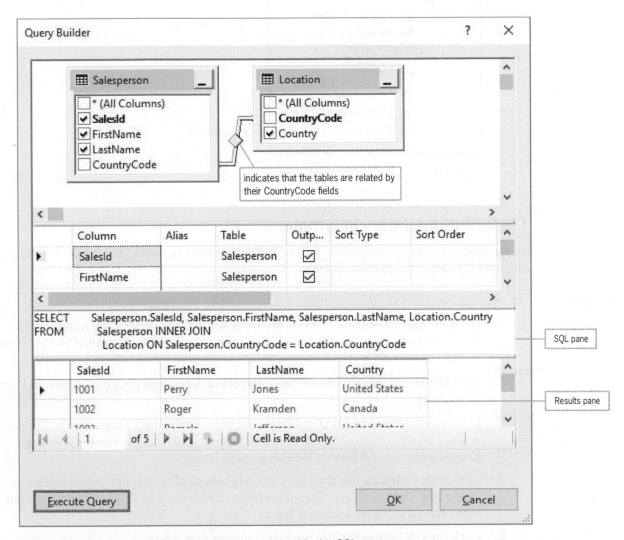

Figure 11-43 Result of executing the query entered in the SQL pane

6. Click the **OK** button to close the Query Builder Dialog box and then click the **Finish** button to close the TableAdapter Configuration Wizard.

7. Save the solution and then close the DataSet Designer window.

8. Expand the Location and Salesperson nodes in the Data Sources window. Notice that in this dataset, the Salesperson entry contains the SalesId, FirstName, and LastName fields from the Salesperson table, as well as the Country field from the Location table. See Figure 11-44.

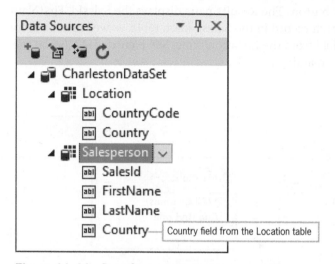

Figure 11-44   Data Sources window

Displaying the Query Information

In the next set of steps, you will use a DataGridView control to display the results of the query that you created in the previous section.

START HERE

To display the results of the query in a DataGridView control:

1. Drag the Salesperson table from the Data Sources window to the middle of the form. Set the SalespersonDataGridView control's AutoSizeColumnsMode property to **Fill**.

2. Click the SalespersonDataGridView control's **task box** and then click **Dock in Parent Container**.

3. In this application, the DataGridView control will only display the records. The user will not be allowed to add, edit, or delete records. Uncheck the **Enable Adding**, **Enable Editing**, and **Enable Deleting** check boxes.

4. Click **Edit Columns** and then click the **Alphabetical** button in the Edit Columns dialog box. Use the HeaderText property to change the first three column headings to **Sales ID**, **First Name**, and **Last Name**.

5. Click the **OK** button to close the Edit Columns dialog box.

6. Change the form's Size property to **575, 235**.

7. Right-click the **Save Data** button (the disk) on the SalespersonBindingNavigator control and then click **Delete**. Use the same process to remove both the **Add new** button (the plus sign) and the **Delete** button (the red *X*).

8. Save the solution and then start the application. See Figure 11-45.

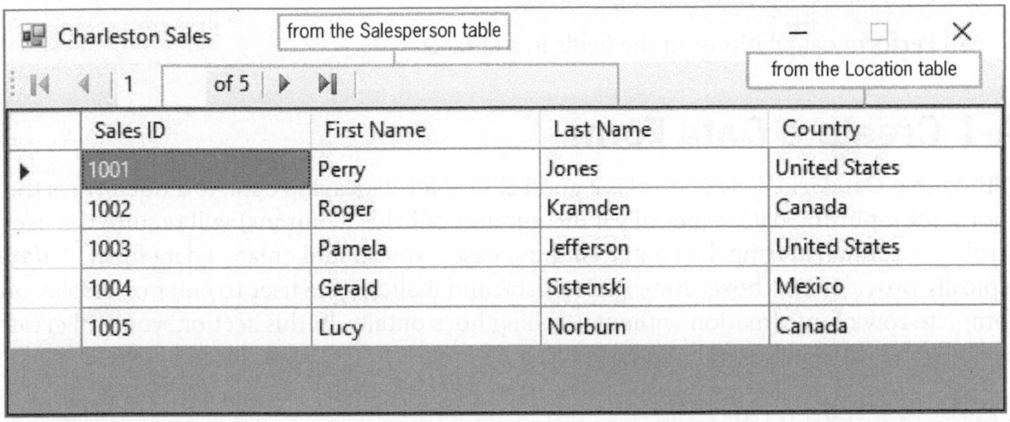

Figure 11-45   Information from both tables displayed in the SalespersonDataGridView control

9. Stop the application and then close the solution.

■ APPLY THE CONCEPTS LESSON

After studying this lesson, you should be able to:

- A-1 Create a data form
- A-2 Bind field objects to existing controls
- A-3 Perform calculations on the fields in a dataset

A-1 Create a Data Form

Although a DataGridView control is a good choice for displaying data, it is not always the best choice for inputting data, especially if the number of fields (columns) will require the user to scroll horizontally during data entry. In those cases, you should create a data form. A **data form** typically provides text boxes for entering data, and it allows the user to enter or display one complete row of information without scrolling horizontally. In this section, you will create a data form for the MyCourses.mdf database file.

START HERE

To create a data form:

1. Open the Course Info Solution.sln file contained in the VB2017\Chap11\Course Info Solution-Data Form folder. Open the designer window.

2. If necessary, open the Data Sources window by clicking **View** on the menu bar, pointing to **Other Windows**, and then clicking **Data Sources**.

3. Permanently display the Data Sources window. Click **Add New Data Source** to display the Choose a Data Source type screen. If necessary, click **Database**.

4. Click the **Next** button to display the Choose a Database Model screen. If necessary, click **Dataset**.

5. Click the **Next** button to display the Choose Your Data Connection screen. Click the **New Connection** button. Verify that Microsoft SQL Server Database File (SqlClient) appears in the Data source box. (If it does not, click the Change button, click Microsoft SQL Server Database File, and then click the OK button.)

6. Click the **Browse** button. Open the VB2017\Chap11\Databases folder, click **MyCourses.mdf**, and then click the **Open** button.

7. Click the **Test Connection** button. The "Test connection succeeded." message appears in a message box. Close the message box.

8. Click the **OK** button to close the Add Connection dialog box. MyCourses.mdf appears in the box next to the New Connection button. Click the **Next** button.

9. Click the **Yes** button to add the MyCourses.mdf file to the application's project folder. Then, click the **Next** button to display the Choose Your Database Objects screen.

10. Expand the **Tables** node and then click the **check box** next to Courses. Click the **Finish** button. The computer adds the MyCoursesDataSet to the Data Sources window. Expand the **Courses** node in the Data Sources window. The dataset contains one table object and five field objects.

11. Click the **Courses** list arrow and then click **Details**. Recall that the ID field is an auto-numbered field, which means that the database will take care of completing the field for each new record. Therefore, you will display the ID field in a label control. Click **ID** in the Data Sources window, click the **list arrow**, and then click **Label**.

12. Now, drag the Courses table to the middle of the form and then release the mouse button. (Do not worry about the exact location.) The computer adds 10 controls to the form: six labels and four text boxes. Each label and text box is associated with a field object in the dataset. See Figure 11-46. (The computer also add the MyCoursesDataSet, CoursesBindingSource, CoursesTableAdapter, TableAdapterManager, and CoursesBindingNavigator objects to the component tray.)

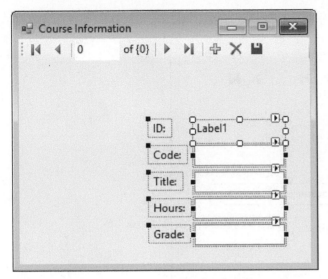

Figure 11-46   Labels and text boxes added to the form

13. Click the **form** to deselect the selected controls.

14. Now, modify the interface as shown in Figure 11-47. Be sure to add the access keys to the labels and also change the names of the text boxes as indicated.

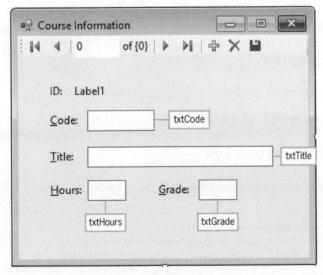

Figure 11-47   Modified interface

15. Lock the controls on the form. Click the **txtCode** control and then set its MaxLength property to **8**. Then, set the MaxLength properties for the txtHours and txtGrade controls to **1**.

16. Set the CharacterCasing properties for the txtCode and txtGrade controls to **Upper**.

17. The application will allow the user to add, edit, and delete records, so you will need to set the database file's Copy to Output Directory property. Temporarily display the Solution Explorer window. Right-click **MyCourses.mdf** and then click **Properties**. Set the Copy to Output Directory property to **Copy if newer**.

18. Save the solution and then start the application. The first record appears in the data form. See Figure 11-48.

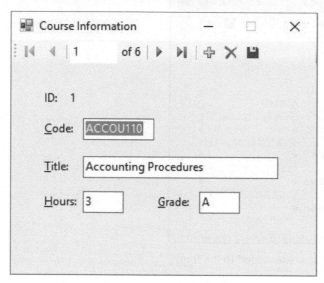

Figure 11-48   First record shown in the data form

19. Use the Move next, Move last, Move previous, and Move first buttons on the BindingNavigator control to view the remaining records.

20. Close the application.

In the next set of steps, you will add the Try...Catch statement to the Save Data button's Click event procedure. You will also code the txtHours_KeyPress procedure to allow the text box to accept only numbers and the Backspace key.

START HERE

To code the procedures and then start and test the application:

1. Auto-hide any open windows except for the form designer window. Open the Code Editor window and locate the CoursesBindingNavigatorSaveItem_Click procedure. Modify the procedure as shown in Figure 11-49.

```
10          Private Sub CoursesBindingNavigatorSaveItem_Click(sender As Object, e As E
11            ┌Try
12                  Me.Validate()
13                  Me.CoursesBindingSource.EndEdit()
14                  Me.TableAdapterManager.UpdateAll(Me.MyCoursesDataSet)
                    MessageBox.Show("Changes saved.", "Course Information",
                                    MessageBoxButtons.OK, MessageBoxIcon.Information)
17            Catch ex As Exception
18                  MessageBox.Show(ex.Message, "Course Information",
19                                  MessageBoxButtons.OK, MessageBoxIcon.Information)
20            └End Try
21          End Sub
```

modify the code as shown here

Figure 11-49   Modified CoursesBindingNavigatorSaveItem_Click procedure

2. Open the code template for the txtHours_KeyPress procedure. Enter the comment and code shown in Figure 11-50.

```
29    ⊟        Private Sub txtHours_KeyPress(sender As Object, e As Key
30               ' Accept only numbers and the Backspace key.
31
              If (e.KeyChar < "0" OrElse e.KeyChar > "9") _
enter this comment and code
33                  AndAlso e.KeyChar <> ControlChars.Back Then
34                  e.Handled = True
35               End If
36           End Sub
```

Figure 11-50 txtHours_KeyPress procedure

3. Save the solution and then start the application.

4. Click the **Add new** button (the plus sign) on the BindingNavigator control. Type **psych100**, press **Tab**, type **General Psychology**, press **Tab**, and then type **3**. The student has not completed the course yet, so you will leave the Grade field empty. Click the **Save Data** button and then close the message box that confirms that the changes were saved.

5. Now, click the **Add new** button and then click the **Code** box. Enter the following record: **art100**, **Ceramics**, **2**, **b**. Click the **Save Data** button and then close the message box.

6. Stop the application and then start it again. Use the BindingNavigator control to locate the PSYCH100 record, which is record 7 in the dataset. Type **C** in the record's Grade field.

7. Locate the ART100 record, which is the last record in the dataset. Press the **Delete** button (the red *X*), click the **Save Data** button, and then close the message box.

8. Stop the application and then start it again. Verify that the PSYCH100 grade was saved and that the ART100 record is no longer in the dataset. Stop the application. Close the Code Editor window and then close the solution.

A-2 Bind Field Objects to Existing Controls

As indicated earlier in Figure 11-19, you can bind an object in a dataset to an existing control on a form. The easiest way to do this is by dragging the object from the Data Sources window to the control. However, you also can click the control and then set one or more properties in the Properties window. The appropriate property (or properties) to set depends on the control you are binding. To bind a DataGridView control, you use the DataSource property. However, you use the DataSource and DisplayMember properties to bind a ListBox control. To bind label and text box controls, you use the DataBindings/Text property.

In the next set of steps, you will use the MyCourses.mdf database file in a different version of the Course Information application. In this version, the information will be displayed in label controls rather than in a DataGridView control.

To bind objects to existing controls:

START HERE

1. Open the Course Info Solution.sln file contained in the VB2017\Chap11\Course Info Solution-Labels folder. Open the designer window and then temporarily display the Solution Explorer window. The application is already connected to the MyCourses.mdf file, and the MyCoursesDataSet has already been created.

2. Permanently display the Data Sources window. Expand the **MyCoursesDataSet** node and then expand the **Courses** node. The dataset contains one table object and five field objects. See Figure 11-51.

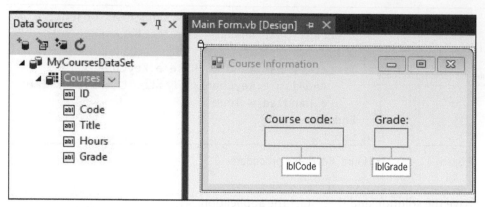

Figure 11-51   Interface and Data Sources window

3. Click **Code** in the Data Sources window, drag the field object to the lblCode control, and then release the mouse button. (Notice that you do not need to change the control type in the Data Sources window to match the existing control's type.) The computer binds the field object to the control and also adds the MyCoursesDataSet, CoursesBindingSource, CoursesTableAdapter, and TableAdapterManager objects to the component tray. Notice that when you drag an object from the Data Sources window to an existing control, the computer does not add a BindingNavigator object to the component tray, nor does it add a BindingNavigator control to the form. You will add the missing control and object in Step 5.

4. Click **Grade** in the Data Sources window and then drag the field object to the lblGrade control. Release the mouse button.

5. You can use the BindingNavigator tool, which is located in the Data section of the toolbox, to add a BindingNavigator control and object to the application. Temporarily display the Toolbox window. Expand the **Data** node and then click **BindingNavigator**. Drag the BindingNavigator tool to the top of the form and then release the mouse button. The computer adds the BindingNavigator1 control to the form and adds the BindingNavigator1 object to the component tray.

6. Temporarily display the Properties window. Set the BindingNavigator1 control's BindingSource property to **CoursesBindingSource**.

7. Right-click the **Delete** button (the red *X*) on the BindingNavigator1 control and then click **Delete**. Now, right-click the **Add new** button (the plus sign) and then click **Delete**.

8. Save the solution and then start the application. The first record appears in the interface. See Figure 11-52.

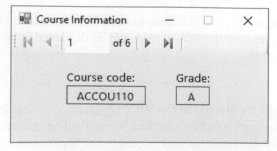

Figure 11-52   Interface showing the first record

9. Use the Move next, Move last, Move previous, and Move first buttons on the BindingNavigator control to view the remaining records.

10. Close the application and then close the solution.

A-3 Perform Calculations on the Fields in a Dataset

In this section, you will use the MyCourses.mdf file in an application that totals the number of credit hours that the student has completed. You can make this calculation by using a loop to accumulate the numbers stored in each record's Hours field.

To open this version of the Course Information application:

START HERE

1. Open the Course Info Solution.sln file contained in the VB2017\Chap11\Course Info Solution-Total Hours folder. Open the designer window. The application is connected to the MyCourses.mdf file. The dataset has already been created and is named MyCoursesDataSet.

2. Start the application. The dataset information appears in the DataGridView control. The dataset contains 14 records and five fields. See Figure 11-53.

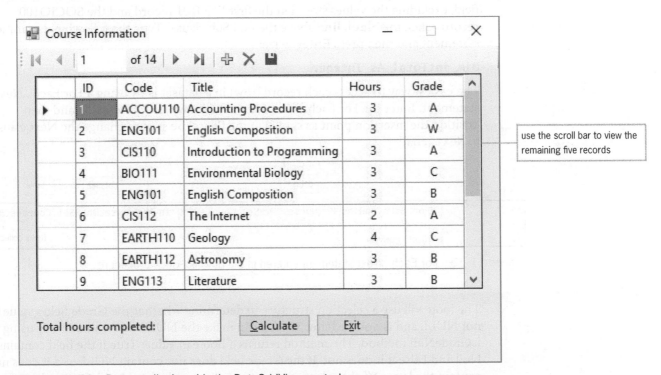

Figure 11-53   Dataset displayed in the DataGridView control

3. Use the scroll bar to view the remaining records. Notice that the Grade field for the first ENG101 record contains W, and the Grade field for the SOCIO100 record is empty. The Hours field for both of these records should not be included in the total number of credit hours completed.

4. Click the **Exit** button.

Figure 11-54 shows the pseudocode for the btnCalc_Click procedure. Recall that an empty Grade field contains NULL.

btnCalc_Click
1. declare intTotal variable for accumulating the number of credit hours completed
2. repeat for each row (record) in the dataset
      if the current row's Grade field is not empty and it does not contain the letter W
         add the hours from the current row's Hours field to the intTotal variable
      end if
   end repeat
3. display the contents of the intTotal variable in the lblTotal control

Figure 11-54 Pseudocode for the btnCalc_Click procedure

START HERE

To code the btnCalc_Click procedure:

1. Open the Code Editor window and locate the btnCalc_Click procedure. The procedure will use an Integer variable named `intTotal` to accumulate the values in the Hours field, excluding the values stored in the first ENG101 record and the SOCIO100 record. Click the **blank line** above the End Sub clause. Type the following declaration statement and then press **Enter** twice:

   `Dim intTotal As Integer`

2. The easiest way to access each record (row) in a dataset is by using a For Each...Next statement. Enter the For Each...Next statement shown in Figure 11-55 and then position the insertion point as shown in the figure. Be sure to change the Next clause to **Next row**.

| dataset | | class | | dataset | | table |

```
15   ┌   For Each row As MyCoursesDataSet.CoursesRow In MyCoursesDataSet.Courses.Rows
16   │   |
17   │   Next row                                                    Rows collection
```

Figure 11-55 For Each...Next statement entered in the btnCalc_Click procedure

3. The loop will use a selection structure to determine whether the Grade field's value is not NULL and is not the letter W. You can make the NULL determination by using the IsGradeNull method. The method returns a Boolean value: True if the field contains Null and False if it does not. If the Grade field does not contain NULL and it does not contain the letter W, the selection structure's True path should add the number of hours stored in the record's Hours field to the `intTotal` accumulator variable. Enter the selection structure shown in Figure 11-56.

```
15   ┌   For Each row As MyCoursesDataSet.CoursesRow In MyCoursesDataSe
16   ┌       ┌If row.IsGradeNull = False AndAlso row.Grade <> "W" Then
     enter this selection structure ┤  │     intTotal += row.Hours
18   │       └End If
19   │   Next row
```

Figure 11-56 Selection structure entered in the loop

4. The last step in the procedure's pseudocode is to display the contents of the `intTotal` variable in the lblTotal control. Insert a **blank line** below the `Next` row clause and then type the assignment statement shown in Figure 11-57.

```
10      Private Sub btnCalc_Click(sender As Object, e As EventArgs) Handles btnCalc.Click
11          ' Display the total number of credit hours completed.
12
13          Dim intTotal As Integer
14
15          For Each row As MyCoursesDataSet.CoursesRow In MyCoursesDataSet.Courses.Rows
16              If row.IsGradeNull = False AndAlso row.Grade <> "W" Then
17                  intTotal += row.Hours
18              End If
19          Next row
20          lblTotal.Text = intTotal.ToString ──── enter this assignment statement
21      End Sub
```

Figure 11-57 Completed btnCalc_Click procedure

5. Save the solution and then start the application. Click the **Calculate** button. The total number of hours completed is 40. See Figure 11-58.

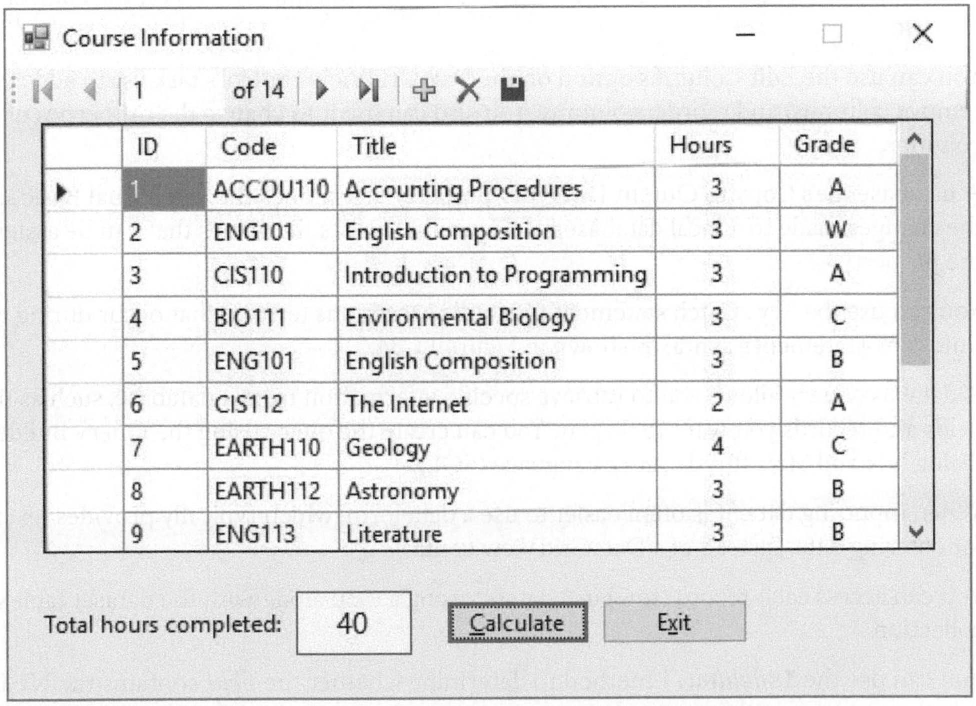

ID	Code	Title	Hours	Grade
1	ACCOU110	Accounting Procedures	3	A
2	ENG101	English Composition	3	W
3	CIS110	Introduction to Programming	3	A
4	BIO111	Environmental Biology	3	C
5	ENG101	English Composition	3	B
6	CIS112	The Internet	2	A
7	EARTH110	Geology	4	C
8	EARTH112	Astronomy	3	B
9	ENG113	Literature	3	B

Course Information

◄◄ ◄ 1   of 14 ► ►► ✚ ✕ 💾

Total hours completed: 40   Calculate   Exit

Figure 11-58 Interface showing the total number of hours completed

6. Click the **Exit** button. Close the Code Editor window and then close the solution.

Summary

- Most businesses store information in computer databases.

- The information in a relational database is stored in one or more tables. Each table is composed of fields (columns) and records (rows).

- Most tables have a primary key that uniquely identifies each record in the table. Some tables also have a foreign key that is used to relate one table to another table.

- You can use the Data Source Configuration Wizard to connect an application to a database file. To start the wizard, open the Data Sources window by clicking View, pointing to Other Windows, and then clicking Data Sources. Then, click Add New Data Source in the Data Sources window.

- For the user to view the information contained in a dataset, you must bind one or more of the objects in the dataset to one or more controls. Figure 11-19 lists different ways of binding table/field objects to controls.

- A DataGridView control displays data in a row (record) and column (field) format, similar to a spreadsheet. To have the columns fill the control's display area, set the control's AutoSizeColumnsMode property to Fill. To anchor the control to the borders of its container (which is typically the form), click the Dock in Parent Container option on the control's task list.

- You can use the Edit Columns option on the DataGridView control's task list to add columns, remove columns, and reorder columns. You also can use it to change the properties of the columns.

- A database file's Copy to Output Directory property determines the way Visual Basic saves the changes made to a local database file. Figure 11-30 lists the values that can be assigned to the property.

- You can use the Try...Catch statement to handle exceptions (errors) that occur during run time. The statement's syntax is shown in Figure 11-34.

- A database query allows you to retrieve specific information from a database, such as the fields and records you want to display. You can create the query using the Query Builder dialog box and Structured Query Language (SQL).

- When inputting data, it is often easier to use a data form, which typically provides text boxes for entering data, instead of a DataGridView control.

- You can access each record (row) in a dataset using a loop along with the dataset table's Rows collection.

- You can use the Is*field*Null method to determine whether the *field* contains the NULL value.

Key Terms

AutoSizeColumnsMode property—determines the way the column widths are sized in a DataGridView control

Binding—the process of connecting an object in a dataset to a control on a form

BindingNavigator control—can be used to add, delete, and save records and also to move the record pointer from one record to another in a dataset

BindingSource object—connects a DataSet object to the bound controls on a form

Bound controls—the controls connected to an object in a dataset

Cell—the intersection of a row and a column in a DataGridView control

Child table—a table linked to a parent table

Computer database—an electronic file that contains an organized collection of related information

Copy to Output Directory property—a property of a database file; determines both when and if the file is copied from the project folder to the project folder's bin\Debug folder

Data form—a form for entering data

Database query—a statement used to retrieve specific information from a database; also called a query

DataGridView control—displays data in a row and column format

Dataset—a copy of the data (database fields and records) that can be accessed by an application

DataSet object—stores the information you want to access from a database

Exception—an error that occurs while an application is running

Field—a single item of information about a person, place, or thing

Foreign key—the field used to link one table to another table

Message property—in a Try...Catch statement, a property of the Catch block's **ex** parameter; contains a description of the error that occurred in the Try block's code

Parent table—a table linked to a child table

Primary key—a field that uniquely identifies each record in a table

Query—a statement used to retrieve specific information from a database; also called a database query

Query Builder dialog box—used to create a query

Record—a group of related fields that contain all of the necessary data about a specific person, place, or thing

Relational databases—databases that store information in tables composed of columns (fields) and rows (records); the information in these databases can be related in different ways

Table—a group of related records

TableAdapter object—connects a database to a DataSet object

TableAdapterManager object—handles saving data to the tables in a dataset

Try...Catch statement—used for exception handling in a procedure

Review Questions

1. Which of the following objects connects a database to a DataSet object?

   a. BindingSource

   b. DataBase

   c. DataGridView

   d. TableAdapter

2. Which of the following is an organized collection of related information stored in a computer file?

   a. database

   b. dataset

   c. field

   d. record

3. Which type of database stores information in tables composed of rows and columns?

   a. columnar

   b. relational

   c. sorted

   d. tabular

4. Which of the following objects provides the connection between a DataSet object and a control on a form?

   a. Bound

   b. Binding

   c. BindingSource

   d. Connecting

5. Which of the following statements retrieves data from the Sales table and stores it in the CompanyDataSet?

   a. `Me.CompanyDataSet.Fill(Me.Sales)`

   b. `Me.SalesBindingSource.Fill(Me.CompanyDataSet)`

   c. `Me.SalesBindingNavigator.Fill(Me.CompanyDataSet.Sales)`

   d. `Me.SalesTableAdapter.Fill(Me.CompanyDataSet.Sales)`

6. If an application contains the `Catch ex As Exception` clause, which of the following can be used to access the exception's description?

   a. `ex.Description`

   b. `ex.Exception`

   c. `ex.Message`

   d. `Exception.Description`

7. The field that links a child table to a parent table is called the _____.

   a. foreign key in the child table

   b. foreign key in the parent table

   c. link key in the parent table

   d. primary key in the child table

8. Which of the following refers to the process of connecting a dataset object to a control in the interface?

   a. assigning

   b. binding

   c. joining

   d. None of the above.

9. Which of the following is true?

   a. Data stored in a relational database can be retrieved both quickly and easily by the computer.

   b. Data stored in a relational database can be displayed in any order.

   c. A relational database stores data in a column and row format.

   d. All of the above.

10. Which of the following SQL data types is associated with the Visual Basic String data type?

    a. char(*n*)   c. varchar(*n*)

    b. string(*n*)   d. Both a and c.

11. Which of the following SQL data types can store the number 12345.67?

    a. decimal(7, 2)   c. decimal(2, 7)

    b. decimal(5, 2)   d. decimal(2, 5)

12. Which of a database file's properties determines if and when the file is copied to the project's bin\Debug folder?

    a. Copy to Debug   c. Copy to Output Directory

    b. Copy to Output   d. Copy to bin\Debug

13. Which of the following is false?

    a. You can use a query to retrieve specific information from a database.

    b. You can write queries using SQL.

    c. You cannot use a query when a database has more than one table.

    d. None of the above.

14. You can use the BindingNavigator control to _____.

    a. add records to a dataset   c. delete records from a dataset

    b. save records in a dataset   d. All of the above.

15. The CompanyDataSet contains a table named Sales and a field named Income. Which of the following loops will accumulate the values in the Income field?

    a.
    ```
    For Each row As CompanyDataSet.Sales.Row
        In CompanyDataSet.Sales.Rows
            Sales.Row += row.Income
    Next row
    ```
    b.
    ```
    For Each row As CompanyDataSet.Sales.Row
        In CompanyDataSet.Sales.Rows
            dblTotal += row.Income
    Next row
    ```
    c.
    ```
    For Each row As CompanyDataSet.Sales.Row
        In CompanyDataSet.Rows
            dblTotal += row.Income
    Next row
    ```
    d.
    ```
    For Each row As CompanyDataSet.Sales
        In CompanyDataSet.Sales.Rows
            dblTotal += row.Income
    Next row
    ```

Exercises

INTRODUCTORY

1. In this exercise, you create an application that keeps track of cookie sales. Create a Windows Forms application. Use the following names for the project and solution, respectively: Cookies Project and Cookies Solution. Save the application in the VB2017\ Chap11 folder.

    a. Figure 11-59 shows the Sales table contained in the VB2017\Chap11\Databases\ Cookies.mdf file. The table contains the numbers of boxes of cookies sold in each of three weeks. The Week field is an auto-numbered field. Open the Data Sources window and click Add New Data Source to start the Data Source Configuration Wizard. Connect the Cookies.mdf file to the application. Include the entire Sales table in the dataset.

    b. Set the Cookies.mdf file's Copy to Output Directory property to "Copy if newer".

    c. Display the dataset information in a DataGridView control and then make the necessary modifications to the control.

    d. Enter an appropriate Try...Catch statement in the SalesBindingNavigatorSaveItem_ Click procedure.

    e. Save the solution and then start the application. Change the Chocolate Chip cookie sales in Week 1 to 205. Then, enter the following record for Week 4: 150, 112, and 76. Save the changes.

    f. Stop the application and then start it again to verify that the changes you made were saved.

Week	Chocolate Chip	Peanut Butter	Pecan Sandies
1	200	150	75
2	185	170	100
3	165	160	120

Figure 11-59 Sales table for Exercise 1 (before any changes)

INTRODUCTORY

2. In this exercise, you create an application that keeps track of music boxes. Create a Windows Forms application. Use the following names for the project and solution, respectively: MusicBox Project and MusicBox Solution. Save the application in the VB2017\Chap11 folder.

    a. Figure 11-60 shows the Boxes table contained in the VB2017\Chap11\Databases\ MusicBoxes.mdf file. The ID field is an auto-numbered field. Open the Data Sources window and click Add New Data Source to start the Data Source Configuration Wizard. Connect the MusicBoxes.mdf file to the application. Include the entire Boxes table in the dataset.

    b. Set the MusicBoxes.mdf file's Copy to Output Directory property to "Copy if newer".

    c. Display the dataset information in a DataGridView control and then make the necessary modifications to the control.

    d. Enter an appropriate Try...Catch statement in the BoxesBindingNavigatorSaveItem_ Click procedure.

    e. Save the solution and then start the application. Change record 9's Source field to Gift. Then, enter the following new record: Round, Purchase, and Music of the Night. Save the changes.

f.   Stop the application and then start it again to verify that the changes you made were saved.

ID	Shape	Source	Song
1	Round	Purchase	As Time Goes By
2	Octagon	Gift	Nadia's Theme
3	Round	Purchase	My Way
4	Rectangle	Purchase	Clair de Lune
5	Octagon	Purchase	Beauty and the Beast
6	Rectangle	Gift	Endless Love
7	Rectangle	Gift	Yesterday
8	Octagon	Purchase	You Light Up My Life
9	Rectangle	Purchase	Edelweiss
10	Rectangle	Gift	Happy Birthday

Figure 11-60   Boxes table for Exercise 2 (before any changes)

3.   In this exercise, you create an application that keeps track of cookie sales. Create a Windows Forms application. Use the following names for the project and solution, respectively: Sales Project and Sales Solution. Save the application in the VB2017\Chap11 folder.

INTRODUCTORY

a.   Figure 11-61 shows the Sales table contained in the VB2017\Chap11\Databases\ Cookies.mdf file. The table contains the numbers of boxes of cookies sold in each of three weeks. The Week field is an auto-numbered field. Open the Data Sources window and click Add New Data Source to start the Data Source Configuration Wizard. Connect the Cookies.mdf file to the application. Include the entire Sales table in the dataset.

b.   Set the Cookies.mdf file's Copy to Output Directory property to "Copy if newer".

c.   Create a data form for the user to enter the sales information. (The Week field's data should appear in a label control.) Lock the controls on the form and then set the tab order.

d.   Rename the text boxes as follows: txtChocolate, txtPeanut, and txtPecan.

e.   Each text box should accept only numbers and the Backspace key. Create an event-handling Sub procedure that will handle the three event procedures.

f.   Enter an appropriate Try...Catch statement in the SalesBindingNavigatorSaveItem_ Click procedure.

g.   Save the solution and then start the application. Change the Peanut Butter sales for Week 1 to 125. Then, enter the following record for Week 4: 100, 100, and 100. Save the changes.

h.   Stop the application and then start it again to verify that the changes you made were saved.

Week	Chocolate Chip	Peanut Butter	Pecan Sandies
1	200	150	75
2	185	170	100
3	165	160	120

Figure 11-61   Sales table for Exercise 3 (before any changes)

INTRODUCTORY

4. Open the MusicBox Solution.sln file contained in the VB2017\Chap11\MusicBox Solution-ListBox folder.

    a. Figure 11-62 shows the Boxes table contained in the VB2017\Chap11\Databases\ MusicBoxes.mdf file. Open the Data Sources window and click Add New Data Source to start the Data Source Configuration Wizard. Connect the MusicBoxes.mdf file to the application. Include the entire Boxes table in the dataset.

    b. Bind the Shape, Source, and Song field objects to the existing labels controls. Then, set the lstId control's DataSource and DisplayMember properties to BoxesBindingSource and ID, respectively. Save the solution and then start the application. Test the application by clicking each ID in the lstIds control.

ID	Shape	Source	Song
1	Round	Purchase	As Time Goes By
2	Octagon	Gift	Nadia's Theme
3	Round	Purchase	My Way
4	Rectangle	Purchase	Clair de Lune
5	Octagon	Purchase	Beauty and the Beast
6	Rectangle	Gift	Endless Love
7	Rectangle	Gift	Yesterday
8	Octagon	Purchase	You Light Up My Life
9	Rectangle	Purchase	Edelweiss
10	Rectangle	Gift	Happy Birthday

Figure 11-62 Boxes table for Exercise 4

INTERMEDIATE

5. Open the Total Cookie Sales Solution.sln file contained in the VB2017\Chap11\Total Cookie Sales Solution folder.

    a. Figure 11-63 shows the Sales table contained in the CookieSales.mdf file. The table contains the numbers of boxes of cookies sold in each of six weeks. The database is already connected to the application and the CookieSalesDataSet has already been created.

    b. Open the Data Sources window and then drag the Sales table to the DataGridView control. Change the control's AutoSizeColumnsMode to Fill. Use the control's task list to disable adding, editing, and deleting records. Also, right-align the numbers in the cookie sales columns.

    c. Lock the controls on the form. Start the application to verify that the six records appear in the DataGridView control. Stop the application.

    d. The Calculate button should display the total sales for each cookie type. Code the btnCalc_Click procedure. (The database does not allow NULLs in any of the fields, so you do not need to check if a field contains the NULL value.)

    e. Save the solution and then start and test the application.

Week	Chocolate Chip	Peanut Butter	Pecan Sandies
1	200	150	75
2	185	170	100
3	165	160	120
4	120	125	110
5	95	80	50
6	101	100	100

Figure 11-63 Sales table for Exercise 5

6. Open the Utilities Solution.sln file contained in the VB2017\Chap11\Utilities Solution-DataGrid folder.

    INTERMEDIATE

    a. Create a SQL Server database named Utilities.mdf.

    b. Add the Bills table definition shown in Figure 11-64 to the database. The Month field's (Is Identity), Identity Increment, and Identity Seed properties are set to True, 1, and 1, respectively. (Recall that you need to expand the Identity Specification property to access these properties.)

    c. After defining the table, click the Update button and then click the Update Database button.

    d. Open the Data Sources window and start the Data Source Configuration Wizard. Connect the Utilities.mdf file to the application. Include the entire Bills table in the dataset.

    e. Set the Utilities.mdf file's Copy to Output Directory property to "Copy if newer".

    f. Drag the Bills table to the form. Set the DataGridView control's AutoSizeColumnsMode property to Fill.

    g. Open the DataGridView control's task list and click Dock in Parent Container. Click Edit Columns. Change the Month column's AutoSizeMode property to ColumnHeader.

    h. Click Electricity in the Edit Columns dialog box, click DefaultCellStyle, click the ... (ellipsis) button, click Format, click the ... (ellipsis) button, click Numeric, and then click the OK button. The Format box now shows N2. Change the Alignment property to MiddleRight and then click the OK button to close the CellStyle Builder dialog box.

    i. Now, format the Water and Gas columns using the Numeric setting with two decimal places. Also, align the values in both columns using the MiddleRight setting. When you are finished setting the properties, close the Edit Columns dialog box.

    j. Change the form's Size property to 330, 200.

    k. Open the Code Editor window and enter an appropriate Try...Catch statement.

    l. Save the solution and then start the application. Enter the three records shown in Figure 11-64. (Recall that the Month field is an auto-numbered field. The numbers 1, 2, and 3 will appear when you click the Save Data button.)

    m. Stop the application and then start it again to verify that the three records were saved.

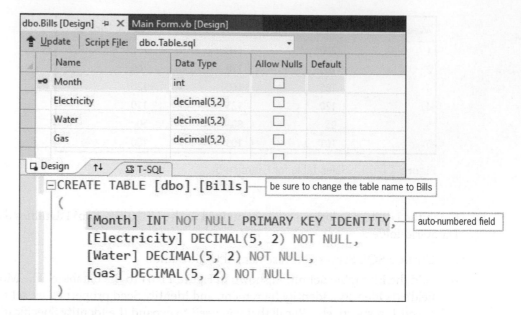

Figure 11-64 Table definition and records for Exercise 6

INTERMEDIATE

7. In this exercise, you modify the Utility Expenses application from Exercise 6. Use Windows to make a copy of the Utilities Solution-DataGrid folder. Rename the copy Utilities Solution-Totals.

 a. Open the Utilities Solution.sln file contained in the VB2017\Chap11\Utilities Solution-Totals folder. Undock the DataGridView control. The interface should now include a Calculate button that displays (in label controls) the following four values: the total cost for electricity, the total cost for water, the total cost for gas, and the total utility cost. Modify the interface and code. Display the totals with a dollar sign and two decimal places. Save the solution and then start and test the application.

 b. Stop the application. Each time the user clicks the Save Data button, the button's Click event procedure should clear the totals from the four labels. Modify the procedure's code.

 c. Save the solution and then start the application. Click the Calculate button. Now, enter the following values for month 4: 55, 20, and 50. Click the Save Data button and then close the message box. The button's Click event procedure clears the contents of the four labels.

 d. Click the Calculate button to verify that the values for month 4 are included in the totals.

ADVANCED

8. Create a Windows Form application for Clancy Boutique. Use the following names for the project and solution, respectively: Clancy Project and Clancy Solution. Save the application in the VB2017\Chap11 folder.

   a. Create the interface shown in Figure 11-65. The interface contains a DataGridView control, a group box, six labels, and two buttons. (The DataGridView tool is located in the Data section of the toolbox.)

   b. Figure 11-66 shows the table definition and records for the Stores table, which is contained in the VB2017\Chap11\Databases\Clancy.mdf file. The Ownership field indicates whether the store is company-owned (C) or a franchisee (F). Connect the database to the application. Include the entire table in the dataset.

   c. Drag the Stores table to the DataGridView control. Use the control's task list to disable adding, editing, and deleting records. The numbers in the Sales column should be right-aligned and displayed with a comma and no decimal places. Center the letters in the Ownership column. Also, be sure that the entire city name appears in the City column. Make the necessary modifications to the control.

   d. Lock the controls on the form and then set the tab order.

   e. The Calculate button should display the total sales made by company-owned stores and the total sales made by franchisees. It should also display the total sales for all of the stores. Code the button's Click event procedure. Display the total sales amounts with a dollar sign and no decimal places.

   f. Save the solution and then start and test the application.

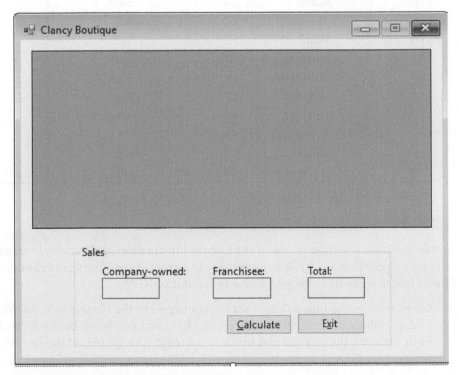

Figure 11-65 Interface for Exercise 8

Name	Data Type	Allow Nulls
⌐○ Store	int	☐
City	varchar(40)	☐
State	char(2)	☐
Sales	int	☐
Ownership	char(1)	☐

Store	City	State	Sales	Ownership
100	San Francisco	CA	236700	C
101	San Diego	CA	125900	C
102	Burbank	CA	96575	F
103	Chicago	IL	135400	C
104	Chicago	IL	108000	F
105	Denver	CO	212600	C
106	Atlanta	GA	123500	C
107	Louisville	KY	178500	C
108	Lexington	KY	167450	F
109	Nashville	TN	205625	C
110	Atlanta	GA	198600	F
111	Denver	CO	45900	F
112	Miami	FL	175300	C
113	Las Vegas	NV	245675	C
114	New Orleans	LA	213400	C
115	Louisville	KY	68900	F
116	Las Vegas	NV	110340	F
118	Indianapolis	IN	97500	C
119	Raleigh	NC	86400	C
120	San Francisco	CA	65975	F

Figure 11-66   Stores table definition and records for Exercise 8

ADVANCED

9. In this exercise, you modify one of the Course Information applications created in this chapter's Apply lesson. Use Windows to make a copy of the Course Info Solution-Total Hours folder. Rename the copy Course Info Solution-GPA.

   a. Open the Course Info Solution.sln file contained in the Course Info Solution-GPA folder. Unlock the controls on the form. Then, add two labels to the form. Position both between the lblTotal and btnCalc controls. Change one of the new label's Text property to GPA:. Change the other new label's name to lblGpa. Lock the controls.

   b. Open the Code Editor window. In addition to displaying the total number of hours completed, the btnCalc_Click procedure should also display the student's GPA. Grades of A, B, C, D, and F are worth 4 points, 3 points, 2 points, 1 point, and no points, respectively. Display the GPA with one decimal place. Modify the procedure's code.

   c. Save the solution and then start and test the application.

ADVANCED

10. In this exercise, you create a two-table SQL Server database. You also create an application that displays the database information in a DataGridView control

    a. Create a Windows Forms application. Use the following names for the project and solution, respectively: Global Project and Global Solution. Save the application in the VB2017\Chap11 folder.

    b. Create a SQL Server database named Global.mdf. Add the Salespeople table definition and records, which are shown in Figure 11-67, to the database. (Remember to click the Update button and then click the Update Database button after defining the table.) Then, add the Sales table definition and records, which are also shown in Figure 11-67, to the database.

    c. Open the Data Sources window and start the Data Source Configuration Wizard. Connect the Global.mdf file to the application. Include both tables in the dataset.

    d. Open the DataSet Designer window by right-clicking GlobalDataSet in the Data Sources window and then clicking Edit DataSet with Designer. Add a relation to the window. Relate both tables by the SalesId field. (The Salespeople table is the parent table, and the Sales table is the child table.)

    e. Right-click Fill,GetData() in the SalespeopleTableAdapter box and then click Configure. Open the Query Builder dialog box. Add the Sales table to the Diagram pane. The application will need to display the SalesId and Name fields from the Salespeople table along with the Sales field from the Sales table. Select the appropriate check box(es). Execute the query to verify that it retrieves the required information. Then, close the Query Builder dialog box and continue configuring the Fill and GetData methods.

    f. Save the solution and then close the GlobalDataSet.xsd window.

Salespeople table and records

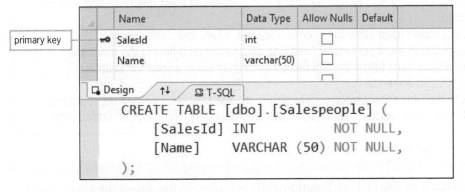

Sales table and records

Figure 11-67 Table definitions and records for Exercise 10

g. Use the DataGridView tool, which is located in the Data section of the toolbox, to add a DataGridView control to the form. Drag the appropriate object from the Data Sources window to the control.

h. The DataGridView control should not allow the user to add, edit, or delete records. When the application is started, its interface should appear similar to the one shown in Figure 11-68. Save the solution and then start and test the application.

Sales ID	Name	Sales
115	Jack Parks	$75,000
201	Jose Guermo	$83,000
363	Sharon Williams	$56,000

Figure 11-68 Global Sales application for Exercise 10

ON YOUR OWN

11. Create a Windows Forms application. Use the following names for the project and solution, respectively: OnYourOwn Project and OnYourOwn Solution. Save the application in the VB2017\Chap11 folder. Plan and design an application of your choice. The only requirement is that you must follow the minimum guidelines listed in Figure 11-69. Before starting the application, be sure to verify the name of the startup form. Save the solution and then start and test the application.

1. You must create a SQL Server database that contains at least one table and at least four fields.
2. The application must allow the user to add, edit, save, and delete records.
3. The application must perform at least one calculation on a field in the database.
4. The interface must follow the GUI design guidelines summarized for Chapters 2 through 11 in Appendix A.
5. Objects that are either coded or referred to in code should be named appropriately.
6. The Code Editor window must contain comments and the three Option statements.

Figure 11-69 Guidelines for Exercise 11

FIX IT

12. Open the VB2017\Chap11\FixIt Solution\FixIt Solution.sln file. Open the Code Editor window. Correct any errors in the code. Start the application. Click the Calculate button. The total on hand should be 125.

Database Queries with SQL

In Chapter 11, you learned how to create a SQL Server database. You also learned how to perform common database tasks, such as editing, adding, deleting, and saving records as well as performing calculations on fields. In this chapter's Focus on the Concepts lesson, you will learn how to perform another common database task: querying. You query a database to filter out specific information that you want to access, perhaps either to display or to use in a calculation. You will create the database queries using Structured Query Language (SQL), which you were briefly introduced to in the *Creating a Database Query* section in Chapter 11's Focus lesson. SQL contains statements that allow you to retrieve and manipulate the data stored in databases created by many different relational database management systems (RDBMSs).

The Apply the Concepts lesson expands on the topics covered in the Focus lesson. More specifically, you will learn how to use SQL to add a calculated field to a dataset. You will also learn how to use the SQL aggregate functions.

FOCUS ON THE CONCEPTS LESSON

Concepts covered in this lesson:

- F-1 SELECT statement
- F-2 Creating a query
- F-3 Parameter queries
- F-4 Saving a query
- F-5 Invoking a query from code

F-1 SELECT Statement

You can pronounce SQL either as *ess-cue-el* or as *sequel*.

The most commonly used statement in **Structured Query Language**, or **SQL**, is the SELECT statement. You use the **SELECT statement** to create database queries. As you learned in Chapter 11, a **database query**, often referred to more simply as a **query**, is a statement that allows you to retrieve specific information from a database. For example, you can use a query to specify the fields and records you want either to display or to use in a calculation.

The basic syntax of the SELECT statement is shown in Figure 12-1 along with some of the operators that can be included in the WHERE clause's condition. Capitalizing the boldfaced keywords in a SELECT statement is optional; however, many programmers do so for clarity.

SELECT Statement

Basic syntax
SELECT *fieldList* **FROM** *table*
    [WHERE *condition*]
    [ORDER BY *field* **[DESC]]**

Operators for the WHERE clause's condition

=	equal to
<>	not equal to
>	greater than
>=	greater than or equal to
<	less than
<=	less than or equal to
AND	all subconditions must be true for the compound condition to evaluate to True
OR	only one of the subconditions needs to be true for the compound condition to evaluate to True
NOT	reverses the truth-value of the condition
LIKE	uses a wildcard character to compare text values; the % wildcard represents zero or more characters and the _ (underscore) wildcard represents one character
IS NULL	compares a value with a NULL value

Figure 12-1 SELECT statement's basic syntax and operators

In the syntax, *fieldList* is one or more field names separated by commas, and *table* is the name of the table containing the fields. The WHERE and ORDER BY clauses are optional parts of the syntax. You use the **WHERE clause**, which contains a *condition*, to limit the records you want to retrieve. Similar to the condition in the If...Then...Else and Do...Loop statements, the condition in a WHERE clause specifies a requirement that must be met for a record to be selected. The **ORDER BY clause** is used to arrange the records in either ascending (the default) or descending order by one or more fields.

Figure 12-2 shows examples of using the SELECT statement to query the Winners table in the Oscars.mdf database.

Winners table in the Oscars.mdf database

Name	Data Type	Allow Nulls	Default
Year	int	☐	
Actor	varchar(50)	☐	
Actress	varchar(50)	☐	
Picture	varchar(50)	☐	
Animated	varchar(50)	☐	

Year	Actor	Actress	Picture	Animated
2008	Daniel Day-Lewis	Marion Cotillard	No Country for Old Men	Ratatouille
2009	Sean Penn	Kate Winslet	Slumdog Millionaire	WALL-E
2010	Jeff Bridges	Sandra Bullock	The Hurt Locker	Up
2011	Colin Firth	Natalie Portman	The King's Speech	Toy Story 3
2012	Jean Dujardin	Meryl Streep	The Artist	Rango
2013	Daniel-Day Lewis	Jennifer Lawrence	Argo	Brave
2014	Matthew McConaughey	Cate Blanchett	12 Years a Slave	Frozen
2015	Eddie Redmayne	Julianne Moore	Birdman	Big Hero 6
2016	Leonardo DiCaprio	Brie Larson	Spotlight	Inside Out
2017	Casey Affleck	Emma Stone	Moonlight	Zootopia

Example 1
```
SELECT Year, Actor, Actress, Picture, Animated FROM Winners
```
selects all of the fields and records from the table

Example 2
```
SELECT Year, Actor, Actress, Picture, Animated FROM Winners
     WHERE Year >= 2014
```
selects all of the fields from records for the year 2014 and later

Example 3
```
SELECT Year FROM Winners WHERE Picture = 'Argo'
```
selects the Year field for the Argo record

Figure 12-2 SELECT statement examples *(continues)*

(continued)

Example 4
SELECT Year, Picture FROM Winners
    WHERE Picture LIKE 'The %'
selects the Year and Picture fields for all records whose Picture field begins with the word
"The" followed by a space and zero or more characters

Example 5
SELECT Year, Animated FROM Winners
    WHERE Year = 2010 OR Year = 2015
    ORDER BY Year DESC
selects the Year and Animated fields for records whose Year field contains either 2010 or 2015
and then arranges the records in descending order by the Year field

---

Figure 12-2   SELECT statement examples

Notice that the word *Argo* in Example 3 appears in single quotes, but the number 2014 in Example 2 does not. The single quotes around the value in the WHERE clause's condition are necessary only when you are comparing a field that contains text with a literal constant. The single quotes are not necessary when you are comparing a numeric field with a literal constant. Text comparisons in SQL are not case sensitive. Therefore, the WHERE clause in Example 3 can also be written as WHERE Picture = 'argo'.

In Example 4, the SELECT statement's WHERE clause contains the SQL **LIKE operator** along with the **%** (percent sign) wildcard, which represents zero or more characters. The statement tells the computer to select the Year and Picture fields for records whose Picture field begins with the word "The" followed by a space and zero or more characters. The LIKE operator can also be used with the _ (underscore) wildcard, which represents one character.

The WHERE clause in Example 5's SELECT statement contains the OR operator. The clause tells the computer to select the specified fields for any record whose Year field contains either 2010 or 2015. The ORDER BY clause in the statement arranges the selected records in descending order by the Year field.

Mini-Quiz 12-1

1. Using the Winners table from Figure 12-2, write a SELECT statement that selects only the Actress field for the year 2010.

2. Using the Winners table from Figure 12-2, write a SELECT statement that selects only the Animated field for records whose Animated field begins with the letter R. Sort the records in ascending order by the Animated field.

3. Using the Winners table from Figure 12-2, write a SELECT statement that selects the Actor and Actress fields for the years 2008 through 2010. Sort the records in descending order by the Year field.

1) SELECT Actress FROM Winners WHERE Year = 2010 2) SELECT Animated FROM Winners WHERE Animated LIKE 'R%' ORDER BY Animated 3) SELECT Actor, Actress FROM Winners WHERE Year >= 2008 AND Year <= 2010 ORDER BY Year DESC

F-2 Creating a Query

In this section, you will use the **Query Builder dialog box**, which you learned about in Chapter 11, to create queries for the examples shown in Figure 12-2. The queries will allow you to observe the way the SELECT statements in those examples retrieve the desired fields and records from the database.

To create queries for the examples in Figure 12-2:

START HERE

1. Open the Oscars Solution.sln file contained in the VB2017\Chap12\Oscars Solution-SELECT folder. Open the designer and Solution Explorer windows. The Oscar Winners application is already connected to the Oscars.mdf database, and the OscarsDataSet is already created.

2. Start the application. The OscarsDataSet contains the 10 records shown in Figure 12-3.

	Year	Actor	Actress	Picture	Animated
▶	2008	Daniel Day-Lewis	Marion Cotillard	No Country for Old Men	Ratatouille
	2009	Sean Penn	Kate Winslet	Slumdog Millionaire	WALL-E
	2010	Jeff Bridges	Sandra Bullock	The Hurt Locker	Up
	2011	Colin Firth	Natalie Portman	The King's Speech	Toy Story 3
	2012	Jean Dujardin	Meryl Streep	The Artist	Rango
	2013	Daniel-Day Lewis	Jennifer Lawrence	Argo	Brave
	2014	Matthew McConaughey	Cate Blanchett	12 Years a Slave	Frozen
	2015	Eddie Redmayne	Julianne Moore	Birdman	Big Hero 6
	2016	Leonardo DiCaprio	Brie Larson	Spotlight	Inside Out
	2017	Casey Affleck	Emma Stone	Moonlight	Zootopia

Oscar Winners — □ ×

Exit

Figure 12-3 Records in the OscarsDataSet

3. Click the **Exit** button. Right-click **OscarsDataSet.xsd** in the Solution Explorer window. The .xsd file, called the dataset's schema file, contains information about the tables, fields, records, and properties included in the OscarsDataSet. Click **Open** to open the DataSet Designer window. See Figure 12-4.

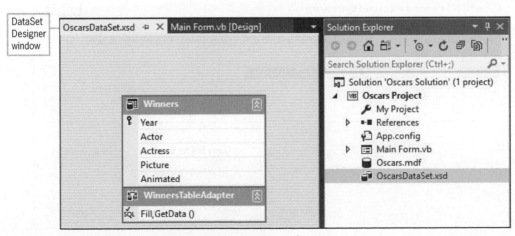

Figure 12-4 DataSet Designer window

4. Right-click **WinnersTableAdapter** in the DataSet Designer window. Point to **Add** on the shortcut menu and then click **Query**. (If Add does not appear on the shortcut menu, click Add Query instead.) Doing this starts the TableAdapter Query Configuration Wizard. The Use SQL statements radio button should be selected on the Choose a Command Type screen, as shown in Figure 12-5.

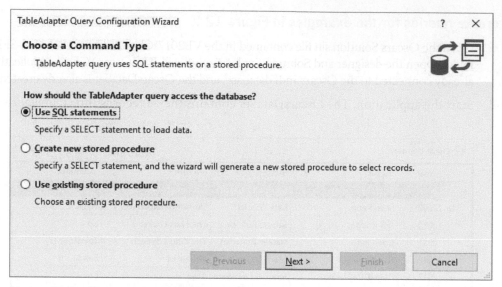

Figure 12-5   Choose a Command Type screen

5. Click the **Next** button to display the Choose a Query Type screen. Verify that the "SELECT which returns rows" radio button is selected.

6. Click the **Next** button to display the Specify a SQL SELECT statement screen. The "What data should the table load?" box contains the default query, which selects all of the fields and records from the table. See Figure 12-6. The default query is automatically executed when the frmMain_Load procedure invokes the WinnersTableAdapter object's Fill method.

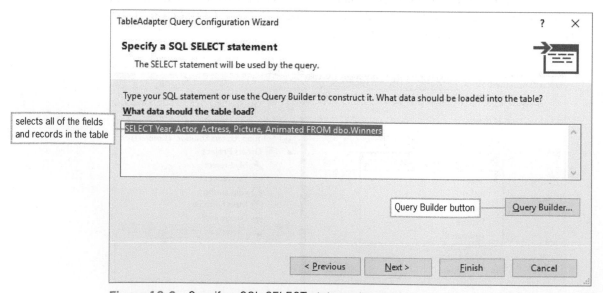

Figure 12-6   Specify a SQL SELECT statement screen

7. You can type a different SELECT statement in the "What data should the table load?" box, or you can use the Query Builder dialog box to construct the statement for you. Click the **Query Builder** button to open the Query Builder dialog box. See Figure 12-7. The table's primary key (Year) appears boldfaced in the Diagram pane.

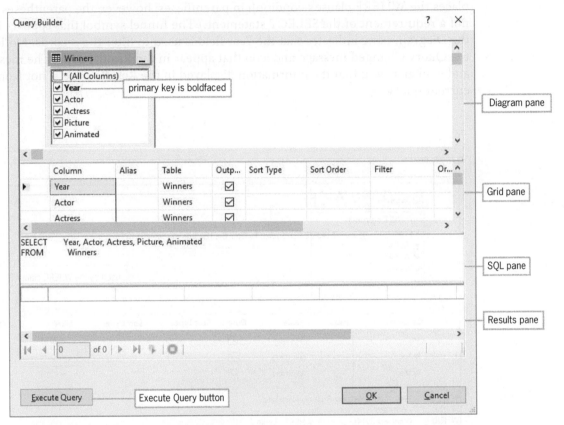

Figure 12-7   Query Builder dialog box

8. The SQL pane contains the same SELECT statement shown in Example 1 in Figure 12-2. The statement selects all of the fields and records from the Winners table. Click the **Execute Query** button to run the query. The query results (10 records) appear in the Results pane. See Figure 12-8. Use the vertical scroll bar to view the remaining records.

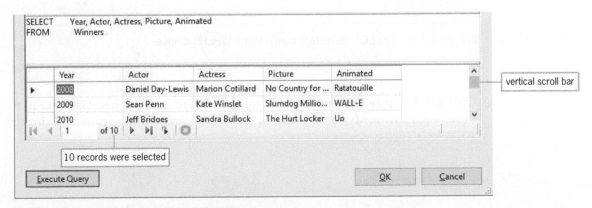

Figure 12-8   Records listed in the Results pane

9. The second example shown earlier in Figure 12-2 selects all of the fields in the Winners table, but only for records for the year 2014 and later. In the Grid pane, click the **blank cell** in the Year field's Filter column. Type **>= 2014** and press **Enter**. See Figure 12-9. The Filter column entry tells the Query Builder to include the WHERE (Year >= 2014) clause in the SELECT statement. (For clarity, the Query Builder places the WHERE clause's condition in parentheses; however, the parentheses are not a requirement of the SELECT statement.) The funnel symbol that appears in the Diagram pane indicates that the Year field is used to filter the records. Notice the Query Changed message and icon that appear in the Results pane. The message and icon alert you that the information displayed in the Results pane is not from the current query.

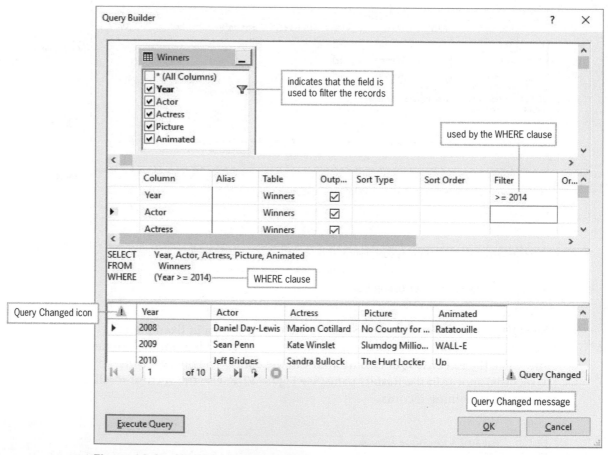

Figure 12-9   SELECT statement containing a WHERE clause

10. Click the **Execute Query** button to run the current query. If necessary, scroll the Results pane to verify that it contains only the records for the years 2014 through 2017.

11. Example 3 in Figure 12-2 selects only the Year field for the Argo record. Delete the **>= 2014** entry from the Year field's Filter column and then click the **blank cell** in the Picture field's Filter column. Type **Argo** and press **Enter**. The Query Builder changes the entry in the Filter column to = 'Argo'. It also enters the WHERE (Picture = 'Argo') clause in the SELECT statement.

12. In the Diagram pane, deselect the **Actor**, **Actress**, **Picture**, and **Animated** check boxes. The Query Builder changes the first line in the SELECT statement to SELECT Year. Click the **Execute Query** button. See Figure 12-10.

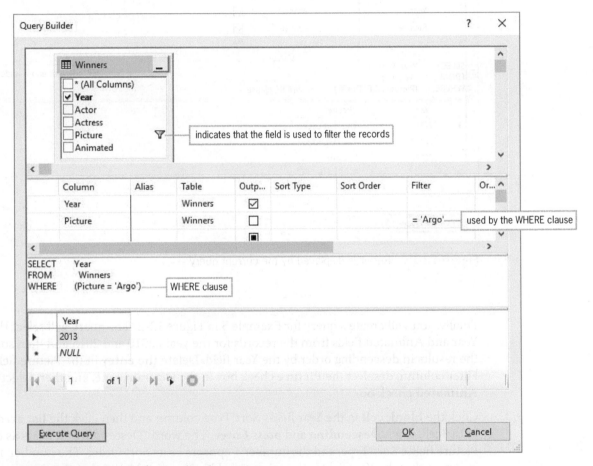

Figure 12-10 Result of executing the current query

13. Next, you will create a query for Example 4 in Figure 12-2. The query will select the Year and Picture fields for all records whose Picture field begins with the word "The" followed by a space and zero or more characters. Select the **Picture** check box in the Diagram pane. Replace the **= 'Argo'** entry in the Grid pane with **LIKE 'The %'** and then press **Enter**. (Be sure to include a space character before the % wildcard.) Click the **Execute Query** button. See Figure 12-11.

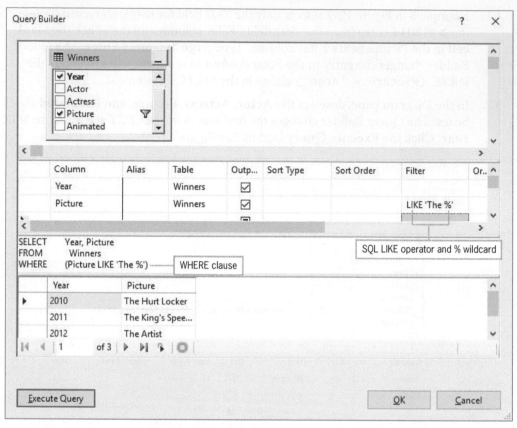

Figure 12-11 Records displayed by the current query

14. Finally, you will create a query for Example 5 in Figure 12-2. The query will select the Year and Animated fields from the records for the years 2010 and 2015 and then sort the results in descending order by the Year field. Delete **the entry** in the Picture field's Filter column, deselect the **Picture** check box in the Diagram pane, and then select the **Animated** check box.

15. Click the **blank cell** in the Year field's Sort Type column and then click the **list arrow** in the cell. Click **Descending** and press **Enter**. The word "Descending" appears as the Picture field's Sort Type, and the number 1 appears as its Sort Order. The number 1 indicates that the Year field is the primary field in the sort. Notice that the Query Builder adds the ORDER BY Year DESC clause to the SELECT statement.

16. In the Year field's Filter column, type **2010 or 2015** and press **Enter**. The Query Builder changes the entry to = 2010 OR = 2015. It also adds the WHERE (Year = 2010 OR Year = 2015) clause to the SELECT statement.

17. Click the **Execute Query** button. See Figure 12-12. (You can use the vertical lines that appear between the column headings in the Grid pane to adjust the width of the columns.)

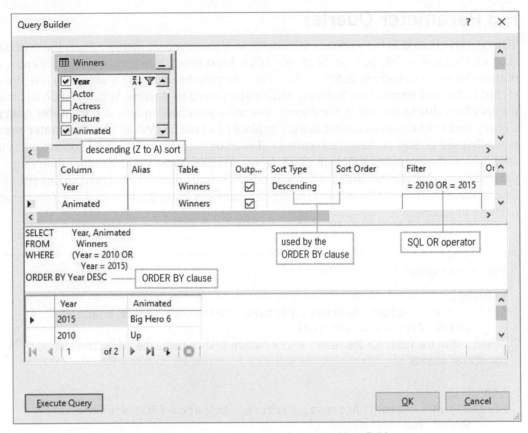

Figure 12-12 Records displayed in descending order by the Year field

18. Click the **Cancel** button in the Query Builder dialog box, and then click the **Cancel** button in the TableAdapter Query Configuration Wizard dialog box.

19. Save the solution. Close the OscarsDataSet.xsd window and then close the solution.

YOU DO IT 1!

Open the You Do It 1 Solution.sln file contained in the VB2017\Chap12\You Do It 1 Solution folder. Use the application to test the SELECT statements from Mini-Quiz 12-1. Close the solution.

F-3 Parameter Queries

The queries created in the previous section retrieve only records matching specific criteria, such as `Picture = 'Argo'` or `Year >= 2014`. Most times, however, you will not know ahead of time the value to include in the criteria. For example, the user may want to retrieve the Argo record today, but retrieve the Slumdog Millionaire record tomorrow. When you do not know the specific value to include in the criteria, you use a parameter query. A **parameter query** is a query that contains a parameter marker in place of a criteria's value. The **parameter marker** typically used in SQL is the @ (at) symbol followed by the name of the field you are querying, as shown in the examples in Figure 12-13. If the WHERE clause contains more than one parameter marker for the same field, you append a unique number (1, 2, and so on) after the field name in each one. For instance, notice the numbers 1 and 2 added to the @Year parameter markers in Example 3.

Parameter Queries

<u>Example 1</u>
```
SELECT Year, Actor, Actress, Picture, Animated FROM Winners
    WHERE Picture = @Picture
```
selects all of the fields for the record whose Picture field contains the value represented by the parameter marker

<u>Example 2</u>
```
SELECT Year, Actor, Actress, Picture, Animated FROM Winners
    WHERE Year >= @Year
```
selects all of the fields for records whose Year field contains a value that is greater than or equal to the value represented by the parameter marker

<u>Example 3</u>
```
SELECT Year, Actor, Actress, Picture, Animated FROM Winners
    WHERE Year >= @Year1 AND Year <= @Year2
```
selects all of the fields for records whose Year field contains a value that is greater than or equal to the value represented by the first parameter marker but less than or equal to the value represented by the second parameter marker

---

Figure 12-13   Examples of parameter queries

Mini-Quiz 12-2

1. Using the Winners table from Figure 12-2, write a parameter query that selects only an actor's Picture field.

2. Using the Winners table from Figure 12-2, write a parameter query that selects only an animated picture's Year field.

3. Using the Winners table from Figure 12-2, write a parameter query that selects the Actor and Actress fields for the year provided by the user.

1) SELECT Picture FROM Winners WHERE Actor = @Actor 2) SELECT Year FROM Winners WHERE Animated = @Animated 3) SELECT Actor, Actress FROM Winners WHERE Year = @Year

In the next set of steps, you will use the Oscar Winners application to test the SELECT statements from Figure 12-13.

To create queries for the examples in Figure 12-13:

START HERE

1. Open the Oscars Solution.sln file contained in the VB2017\Chap12\Oscars Solution-Parameter Queries folder. The Oscar Winners application is already connected to the Oscars.mdf database, and the OscarsDataSet is already created.

2. Right-click **OscarsDataSet.xsd** in the Solution Explorer window and then click **Open** to open the DataSet Designer window. (You can also right-click OscarsDataSet in the Data Sources window and then click Edit DataSet with Designer.)

3. Right-click **WinnersTableAdapter** in the DataSet Designer window. Point to **Add** on the shortcut menu, and then click **Query** to start the TableAdapter Query Configuration Wizard. (If Add does not appear on the shortcut menu, click Add Query instead.)

4. Verify that the Use SQL statements radio button is selected on the Choose a Command Type screen. Click the **Next** button to display the Choose a Query Type screen. Verify that the "SELECT which returns rows" radio button is selected. Click the **Next** button to display the Specify a SQL SELECT statement screen. Click the **Query Builder** button to open the Query Builder dialog box.

5. First, you will create a parameter query that selects a record based on the value in its Picture field. In the Grid pane, click the **blank cell** in the Picture field's Filter column. Type **@Picture** and press **Enter**. The Query Builder changes the entry in the Filter column to = @Picture. It also adds the WHERE (Picture = @Picture) clause to the SELECT statement.

6. Click the **Execute Query** button to run the query. The Query Parameters dialog box opens. Type **Argo** in the Value column. See Figure 12-14.

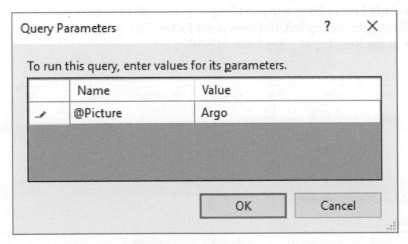

Figure 12-14 Query Parameters dialog box

7. Click the **OK** button to close the Query Parameters dialog box. The Argo record appears in the Results pane. See Figure 12-15.

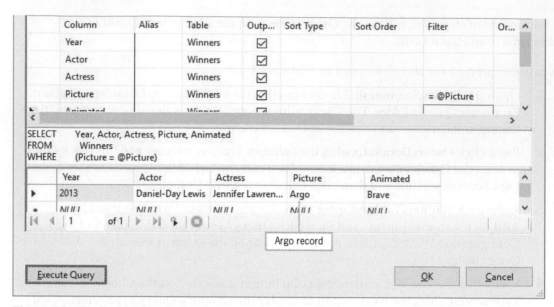

Figure 12-15   Result of executing the current parameter query

8. Now, you will use the query to select the Slumdog Millionaire record. Click the **Execute Query** button, type **Slumdog Millionaire** in the Value column, and then press **Enter**. The Slumdog Millionaire record appears in the Results pane.

9. Next, you will create a query for Example 2 from Figure 12-13. The query will select all of the fields for records whose Year field contains a value that is greater than or equal to the value provided by the user. Delete = **@Picture** from the Picture field's Filter column. Type >= **@Year** in the Year field's Filter column and then press **Enter**. The Query Builder changes the entry in the Filter column to >= @Year. It also changes the WHERE clause to WHERE (Year >= @Year).

10. Click the **Execute Query** button to run the query. Type **2016** in the Value column of the Query Parameters dialog box and then press **Enter**. The records for years 2016 and 2017 appear in the Results pane. See Figure 12-16.

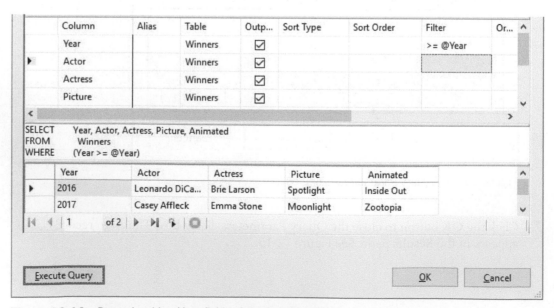

Figure 12-16   Records with a Year field value of at least 2016

11. Now, you will use the query to select records for the year 2013 and later. Click the **Execute Query** button, type **2013** in the Value column, and then click the **OK** button. The records for the years 2013 through 2017 appear in the Results pane.

12. Finally, you will create a query for Example 3 from Figure 12-13. The query will select all of the fields for records whose Year field contains a value that is greater than or equal to the first value provided by the user, but less than or equal to the second value the user provides. Change the entry in the Year field's Filter column to >= **@Year1 and <= @Year2** and press **Enter**. The Query Builder changes the entry in the Filter column to >= @Year1 AND <= @Year2. It also changes the WHERE clause to WHERE (Year >= @Year1 AND Year <= @Year2).

13. Click the **Execute Query** button. Type **2010** in the Value column for @Year1, type **2012** in the Value column for @Year2, and then press **Enter**. The records for the years 2010 through 2012 appear in the Results pane. See Figure 12-17. (You can use the vertical lines that appear between the column headings in the Grid pane to adjust the width of the columns.)

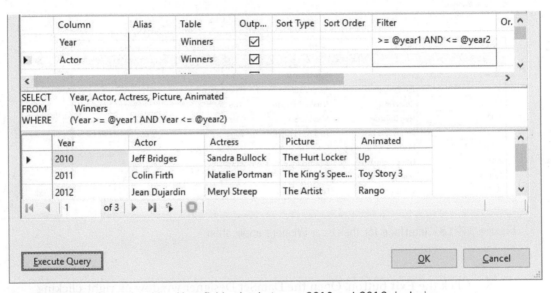

Figure 12-17   Records with a Year field value between 2010 and 2012, inclusive

14. Click the **Cancel** button in the Query Builder dialog box and then click the **Cancel** button in the TableAdapter Query Configuration Wizard dialog box. Save the solution. Close the OscarsDataSet.xsd window and then close the solution.

YOU DO IT 2!

Open the You Do It 2 Solution.sln file contained in the VB2017\Chap12\You Do It 2 Solution folder. Use the application to test the parameter queries from Mini-Quiz 12-2. Close the solution.

F-4 Saving a Query

For an application to use a query during run time, you will need to save the query and then invoke it from code. You save a query that contains the SELECT statement by associating the query with one or more methods. The TableAdapter Query Configuration Wizard provides an easy way to perform this task.

START HERE

To save a query:

1. Open the Oscars Solution.sln file contained in the VB2017\Chap12\Oscars Solution-Save Query folder. The Oscar Winners application is already connected to the Oscars.mdf database, and the OscarsDataSet is already created.

2. Start the application. See Figure 12-18. The application allows the user to display either all of the records in the dataset or only the record for the year entered in the txtYear control.

Figure 12-18 Interface for the Oscar Winners application

3. Click the **Exit** button. Open the DataSet Designer window by right-clicking **OscarsDataSet.xsd** in the Solution Explorer window and then clicking **Open**.

4. Right-click **WinnersTableAdapter** in the DataSet Designer window. Point to **Add** on the shortcut menu, and then click **Query** to start the TableAdapter Query Configuration Wizard. (If Add does not appear on the shortcut menu, click Add Query instead.)

5. Verify that the Use SQL statements radio button is selected. Click the **Next** button to display the Choose a Query Type screen. Verify that the "SELECT which returns rows" radio button is selected. Click the **Next** button to display the Specify a SQL SELECT statement screen. The "What data should the table load?" box contains the default query, which selects all of the fields and records in the table. Recall that the default query is automatically executed when the frmMain_Load procedure invokes the WinnersTableAdapter object's Fill method.

6. Click the **Query Builder** button to open the Query Builder dialog box. You will create a parameter query that displays the Oscar winners for the year entered in the txtYear control. In the Grid pane, type **@Year** in the Year field's Filter column and then press **Enter**. The Query Builder changes your entry to = @Year. It also adds the WHERE (Year = @Year) clause to the SELECT statement.

7. Click the **Execute Query** button to run the query. The Query Parameters dialog box opens. Type **2010** in the Value column and then press **Enter**. The 2010 record appears in the Results pane.

8. Now that you know that the query works correctly, you can save it. Click the **OK** button to close the Query Builder dialog box. The parameter query appears in the "What data should the table load?" box. See Figure 12-19.

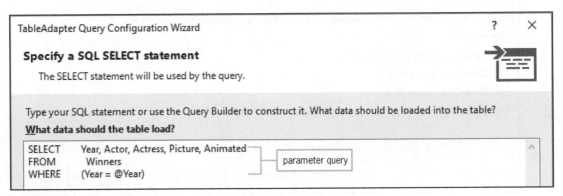

Figure 12-19   Parameter query in the Specify a SQL SELECT statement screen

9. Click the Next button to display the Choose Methods to Generate screen. If necessary, select the **Fill a DataTable** and **Return a DataTable** check boxes. Change the Fill a DataTable method's name from FillBy to **FillByYear**. Change the Return a DataTable method's name from GetDataBy to **GetDataByYear**. See Figure 12-20. The FillByYear and GetDataByYear methods are associated with the parameter query that you created, which means you can use them to invoke the query during run time.

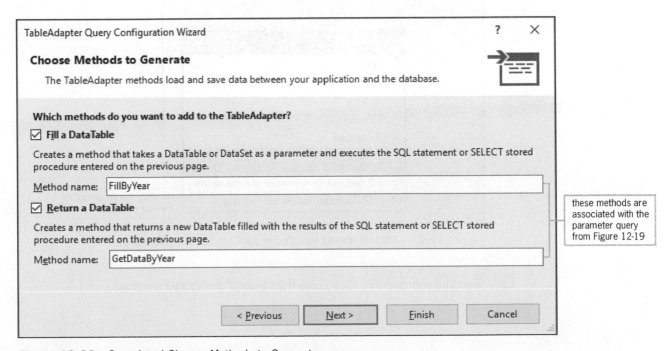

Figure 12-20   Completed Choose Methods to Generate screen

10. Click the **Next** button to display the Wizard Results screen. See Figure 12-21.

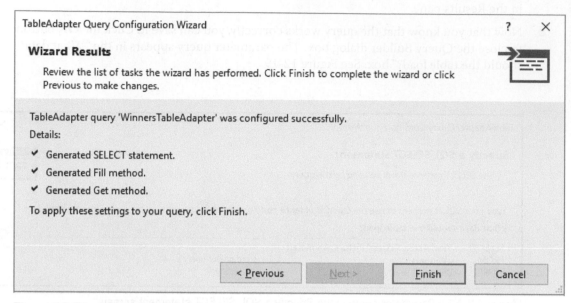

Figure 12-21   Wizard Results screen

11. Click the **Finish** button. The FillByYear and GetDataByYear methods appear in the DataSet Designer window, as shown in Figure 12-22.

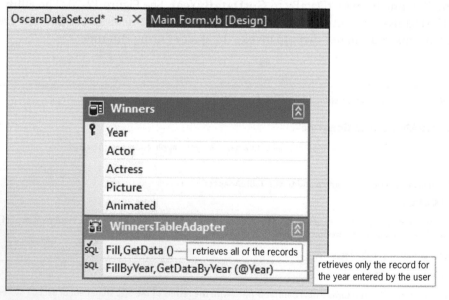

Figure 12-22   Method names included in the DataSet Designer window

12. Save the solution and then close the OscarsDataSet.xsd window.

F-5 Invoking a Query from Code

The Display button in the Oscar Winners application is responsible for invoking the appropriate query: either the default Fill query (if the All radio button is selected) or the FillByYear query (if the Year radio button is selected). You can invoke a query during run time by entering its associated Fill method in a procedure's code. In this application, you will enter the methods in the btnDisplay_Click procedure.

To code the btnDisplay_Click procedure:

START HERE

1. Open the Code Editor window and locate the btnDisplay_Click procedure. Click the **blank line** above the End Sub clause.

2. If the All radio button is selected in the interface, the procedure will use the WinnersTableAdapter object's default Fill method to select all of the records. Enter the lines of code shown in Figure 12-23 and then position the insertion point as shown in the figure.

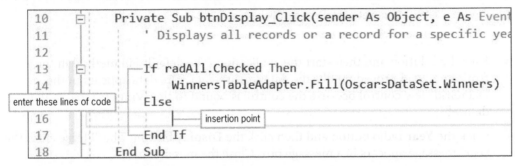

```
10    Private Sub btnDisplay_Click(sender As Object, e As Event
11        ' Displays all records or a record for a specific yea
12
13    If radAll.Checked Then
14        WinnersTableAdapter.Fill(OscarsDataSet.Winners)
      Else          [enter these lines of code]
16            [insertion point]
17    End If
18    End Sub
```

Figure 12-23 Code entered in the procedure

3. If the Year radio button is selected, the procedure will use the WinnersTableAdapter object's FillByYear method to select the record whose Year field matches the year number entered in the txtYear control. First, the procedure will determine whether the control contains a value. If it does not contain a value, the procedure will display an appropriate message. Enter the additional lines of code indicated in Figure 12-24, and then position the insertion point as shown in the figure.

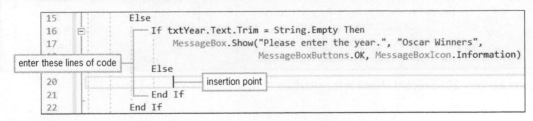

```
15    Else
16        If txtYear.Text.Trim = String.Empty Then
17            MessageBox.Show("Please enter the year.", "Oscar Winners",
                              MessageBoxButtons.OK, MessageBoxIcon.Information)
      [enter these lines of code]    Else
20            [insertion point]
21        End If
22    End If
```

Figure 12-24 Additional code entered in the procedure

4. The Year field in the database has the SQL int data type, so the procedure will need to convert the text box entry to an integer. Enter the following lines of code:

```
Dim intYear As Integer
Integer.TryParse(txtYear.Text.Trim, intYear)
```

5. Next, the procedure will invoke the WinnersTableAdapter object's FillByYear method. The method is associated with a parameter query, so it will need to include the parameter information. Type the additional line of code indicated in Figure 12-25.

```vb
10      Private Sub btnDisplay_Click(sender As Object, e As EventArgs) Handles btnDisp
11          ' Displays all records or a record for a specific year.
12
13          If radAll.Checked Then
14              WinnersTableAdapter.Fill(OscarsDataSet.Winners)
15          Else
16              If txtYear.Text.Trim = String.Empty Then
17                  MessageBox.Show("Please enter the year.", "Oscar Winners",
18                                  MessageBoxButtons.OK, MessageBoxIcon.Information)
19              Else
20                  Dim intYear As Integer
21                  Integer.TryParse(txtYear.Text.Trim, intYear)
22                  WinnersTableAdapter.FillByYear(OscarsDataSet.Winners, intYear)
23              End If
24          End If
25      End Sub
```

enter this line of code — line 22

contains the year number for the parameter query

Figure 12-25 Completed btnDisplay_Click procedure

6. Save the solution and then start the application. The default Fill method in the frmMain_Load procedure fills the dataset with data. The data appears in the DataGridView control because the control is bound to the Winners table in the dataset.

7. Click the **Year** radio button and then click the **Display** button. The "Please enter the year." message appears in a message box. Close the message box.

8. Click the **text box** located below the Year radio button. Type **2013** and then click the **Display** button. The btnDisplay_Click procedure invokes the FillByYear method, which retrieves only the record for the year 2013. The record appears in the DataGridView control, as shown in Figure 12-26.

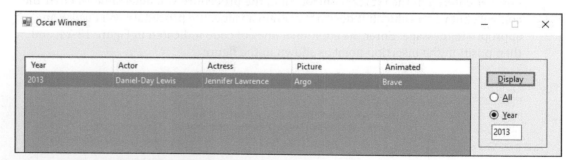

Figure 12-26 2013 record shown in the interface

9. Click the **All** radio button and then click the **Display** button. The btnDisplay_Click procedure invokes the default Fill method, which retrieves all of the records from the dataset. The records appear in the DataGridView control.

10. Click the **Exit** button. Close the Code Editor window and then close the solution.

APPLY THE CONCEPTS LESSON

After studying this lesson, you should be able to:

- A-1 Add a calculated field to a dataset
- A-2 Use the SQL aggregate functions
- A-3 Professionalize your application's interface

A-1 Add a Calculated Field to a Dataset

You can use the SELECT statement to add a calculated field to a dataset. A **calculated field** is a field whose values are the result of a calculation involving one or more of the dataset's existing fields. Although the calculated field is included in the dataset, it is not stored in the database. Instead, it is calculated each time the dataset is accessed.

In the next set of steps, you will create a calculated field for the Ellington Company application. The company has three stores, which are located in the following cities in Florida: Jacksonville, Miami, and Tampa. The company records each store's monthly sales amount in the Sales2019 table, which is contained in the Ellington.mdf database. The sales amounts for the first six months of 2019 are shown in Figure 12-27.

Name	Data Type	Allow Nulls	Default
⚷ Month	int	☐	
Jacksonville	int	☐	
Miami	int	☐	
Tampa	int	☐	

Month	Jacksonville	Miami	Tampa
1	67000	45000	43500
2	69500	43600	47250
3	65900	46500	45000
4	64250	47000	46750
5	63000	45000	49500
6	62600	46700	50200

Figure 12-27 Sales2019 table in the Ellington.mdf database

In addition to displaying the table data shown in Figure 12-27, the application will also display the total of each month's sales. To accomplish this, you will need to create a calculated field that adds together the monthly sales amounts for each of the three stores.

To create a calculated field:

START HERE

1. Open the Ellington Solution.sln file contained in the VB2017\Chap12\Ellington Solution folder. Open the designer window. The Ellington Company application is already connected to the Ellington.mdf database, and the EllingtonDataSet is already created.

2. Permanently display the Data Sources window. (If the Data Sources window is not open, click View, point to Other Windows, and then click Data Sources.) Expand the **EllingtonDataSet** node and then expand the **Sales2019** node.

3. Open the DataSet Designer window by right-clicking **EllingtonDataSet** in the Data Sources window and then clicking **Edit DataSet with Designer**. (You can also open the window by right-clicking EllingtonDataSet.xsd in the Solution Explorer window and then clicking Open.) See Figure 12-28.

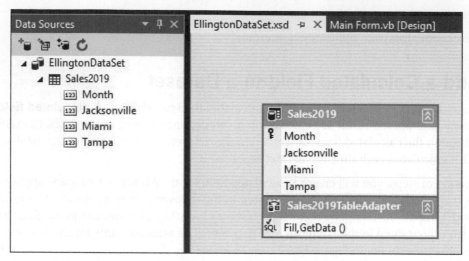

Figure 12-28   Data Sources and DataSet Designer windows

4. Right-click **Fill,GetData ()** in the DataSet Designer window and then click **Configure**. The default SELECT statement appears in the Enter a SQL Statement screen. Recall that this is the statement that the form's Load event procedure uses to fill the dataset with data. You will need to modify this statement to include a calculated field. In this case, the calculated field in each record should contain the total sales made in that month. Modify the SELECT statement as shown in Figure 12-29. The modification tells the computer to add together the values contained in a record's Jacksonville, Miami, and Tampa fields; it should then create a Total field and store the sum in that field.

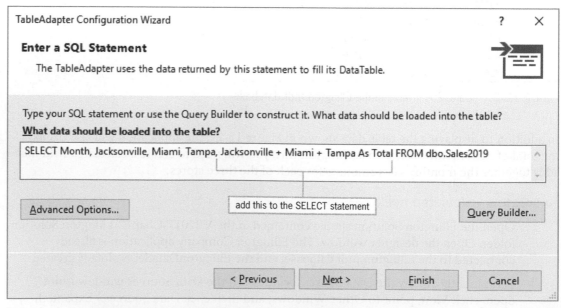

Figure 12-29   Modified SELECT statement

5. Click the **Next** button to display the Choose Methods to Generate screen. The statement in Figure 12-29 should be the default SELECT statement, so you will associate it with the default Fill and GetData methods. Click the **Next** button to display the Wizard Results screen. See Figure 12-30.

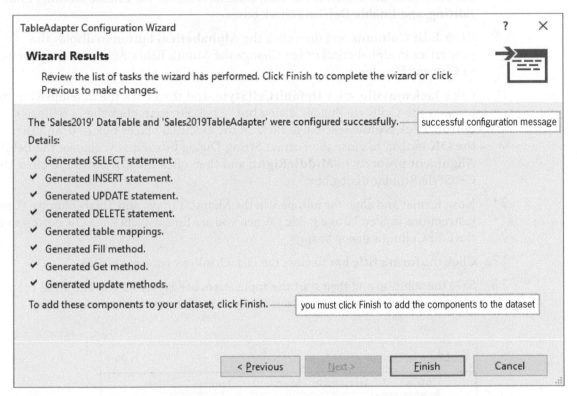

Figure 12-30   Wizard Results screen

6. Click the **Finish** button. Notice that the calculated field (Total) is added to the Sales2019 table in the EllingtonDataSet. See Figure 12-31.

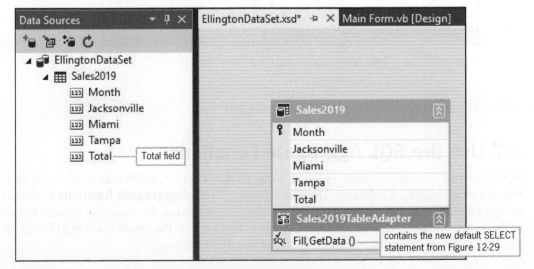

Figure 12-31   Total field added to the table in the dataset

7. Save the solution and then close the EllingtonDataSet.xsd window. If necessary, expand the **Sales2019** node in the Data Sources window.

8. Drag the **Sales2019** table to the DataGridView control. Set its AutoSizeColumnsMode to **Fill**. Click its **task box** and then click **Dock in Parent Container**. Notice that the last column in the control is the Total column. Deselect the **Enable Adding, Enable Editing**, and **Enable Deleting** check boxes.

9. Click **Edit Columns** and then click the **Alphabetical** button to display the properties in alphabetical order. Change the Month field's AutoSizeMode property to **ColumnHeader**.

10. Click **Jacksonville**, click **DefaultCellStyle**, and then click the **...** (ellipsis) button to open the CellStyle Builder dialog box. Click **Format**, click the **...** (ellipsis) button, click **Numeric**, change the 2 in the Decimal places box to **0**, and then click the **OK** button to close the Format String Dialog box. Finally, change the field's Alignment property to **MiddleRight**, and then click the **OK** button to close the CellStyle Builder dialog box.

11. Now, format and align the numbers in the Miami, Tampa, and Total columns. (Use the instructions in Step 10 as a guide.) When you are finished, click the **OK** button to close the Edit Columns dialog box.

12. Click the **form's title bar** to close the DataGridView control's task list.

13. Save the solution and then start the application. See Figure 12-32. The Total column (field) contains the total of the sales amounts in each row (record).

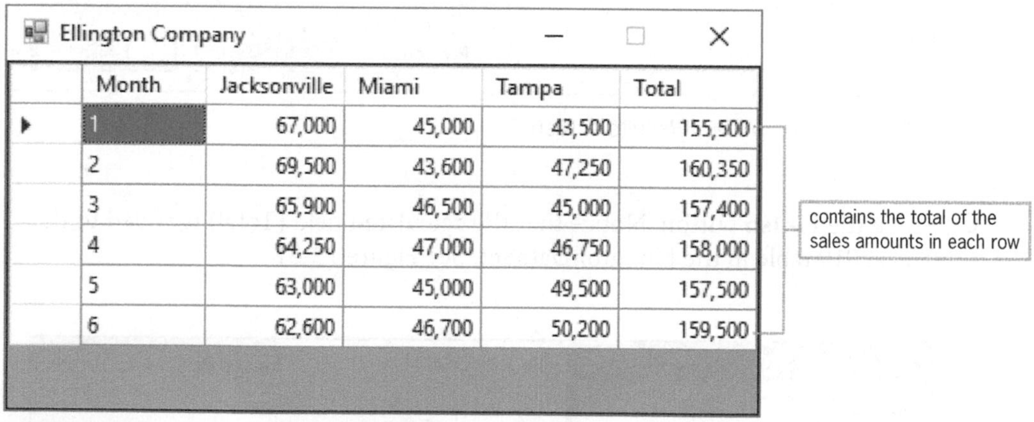

Figure 12-32 Calculated field displayed in the interface

14. Close the application and then close the solution.

A-2 Use the SQL Aggregate Functions

SQL provides several functions—such as AVG, COUNT, MAX, MIN, and SUM—that you can use when querying a dataset. These functions are called **aggregate functions** because they return a single value from a group of values. The SUM function, for example, returns the sum of the values in the group, whereas the MIN function returns the smallest value in the group. Figure 12-33 lists the most commonly used aggregate functions.

SQL Aggregate Functions

Function	Purpose
AVG	returns the average of the values in a group
COUNT	returns the number of values in a group
MAX	returns the maximum value in a group
MIN	returns the minimum value in a group
SUM	returns the sum of the values in a group

Figure 12-33   Most commonly used aggregate functions

In the next set of steps, you will use the SUM aggregate function in a slightly different version of the Ellington Company application from the previous section.

To use the SUM aggregate function:

START HERE

1. Open the Ellington Solution.sln file contained in the VB2017\Chap12\Ellington Solution-Aggregate folder. Open the designer window. The application is the same as the one in the previous section. However, six labels have been added to the interface, as shown in Figure 12-34. Three of the labels will display the total sales made in each of the three stores during the first six months of 2019.

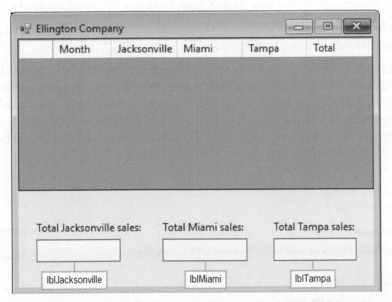

Figure 12-34   Labels added to the Ellington Company interface

2. Permanently display the Data Sources window. Expand the **EllingtonDataSet** node and then expand the **Sales2019** node.

3. Open the DataSet Designer window by right-clicking **EllingtonDataSet** in the Data Sources window and then clicking **Edit DataSet with Designer**. See Figure 12-35. The Sales2019TableAdapter is associated with the default SELECT statement, which displays the appropriate data in the DataGridView control. (The default SELECT statement is shown earlier in Figure 12-29.)

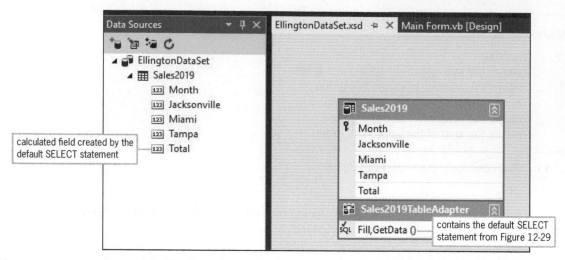

Figure 12-35 Data Sources and DataSet Designer windows

4. Now, you will add a second TableAdapter to the project. This one will be associated with a SELECT statement that uses the SUM aggregate function to total each store's sales amounts. Right-click an **empty area** in the DataSet Designer window. Point to **Add** and then click **TableAdapter**. ElligtonConnectionString appears in the Choose Your Data Connection screen; the new TableAdapter can use the same connection.

5. Click the **Next** button to display the Choose a Command Type screen. Verify that the Use SQL statements radio button is selected.

6. Click the **Next** button to display the Enter a SQL Statement screen. Enter the SELECT statement shown in Figure 12-36. The statement tells the computer to add together all of the values in the Jacksonville field (group) and store the sum in the TotalJack field. It also tells the computer to add together all of the values in the Miami field and all of the values in the Tampa field and store the sums in the TotalMiami and TotalTampa fields, respectively.

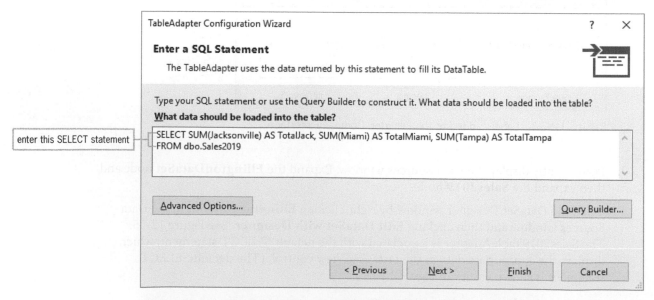

Figure 12-36 SELECT statement containing the SUM aggregate function

7. Click the **Next** button to display the Choose Methods to Generate screen. Change the Fill method's name to **FillByStore**. Change the GetData method's name to **GetDataByStore**. Click the **Next** button to display the Wizard Results screen and then click the **Finish** button.

8. Right-click **DataTable1**, which appears at the top of the new TableAdapter object, and then click **Rename**. Type **Store2019** and press **Enter**. Then, right-click **DataTable1TableAdapter**, click **Rename**, type **Store2019TableAdapter**, and press **Enter**.

9. Expand the **Store2019** node in the Data Sources window. See Figure 12-37.

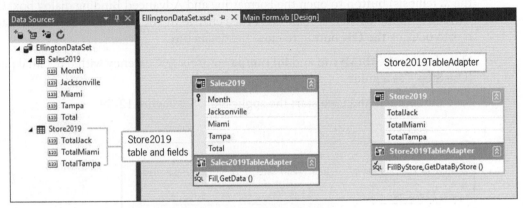

Figure 12-37   Store2019 table and Store2019TableAdapter

10. Save the solution and then close the EllingtonDataSet.xsd window.

11. Expand the **Store2019** node in the Data Sources window. Drag the **TotalJack** field from the Data Sources window to the lblJacksonville control and then release the mouse button. Drag the **TotalMiami** and **TotalTampa** fields from the Data Sources window to the lblMiami and lblTampa controls, respectively.

12. Save the solution and then start the application. Each store's total sales amount appears in its respective label control. See Figure 12-38.

Ellington Company

Month	Jacksonville	Miami	Tampa	Total
1	67,000	45,000	43,500	155,500
2	69,500	43,600	47,250	160,350
3	65,900	46,500	45,000	157,400
4	64,250	47,000	46,750	158,000
5	63,000	45,000	49,500	157,500
6	62,600	46,700	50,200	159,500

Total Jacksonville sales: 392250
Total Miami sales: 273800
Total Tampa sales: 282200

Figure 12-38   Label controls showing the total sales for each store

13. Close the application.

A-3 Professionalize Your Application's Interface

The interface shown in Figure 12-38 would look more professional if each store's total sales amount was formatted with a dollar sign and a thousands separator.

START HERE

To format the sales amounts:

1. Click the **lblJacksonville** control. Temporarily display the Properties window (if necessary). Click **(Data Bindings)**, which appears at the top of the Properties list. Click the **plus box** that appears next to the property and then click **(Advanced)**. Click the **...** (ellipsis) button to open the Formatting and Advanced Binding dialog box. Click **Currency** in the Format type box and then change the number in the Decimal places box to **0**. Click the **OK** button to close the dialog box.

2. Now, format the **lblMiami** and **lblTampa** controls to Currency with 0 decimal places. (Use Step 1 as a guide.)

3. Save the solution and then start the application. See Figure 12-39.

Total Jacksonville sales: Total Miami sales: Total Tampa sales:

$392,250 $273,800 $282,200

Figure 12-39 Formatted total sales amounts

4. Stop the application and then close the solution.

Summary

- A database query, referred to more simply as a query, allows you to retrieve specific information from a database.

- You use the SQL SELECT statement to query a database. The statement's syntax is shown in Figure 12-1.

- You use the SELECT statement's WHERE clause to limit the records you want to access. When comparing a text field with a literal constant, the literal constant must be enclosed in single quotes.

- You can use the SQL LIKE operator to compare text values in a SELECT statement's WHERE clause. The operator can be combined with the following two wildcards: % (percent sign) and _ (underscore). The % wildcard represents zero or more characters, and the _ wildcard represents one character.

- You use the SELECT statement's ORDER BY clause to sort the selected records.

- To open the DataSet Designer window, right-click the name of the dataset's schema file in the Solution Explorer window and then click Open. The schema filename ends with .xsd. Or, right-click the dataset's name in the Data Sources window and then click Edit DataSet with Designer.

- To start the TableAdapter Query Configuration Wizard, open the DataSet Designer window and then right-click the table adapter's name. Point to Add on the shortcut menu and then click Query. (If Add does not appear on the shortcut menu, click Add Query instead.)

- To open the Query Builder dialog box, start the TableAdapter Query Configuration Wizard. Click the Next button to display the Choose a Query Type screen, and then click the Next button to display the Specify a SQL SELECT statement screen. Click the Query Builder button.

- To create a parameter query, use a parameter marker in place of the criteria's value. In SQL, the parameter marker is the @ (at) symbol followed by the name of the field you are querying. If the field appears more than once in the WHERE clause, append a number (1, 2, and so on) to the field name in the parameter marker.

- To save a query that contains the SELECT statement, use the TableAdapter Query Configuration Wizard to associate the query with one or more methods.

- You invoke a saved query from code by entering the Fill method associated with the query in a procedure.

- You can use the SELECT statement to add a calculated field to a dataset.

- SQL provides the following aggregate functions: AVG, COUNT, MAX, MIN, and SUM. These functions return a single value from a group of values.

- You can use the DataSet Designer window to add a new TableAdapter to a project.

- To format the data displayed in a bound label control, click (Data Bindings) in the control's Properties list. Click the plus box next to the property, click (Advanced), and then click the ... (ellipsis) button to open the Formatting and Advanced Binding dialog box.

Key Terms

%—the percent sign wildcard used along with the LIKE operator in a SELECT statement's WHERE clause; represents zero or more characters

_—the underscore wildcard used along with the LIKE operator in a SELECT statement's WHERE clause; represents one character

Aggregate functions—functions that return a single value from a group of values, such as the following SQL functions: AVG, COUNT, MIN, MAX, and SUM

Calculated field—a field that is the result of using one or more existing fields in a calculation

Database query—a statement used to retrieve specific information from a database; also called a query

LIKE operator—used with a wildcard character in a SELECT statement's WHERE clause

ORDER BY clause—used in a SELECT statement to sort the selected records

Parameter marker—used in place of a criteria's value in a parameter query; in SQL, the parameter marker is the @ (at) symbol followed by the name of the field you are querying and an optional number; the number is necessary only when the WHERE clause contains more than one parameter marker for the same field

Parameter query—a query that contains a parameter marker in place of a criteria's value

Query—a statement used to retrieve specific information from a database; also called a database query

Query Builder dialog box—used to create a query

SELECT statement—the SQL statement that allows you to specify the fields and records to select as well as the order in which the fields and records appear when displayed

SQL—an acronym for Structured Query Language

Structured Query Language—SQL; a set of statements that allows you to access and manipulate the data stored in a database

WHERE clause—used in a SELECT statement to limit the records to be selected

Review Questions

1. SQL stands for _____.

   a. Select Query Language

   b. Semi-Quick Language

   c. Structured Quick Language

   d. Structured Query Language

2. Which of the following will select the State and Sales fields from the Stores table?

   a. `SELECT State AND Sales FROM Stores`

   b. `SELECT State OR Sales FROM Stores`

   c. `SELECT State, Sales FROM Stores`

   d. `SELECT ONLY State, Sales FROM Stores`

3. Which of the following will select the SSN field from the PayInfo table and then sort the records in descending order by the SSN field?

   a. `SELECT SSN FROM PayInfo DESC`

   b. `SELECT SSN FROM PayInfo ORDER BY SSN DESC`

   c. `SELECT SSN FROM PayInfo WHERE SSN DESC`

   d. `SELECT SSN FROM PayInfo SORT SSN DESC`

4. Which of the following will select the Id and Status fields for records whose Status field contains only the letter F?

   a. `SELECT Id, Status FROM Employ WHERE Status = 'F'`

   b. `SELECT Id, Status FROM Employ ORDER BY Status = 'F'`

   c. `SELECT Id, Status FROM Employ FOR Status = 'F'`

   d. `SELECT Id, Status FROM Employ SELECT Status = 'F'`

5. Which of the following will select the State and Capital fields for the Kansas and Kentucky records?

   a. `SELECT State, Capital FROM States WHERE State LIKE 'K_'`

   b. `SELECT State, Capital FROM States WHERE State LIKE 'K*'`

   c. `SELECT State, Capital FROM States WHERE State LIKE 'K%'`

   d. `SELECT State, Capital FROM States WHERE State LIKE 'K#'`

6. Which of the following will select the State and Capital fields for states with populations that exceed 5,000,000? (The Population field is numeric.)

   a. `SELECT State, Capital FROM States WHERE Population > 5000000`

   b. `SELECT State, Capital FROM States WHERE Population > '5000000'`

   c. `SELECT State, Capital FROM States WHERE Population > "5000000"`

   d. `SELECT State, Capital FROM States SELECT Population > 5000000`

7. In a SELECT statement, which clause is used to limit the records that will be selected?

   a. LIMIT   c. ONLY

   b. ORDER BY   d. WHERE

8. What does the funnel symbol that appears next to a field's name in the Query Builder dialog box indicate?

   a. The field is used in a SELECT statement's ORDER BY clause.

   b. The field is used in a SELECT statement's WHERE clause.

   c. The field is the primary key.

   d. The field is the foreign key.

9. The SQL SELECT statement performs case-sensitive comparisons.

   a. True   b. False

10. When used in a parameter query, which of the following WHERE clauses will select the records for employees working more than 40 hours?

   a. `WHERE Hours > @Hours`

   b. `WHERE Hours > !Hours`

   c. `WHERE Hours > #Hours`

   d. `WHERE Hours > %Hours`

11. Which of the following calculates the average of the values in the OnHand field?

   a. `SELECT AVERAGE(OnHand) AS Available FROM dbo.Inventory`

   b. `SELECT OnHand.AVG AS Available FROM dbo.Inventory`

   c. `SELECT AVG(OnHand) AS Available FROM dbo.Inventory`

   d. `SELECT AVG.OnHand AS Available FROM dbo.Inventory`

12. Which of the following calculates a 10% commission on the values in the Sales field and then stores the results in the Commission field?

   a. `SELECT Year, Sales, Commission = Sales * 0.1 FROM dbo.TrentSales`

   b. `SELECT Year, Sales, AS Commission = Sales * 0.1 FROM dbo.TrentSales`

   c. `SELECT Year, Sales, Sales * 0.1 = Commission FROM dbo.TrentSales`

   d. `SELECT Year, Sales, Sales * 0.1 AS Commission FROM dbo.TrentSales`

Exercises

1. The Magazine table contains three fields. The Cost field is numeric. The Code and Name fields contain text.

    a. Write a SQL SELECT statement that arranges the records in descending order by the Cost field.

    b. Write a SQL SELECT statement that selects only the Name and Cost fields from records having a code of PG10.

    c. Write a SQL SELECT statement that selects only the Name and Cost fields from records having a cost of $3 or more.

    d. Write a SQL SELECT statement that selects the Visual Basic record.

    e. Write a SQL SELECT statement that selects only the Name field from records whose magazine name begins with the letter C.

    f. Write a SQL SELECT statement that selects only the Name field from records whose magazine name contains two characters.

    g. Write a SQL SELECT statement that selects only the Name and Cost fields from records whose cost is from $4 to $6, inclusive.

    h. Write a SQL SELECT statement that selects only records for the Code provided by the user.

    i. Write a SQL SELECT statement that selects only records that cost at least as much as the amount provided by the user.

    j. Write a SQL SELECT statement that selects only records that cost more than the first amount provided by the user but less than the second amount he or she provides.

    k. Open the Harken Solution.sln file contained in the VB2017\Chap12\Harken Solution folder. The application is already connected to the Harken.mdf database, and the HarkenDataSet has already been created. Start the application to view the records contained in the dataset and then stop the application. Open the DataSet Designer window and then start the TableAdapter Query Configuration Wizard. Open the Query Builder dialog box. Use the dialog box to test your SELECT statements from Steps a through j.

2. The Employees table contains six fields. The EmpNum, Rate, and DeptCode fields are numeric. The LastName, FirstName, and Status fields contain text. The Status field contains either the letter F (for full time) or the letter P (for part time). The DeptCode field identifies the employee's department: 1 for Accounting, 2 for Advertising, 3 for Personnel, and 4 for Inventory.

    a. Write a SQL SELECT statement that selects all of the fields and records in the table and then sorts the records in ascending order by the DeptCode field.

    b. Write a SQL SELECT statement that selects only the EmpNum, LastName, and FirstName fields from all of the records.

    c. Write a SQL SELECT statement that selects only the records for full-time employees.

    d. Write a SQL SELECT statement that selects the EmpNum, Rate, and DeptCode fields for employees in the Personnel department.

e. Write a SQL SELECT statement that selects the EmpNum, LastName, and FirstName fields for employees whose last name is Smith.

f. Write a SQL SELECT statement that selects the EmpNum, LastName, and FirstName fields for employees whose last name begins with the letter S.

g. Write a SQL SELECT statement that selects only the first and last names for part-time employees and then sorts the records in descending order by the LastName field.

h. Write a SQL SELECT statement that selects the records for employees earning more than $15 per hour and sorts them in ascending order by the Rate field.

i. Write a SQL SELECT statement that selects the records for employees whose Rate field contains a value that is at least $12 but not more than $15.

j. Write a SQL SELECT statement that selects the records for employee numbers 103 and 109.

k. Write a SQL SELECT statement that selects the records matching the Status provided by the user.

l. Write a SQL SELECT statement that selects the records whose Rate field value is greater than the first amount provided by the user but less than the second amount he or she provides.

m. Write a SQL SELECT statement that selects records that match both the Status and the DeptCode provided by the user. (For example, if the user provides P and 1, the statement should select only part-time employees in the Accounting department.)

n. Open the Incor Solution.sln file contained in the VB2017\Chap12\Incor Solution folder. The application is already connected to the Incor.mdf database, and the IncorDataSet has already been created. Start the application to view the records contained in the dataset and then stop the application. Open the DataSet Designer window and then start the TableAdapter Query Configuration Wizard. Open the Query Builder dialog box. Use the Query Builder dialog box to test your SELECT statements from Steps a through m.

o. Now, use the Query Builder dialog box to create a statement that selects only the LastName and FirstName fields for employees whose last name begins with the letter J. Sort the records in ascending order by the last name. If two or more employees have the same last name, those records should be sorted in ascending order by the first name. (You can complete the Sort Type box for more than one field.) What SQL statement appears in the SQL pane?

p. Finally, use the Query Builder dialog box to create a statement that selects the records for all part-time employees earning more than $11 per hour. (You can complete the Filter box for more than one field.) What SQL statement appears in the SQL pane?

3. Open the Adalene Solution.sln file contained in the VB2017\Chap12\Adalene Solution folder. The application is already connected to the Adalene.mdf file, and the AdaleneDataSet has already been created. Start the application to view the records in the dataset and then stop the application. The Adalene Fashions application should allow the user to display all of the information in the dataset, only the information for company-owned stores, or only the information for franchisees. Create the appropriate queries and then use them to code the btnDisplay_Click procedure. Save the solution and then start and test the application.

INTERMEDIATE

INTERMEDIATE   4. Open the Opals Solution.sln file contained in the VB2017\Chap12\Opals Solution folder. The application is already connected to the Opals.mdf file, and the OpalsDataSet has already been created. The Product table in the database is shown in Figure 12-40. Create a query that calculates the total sales amount for each item. After creating the query, display the Product table (which will now contain the calculated field) in a DataGridView control, as shown in Figure 12-41. Save the solution and then start and test the application.

Name	Data Type	Allow Nulls	Default
ID	varchar(5)	☐	
Name	varchar(50)	☐	
Price	int	☐	
Sold	int	☐	

ID	Name	Price	Sold
F120	Full Headboard	60	7
F345	Full Bed	110	10
K120	King Headboard	120	45
K345	King Bed	200	57
K78	King Pillows	45	35
Q120	Queen Headboard	75	38
Q345	Queen Bed	150	35
S78	Standard Pillows	10	59
TW120	Twin Headboard	50	24
TW345	Twin Bed	75	24

Figure 12-40   Product table in the Opals.mdf database

ID	Name	Price	Sold	Total Sales
F120	Full Headboard	60	7	$420
F345	Full Bed	110	10	$1,100
K120	King Headboard	120	45	$5,400
K345	King Bed	200	57	$11,400
K78	King Pillows	45	35	$1,575
Q120	Queen Headboard	75	38	$2,850
Q345	Queen Bed	150	35	$5,250
S78	Standard Pillows	10	59	$590
TW120	Twin Headboard	50	24	$1,200
TW345	Twin Bed	75	24	$1,800

Figure 12-41   DataGridView control showing the total sales for each item

5. Open the Games Solution.sln file contained in the VB2017\Chap12\Games Solution folder. Start the application to view the records, and then click the Exit button. In addition to displaying all of the records, the application should allow the user to display only the games for a specific platform, only the games with a specific rating, only the games that are marked as new, or only the games that are marked as used. Complete the application. Save the solution and then start and test the application.

ADVANCED

6. In this exercise, you modify the Games application from Exercise 5. Use Windows to make a copy of the Games Solution folder. Rename the copy Games Solution-Total. The frmMain_Load procedure should display (in a label control) the total value of the games sold in the store. Display the value with a dollar sign and two decimal places. Complete the application. Save the solution and then start and test the application.

ADVANCED

7. In this exercise, you modify the Adalene Fashions application from Exercise 3. Use Windows to make a copy of the Adalene Solution folder. Rename the copy Adalene Solution-TotalSales. Modify the interface as shown in Figure 12-42. In addition to displaying the records in the dataset, the frmMain_Load procedure should display the total sales made by company-owned stores, the total sales made by franchisees, and the total sales made by both types of stores. Create appropriate queries; use a SQL aggregate function to make each calculation. Save the solution and then start and test the application.

ADVANCED

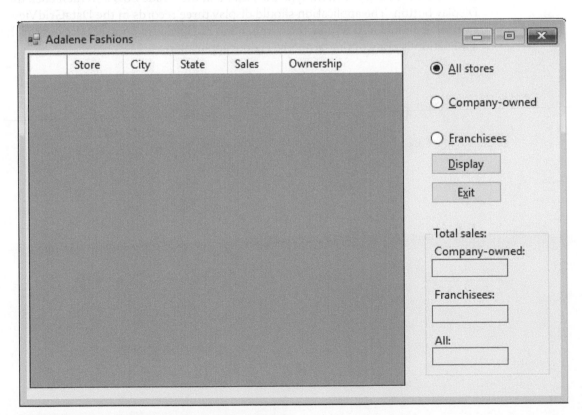

Figure 12-42 Modified Adalene Fashions interface

ON YOUR OWN

8. Create a Windows Forms application. Use the following names for the project and solution, respectively: OnYourOwn Project and OnYourOwn Solution. Save the application in the VB2017\Chap12 folder. Plan and design an application of your choice. The only requirement is that you must follow the minimum guidelines listed in Figure 12-43. Before starting the application, be sure to verify the name of the startup form. Save the solution and then start and test the application.

1. You must create a SQL Server database that contains at least one table and at least four fields.
2. The application must use at least one SELECT statement in addition to the default SELECT statement.
3. The interface must follow the GUI design guidelines summarized for Chapters 2 through 12 in Appendix A.
4. Objects that are either coded or referred to in code should be named appropriately.
5. If you are entering any code in the Code Editor window, then the window must contain comments and the three Option statements.

Figure 12-43   Guidelines for Exercise 8

FIX IT

9. Open the VB2017\Chap12\FixIt Solution\FixIt Solution.sln file. Start the application. Click the Grade radio button, type the letter a in the Grade box, and then click the Display button. The application should display three records in the DataGridView control. It should also display the number 3 in the lblCount control. Notice that the application is not working properly. Fix the application.

Web Site Applications

In this chapter's Focus on the Concepts lesson, you will learn how to create Web Site applications using Visual Studio along with a technology called ASP.NET. The applications you create will contain both static and dynamic Web pages. The pages can be viewed using any browser, such as Microsoft Edge, Google Chrome, Mozilla Firefox, and Safari. However, the figures in this chapter show how the pages look in Microsoft Edge. The Apply the Concepts lesson expands on the topics covered in the Focus lesson.

■ FOCUS ON THE CONCEPTS LESSON

Concepts covered in this lesson:

- F-1 Basic web terminology
- F-2 Creating a Web Site application
- F-3 Starting a Web application
- F-4 Modifying the Site.master page
- F-5 Personalizing the Default.aspx page
- F-6 Personalizing the About.aspx page
- F-7 Testing with different browsers
- F-8 Closing and opening a Web Site application

F-1 Basic Web Terminology

The Internet is the world's largest computer network, connecting millions of computers located all around the world. One of the most popular features of the Internet is the World Wide Web, often referred to simply as the Web. The Web consists of documents called **Web pages** that are stored on Web servers. A **Web server** is a computer that contains special software that "serves up" Web pages in response to requests from client computers. A **client computer** is a computer that requests information from a Web server. The information is requested and subsequently viewed through the use of a program called a Web browser or, more simply, a **browser**. Examples of popular browsers include Microsoft Edge, Google Chrome, Mozilla Firefox, and Safari.

Many Web pages are static. A **static Web page** is a document whose purpose is merely to display information to the viewer. Figure 13-1 shows an example of a static Web page that displays a store's name, address, and telephone number.

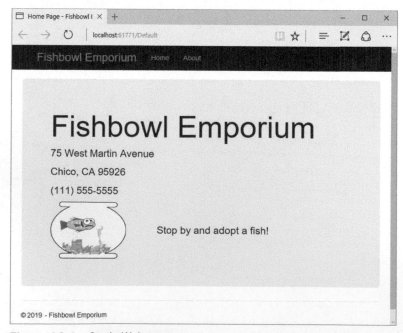

Figure 13-1 Static Web page

Unlike a static Web page, a **dynamic Web page** is interactive in that it can accept information from the user and also retrieve information for the user. Examples of dynamic Web pages include forms for purchasing merchandise online and for submitting online résumés. Figure 13-2 shows a dynamic Web page that calculates the number of gallons of water a rectangular aquarium holds. To use the Web page, you enter the length, width, and height of the aquarium and then click the Submit button. The button's Click event procedure displays the corresponding number of gallons on the Web page.

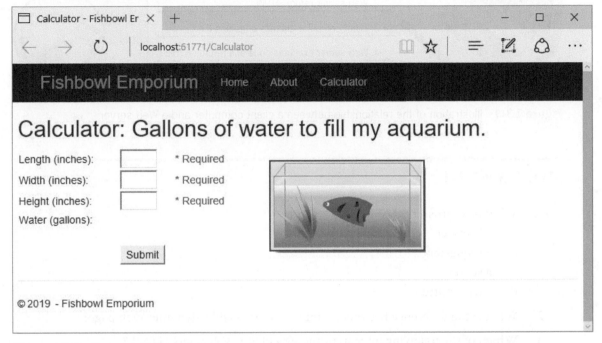

Figure 13-2 Dynamic Web page

The Web applications created in this chapter use a technology called ASP.NET. **ASP** stands for "active server page" and refers to the type of Web page created by the ASP technology. All ASP pages contain HTML (Hypertext Markup Language) tags that tell the client's browser how to render the page on the computer screen. For example, the instruction `<h1>Hello</h1>` uses the opening `<h1>` tag and its closing `</h1>` tag to display the word "Hello" as a heading on the page. Many ASP pages also contain ASP tags that specify the controls to include on the page. In addition to the HTML and ASP tags, dynamic ASP pages contain code that tells the objects on the page how to respond to the user's actions. In this chapter, you will write the appropriate code using the Visual Basic programming language.

When a client computer's browser sends a request for an ASP page, the Web server locates the page and then sends the appropriate HTML instructions to the client. The client's browser uses the instructions to render the Web page on the computer screen. If the Web page is a dynamic one, like the Web page shown in Figure 13-2, the user can interact with the page by entering data. In most cases, the user then clicks a button on the Web page to submit the page and its data to the server for processing. Using Web terminology, the information is "posted back" to the server; this event is referred to as a **postback**.

When the server receives the information, it executes the Visual Basic code associated with the Web page. It then sends back the appropriate HTML to the client for rendering in the browser window. The returned information includes the result of processing the code and data. Notice that the Web page's HTML is interpreted and executed by the client computer, whereas the program code is executed by the Web server. Figure 13-3 illustrates the relationship between the client computer and the Web server.

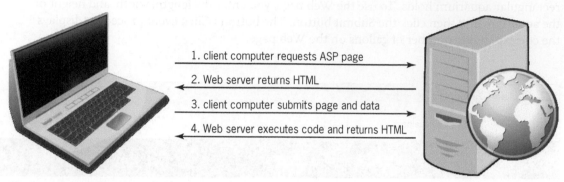

1. client computer requests ASP page
2. Web server returns HTML
3. client computer submits page and data
4. Web server executes code and returns HTML

Figure 13-3 Illustration of the relationship between a client computer and a Web server

Mini-Quiz 13-1

1. What is Microsoft Edge?
   a. a browser
   b. a requester
   c. a server
   d. a transmitter

2. What is the difference between a static Web page and a dynamic Web page?

3. Which of the following interprets and executes a Web page's HTML?

   a. the client computer
   b. the Web server

1) a. 2) Both types of Web pages display information. However, a dynamic Web page can interact with the viewer. 3) a.

F-2 Creating a Web Site Application

In previous chapters, you used the Windows Forms App (.NET Framework) template to create your Windows Forms applications. Visual Basic also provides templates for creating Web applications. The templates contain files that are designed to make the creation of a Web application a fairly simple matter. Figure 13-4 lists the names and purposes of four of the files included in the ASP.NET Web Forms Site template, which you will use in this lesson to create a Web site application for the Fishbowl Emporium store. The application will contain three Web pages: two static and one dynamic. You will create both static Web pages in this lesson and create the dynamic Web page in the Apply the Concepts lesson.

Filename	Purpose
Site.master	creates a consistent layout for the pages in your application (for example, the same color, header, footer, and buttons)
Default.aspx	serves as the home page
About.aspx	contains information about the website, such as its history or purpose
Contact.aspx	provides contact information, such as a phone number or e-mail address

Figure 13-4   Four of the files included in the ASP.NET Web Forms Site template

To create the Web site application:

START HERE

1. If necessary, start Visual Studio 2017. Permanently display the Solution Explorer window and auto-hide the Toolbox window.

2. Click **File** on the menu bar and then click **New Web Site** to open the New Web Site dialog box. If necessary, click **Visual Basic** in the Installed Templates list. Click **ASP.NET Web Forms Site** in the middle column of the dialog box.

3. If necessary, change the entry in the Web location box to **File System**. The File System selection allows you to store your Web site application in any folder on either your computer or a network drive.

4. In this chapter, you will be instructed to store your applications in the VB2017\Chap13 folder on the E drive. However, you should use the letter for the drive where your data is stored, which might not be the E drive. In the box that appears next to the Web location box, replace the existing text with **E:\VB2017\Chap13\Fishbowl**. See Figure 13-5.

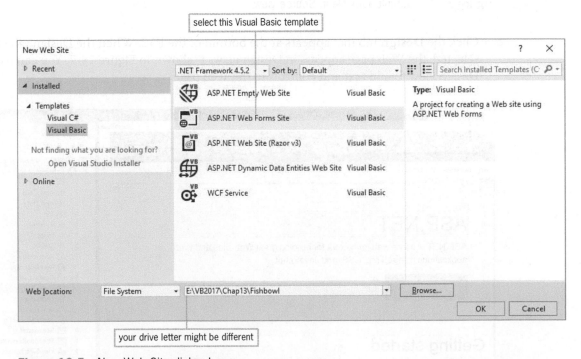

Figure 13-5   New Web Site dialog box

5. Click the **OK** button to close the dialog box. The computer uses the selected template to create a Web site application named Fishbowl. The template includes the files listed in the Solution Explorer window. If necessary, click the **Source** tab. The Default.aspx window shows the contents of the Default.aspx file in Source view. This view reveals the HTML and ASP tags that tell a browser how to render the Web page. The tags were automatically generated when you created the application. If necessary, auto-hide the Properties window. See Figure 13-6.

To display line numbers, click Tools, click Options, expand the Text Editor node, click All Languages, and then click Line numbers until a check mark appears next to the option.

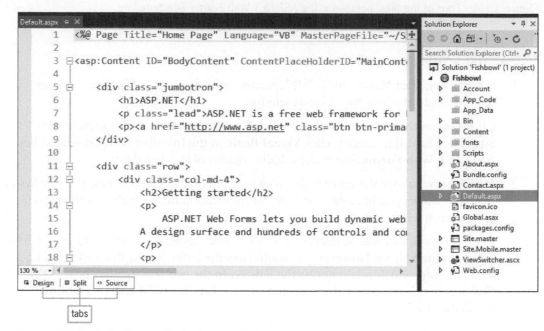

Figure 13-6 Default.aspx file in Source view

6. Click the **Design** tab that appears at the bottom of the IDE. When the Design tab is selected, the Web page appears in Design view, as shown in Figure 13-7. You can use Design view to add text and controls to the Web page.

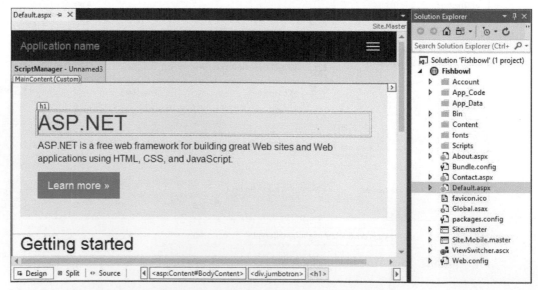

Figure 13-7 Default.aspx Web page in Design view

7. Click the **Split** tab to split the Default.aspx window into two parts. The upper half displays the Web page in Source view, and the lower half displays it in Design view.

8. Click the **Design** tab to return to Design view. Click **View** on the menu bar and then point to **Toolbars**. If the Formatting option is not checked, click **Formatting**; otherwise, click **View** to close the menu. The Formatting toolbar appears below the Standard toolbar. See Figure 13-8. (If the Formatting toolbar appears next to the Standard toolbar, rather than below it, position your mouse pointer on the beginning of the Formatting toolbar until it turns into a move pointer, which looks like horizontal and vertical lines with arrowheads at each end. Hold down the left mouse button as you drag the Formatting toolbar below the Standard toolbar, and then release the mouse button.)

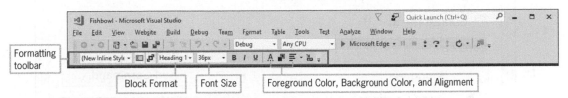

Figure 13-8 Formatting toolbar

F-3 Starting a Web Application

You can start a Web application either with or without the debugging option. In this chapter, you will start your Web applications without the option. The advantage of doing this is that you will not need to remember to stop the application each time you close the browser window after starting the application.

You can start an application without the debugging option either by pressing Ctrl+F5 or by clicking the Start Without Debugging option on the Debug menu. The method you use—the shortcut keys or the menu option—is a matter of personal preference. If you prefer to use a menu option, you might need to add the Start Without Debugging option to the Debug menu because the option is not automatically included on the menu. You can add the option to the menu by performing the next set of steps. If you prefer to use the Ctrl+F5 shortcut keys, you can skip the next set of steps.

To add the option to the Debug menu:

START HERE

1. First, you will determine whether your Debug menu already contains the option. Click **Debug** on the menu bar. If the menu contains the Start Without Debugging option, close the menu by clicking **Debug** again, and then skip the remaining steps in this set of steps.

2. If the Debug menu does *not* contain the Start Without Debugging option, close the menu by clicking **Debug** again. Click **Tools** on the menu bar and then click **Customize** to open the Customize dialog box.

3. Click the **Commands** tab. The Menu bar radio button should be selected. Click the **down arrow** in the Menu bar list box. Scroll down the list until you see Debug, and then click **Debug**.

4. Click the **Add Command** button to open the Add Command dialog box, and then click **Debug** in the Categories list. Scroll down the Commands list until you see Start Without Debugging, and then click **Start Without Debugging**. Click the **OK** button to close the Add Command dialog box.

5. Click the **Move Down** button until the Start Without Debugging option appears below the Start / Continue option. See Figure 13-9.

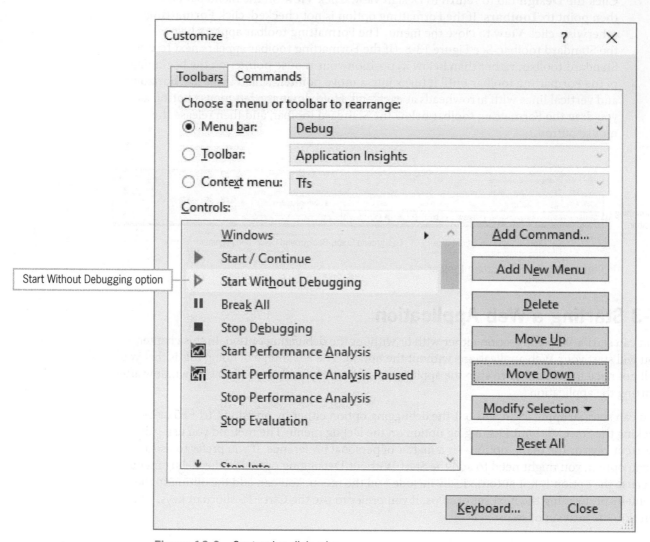

Start Without Debugging option

Figure 13-9   Customize dialog box

6. Click the **Close** button to close the Customize dialog box.

When you start a Web application, the computer creates a temporary Web server (on your local machine) that allows you to view your Web page in a browser. Keep in mind, however, that your Web page will need to be placed on an actual Web server for others to view it.

START HERE

To start the Web application:

1. Start the application either by pressing **Ctrl+F5** or by clicking the **Start Without Debugging** option on the Debug menu. Your browser requests the Default.aspx page from the Web server. The server locates the page and then sends the appropriate HTML instructions to your default browser for rendering on the screen. Figure 13-10 shows the Default.aspx page created by the template you are using. The page is displayed in Microsoft Edge and might appear slightly different in a different browser.

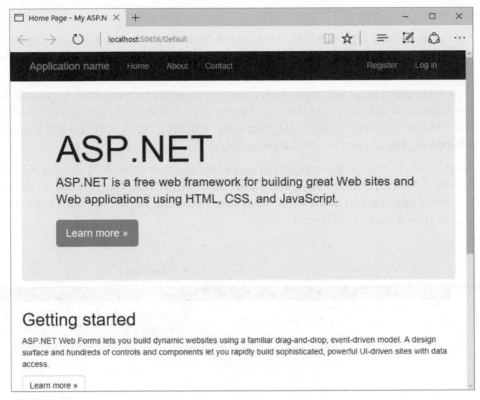

Figure 13-10   Default.aspx page created by the template

2. Click **About** to display the About page that comes with the template. Click **Contact**, then click **Register**, and then click **Log in** to display those pages.

3. Close the **browser** window. In the next section, you will personalize the Web application for the Fishbowl Emporium store.

F-4 Modifying the Site.master Page

Before adding any text or controls to the .aspx pages, you will make the changes indicated in Figure 13-11 to the Site.master page. Any changes made to that page will affect all of the .aspx pages in the Web application. You will also replace the My ASP.NET Application text in the Site.master page's footer with Fishbowl Emporium.

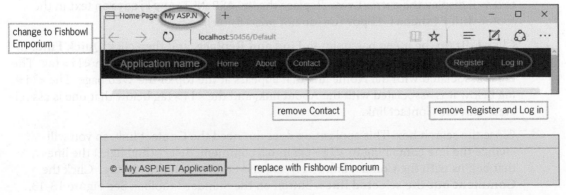

Figure 13-11   Site.master page changes

START HERE **To make changes to the Site.master page:**

1. Close the Default.aspx window. Double-click **Site.master** in the Solution Explorer window to open the Site.master page. If necessary, click the **Source** tab. Auto-hide the Solution Explorer window.

2. First, you will change the application name that appears on each Web page's tab in the browser window. Locate the `<title>` tag, which is at the beginning of Line 9 in the Site.master window. Select (highlight) My ASP.NET Application and then type **Fishbowl Emporium** (but do not press Enter).

3. Next, you will change the application name that appears on each Web page. Click **Edit** on the menu bar, point to **Find and Replace**, and then click **Quick Find**. In the search box, type **application name**. The Quick Find option highlights the Application name text in the `<a>` tag. See Figure 13-12.

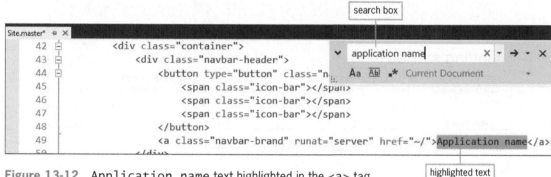

Figure 13-12   Application name text highlighted in the `<a>` tag

4. Close the search box. The Application name text should still be selected. Replace the selected text with **Fishbowl Emporium** (do not press Enter).

5. Click the **Design** tab at the bottom of the IDE. In the Fishbowl Emporium text that appears below the Site.master tab, click **immediately before the letter E**. Click the **Font Size** arrow on the Formatting toolbar and then click **x-large (24 pt)**.

6. Now, you will change the text that appears in each page's footer. Click the **Source** tab. Click **Edit** on the menu bar, point to **Find and Replace**, and then click **Quick Find**. In the search box, type **footer**. The Quick Find option highlights the `<footer>` tag. Close the search box. The `<p>` tag below the `<footer>` tag specifies the text that will appear at the bottom of each Web page. The DateTime.Now.Year entry in the footer text will display the current year. Replace the My ASP.NET Application text in the footer with **Fishbowl Emporium** (do not press Enter).

7. Click **Edit** on the menu bar, point to **Find and Replace**, and then click **Quick Find**. In the search box, type **Home**. The Quick Find option highlights Home in an `<li>` tag. The tag is associated with the Home link that appears at the top of the Web page. The `<li>` tag below it is associated with the About link, and the `<li>` tag below that one is associated with the Contact link.

8. Close the search box. This application does not need the Contact link, so you will change the line containing its `<li>` tag into a comment. Select (highlight) the line that begins with the Contact link's `<li>` tag and ends with its `</li>` tag. Click the **Comment out the selected lines.** button on the Standard toolbar. See Figure 13-13. The `<%` and `%>` tags indicate the beginning and the end, respectively, of a comment.

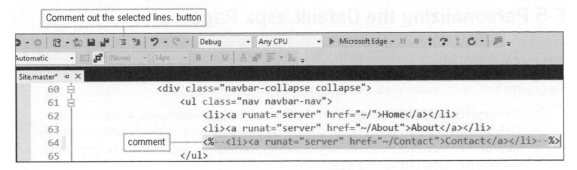

Figure 13-13 Contact `<li>` tag changed into a comment

9. If necessary, scroll down the Site.master window until you see the `<li>` tags for the Register and Log in links. Here too, the application will not need these links, so you will change them to comments. Highlight (select) the lines of code beginning with the `<li>` tag for the Register link and ending with the `</li>` tag for the Log in link. Click the **Comment out the selected lines.** button on the Standard toolbar. See Figure 13-14.

```
<AnonymousTemplate>
    <ul class="nav navbar-nav navbar-right">
        <%--<li><a runat="server" href="~/Account/Register">Register</a></li>
        <li><a runat="server" href="~/Account/Login">Log in</a></li>--%>
    </ul>
```
beginning comment tag   ending comment tag

Figure 13-14 Register and Log in `<li>` tags changed into comments

10. Save the application and then close the **Site.master** window. Temporarily display the Solution Explorer window. Open the Default.aspx page by double-clicking **Default.aspx**.

11. Now, you will start the application to view the changes you made to the Site.master page. Start the application either by pressing **Ctrl+F5** or by clicking **Start Without Debugging** on the Debug menu. Fishbowl Emporium appears as the application's name on the Web page. Some of the name also appears on the application's tab in the browser window. In addition, the Web page no longer contains the Contact, Register, and Log in links. Scroll down the page to view its footer, which now includes the application's name. See Figure 13-15.

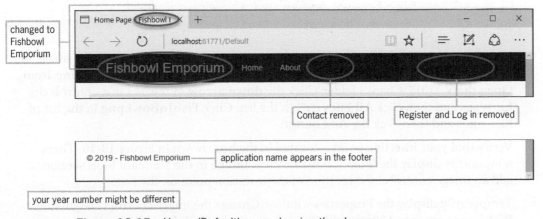

changed to Fishbowl Emporium

Contact removed

Register and Log in removed

© 2019 - Fishbowl Emporium — application name appears in the footer

your year number might be different

Figure 13-15 Home (Default) page showing the changes

12. Close the **browser** window.

F-5 Personalizing the Default.aspx Page

In this section, you will create the first static Web page for the Fishbowl Emporium store. The page is shown earlier in Figure 13-1.

START HERE

To create the first static Web page:

1. If necessary, click the **Design** tab at the bottom of the Default.aspx window. (If the Default.aspx window is not open, double-click Default.aspx in the Solution Explorer window.) Notice that Fishbowl Emporium appears as the page's title. The page inherited the title from the Site.master page.

2. Select the **ASP.NET** text that appears in the MainContent (Custom) area of the page. Type **Fishbowl Emporium** and press **Enter**.

3. Now, enter the address and phone number shown in Figure 13-16 and then position the insertion point as shown in the figure.

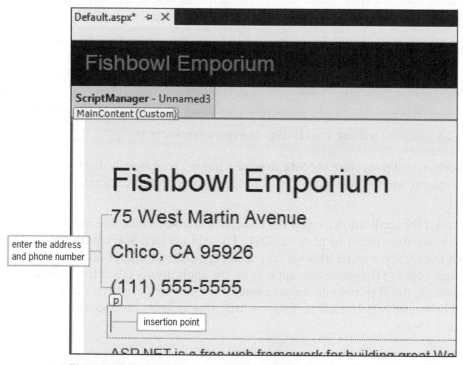

Figure 13-16 Address and phone number entered on the page

4. Before you can add the fishbowl image to the Web page, you need to add the image file to the application. Click **Website** on the menu bar and then click **Add Existing Item**. Open the VB2017\Chap13 folder. Click the **down arrow** in the box that controls the file types and then click **All Files (*.*)** in the list. Click **FishInBowl.png** in the list of filenames and then click the **Add** button.

5. Verify that your insertion point is located in the box shown in Figure 13-16. Then, temporarily display the toolbox. Double-click **Image** in the Standard tools section to add an image control at the location of the insertion point on the page.

6. Temporarily display the Properties window. Change the image control's Height and Width properties to **120px** and **160px**, respectively. Click **ImageUrl** in the Properties list, and then click the **...** (ellipsis) button to open the Select Image dialog box. Click **FishInBowl.png** in the Contents of folder section and then click the **OK** button.

7. Click to the **right of the image control** and then press the **Spacebar** 10 times. Type **Stop by and adopt a fish!** (but do not press Enter).

8. Now, select all of the information that appears below the image on the Web page, beginning with the text that starts with "ASP.NET is a free web framework" and ending with the text that appears above the footer. Press the **Delete** key.

9. Save and then start the application. See Figure 13-17.

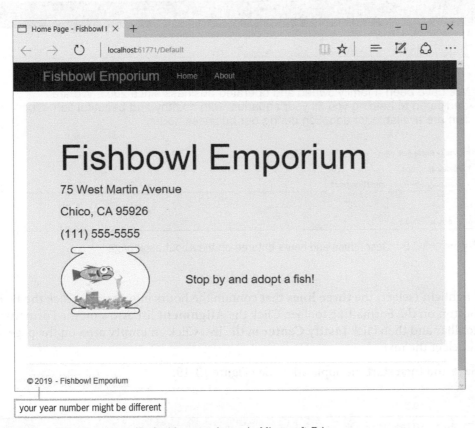

your year number might be different

Figure 13-17   Home (Default) page shown in Microsoft Edge

10. Close the **browser** window.

F-6 Personalizing the About.aspx Page

The About.aspx page created by the template will be the second static Web page included in the application. You will personalize the page in the next set of steps. The page will contain a brief description of the store's owners and operators as well as the store's hours of operation.

To personalize the About.aspx page:

START HERE

1. Close the **Default.aspx** window. Temporarily display the Solution Explorer window and then double-click **About.aspx**. If necessary, click the **Source** tab.

2. In the first line, change the page title from "About" to **"About Us"**.

3. Click the **Design** tab. Notice that the page inherits the application's name and footer from the Site.master page.

4. Delete the **.** (period) in the first line of the MainContent (Custom) section.

5. Now, select (highlight) the remaining **two lines of text** in the MainContent (Custom) section. Replace the selected text with the description and hours information shown in Figure 13-18. (When typing the description text, press the Enter key only after typing the last sentence.)

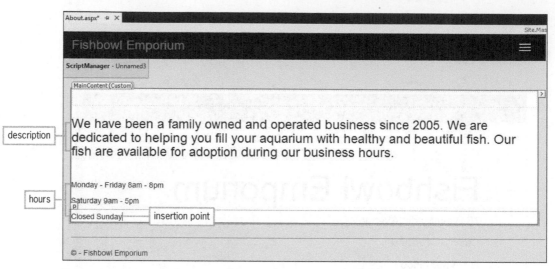

Figure 13-18 Description and hours entered on the About.aspx page

6. Highlight (select) the **three lines** that contain the hours information. Click the **B** (Bold) button on the Formatting toolbar. Click the **Alignment** list arrow on the Formatting toolbar and then click **Justify Center** in the list. Click an **empty area** on the page to deselect the text.

7. Save and then start the application. See Figure 13-19.

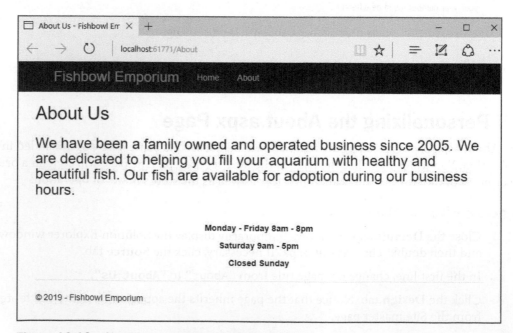

Figure 13-19 About Us page shown in Microsoft Edge

8. Click **Home** to display the Default (Home) page, and then click **About** to display the About Us page. Click **Fishbowl Emporium** to display the Default (Home) page. Close the browser window.

F-7 Testing with Different Browsers

While you are creating a Web site application, it is helpful to see how the Web pages look in different browsers. This is because some Web pages will look slightly different depending on the browser. It is very easy to change browsers from within the Visual Basic IDE. You just need to click the list arrow on the Standard toolbar's Start *<browser>* button, which is shown in Figure 13-20. The name on the button will be the name of your default browser. You then select the desired browser from the list of browsers available on your computer. When you start a Web application, the Web pages will appear in the selected browser window. You can also use the Browse With option to add, remove, or set the default browser. Of course, to add a browser, you must have downloaded the browser onto your computer and also installed it.

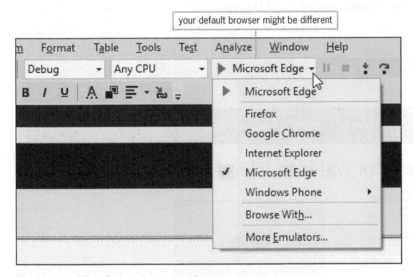

Figure 13-20 Start *<browser>* button

F-8 Closing and Opening a Web Site Application

To close and then open a Web Site application:

START HERE

1. Click **File** on the menu bar and then click **Close Solution**. Temporarily display the Solution Explorer window to verify that the Fishbowl application is closed.

2. Click **File** on the menu bar and then click **Open Web Site**. If necessary, open the VB2017\Chap13 folder. Click **Fishbowl** and then click **Open**. Temporarily display the Solution Explorer window to verify that the Fishbowl application is open.

3. Click **File** on the menu bar and then click **Close Solution**.

APPLY THE CONCEPTS LESSON

After studying this lesson, you should be able to:

- A-1 Repurpose an existing Web page
- A-2 Add a table and controls to a Web page
- A-3 Code a control on a Web page
- A-4 Use a validation control

A-1 Repurpose an Existing Web Page

In addition to the two static Web pages created in this chapter's Focus on the Concepts lesson, the Fishbowl Emporium application will contain one dynamic Web page named Calculator.aspx. The page, which is shown in Figure 13-21, provides areas for the user to enter the length, width, and height of an aquarium. When the user clicks the Submit button, the page calculates and displays the number of gallons of water needed to fill the aquarium.

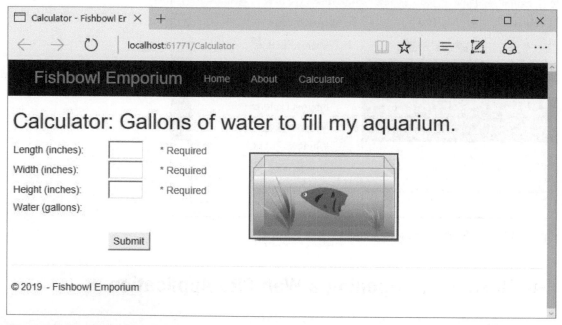

Figure 13-21   Dynamic Calculator.aspx page

In addition to the Home and About links, the Calculator.aspx page contains a Calculator link, a table, four labels, three text boxes, an image, three validation controls, and a button. Rather than adding a new Web page to the application, you can use one of the unused pages created by the ASP.NET Web Forms Site template. In this case, you will repurpose the Contact.aspx page.

START HERE   **To repurpose the Contact.aspx page:**

1. Click **File** on the menu bar and then click **Open Web Site**. If necessary, open the VB2017\Chap13 folder. Click **Fishbowl** and then click **Open**. If necessary, close any open .aspx windows.

2. Temporarily display the Solution Explorer window. Right-click **Contact.aspx** and then click **Rename**. Change the file's name to **Calculator.aspx** and press **Enter**. The Calculator.aspx window opens and displays the Calculator.aspx page. If necessary, click the **Source** tab. Click the window's **Auto Hide** button to permanently display the window. (If the Calculator.aspx window does not open, double-click Calculator.aspx in the Solution Explorer window.)

3. In the first line of text, change the page's title from "Contact" to **"Calculator"**.

4. Before making any further modifications to the Calculator.aspx page, you will tell the Site.master page to display the Calculator link and also to open the Calculator.aspx file when the link is clicked. Temporarily display the Solution Explorer window and then double-click **Site.master**. If necessary, click the **Source** tab.

5. Scroll down the Site.master window until you locate the <li> tag for the Contact link, which appears on Line 64. In the Focus lesson, you made the line that contains this tag into a comment. Click the **line that contains the tag** and then click the **Uncomment the selected lines.** button on the Standard toolbar. The button is located next to the "Comment out the selected lines." button that you used in the Focus lesson. Change both occurrences of the word Contact to **Calculator**. See Figure 13-22.

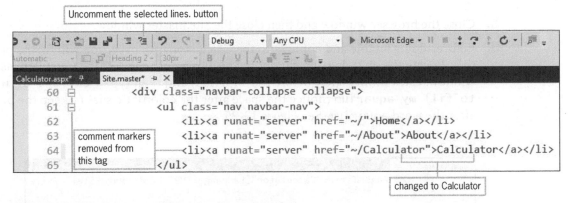

Figure 13-22 Changes made to the Site.master page

6. Save and then start the application. See Figure 13-23. Notice that the Calculator link appears on the Home (Default) page.

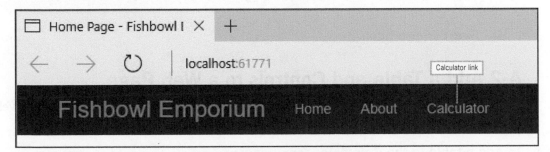

Figure 13-23 Calculator link shown on the Home (Default) page

7. Click the **Calculator** link to display the Calculator page. See Figure 13-24. (For now, do not be concerned about the period that follows the word Calculator.)

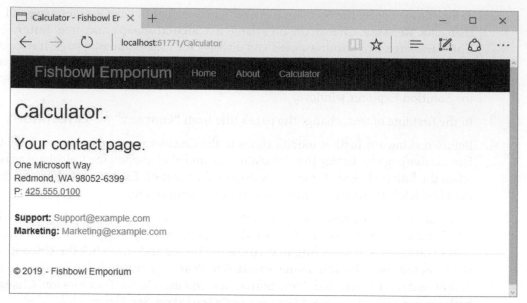

Figure 13-24 Calculator page

8. Close the browser window and then close the Site.master window.

9. Before adding a table and controls to the Calculator.aspx page, you will fix the page's title. Locate the <h2> tag, which is at the beginning of Line 4 in the Calculator.aspx window. Click immediately before the **.** (period) and then type **: Gallons of water to fill my aquarium** (notice the space after the colon). Be sure to keep the period after the word **aquarium**. See Figure 13-25.

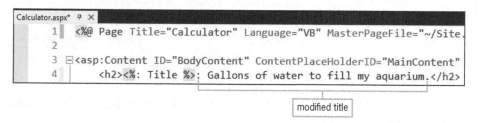

Figure 13-25 Modified title for the Calculator.aspx page

10. Save the application.

A-2 Add a Table and Controls to a Web Page

In this section, you will add a table to the Calculator.aspx page. Tables are often used on Web pages to make it easier to align the controls on the page.

START HERE **To add a table to the Calculator.aspx page:**

1. Click the **Design** tab. Select (highlight) all of the text that appears below the page's title, beginning with the "Your contact page." line and ending with the Marketing Web address. Press **Delete**.

2. Click immediately after the **.** (period) in the page's title and then press **Enter**.

3. Click **Table** on the menu bar and then click **Insert Table** to open the Insert Table dialog box. In the Size section of the dialog box, change the number of rows to **6** and change the number of columns to **3**. Click the **OK** button to close the dialog box.

4. Position your mouse pointer on the line that divides the first and second columns in the table, as shown in Figure 13-26. A screen tip box appears and displays the width of the column in pixels. Use your mouse pointer to drag the line to the left until the first column is **135px** wide, and then release the mouse button.

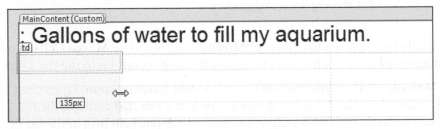

Figure 13-26   Column width box shown on the Web page

5. Position your mouse pointer on the line that divides the second and third columns. Drag the line to the left until the second column is **135px** wide, and then release the mouse button.

6. Click the **cell located in the first row, first column in the table**. Type **Length (inches):** and then press **Tab** to move the insertion point into the second column in the first row. Permanently display the toolbox. If necessary, expand the Standard node. Click the **TextBox tool** and then drag a text box to the location of the insertion point. Release the mouse button.

7. Temporarily display the Properties window. Unlike the controls on a Windows Form, the controls on a Web page have an ID property rather than a Name property. The ID property is located at the top of the Properties list. Change the TextBox1 control's ID property to **txtLength**. Change its Width property to **50px**.

8. Now, click the **first cell in the table's second row**. Type **Width (inches):** and press **Tab**. Drag a text box into the cell located in the current row's second column, and then change its ID and Width properties to **txtWidth** and **50px**, respectively.

9. Next, click the **first cell in the table's third row**. Type **Height (inches):** and press **Tab**. Drag a text box into the cell located in the current row's second column, and then change its ID and Width properties to **txtHeight** and **50px**, respectively.

10. Click the **first cell in the table's fourth row**. Type **Water (gallons):** and press **Tab**. This time, drag a label into the cell located in the current row's second column and then change its ID property to **lblGallons**. Also, remove **the contents of its Text property**.

11. Click the **cell located in the second column of the last (sixth) row**. Drag a button control into the cell. Change the button's ID and Text properties to **btnSubmit** and **Submit**, respectively.

12. Click the **first cell in the table's third column**. Then, select (highlight) only the six cells in the third column. (You can do this by pressing and holding down your left mouse button as you drag the mouse pointer down the third column.) When the six cells are selected, release the mouse button. See Figure 13-27.

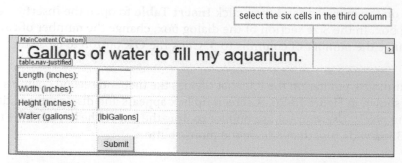

select the six cells in the third column

Figure 13-27 Table showing the six selected cells

13. Click **Table** on the menu bar, point to **Modify**, and then click **Merge Cells**. Now, click the **Image tool** in the toolbox and then drag an image control into the third column.

14. Click **Website** on the menu bar and then click **Add Existing Item**. Open the VB2017\Chap13 folder. Click the **down arrow** in the box that controls the file types and then click **All Files (*.*)** in the list. Click **Aquarium.png** in the list of filenames and then click the **Add** button.

15. If necessary, click the image control in the table. Temporarily display the Properties window. Click **ImageUrl** in the Properties list, and then click the **...** (ellipsis) button to open the Select Image dialog box. Click **Aquarium.png** in the Contents of folder section and then click the **OK** button.

16. Auto-hide the toolbox and then click the **Calculator.aspx** tab. Save and then start the application. See Figure 13-28.

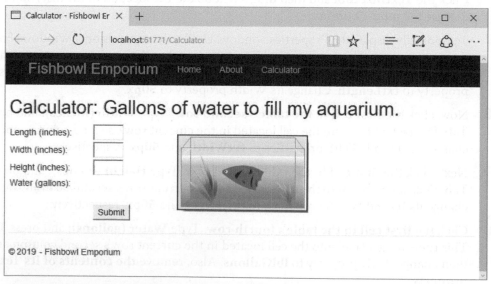

Figure 13-28 Calculator page displayed in Microsoft Edge

17. Close the browser window.

A-3 Code a Control on a Web Page

When the user clicks a button on a Web page, a postback occurs and the button's Click event procedure is automatically sent to the server for processing. In the following set of steps, you will code the btnSubmit_Click procedure to calculate and display the number of gallons of water needed to fill an aquarium. The procedure's pseudocode is shown in Figure 13-29.

---

btnSubmit_Click
1. declare dblLength, dblWidth, and dblHeight to store aquarium's length (in inches), width (in inches), and height (in inches)
2. declare dblVolume to store the aquarium's volume in cubic inches
3. declare dblGallons to store the number of gallons of water
4. store aquarium's length, width, and height in dblLength, dblWidth, and dblHeight
5. calculate the rectangular aquarium's volume in cubic inches by multiplying its length (dblLength) by its width (dblWidth) and then multiplying the result by its height (dblHeight); store the result in dblVolume
6. calculate the number of gallons of water by dividing the aquarium's volume in cubic inches (dblVolume) by 231; store the result in dblGallons (There are 231 cubic inches in one gallon.)
7. display the number of gallons of water (dblGallons) in lblGallons

---

Figure 13-29   Pseudocode for the btnSubmit_Click procedure

To code and then test the btnSubmit_Click procedure: START HERE

1. Right-click the **Submit** button and then click **View Code** on the context menu. The Calculator.aspx.vb window opens. Recall that the .vb extension on a filename indicates that the file contains Visual Basic code. In this case, the file is referred to as the code-behind file because it contains code that supports the Web page.

2. Type the comments and Option statements shown in Figure 13-30. Replace <your name> and <current date> with your name and the current date, respectively.

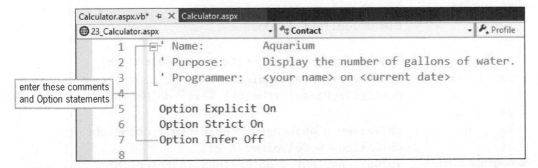

Calculator.aspx.vb*	X	Calculator.aspx		
23_Calculator.aspx			Contact	Profile

```
1      ' Name:          Aquarium
2      ' Purpose:       Display the number of gallons of water.
3      ' Programmer:    <your name> on <current date>
4
5      Option Explicit On
6      Option Strict On
7      Option Infer Off
8
```

enter these comments and Option statements

Figure 13-30   Comments and Option statements

3. Open the btnSubmit_Click procedure. Type the following comment and then press **Enter** twice:

   ' Displays the number of gallons of water.

4. The first three steps in the pseudocode declare the procedure's variables. Enter the following Dim statements. Press **Enter** twice after typing the last Dim statement.

```
Dim dblLength As Double
Dim dblWidth As Double
Dim dblHeight As Double
Dim dblVolume As Double
Dim dblGallons As Double
```

5. The fourth step in the pseudocode stores the three input items in variables. Enter the following three TryParse methods. Press **Enter** twice after typing the last TryParse method.

```
Double.TryParse(txtLength.Text, dblLength)
Double.TryParse(txtWidth.Text, dblWidth)
Double.TryParse(txtHeight.Text, dblHeight)
```

6. The fifth step in the pseudocode calculates the volume of the rectangular aquarium in cubic inches. Enter the following assignment statement:

```
dblVolume = dblLength * dblWidth * dblHeight
```

7. The sixth step in the pseudocode calculates the number of gallons of water needed to fill the rectangular aquarium. Enter the following assignment statement:

```
dblGallons = dblVolume / 231
```

8. The last step in the pseudocode displays the number of gallons of water in the lblGallons control. Enter the additional assignment statement indicated in Figure 13-31.

```
12      Private Sub btnSubmit_Click(sender As Object, e As
13          ' Displays the number of gallons of water.
14
15          Dim dblLength As Double
16          Dim dblWidth As Double
17          Dim dblHeight As Double
18          Dim dblVolume As Double
19          Dim dblGallons As Double
20
21          Double.TryParse(txtLength.Text, dblLength)
22          Double.TryParse(txtWidth.Text, dblWidth)
23          Double.TryParse(txtHeight.Text, dblHeight)
24
25          dblVolume = dblLength * dblWidth * dblHeight
26          dblGallons = dblVolume / 231
```
enter this assignment statement ——lblGallons.Text = dblGallons.ToString("N1")
```
28      End Sub
```

Figure 13-31   Completed btnSubmit_Click procedure

9. Save and then start the application. Your browser requests the Calculator.aspx page from the server. The server locates the page and then sends the appropriate HTML instructions to your browser for rendering on the screen.

10. Click the **Length (inches)** box, type **20.5**, and then press **Tab**. Type **10.5** in the Width box, press **Tab**, and then type **12.5** in the Height box.

11. Click the **Submit** button, which submits the Web page and data to the server along with a request for additional services. At this point, a postback has occurred. The server processes the code contained in the btnSubmit_Click procedure and then sends the appropriate HTML to your browser for rendering on the screen. As Figure 13-32 indicates, the aquarium needs 11.6 gallons of water.

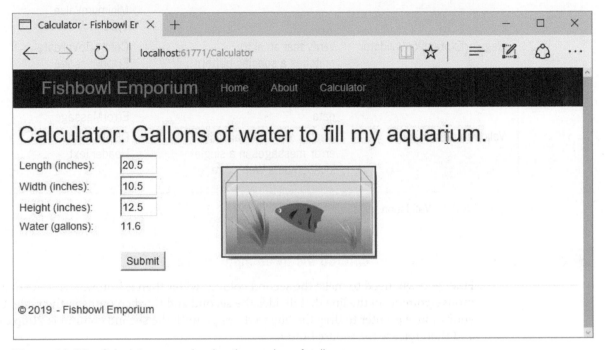

Figure 13-32 Calculator page showing the number of gallons

12. Close the browser window and then close the Calculator.aspx.vb window.

A-4 Use a Validation Control

The Validation section of the toolbox provides several **validation tools** for validating user input. The name, purpose, and important properties of each validation tool are listed in Figure 13-33. In the Fishbowl Emporium application, you will use RequiredFieldValidator controls to verify that the user entered the three input items.

Name	Purpose	Properties
CompareValidator	compare an entry with a constant value or with a control's property	ControlToCompare ControlToValidate ErrorMessage Operator Type ValueToCompare
CustomValidator	verify that an entry passes the specified validation logic	ClientValidationFunction ControlToValidate ErrorMessage

Figure 13-33 Validation tools *(continues)*

(continued)

Name	Purpose	Properties
RangeValidator	verify that an entry is within the specified minimum and maximum values	ControlToValidate ErrorMessage MaximumValue MinimumValue Type
RegularExpressionValidator	verify that an entry matches a specific pattern	ControlToValidate ErrorMessage ValidationExpression
RequiredFieldValidator	verify that a control contains data	ControlToValidate ErrorMessage
ValidationSummary	display all of the validation error messages in a single location on a Web page	DisplayMode HeaderText

Figure 13-33   Validation tools

START HERE

To verify that the user entered the three input items:

1. First, you will need to make the second column wider than it is now. Position your mouse pointer on the line that divides the second and third columns in the table. Use your mouse pointer to drag the line to the right until the second column is **200px** wide, and then release the mouse button.

2. Permanently display the Toolbox window. If necessary, expand the Validation section.

3. Click **to the immediate right of the txtLength control** and then press the **Spacebar** five times.

4. Click the **RequiredFieldValidator** tool and then drag your mouse pointer to the location of the insertion point. Release the mouse button. A RequiredFieldValidator control appears on the Web page.

5. Temporarily display the Properties window. Set the RequiredFieldValidator1 control's ControlToValidate property to **txtLength**. Then, set its ErrorMessage property to *** Required** (notice the asterisk and the space character before the word Required). Click **ForeColor** in the Properties window, click the **...** (ellipsis) button, click a **red hexagon,** and then click the **OK** button to close the More Colors dialog box.

6. Click **to the immediate right of the txtWidth control** and then press the **Spacebar** five times. Drag a required field validator control to the location of the insertion point. Set the RequiredFieldValidator2 control's ControlToValidate and ErrorMessage properties to **txtWidth** and *** Required**, respectively. Also, set its ForeColor property using the same **red hexagon** used in Step 5. Click the **OK** button to close the More Colors dialog box.

7. Click **to the immediate right of the txtHeight control** and then press the **Spacebar** five times. Drag a required field validator control to the location of the insertion point. Set the RequiredFieldValidator3 control's ControlToValidate and ErrorMessage properties to **txtHeight** and *** Required**, respectively. Also, set its ForeColor property using the same **red hexagon** used in Step 5. Click the **OK** button to close the More Colors dialog box.

8. Click the **Calculator.aspx** tab and then auto-hide the Toolbox window.

9. Save and then start the application. Click the **Submit** button without entering any values. Each RequiredFieldValidator control displays the "* Required" message, as shown in Figure 13-34.

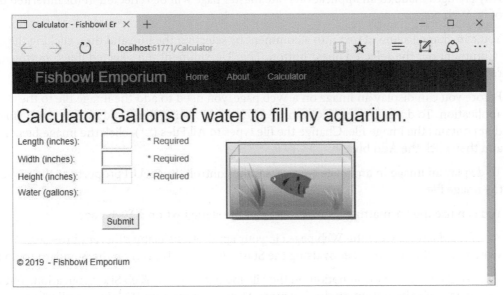

Figure 13-34 Error messages displayed by the RequiredFieldValidator controls

10. Type **16** in the Length box and then press **Tab** to move the insertion point into the Width box. Notice that the "* Required" message next to the Length box disappears.

11. Type **8** and **10** in the Width and Height boxes, respectively, and then click the **Submit** button. The Web page indicates that 5.5 gallons of water are needed to fill the aquarium.

12. Close the browser window. Click **File** and then click **Close Solution**.

Summary

- The Web is one of the most popular features of the Internet. It consists of Web pages that are stored on Web servers.

- A client computer's browser requests information from a Web server. The information returned by the Web server is then displayed in the browser.

- A Web page's HTML is interpreted and executed by a client computer. A Web page's code is executed by a Web server.

- To create a Web Site application, click File and then click New Web Site. If necessary, click Visual Basic in the Installed Templates list. Click ASP.NET Web Forms Site in the New Web Site dialog box. If necessary, change the entry in the Web location box to File System. In the box that appears next to the Web location box, enter the location where you want the application saved. Also, enter the application's name. Click the OK button to close the New Web Site dialog box.

- You can use the tabs at the bottom of a .aspx window to view a Web page in Design view, Split view, or Source view.

- To start a Web Site application, either press Ctrl+F5 or click the Start Without Debugging option on the Debug menu.

- Any changes made to an application's Site.master page will be reflected in (or inherited by) all of its Web pages.

- You can change a line of text into a comment by selecting the line and then clicking the "Comment out the selected lines." button. The "Uncomment the selected lines." button removes the comment markers from the selected line.

- Before you can display an image on a Web page, you need to add the image file to the application. To do this, you click Website, click Add Existing Item, and then open the folder that contains the image file. Change the file types to All Files (*.*), click the image filename, and then click the Add button.

- To display an image in an image control, set the control's ImageUrl property to the name of the image file.

- You can use the Formatting toolbar to format the static text on a Web page.

- You should always view the Web pages in your applications using different browsers. You can switch to a different browser by using the Start *<browser>* button on the Standard toolbar.

- You use the Close Solution option on the File menu to close a Web Site application. You use the Open Web Site option on the File menu to open an existing Web Site application.

- Web controls have an ID property rather than a Name property. You use the ID property to refer to the control in code.

- To code a control on a Web page, enter the code in the page's Code Editor window.

- The toolbox provides validation tools that you can use to validate the user input on a Web page.

Key Terms

ASP—stands for "active server page"

Browser—a program that allows a client computer to request and view Web pages

Client computer—a computer that requests information from a Web server

Dynamic Web page—an interactive document that can accept information from the user and also retrieve information for the user

Postback—occurs when the information on a dynamic Web page is sent (posted) back to a server for processing

Static Web page—a noninteractive document whose purpose is merely to display information to the viewer

Validation tools—the tools contained in the Validation section of the toolbox; used to validate user input on a Web page

Web pages—the documents stored on Web servers

Web server—a computer that contains special software that "serves up" Web pages in response to requests from client computers

Review Questions

1. A computer that requests an ASP page from a Web server is called a
   _____ computer.

   a. browser   c. requesting

   b. client   d. server

2. Which of the following is a program that uses HTML to render a Web page on the
   computer screen?

   a. browser   c. server

   b. client   d. renderer

3. An online form used to purchase a product is an example of which type of Web page?

   a. dynamic   b. static

4. Which of the following is responsible for processing a Web page's HTML instructions?

   a. client computer   b. Web server

5. Which of the following occurs when a user clicks a Submit button on a Web page?

   a. backpost   c. postback

   b. clientpost   d. serverpost

6. In code, you refer to a control on a Web page by using which of the following
   properties?

   a. Caption   c. Name

   b. ID   d. Text

7. The Visual Basic code in a Web page is processed by which of the following?

   a. client computer   b. Web server

8. Which of the following controls is used to verify that a control on a Web page contains
   data?

   a. FieldValidator   c. RequiredFieldValidator

   b. RequiredField   d. RequiredValidator

9. Which of the following controls is used to verify that an entry on a Web page is within
   minimum and maximum values?

   a. MinMaxValidation   c. EntryValidator

   b. MaxMinValidation   d. RangeValidator

Exercises

1. In this exercise, you create two static Web pages for Spa Monique. Figures 13-35 and 13-36 show the completed pages displayed in Microsoft Edge. Keep in mind that the year displayed on your pages might be different than the one shown in the figures.

   a. Use the New Web Site option on the File menu to create a Web Site application named Spa. (Be sure to select the Visual Basic ASP.NET Web Forms Site template.) Save the application in the VB2017\Chap13 folder.

   b. Open the Site.master page in Source view. Replace My ASP.NET Application in the <title> tag with Spa Monique. Also, replace Application name in the <a> tag with Spa Monique. In addition, replace My ASP.NET Application in the page's footer with Spa Monique.

   c. Locate the About <li> tag. Replace both occurrences of About with Massages. In the Solution Explorer window, change the About.aspx filename to Massages.aspx. Press Enter after typing the name.

   d. Click the Site.master tab. Save the application and then (if necessary) close the Massages.aspx window.

   e. In the Site.master window, locate the Contact <li> tag and change it to a comment. Also, locate the Register and Login <li> tags and change both tags to comments.

   f. Click the Design tab. Click immediately before the letter M in the Spa Monique text that appears below the Site.master tab. Change the text's font size to xx-large (36pt). Save the application and then close the Site.master window.

   g. Now, you will customize the Default.aspx page. If necessary, click the Design tab to show the Default.aspx page in Design view. Use the Add Existing Item option on the Website menu to add the Spa.png file to the application. The file is contained in the VB2017\Chap13 folder. [Be sure to change the file type box to All Files (*.*).]

   h. Select the ASP.NET text that appears in the MainContent (Custom) area of the page. Type Spa Monique of Glen Springs but do not press Enter. Use the Alignment button to center the text.

   i. Delete the Learn more button and all of the information (except the footer) below it.

   j. Replace the sentence that appears below the heading with the two sentences shown in Figure 13-35. Center the sentences horizontally on the page. Then, select the sentences and change their font size to x-large (24pt). Also, change their font color to purple. (Select any purple hexagon in the More Colors dialog box.)

   k. Click immediately after the ! (exclamation point) and then press Enter. Add an image control to the page. Use the control's ImageUrl property to display the image stored in the Spa.png file. Save and then start the application to view the Default.aspx page in a browser window. (Be sure to use either Ctrl+F5 or the Start Without Debugging option on the Debug menu.) Close the browser window and then close the Default.aspx window.

   l. Now, you will customize the Massages.aspx page. Double-click Massages.aspx in the Solution Explorer window. If necessary, click the Source tab. In the first line, change the page title from "About" to "Massages". Delete the . (period) in the <h2> tag, and then delete the entire line that contains the <h3> tag.

   m. Click the Design tab. Select the "Use this area to provide additional information." sentence and then press Delete.

   n. Click Table on the menu bar and then click Insert Table. The table will need two columns and six rows. The first column should be 140px wide.

o. In the first cell in the first row, type Types. Select Types and then click the B (Bold) and U (Underline) buttons on the Formatting toolbar.

p. In the cell below Types, type Swedish and press Tab. Then, type 50 minutes $100. Use the information shown in Figure 13-36 to complete the table.

q. Save and then start the application. Click Home and then click Massages. Close the browser window and then close the solution.

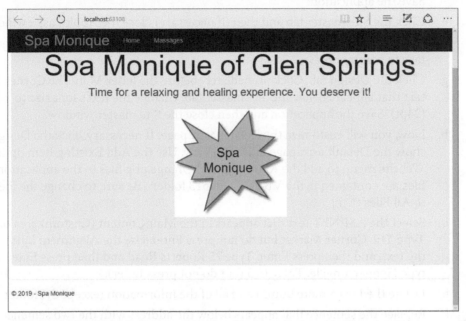

Figure 13-35 Default.aspx page for Spa Monique displayed in Microsoft Edge

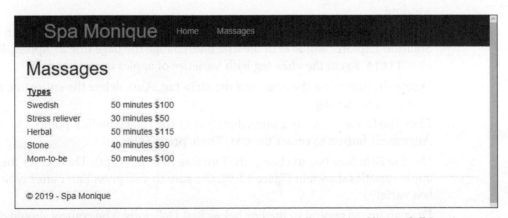

Figure 13-36 Massages.aspx page for Spa Monique displayed in Microsoft Edge

2. In this exercise, you create three static Web pages for The Corner Market. Figures 13-37, 13-38, and 13-39 show the completed pages displayed in Microsoft Edge. Keep in mind that the year displayed on your pages might be different than the one shown in the figures.

INTRODUCTORY

a. Use the New Web Site option on the File menu to create a Web Site application named Market. (Be sure to select the Visual Basic ASP.NET Web Forms Site template.) Save the application in the VB2017\Chap13 folder.

b. Open the Site.master page in Source view. Replace My ASP.NET Application in the <title> tag with The Corner Market. Also, replace Application name in the <a> tag with The Corner Market. In addition, replace My ASP.NET Application in the page's footer with The Corner Market.

c. Locate the About and Contact <li> tags. Replace both occurrences of About with Apples, and replace both occurrences of Contact with Oranges.

d. In the Solution Explorer window, change the About.aspx filename to Apples.aspx. Save the application.

e. Click the Site.master tab and then (if necessary) close the Apples.aspx window.

f. In the Site.master window, locate the Register and Login <li> tags. Change both tags to comments.

g. Click the Design tab. Click immediately before the letter M in The Corner Market text that appears below the Site.master tab. Change the text's font size to x-large (24pt). Save the application and then close the Site.master window.

h. Now, you will customize the Default.aspx page. If necessary, click the Design tab to show the Default.aspx page in Design view. Use the Add Existing Item option on the Website menu to add the Apple.png and Orange.png files to the application. The files are contained in the VB2017\Chap13 folder. [Be sure to change the file type box to All Files (*.*).]

i. Select the ASP.NET text that appears in the MainContent (Custom) area of the page. Type The Corner Market but do not press Enter. Use the Alignment button to center the text, and then press Enter. Type 75 Roberts Road and then press Enter. Then, type Hendersonville, TN 37075 (but do not press Enter).

j. Delete the Learn more button and all of the information (except the footer) below it.

k. Replace the sentence that appears below the address with the two sentences shown in Figure 13-37. Save and then start the application to view the Default.aspx page in a browser window. Close the browser window and then close the Default.aspx window.

l. Now, you will customize the Apples.aspx page. Double-click Apples.aspx in the Solution Explorer window. In the first line, change the page title to Apples. Replace <%: Title %>. in the <h2> tag with Varieties of apples in stock today!.

m. Delete the entire line that contains the <h3> tag. Also, delete the entire line that contains the <p> tag.

n. Click the Design tab. Click immediately after the ! (exclamation point). Use the Alignment button to center the text. Then, press Enter.

o. Use the Font Size box to change the font size to large (18pt). Then, enter the five apple varieties shown in Figure 13-38. (Be sure to also press Enter after typing the last variety.)

p. Drag an image control to the line below Red Delicious. The control should display the contents of the Apple.png file.

q. Save and then start the application to view the Apples.aspx page in a browser window. Close the browser window and then close the Apples.aspx window.

r. Use Windows to open the VB2017\Chap13\Market folder. Make a copy of the Apples.aspx file. Change the name of the copied file to Oranges.aspx. Also, make a copy of the Apples.aspx.vb file. Change the name of the copied file to Oranges.aspx.vb.

s. Click Website on the Visual Basic menu bar and then click Add Existing Item. Change the file type box to All Files (*.*). Click Oranges.aspx and then Ctrl+click Oranges.aspx.vb. Click the Add button.

t. Double-click Oranges.aspx in the Solution Explorer window. In the first line, change the page title to `"Oranges"`. Also, change `"Apples.aspx.vb"` in the first line to `"Oranges.aspx.vb"`.

u. Next, modify the Oranges.aspx page so that it looks like the one shown in Figure 13-39.

v. Save and then start the application. Click Home, click Apples, and then click Oranges. Close the browser window and then close the solution.

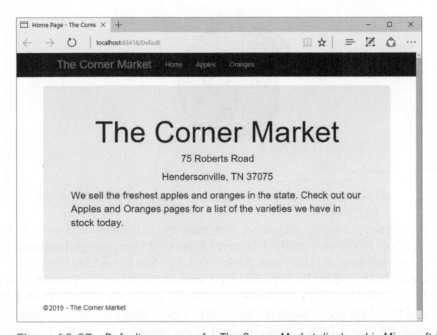

Figure 13-37 Default.aspx page for The Corner Market displayed in Microsoft Edge

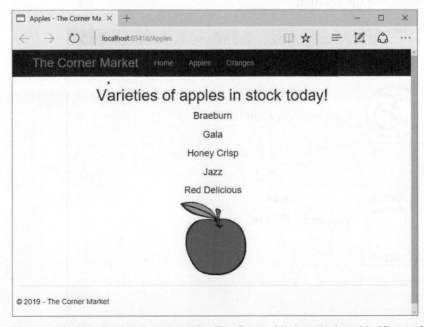

Figure 13-38 Apples.aspx page for The Corner Market displayed in Microsoft Edge

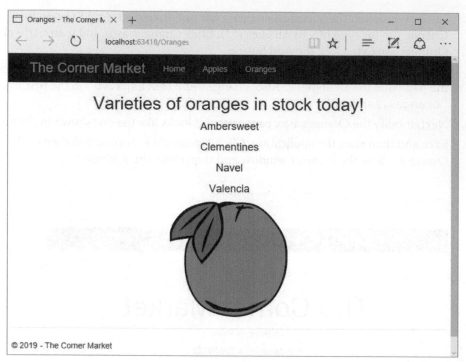

Figure 13-39 Oranges.aspx page for The Corner Market displayed in Microsoft Edge

INTERMEDIATE

3. In this exercise, you create a dynamic Web page that calculates the area of a circle. Use the New Web Site option on the File menu to create a Web Site application named Circle. (Be sure to select the Visual Basic ASP.NET Web Forms Site template.) Save the application in the VB2017\Chap13 folder. Figure 13-40 shows the Default.aspx page in Design view, and Figure 13-41 shows a sample run of the page in Microsoft Edge. The image of the circle is contained in the VB2017\Chap13\Circle.png file. Create the page and then code the Submit button. Use 3.14 as the value for Pi. Display the area with one decimal place. Save and then start and test the application. Close the browser window and then close the solution.

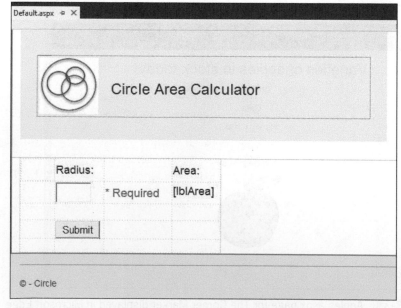

Figure 13-40 Default.aspx page for the Circle application displayed in Design view

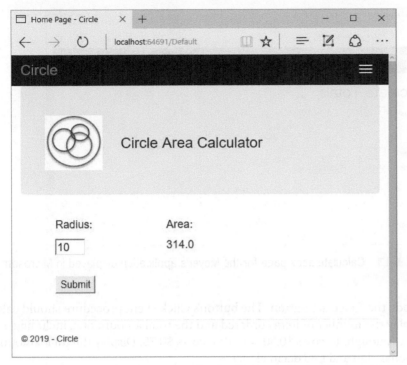

Figure 13-41 Default.aspx page for the Circle application displayed in Microsoft Edge

4. In this exercise, you create two Web pages for Meyer's Purple Bakery: a static page and a dynamic page.

   a. Use the New Web Site option on the File menu to create a Web Site application named Meyer. (Be sure to select the Visual Basic ASP.NET Web Forms Site template.) Save the application in the VB2017\Chap13 folder.

   b. Figures 13-42 and 13-43 show the Default.aspx and Calculate.aspx pages, respectively, in Microsoft Edge. The image of the chef's hat is contained in the VB2017\Chap13\Chef.png file. Create both pages.

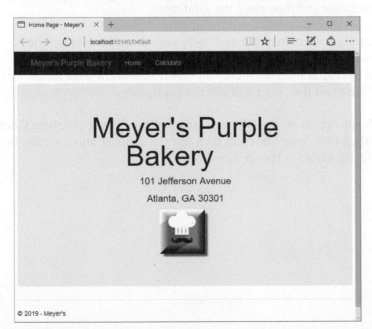

Figure 13-42 Default.aspx page for the Meyer's application displayed in Microsoft Edge

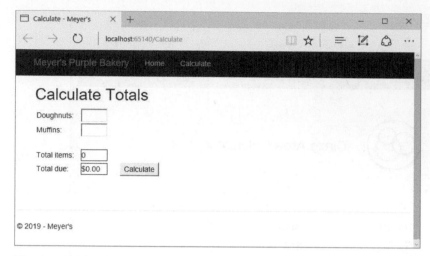

Figure 13-43 Calculate.aspx page for the Meyer's application displayed in Microsoft Edge

c. Next, code the Calculate button. The button's Click event procedure should calculate and display the number of items ordered and the total amount due, including a 5% sales tax. A doughnut costs $0.50; a muffin costs $0.75. Display the total amount due with a dollar sign and two decimal places.

d. Save and then start and test the application. Close the browser window and then close the solution.

ADVANCED 5. In this exercise, you modify the application from Exercise 2. Use Windows to make a copy of the Market folder. Rename the copy MarketAdvanced. Use the Open Web Site option on the File menu to open the MarketAdvanced application. The Corner Market now offers four different varieties of peaches: Blushing Star, Crest Haven, Madison, and Summer Pearl. Create a Web page named Peaches.aspx. Include the image stored in the VB2017\Chap13\Peach.png file on the page. Then, make the appropriate modifications to the Site.master and Default.aspx pages. Save and then start and test the application. Close the browser window and then close the solution.

ON YOUR OWN 6. Create a Web Site application named OnYourOwn. Save the application in the VB2017\Chap13 folder. Plan and design an application of your choice. The only requirement is that the application must contain at least one static page and at least one dynamic page. Save and then start and test the application.

FIX IT 7. Use the Open Web Site option on the File menu to open the FixIt application. Click File, click Save All, and then click Save. Start and then test the application. Close the browser window and then fix the errors in the application.

APPENDIX A

GUI Design Guidelines

Chapter 2

Organizing the Interface

- Organize the user interface so that the information flows either vertically (top to bottom) or horizontally (left to right).

Grouping Controls

- Group related controls together using either white (empty) space or one of the tools from the Containers section of the toolbox.

Identifying Controls

- Use a label to identify each text box in the user interface. Also use a label to identify other label controls that display program output. The label text should be meaningful, consist of one to three words only, and appear on one line. Left-align the text within the label and position the label either above or to the left of the control it identifies. Enter the label text using sentence capitalization, and insert a colon (:) following the label text.

Identifying Buttons

- Display a meaningful caption on the face of each button. The caption should indicate the action the button will perform when clicked. Enter the caption using sentence capitalization. Place the caption on one line and use from one to three words only.

Aligning Buttons

- When a group of buttons are stacked vertically, all buttons in the group should be the same height and width. When a group of buttons are positioned horizontally, all buttons in the group should be the same height; their widths can vary if necessary. In a group of buttons, the most commonly used button is typically placed first in the group.

Aligning Control Borders

- Align the borders of the controls wherever possible to minimize the number of different margins appearing in the interface.

Using Graphics

- Use graphics sparingly. If the graphic is used solely for aesthetics, use a small graphic and place it in a location that will not distract the user.

Choosing Font Types, Styles, and Sizes

- Use only one font type (typically Segoe UI) for all of the text in the interface.
- Use no more than two different font sizes in the interface.
- Avoid using italics and underlining because both font styles make text difficult to read.
- Limit the use of bold text to titles, headings, and key items that you want to emphasize.

Using Color

- Build the interface using black, white, and gray. Only add color if you have a good reason to do so.
- Use white, off-white, or light gray for the background. Use black for the text.
- Limit the number of colors in an interface to three, not including white, black, and gray. The colors you choose should complement each other.
- Never use color as the only means of identification for an element in the interface.

Setting the BorderStyle Property

- Keep the BorderStyle property of text boxes at the default setting: Fixed3D.
- Keep the BorderStyle property of identifying labels at the default setting: None.
- Use FixedSingle for the BorderStyle property of labels that display program output, such as the result of a calculation.
- Avoid setting a label control's BorderStyle property to Fixed3D because in Windows applications, a control with a three-dimensional appearance implies that it can accept user input.

Setting the AutoSize Property

- Keep the AutoSize property of identifying labels at the default setting: True.
- In most cases, use False for the AutoSize property of label controls that display program output.

Setting the TextAlign Property

- Use the TextAlign property to specify the alignment of the text within a label control.

Assigning Access Keys

- Assign a unique access key to each control that can accept user input.

- When assigning an access key to a control, use the first letter of the control's caption or identifying label, unless another letter provides a more meaningful association. If you cannot use the first letter and no other letter provides a more meaningful association, then use a distinctive consonant. As a last choice, use a vowel or a number.

Setting the Tab Order

- Assign a TabIndex value (starting with 0) to each control in the interface, except for controls that do not have a TabIndex property. The TabIndex values should reflect the order in which the user will want to access the controls.

Providing Keyboard Access to a Text Box

- Assign an access key to the text box's identifying label, and then set the identifying label's TabIndex value so it is one number less than the text box's TabIndex value.

Chapter 4

Check Boxes

- Use check boxes to allow the user to select any number of choices from a group of one or more independent and nonexclusive choices.

- The text in the check box's Text property should be entered using sentence capitalization.

- Assign a unique access key to each check box in an interface.

Radio Buttons

- Use radio buttons to limit the user to one choice in a group of related but mutually exclusive choices.

- The minimum number of radio buttons in a group is two, and the recommended maximum number is seven.

- The text in the radio button's Text property should be entered using sentence capitalization.

- Assign a unique access key to each radio button in an interface.

- Use a container (such as a group box) to create separate groups of radio buttons. Only one button in each group can be selected at any one time.

- Designate a default radio button in each group of radio buttons.

Group Boxes

- Use sentence capitalization for the optional identifying label, which is entered in the group box's Text property.

Chapter 5

List Boxes

- Use a list box only when you need to offer the user at least three different choices.
- Don't overwhelm the user with a lot of choices at the same time. Instead, display from three to eight items and let the user employ the scroll bar to view the remaining ones.
- Use a label control to provide keyboard access to the list box. Set the label's TabIndex property to a value that is one number less than the list box's TabIndex value.
- List box items are either arranged by use, with the most used entries appearing first in the list, or sorted in ascending order.
- If a list box allows the user to make only one selection, a default item is typically selected when the interface first appears. The default item should be either the item selected most frequently or the first item in the list. However, if a list box allows more than one selection at a time, you do not select a default item.

Default Buttons

- The default button should be the button that is most often selected by the user, except in cases where the tasks performed by the button are both destructive and irreversible.
- If a form contains a default button, it typically is the first button. A form can have only one default button.

Chapter 6

Combo Boxes

- Use a label control to provide keyboard access to a combo box. Set the label's TabIndex property to a value that is one number less than the combo box's TabIndex value.
- Combo box items are either arranged by use, with the most used entries appearing first in the list, or sorted in ascending order.

MessageBox.Show Method

- Use sentence capitalization for the *text* argument, but use book title capitalization for the *caption* argument.
- Display the Exclamation icon to alert the user that he or she must make a decision before the application can continue. You can phrase the message as a question. Message boxes that contain the Exclamation icon typically contain more than one button.
- Display the Information icon along with an OK button in a message box that displays an informational message.
- Display the Stop icon to alert the user of a serious problem that must be corrected before the application can continue.
- The default button in the message box should represent the user's most likely action as long as that action is not destructive.

Chapter 9

Menus

- Menu title captions should be one word, with only the first letter capitalized. Each menu title should have a unique access key.

- Menu item captions can be from one to three words. Use book title capitalization, and assign a unique access key to each menu item on the same menu.

- Assign unique shortcut keys to commonly used menu items.

- If a menu item requires additional information from the user, place an ellipsis (...) at the end of the item's caption, which is entered in the item's Text property.

- Follow the Windows standards for the placement of menu titles and items.

- Use a separator bar to separate groups of related menu items.

Additional Topics

This appendix contains additional topics that can be covered along with (or after) the specified chapter.

Topics covered in this appendix:

- ◎ Chapter 1: Splash Screen
- ◎ Chapter 1: Timer Control
- ◎ Chapter 1: PrintForm Control
- ◎ Chapter 3: InputBox Function
- ◎ Chapter 4: Using TryParse to Validate Data
- ◎ Chapter 4: Common Errors in Selection Structures
- ◎ Chapter 4: Swapping Numeric Values
- ◎ Chapter 7: Random Double Numbers
- ◎ Chapter 7: Aligning Columns
- ◎ Chapter 8: LINQ with Arrays
- ◎ Chapter 8: Structures

Chapter 1: Splash Screen

Some applications begin by displaying a splash screen, which is simply a form that introduces the application and holds the user's attention while the rest of the application is being read into the computer's main memory. You can use Visual Basic's Splash Screen template to create the splash screen. Or, you can create one from scratch by using a Windows form. In the next set of steps, you will use the Splash Screen template.

To use the Splash Screen template: START HERE

1. Open the Splash Solution.sln file contained in the VB2017\AppB\Splash Solution folder. Open the Solution Explorer window. If the designer window is not open, right-click **Main Form.vb** and then click **Open**.

2. Click **Project**, click **Add New Item**, expand the **Common Items** node (if necessary), and then click **Windows Forms**. Click **Splash Screen** in the middle column. Change the file's name to **Splash Form.vb** and then click the **Add** button.

3. Click the **Application Title** text on the splash screen form. Temporarily display the Properties window and then set the ApplicationTitle object's Text property to **Welcome to my application!**.

4. Right-click **My Project** in the Solution Explorer window and then click **Open** to open the Project Designer window. Change the name in the Startup form box to **frmMain**.

5. Locate the Splash screen box in the Project Designer window. Click the **list arrow** and then click **Splash_Form**.

6. Save the solution and then close the Project Designer window. Start the application. The splash screen appears first. Then, after several seconds, the splash screen disappears and the Main Form appears.

7. Click the **Close** button on the Main Form's title bar to close the application. Close the solution.

Chapter 1: Timer Control

The purpose of a **timer control** is to process code at one or more regular intervals. The length of each interval is specified in milliseconds and entered in the timer's Interval property. A millisecond is 1/1000 of a second; in other words, there are 1,000 milliseconds in a second. The timer's state—either running or stopped—is determined by its Enabled property, which can be set to either the Boolean value True or the Boolean value False. When its Enabled property is set to True, the timer is running; when it is set to False (the default), the timer is stopped.

If the timer is running, its Tick event occurs each time an interval has elapsed. Each time the Tick event occurs, the computer processes any code contained in the Tick event procedure. If the timer is stopped, the Tick event does not occur and, therefore, any code entered in the Tick event procedure is not processed.

To use a timer control: START HERE

1. Open the Timer Solution.sln file contained in the VB2017\AppB\Timer Solution folder. Open the Solution Explorer window. If the designer window is not open, right-click **Main Form.vb** and then click **Open**.

2. Temporarily display the Toolbox window. Expand the Components node in the toolbox and then click **Timer**. Drag the Timer tool to the form and then release the mouse button. A timer control appears in the component tray located at the bottom of the IDE.

3. Set the timer control's Name property to **tmrBlink**. Also, set its Interval and Enabled properties to **1000** and **True**, respectively. (1000 milliseconds is equivalent to 1 second.)

4. Open the Code Editor window and then open the code template for the tmrBlink_Tick procedure. Type the following assignment statement and then press **Enter**. (You will learn about the Not logical operator in Chapter 4. The operator changes True to False and changes False to True.)

   ```
   picSmile.Visible = Not picSmile.Visible
   ```

5. Save the solution and then start the application. A blinking picture box appears on the form. Click the **Close** button on the form's title bar. Close the Code Editor window and then close the solution.

Chapter 1: PrintForm Control

Visual Basic provides the **PrintForm tool** for printing an interface from code. The tool is contained in the Visual Basic PowerPacks section of the toolbox. If your toolbox does not contain the PowerPacks section, the next set of steps will show you how to add the section to your toolbox.

When you drag the PrintForm tool to a form, a print form control appears in the component tray located at the bottom of the IDE. You can use the control to send the printout to a file, the Print preview window, or directly to the printer.

START HERE

To use a print form control:

1. Open the PrintForm Solution.sln file contained in the VB2017\AppB\PrintForm Solution folder. Open the Solution Explorer window. If the designer window is not open, right-click **Main Form.vb** and then click **Open**.

2. Permanently display the toolbox. Scroll down the toolbox to see if it contains the Visual Basic PowerPacks section. If it does, you can skip to Step 10 in this set of steps.

3. If your toolbox does not contain the PowerPacks section, close the solution and exit Visual Studio. Then, use Windows to open the VB2017\AppB folder. Double-click **vb_vbpowerpacks.exe**. (Depending on your computer system, you may need to right-click **vb_vbpowerpacks.exe** and then click **Run as administrator**.)

4. Select the **I agree to the License Terms and Privacy Policy.** check box. Either select or deselect the **check box** that asks if you want to join the Visual Studio Experience Improvement program. Click **Install**. Then, click the **Yes** button.

5. When the "Setup Successful!" message appears, click the **Close** button. Start Visual Studio and open the PrintForm Solution.sln file.

6. Right-click the **Toolbox** window and then click **Add Tab**. Type **Visual Basic PowerPacks** and press **Enter**.

7. Right-click the **Visual Basic PowerPacks** tab and then click **Choose Items**. If necessary, click the **.NET Framework Components** tab in the Choose Toolbox Items dialog box.

8. In the Filter box, type **powerpacks**. Select Version 12's **PrintForm** control, as shown in Figure B-1. (Although this appendix uses only the PrintForm control, you can also select Version 12's DataRepeater, LineShape, OvalShape, and RectangleShape controls.)

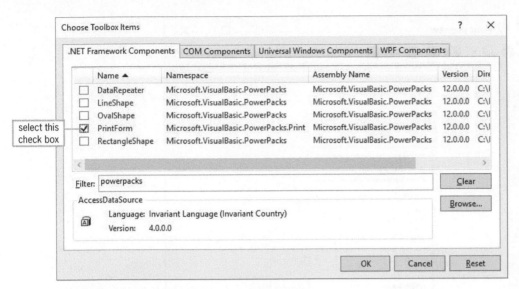

Figure B-1 Choose Toolbox Items dialog box

9. Click the **OK** button to close the Choose Toolbox Items dialog box.

10. If necessary, expand the Visual Basic PowerPacks node in the toolbox. See Figure B-2. (Your Visual Basic PowerPacks section may contain additional tools.)

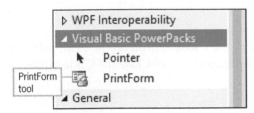

Figure B-2 Visual Basic PowerPacks section in the toolbox

11. Click **PrintForm** and then drag your mouse pointer to the form. Release the mouse button. A print form control appears in the component tray.

12. In the Properties window, set the control's PrintAction property to **PrintToPreview**.

13. Open the Code Editor window and then open the code template for the btnPrint_Click procedure. Enter the comment and code shown in Figure B-3.

```
6      Private Sub btnPrint_Click(sender As Object, e As Ev
7          ' Print the sales receipt without the buttons.
8
9          btnPrint.Visible = False
10         btnExit.Visible = False
11         PrintForm1.Print()
12         btnPrint.Visible = True
13         btnExit.Visible = True
14     End Sub
```

enter this comment and code

Figure B-3 btnPrint_Click procedure

14. Save the solution and then start the application. Click the **Print** button. A printout of the interface appears in the Print preview window. (It may take a few seconds for the window to open.) Click the **Zoom** button's list arrow and then click **75%**. See Figure B-4.

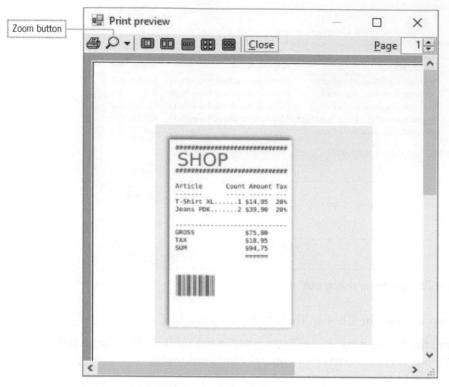

Figure B-4 Print preview window

15. You won't need to print the sales receipt, so click the **Close** button on the Print preview window's toolbar. Click the **Exit** button to end the application. Close the Code Editor window and then close the solution.

Chapter 3: InputBox Function

The **InputBox function** displays an input dialog box, which is one of the standard dialog boxes available in Visual Basic. An input dialog box allows an application to interact with a user while an application is running.

An example of an input dialog box is shown in Figure B-5. The message in the dialog box should prompt the user to enter the appropriate information in the input area. The user closes the dialog box by clicking the OK button, Cancel button, or Close button. The value returned by the InputBox function depends on the button the user chooses. If the user clicks the OK button, the function returns the value contained in the input area of the dialog box; the return value is always treated as a string. If the user clicks either the Cancel button in the dialog box or the Close button on the dialog box's title bar, the function returns an empty (or zero-length) string.

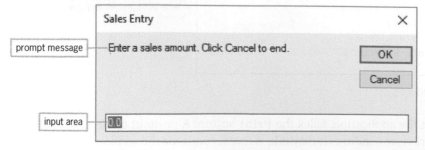

Figure B-5 Example of an input dialog box

Figure B-6 shows the basic syntax of the InputBox function along with examples of using it. The *prompt* argument contains the message to display inside the dialog box. The optional *title* and *defaultResponse* arguments control the text that appears in the dialog box's title bar and input area, respectively. If you omit the *title* argument, the project name appears in the title bar. If you omit the *defaultResponse* argument, a blank input area appears when the dialog box opens.

Using the InputBox Function

Note: The InputBox function's syntax also includes optional *XPos* and *YPos* arguments for specifying the dialog box's horizontal and vertical positions, respectively. If both arguments are omitted, the dialog box appears centered on the screen.

Basic syntax
InputBox(*prompt*[, *title*] [, *defaultResponse*]**)**

Example 1
```
strSales =
    InputBox("Enter a sales amount. Click Cancel to end.",
    "Sales Entry", "0.0")
```
Displays the input dialog box shown in Figure B-5. When the user closes the dialog box, the assignment statement assigns the function's return value to the strSales variable.

Example 2
```
strCity = InputBox("City name:", "City")
```
Displays an input dialog box that shows "City name:" as the prompt, "City" in the title bar, and an empty input area. When the user closes the dialog box, the assignment statement assigns the function's return value to the strCity variable.

Example 3
```
Const strPROMPT As String = "Enter the discount rate:"
Const strTITLE As String = "Discount Rate"
strRate = InputBox(strPROMPT, strTITLE, ".00")
```
Displays an input dialog box that shows the contents of the strPROMPT constant as the prompt, the contents of the strTITLE constant in the title bar, and .00 in the input area. When the user closes the dialog box, the assignment statement assigns the function's return value to the strRate variable.

Example 4
```
Integer.TryParse(InputBox("How old are you?",
    "Discount Verification"), intAge)
```
Displays an input dialog box that shows "How old are you?" as the prompt, "Discount Verification" in the title bar, and an empty input area. When the user closes the dialog box, the TryParse method converts the function's return value from String to Integer and then stores the result in the intAge variable.

Figure B-6 Basic syntax and examples of the InputBox function

The *prompt*, *title*, and *defaultResponse* arguments can be string literals, String named constants, or String variables. The Windows standard is to use sentence capitalization for the prompt but book title capitalization for the title. The capitalization (if any) you use for the defaultResponse depends on the text itself. In most cases, you assign the value returned by the InputBox function to a String variable.

START HERE **To use an input dialog box:**

1. Open the InputBox Solution.sln file contained in the VB2017\AppB\InputBox Solution folder. Open the Solution Explorer window. If the designer window is not open, right-click **Main Form.vb** and then click **Open**.

2. Open the Code Editor window and then open the code template for the btnGetName_Click procedure. Enter the comment and code shown in Figure B-7.

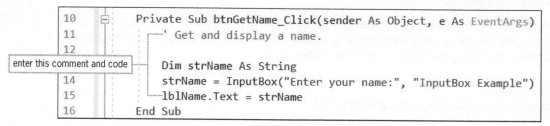

```
10    Private Sub btnGetName_Click(sender As Object, e As EventArgs)
11        ' Get and display a name.
12
          Dim strName As String
14        strName = InputBox("Enter your name:", "InputBox Example")
15        lblName.Text = strName
16    End Sub
```

enter this comment and code

Figure B-7   btnGetName_Click procedure

3. Save the solution and then start the application. Click the **Get name** button. The input dialog box shown in Figure B-8 opens.

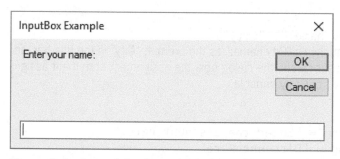

InputBox Example   ✕

Enter your name: [OK]

                                               [Cancel]

| |

Figure B-8   Input dialog box

4. Type your name in the input area of the dialog box and then click the **OK** button. Your name appears in the label control on the form. Click the **Exit** button. Close the Code Editor window and then close the solution.

Chapter 4: Using TryParse to Validate Data

In Chapter 3, you learned how to use the **TryParse method** to convert a string to a number of a specified data type. Recall that if the conversion is successful, the TryParse method stores the number in the variable specified in the method's *numericVariable* argument; otherwise, it stores the number 0 in the variable. What you did not learn in Chapter 3 was that in addition to storing a number in the variable, the TryParse method also returns a Boolean value that indicates whether the conversion was successful (True) or unsuccessful (False). You can assign the value returned by the TryParse method to a Boolean variable, as shown in the syntax and example in Figure B-9. You can then use a selection structure to take the appropriate action based on the result of the conversion.

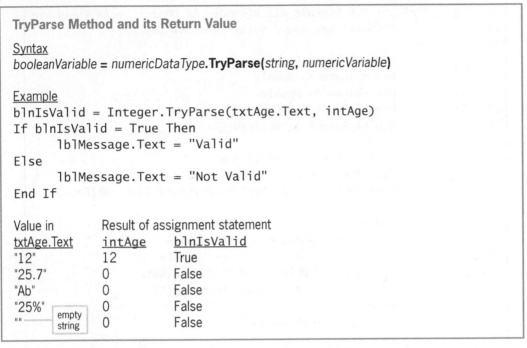

TryParse Method and its Return Value

<u>Syntax</u>
booleanVariable = *numericDataType*.**TryParse**(*string*, *numericVariable*)

<u>Example</u>
```
blnIsValid = Integer.TryParse(txtAge.Text, intAge)
If blnIsValid = True Then
      lblMessage.Text = "Valid"
Else
      lblMessage.Text = "Not Valid"
End If
```

Value in txtAge.Text	Result of assignment statement	
	intAge	blnIsValid
"12"	12	True
"25.7"	0	False
"Ab"	0	False
"25%"	0	False
"" empty string	0	False

Figure B-9   Syntax and an example of using the TryParse method's return value

The TryParse method in the assignment statement in Figure B-9 will attempt to convert the string stored in the txtAge.Text property to a number that has the Integer data type. If the conversion is successful, the method stores the integer in the intAge variable and also returns the Boolean value True. If the conversion is not successful, the method stores the number 0 in the intAge variable and returns the Boolean value False. The assignment statement assigns the TryParse method's return value (either True or False) to the blnIsValid variable. The selection structure in the figure uses the value in the blnIsValid variable to determine the appropriate message to display.

To use the Boolean value returned by the TryParse method:

START HERE

1. Open the TryParse Solution.sln file contained in the VB2017\AppB\TryParse Solution folder. Open the Solution Explorer window. If the designer window is not open, right-click **Main Form.vb** and then click **Open**.

2. Open the Code Editor window and locate the btnCalc_Click procedure. Before modifying the code to use the Boolean value returned by the TryParse method, you will observe how the procedure currently works. Start the application. Type **10** in the Old pay box and then click the **Calculate** button. Rather than alerting the user that the Raise rate box is empty, the procedure displays the old pay amount ($10.00) in the New pay box.

3. Type **a** in the Raise rate box and then click the **Calculate** button. Even though the raise rate is invalid, the procedure displays the old pay amount ($10.00) in the New pay box. Click the **Exit** button.

4. Use the code shown in Figure B-10 to modify the btnCalc_Click procedure. The modifications are shaded in the figure.

```
14      Private Sub btnCalc_Click(sender As Object, e As EventArgs)
15          ' Calculates and displays the new pay.
16
17          Dim dblOld As Double
18          Dim dblRate As Double
19          Dim dblNew As Double
20          Dim blnOldOk As Boolean
21          Dim blnRateOk As Boolean
22
23          ' Convert the input to numbers.
24          blnOldOk = Double.TryParse(txtOld.Text, dblOld)
25          blnRateOk = Double.TryParse(txtRate.Text, dblRate)
26
27          ' Determine whether the conversions were successful.
28          If blnOldOk AndAlso blnRateOk Then
29              ' Calculate and display the new pay.
30              dblNew = dblOld + dblOld * dblRate
31              lblNew.Text = dblNew.ToString("C2")
32          Else
33              lblNew.Text = "N/A"
34          End If
35      End Sub
```

Figure B-10   Modified btnCalc_Click procedure

5. Save the solution and then start the application. Type **10** in the Old pay box and then click the **Calculate** button. Because no raise rate was entered, the procedure displays the "N/A" message in the New pay box.

6. Type **.05** in the Raise rate box and then click the **Calculate** button. The procedure displays $10.50 as the new pay amount, which is correct.

7. Change the old pay to the letter **a** and then click the **Calculate** button. The procedure displays the "N/A" message, which is correct.

8. Click the **Exit** button. Close the Code Editor window and then close the solution.

Chapter 4: Common Errors in Selection Structures

Figure B-11 lists four common errors made when writing selection structures.

Common Errors in Selection Structures

1. Using a compound condition rather than a nested selection structure.
2. Reversing the decisions in the outer and nested selection structures.
3. Using an unnecessary nested selection structure.
4. Including an unnecessary comparison in a condition.

Figure B-11   Common errors in selection structures

It is easier to understand the errors listed in Figure B-11 by viewing them in a procedure. The first three errors will be illustrated using a procedure that displays the daily fee for renting a car. The daily fee is $55; however, there is an additional charge for renting a luxury car. The additional charge, either $20 or $30, depends on whether the customer belongs to the

Car Rental Club. Notice that the car's classification determines whether the renter is charged an additional amount. If the car is classified as a luxury vehicle, then whether the customer is a club member determines the appropriate additional amount. In this case, the decision regarding the car's classification is the primary decision, while the decision regarding the customer's membership status is the secondary decision. The pseudocode shown in Example 1 in Figure B-12 contains the correct selection structures for this procedure. The selection structures in Examples 2 through 4 illustrate the first three errors.

Example 1—pseudocode (correct)
1. daily fee = 55
2. if luxury car
        if club member
            add 20 to the daily fee
        else
            add 30 to the daily fee
        end if
   end if
3. display the daily fee

The selection structures indicate that a hierarchy exists between the car classification and the membership decisions. The decision regarding the car classification must be made first. The membership decision is necessary only when the car classification decision evaluates to True.

Example 2—pseudocode (first error)
1. daily fee = 55
2. if luxury car and club member
        add 20 to the daily fee
   else
        add 30 to the daily fee
   end if
3. display the daily fee

uses a compound condition instead of a nested selection structure

The compound condition indicates that only club members who are renting a luxury car are charged $20 extra; everyone else is charged $30 extra. If a customer is renting a standard vehicle, this selection structure will incorrectly charge him or her an additional $30.

Example 3—pseudocode (second error)
1. daily fee = 55
2. if club member
        if luxury car
            add 20 to the daily fee
        else
            add 30 to the daily fee
        end if
   end if
3. display the daily fee

reverses the outer and nested decisions

The selection structures indicate that a hierarchy exists between the car classification and the membership decisions. The decision regarding the membership must be made first. The car classification decision is necessary only when the membership decision evaluates to True. These selection structures will incorrectly charge a club member renting a standard vehicle an extra $30, and it will not charge anything extra to a nonmember renting a luxury vehicle.

Example 4—pseudocode (third error)
1. daily fee = 55
2. if luxury car
        if club member
            add 20 to the daily fee
        else
            if nonmember
                add 30 to the daily fee
            end if
        end if
   end if
3. display the daily fee

unnecessary nested selection structure

The third selection structure is unnecessary because the second selection structure's condition already determines the membership status. Although these selection structures produce the correct results, they do so less efficiently.

Figure B-12 Correct and incorrect pseudocode for the car rental procedure

The fourth error listed in Figure B-11 will be illustrated using a procedure that displays the price of an item. The item price is based on the quantity purchased, as shown in Figure B-13. Example 1 in the figure shows the correct selection structures for this procedure; the selection structures in Example 2 illustrate the fourth error. Although Example 2's selection structures produce the correct results, they do so in a less efficient manner than the ones shown in Example 1.

Information

Quantity purchased	Price per item
Less than or equal to 0	$0.00
1–99	$9.50
100 or more	$7.75

Example 1—pseudocode (correct)
1. if quantity <= 0
        price = 0
    else
        if quantity < 100
            price = 9.50
        else
            price = 7.75
        end if
    end if
2. display the price

Example 2—pseudocode (fourth error)
1. if quantity <= 0
        price = 0   unnecessary comparison because the quantity has to be greater than 0 for this nested structure to be processed
    else
        if quantity > 0 and quantity < 100
            price = 9.50
        else
            price = 7.75
        end if
    end if
2. display the price

Figure B-13   Correct and incorrect pseudocode for the item price procedure

Chapter 4: Swapping Numeric Values

Figure B-14 shows a sample run of an application that displays the lowest and highest of two scores entered by the user. It also shows the code entered in the btnDisplay_Click procedure. The condition in the If clause compares the contents of the intScore1 variable with the contents of the intScore2 variable. If the value in the intScore1 variable is greater than the value in the intScore2 variable, the condition evaluates to True and the three instructions in the If...Then...Else statement's true path swap both values. Swapping the values places the smaller number in the intScore1 variable and places the larger number in the intScore2 variable. If the condition evaluates to False, on the other hand, the true path instructions are skipped over because the intScore1 variable already contains a number that is smaller than (or possibly equal to) the number stored in the intScore2 variable.

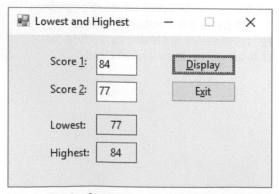

Figure B-14   Sample run and btnDisplay_Click procedure (continued)

(continued)

```
Private Sub btnDisplay_Click(sender As Object, e
    ' Display the lowest and highest scores.

    Dim intScore1 As Integer
    Dim intScore2 As Integer
    Dim intTemp As Integer

    Integer.TryParse(txtScore1.Text, intScore1)
    Integer.TryParse(txtScore2.Text, intScore2)

    ' Swap scores (if necessary).
    If intScore1 > intScore2 Then
        intTemp = intScore1
        intScore1 = intScore2
        intScore2 = intTemp
    End If

    ' Display lowest and highest scores.
    lblLow.Text = intScore1.ToString
    lblHigh.Text = intScore2.ToString
End Sub
```

Figure B-14   Sample run and btnDisplay_Click procedure

The first instruction in the If...Then...Else statement's true path assigns the intScore1 variable's value to the intTemp variable. If you do not store that value in the intTemp variable, it will be lost when the computer processes the next statement, intScore1 = intScore2, which replaces the contents of the intScore1 variable with the contents of the intScore2 variable. Finally, the intScore2 = intTemp instruction assigns the intTemp variable's value to the intScore2 variable; this completes the swap. Figure B-15 illustrates the concept of swapping, assuming the user enters the numbers 84 and 77 in the Score 1 and Score 2 boxes, respectively.

	intScore1	intScore2	intTemp
values stored in the variables immediately before the intTemp = intScore1 statement is processed	84	77	0
result of the intTemp = intScore1 statement	84	77	84
result of the intScore1 = intScore2 statement	77	77	84
result of the intScore2 = intTemp statement	77	84	84

Figure B-15   Illustration of the swapping concept   the values were swapped

Chapter 7: Random Double Numbers

In Chapter 7's Apply the Concepts lesson, you learned how to use Visual Basic's pseudo-random number generator to generate random integers. Figure B-16 shows the syntax and examples of using the generator to generate random Double numbers.

Generating Random Double Numbers

Syntax
To create a random number that is greater than or equal to 0.0 but less than 1.0:
Dim *randomObject* **As New Random**
randomObject.**NextDouble**

To create a random number that is greater than or equal to a minimum value but less than a maximum value:
Dim *randomObject* **As New Random**
(*maxValue* − *minValue* + 1) * *randomObject*.**NextDouble** + *minValue*

Example 1
```
Dim randGen As New Random
dblNum = randGen.NextDouble
```
The Dim statement creates a Random object named randGen. The randGen.NextDouble expression generates a random Double number that is greater than or equal to 0.0 but less than 1.0. The assignment statement assigns the random Double number to the dblNum variable.

Example 2
```
Dim randGen As New Random
dblNum = (25 - 5 + 1) * randGen.NextDouble + 5
```
The Dim statement creates a Random object named randGen. The (25 - 5 + 1) * randGen.NextDouble + 5 expression generates a random number that is greater than or equal to 5.0 but less than 25.0.

Figure B-16 Syntax and examples of generating random Double numbers

Chapter 7: Aligning Columns

In Chapter 7's Focus on the Concepts lesson, you learned how to use the PadLeft and PadRight methods to pad a string with a character until the string is a specified length. Each method's syntax is shown in Figure B-17. Recall that when processing the methods, the computer first makes a temporary copy of the *string* in memory; it then pads the copy only. The *totalChars* argument in each syntax is an integer that represents the total number of characters you want the string's copy to contain. The optional *padCharacter* argument is the character that is used to pad the string until the desired number of characters is reached. If the *padCharacter* argument is omitted, the default padding character is the space character. You can use the PadLeft and PadRight methods to align columns of information, as shown in the examples included in Figure B-17.

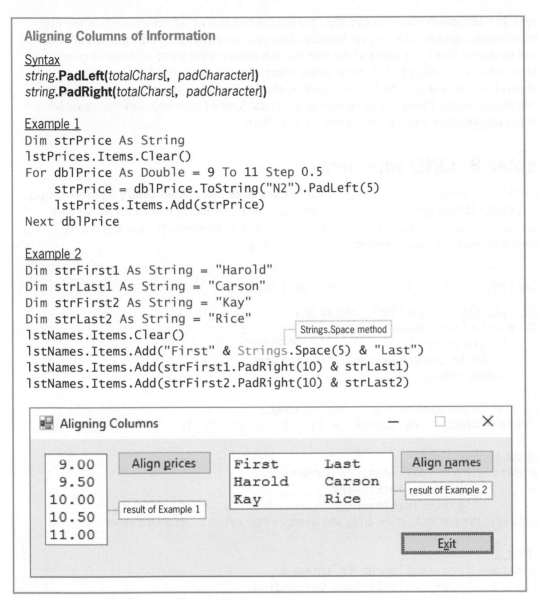

Aligning Columns of Information

<u>Syntax</u>
string.**PadLeft**(*totalChars*[, *padCharacter*])
string.**PadRight**(*totalChars*[, *padCharacter*])

<u>Example 1</u>
```
Dim strPrice As String
lstPrices.Items.Clear()
For dblPrice As Double = 9 To 11 Step 0.5
    strPrice = dblPrice.ToString("N2").PadLeft(5)
    lstPrices.Items.Add(strPrice)
Next dblPrice
```

<u>Example 2</u>
```
Dim strFirst1 As String = "Harold"
Dim strLast1 As String = "Carson"
Dim strFirst2 As String = "Kay"
Dim strLast2 As String = "Rice"
lstNames.Items.Clear()
lstNames.Items.Add("First" & Strings.Space(5) & "Last")
lstNames.Items.Add(strFirst1.PadRight(10) & strLast1)
lstNames.Items.Add(strFirst2.PadRight(10) & strLast2)
```

Strings.Space method

result of Example 1

result of Example 2

Figure B-17 Examples of aligning columns of information

Example 1's code aligns a column of numbers by the decimal point. Notice that you first format each number in the column to ensure that each has the same number of digits to the right of the decimal point. You then use the PadLeft method to insert spaces at the beginning of the number (if necessary); this right-aligns the number within the column. Because each number has the same number of digits to the right of the decimal point, aligning each number on the right will align each by its decimal point. You also need to set the lstPrices control's Font property to a fixed-spaced font, such as Courier New. A fixed-space font uses the same amount of space to display each character.

Example 2's code shows how you can align the second column of information when the first column contains strings with varying lengths. First, you use either the PadRight or PadLeft method to ensure that each string in the first column contains the same number of characters. You then concatenate the padded string to the information in the second column. Example 2 also shows how you can use the Strings.Space method to include a specific number of space characters in a string. The method's syntax is `Strings.Space(number)`, in which *number* is an integer representing the number of spaces to include.

Chapter 8: LINQ with Arrays

Built into Visual Basic is a query language called **Language-Integrated Query** or, more simply, **LINQ**. A **query language** allows you to retrieve specific information from a variety of data sources, such as arrays, collections, and databases. Figure B-18 shows the basic syntax of LINQ when used to select (retrieve) information from an array.

Using LINQ to Retrieve Information from an Array

<u>Basic syntax (Be sure to set Option Infer to On.)</u>
Dim *variable* = **From** *element* **In** *array*
    [**Where** *condition*]
    [**Order By** *element* [**Ascending** | **Descending**]] ← default sort order
    Select *element*

Note: All of the examples refer to the following array:
`Private intNums() As Integer = {10, 8, 5, 12, 7, 3}`

<u>Example 1</u>
```
Dim data = From intElement In intNums
           Order By intElement
           Select intElement
```
selects all of the elements in the array and arranges their values in ascending order

<u>Example 2</u>
```
Dim data = From intElement In intNums
           Order By intElement Descending
           Select intElement
```
selects all of the elements in the array and arranges their values in descending order

<u>Example 3</u>
```
Dim data = From intElement In intNums
           Where intElement > 8
           Select intElement
```
selects only the array elements that contain a value that is greater than 8

<u>Example 4</u>
```
Dim data = From intElement In intNums
           Where intElement Mod 2 = 0
           Order By intElement
           Select intElement
```
selects only the array elements that contain an even number and arranges their values in ascending order

---

Figure B-18 Basic LINQ syntax and examples for retrieving information from an array

To test the examples shown in Figure B-18:

START HERE

1. Open the Linq Array Solution.sln file contained in the VB2017\AppB\Linq Array Solution folder. Open the designer window.

2. Open the Code Editor window and locate the btnEx1_Click procedure. Click the **blank line** above the `lstNums.Items.Clear` statement. Then, enter the code shown in Example 1 in Figure B-18.

3. Locate the btnEx2_Click procedure. Click the **blank line** above the `lstNums.Items.Clear` statement and then enter the code shown in Example 2 in Figure B-18.

4. Locate the btnEx3_Click procedure. Click the **blank line** above the `lstNums.Items.Clear` statement and then enter the code shown in Example 3 in Figure B-18.

5. Locate the btnEx4_Click procedure. Click the **blank line** above the `lstNums.Items.Clear` statement and then enter the code shown in Example 4 in Figure B-18.

6. Save the solution and then start the application. Click the **Example 1** button. The numbers stored in the array appear in ascending order in the list box. See Figure B-19.

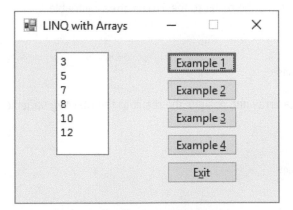

Figure B-19   Result of processing Example 1's code

7. Click the **Example 2** button. The array values appear in descending order in the list box.

8. Click the **Example 3** button. The two array values that are greater than 8 (in this case, the numbers 10 and 12) appear in the list box.

9. Click the **Example 4** button. The three even numbers in the array (8, 10, and 12) appear in ascending order in the list box.

10. Click the **Exit** button. Close the Code Editor window and then close the solution.

LINQ Aggregate Operators

LINQ also provides several aggregate operators—such as Average, Count, Max, Min, and Sum—that you can use when querying an array. An **aggregate operator** returns a single value from a group of values. The Sum operator, for example, returns the sum of the values in the group, whereas the Min operator returns the smallest value in the group. You include an aggregate operator in a LINQ statement using the syntax shown in Figure B-20. The figure also includes examples of using the syntax.

LINQ Aggregate Operators

Syntax
[**Dim**] *variable* [**As** *dataType*] =
  Aggregate *element* **In** *array*
  [**Where** *condition*]
  Select *element* **Into** *aggregateOperator*

Note: All of the examples refer to the following array:
```
Private intNums() As Integer = {10, 8, 5, 12, 7, 3}
```

Example 1
```
Dim intTotal As Integer =
    Aggregate number In intNums
    Select number Into Sum
```
calculates the total of the values in the array and assigns the result to the `intTotal` variable

Example 2
```
Dim intHighest As Integer =
    Aggregate number In intNums
    Select number Into Max
```
finds the highest value in the array and assigns the result to the `intHighest` variable

Example 3
```
Dim dblAvg As Double =
    Aggregate number In intNums
    Select number Into Average
```
calculates the average of the values in the array and assigns the result to the `dblAvg` variable

Example 4
```
Dim intCountOdd As Integer =
    Aggregate number In intNums
    Where number Mod 2 = 1
    Into Count
```
counts the number of odd numbers in the array and assigns the result to the `intCountOdd` variable (The Count operator is the only operator that does not need the Select clause.)

Figure B-20   Syntax and examples of the LINQ aggregate operators

START HERE

To test the examples shown in Figure B-20:

1. Open the Linq Aggregate Array Solution.sln file contained in the VB2017\AppB\Linq Aggregate Array Solution folder. Open the designer window.

2. Open the Code Editor window and locate the btnEx1_Click procedure. Click the **blank line** above the assignment statement and then enter the code shown in Example 1 in Figure B-20.

3. Locate the btnEx2_Click procedure. Click the **blank line** above the assignment statement and then enter the code shown in Example 2 in Figure B-20.

4. Locate the btnEx3_Click procedure. Click the **blank line** above the assignment statement and then enter the code shown in Example 3 in Figure B-20.

5. Locate the btnEx4_Click procedure. Click the **blank line** above the assignment statement and then enter the code shown in Example 4 in Figure B-20.

6. Save the solution and then start the application. Click the **Example 1** button. The sum of the numbers in the array appears in the lblResult control. See Figure B-21.

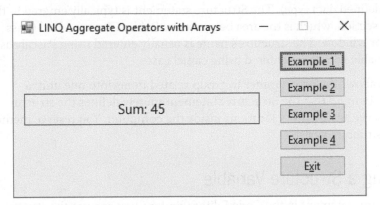

Figure B-21   Result of processing Example 1's code

7. Click the **Example 2** button. The "Highest number: 12" message appears in the lblResult control.

8. Click the **Example 3** button. The "Average number: 7.5" message appears in the lblResult control.

9. Click the **Example 4** button. The "Number of odd numbers: 3" message appears in the lblResult control.

10. Click the **Exit** button. Close the Code Editor window and then close the solution.

Chapter 8: Structures

The data types used in previous chapters, such as Integer and Double, are built into the Visual Basic language. You also can create your own data types by using the **Structure statement**, whose syntax is shown in Figure B-22. Data types created by the Structure statement are referred to as **user-defined data types** or **structures**.

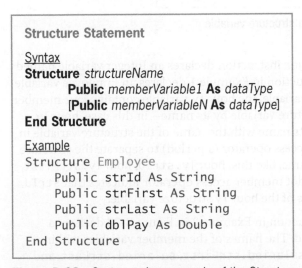

Figure B-22   Syntax and an example of the Structure statement

The structures you create are composed of members that are defined between the Structure and End Structure clauses. The members can be variables, constants, or procedures. However, in most cases, the members will be variables; such variables are referred to as **member variables**. The *dataType* in the member variable definition identifies the type of data the member variable will store, and it can be any of the standard data types available in Visual Basic; it can also be another structure (user-defined data type). The Structure statement is typically entered in the form class's declarations section, which is the area between the Public Class and End Class clauses in the Code Editor window. The structure's name is usually entered using Pascal case, whereas the member variable names are entered using camel case.

The Structure statement allows the programmer to group related items into one unit: a structure. However, keep in mind that the Structure statement merely defines the structure members. It does not reserve any memory locations inside the computer. You reserve memory locations by declaring a structure variable.

Declaring and Using a Structure Variable

After entering the Structure statement in the Code Editor window, you can use the structure to declare a variable. Variables declared using a structure are often referred to as **structure variables**. The syntax for creating a structure variable is shown in Figure B-23. The figure also includes examples of declaring structure variables using the Employee structure from Figure B-22.

Declaring a Structure Variable

Syntax
{**Dim** | **Private**} *structureVariable* **As** *structureName*

Example 1
```
Dim hourly As Employee
```
declares a procedure-level Employee structure variable named `hourly`

Example 2
```
Private salaried As Employee
```
declares a class-level Employee structure variable named `salaried`

Figure B-23 Syntax and examples of declaring a structure variable

Similar to the way the `Dim intAge As Integer` instruction declares an Integer variable named `intAge`, the `Dim hourly As Employee` instruction in Example 1 declares an Employee variable named `hourly`. However, unlike the `intAge` variable, the `hourly` variable contains four member variables. In code, you refer to the entire structure variable by its name—in this case, `hourly`. You refer to a member variable by preceding its name with the name of the structure variable in which it is defined. You use the dot member access operator (a period) to separate the structure variable's name from the member variable's name, like this: `hourly.strId`, `hourly.strFirst`, `hourly.strLast`, and `hourly.dblPay`. The dot member access operator indicates that `strId`, `strFirst`, `strLast`, and `dblPay` are members of the `hourly` structure variable.

The `Private salaried As Employee` instruction in Example 2 in Figure B-23 declares a class-level Employee variable named `salaried`. The names of the member variables within the `salaried` variable are `salaried.strId`, `salaried.strFirst`, `salaried.strLast`, and `salaried.dblPay`.

The member variables in a structure variable can be used just like any other variables. You can assign values to them, use them in calculations, display their contents, and so on. Figure B-24 shows various ways of using the member variables created by the statements shown in Figure B-23.

Using a Member Variable

<u>Example 1</u>
```
hourly.strFirst = "Caroline"
```
assigns the string "Caroline" to the `hourly.strFirst` member variable

<u>Example 2</u>
```
hourly.dblPay *= 1.05
```
multiplies the contents of the `hourly.dblPay` member variable by 1.05 and then assigns the result to the member variable; you can also write the statement as `hourly.dblPay = hourly.dblPay * 1.05`

<u>Example 3</u>
```
lblSalary.Text = salaried.dblPay.ToString("C2")
```
formats the value contained in the `salaried.dblPay` member variable and then displays the result in the lblSalary control

---

Figure B-24   Examples of using a member variable

Programmers use structure variables when they need to pass a group of related items to a procedure for further processing. This is because it is easier to pass one structure variable rather than many individual variables. Programmers also use structure variables to store related items in an array, even when the members have different data types. In the next two sections, you will learn how to pass a structure variable to a procedure and also how to store a structure variable in an array.

Passing a Structure Variable to a Procedure

The sales manager at Norbert Pool & Spa Depot wants you to create an application that determines the amount of water required to fill a rectangular pool. To perform this task, the application will need to calculate the volume of the pool. You calculate the volume by first multiplying the pool's length by its width and then multiplying the result by the pool's depth. Assuming the length, width, and depth are measured in feet, this gives you the volume in cubic feet. To determine the number of gallons of water, you multiply the number of cubic feet by 7.48 because there are 7.48 gallons in one cubic foot.

To open and then test the Norbert Pool & Spa Depot application:

START HERE

1. Open the Norbert Solution.sln file contained in the VB2017\AppB\Norbert Solution folder. Open the designer window.

2. Start the application. Type **100** in the Length box, type **30** in the Width box, and type **4** in the Depth box. Click the **Calculate** button. The required number of gallons appears in the interface. See Figure B-25.

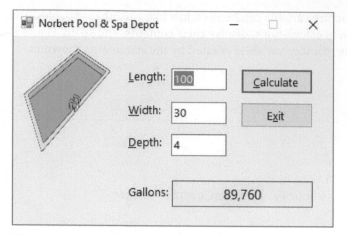

Figure B-25 Interface showing the required number of gallons

3. Click the **Exit** button to end the application, and then open the Code Editor window.

Figure B-26 shows the GetGallons function and the btnCalc_Click procedure. The procedure calls the function, passing it three variables *by value*. The function uses the values to calculate the number of gallons required to fill the pool. The function returns the number of gallons as a Double number to the procedure, which assigns the value to the dblGallons variable.

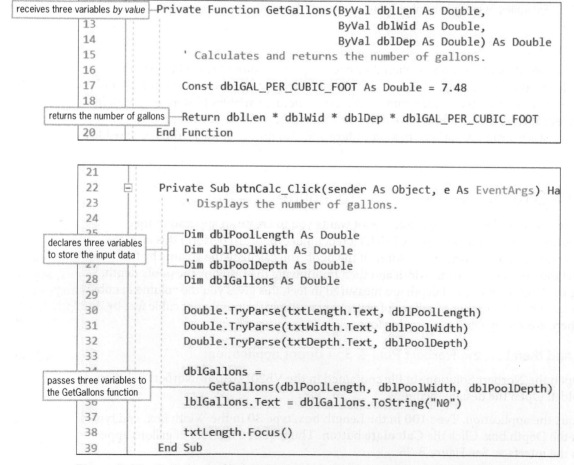

Figure B-26 Code for the Norbert Pool & Spa Depot application (without a structure)

A more convenient way of coding the application is to use a structure to group together the input items: length, width, and depth. It is logical to group the three items because they are related; each represents one of the three dimensions of a rectangular pool. A descriptive name for the structure would be Dimensions.

To use a structure in the application:

START HERE

1. First, you will declare the structure in the form class's declarations section. Click the **blank line** immediately below the Public Class clause, and then press **Enter** to insert another blank line. Enter the following Structure statement:

```
Structure Dimensions
    Public dblLength As Double
    Public dblWidth As Double
    Public dblDepth As Double
End Structure
```

2. Locate the btnCalc_Click procedure. The procedure will use a structure variable (rather than three separate variables) to store the input items. Replace the first three Dim statements with the following Dim statement:

```
Dim poolSize As Dimensions
```

3. Next, you will store each input item in its corresponding member in the structure variable. In the three TryParse methods, change dblPoolLength, dblPoolWidth, and dblPoolDepth to **poolSize.dblLength**, **poolSize.dblWidth**, and **poolSize.dblDepth**, respectively.

4. Instead of sending three separate variables to the GetGallons function, the procedure now needs to send only one variable: the structure variable. When you pass a structure variable to a procedure, all of its members are passed automatically. Although passing one structure variable rather than three separate variables may not seem like a huge advantage, consider the convenience of passing one structure variable rather than 10 separate variables. Change the statement that invokes the GetGallons function to **dblGallons = GetGallons(poolSize)**. Don't be concerned about the squiggle (jagged line) that appears below GetGallons(poolSize) in the statement. It will disappear when you modify the GetGallons function in the next step.

5. Locate the GetGallons function. The function will now receive a Dimensions structure variable rather than three Double variables. Like the Double variables, the structure variable will be passed *by value* because the function does not need to change any member's value. Replace the three parameters in the function header with **ByVal pool As Dimensions.**

6. The function will now use the members of the structure variable to calculate the number of gallons. Change the Return statement as follows:

```
Return pool.dblLength * pool.dblWidth *
    pool.dblDepth * dblGAL_PER_CUBIC_FOOT
```

Figure B-27 shows the Structure statement, the GetGallons function, and the btnCalc_Click procedure. The procedure calls the function, passing it a structure variable *by value*. The function uses the values contained in the structure variable to calculate the number of gallons required to fill the pool. The function returns the number of gallons as a Double number to the procedure, which assigns the value to the dblGallons variable.

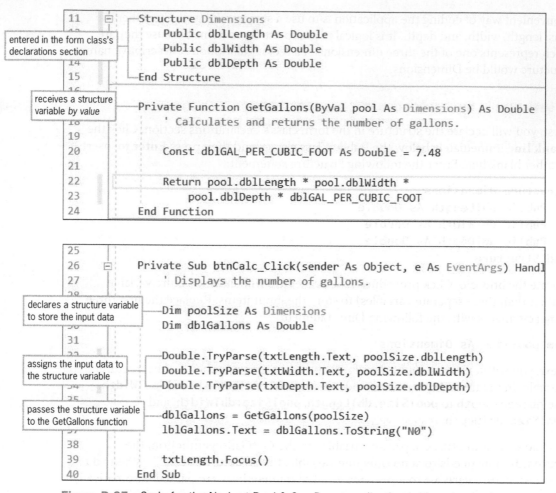

entered in the form class's declarations section

```
11          Structure Dimensions
                Public dblLength As Double
                Public dblWidth As Double
                Public dblDepth As Double
14
15          End Structure
16
```

receives a structure variable *by value*

```
            Private Function GetGallons(ByVal pool As Dimensions) As Double
                ' Calculates and returns the number of gallons.
18
19
20              Const dblGAL_PER_CUBIC_FOOT As Double = 7.48
21
22              Return pool.dblLength * pool.dblWidth *
23                  pool.dblDepth * dblGAL_PER_CUBIC_FOOT
24          End Function
```

```
25
26          Private Sub btnCalc_Click(sender As Object, e As EventArgs) Handl
27              ' Displays the number of gallons.
28
```

declares a structure variable to store the input data

```
            Dim poolSize As Dimensions
            Dim dblGallons As Double
31
```

assigns the input data to the structure variable

```
            Double.TryParse(txtLength.Text, poolSize.dblLength)
            Double.TryParse(txtWidth.Text, poolSize.dblWidth)
            Double.TryParse(txtDepth.Text, poolSize.dblDepth)
```

passes the structure variable to the GetGallons function

```
            dblGallons = GetGallons(poolSize)
            lblGallons.Text = dblGallons.ToString("N0")
38
39              txtLength.Focus()
40          End Sub
```

Figure B-27 Code for the Norbert Pool & Spa Depot application (with a structure)

START HERE

To test the modified code:

1. Save the solution and then start the application. Type **100**, **30**, and **4** in the Length, Width, and Depth boxes, respectively. Press **Enter** to select the Calculate button. The required number of gallons (89,760) appears in the interface, as shown earlier in Figure B-25.

2. Click the **Exit** button. Close the Code Editor window and then close the solution.

Creating an Array of Structure Variables

As mentioned earlier, another advantage of using a structure is that a structure variable can be stored in an array, even when its members have different data types. The Paper Warehouse application from Chapter 8's Apply the Concepts lesson can be used to illustrate this concept. The application displays the price corresponding to the item ID entered by the user. The price list is shown in Figure B-28.

Item ID	Price ($)
A45G	8.99
J63Y	12.99
M93K	5.99
C20P	13.50
F77T	7.25

Figure B-28   Paper Warehouse price list

As you may remember, you coded the application in two ways. First, you used two parallel one-dimensional arrays: one having the String data type and the other having the Double data type. You then used a two-dimensional String array. In this appendix, you will code the application using a one-dimensional array of structure variables. (Notice that there are many different ways of solving the same problem.) Each structure variable will contain two member variables: a String variable for the ID and a Double variable for the price.

To use an array of structure variables in the Paper Warehouse application:

START HERE

1. Open the Paper Solution.sln file contained in the VB2017\AppB\Paper Solution folder. See Figure B-29.

Figure B-29   Interface for the Paper Warehouse application

2. Open the Code Editor window. First, you will declare the ProductInfo structure, which will contain two members: one for the item ID and one for the price. Click the **blank line** immediately below the ' Declare structure. comment. Then, enter the following Structure statement:

```
Structure ProductInfo
    Public strId As String
    Public dblPrice As Double
End Structure
```

3. The procedure will store the price list in a one-dimensional array of ProductInfo structure variables. Click the **blank line** below the ' Declare array of structure variables. comment. Type the following statement and then press **Enter**:

```
Private priceList(4) As ProductInfo
```

The frmMain_Load procedure will be responsible for storing the five IDs and prices in the priceList array. Keep in mind that each element in the array is a structure variable, and each structure variable contains two member variables: strId and dblPrice. You refer to a member variable in an array element using the syntax shown in Figure B-30. The figure also indicates how you would refer to some of the member variables contained in the priceList array. For example, to refer to the strId member contained in the first array element, you use priceList(0).strId. Similarly, you use priceList(4).dblPrice to refer to the dblPrice member contained in the last array element.

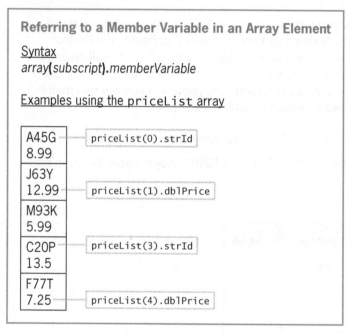

Figure B-30 Syntax and examples of referring to member variables in an array

START HERE

To continue coding the application:

1. Open the form's Load event procedure. Type the following comment and then press **Enter** twice:

    ```
    ' Fill array with IDs and prices.
    ```

2. Enter the following assignment statements:

    ```
    priceList(0).strId = "A45G"
    priceList(0).dblPrice = 8.99
    priceList(1).strId = "J63Y"
    priceList(1).dblPrice = 12.99
    priceList(2).strId = "M93K"
    priceList(2).dblPrice = 5.99
    priceList(3).strId = "C20P"
    priceList(3).dblPrice = 13.5
    priceList(4).strId = "F77T"
    priceList(4).dblPrice = 7.25
    ```

3. Locate the btnGet_Click procedure. The procedure will use a loop to search each element in the array, comparing the value contained in the current element's strId member with the value stored in the strSearchId variable. The loop should stop

searching either when the end of the array is reached or when the ID is found. Click the **blank line** above the End Sub clause and then enter the following Do loop:

```
Do Until intSub = priceList.Length OrElse
        priceList(intSub).strId = strSearchId
    intSub += 1
Loop
```

4. Insert a **blank line** below the Loop clause. The procedure will use a selection structure to determine why the loop ended and then take the appropriate action. If the value contained in the intSub variable is less than the number of array elements, the loop ended because the ID was located in the array. In that case, the selection structure's true path should display the corresponding price in the lblPrice control; otherwise, its False path should display an appropriate message. Enter the selection structure shown in Figure B-31.

```
29    |       Loop
30    ⊟      If intSub < priceList.Length Then ──────
31    |           lblPrice.Text = priceList(intSub).dblPrice.ToString("C2")
32    |       Else                                                              ── enter this selection structure
33    |           MessageBox.Show("ID not found", "Paper Warehouse",
34    |                           MessageBoxButtons.OK, MessageBoxIcon.Information)
35    |       End If ───────
```

Figure B-31   Selection structure entered in the btnGet_Click procedure

Figure B-32 shows the form class's declarations section, the btnGet_Click procedure, and the frmMain_Load procedure.

```
9    ⊟Public Class frmMain
10   |      ' Declare structure. ──────
11   ⊟      Structure ProductInfo
12   |          Public strId As String                    form class's
13   |          Public dblPrice As Double                 declarations section
14   |      End Structure
15   |      ' Declare array of structure variables.
16   |      Private priceList(4) As ProductInfo ──────
```

```
17   |
18   ⊟      Private Sub btnGet_Click(sender As Object, e As EventArgs) Handles btnGet.──── btnGet_Click procedure
19   |          Dim strSearchId As String
20   |          Dim intSub As Integer
21   |
22   |          strSearchId = txtId.Text.Trim.ToUpper
23   |
24   |          ' Search the priceList array until the
25   |          ' end of the array or the ID is found.
26   ⊟          Do Until intSub = priceList.Length OrElse
27   |                  priceList(intSub).strId = strSearchId
28   |              intSub += 1
29   |          Loop
30   ⊟          If intSub < priceList.Length Then
31   |              lblPrice.Text = priceList(intSub).dblPrice.ToString("C2")
32   |          Else
33   |              MessageBox.Show("ID not found", "Paper Warehouse",
34   |                              MessageBoxButtons.OK, MessageBoxIcon.Information)
35   |          End If
36   |      End Sub
```

Figure B-32   Code for the Paper Warehouse application using an array of structure variables *(continued)*

(continued)

```
frmMain_Load procedure    Private Sub frmMain_Load(sender As Object, e As EventArgs) Handles Me.Load
51                          ' Fill array with IDs and prices.
52
53                          priceList(0).strId = "A45G"
54                          priceList(0).dblPrice = 8.99
55                          priceList(1).strId = "J63Y"
56                          priceList(1).dblPrice = 12.99
57                          priceList(2).strId = "M93K"
58                          priceList(2).dblPrice = 5.99
59                          priceList(3).strId = "C20P"
60                          priceList(3).dblPrice = 13.5
61                          priceList(4).strId = "F77T"
62                          priceList(4).dblPrice = 7.25
63
64                      End Sub
```

Figure B-32   Code for the Paper Warehouse application using an array of structure variables

START HERE

To test the application's code:

1. Save the solution and then start the application. Type **m93k** in the ID box and then click the **Get price** button. $5.99 appears in the Price box. See Figure B-33.

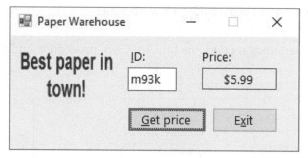

Figure B-33   Interface showing the price for item M93K

2. Type **a45h** in the ID box and then click the **Get price** button. The "ID not found" message appears in a message box. Close the message box.

3. Click the **Exit** button. Close the Code Editor window and then close the solution.

Key Terms

Aggregate operator—an operator that returns a single value from a group of values; examples of aggregate operators in LINQ include Average, Count, Max, Min, and Sum

InputBox function—displays an input dialog box that contains a prompt message, an input area, and OK and Cancel buttons; allows an application to communicate with the user during run time

Language-Integrated Query—the query language built into Visual Basic; used to retrieve information from a variety of data sources; also called LINQ

LINQ—the acronym for the Language-Integrated Query language

Member variables—the variables contained in a structure

PrintForm tool—a tool for printing an interface from code; included in Visual Basic's Power Packs

Query language—allows you to retrieve specific information from different data sources

Structure statement—used to create user-defined data types, called structures

Structure variables—variables declared using a structure as the data type

Structures—data types created by the Structure statement; allow the programmer to group related items into one unit; also called user-defined data types

Timer control—used to process code at one or more regular intervals; the intervals are measured in milliseconds; the code is entered in the control's Tick event procedure

TryParse method—converts a string to a number of a specified data type; returns a Boolean value that indicates whether the conversion was successful (True) or unsuccessful (False)

User-defined data types—data types created by using the Structure statement; also called structures

Finding and Fixing Program Errors

Concepts covered in this appendix:

- ◎ Syntax errors and the Error List window
- ◎ Logic errors and stepping through code
- ◎ Logic errors and setting breakpoints
- ◎ Run time errors

Syntax Errors and the Error List Window

A syntax error occurs when you break one of a programming language's rules. Most syntax errors are a result of typing errors that occur when entering instructions, such as typing `Intger` instead of `Integer`. The Code Editor detects syntax errors as you enter the instructions. However, if you are not paying close attention to your computer screen, you may not notice the errors. In the next set of steps, you will observe what happens when you start an application that contains a syntax error.

To start debugging the Total Sales Calculator application:

START HERE

1. Open the Total Sales Solution.sln file contained in the VB2017\AppC\Total Sales Solution folder. Open the designer window. The application calculates and displays the total of the sales amounts entered by the user. See Figure C-1.

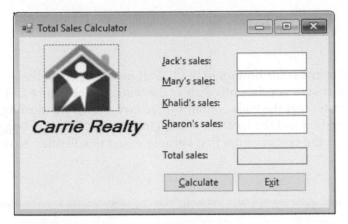

Figure C-1 Interface for the Total Sales Calculator application

2. Open the Code Editor window. Figure C-2 shows the code entered in the btnCalc_Click procedure. The red jagged lines, called squiggles, alert you that three lines of code contain a syntax error. The green squiggle warns you of a potential problem in your code.

```
14      Private Sub btnCalc_Click(sender As Object, e As EventArg
15          ' Calculates and displays the total sales.
16
17          Dim intJack As Integer
18          Dim intMary As Integer
19          Dim intKhalid As Integer
20          Dim intSharon As Integer
21          Dim intTotal As Intger          syntax error
22
23          Integer.TryParse(txtJack.Text, intJack      syntax error
24          Integer.TryParse(txtMary.Text, intMary)
25          Integer.TryParse(txtKhalid.Text, intKhalid)
26          Integer.TryParse(txtSharon.Text, intSharon)
27
28  syntax error  intTotal = intJack + intMary + intKhalid + intSharon
29          lblTotal.Text = intTotal.ToString("C0")
30      End Sub
                                    warning
```

Figure C-2 btnCalc_Click procedure in the Total Sales Calculator application

3. Press **F5** to start the application. The dialog box shown in Figure C-3 appears. Click the **No** button.

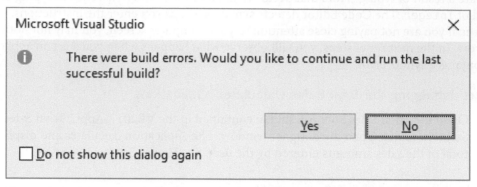

Microsoft Visual Studio   ✕

ℹ   There were build errors. Would you like to continue and run the last
    successful build?

                                              Yes   No

☐ Do not show this dialog again

Figure C-3   Dialog box

4. The Error List window opens at the bottom of the IDE. If necessary, click the window's **Auto Hide** button to permanently display the window. See Figure C-4. The Error List window indicates that the code contains three errors and one warning, and it provides both a description and the location of each in the code. When debugging your code, always correct the syntax errors first because doing so will often remove any warnings.

Error List   ▾ ⌑ ✕

| Entire Solution | ▾ | ⊗ 3 Errors | ⚠ 1 Warning | ⓘ 0 Messages | Build + IntelliSense | ▾ | Search Error List | 🔎 ▾ |

	Code	Description	Project	File	Line	Suppression St... ▼
⊗	BC30198	')' expected.	Total Sales Project	Main Form.vb	23	Active
⊗	BC30002	Type 'Intger' is not defined.	Total Sales Project	Main Form.vb	21	Active
⊗	BC30451	'inTotal' is not declared. It may be inaccessible due to its protection level.	Total Sales Project	Main Form.vb	28	Active
⚠	BC42104	Variable 'intTotal' is used before it has been assigned a value. A null reference exception could result at runtime.	Total Sales Project	Main Form.vb	29	Active

Figure C-4   Error List window

Note: You can change the size of the Error List window by positioning your mouse pointer on the window's top border until the mouse pointer becomes a vertical line with an arrow at the top and bottom. Then, press and hold down the left mouse button while you drag the border either up or down.

5. The Error List window indicates that there is a missing parenthesis in the statement on Line 23. Double-click the **first error's description** in the Error List window. The Code Editor positions the blinking insertion point at the end of the first TryParse method. Hover your mouse pointer over the red squiggle that appears next to the blinking insertion point. See Figure C-5. The error message box alerts you that the Code Editor is expecting an ending parenthesis on this line.

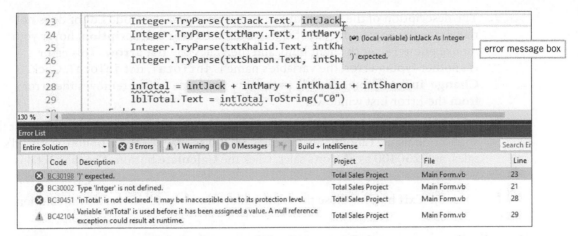

Figure C-5 Result of double-clicking the error description for Line 23

6. Type **)**. The Code Editor removes the error from the Error List window.

7. Now, double-click the **error description for Line 21**. A LightBulb indicator appears in the margin. Hover your mouse pointer over the light bulb until a list arrow appears, and then click the **list arrow**. A list of suggestions for fixing the error appears. See Figure C-6.

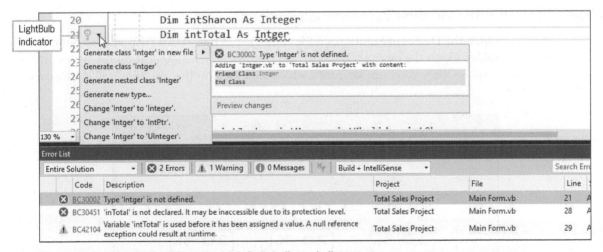

Figure C-6 Result of clicking the LightBulb indicator's list arrow

8. The error in Line 21 is simply a typing error; the programmer meant to type Integer rather than Intger. You can either type the missing letter e yourself or click the appropriate suggestion in the list. Click **Change 'Intger' to 'Integer'.** in the list. The Code Editor makes the change in the Dim statement and also removes both the error and the warning from the Error List window.

9. The description of the remaining error indicates that the Code Editor does not recognize the name `inTotal`. Double-click the **error's description**, hover your mouse pointer over the light bulb, and then click the **list arrow**. This error is another typing error; the variable's name is `intTotal`, not `inTotal`. Click **Change 'inTotal' to 'intTotal'.** in the list. The Code Editor removes the error from the Error List window.

10. Close the Error List window. Save the solution and then start the application. Test the application using **125600** as Jack's sales, **98700** as Mary's sales, **165000** as Khalid's sales, and **250400** as Sharon's sales. Click the **Calculate** button. The sales total is $639,700.

11. Click the **Exit** button. Close the Code Editor window and then close the solution.

Logic Errors and Stepping Through Code

Unlike syntax errors, logic errors are much more difficult to find because they do not trigger an error message from the Code Editor. A logic error can occur for a variety of reasons, such as forgetting to enter an instruction or entering the instructions in the wrong order. Some logic errors occur as a result of calculation statements that are correct syntactically but incorrect mathematically. For example, consider the statement `dblSum = dblNum1 * dblNum2`, which is supposed to calculate the sum of two numbers. The statement's syntax is correct, but it is incorrect mathematically because it uses the multiplication operator rather than the addition operator. In the next section, you will debug an application that contains a logic error.

START HERE

To debug the Discount Calculator application:

1. Open the Discount Solution.sln file contained in the VB2017\AppC\Discount Solution folder. Open the designer window. See Figure C-7. The application calculates and displays three discount amounts, which are based on the price entered by the user.

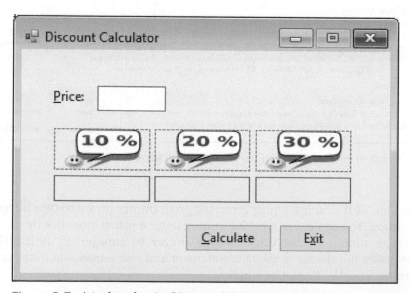

Figure C-7 Interface for the Discount Calculator application

2. Open the Code Editor window. Figure C-8 shows the btnCalc_Click procedure.

```
14    ⊟      Private Sub btnCalc_Click(sender As Object, e A:
15                  ' Calculates and displays discounts.
16
17             Dim decPrice As Decimal
18             Dim decDiscount10 As Decimal
19             Dim decDiscount20 As Decimal
20             Dim decDiscount30 As Decimal
21
22             decDiscount10 = decPrice * 0.1D
23             decDiscount20 = decPrice * 0.2D
24             decDiscount30 = decPrice * 0.3D
25
26             lbl10.Text = decDiscount10.ToString("N2")
27             lbl20.Text = decDiscount20.ToString("N2")
28             lbl30.Text = decDiscount30.ToString("N2")
29         End Sub
```

Figure C-8 btnCalc_Click procedure in the Discount Calculator application

3. Start the application. Type **100** in the Price box and then click the **Calculate** button. The interface shows that each discount is 0.00, which is incorrect. Click the **Exit** button.

4. You will use the Debug menu to run the Visual Basic debugger, which is a tool that helps you locate the logic errors in your code. Click **Debug** on the menu bar. The menu's Step Into option will start your application and allow you to step through your code. It does this by executing the code one statement at a time, pausing immediately before each statement is executed. Click **Step Into**.

5. Type **100** in the Price box and then click the **Calculate** button. The debugger highlights the first instruction to be executed, which is the btnCalc_Click procedure header. It also pauses the code's execution. In addition, an arrow points to the procedure header and the LightBulb indicator appears. See Figure C-9.

```
         13
   ⇨     14 💡 ⊟    Private Sub btnCalc_Click(sender As Object, e
         15                ' Calculates and displays discounts.
         16
         17             Dim decPrice As Decimal
```

Figure C-9 Procedure header highlighted while code execution is paused

6. You can use either the Debug menu's Step Into option or the F8 key on your keyboard to tell the computer to execute the highlighted instruction. Press the **F8** key. After the computer processes the procedure header, the debugger highlights the next statement to be processed, which is the decDiscount10 = decPrice * 0.1D statement. It then pauses execution of the code. (The Dim statements are skipped over because they are not considered executable by the debugger.)

7. While the execution of a procedure's code is paused, you can view the contents of controls and variables that appear in the highlighted statement and also in the statements that precede it in the procedure. Before you view the contents of a control or variable, however, you should consider the value you expect to find. Before the highlighted statement is processed, the decDiscount10 variable should contain its initial value, 0. (Recall that the Dim statement initializes numeric variables to 0.) Place your mouse pointer on decDiscount10 in the highlighted statement. The variable's name and current value appear in a small box, as shown in Figure C-10. At this point, the decDiscount10 variable's value is correct.

```
17            Dim decPrice As Decimal
18            Dim decDiscount10 As Decimal
19            Dim decDiscount20 As Decimal
20            Dim decDiscount30 As Decimal
21
⇨  22        ▶| decDiscount10 = decPrice * 0.1D
23            decDisco ⬤ decDiscount10 0 ⊟ |e * 0.2D
24            decDiscount30 = decPrice * 0.3D
```

variable's name and value

Figure C-10 Value stored in decDiscount10 before the highlighted statement is executed

8. Now, consider the value you expect to find in the decPrice variable. Before the highlighted statement is processed, the variable should contain the number 100, which is the value you entered in the Price box. Place your mouse pointer on decPrice in the highlighted statement. The variable contains 0, which is its initial value. The value is incorrect because no statement above the highlighted statement assigns the Price box's value to the decPrice variable. In other words, a statement is missing from the procedure.

9. Click **Debug** on the menu bar and then click **Stop Debugging** to stop the debugger. (Or, you can click the Stop Debugging button, which is a red square, on the Standard toolbar.) Click the **blank line** below the last Dim statement and then press **Enter** to insert another blank line. Type the following TryParse method and then press **Enter**:

```
Decimal.TryParse(txtPrice.Text, decPrice)
```

10. Save the solution. Click **Debug** on the menu bar and then click **Step Into**. Type **100** in the Price box and then click the **Calculate** button. Press **F8** to process the procedure header. The debugger highlights the TryParse method and then pauses execution of the code.

11. Before the TryParse method is processed, the txtPrice.Text property should contain 100, which is the value you entered in the Price box. Place your mouse pointer on txtPrice.Text in the TryParse method. The box shows that the Text property contains the expected value. The 100 is enclosed in quotation marks because Visual Basic treats the contents of a text box as a string.

12. The decPrice variable should contain its initial value, 0. Place your mouse pointer on decPrice in the TryParse method. The box shows that the variable contains the expected value.

13. Press **F8** to process the TryParse method. The debugger highlights the
`decDiscount10 = decPrice * 0.1D` statement before pausing execution of the
code. Place your mouse pointer on `decPrice` in the TryParse method, as shown in
Figure C-11. Notice that after the method is processed by the computer, the `decPrice`
variable contains the number 100, which is correct.

```
22        ▶ Decimal.TryParse(txtPrice.Text, decPrice)
23                                              ⬤ decPrice 100 ⊟
⬄  24            decDiscount10 = decPrice * 0.1D
25            decDiscount20 = decPrice * 0.2D
                                              variable's name and value
```

Figure C-11   Value stored in `decPrice` after the TryParse method is executed

14. Before the highlighted statement is processed, the `decDiscount10` variable should
contain its initial value, and the `decPrice` variable should contain the value assigned
to it by the TryParse method. Place your mouse pointer on `decDiscount10` in the
highlighted statement. The box shows that the variable contains 0, which is correct.
Place your mouse pointer on `decPrice` in the highlighted statement. The box shows
that the variable contains 100, which also is correct.

15. After the highlighted statement is processed, the `decPrice` variable should still contain
100. However, the `decDiscount10` variable should contain 10, which is 10% of 100.
Press **F8** to execute the highlighted statement, and then place your mouse pointer on
`decDiscount10` in the statement. The box shows that the variable contains 10.0, which
is correct. On your own, verify that the `decPrice` variable in the statement contains the
appropriate value (100).

16. To continue program execution without using the debugger, click **Debug** on the menu
bar and then click **Continue**. This time, the correct discount amounts appear in the
interface. See Figure C-12.

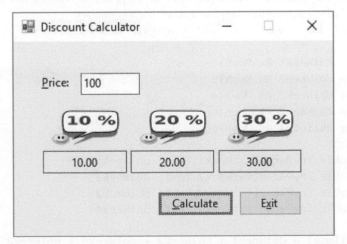

Figure C-12   Sample run of the Discount Calculator application

17. Click the **Exit** button. Close the Code Editor window and then close the solution.

Logic Errors and Setting Breakpoints

Stepping through code one line at a time is not the only way to search for logic errors. You also can use a breakpoint to pause execution at a specific line in the code. You will learn how to set a breakpoint in the next set of steps.

To begin debugging the Hours Worked application:

1. Open the Hours Worked Solution.sln file contained in the VB2017\AppC\Hours Worked Solution folder. Open the designer window. See Figure C-13. The application calculates and displays the total number of hours worked in four weeks.

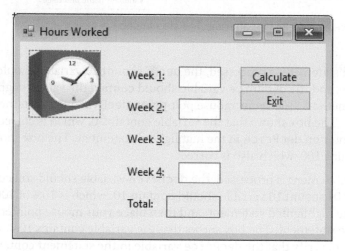

Figure C-13 Interface for the Hours Worked application

2. Open the Code Editor window and locate the btnCalc_Click procedure. See Figure C-14.

```
14      Private Sub btnCalc_Click(sender As Object, e As EventArgs
15          ' Calculates and displays the total number
16          ' of hours worked during 4 weeks.
17
18          Dim dblWeek1 As Double
19          Dim dblWeek2 As Double
20          Dim dblWeek3 As Double
21          Dim dblWeek4 As Double
22          Dim dblTotal As Double
23
24          Double.TryParse(txtWeek1.Text, dblWeek1)
25          Double.TryParse(txtWeek2.Text, dblWeek2)
26          Double.TryParse(txtWeek3.Text, dblWeek2)
27          Double.TryParse(txtWeek4.Text, dblWeek4)
28
29          dblTotal = dblWeek1 + dblWeek2 + dblWeek3 + dblWeek4
30          lblTotal.Text = dblTotal.ToString("N1")
31      End Sub
```

Figure C-14 btnCalc_Click procedure in the Hours Worked application

3. Start the application. Type **10.5, 25, 33**, and **40** in the Week 1, Week 2, Week 3, and Week 4 boxes, respectively, and then click the **Calculate** button. The interface shows that the total number of hours is 83.5, which is incorrect; it should be 108.5. Click the **Exit** button.

The statement that calculates the total number of hours worked is not giving the correct result. Rather than having the computer pause before processing each line of code in the procedure, you will have it pause only before processing the calculation statement. You can do this by setting a breakpoint on the statement.

To finish debugging the application:

START HERE

1. Click anywhere within the **calculation statement**. Click **Debug** on the menu bar and then click **Toggle Breakpoint**. (You can also set a breakpoint by clicking in the gray margin that appears to the left of the statement.) The debugger highlights the statement and places a circle next to it, as shown in Figure C-15.

```
28
29 ♀    dblTotal = dblWeek1 + dblWeek2 + dblWeek3 + dblWeek4
30       lblTotal.Text = dblTotal.ToString("N1")
31    End Sub
```

Figure C-15   Breakpoint set in the btnCalc_Click procedure

2. Start the application. Type **10.5, 25, 33**, and **40** in the Week 1, Week 2, Week 3, and Week 4 boxes, respectively, and then click the **Calculate** button. The computer begins processing the code contained in the btnCalc_Click procedure. It stops processing when it reaches the breakpoint statement, which it highlights. The highlighting indicates that the statement is the next one to be processed. Notice that a yellow arrow now appears in the red dot next to the breakpoint. See Figure C-16.

```
28
29 ♀    dblTotal = dblWeek1 + dblWeek2 + dblWeek3 + dblWeek4
30       lblTotal.Text = dblTotal.ToString("N1")
31    End Sub
```

Figure C-16   Result of the computer reaching the breakpoint

3. Before viewing the values contained in each variable in the highlighted statement, consider the values you expect to find. Before the calculation statement is processed, the dblTotal variable should contain its initial value (0). Place your mouse pointer on dblTotal in the highlighted statement. The box shows that the variable's value is 0, which is correct. (You can verify the variable's initial value by placing your mouse pointer on dblTotal in its declaration statement.)

4. The other four variables should contain the numbers 10.5, 25, 33, and 40, which are the values you entered in the text boxes. On your own, view the values contained in the dblWeek1, dblWeek2, dblWeek3, and dblWeek4 variables. Notice that two of the variables (dblWeek1 and dblWeek4) contain the correct values (10.5 and 40). The dblWeek2 variable, however, contains 33 rather than 25, and the dblWeek3 variable contains its initial value (0) rather than the number 33.

5. Two of the TryParse methods are responsible for assigning the text box values to the dblWeek2 and dblWeek3 variables. Looking closely at the four TryParse methods in the procedure, you will notice that the third one is incorrect. After converting the contents of the txtWeek3 control to a number, the method should assign the number to the dblWeek3 variable rather than to the dblWeek2 variable. Click **Debug** on the menu bar and then click **Stop Debugging**.

6. Change `dblWeek2` in the third TryParse method to **dblWeek3**.

7. Click the **breakpoint circle** in the gray margin to remove the breakpoint.

8. Save the solution and then start the application. Type **10.5, 25, 33**, and **40** in the Week 1, Week 2, Week 3, and Week 4 boxes, respectively, and then click the **Calculate** button. The interface shows that the total number of hours is 108.5, which is correct. See Figure C-17.

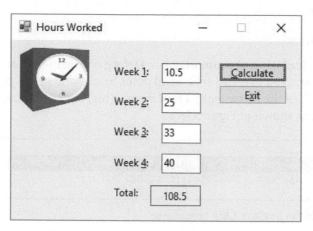

Figure C-17   Sample run of the Hours Worked application

9. Click the **Exit** button. Close the Code Editor window and then close the solution.

Run Time Errors

In addition to syntax and logic errors, programs also can have run time errors. A run time error is an error that occurs while an application is running. As you will observe in the following set of steps, an expression that attempts to divide a value by the number 0 will result in a run time error if the expression's numerator and/or denominator has the Decimal data type.

START HERE ▶

To use the Quotient Calculator application to observe a run time error:

1. Open the Quotient Solution.sln file contained in the VB2017\AppC\Quotient Solution folder. Open the designer window. See Figure C-18. The interface provides two text boxes for the user to enter two numbers. The Calculate button's Click event procedure divides the number in the txtNumerator control by the number in the txtDenominator control and then displays the result, called the quotient, in the lblQuotient control.

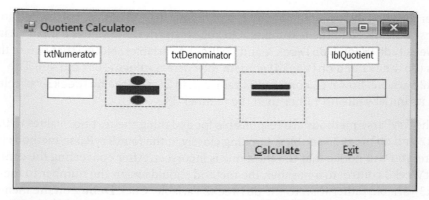

Figure C-18   Interface for the Quotient Calculator application

2. Open the Code Editor window. Figure C-19 shows the btnCalc_Click procedure.

```
14    Private Sub btnCalc_Click(sender As Object, e As EventArgs)
15        ' Display the result of dividing two numbers.
16
17        Dim decNumerator As Decimal
18        Dim decDenominator As Decimal
19        Dim decQuotient As Decimal
20
21        Decimal.TryParse(txtNumerator.Text, decNumerator)
22        Decimal.TryParse(txtDenominator.Text, decDenominator)
23
24        decQuotient = decNumerator / decDenominator
25        lblQuotient.Text = decQuotient.ToString("N2")
26    End Sub
```

Figure C-19   btnCalc_Click procedure in the Quotient Calculator application

3. Start the application. Type **100** and **5** in the txtNumerator and txtDenominator controls, respectively, and then click the **Calculate** button. The interface shows that the quotient is 20.00, which is correct.

4. Delete the 5 from the txtDenominator control and then click the **Calculate** button. A run time error occurs. The Exception Unhandled window indicates that the highlighted statement, which also has an arrow pointing to it, is attempting to divide by zero. See Figure C-20.

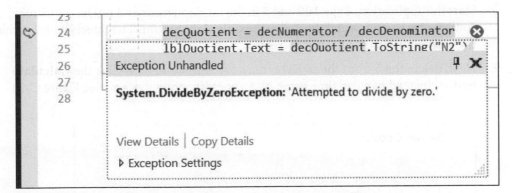

Figure C-20   Run time error caused by attempting to divide by zero

When the txtDenominator control is empty, or when it contains a character that cannot be converted to a number, the second TryParse method in the procedure stores the number 0 in the decDenominator variable. When that variable contains the number 0, the statement that calculates the quotient will produce a run time error because the variable is used as the denominator in the calculation. To prevent this error from occurring, you will need to tell the computer to calculate and display the quotient only when the decDenominator variable does not contain the number 0; otherwise, it should display the "N/A" message. You can do this using a selection structure, which is covered in Chapter 4 of this book.

START HERE

To add a selection structure to the btnCalc_Click procedure:

1. Click **Debug** on the menu bar and then click **Stop Debugging**.

2. Enter the selection structure shown in Figure C-21. Be sure to move the statements that calculate and display the quotient into the selection structure's true path as shown in the figure.

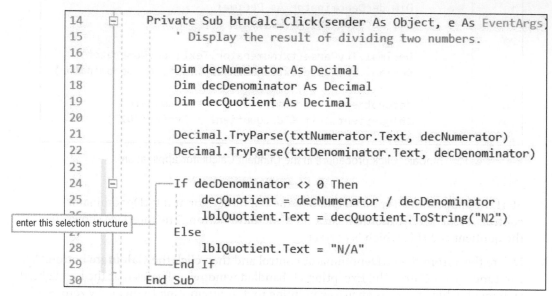

Figure C-21 Selection structure entered in the procedure

3. Start the application. Type **100** and **5** in the txtNumerator and txtDenominator controls, respectively, and then click the **Calculate** button. The interface shows that the quotient is 20.00, which is correct.

4. Next, delete the 5 from the txtDenominator control and then click the **Calculate** button. Instead of a run time error, N/A appears in the interface. See Figure C-22.

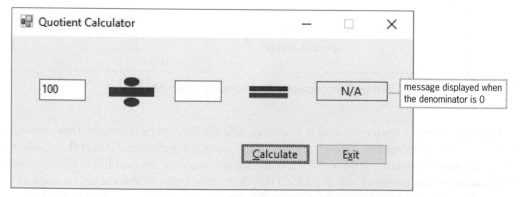

Figure C-22 Result of including the selection structure in the btnCalc_Click procedure

5. Click the **Exit** button. Close the Code Editor window and then close the solution.

Summary

- To find the syntax errors in a program, look for squiggles (jagged lines) in the Code Editor window. Or, start the application and then look in the Error List window.

- To find the logic errors in a program, either step through the code in the Code Editor window or set a breakpoint.

- To step through your code, use either the Step Into option on the Debug menu or the F8 key on your keyboard.

- To set a breakpoint, click the line of code on which you want to set the breakpoint and then use the Toggle Breakpoint option on the Debug menu. In addition, you can click in the gray margin that appears to the left of the statement.

- To remove a breakpoint, click the breakpoint circle in the gray margin. Or, click Debug on the menu bar and then click Toggle Breakpoint.

- You can use a selection structure to determine whether a variable contains the number 0.

Review Questions

1. The process of locating and fixing any errors in a program is called _____.

   a. bug-proofing   c. debugging

   b. bug-eliminating   d. error removal

2. While stepping through code, the debugger highlights the statement that

   _____.

   a. was just executed   c. contains the error

   b. will be executed next   d. None of the above.

3. Logic errors are listed in the Error List window.

   a. True   b. False

4. Which key is used to step through code?

   a. F5   c. F7

   b. F6   d. F8

5. While stepping through the code in the Code Editor window, you can view the contents of controls and variables that appear in the highlighted statement only.

   a. True   b. False

6. You use _____ to pause program execution at a specific line in the code.

   a. a breakpoint

   b. the Error List window

   c. the Step Into option on the Debug menu

   d. the Stop Debugging option on the Debug menu

7. The statement `Constant dblRATE As Double` is an example of a _____.

    a. correct statement   c. syntax error

    b. logic error   d. run time error

8. When entered in a procedure, which of the following statements will result in a syntax error?

    a. `Me.Clse()`

    b. `Integer.TryPars(txtHours.Text, intHours)`

    c. `Dim decRate as Decimel`

    d. All of the above.

Exercises

INTRODUCTORY

1. Open the Commission Calculator Solution.sln file contained in the VB2017\AppC\Commission Calculator Solution folder. Use what you learned in the appendix to debug the application.

INTRODUCTORY

2. Open the New Pay Solution.sln file contained in the VB2017\AppC\New Pay Solution folder. Use what you learned in the appendix to debug the application.

INTRODUCTORY

3. Open the Hawkins Solution.sln file contained in the VB2017\AppC\Hawkins Solution folder. Use what you learned in the appendix to debug the application.

INTRODUCTORY

4. Open the Allenton Solution.sln file contained in the VB2017\AppC\Allenton Solution folder. Use what you learned in the appendix to debug the application.

INTERMEDIATE

5. Open the Martins Solution.sln file contained in the VB2017\AppC\Martins Solution folder. Use what you learned in the appendix to debug the application.

INTERMEDIATE

6. Open the Average Score Solution.sln file contained in the VB2017\AppC\Average Score Solution folder. Use what you learned in the appendix to debug the application.

ADVANCED

7. Open the Beachwood Solution.sln file contained in the VB2017\AppC\Beachwood Solution folder. Use what you learned in the appendix to debug the application.

ADVANCED

8. Open the Framington Solution.sln file contained in the VB2017\AppC\Framington Solution folder. Use what you learned in the appendix to debug the application.

Visual Basic 2017 Cheat Sheet

Statements

Assignment

object.property = expression
variable = expression

Named Constant Declaration

[**Private**] **Const** *constantName* **As** *dataType = expression*

Variable Declaration

[**Dim** | **Private** | **Static**] *variableName* **As** *dataType* [*= initialValue*]

Option Explicit

when set to On, prevents the computer from creating an undeclared variable: **Option Explicit** [**On** | **Off**]

Option Strict

when set to On, prevents the computer from making implicit type conversions that may result in a loss of data: **Option Strict** [**On** | **Off**]

Option Infer

when set to Off, prevents the computer from inferring a variable's data type: **Option Infer** [**On** | **Off**]

Do...Loop

Pretest loop

Do {While | Until} *condition*
> *loop body instructions to be processed either while the condition is true or until the condition becomes true*

Loop

Posttest loop

Do
> *loop body instructions to be processed either while the condition is true or until the condition becomes true*

Loop {While | Until} *condition*

For Each...Next

For Each *elementVariable* **As** *dataType* **In** *group*
> *loop body instructions*

Next *elementVariable*

For...Next

For *counter* [**As** *dataType*] = *startValue* **To** *endValue* [**Step** *stepValue*]
> *loop body instructions*

Next *counter*

If the stepValue is a	The loop body is processed when the	The loop ends when the
positive number	*counter*'s value $<=$ *endValue*	*counter*'s value $>$ *endValue*
negative number	*counter*'s value $>=$ *endValue*	*counter*'s value $<$ *endValue*

If...Then...Else

If *condition* **Then**
> *statement block to be processed when the condition is true*

[**ElseIf** *condition2*
> *statement block to be processed when the first condition is false and condition2 is true*]

[**Else**
> *statement block to be processed when all previous conditions are false*]

End If

Select Case

Select Case *selectorExpression*
>   **Case** *expressionList1*
>   *instructions for the first Case*
>   [**Case** *expressionList2*
>   *instructions for the second Case*]
>   [**Case** *expressionListN*
>   *instructions for the Nth Case*]
>   [**Case Else**
>   *instructions for when the selectorExpression does not match any of the expressionLists*]

End Select

Specifying a range of values
Case *smallest value in the range* **To** *largest value in the range*
Case Is *comparisonOperator value*

Try...Catch

Try
      one or more statements that might generate an exception
Catch ex As Exception
      one or more statements to execute when an exception occurs
End Try

Counters and Accumulators

Updating a Counter

counterVariable = counterVariable {+ | −} constantValue
counterVariable {+= | −=} constantValue

Updating an Accumulator

accumulatorVariable = accumulatorVariable {+ | −} value
accumulatorVariable {+= | −=} value

Rules for Naming Objects

Naming rules (these are required by Visual Basic)

1. Each object must have a unique name.
2. Each name must begin with a letter and contain only letters, numbers, and the underscore character.

Naming conventions used in this book

1. Each name will begin with an ID of three (or more) characters that represents the object's type—for example, *frm* for a form, *btn* for a button, and *txt* for a text box.
2. The remaining characters after the ID will indicate the object's purpose.
3. Each name will be entered using camel case: the ID will be in lowercase, and the first letter in each subsequent word in the name will be capitalized.

Data Types

Boolean	a logical value (True, False)
Char	one character
Decimal	a number with a decimal place (29 significant digits)
Double	a number with a decimal place (15 significant digits)
Integer	an integer
String	text; 0 to approximately 2 billion characters

Rules for Naming Variables

Naming rules (these are required by Visual Basic)

1. Each variable declared in a procedure must have a unique name.
2. Each name must begin with a letter and contain only letters, numbers, and the underscore character.
3. The recommended maximum number of characters to use for a name is 32.
4. The name cannot be a reserved word, such as Sub or Double.

Naming conventions used in this book

1. Each name will begin with an ID of three (or more) characters that represents the variable's data type. The IDs are listed here: bln for Boolean, dec for Decimal, dbl for Double, int for Integer, and str for String.
2. The remaining characters after the ID will indicate the variable's purpose.
3. Each name will be entered using camel case: the ID will be in lowercase, and the first letter in each subsequent word in the name will be capitalized.

Type Conversion Rules

1. Strings will not be implicitly converted to numbers.
2. Numbers will not be implicitly converted to strings.
3. Wider data types will not be implicitly demoted to narrower data types.
4. Narrower data types will be implicitly promoted to wider data types.

Operators and Precedence

^	exponentiation (raises a number to a power)	1
−	negation (reverses the sign of a number)	2
*, /	multiplication and division	3
\	integer division	4
Mod	modulus (remainder) arithmetic	5
+, −	addition and subtraction	6
&	concatenation	7
=, <>	equal to, not equal to	8
>, >=	greater than, greater than or equal to	8
<, <=	less than, less than or equal to	8
Not	reverses the truth-value of the condition; True becomes False, and False becomes True	9
And	all subconditions must be true for the compound condition to evaluate to True	10
AndAlso	same as the And operator, except performs short-circuit evaluation	10
Or	only one of the subconditions needs to be true for the compound condition to evaluate to True	11
OrElse	same as the Or operator, except performs short-circuit evaluation	11
Xor	one and only one of the subconditions can be true for the compound condition to evaluate to True	12

Arithmetic Assignment Operators

variableName arithmeticAssignmentOperator value

Operator	Purpose
+=	addition assignment
−=	subtraction assignment
*=	multiplication assignment
/=	division assignment

Truth Tables for the Logical Operators

Not Operator

value of *condition*	value of Not *condition*
True	False
False	True

AndAlso Operator

subcondition1	subcondition2	subcondition1 AndAlso subcondition2
True	True	True
True	False	False
False	(not evaluated)	False

OrElse Operator

subcondition1	subcondition2	subcondition1 OrElse subcondition2
True	(not evaluated)	True
False	True	True
False	False	False

And Operator

subcondition1	subcondition2	subcondition1 And subcondition2
True	True	True
True	False	False
False	True	False
False	False	False

Or Operator

subcondition1	subcondition2	subcondition1 Or subcondition2
True	True	True
True	False	True
False	True	True
False	False	False

Xor Operator

subcondition1	subcondition2	subcondition1 Xor subcondition2
True	True	False
True	False	True
False	True	True
False	False	False

Planning Steps

1. Identify the application's purpose.
2. Identify the items that the user must provide.
3. Identify the items that the application must provide.
4. Determine how the user and the application will provide their respective items.
5. Draw a sketch of the user interface.

Format Menu Options

Align	align two or more controls by their left, right, top, or bottom borders
Make Same Size	make two or more controls the same width and/or height
Horizontal Spacing	adjust the horizontal spacing between two or more controls
Vertical Spacing	adjust the vertical spacing between two or more controls
Center in Form	center one or more controls either horizontally or vertically on the form
Order	specify the layering of one or more controls on the form
Lock Controls	lock the controls in place on the form

Printing

Print the Interface during Design Time

Make the designer window the active window. Click Start on the Windows 10 taskbar. Click Windows Accessories on the Start menu and then click Snipping Tool. Click the New button. Hold down your left mouse button as you drag your mouse pointer around the form, and then release the mouse button. Click File on the Snipping Tool's menu bar and then click Print. Select the appropriate printer and then click Print. Close the Snipping tool.

Print the Interface during Run Time

Add a PrintForm control (object) to the component tray. Set the control's PrintAction property in the Properties window. Or, you can set the property from code by using the *object*.**PrintAction = Printing.PrintAction.***destination* statement. In the statement, *destination* can be `PrintToPreview` or `PrintToPrinter`. Use the *object*.**Print()** statement to start the printing task.

Print the Code during Design Time

Make the Code Editor window the active window. Click the Print option on the File menu and then click the OK button.

Generate Random Numbers

Integers

Dim *randomObject* **As New Random**
randomObject.**Next**(*minValue*, *maxValue*)

Double Numbers

Dim *randomObject* **As New Random**
(*maxValue* − *minValue* + **1**) * *randomObject*.**NextDouble** + *minValue*

Methods

Financial Class Methods

Financial.DDB	calculate the depreciation of an asset for a specific time period using the double-declining balance method
Financial.FV	calculate the future value of an annuity based on periodic fixed payments and a fixed interest rate
Financial.IPmt	calculate the interest payment for a given period of an annuity based on periodic fixed payments and a fixed interest rate
Financial.IRR	calculate the internal rate of return for a series of periodic cash flows (payments and receipts)
Financial.Pmt	calculate the payment for an annuity based on periodic fixed payments and a fixed interest rate
Financial.PPmt	calculate the principal payment for a given period of an annuity based on periodic fixed payments and a fixed interest rate
Financial.PV	calculate the present value of an annuity based on periodic fixed payments to be paid in the future and a fixed interest rate
Financial.SLN	calculate the straight-line depreciation of an asset for a single period
Financial.SYD	calculate the sum-of-the-years' digits depreciation of an asset for a specified period

Financial.Pmt Method

Financial.Pmt(*Rate, NPer, PV*)

Focus

object.**Focus**()

Math.Round

Math.Round(*value*[, *digits*])

MessageBox.Show

MessageBox.Show(*text, caption, buttons, icon*[, *defaultButton*])
dialogResultVariable = **MessageBox.Show**(*text, caption, buttons, icon*[, *defaultButton*])

Argument	Meaning
text	text to display in the message box; use sentence capitalization
caption	text to display in the message box's title bar; use book title capitalization
buttons	buttons to display in the message box; can be one of the following constants: MessageBoxButtons.AbortRetryIgnore MessageBoxButtons.OK (default setting) MessageBoxButtons.OKCancel MessageBoxButtons.RetryCancel MessageBoxButtons.YesNo MessageBoxButtons.YesNoCancel
icon	icon to display in the message box; typically, one of the following constants: MessageBoxIcon.Exclamation MessageBoxIcon.Information MessageBoxIcon.Stop

Argument   Meaning
defaultButton   button automatically selected when the user presses Enter; can be one of the
               following constants:
               `MessageBoxDefaultButton.Button1` (default setting)
               `MessageBoxDefaultButton.Button2`
               `MessageBoxDefaultButton.Button3`

MessageBox.Show method's return values

Integer	DialogResult value	Meaning
1	`DialogResult.OK`	user chose the OK button
2	`DialogResult.Cancel`	user chose the Cancel button
3	`DialogResult.Abort`	user chose the Abort button
4	`DialogResult.Retry`	user chose the Retry button
5	`DialogResult.Ignore`	user chose the Ignore button
6	`DialogResult.Yes`	user chose the Yes button
7	`DialogResult.No`	user chose the No button

SelectAll

textbox.**SelectAll**()

ToString

formats a number: *numericVariable*.**ToString**[(*formatString*)]

TryParse

converts a string to a number
numericDataType.**TryParse**(*string, numericVariable*)
booleanVariable = *dataType*.**TryParse**(*string, numericVariable*)

Functions
InputBox

gets data from the user: **InputBox**(*prompt*[, *title*][, *defaultResponse*])

Independent Sub Procedure

Private Sub *procedureName*([*parameterList*])
        statements
End Sub

Invoking an independent Sub procedure
procedureName([*argumentList*])

Function Procedure

Private Function *procedureName*([*parameterList*]) **As** *dataType*
        statements
        Return *expression*
End Function

Internally Document the Code

Start the comment with an apostrophe followed by an optional space.

Control the Characters Accepted by a Text Box

<u>Example</u>

```
Private Sub txtAge_KeyPress(sender As Object,
e As KeyPressEventArgs) Handles txtAge.KeyPress
        ' Accept only numbers and the Backspace key.
        If (e.KeyChar < "0" OrElse e.KeyChar > "9") AndAlso
            e.KeyChar <> ControlChars.Back Then
                e.Handled = True
        End If
End Sub
```

Prevent a Form from Closing (FormClosing Event Procedure)

```
e.Cancel = True
```

Working with Strings

Accessing characters

string.**Substring**(*startIndex*[**,** *numCharsToAccess*])

Aligning the characters

string.**PadLeft**(*totalChars*[**,** *padCharacter*])
string.**PadRight**(*totalChars*[**,** *padCharacter*])

Character array

string(*index*)

Comparing Using Pattern Matching

string **Like** *pattern*

Pattern-matching characters	Matches in string
?	any single character
*	zero or more characters
#	any single digit (0 through 9)
[characterList]	any single character in the characterList (for example, "[A5T]" matches A, 5, or T, whereas "[a–z]" matches any lowercase letter)
[!characterList]	any single character not in the characterList (for example, "[!A5T]" matches any character other than A, 5, or T, whereas "[!a–z]" matches any character that is not a lowercase letter)

Concatenation

string **&** *string* [...**&** *string*]

Converting to Uppercase or Lowercase

string.**ToUpper**
string.**ToLower**

Determining the Number of Characters

string.**Length**

Inserting Characters

string.**Insert**(*startIndex, value*)

Removing Characters

string.**Remove**(*startIndex*[, *numCharsToRemove*])
string.**Trim**[(*trimChars*)]
string.**TrimStart**[(*trimChars*)]
string.**TrimEnd**[(*trimChars*)]

Replacing Characters

string.**Replace**(*oldValue, newValue*)

Searching

string.**Contains**(*subString*)
string.**IndexOf**(*subString*[, *startIndex*])

Strings.Space

returns a string containing the specified number of space characters: **Strings.Space**(*number*)

List/Combo Boxes

Add Items

Use the String Collection Editor dialog box or the Items collection's Add method.
object.**Items.Add**(*item*)

Clear Items

object.**Items.Clear**()

Determine the Number of Items

object.**Items.Count**

Determine the Selected Item

object.**SelectedItem**
object.**SelectedIndex**

Perform a Task When the Selected Item Changes

Code the SelectedValueChanged or SelectedIndexChanged events.

Remove Items

object.**Items.Remove**(*item*)
object.**Items.RemoveAt**(*index*)

Select an Item

object.**SelectedItem** = *item*
object.**SelectedIndex** = *itemIndex*

One-Dimensional Arrays

Array Declaration

{**Dim** | **Private** | **Static**} *arrayName*(*highestSubscript*) **As** *dataType*
{**Dim** | **Private** | **Static**} *arrayName*() **As** *dataType* = {*initialValues*}

Highest Subscript

arrayName.**GetUpperBound**(0)
arrayName.**Length** – 1

Number of Elements

arrayName.**Length**
arrayName.**GetUpperBound**(0) + 1

Reversing

Array.Reverse(*arrayName*)

Sorting (Ascending Order)

Array.Sort(*arrayName*)

Traversing

```
Dim strCities() As String = {"Boston", "Chicago",
                             "Louisville", "Tampa"}
```

Example 1—For…Next

```
Dim intHigh As Integer = strCities.GetUpperBound(0)
For intSub As Integer = 0 To intHigh
    lstCities.Items.Add(strCities(intSub))
Next intSub
```

Example 2—Do…Loop

```
Dim intHigh As Integer = strCities.Length - 1
Dim intSub As Integer
Do While intSub <= intHigh
    lstCities.Items.Add(strCities(intSub))
    intSub += 1
Loop
```

Example 3—For Each...Next

```
For Each strCity As String In strCities
    lstCities.Items.Add(strCity)
Next strCity
```

Using LINQ with an Array
Basic Syntax (Be sure to set Option Infer to On.)

Dim *variable* = **From** *element* **In** *array*
  [**Where** *condition*]
  [**Order By** *element* [**Ascending** | **Descending**]
  Select *element*

Aggregate Operators (Average, Count, Max, Min, and Sum)

[**Dim**] *variable* [**As** *dataType*] =
  Aggregate *element* **In** *array*
  [**Where** *condition*]
  Select *element* **Into** *aggregateOperator*

Two-Dimensional Arrays
Array Declaration

{**Dim** | **Private** | **Static**} *arrayName*(*highestRowSub, highestColumnSub*) **As** *dataType*
{**Dim** | **Private** | **Static**} *arrayName*(,) **As** *dataType* = {{*initialValues*}, ...{*initialValues*}}

Highest Column Subscript

arrayName.**GetUpperBound**(**1**)

Highest Row Subscript

arrayName.**GetUpperBound**(**0**)

Traversing

```
Dim strMonths(,) As String = {{"Jan", "31"},
                 {"Feb", "28 or 29"},
                 {"Mar", "31"},
                 {"Apr", "30"}}
```

Example 1—For...Next (displays contents row by row)

```
Dim intHighRow As Integer = strMonths.GetUpperBound(0)
Dim intHighCol As Integer = strMonths.GetUpperBound(1)
For intRow As Integer = 0 To intHighRow
    For intCol As Integer = 0 To intHighCol
        lstMonths.Items.Add(strMonths(intRow, intCol))
    Next intCol
Next intRow
```

Example 2—Do...Loop (displays contents column by column)

```
Dim intHighRow As Integer = strMonths.GetUpperBound(0)
Dim intHighCol As Integer = strMonths.GetUpperBound(1)
Dim intRow As Integer
Dim intCol As Integer
Do While intCol <= intHighCol
    intRow = 0
    Do While intRow <= intHighRow
        lstMonths.Items.Add(strMonths(intRow, intCol))
        intRow += 1
    Loop
    intCol += 1
Loop
```

Example 3—For Each...Next (displays contents row by row)

```
For Each strElement As String In strMonths
    lstMonths.Items.Add(strElement)
Next strElement
```

Sequential Access Files

Close a File

streamWriterVariable.**Close()**
streamReaderVariable.**Close()**

Open a File and Create a StreamReader Object

IO.File.OpenText(*fileName***)**

Open a File and Create a StreamWriter Object

IO.File.method(*fileName***)**

method	Description
CreateText	opens a sequential access file for output
AppendText	opens a sequential access file for append

Declare StreamWriter and StreamReader Variables

{**Dim** | **Private**} *streamWriterVariable* **As IO.StreamWriter**
{**Dim** | **Private**} *streamReaderVariable* **As IO.StreamReader**

Determine Whether a File Exists

IO.File.Exists(*fileName***)**

Read Data from a File

streamReaderVariable.**ReadLine**
streamReaderVariable.**ReadToEnd**

Determine Whether a File Contains Another Character to Read

streamReaderVariable.**Peek**

Write Data to a File

streamWriterVariable.**Write**(*data*)
streamWriterVariable.**WriteLine**(*data*)

Structures

Declare a Structure Variable

{**Dim** | **Private**} *structureVariable* **As** *structureName*

Declare an Array of Structure Variables

Use the structure's name as the array's dataType.

Definition

Structure *structureName*
      Public *memberVariable1* **As** *dataType*
      [**Public** *memberVariableN* **As** *dataType*]
End Structure

Member Variable within a Structure Variable

structureVariable.*memberVariable*

Member Variable within an Array of Structure Variables

array(*subscript*)*.memberVariable*

SQL Server Databases

Visual Basic and SQL Data Types

Visual Basic	SQL
Boolean	bit
Decimal	decimal(*p, s*)
Double	float
Integer	int
String	char(*n*), varchar(*n*)

Create a SQL Server Database

1. Open a solution file.
2. Click Project on the menu bar and then click Add New Item. Expand the Installed node and then expand the Common Items node. Click Data. Click Service-based Database. Change the name in the Name box; use .mdf as the filename extension. Click the Add button.
3. Right-click the database filename in the Solution Explorer window and then click Open to open the Server Explorer window. Expand the Data Connections node in the Server Explorer window and then expand the database filename node.
4. To add a table to the database, right-click Tables in the Server Explorer window and then click Add Table. Change the table's name in the T-SQL pane. Then, define the fields.

5. Click the Update button and then click the Update Database button.
6. To add records to the table, expand the Tables node in the Server Explorer window and then expand the table name's node. Right-click the table name and then click Show Table Data. Add the records and then save the solution.

Relate Two Tables

1. Create a SQL Server database that contains two tables.
2. Right-click the name of the dataset in the Data Sources window. Click Edit DataSet with Designer to open the DataSet Designer window.
3. Right-click an empty area of the DataSet Designer window, point to Add, and then click Relation to open the Relation dialog box. Select the appropriate parent and child table. Then, select the appropriate primary key and foreign key. Click the OK button to close the Relation dialog box. Save the solution.

Connect an Application to a SQL Server Database

1. Open the application's solution file.
2. If necessary, open the Data Sources window by clicking View on the menu bar, pointing to Other Windows, and then clicking Data Sources.
3. Click Add New Data Source in the Data Sources window to start the Data Source Configuration Wizard, which displays the Choose a Data Source Type screen. If necessary, click Database.
4. Click the Next button, and then continue using the wizard to specify the data source and the name of the database file. The data source for a SQL Server database is Microsoft SQL Server Database File (SqlClient).

Bind an Object in a Dataset

To have the computer create a control and then bind an object to it:

In the Data Sources window, click the object you want to bind. If necessary, use the object's list arrow to change the control type. Drag the object to an empty area on the form, and then release the mouse button.

To bind an object to an existing control:

In the Data Sources window, click the object you want to bind. Drag the object to the control on the form and then release the mouse button. Alternatively, you can click the control on the form and then use the Properties window to set the appropriate property or properties. (Refer to the A-2 Bind Field Objects to Existing Controls section in Chapter 11's Apply the Concepts lesson.)

Copy to Output Directory Property

Property setting	Meaning
Do not copy	The file in the project folder is not copied to the bin\Debug folder when the application is started.
Copy always	The file in the project folder is copied to the bin\Debug folder each time the application is started.
Copy if newer	When an application is started, the computer compares the date on the file in the project folder with the date on the file in the bin\Debug folder. The file from the project folder is copied to the bin\Debug folder only when its date is newer.

SQL

Selecting Fields and Records

SELECT *fieldList* **FROM** *table*

      [**WHERE** *condition*]

      [**ORDER BY** *field* [**DESC**]]

Operators for the WHERE Clause's Condition

=	equal to
<>	not equal to
>	greater than
>=	greater than or equal to
<	less than
<=	less than or equal to
AND	all subconditions must be true for the compound condition to evaluate to True
OR	only one of the subconditions needs to be true for the compound condition to evaluate to True
NOT	reverses the truth-value of the condition
LIKE	uses a wildcard character to compare text values; the % wildcard represents zero or more characters and the _ (underscore) wildcard represents one character
IS NULL	compares a value with a NULL value

SQL Aggregate Functions

AVG	returns the average of the values in a group
COUNT	returns the number of values in a group
MAX	returns the maximum value in a group
MIN	returns the minimum value in a group
SUM	returns the sum of the values in a group

Classes

Define a Class

Public Class *className*

      attributes section

      behaviors section

End Class

Instantiate an Object

<u>Syntax–Version 1</u>

{**Dim** | **Private**} *variable* **As** *className*
variable = **New** *className*

<u>Syntax–Version 2</u>

{**Dim** | **Private**} *variable* **As New** *className*

Create a Property Procedure

Public [**ReadOnly** | **WriteOnly**] **Property** *propertyName*[(*parameterList*)] **As** *dataType*

    Get
       [*instructions*]
       Return *privateVariable*
    End Get
    Set(value As *dataType*)
       [*instructions*]
       privateVariable = {**value** | *defaultValue*}
    End Set
End Property

Create a Constructor

Public Sub New([*parameterList*]**)**
      instructions to initialize the class's Private variables
End Sub

Create a Method That Is Not a Constructor

Public {**Sub** | **Function**} *methodName*(**[**parameterList**]**) [**As** *dataType*]
    instructions
End {**Sub** | **Function**}

Create an Auto-Implemented Property

Public Property *propertyName* **As** *dataType*

Most Commonly Used Properties

Form

AcceptButton	specify a default button that will be selected when the user presses the Enter key
BackColor	specify the background color of the form
CancelButton	specify a cancel button that will be selected when the user presses the Esc key
ControlBox	indicate whether the form contains the Control box and Minimize, Maximize, and Close buttons
Font	specify the font to use for text
FormBorderStyle	specify the appearance and behavior of the form's border
MaximizeBox	specify the state of the Maximize button
MinimizeBox	specify the state of the Minimize button
Name	give the form a meaningful name (use frm as the ID)
StartPosition	indicate the starting position of the form
Text	specify the text that appears in the form's title bar and on the taskbar

Button

Enabled	indicate whether the button can respond to the user's actions
Font	specify the font to use for text
Image	specify the image to display on the button's face
ImageAlign	indicate the alignment of the image on the button's face
Name	give the button a meaningful name (use btn as the ID)
Text	specify the text that appears on the button's face; the text should be entered using sentence capitalization and include an access key

CheckBox

Checked	indicate whether the check box is selected or unselected
Font	specify the font to use for text
Name	give the check box a meaningful name (use chk as the ID)
Text	specify the text that appears inside the check box; the text should be entered using sentence capitalization and include a unique access key

ComboBox

DropDownStyle	indicate the style of the combo box
Font	specify the font to use for text
Name	give the combo box a meaningful name (use cbo as the ID)
SelectedIndex	get or set the index of the selected item
SelectedItem	get or set the value of the selected item
Sorted	specify whether the items in the list portion should appear in the order they are entered or in sorted order (When sorted, the items appear in dictionary order based on their leftmost characters.)
Text	get or set the value that appears in the text portion

DataGridView

AutoSizeColumnsMode	control the way the column widths are sized
DataSource	indicate the source of the data to display in the control
Dock	define which borders of the control are bound to its container

GroupBox

Name	give the group box a meaningful name (use grp as the ID)
Text	specify the text that appears in the upper-left corner of the group box

Label

AutoSize	enable/disable automatic sizing; labels that display program output typcally have their AutoSize property set to False; identifying labels should have the default property setting (True)
BackColor	specify the label's background color

BorderStyle	specify the appearance of the label's border; labels that display program output typcally have their BorderStyle property set to FixedSingle; identifying labels should have the default property setting (None)
Font	specify the font to use for text
ForeColor	specify the color of the text inside the label
Name	give the label a meaningful name (use lbl as the ID)
Text	specify the text that appears inside the label; if the label identifies another control that can accept user input, the text should be entered using sentence capitalization and include an access key
TextAlign	specify the position of the text inside the label

ListBox

Font	specify the font to use for text
Name	give the list box a meaningful name (use lst as the ID)
SelectedIndex	get or set the index of the selected item
SelectedItem	get or set the value of the selected item
SelectionMode	indicate whether the user can select zero items, one item, or more than one item at a time; the default is one item
Sorted	specify whether the items in the list should appear in the order they are entered or in sorted order (When sorted, the items appear in dictionary order based on their leftmost characters. Dictionary order means that numbers appear before letters, and a lowercase letter appears before its uppercase equivalent.)

PictureBox

Image	specify the image to display
Name	give the picture box a meaningful name (use pic as the ID)
SizeMode	specify how the image should be displayed
Visible	hide/display the picture box

RadioButton

Checked	indicate whether the radio button is selected or unselected
Font	specify the font to use for text
Name	give the radio button a meaningful name (use rad as the ID)
Text	specify the text that appears inside the radio button; the text should be entered using sentence capitalization and include an access key

TextBox

BackColor	specify the text box's background color
CharacterCasing	while the text is being entered into the text box, specify whether the text should remain as typed or be converted to either uppercase or lowercase
Font	specify the font to use for text

ForeColor	specify the color of the text inside the text box
Name	give the text box a meaningful name (use txt as the ID)
MaxLength	specify the maximum number of characters the text box will accept
Multiline	specify whether the text box can span more than one line
PasswordChar	specify the character to display when entering a password
ReadOnly	specify whether the text can be edited
ScrollBars	indicate whether scroll bars appear on the text box (used with a multiline text box)
TabStop	indicate whether the text box can receive the focus when the user presses the Tab key
Text	get or set the text that appears inside the text box

Timer

Name	give the timer a meaningful name (use tmr as the ID)
Enabled	when set to True, the timer is running; when set to False, the timer is stopped
Interval	controls the length of each interval between when the Tick event occurs; specified in milliseconds

Case Projects

Your Special Day Catering (Chapters 1–3)

Create an application for Your Special Day Catering. The interface should allow the user to enter the customer ID, the bride's name, the groom's name, and the date of the wedding reception. It should also allow the user to enter the number of beef dinners, the number of chicken dinners, and the number of vegetarian dinners ordered for the reception. The interface should display the total number of dinners ordered, the subtotal (which is the total price of the order without sales tax), the sales tax, and the total price of the order with sales tax. Each dinner costs $26.75, and the sales tax rate is 5%. Include an image in the interface. (You can find many different images on the Open Clip Art Library Web site at *openclipart.org*.)

Crispies Bagels and Bites (Chapters 1–3)

Create an application for Crispies Bagels and Bites. The interface should allow the salesclerk to enter the number of bagels, donuts, and cups of coffee a customer orders. Bagels are 99¢, donuts are 75¢, and coffee is $1.20 per cup. The application should calculate and display the subtotal (which is the total price of the order without sales tax), the sales tax, and the total due. The sales tax rate is 6%. Include an image in the interface. (You can find many different images on the Open Clip Art Library Web site at *openclipart.org*.)

Filmore's Fast Food (Chapters 1–4)

Create an application for Filmore's Fast Food restaurant. The restaurant sells hot dogs for $1.25, hamburgers for $2.50, fish sandwiches for $2.97, fries for $0.99, and fountain drinks for $1.49. Create an interface that allows the user to enter a customer's order. The customer can choose only one of the following: a hot dog, a hamburger, or a fish sandwich. However, he or she can also order only fries, only a fountain drink, or both fries and a fountain drink. The application should calculate and display the total due, which should include a 5% sales tax. (For example, if the customer orders only fries, the total due is $1.04. If he or she orders a hot dog and a drink, the total due is $2.88.)

Savings Calculator (Chapters 1–5)

Research Visual Basic's Financial.FV (Future Value) method. Create an application that allows the user to enter the amount a customer plans to deposit in a savings account each month, and whether the money will be deposited at either the beginning or the end of the month. The application should calculate and display the value of the account at the end of 5 years, 10 years, 15 years, 20 years, and 25 years. The interest rate is 3% and is compounded monthly.

Mortgage Calculator (Chapters 1–6)

Create an application that calculates and displays four monthly mortgage payments. The application should use the loan amount and annual interest rate provided by the user, along with terms of 15 years, 20 years, 25 years, and 30 years. Use a combo box to get the annual interest rate, which should range from 2% through 8% in increments of 0.5%. The application should also display the total amount paid at the end of 15 years, 20 years, 25 years, and 30 years.

High Total Game (Chapters 1–7)

The High Total game requires two players. The application's interface should allow the user to enter each player's name. When the user clicks a button, the button's Click event procedure should generate two random numbers for player 1 and two random numbers for player 2. The random numbers should be in the range of 1 through 20, inclusive. The procedure should display the four numbers in the interface. It should also total the numbers for each player and then display both totals in the interface. If both totals are the same, the application should display the message "Tie". If player 1's total is greater than player 2's total, it should display the message "*player 1's name* won". If player 2's total is greater than player 1's total, it should display the message "*player 2's name* won". The application should keep track of the number of times player 1 wins, the number of times player 2 wins, and the number of ties. The interface should also include a button that allows the user to reset the counters and interface for a new game.

Math Practice (Chapters 1–7)

Create an application that can be used to practice adding, subtracting, multiplying, and dividing numbers. The application should display a math problem on the screen and then allow the student to enter the answer and also verify that the answer is correct. The application should give the student as many chances as necessary to answer the problem correctly. The math problems should use random integers from 1 through 20, inclusive. The subtraction problems should never ask the student to subtract a larger number from a smaller one. The division problems should never ask the student to divide a smaller number by a larger number. Also, the answer to the division problems should always result in a whole number. The application should keep track of the number of correct and incorrect responses made by the student. The interface should include a button that allows the user to reset the counters for a different student.

Tax-Deductible Calculator (Chapters 1–7)

Create an interface that provides text boxes for entering the following business expenses: lodging, travel, meals, and entertainment. Lodging and travel are 100% tax deductible; meals and entertainment are only 50% tax deductible. The application should calculate and display the total expenses, the amount that is tax deductible, and the percentage that is tax deductible. Each text box should accept only numbers, one period, and the Backspace key. (Notice that each text box should not allow the user to enter more than one period.)

Shopping Cart (Chapters 1–9)

The shopping cart application should list the names of 10 different DVDs in a list box and store the associated prices in a one-dimensional array. (Use at least four different prices for the DVDs.) To purchase a DVD, the user needs to click its name in the list box and then click an Add to cart button. The button's Click event procedure should display the DVD's name and price in another list box, which will represent the shopping cart. A DVD can appear more than once in the shopping cart. The interface should also provide a Remove from cart button. (Research the Items collection's Remove and RemoveAt methods for a list box. Or, complete Exercise 17 in Chapter 5.) It should also provide a button that clears the shopping cart and prepares the application for the next customer's order. The application should display the subtotal (which is the cost of the items in the shopping cart), the sales tax, the shipping charge, and the total cost. The sales tax rate is 4%. The shipping charge is $1 per DVD, up to a maximum shipping charge of $5. (It may help to complete the Chapter 7: Aligning Columns section in Appendix B.)

Airplane Seats (Chapters 1–9)

Create an interface that contains a list box with the following 18 items: 1A, 1B, 1C, 2A, 2B, 2C, 3A, 3B, 3C, 4A, 4B, 4C, 5A, 5B, 5C, 6A, 6B, and 6C. Each item represents a seat designation on an airplane. When the user clicks a list box item, the application should display the seat designation, passenger's name, and ticket price. The application should use both a sequential access file and a two-dimensional array for the passenger information. You can create the sequential access file by using the New File option on the File menu. The file should contain 18 seat designations, passenger names, and ticket prices.

Theater Seats (Chapters 1–10)

Create an interface that contains a list box with the following 10 items: A1, B1, A2, B2, A3, B3, A4, B4, A5, and B5. Each item represents a seat number in a theater. When the user clicks a list box item, the application should display the seat number, theater patron's name, and ticket price. The application should use a sequential access file, a class, and a one-dimensional array. You can create the sequential access file by using the New File option on the File menu. The file should contain 10 seat numbers, patron names, and ticket prices.

Jefferson Realty (Chapters 1–12)

Create a SQL Server database that contains one table named Homes. The table should contain 10 records, each having five fields. The ID field should be an auto-numbered field. The ZIP code field should contain text. Be sure to use at least three different ZIP codes. The number of bedrooms, number of bathrooms, and price fields should be numeric. Create an application that displays the contents of the database in a DataGridView control. The user should not be allowed to add, edit, delete, or save records. The application should allow the user to display the records for a specific number of bedrooms, a specific number of bathrooms, or a specific ZIP code. When the interface appears, it should display the average home price for the entire database.

Rosette Catering (Chapters 1–13)

Create a Web Site application for Rosette Catering. The interface should allow the user to enter the customer ID, the bride's name, the groom's name, and the date of the wedding reception. It should also allow the user to enter the number of chicken dinners, the number of pasta dinners, and the number of vegetarian dinners ordered for the reception. The interface should display the total number of dinners ordered, the total price of the order without sales tax, the sales tax, and the total price of the order with sales tax. Each dinner costs $21, and the sales tax rate is 3%. Include an image in the interface. (You can find many different images on the Open Clip Art Library Web site at *openclipart.org*.)

Index

Note: Page numbers in **boldface** type indicate where key terms are defined.